Introduction to

PUBLIC LAW

Readings on the Law, State, and Citizen

edited by

NICK E. MILANOVIC

Department of Law and Legal Studies
Carleton University

CANADIAN LEGAL STUDIES SERIES

Captus Press

Canadian Legal Studies Series
Introduction to Public Law: Readings on the Law, State,
and Citizen

Captus Press Inc.
Units 14 & 15
1600 Steeles Avenue West
Concord, ON   L4K 4M2
Telephone: (416) 736–5537
Fax: (416) 736–5793
Email: Info@captus.com
Internet: http://www.captus.com

Library and Archives Canada Cataloguing in Publication

Introduction to public law (2015)
    Introduction to public law : readings on the law, state,
and citizen / edited by Nikola E. Milanovic, Department of
Law, Carleton University.

(Canadian legal studies series)
"Evolves from Introduction to public law : readings on the state,
    the administrative process, and basic values, compiled and
    written by Prof. David Elliott"—Preface.

Includes bibliographical references.
ISBN 978-1-55322-300-9

    1. Public law—Canada.   I. Milanovic, Nikola E., editor
II. Series: Canadian legal studies series

KE4120.I5718 2015   342.71   C2014-907223-6
KF4482.I5718 2015

Canada   *We acknowledge the financial support of the Government of Canada through the Canada Book Fund (CBF) for our publishing activities.*

0 9 8 7 6 5 4 3 2 1
Printed and bound in Canada

Table of Contents

Preface

This volume was designed especially for students taking introductory public law courses at the Department of Law and Legal Studies at Carleton University. It is meant for students enrolled in Law, State & Citizen, which focuses on administrative law and the *Charter of Rights and Freedoms*. It accompanies the forthcoming companion volume *Introduction to Public Law: Law, State & Constitution*, which is also designed for students enrolled in Law, State & Constitution, and centres on constitutional law and the federal system.

This book evolves from *Introduction to Public Law: Readings on the State, the Administrative Process, and Basic Values*, compiled and written by Prof. David Elliott at the Law Department of Carleton University. The publisher and the editor

thank Prof. Elliott for granting permission to use his work in this new volume.

The editor also acknowledges the authors and publishers who have kindly granted permission to publish their works herein. Not all reproduced extracts contain the original footnotes or endnotes or note numbering. Due to permission constraints, the editor has not altered over-inclusive or under-inclusive uses of gender in original extracts.

The editor gratefully recognizes the valuable assistance of Captus Press and its staff, my colleagues, and my assistant Ms. Christina Decarie for their valuable contributions and hard work on my behalf. Thank you, also, to the students, who help make this subject a pleasure and a challenge to teach.

Ottawa, Ontario
September 2014

Introductory Note

David W. Elliott

These materials are concerned with public law, the law that relates primarily to the relationship between the state and society. They address some theoretical aspects of the state; the operation and control of the administrative process; the protection of basic values by the *Charter* and other means; and the role of law and courts in all these areas. Although the main emphasis is on Canada, the material is not confined to our borders. States and legal systems are not islands, but parts of a single, complex and highly interconnected world. A public international law section addresses this larger world specifically.

What should *you* be looking for in these materials? That is for you, the student, to decide. But for those who seek an introductory picture of law and the state, a few suggestions are offered. First, look beneath the surface detail for underlying frameworks. What is the key objective and function of a given state structure? What is the main purpose of the statute you are examining? How was it designed? How did the administrator try to implement it? What was the end result of that judicial decision? How did the judge try to justify it?

Second, study law about the state in its *context*. State power is not the only kind of power, and formal laws are not the only social norms. Consider the non-legal forces — voluntary, coercive, corporate, non-corporate, domestic, or international — that share the stage with the state. Look for the historical, social, economic, conceptual, and political factors that act on law and are influenced by law. Ask who benefits from individual laws, and who is burdened by them.

Third, look for broad themes and patterns. These won't appear in gold frames or neon lights. You will need to search creatively, and ask big questions. For example, how well are the theoretical models and goals in the first chapter realized in the law about the state? How are issues such as equality addressed in law and in practice? To what extent are law and state concerned with the linked issues of power, community, and human dignity? What role do law and courts play — and what role should they play — in addressing these issues?

Fourth, look for the values and preferences on which the law and the state are both built. What the scholar John Hogarth once said about sentencing is true of all law: it is a human process.

Finally, be critical. After exploring all available evidence, and assessing all contending arguments, it is up to you and others to decide if present laws and state structures are adequate, or if they should be changed, and why. Public law should be the public's law: it shapes us all; shouldn't we all be shaping it?

Law, State, and Social Goals and Techniques

(a) Social Goals and the State

David W. Elliott

SOCIAL GOALS[1]

The state is not a natural landmark like Mount Robson. Like law, it is a human creation, whose role and significance can vary with the era and social goals of the individual observer. Although our focus here is on the state, law and society are clearly important as well.

For the ancient Greeks, the "state" was not distinct from society as a whole.[2] In early Christian and feudal times, the state was considered an earthly adjunct to the more important City of God.[3] Secular law was a pale and fallible imitation of the "natural law" of superior moral norms. Later philosophers evolved more secular explanations for the state. These often varied with the importance they attached to one or more of the following main social goals: furthering collective interests; protecting private interests; securing control by citizens; and promoting equality. At times, too, other social concerns have dominated.

Collective Interests and the State

Thomas Hobbes' state was an instrument for ensuring human survival and physical security.[4] This collectivist "law and order" goal remains a basic rationale for states to this day. In Canada it can be seen in the "Peace, order, and good Government" clause in the *Constitution Act, 1867*; in section 1 of the *Canadian Charter of Rights and Freedoms*; in our criminal law and our law of torts; and in the arguments for efficiency in administrative law. Other thinkers who stressed state collective potential include Jeremy Bentham, who sought to harness legislation in maximizing human happi-

ness,[5] and Roscoe Pound, with his optimistic school of social engineering.[6] With the 20th century came the modern welfare and regulatory state. In Canada, concern for social welfare was heightened by economic disruption from two world wars and a devastating depression. Proclaimed during the depression, the C.C.F. party's founding *Regina Manifesto* said state resources should be used to improve economic and social conditions for all citizens.[7] Two American writers, Henry Hart and Albert Sacks, were among the first to describe systematically the wealth of control options available to the regulatory state;[8] in Canada they were followed by writers such as William Stanbury[9] and Michael Trebilcock.[10]

Private Interests and the State

Other approaches to the state stress its relationship to private interests. Private interests can be seen in a negative or a positive sense in relation to the state. In the negative sense, private interests are a zone within which law, state, and society as a whole do not or should not interfere. This is the sense referred to in John Stuart Mill's essay on liberty.[11] Until the enactment of the *Charter*, it was the main sense in which private interests were protected in Canada. In a rather similar vein, pluralists such as Robert Dahl see the state as a relatively neutral forum that permits competition and accommodation between many varied private social interests.[12]

In the positive sense, rights are interests that are or should be enforceable against the state. This idea has roots both in natural law and the social contract notion of John Locke.[13] It is embodied in both the French and the American constitutions of the 18th century. With the enactment of the *Constitution Act, 1982*, the constitutional rights-based approach gained a central role in Canada, affecting civil liberties and certain group cultural interests, but expanding well beyond into such fields as criminal and administrative law.

Citizen Control[14] and the State

Another approach to law and the state focuses on citizen control of government, sometimes referred to as "democracy". Most people have heard of the government of the ancient Greek city states, in which "all" citizens — excluding women and slaves![15] — could participate directly in the affairs of society.[16] Even assuming that the Greeks had achieved universal direct participation, the feat cannot be duplicated in larger, more complex societies. Most modern citizen control can be carried on only through representatives. At a minimum, though, this indirect control should be:

(a) general, involving virtually all adult citizens; and

(b) effective, permitting the citizens to control their representatives, and the representatives to control government.

In the British constitutional system, the chief vehicle for citizen control is Parliament. Parliament gained a large measure of effectiveness before it acquired much generality. Its supremacy over the other branches of government was established in the 17th century,[17] the period in which Locke advocated an even more ultimate form of citizen control, the right of rebellion against a government that fails in its most fundamental obligations.[18]

Generality of control was strongly supported by Mill, who argued that a wide pool of opinion is vital to both truth and good government.[19] The base of citizen control widened slowly in the 19th and 20th centuries. In Canada women did not gain the right to vote in federal elections in 1918;[20] registered Indians did not gain it until 1960.[21]

Full or classical parliamentary sovereignty reached a peak in late 19th and early 20th century Britain.[22] Unlike Britain, though, Canada has always had a system of limited parliamentary sovereignty, subject to some legal constraints in the Constitution. In 1982, with the enactment of the *Charter*, constitutional limits became more important. Meanwhile, the early 20th century enlargement of the franchise was offset by the growth of strong executives and strict political party discipline. Parliamentary sovereignty's potential as an effective vehicle for citizen control declined. Many recent initiatives, from citizen participation initiatives to the *Charter* itself, have been attempts to compensate for this decline.

Equality and the State

Another main perspective is that the state should follow the goal of equality. Karl Marx felt that the state did *not* promote equality; instead the state was "the form in which the individuals of a ruling class assert their common interests."[23] The traditional approach to Marx's writings sees the state in capitalist society as an instrument through which the bourgeoisie maintain their economic domination of the working class. More recent interpretations argue that Marx did not perceive the state as a mere agent of the ruling class, but rather as acting independently to unite the various competing factions of capital while at the same time seeking to forge compromises with subordinate classes. In doing so, it encourages the consent of the dominated. In this perspective, the state in capitalist society has relative autonomy from both the ruling class and the class struggle within civil society.[24]

Sociologists such as John Porter[25] and Wallace Clement[26] have stressed élite power more than class domination, and have said that élite power is both economic and political. Antonio Gramsci said ruling class domination is enforced not only through economic relations and the state, but also through institutions such as the media, schools, and the family.[27] Gramsci and other Marxist writers claim that many features of modern democratic states, such as representation, principles of justice, and notions of basic rights, are involved in the production, reproduction, and mobilization of hegemony, that is, rule by a dominant social group that is supported by both coercion and induced consent. Alan Hunt explores the implications of Gramsci's concepts of hegemony and counter-hegemony for the understanding of law.[28] Hunt says Gramsci locates law at the intersection between state and civil society because it involves processes that are both coercive and produce consent. As such, law is an area of struggle that is responsive and can be transformed by movements within civil society.

Focusing on another aspect of law's legitimation role, Harry Glasbeek and Michael Mandel say the abstract legal guarantees of the *Canadian*

Charter of Right and Freedoms serve to distract Canadian working classes from the severe economic inequalities in the country.[29] Non-Marxist Michel Foucault would carry the concepts of power relationships and domination still further, arguing that they are a part of virtually *all* human social relations.[30]

Others are somewhat more optimistic. For example, E.P. Thompson argues that although the rule of law did function as a legitimizing device in 18th century England, it provided concrete benefits for lower classes and instilled in them a desire for greater justice.[31] C.B. McPherson saw the end of economic scarcity as an opportunity for Western democracies to curb the excesses of market capitalism.[32] Neil MacCormick claims that economic egalitarianism is a necessary condition of individual freedom, attainable by such tools as progressive taxation and a guaranteed minimum income.[33] Meanwhile, supporters of welfare programs see these as throwing state lifelines to at least some souls at the bottom of the ladder.

Most of the above writers have focused on economic inequality. Two of the most important goals of the 20th century have been to achieve greater racial and gender equality. These and other non-economic equality goals have been pursued in Canada through human rights codes, bills of rights, and the *Charter*. Of special interest here is the feminist movement. Here Annie Bunting stresses the importance of equality,[34] and writers such as Kathleen Lahey argue that "formal" equality is not enough, and that law and the state must also take account of circumstances unique to women.[35]

Other Social Goals and the State

Ethnic and cultural concerns can constitute either a collective interest or a quasi-private group interest, depending on whether they are desired for the population at large, or a particular segment. They may seek protective measures from the state, or more positive state action. In 1774, some of the distinct cultural interests of French-speaking Canadians were given constitutional protection in the *Quebec Act*, and at Confederation their interests and regional differences were acknowledged in the cultural powers given to the provinces. In this century, the Canadian state regulates the communications industry to try to protect Canadian culture against domination by the United States. French-speaking Canadians in Quebec, Aboriginal peoples, and other minority ethnic groups seek additional constitutional protection from control by the majority. Some want more than protective measures, and demand varying degrees of independence from the majority. Indeed, a significant minority of Quebeckers favour the creation of a separate state of Quebec.

Another special concern is a desire by some to shift the state's focus from economic growth to less material goals, such as promoting environmental conservation[36] or fostering human learning and contemplation.[37] This desire has been influenced by a rediscovery of the traditional philosophies of Aboriginal cultures. As stressed by writers such as Leroy Littlebear, they attach great importance to maintaining harmony with nature.[38]

SOCIAL TECHNIQUES

Some modern philosophers take a less directly normative approach. Instead of associating the state with specific social goals, they have tried to identify characteristic techniques of the state and social phenomena associated with it. Max Weber, for example, described the state as a compulsory political organization with a monopoly on the legitimate use of force in a particular territory.[39] For Michel Foucault, "government" extends far beyond the state and political structures, and encompasses social control in general. He saw state apparatus as little more than one of the many social forums through which institutions and individuals control others.[40] Approaches that focus on social techniques tend to suggest that the state and state law may be far less distinct than traditionally thought.

SOCIAL CONTEXT

It is worth reminding ourselves that the state is a human construct, existing in a social as well as a legal context. Thus, understanding a state and its goals requires a familiarity with its history, and with the economic and political climate around it.[41] It requires an awareness of the relationship between the state and its citizens, and of the general attributes of citizenship.[42] Finally, it requires an awareness of the broader global context that plays an ever-greater role in domestic national life.[43] No person is an island, and neither is the modern state.

Notes

1. See also "Public Law, The State, and the Courts" in David W. Elliott, ed. *Introduction to Public Law:*

Sourcebook, 6th ed. (North York, Ont.: Captus Press, 2003) Ch. 1.

2. Westel Woodbury Willoughby, *The Political Theories of the Ancient World* [1903] (Freeport, N.Y.: Books for Libraries, 1969) at 62–63.

3. See C.J. Friedrich, *The Philosophy of Law in Historical Perspective*, 2d ed. (Chicago: University of Chicago Press, 1963) ch. IV.

4. Thomas Hobbes, *Leviathan* [1651], ed. M. Oakshott (Oxford: Blackwell, 1947).

5. J. Bentham, *A Fragment on Government* and *An Introduction to the Principles of Morals and Legislation* [1776 and 1789, respectively] by W. Harrison (Oxford: Oxford University Press, 1948) at 113.

6. R. Pound, *Social Control Through Law* (New Haven, Conn.: Yale University Press, 1942).

7. J.T. Morely, "Co-operative Commonwealth Federation" in J.H. Marsh, ed. *The Canadian Encyclopedia: Year 2000 Edition* (Toronto: McClelland & Stewart, 1999) at 564.

8. Henry Hart Jr. and Albert Sacks, *The Legal Process: Basic Problems in the Making and Application of Law* (Westbury, N.Y.: The Foundation Press, 1994, from 1958 tentative ed.).

9. W.T. Stanbury, *Business-Government Relations in Canada* (Toronto: Methuen, 1986).

10. M. Trebilcock et al., for Economic Council of Canada, *The Choice of Governing Instrument* (Ottawa: Supply and Services Canada, 1982); and Canada, Law Reform Commission of Canada, *Working Paper 51* (Ottawa: Supply and Services Canada, 1986).

11. J.S. Mill, *On Liberty; Representative Government; The Subjection of Women: Three Essays* [1859, 1861, and 1869, respectively], Introduction by M.G. Fawcett (London: Oxford University Press, 1966), and extracts below.

12. For example, R.A. Dahl, *Polyarchy, Participation and Opposition* (New Haven, Conn.: Yale University Press, 1971); and *Dilemmas of Pluralist Democracy: Autonomy vs. Control* (New Haven, Conn.: Yale University Press, 1982).

13. John Locke, *Two Treatises of Government: The Second Treatise* [1690] by P. Laslett (Cambridge, Mass.: Cambridge University Press, 1967), and extract below.

14. See also "Public Law, The State, and the Courts," *supra* note 1 at 4.

15. See B. Russell, *A History of Western Philosophy* [1946] (London: Counterpoint, 1984) at 30.

16. D.D. Kagan, *The Greek Dialogue: History of Greek Political Thought from Homer to Polybius* (New York: The Free Press, 1965) at 73–90.

17. R. Blake, "Mother of Parliaments: The Development of the Lords and Commons over Seven Centuries" in ed. R. Blake, *The English World: History, Character and People* (New York: Abrams, 1982) at 93–95.

18. *Two Treatises of Government: The Second Treatise* [1690] *supra* note 13 at 430–31, and extracts below.

19. *On Liberty; Representative Government; The Subjection of Women: Three Essays*, *supra* note 11. See also extracts below.

20. J. Stoddart (revision) and L. MacPherson, "Women and the Law," in J.H. Marsh, ed. *The Canadian Encyclopedia: Year 2000 Edition* (Toronto: McClelland & Stewart, 1999) at 2528. Women spouses of members of the armed forces were enfranchised in 1917, and then the vote was broadened to most adult women in 1918. Women could not vote in Quebec until 1940, and registered Indian women (and men) could not vote in federal elections until 1960. Other milestones: 1916: the extension of the franchise to women in the provinces of Alberta, Saskatchewan, and Manitoba; 1930: *Edwards v. Canada (A.G.)*, [1930] 1 D.L.R. 98 (J.C.P.C.), holding that women are "persons" for the purposes of appointment to the Senate; 1957: the swearing in of Ms. Ellen Fairclough as the first woman federal Cabinet Minister; 1981: Canada's ratification of the United Nations *Convention on the Elimination of all Forms of Discrimination Against Women*; 1982: the appointment of Madame Justice Bertha Wilson as the first woman justice of the Supreme Court of Canada; 1985: the coming into force of the equality provisions of the *Canadian Charter of Rights and Freedoms*; 1993: the selection of Kim Campbell as the first woman Prime Minister of Canada; and 2000: the appointment of Beverley McLachlin as the first woman Chief Justice of the Supreme Court of Canada.

21. J.C. Courtney, "Franchise," in *The Canadian Encyclopedia: Year 2000 Edition*, ibid., 908. Inuit were granted the right to vote in federal elections in 1950. Registered Indians were unable to vote in Quebec provincial elections until 1969.

22. It is well described in Albert Venn Dicey, *An Introduction to the Study of the Law of the Constitution* [1908], 10th ed. (London: MacMillan, 1965) Ch. 1. See *Dicey's View* in Chapter 6(b), below. Note that the British Parliament no longer has full legal supremacy; since 1972 Britain has been a member of the European Economic Community or (since 1993) its successor the European Union. At least as long as Britain is a member of the Union, where there is a conflict between Union laws and British laws, the former prevail: see *R. v. Secretary of State for Transport, ex parte Factortame Ltd. (No.2)*, [1991] 1 A.C. 603, 643 (H.L.).

23. Karl Marx, "The Materialist Conception of History" in T. Bottomore, trans. *Karl Marx* (New York: McGraw-Hill, 1956) at 225–27. See also extracts below.

24. For a survey of some late 20th century Marxist approaches to law, state, and society, see D.K. Stasiulus, "Democracy and the Canadian State" in D. Forcese and S. Richer, eds., *Social Issues: Sociological Views of Canada*, 2d ed. (Toronto: Prentice-Hall, 1988) at 223.

25. J. Porter, *The Vertical Mosaic* (Toronto: University of Toronto Press, 1964). See also C.W. Mills, *The Power Elite* (New York: Oxford University Press, 1956); and R. Helmes-Hayes and J. Curtis, eds. *The Vertical Mosaic Revisited* (Toronto: University of Toronto Press, 1998).

26. W. Clement, *Class, Power and Property* (Toronto: Methuen, 1983). Cf. W. Clement and J. Myles, *Relations of Ruling: Class and Gender in Postindustrial Societies* (Montreal & Kingston: McGill-Queen's University Press, 1994).

27. Antonio Gramsci, *Selections from the Prison Notebooks of Antonio Gramsci*, ed. and trans. Quentin Hoare and Geoffrey Nowell-Smith (London: Lawrence & Wishart, 1971) at 12–13 (referring to social hegemony and state domination). See extracts cited in Hunt article *infra* note 28 and M. Cain, "Gramsci: The State and the Place of Law" in D. Sugarman, ed., *Legality, Ideology and The State* (London: Academic Press, 1983) at 96 (noting that Gramsci sometimes referred to "the state" in a broader sense, to include both government and civil society).

28. A. Hunt, "Rights and Social Movements Counter-hegemonic Strategies" in A. Hunt, *Explorations in Law and Society: Towards a Constitutive Theory of Law* (New York: Routledge, 1993) at 227, and extracts below.

29. H. Glasbeek and M. Mandel, "The Legalization of Politics in Advanced Capitalism" in R. Martin, [guest] ed., *Critical Perspectives on the Constitution* [Socialist Studies Series] (Winnipeg, Man.: Society for Socialist Studies, 1984) 84 at 93–108. See also A.C. Hutchinson and P. Monahan, "Democracy and the Rule of Law" in eds. A.C. Hutchinson and P. Monahan, *The Rule of Law: Ideal or Ideology* (Toronto: Carswell, 1987) at 97.

30. See generally, M. Foucault, *Discipline and Punish: The Birth of the Prison* [1975], trans. A. Sheridan (New York: Pantheon Books, 1977).

31. E.P. Thompson, *Whigs and Hunters: The Origins of the Black Act* (London: Allen Lane, 1975). See *Thompson's View* in Chapter 6(b), below.

32. C.B. McPherson, *The Real World of Democracy* (Oxford: Clarendon Press, 1966).

33. N.M. MacCormick, *Legal Right and Social Democracy* (Oxford: Oxford University Press, 1982).

34. A. Bunting, "Feminism, Foucault, and Law as Power/Knowledge" (1992) 30 Alta. L. Rev. 829. See extracts below.

35. K.A. Lahey, "On Silences, Screams and Scholarship: An Introduction to Feminist Legal Theory," in R.F. Devlin, ed., *Canadian Perspectives on Legal Theory* (Toronto: Emond Montgomery, 1991); K.A. Lahey, *Are We 'Persons' Yet?: Law and Sexuality in Canada* (Toronto: University of Toronto Press, 1999). See also R. Hamilton, *Gendering the Vertical Mosaic: Feminist Perspectives in Canadian Society* (Toronto: Copp Clark, 1996); and P. Armstrong, *Feminism, Political Economy and the State: Contested Terrain* (Toronto: Canadian Scholar's Press, 1999).

36. For example, D.T. Suzuki, *Time to Change: Essays* (Don Mills, Ont.: Stoddart, 1994); B. Mitchell, *Environmental Change and Challenge: A Canadian Perspective* (Toronto: Oxford University Press, 1997).

37. C. Taylor, "The Agony of Economic Man" in L. Lapierre et al., eds., *Essays on the Left* (Toronto: McClelland & Stewart, 1971). Taylor criticized the modern obsession with production, consumption, and technology. As an alternative, he proposed a socialistic society dedicated to learning, imagining, and thinking.

38. Leroy Little Bear, "The Aboriginal Peoples' Standard" in J. Rick Ponting, ed., *Arduous Journey: Canadian Indians and Decolonization* (Toronto: McClelland & Stewart, 1986) at 245–47. See extracts below. See also A. Hungry Wolf, *Teachings of Nature* (Skookumchuck, BC: Good Medicine Books, 1989); and B. Bryan, "Property as Ontology: On Aboriginal and English Understandings of Ownership" (2000) 13 Can. J.L. & Juris. 3.

39. Max Weber, *Economy and Society: An Outline of Interpretive Sociology* [from German 4th ed., 1956], ed. and trans. G. Roth and C. Wittich et al. (New York: Bedminster Press, 1968) at 54. See extracts below.

40. For example, Foucault listed state apparatuses such as the police alongside "specialized" institutions such as penitentiaries, "pre-existing authorities" such as the family, institutions such as schools and hospitals, as examples of bodies that exercise the non-coercive or semi-coercive kind of power of control he called "discipline": M. Foucault, *Discipline and Punish: The Birth of the Prison*, transl. A. Sheridan (New York: Pantheon Books, 1977) at 215. See extracts from A. Bunting, "Feminism, Foucault, and Law as Power/Knowledge" (1992) 30 Alta. L. Rev. 829, below, and cf. the political theory of Antonio Gramsci, referred to above.

41. For introductory texts on the historical, economic, and political context in Canada, see, respectively, J.L. Finlay and D.N. Sprague, *The Structure of Canadian History*, 6th ed. (Scarborough, Ont.: Prentice Hall Allyn and Bacon Canada, 2000); John C. Strick, *The Public Sector in Canada: Programs, Finance and Policy* (Toronto: Thompson Educational Publishing, 1999); and Rand Dyck, *Canadian Politics: Critical Approaches*, 4th ed. (Scarborough, Ont.: Thomson Nelson, 2004).

42. There are many possible different approaches to the concept of citizenship. The civic republican approach, derived from the ancient Romans and Greeks, stresses the importance of citizen participation in the public affairs of the state: D.K. Heater, *Citizenship: The Civic Ideal in World History, Politics and Education* (London: Longman, 1990); C.R. Sunstein, *The Partial Constitution* (Cambridge, Mass.: Harvard University Press, 1993). The classical liberal approach stresses the autonomy of the individual, and views a citizen's relationship to the state mainly from the perspective of this autonomy: J.S. Mill, *On Liberty; Representative Government; The Subjection of Women: Three Essays* [1859, 1861, and 1869, respectively], Introduction by M.G. Fawcett (London: Oxford University Press, 1966), and extracts below. An evolutionary approach suggested by writer T.H. Marshall sees citizenship as an historical development from civil liberty rights alone, to civil liberty and political democratic rights, to a later stage in which these are supplemented by rights to social benefits: T.H. Marshall, "Citizenship and Social Class" in David Held et al., eds., *States and Societies* (Oxford: Basil Blackwell, 1985) at 248–60 and M. Bulmer and A.M. Rees, *Citizenship Today; The Contemporary Relevance of T.H. Marshall* (London: UCL Press, 1996). Another evolutionary approach, that of Jürgen Habermas, envisages an historical movement from ethnic-based associations to a potentially universal citizenship based on a shared commitment to participation in democratic institutions: Jürgen Habermas, "Citizenship and National Identity (1990)," in *Between Facts and Norms*, trans. W. Rehg (Cambridge, Mass.: MIT Press, 1996) at 491 *et seq.*

43. See extracts in Chapter 12, below.

(b) Leviathan†

Thomas Hobbes

NOTE

Can you see why Thomas Hobbes could be said to favour a collectivist view of the role of the state? Hobbes, a leading 17th century English philosopher, was tutor to the son of the Earl of Devonshire, a close advisor to King Charles I. Not surprisingly, Hobbes sided with the Stuart monarchy during the English civil wars: see, for example, Johann P. Sommerville, *Thomas Hobbes: Political Ideas in Historical Context* (London and New York: St. Martin's Press, 1992). Compare and contrast

---

† Excerpts from Thomas Hobbes's *Leviathan* [1651], edited with an introduction by Michael Oakshott (Oxford, England: Basil Blackwell Ltd., 1947) at 82, 109, and 111–13. [Commentary note by David W. Elliott.]

this extract from Hobbes with the extract from another eminent 17th century English philosopher, John Locke. Locke, who emphasized private rights against the state, sided with anti-Stuart forces in Parliament: see Graham Faiella, *John Locke, Champion of Modern Democracy* (New York, N.Y.: Rosen Pub. Group, 2006). Do the two philosophers' different backgrounds help explain their approaches to the state?

In effect, the theories of state in this chapter are models that highlight what each author considered most important. Their subjectivity should caution us against finding in any single theory a monopoly on truth; their diversity should encourage us to widen our own perspectives.

EXTRACT

[When mankind is in its natural condition, there is] ... continual fear, and danger of violent death; and the life of man, solitary, poor, nasty, brutish, and short.

. . . .

The final cause, end, or design of men, who naturally love liberty, and dominion over others, in the introduction of that restraint upon themselves, in which we see them live in commonwealths, is the foresight of their own preservation, and of a more contented life thereby; that is to say, of getting themselves out from that miserable condition of war, which is necessarily consequent, as hath been shown (Chapter XIII), to the natural passions of men, when there is no visible power to keep them in awe, and tie them by fear of punishment to the performance of their covenants, and observation of those laws of nature set down in the fourteenth and fifteenth chapters.

For the laws of nature, as *justice, equity, modesty, mercy*, and, in sum, *doing to others, as we would be done to*, of themselves, without the terror of some power, to cause them to be observed, are contrary to our natural passions, that carry us to partiality, pride, revenge, and the like. And covenants, without the sword, are but words, and of no strength to secure a man at all....

. . . .

... [T]he agreement of [human beings, as opposed to other social animals] is by covenant only, which is artificial: and therefore it is no wonder if

there be somewhat else required, besides covenant, to make their agreement constant and lasting; which is a common power, to keep them in awe, and to direct their actions to the common benefit.

The only way to erect such a common power, as may be able to defend them from the invasion of foreigners, and the injuries of one another, and thereby to secure them in such sort, as that by their own industry, and by the fruits of the earth, they may nourish themselves and live contentedly; is, to confer all their power and strength upon one man, or upon one assembly of men, that may reduce all their wills, by plurality of voices, unto one will: which is as much as to say, to appoint one man, or assembly of men, to bear their person; and every one to own, and acknowledge himself to be author of whatsoever he that so beareth their person, shall act, or cause to be acted, in those things which concern the common peace and safety; and therein to submit their wills, everyone to his will, and their judgments, to his judgment. This is more than consent, or concord; it is a real unity of them all, in one and the same person, made by covenant of every man with every man, in such manner, as if every man should say to every man, *I authorize and give up my right of governing myself, to this man, or to this assembly of men, on this condition, that thou give up thy right to him, and authorize all his actions in like manner.* This done, the multitude so united in one person, is called a COMMONWEALTH, in Latin CIVITAS. This is the generation of that great LEVIATHAN, or rather, to speak more reverently, of that *mortal god*, to which we owe under the *immortal God*, our peace and defence. For by this authority, given him by every particular man in the commonwealth, he hath the use of so much power and strength conferred on him, that by terror thereof, he is enabled to perform the wills of them all, to peace at home, and mutual aid against their enemies abroad. And in him consisteth the essence of the commonwealth; which, to define it, is *one person, of whose acts a great multitude, by mutual covenants one with another, have made themselves everyone the author, to the end he may use the strength and means of them all, as he shall think expedient, for their peace and common defence.*

And he that carrieth this person, is called SOVEREIGN, and said to have sovereign power; and every one besides, his SUBJECT.

The attaining to this sovereign power, is by two ways. One, by natural force; as when a man maketh his children, to submit themselves, and their children, to his government, as being able to destroy them if they refuse; or by war subdueth his enemies to his will, giving them their lives on that condition. The other, is when men agree amongst themselves to submit to some man, or assembly of men, voluntarily, on confidence to be protected by him against all others. This latter, may be called a political commonwealth, or commonwealth by *institution*; and the former, a commonwealth by *acquisition*....

(c)   The Second Treatise on Civil Government†

John Locke

95. Men being, as has been said, by nature all free, equal, and independent, no one can be put out of this estate and subjected to the political power of another without his consent, which is done by agreeing with other men, to join and unite into a community for their comfortable, safe, and peaceable living one amongst another, in a secure enjoyment of their properties, and a greater security against any that are not of it.... When any number of men have so consented to make one community or government, they are thereby presently incorporated, and make one body politic, wherein the majority have a right to act and conclude the rest.

.   .   .   .

124. The great and chief end, therefore, of men uniting into commonwealths, and putting themselves under government, is the preservation of their property; to which in the state of Nature there are many things wanting.

.   .   .   .

142. These are the bounds which the trust that is put in them by the society and the Law of God and Nature have set to the legislative power of every commonwealth, in all forms of government. First: They are to govern by promulgated established laws, not to be varied in particular cases, but to have one rule for the rich and poor, for the favourite at Court, and the countryman at plough. Secondly: These laws also ought to be designed for no other end ultimately but the good of the people. Thirdly: They must not raise taxes on the property of the people without the consent of the people given by themselves, or their deputies.... Fourthly: Legislative neither must nor can transfer the power of making laws to anybody else, or place it anywhere but where the people have.

.   .   .   .

222. ... [W]henever the legislators endeavour to take away and destroy the Property of the people, or to reduce them to slavery under arbitrary power, they put themselves in a state of war with the people, who are thereupon absolved from any further obedience, and are left to the common refuge which God hath provided for all men against force and violence. Whensoever, therefore, the legislative shall transgress this fundamental rule of society, and ... endeavour to grasp themselves, or put into the hands of any other, an absolute power over the lives, liberties, and estates of the people, who have a right to resume their original liberty, and, by the establishment of a new legislative (such as they shall think fit) provide for their own safety and security, which is the end for which they are in society. What I have said here, concerning the legislative in general holds true also concerning the supreme executor, who having a double trust put in him, both to have a part in the legislative, and the supreme execution of the law, acts against both, when he goes about to set up his own arbitrary will as the law of the society.

---

† Excerpts from John Locke, *Two Treatises of Government: The Second Treatise* [1690] (Buffalo: Prometheus Books, 1986) at 54–55, 70, 79–80, and 119.

(d)   On Liberty; Representative Government†

J.S. Mill

NOTE

Can you see a common thread in Mill's arguments for freedom of expression, representative government, and extending the franchise to women? Does Mill base these arguments on inherent individual rights, or on a notion of the common good of society? For evidence of the contemporary influence of Mill's work, see the discussion of the rationales for freedom of expression in *Irwin Toy Ltd. v. Quebec (A.G.)*, [1989] 1 S.C.R. 927 (reproduced in Chapter 9), and the reference to Mill's harm principle in *R. v. Malmo Levine*, [2003] 3 S.C.R. 571, esp. at para. 244; and Wayne L. Sumner, *The Hateful and the Obscene: Studies in the Limits of Free Expression* (Toronto: University of Toronto Press, 2004), considering Mill's harm principle in regard to hate propaganda and obscenity.

EXTRACT

ON LIBERTY

. . . .

The object of this Essay is to assert one very simple principle, as entitled to govern absolutely the dealings of society with the individual in the way of compulsion and control, whether the means used be physical force in the form of legal penalties, or the moral coercion of public opinion. That principle is, that the sole end for which mankind are warranted, individually or collectively, in interfering with the liberty of action of any of their number, is self-protection. That the only purpose for which power can be rightfully exercised over any member of a civilized community, against his will, is to prevent harm to others. His own good, either physical or moral, is not a sufficient warrant. He cannot rightfully be compelled to do or forbear because it will be better for him to do so, because it will make him happier, because, in the opinions of others, to do so would be wise, or even right. These are good reasons for remonstrating with him, or reasoning with him, or persuading him, or entreating him, but not for compelling him, or visiting him with any evil in case he do otherwise. To justify that, the conduct from which it is desired to deter him, must be calculated to produce evil to some one else. The only part of the conduct of any one, for which he is amenable to society, is that which concerns others. In the part which merely concerns himself, his independence is, of right, absolute. Over himself, over his own body and mind, the individual is sovereign.

. . . .

... [T]here is a sphere of action in which society, as distinguished from the individual, has, if any, only an indirect interest; comprehending all that portion of a person's life and conduct which affects only himself, or if it also affects others, only with their free, voluntary, and undeceived consent and participation. When I say only himself, I mean directly, and in the first instance: for whatever affects himself, may affect others through himself; and the objection which may be grounded on this contingency will receive consideration in the sequel. This, then, is the appropriate region of human liberty. It comprises, first, the inward domain of consciousness; demanding liberty of conscience, in the most comprehensive sense; liberty of thought and feeling; absolute freedom of opinion and sentiment on all subjects, practical or speculative, scientific, moral, or theological. The liberty of expressing and publishing opinions ... [is included here too]. Secondly, the principle requires liberty of tastes and pursuits; of framing the plan of our life to suit our own character; of doing as we like, subject to such consequences as may follow: without impediment from our fellow creatures, so long as what we do does not harm them, even though they should think our conduct foolish, perverse, or wrong. Thirdly, from this liberty of each

† Excerpts from J.S. Mill, "On Liberty" [1859] and "Representative Government" [1861] in *On Liberty; Representative Government; The Subjection of Women: Three Essays*, Introduction by M.G. Fawcett (London, England: Oxford University Press, 1960) at 14–15, 17–18, 57, 92–94, 186–87, 198, and 290–91. Reproduced by permission of Oxford University Press. [Commentary note by David W. Elliott.]

individual, follows the liberty, within the same limits, of combination among individuals; freedom to unite, for any purpose not involving harm to others: the persons combining being supposed to be of full age, and not forced or deceived.

No society in which these liberties are not, on the whole, respected, is free, whatever may be its form of government; and none is completely free in which they do not exist absolute and unqualified. The only freedom which deserves the name, is that of pursuing our own good in our own way, so long as we do not attempt to deprive others of theirs, or impede their efforts to obtain it. Each is the proper guardian of his own health, whether bodily, or mental and spiritual. Mankind are greater gainers by suffering each other to live as seems good to themselves, than by compelling each to live as seems good to the rest.

. . . .

It still remains to speak of one of the principal causes which make diversity of opinion advantageous.... We have hitherto considered only two possibilities: that the received opinion may be false, and some other opinion, consequently, true; or that, the received opinion being true, a conflict with the opposite error is essential to a clear apprehension and deep feeling of its truth. But there is a commoner case than either of these; when the conflicting doctrines, instead of being one true and the other false, share the truth between them; and the nonconforming opinion is needed to supply the remainder of the truth, of which the received doctrine embodies only a part. Popular opinions, on subjects not palpable to sense, are often true, but seldom or never the whole truth. They are a part of the truth; sometimes a greater, sometimes a smaller part, but exaggerated, distorted, and disjoined from the truths by which they ought to be accompanied and limited.

. . . .

What, then, is the rightful limit to the sovereignty of the individual over himself? Where does the authority of society begin? How much of human life should be assigned to individuality, and how much to society?

Each will receive its proper share, if each has that which more particularly concerns it. To individuality should belong the part of life in which it is chiefly the individual that is interested; to society, the part which chiefly interests society.

Though society is not founded on a contract, and though no good purpose is answered by inventing a contract in order to deduce social obligations from it, every one who receives the protection of society owes a return for the benefit, and the fact of living in society renders it indispensable that each should be bound to observe a certain line of conduct towards the rest. This conduct consists, first, in not injuring the interests of one another; or rather certain interests, which either by express legal provision or by tacit understanding, ought to be considered as rights; and secondly, in each person's bearing his share (to be fixed on some equitable principle) of the labours and sacrifices incurred for defending the society or its members from injury and molestation. These conditions society is justified in enforcing at all costs to those who endeavour to withhold fulfilment. Nor is this all that society may do. The acts of an individual may be hurtful to others, or wanting in due consideration for their welfare, without going the length of violating any of their constituted rights. The offender may then be justly punished by opinion, though not by law. As soon as any part of a person's conduct affects prejudicially the interests of others, society has jurisdiction over it, and the question whether the general welfare will or will not be promoted by interfering with it, becomes open to discussion. But there is no room for entertaining any such question when a person's conduct affects the interests of no persons besides himself, or needs not affect them unless they like (all the persons concerned being of full age, and the ordinary amount of understanding). In all such cases there should be perfect freedom, legal and social, to do the action and stand the consequences.

. . . .

... [N]either one person, nor any number of persons, is warranted in saying to another human creature of ripe years, that he shall not do with his life for his own benefit what he chooses to do with it. He is the person most interested in his own wellbeing: the interest which any other person, except in cases of strong personal attachment, can have in it, is trifling, compared with that which he himself has.... Considerations to aid his judgement, exhortations to strengthen his will, may be offered to him, even obtruded on him, by others; but he himself is the final judge. All errors which he is likely to commit against advice and warning, are far outweighed by the evil of allowing others to constrain him to what they deem his good.

. . . .

REPRESENTATIVE GOVERNMENT

The ideally best form of government ... does not mean one which is practicable or eligible in all states of civilization, but the one which, in the circumstances in which it is practicable and eligible, is attended with the greatest amount of beneficial consequences, immediate and prospective. A completely popular government is the only polity which can make out any claim to this character....

Its superiority in reference to present well-being rests upon two principles, of as universal truth and applicability as any general propositions which can be laid down respecting human affairs. The first is, that the rights and interests of every or any person are only secure from being disregarded, when the person interested is himself able, and habitually disposed, to stand up for them. The second is, that the general prosperity attains a greater height, and is more widely diffused, in proportion to the amount and variety of the personal energies enlisted in promoting it.

Putting these two propositions into a shape more special to their present application; human beings are only secure from evil at the hands of others, in proportion as they have the power of being, and are, self-*protecting*; and they only achieve a high degree of success in their struggle with Nature, in proportion as they are self-*dependent*, relying on what they themselves can do, either separately or in concert, rather than on what others do for them.

. . . .

From these accumulated considerations it is evident, that the only government which can fully satisfy all the exigencies of the social state, is one in which the whole people participate; that any participation, even in the smallest public function, is useful; that the participation should everywhere be as great as the general degree of improvement of the community will allow; and that nothing less can be ultimately desirable than the admission of all to a share in the sovereign power of the state. But since all cannot, in a community exceeding a single small town, participate personally in any but some very minor portions of the public business, it follows that the ideal type of a perfect government must be representative.

. . . .

In the preceding argument for universal, but graduated suffrage, I have taken no account of difference of sex. I consider it to be as entirely irrelevant to political rights, as difference in height, or in the colour of the hair. All human beings have the same interest in good government; the welfare of all is alike affected by it, and they have equal need of a voice in it to secure their share of its benefits. If there be any difference, women require it more than men, since, being physically weaker, they are more dependent on law and society for protection.

Mankind have long since abandoned the only premises which will support the conclusion that women ought not to have votes. No one now holds that women should be in personal servitude; that they should have no thought, wish, or occupation, but to be the domestic drudges of husbands, fathers, or brothers. It is allowed to unmarried, and wants but little of being conceded to married women, to hold property, and have pecuniary and business interests, in the same manner as men. It is considered suitable and proper that women should think, and write, and be teachers. As soon as these things are admitted, the political disqualification has no principle to rest on. The whole mode of thought of the modern world is, with increasing emphasis, pronouncing against the claim of society to decide for individuals what they are and are not fit for, and what they shall and shall not be allowed to attempt. If the principles of modern politics and political economy are good for anything, it is for proving that these points can only be rightly judged of by the individuals themselves....

10

(e) Writings in Sociology and Social Philosophy†

Karl Marx

PREFACE TO CONTRIBUTION TO CRITIQUE OF POLITICAL ECONOMY

I was led by my studies to the conclusion that legal relations as well as forms of State could neither be understood by themselves, nor explained by the so-called general progress of the human mind but that they are rooted in the material conditions of life ... and that the anatomy of civil society is to be sought in political economy.... The general conclusion at which I arrived and which, once reached, continued to serve as the guiding thread in my studies, may be formulated briefly as follows: In the social production which men carry on they enter into definite relations that are indispensable and independent of their will; these relations of production correspond to a definite stage of development of their material powers of production. The totality of these relations of production constitutes the economic structure of society — the real foundation, on which legal and political superstructures arise and to which definite forms of social consciousness correspond. The mode of production of material life determines the general character of the social, political, and spiritual processes of life. It is not the consciousness of men that determines their being, but, on the contrary, their social being determines their consciousness. At a certain stage of their development, the material forces of production in society come in conflict with the existing relations of production, or — what is but a legal expression for the same thing — with the property relations within which they had been at work before. From forms of development of the forces of production these relations turn into their fetters. Then occurs a period of social revolution. With the change of the economic foundation the entire immense superstructure is more or less rapidly transformed.... The bourgeois relations of production are the last antagonistic form of the social process of production; not in the sense of individual antagonisms, but of conflict arising from conditions surrounding the life of individuals in society. At the same time the productive forces developing in the womb of bourgeois society create the material conditions for the solution of that antagonism. With this social formation, therefore, the prehistory of human society comes to an end.

. . . .

GERMAN IDEOLOGY

Since the State is the form in which the individuals of a ruling class assert their common interests, and in which the whole civil society of an epoch is epitomized, it follows that the State acts as an intermediary for all community institutions, and that these institutions receive a political form. Hence the illusion that law is based on will, and indeed on will divorced from its real basis — on *free* will. Similarly, law is in its turn reduced to the actual laws.

. . . .

In historical fact the theorists who considered *force* as the basis of law were directly opposed to those who saw *will* as the basis of law. If force is taken to be the basis of law, as by Hobbes, law and legislative instruments are only a symptom or expression of *other* conditions upon which the State power exists. The material life of individuals, which certainly does not depend on their mere "will," their mode of production and their form of intercourse, which reciprocally influence each other, are the real basis of the State....

---

† Excerpts from Karl Marx, "Preface to Contribution to Critique of Political Economy" [1859] and "German Ideology" [1845–46] in T.B. Bottomore, ed. and trans., *Selected Writings in Sociology and Social Philosophy* (New York: McGraw-Hill, 1964) at 51–53, 223, and 225. Reproduced with permission of The McGraw-Hill Companies.

(f) Economy and Society: An Outline of Interpretive Sociology†

Max Weber

A "ruling organization" will be called "political" insofar as its existence and order is continuously safeguarded within a given *territorial* area by the threat and application of physical force on the part of the administrative staff. A compulsory political organization with continuous operation ... will be called a "state" insofar as its administrative staff successfully upholds the claim to the *monopoly* of the *legitimate* use of physical force in the enforcement of its order.

... The primary formal characteristics of the modern state are as follows: It possesses an administrative and legal order subject to change by legislation, to which the organized activities of the administrative staff, which are also controlled by regulations, are oriented. This system of order claims binding authority, not only over the members of the state, the citizens, most of whom have obtained membership by birth, but also to a very large extent over all action taking place in the area of its jurisdiction. It is thus a compulsory organization with a territorial basis. Furthermore, today, the use of force

is regarded as legitimate only so far as it is either permitted by the state or prescribed by it.... The claim of the modern state to monopolize the use of force is as essential to it as its character of compulsory jurisdiction and continuous operation.

Conceptually the "state" is ... not indispensable to any economic activity. But an economic system, especially of the modern [capitalist] type, could certainly not exist without a legal order with the very special features which could not develop except in the frame of a public legal order.... The tempo of modern business communications requires a promptly and predictably functioning legal system, i.e., one which is guaranteed by the strongest coercive power.... The universal predominance of the market consociation requires on one hand a legal system the functioning of which is *calculable* in accordance with rational rules. On the other hand, the constant expansion of the market ... has favoured the monopolization and regulation of all "legitimate" coercive power by *one* universalist coercive institution....

(g) Rights and Social Movements Counter-Hegemonic Strategies‡

Alan Hunt

GRAMSCI: INTRODUCTORY REMARKS

There has been surprisingly little explicit attention paid to the implications of Gramsci's theoretical and political thought for the understanding of law.

Gramsci's unique contribution to Marxist theory stems from his criticism of the economistic versions of Marxism that had become institutionalized by the beginning of the twentieth century. This led him to a central concern with ideology. The most distinctive feature of Gramsci's account of ideology was the

† Excerpts from Max Weber, *Economy and Society: An Outline of Interpretive Sociology* [from German 4th ed., 1956], ed. and trans. by G. Roth and C. Wittich et al. (New York: Bedminster Press, 1968) at 54, 56, and 336–37. Reproduced with permission of University of California Press.

‡ (Autumn 1990) 17:3 J.L. & and Society at 310–17. Journal of Law and Society by Blackwell Publishing Ltd. Reproduced with permission of Blackwell Publishing Ltd. via Copyright Clearance Center.

break with Marx's conception of ideology as "ideology," that is, as a *Weltanschauung*, a coherent worldview, intellectually developed and at the same time informing the consciousness of active social classes.

The work that Gramsci does on Marx's concept of ideology is fivefold. Focus is shifted from the intellectual plane of philosophical systems to the formation of popular consciousness of common sense. Second, there is less emphasis on ideology as "system," as integrated or coherent. Third, ideological struggle is viewed, not as titanic struggles between rival *Weltanschauungen*, but as practical engagements about shifts and modifications in "common sense," or popular consciousness. Fourth, is the emphasis on ideologies as active processes that "'organize' human masses and create the terrain on which men [*sic*] move, acquire consciousness of their position, struggle, etc." (Gramsci 1971: 377).[1] Fifth, his conception of ideology is positive while Marx's was negative. For Marx ideology blocked and distorted, while for Gramsci it provided the very mechanisms through which participation in social life was possible.

HEGEMONY: FROM IDEOLOGY TO POLITICAL STRATEGY

The far-reaching implications of Gramsci's development of the concept of hegemony is that, on the one hand, it makes it possible to grasp the connection between the ways in which social consciousnesses are formed and the exercise of political (or class) rule under conditions of high level of popular consent. On the other hand, it provides the key to the strategy of revolutionary political change in "the West." Gramsci's concept of hegemony was developed as he grappled with this dual project of elaborating the mechanisms whereby modern capitalism succeeded in securing its continued role under conditions of relative social stability, while he searched for appropriate political strategies capable of securing the opening up of a transition to socialism under these characteristic conditions of capitalist rule in "the West."

Hegemony is the process that generates

> the 'spontaneous' consent given by the great mass of the population to the general direction imposed on social life by the dominant fundamental group [historical bloc]. (1971: 12)

Hegemony is thus an active process involving the production, reproduction, and mobilization of popular consent. But it should be noticed that Gramsci's focus is on the securing of "leadership" and "direction" by the dominant bloc rather than upon the more passive idea of consent itself.

The hegemonic or historical bloc can never constitute its leadership by simply articulating the immediate interests of its own constituents. One of the most important corollaries of Gramsci's conception of hegemony is that for a hegemonic project to be dominant it must address and incorporate, if only partially, some aspects of the aspirations, interests, and ideology of subordinate groups. This "incorporative hegemony" creates the opportunity to move away from the sometimes narrow class-reductionism of Marx's account of politics (that is, the ruling class conceived as deploying the instrumentality of state and law to advance, impose, and protect its own class interests).

A number of quite distinctive mechanisms are involved in the processes whereby "incorporative hegemony" installs the presence of subordinate interests within the dominant hegemony. First, a successful hegemony needs to incorporate values and norms that contribute to securing the minimum standards of social life. Second, the process by which, as a result of actual struggle or the apprehension of it, a dominant bloc engages in a more or less self-conscious "compromise" to incorporate some element of the interests of a subordinate group. Frequently a "compromise" is inflected toward the interests and values of the dominant bloc. An important example of this process is the way in which the institutionalization of welfare provisions has been incorporated not in the form of generalized or universal rights, but in forms that tend toward the degradation of the "client" who is transformed in minute ways into a supplicant.

A third and more complex process is the way in which a dominant hegemony will articulate values and norms in such a way that they take on significant trans-class appeal. While, for example, the content of law in capitalist societies protects and legitimizes property relations, it is of considerable significance that the most visible form of property law, in the criminal law of theft, provides both protection and legitimation for the widest form of "private property" in consumption goods. The effect is not only to obscure the fundamental distinction between capital and consumption goods, but even more importantly, it valorizes property in the most general form in which it is held by the whole population.

Gramsci identified a number of different stages or levels of hegemony. These have special relevance with respect to the formation of counter-hegemony, that is, the process by which subordinate classes challenge the dominant hegemony and seek to supplant it by articulating an alternative hegemony. The most salient aspect is that subordinate groups will tend to articulate only their immediate interests. His most important illustration was that trade unions tend first to succeed in gaining influence over the immediate circle of those sharing common circumstances of work; in so doing they articulate a "corporate consciousness" that focuses on their shared interests, but this may coexist with the presence of a rivalry against some other group of workers (for example, maintenance of wage differentials *vis-à-vis* some other group, or men over women, or skilled over unskilled, and so on). An important feature of Gramsci's antieconomism was his insistence on the political and intellectual limitations of corporatist consciousness. While Gramsci was at pains to stress that the "stages" that he identified were not simply sequential or developmental, his second stage, "class economic-corporate," widened the scope of consciousness to focus on the common interests of the class and thus required deliberate strategies to overcome sectional interests.

The most important and distinctive stage is that of "hegemonic consciousness," whose key characteristic is the emergence of political and ideological projects that seek to develop the capacity to integrate purely class aspirations with the achievement of leadership over other subordinate groups by taking up and integrating the interests of those other groups and classes along with those of the working class, which was his primary point of reference. Such a project implied the necessity of foregoing or at least varying immediate class interests in order to bind in more closely other social forces. Illustrations of such hegemonic practices would be the need to challenge long-established trade unions' chauvinist practices, which excluded or marginalized women workers, or to restrict wage demands in order to construct alliances with consumers or with other classes. The general characteristic of hegemonic practices is the increasingly conscious projection of a subordinate class to aspire to national leadership by seeking a common articulation of popular interests and of popular culture; for this project Gramsci coined the concept of the "national-popular."

Gramsci's treatment of hegemony is premised on his traditional Marxist preoccupation with the primacy of the working class and the concern with the Leninist problematic of "the Party" as the agent of hegemonic transformation. I want to suggest that the concept of hegemony remains pertinent even when one displaces the traditional Marxist unitary agency of the class/party. A contemporary politics oriented toward social transformation through a more pluralistic conception of agency will still require expression at the level of the nation/state through the medium of political parties even though one conceives of such a party representing hegemonic projects forged within civil society and constituted through alliances and coalitions of social movements. This displacement of the unitary conception of party/class suggests that it may be valuable to make use of a concept of "local hegemony." This is a potentially useful "new" concept specifying the construction of some hegemonic project within some particular area or region of social life. For example, one could readily envisage the realization of a radically transformed sexual division of labor as a hegemonic project of women's movements, but one that is not necessarily linked to any specific form of political transformation.

WHAT IS COUNTER-HEGEMONY?

One of the more important themes that marks more clearly than any other Gramsci's theoretical (if not political) rupture with the Marxism of both Marx and, more significantly, of Lenin is the contention that in "the West" the working class must first become "hegemonic" in the sense of securing a generalized leadership over a decisive majority, including classes and social groups outside the working class. Gramsci identifies the conditions under which hegemony is attained when

> one's own corporate interests ... transcend the corporate limits of the purely economic class, and can and must become the interests of other subordinate social groups. This ... marks the decisive passage from the structure to the sphere of complex superstructures ... bringing about not only a unison of economic and political aims, but also an intellectual and moral unity, posing all the questions around which struggle rages not on a corporate but on a 'universal' plane, and thus creating the hegemony of a fundamental group over a series of subordinate groups. (1971: 181–82)

I will return below to elaborate on Gramsci's suggestion that the achievement of hegemony requires a transition from the posing of issues in "corporate" terms to their transformation onto a "universal" plane.

It is important to stress that counter-hegemony is not some purely oppositional project conceived of as if it were constructed "elsewhere," fully finished and then drawn into place, like some Trojan horse of the mind, to do battle with the prevailing dominant hegemony. Without such an understanding the quest for counter-hegemony can only be a continuation of that which the concept seeks to displace, namely, the search for a unitary political subject that needs simply to achieve consciousness of itself to be able to challenge the dominant hegemony.

The alternative to this scenario is a conception of counter-hegemony that has to start from that which exists, which involves starting from "where people are at." Such a conception of counter-hegemony requires the "reworking" or "refashioning" of the elements that are constitutive of the prevailing hegemony. Gramsci himself made this important point in the following way:

> [I]t is not a question of introducing from scratch a scientific form of thought into everyone's individual life, but of renovating and making 'critical' an already existing activity. (quoted in Larrain 1983: 84)

This is real, practical activity that involves a number of different elements whose mixture can only be identified concretely, but some of whose characteristics can be sketched. One step is to "supplement" that which is already in place; to add to or extend an existing discourse.

Beyond this first step, characterized by the paradox that it is necessary to struggle to achieve that which is already proclaimed within the hegemonic discourse, is the importance of opening up its "silences." The struggle for votes for women attests to both the difficulty and the importance of the opening up of the discourse of "manhood" suffrage that dominated so much of the nineteenth century to the exclusion of half the population.

The most significant stage in the construction of counter-hegemony comes about with the putting into place of discourses, which while still building on the elements of the hegemonic discourses, introduce elements which transcend that discourse. The struggle for trade union rights is a classical exemplification; starting on the terrain of traditional elements of individual rights (of speech and association) this struggle inserted the [transcendent] presence of social and collective rights. And this example serves to illustrate another very important issue. A Leftist reading of counter-hegemony often involves strategies that are directed at negating or reversing the existing hegemony; for example, in the rights debate one encounters the opposition between individual and collective rights in a form in which "individual rights" are opposed in order to replace them by "social" or "collective" rights. The emphasis on counter-hegemony as a [transcendent] project involves a

line of thought that does not negate that which exists, but strives to construct, in Gramsci's terms, "good sense" from "common sense" and in this way to prioritize or valorize those elements or features that are "new." The effect of such a process ends up with the dying away or exhaustion of elements once dominant. In the eighteenth century and through the first half of the nineteenth, the connection between the franchise and property constituted the common sense of the dominant political discourse; the struggle for the extension of the franchise created a context in which any attempt made today to reestablish a link between the right to vote and a property qualification would seem entirely anachronistic and to fly in the face of common sense.

The insistence on the *contested* nature of hegemony applies with even greater force to counter-hegemony. It follows that the process is never either incremental or evolutionary, but it involves both changes of direction, that is, advances and retreats, as well as changes in pace. Gramsci effectively displaces the notion of "crisis" from the economic realm and redirects attention to the importance of "hegemonic crisis." The political and theoretical significance of this innovation is that capitalism is no longer conceived as having any necessary economic tendency to "break down"; in its place, attention is directed to the circumstances under which a dominant bloc may experience a "hegemonic crisis" either as a result of some circumstances internal to its own project or as a result of a rapid advance of counter-hegemonic forces that has the result of undermining the previously secured leadership of the dominant bloc such that it is no longer able to rule in the old way.

It is probably necessary to go beyond Gramsci's own account of hegemonic crisis and to suggest another possibility. The contest of hegemonic projects can result in circumstances in which they "block" each other. One form of such a blockage could be the kind of circumstances in which no historical bloc is able to achieve hegemony and which thus opens up the opportunity for the kind of exceptional outcome that Gramsci labeled "Caesarism." But another scenario could be where one element of the dominant hegemony may be of such paramount significance that it blocks or inhibits change and development within the dominant hegemony itself. For example, the priority within Catholic theology of the injunction against birth control impedes any process of doctrinal modernization over the whole range of reproductive and familial policies. Alternatively the strength and near fixity of some element in the dominant hegemony may have such wide-ranging repercussions as to block the development of a counter-hegemonic project; for example, the centrality that Islam accorded to gender segregation may have succeeded, for the present at least, in blocking the modernizing and secularizing thrust unleashed during the overthrow in 1979 of the Shah in Iran.

This consideration of "blocked hegemony" leads to the suggestion that one possible objection to the pursuit of a rights strategy, at least in the United States, is that the association established within the dominant hegemony between "liberty" and "rights" has such a central role so as to block the extension of a discourse of rights to the kind of broadening that would encompass social and collective rights and thus to impede significantly, if not block, a progressive rights strategy. These reflections on "blocked hegemony" are tentative and for this reason I will not pursue this potential objection further, save to suggest that it may be worthy of future consideration.

Although neither hegemony nor counter-hegemony is a concept used by Foucault, a Foucauldian approach can be helpful in emphasizing the "small" or microconstituents that constitute "shifts" in the dominant hegemony or in a developing counter-hegemony. Where I suggest Foucault is lacking is in his almost complete failure to address the strategic question of the cumulative connections between the elements of micropolitics that are essential if a counter-hegemony is to succeed in displacing an existing hegemonic bloc. For Gramsci the realization of counter-hegemony is necessarily a "project" involving intention and agency on the part of specific social actors. This role he assigned to "the Modern Prince," his coded reference to "the Party." There is no necessity that this role be attributed to a single party nor to make any particular assumptions about the relationship between parties and classes. But what is important is the contention that political parties exemplify a "strategic" capacity; it is for this reason that this chapter concerns itself with "counter-hegemonic strategies." Strategies involve the idea of a special role for social agents that sustain a commitment to a self-conscious reflexivity about the conditions and possibilities of transformative politics.

One of the most important features of any such strategic project is the concern to find ways of going beyond the limited expression of the immediate interests of social groups, Gramsci's "corporate stage," such that they connect up with and find ways of articulating the aspirations of wider constituencies.

GRAMSCI: LAW BETWIXT STATE AND CIVIL SOCIETY

It is not my intention to embark on a consideration of Gramsci's suggestive but tantalizingly underdeveloped comments on law. Rather my present concerns are to comment on a number of its features that are pertinent to a consideration of the connection between hegemony and rights strategies.

The first feature to be noted is the location that Gramsci attributes to law within his social topography. He locates hegemony at the intersection of state and civil society. This is precisely the location in which he places law. Law combines coercion and consent or persuasion. Law is closely tied to the processes of securing an equilibrium between "state" and "civil society"; on the one hand, law lends authoritative legitimations to the norms and projects through which the state seeks to govern civil society; but, on the other hand, law has a degree of responsiveness to civil society where state law provides a facilitative framework for private transactions and those dimensions of public law that provide mechanisms of public accountability and surveillance.

One of Gramsci's most distinctive motifs is the connection that he points to between "law" and "education." He suggests that law "renders the ruling group homogeneous" (1971: 195). The leadership of the hegemonic bloc is never automatic, but rather it constantly needs to secure its own coherence and unity. Legal norms, and the values that underlie these norms, are not only mobilized and reinforced, but they are linked and connected in a way that helps to secure their coherence. Gramsci gives a different inflection to the educative role of law when he refers to the idea that law serves the role of "assimilating the entire grouping to its most advanced fraction" and that it results in a "social conforming" (1971: 195). This is a more conventional sense of education since it involves the idea of transmission from an originating subject, from the hegemonic bloc to its allies. This I suggest is exactly the same process that Foucault calls a "discursive formation"; it puts in place a set of values, renders them coherent, but most importantly, they become *material* in providing an active framework in the sense that what law proscribes as self-evidently "wrong" and what it valorizes tend to become perceived as how things should be.

The feature of Gramsci's comments on law that connects most closely with my present concern is the very specific way in which he envisaged the "struggle over law" developing in the struggle for socialism. He conceived the struggle for the control of law as involving the need for subordinate classes to become "legislators" by achieving authoritative, norm-creating capacity (1971: 265–66). What is needed in order to develop this line of thought is not so much the focus on the struggle for substantive law reform, but rather to focus on the connection between law as an arena of struggle and the development of hegemonic structures in which law reform has a part to play. The

remaining sections of this chapter seek to contribute to just such a strategic line of enquiry.

Note

1. [The references in the text to "Gramsci (1971)" and "(1971)" are from eds./trans. Quentin Hoare and Geoffrey Nowell-Smith, *Selections from the Prison Notebooks of Antonio Gramsci* (London: Lawrence & Wishart, 1971).]

(h) General Idea of the Revolution in the Nineteenth Century†

Pierre-Joseph Proudhon

NOTE

Many conventional liberal political theorists, such as Locke and Mill, placed the role of the State at the centre of their writings. Even revolutionary theorists, such as Marx and Gramsci, focused on the role, nature, and place of the State in society. The concept of the State has always been a central yet contested notion, so it is perhaps not surprising that some reject the State entirely. Pierre-Joseph Proudhon was a nineteenth century social theorist who famously declared *"La propriété, c'est le vol!* (Property is theft!): Pierre-Joseph Proudhon, *What is Property? An Inquiry into the Principle of Right and of Government* [1840], translated by Benj. R. Tucker (New York: Humboldt Publishing Company, 1890). Anarchists like Proudhon reject a place for the law, government, or State authority as a means of establishing order in society: Ian McLean and Alistair McMillan, *Oxford Concise Dictionary of Politics* (Oxford: Oxford University Press, 2003) at 14. Instead, anarchists prefer the mutualism of a self-regulated society and freely associated groups to a social order enforced by the State: Tom Bottomore (ed.), *A Dictionary of Marxist Thought*, (Cambridge: Harvard University Press, 1983) at 18–19. What implications do these ideas hold for governmental authority, law, and constitutional order? Can a peaceful and well-ordered modern society ever exist without the

coercion imposed by the State? When reading the following passage, consider whether the State is truly based on a contract between individuals that creates a sovereign, or on a contract between individuals and the sovereign directly that seeks to preserve domestic tranquillity.

EXTRACT

1.   THESIS. — ABSOLUTE AUTHORITY.

.   .   .   .

The first form under which the principle [of government] is manifested is that of absolute power. This is the purest, the most rational, the most efficient, the most straightforward, and taken altogether, the least immoral and the least disagreeable form of government.

But absolute power, in its simplest expression, is odious to reason and to liberty: the feeling of the people is always aroused against it: following feeling, revolt makes its protest heard. Then the principle of authority is forced to retire: it retires step by step, by a series of concessions, each one more insufficient than the other, of which the last, pure democracy, or direct government, ends in the impossible and the absurd. The first term of the series then being Abso-

† Excerpts from Pierre-Joseph Proudhon, *General Idea of the Revolution in the Nineteenth Century* [1851], translated by John Beverly Robinson (London, U.K.: Freedom Press, 1923).

lutism, the last fateful term is Anarchy, in every sense.

We are about to pass in review, one after the other, the principal terms of this great evolution.

Humanity asks its masters: Whence these pretensions of yours to reign over me and govern me?

They answer: Because society cannot dispense with order: because in a society it is necessary there should be some who obey and labor, while others give orders and directions: because, individual faculties being unequal, interests opposite, passions antagonistic, the advantage of one opposed to the general advantage, some authority is needed which shall assign the boundaries of rights and duties, some arbiter who will cut short conflicts, some public force which will put into execution the judgments of the sovereign. The power of the State is just this discretionary authority, this arbiter who renders to each what is his, this force which assures that the peace shall be respected. Government, in a word, is the principle and guaranty of social order: that is what both nature and common sense tell us.

This explanation has been repeated since the origin of societies. It is the same at all epochs, and in the mouth of all powers. ...

Thus Government, in its unmodified nature, presents itself as the absolute, necessary, *sine qua non* condition of order. For that reason it always aspires toward absolutism, under all disguises; in fact, according to the principle, the stronger the Government, the nearer order approaches perfection. These two notions then, government and order, are in the relation to each other of cause of effect: the cause is Government, the effect is Order. It is thus that primitive societies have reasoned. ...

But this reasoning is none the less false ... [T]here are many ways of conceiving order; but who has proved to us that order in a society is what its masters choose to call it?

. . . .

... Well, sovereigns, with your crowns, robes and fasces, that is precisely what is meant by the social question; and you think to solve it with club and bayonet! Saint Simon was quite right in regarding the words government and military as synonyms. Government cause order in society? It is like Alexander untying the Gordian knot with his sword!

Who then, shepherds of the public, authorizes you to think that the problem of opposition of interests and inequality of faculties cannot be solved; that the distinction of classes necessarily springs from it; and that, in order to maintain this natural and provi-

dential distinction, force is necessary and legitimate? I affirm, on the contrary, and all they whom the world calls Utopians, because they oppose your tyranny, affirm, with me, that the solution can be found. Some believe that they have found it in the community, others in association, yet others in the industrial series. For my part, I say that it is found in the organization of economic forces, under the supreme law of Contract. Who can assure you that none of these hypotheses is true?

. . . .

Consider, moreover, that if the social contract can be solved between two producers, — and who doubts terms? — it can as well be solved among millions, as it relates always to a similar engagement; and that the number of signatures adds nothing to it, while making it more and more effective. Your plea of inability then does not exist, it is ridiculous, and you are left without excuse.

However that may be, listen, men of power, to the words of the Producer, the proletarian, the slave, of him whom you expect to force to work for you: I demand neither the goods nor the money of anybody; and I am not disposed to allow the fruit of my labor to become the prey of another. I, also, want order, as much as they who are continually upsetting it by their alleged government; but I want it as the result of my free choice, a condition for my labor, a law of my reason. I will not submit to it coming from the will of another, and imposing sacrifice and servitude upon me as preliminary conditions.

2. LAWS.

What with the impatience of the people, and the imminence of revolt, the Government must yield. It has promised institutions and laws; it has declared that its most fervent desire was that each one should enjoy the fruit of his labor under his own vine and fig tree. This was a necessity of its position. From the time that the Government presented itself as the judge of what was right, as the sovereign arbiter of destinies, it could not pretend to drive men at its own good pleasure. King, President, Directory, Committee, Popular Assembly, it matters not: power must have rules of conduct: how can it establish discipline among its subjects without them? How can citizens conform to orders, if they are not notified of what the orders are; or if the orders are revoked when scarcely announced; if they change from day to day, from hour to hour?

So the Government must make laws; that is to say, place limits for itself; for whatever is a rule for the citizen is a limit for the ruler. It must make as many laws as it finds interests; and, as interests are innumerable, relations arising from one another multiply to infinity, and antagonism is endless, law-making must go on without stopping. Laws, decrees, edicts, ordinances, resolutions, will fall like hail upon the unfortunate people. After a time the political ground will be covered with a layer of paper, which the geologists will put down among the vicissitudes of the earth as the papyraceous formation. The Convention in three years one month and four days passed eleven thousand six hundred laws and decrees: the Constituent and Legislative Assemblies passed as many: the Empire and the Governments that followed continued the work. at present, the Bulletin of Laws contains, it is said, more than fifty thousand: if our representatives do their duty, this enormous figure will soon be doubled. Do you suppose that the people, or even the Government itself, can keep their reason in this labyrinth?

Certainly we are already far from the primitive institution. It is said that the Government fills the part of father in Society; but what father ever made an agreement with his family, or granted a charter to his children, or arranged a balance of power between himself and their mother? The head of a family is inspired by his heart in his government: he does not rob his children; he supports them by his labor: guided by his love, he thinks only of their interests and circumstances: his will is their law, and all, mother and children, have confidence in it. The little State would be doomed if paternal action encountered the least opposition, if it were limited in its prerogatives or determined in advance in its effects. What! can it be true that Government is not a father to the people, since it submits to regulations, compromises with its subjects, and makes itself the slave of a rule, which, whether divine or popular, is not its own?

If this is so, I do not see why I myself should submit to this law. Who guarantees to me its justice, its sincerity? Whence comes it? Who made it? Rousseau teaches in unmistakeable terms, that in a government really democratic and free the citizen, in obeying the law, obeys only his own will. But the law has been made without my participation, despite my absolute disapproval, despite the injury which it inflicts upon me. The State does not bargain with me: it gives me nothing in exchange: it simply practises extortion upon me. Where then is the bond of conscience, reason, passion or interest which binds me?

But what do I say? Laws for one who thinks for himself, and who ought to answer only for his own actions; laws for one who wants to be free, and feels himself worthy of liberty? I am ready to bargain, but I want no laws. I recognize none of them: I protest against every order which it may please some power, from pretended necessity, to impose upon my free will. Laws! We know what they are, and what they are worth! Spider webs for the rich and powerful, steel chains for the weak and poor, fishing nets in the hands of the Government.

You say that you will make but few laws; that you will make them simple and good. That is indeed an admission. ...

Few laws! Excellent laws! It is impossible. Must not the Government regulate all interests, and judge all disputes; and are not interests, by the nature of society, innumerable; are not relations infinitely variable and changeable? How then is it possible to make few laws? How can they be simple? How can the best law be anything but detestable?

You talk of simplification. But if you can simplify in one point, you can simplify in all. Instead of a million laws, a single law will suffice. What shall this law be? *Do not to others what you would not they should do to you: do to others as you would they should do to you.* That is the law and the prophets.

But it is evident that this is not a law; it is the elementary formula of justice, the rule of all transactions. Legislative simplification then leads us to the idea of contract, and consequently to the denial of authority. In fact, if there is but a single law, if it solves all the contradictions of society, if it is admitted and accepted by everybody, it is sufficient for the social contract. In promulgating it you announce the end of government. What prevents you then from making this simplification at once?

. . . .

EPILOGUE

. . . .

... To be **Governed** is to be kept in sight, inspected, spied upon, directed, law-driven, numbered, enrolled, indoctrinated, preached at, controlled, estimated, valued, censured, commanded, by creatures who have neither the right, nor the wisdom, nor the virtue to do so.... To be **Governed** is to be at every operation, at every transaction, noted, registered, enrolled, taxed, stamped, measured, numbered, assessed, licensed, authorized, admonished, forbidden, reformed, corrected, punished. It is, under the pretext of public utility, and in the name of the general interest, to be placed under contribution, trained, ransomed, exploited, monopolized, extorted, squeezed, mystified, robbed; then, at the slightest resistance, the first word of complaint, to be repressed, fined, despised, harassed, tracked, abused, clubbed, disarmed, choked, imprisoned, judged, condemned, shot, deported, sacrificed, sold, betrayed; and, to crown all, mocked, ridiculed, outraged, dishonored. That is government; that is its justice; that is its morality. And to think that there are democrats among us who pretend that there is any good in government; Socialists who support this ignominy, in the name of Liberty, Equality, and Fraternity; proletarians who proclaim their candidacy for the Presidency of the Republic! Hypocrisy! ...

Administrative Law Structure and Action

(a) Administrative Law Structure and Action

David W. Elliott

INTRODUCTION

Definitions

Administrative law is the law that relates to the administrative process. The administrative process includes those bodies that exercise statutory, prerogative, or other governmental power[1] on behalf of the state.[2] Administrative law usually operates at a more specific, day-to-day level than constitutional law, which deals with the ground rules of government and society. But administrative law must still operate within the framework of constitutional law, and both are aspects of public law, the law relating to the state and its relationship with society. And the state? We have already seen that there are as many ways of viewing the state as there are social goals and philosophies.[3] For this discussion, the state will be defined as the institution that exercises sovereign power and purports to act on behalf of the "public" in a given geographical area. It will be equated, roughly, with government.

Themes

Administrative law has two sides, one concerned with doing the jobs of government efficiently, and the other with doing them fairly. The first is the "positive" side, concerned with the performance of government action, and the second is the "negative" or control side, concerned to ensure that government does what it is supposed to do, without causing undue harm. Both sides are vital to administrative law; indeed, the underlying challenge of administrative law is to find the best balance between the two. Embedded in this policy challenge are institutional questions. For example, who in government should set the balance on a daily basis? And who should control it?

Theories

How this balance is set will vary with the immediate context, prevailing social needs, and the social goals of the observer. Although the first two factors are amenable to empirical study, the last is partly a matter of subjective opinion. Administrative law — like virtually all other fields of law — is coloured by the values of those who describe it. Sometimes these values are expressed in unarticulated preferences, as when a writer describes a court action as "interventionist" or "robust", without saying why. At other times, they may take the more elaborate form of competing concepts or theories of state, law, or power. Some of the possible theoretical approaches will be identified here.[4]

First, a person's view of the balance between fairness and efficiency may be influenced by his or her concept of the main role of the state. In the last chapter, we saw several possible key state roles. For example, depending on the philosopher, the state may be seen as a facilitator of collective interests, of private interests, of citizen control, or of equality. From this, one can see how supporters of a strong collectivist state[5] could set the balance differently from those who are not.

Second, administrative law approaches can vary according to an observer's concept of law. It may not be difficult to get consensus on a lowest-common-denominator description of law. For example, law can be referred to as a body of rules enforceable in the courts.[6] But people are likely to feel that there is more than this to law. And at this point, consensus tends to break down.

On one side is the philosophical perspective of legal positivism. This approach stresses the primacy of statutes, and tends to allocate an auxiliary, interpretive role to courts.[7] That view must be qualified in Canada, where ordinary statutes are subordinate to formal written constitutional documents.[8] But virtually all positivists insist on the legal importance of statutory texts. They are also likely to reject the proposition that courts can invalidate legislation on the basis of moral principles that lie beyond the text of any written constitutional enactment.[9]

Opposing positivism are two alternative perspectives, one linked to "natural law" and the other based on legal "realism". The first of these views is that judges and others can rely on a set of unwritten, but distinct and objective, principles to invalidate offending government decisions and laws.[10] These principles used to be attributed to a universal law of nature or divine wisdom.[11] Today, they are more likely to be found in traditional, constitutional, moral, or common sense notions of fairness and reasonableness.[12] The natural law approach says that judges must be free to look beyond written texts — whether statutory or constitutional — in order to administer these higher principles of justice.[13]

The third perspective is both anti-positivist and anti-natural law in character. This is the realist notion that law is the expression of social and power relationships, which are often disguised as objective norms.[14] Legal realism distrusts objective-sounding legal categories. It focuses on the social context that surrounds legal rules.[15]

These contrasting perspectives can support different approaches to the role of courts in administrative law. Until the 1970s, for example, most judicial review of non-procedural administrative action[16] could be described as a specialized form of statutory interpretation, supplemented by rebuttable presumptions against certain kinds of arbitrary behaviour.[17] Today, courts stress not only legislative intent but also their own responsibility to uphold the rule of law.[18] Statutory wording is still important, but courts pay much more attention to identifying and weighing competing contextual factors, such as administrative expertise.[19] In recent years, they have asserted the power to invalidate administrative decisions and enabling legislation

that violate unwritten legal constitutional norms.[20] Have realism and natural law gained ground on positivism?

A third set of differences can result from different concepts of power allocation and control within government. Traditionalists tend to emphasize the roles of the traditional power centres — the legislature and the courts.[21] Pluralists will draw attention to centres of law-making and control within the administrative process[22] and to instruments of governance outside government.[23] Functionalists will stress that powers should be allocated according to the branch or unit of government that is best suited to perform a particular task.[24]

Individual theorists may draw on more than one of the above approaches in formulating concepts, theories, or critical outlooks on administrative law. One such writer was the 19th century constitutional lawyer Albert Venne Dicey. Dicey's formulations of sovereignty of Parliament and the rule of law have had an enduring if controversial impact on Canadian law.[25] Another was Canadian academic John Willis, who wrote in the early and middle part of the 20th century. Willis strongly opposed Dicey's emphasis on legal rules and on traditional control bodies such as the courts. Instead, Willis preferred a realist, functionalist, and pluralist approach to administrative law.[26]

When you look at the administrative law structures, principles, and proposals examined in the following pages and chapters, keep in mind their subjective component. Theories attempt to represent aspects of reality, but administrative and constitutional reality has an inevitable foundation in personal values. Which of the theories and values above seem to underlie the main current approaches in Canada to balancing fairness and efficiency? Which of these has been getting more significant in recent decades? Which, in your view, should be most important?

Structure

Administrative law is concerned mainly with the executive branch of government. The executive is the branch of government whose characteristic function is to initiate and administer policy and law and to administer the assets of the state. It can be contrasted with the legislative branch, whose characteristic functions are to represent the interests of the electorate, to monitor the executive branch, and to formally enact law; and with those of the judiciary, to resolve disputes according to law and to interpret and develop law. Despite these differences, though, there are significant overlaps between all three branches, especially the executive and legislative branches.

The main components of the executive branch are the cabinet and the individual ministers of the Crown, central bodies to coordinate government policy, finance, and employment,[27] the traditional departments or ministries,[28] a large number of independent agencies,[29] Crown corporations,[30] and municipal corporations.[31]

Because Canada is a federal system, we have 14 separate executives: one at the federal level, 10 at the provincial level, and one each for the three territories. Municipal governments, including municipal executives, are subject to the control of parent provincial or territorial governments. The shape of individual executives may differ considerably from one jurisdiction to another.

But administrative law is not concerned only with the executive branch. It extends to the operation of legislation and policies outside governmental institutional structures, and to a variety of private or semi-private organizations that carry out public responsibilities under or subject to statute.[32] Where it is unclear how "public" an organization's powers are, it may also be unclear how far the principles of administrative law apply.

Constitutional Basics

Four constitutional principles are considered especially important to administrative law. First, government action must be authorized either by statute or (in a very small number of situations) by the royal prerogative. Beyond this, all government action penalizing or capable of negatively affecting individuals (i.e., virtually all government action) must be authorized by statute.[33] This is another way of expressing the democratic goals of representative and responsible government — that citizens should have some ultimate say in the decisions that affect them most crucially. Representative and responsible government are imperfect mechanisms, and part of the challenge in administrative law is how to deal with their imperfections. Meanwhile, though, they remain as fundamental assumptions on which our system of government is based.

Second, government action must comply with the formal part of the Canadian constitution.[34] For many years the Constitution has existed at the margins of administrative law, outlining the boundaries of our federal system. Now, though, with the addition of the *Charter*[35] we have a new constitu-

tional document that affects some areas of administrative law[36] and may extend to more in future.

Third, the statutory, prerogative, and constitutional law that authorizes or limits government action is subject to interpretation by the judiciary. In the course of their interpretation, the courts may impose additional implied restrictions from the common law. An example of these restrictions is the rules of natural justice.[37]

Fourth, those who work for government may still retain the capacity and restrictions of private individuals. Like other individuals they are free to do anything that is not forbidden by law. However, if they have acted outside their statutory authorization, they may be subject to private law actions (for example, in tort) on the same basis as other private individuals.[38]

GOVERNMENT AND ADMINISTRATION AS A PROCESS

Government is not just structure and principles — it is an ongoing process. One way to visualize that process, and the place of administrative law in it, is to look at government as a series of interrelated mandates. The voting public and the Constitution give a general mandate to the political head of the executive — the first minister and the cabinet. With the help of other parts of the executive branch, the first minister and cabinet respond to this mandate by initiating policy. Their policy is then transformed into law by the legislature. The legislature enacts specific statutes, which take the form of either rules addressed directly to the public or direct mandates addressed to the executive branch. The mandates to the executive result in administrative actions that affect the public.

Theoretically, this process completes a full circle in which the legislation and administrative action that shapes our lives has — in a general sense — been authorized by the general public as voters. The essence of courts' role in administrative law is to help ensure the integrity of the process. Their job is to determine, when asked, the extent to which the actions of the executive are authorized by legislation[39] or by the Constitution.

But the idea of a chain of mandates is only a model. To have any claim on reality, it needs qualification. First, at the initial stage, there are more inputs at work than electoral results and constitutional requirements. For example, interest groups and developments in federal-provincial relations or the international community may wield considerable non-electoral influence on government policy. Elections may have involved issues that were too broad to have much bearing on a specific policy problem. Once elected, political leaders often change their minds on policy priorities.

Second, the legislative branch has less power and responsibility than the formal model suggests. The executive branch not only initiates most policy but makes all subordinate legislation[40] and does most of the job of creating statutes. Even courts "make" law when they apply it to new situations.

Third, as noted earlier,[41] not all mandates are directed to bodies within the executive branch of government. Quasi-governmental or non-governmental bodies, such as professional associations, arbitrators, and universities, often exercise public statutory powers or discharge public duties.

The discrepancies between the formal model and these qualifications raise important questions. For example, if there are weaknesses in the electoral and legislative roles, should we be trying to strengthen non-electoral and non-parliamentary forms of control over the administrative process, such as *Charter* control or greater direct citizen participation in agencies and other government bodies? Or should we be trying to strengthen the electoral process and Parliament itself?[42] If part of the administrative process exists outside the executive branch of government, it must be asked how far administrative law principles should apply to these bodies. Existing principles of administrative law judicial control generally stop at the boundaries of public statutory power. Should they be re-designed to apply to all significant exercises of power, in the "non-governmental" parts of society as well? On the other hand, traditionalists might argue that non-governmental power is best regulated by Parliament and the administrative process, not the courts.

HISTORICAL DEVELOPMENT

At the beginning of the 19th century, the state was a relatively limited operation.[43] In the Canadian colonies most local government functions were carried out by unpaid, part-time, lower-level officers of the ordinary courts called justices of the peace. Where they did not do the work directly, the justices generally appointed or confirmed the appointment of other officials who did. As in Britain, the role of the state was seen in mainly negative terms: defence, internal peace and order (more in the hands of the

judiciary than the executive), providing such basic services as road repair and drainage, and raising the revenue to support these functions. Transportation was becoming increasingly important in both places, and by the 1820s Upper Canada, especially, was actively involved in canal-building.

In the century and a half that followed, Canada experienced a massive expansion in the role of the state in society. Government moved from the mainly negative role described above to the more positive roles of the regulatory, entrepreneurial, and welfare state.[44] Hobbes' collective state[45] was becoming a vast modern reality.

In Canada today, statutes and subordinate legislation affect virtually every aspect of our lives. Government regulates almost all private industry, from mining to communications to professional services. Through legislation, government sets standards, licenses, taxes, defends, expropriates, offers incentives and guarantees, protects, runs basic services, competes with some private enterprise, educates, inoculates, and imposes penalties. As seen, Canada has not one, but 14 legislatures engaged in the business of formal law-making. The volume is augmented still further by the by-laws of thousands of municipal corporations and by the myriad other kinds of subordinate legislation of the executive branch.

As well as enacting more laws, government has tended to spend more money. In 1867, Canadian government spending accounted for between four and 7% of the country's gross domestic product.[46] In 1916, it was 15.5%; in 1950 it was 21.3%; and in 1990, it was 47.8% of the GDP.[47] The cost cutting of the 1990s reduced this sharply, to below 40%.[48] However, by 2004 the proportion was at 41.1% of the GDP,[49] and there were indications that it would continue to rise in subsequent years.[50]

There was also a general increase in the number of government employees, especially in the executive branch of government. Government officers were required to implement most statutes and to exercise subordinate law-making powers. Even after the cutbacks of the 1990s, the total number of employees in federal, provincial, and territorial government entities constituted over one in six members of the Canadian labour force.[51]

Moreover, employment figures fall short of illustrating the true reach of Canadian government. How many additional jobs, for example, depend on government contracts? On government licences or tax expenditure incentives? On government trade tariffs or marketing programs? On government loans or assurances? How many individuals are dependent on unemployment insurance cheques? On welfare payments? On state-subsidized medical plans?

Globalization pressures and deficit and debt concerns resulted in a reduction in public employment and spending during the 1990s. However, by the beginning of the new century, most governments had won their deficit (but not debt) struggles, and were talking less of future cutbacks. There were renewed calls for increased spending in areas such as health care, and for a heightened government presence in combatting such varied ills as drinking water contamination, smog, drug trafficking, organized crime, and international terrorism. Leviathan was a little leaner, but still very much a reality.[52]

POLICY AND STRUCTURAL OPTIONS

In dealing with any given social problem, government policy-makers can choose from a great variety of different policy, structural, and compliance options in deciding how to respond to social problems. The discussion of policy options here is based on the work of two American writers, Henry Hart and Albert Sacks.[53]

Policy Options

Government policy-makers have three basic options: to do nothing, to apply coercive measures, or to resort to non-coercive measures. Doing nothing is not always the least expensive option: if there is already a bureaucratic structure in place, it may be costly to dismantle, as the proponents of deregulation have discovered.

Coercive government measures are sometimes addressed directly to the general public, requiring little government administration except to police or punish cases of non-compliance.[54] Usually a bureaucracy is required to administer the measures initially as well. This is also the case with the many government policy measures that are non-coercive.[55]

As Hart and Sacks point out, one especially important form of coercive technique is the licence.[56] A licence is a requirement of a government permission in order to carry out a desired activity. A licence generally involves individual case-by-case assessment, and usually requires large numbers of officials. Until granted, it can hold up potentially useful activity. It is generally issued on a case-by-case basis that attracts arguments that court-like protections should be imposed. This, in turn,

leads to greater formality and further delays. Failure to obtain a necessary licence or breach of the terms of an existing licence can result in penalties. The prevalence and coercive aspect of the licence might be regarded as a potential threat to individual freedom. For all these reasons, the licence may well be inappropriate where the desired government objective is considered less urgent, or where non-coercive alternatives are readily available.

On the other hand, the licence is useful in schemes for rationing limited resources, controlling monopolistic enterprises, and regulating activity on a case-by-case basis in the interests of safety or some other pressing objective. As well, it provides an effective means of collecting information and revenue. It is little wonder that the licence is the most popular single policy option used in Canada today.

Structural Options

Wherever policy makers have decided on a governmental body to help administer a measure, they must decide how to structure the body and its powers. In the first place, they must decide whether to subject the new body to the same controls as a traditional government department, or to give it greater independence. A traditional department is a hierarchical organization that is subject to the direct political control and responsibility of an elected cabinet minister, has a chief career officer known as a Deputy Minister, is funded from parliamentary estimates, and is subject to competitive examinations and a merit-based approach to hiring and promotion.[57] Today, however, much of the administrative process consists of independent agencies,[58] Crown corporations, and — at the provincial level — municipal corporations. These government bodies all exist at arms' length from direct ministerial control and the other constraints of traditional departments.

For independent agencies,[59] a driving force has been the popularity of the licence as a policy option. Wherever government awards, reconsiders, or revokes a licence, there is a general expectation that it will do so fairly, with minimum political interference. In response, agencies with adjudicatory and regulatory functions are given varying degrees and kinds of autonomy from direct ministerial and central government controls. Similarly, autonomy is considered important for bodies created to investigate government wrongdoing. These are all cases, though, where policy makers have decided to keep the adjudicating, regulating, or investigating functions within the general framework of the executive branch of government, rather than handing them over to ordinary courts.

In the case of Crown corporations, independence has been considered necessary to enable organizations with commercial or industrial functions to compete more effectively with private sector counterparts, and to reach financial targets with a degree of freedom from political constraints. Again, the Crown corporation remains part of the executive branch, although at a greater distance than the traditional department. Relative autonomy is also important for municipal corporations, where it helps to protect the electoral accountability of municipal political leaders.

As well as for serving goals of impartiality, efficiency, and local accountability, independence may be employed in the interests of hiring, spending, or organizational flexibility. For example, where adjudicatory functions are created, it is generally considered important to create non-hierarchical, relatively autonomous structures that facilitate direct participation by interested parties.

On the other hand, governments retain responsibility for all members of the executive branch, however autonomous. Some form of ministerial or central control will remain necessary in the interests of national or provincial policy and electoral accountability, and supplementary forms of control may be needed as well.

Policy makers may also choose to give the body adjudicatory functions. This is an almost inevitable result of a decision to employ some form of licence. The more adjudicatory the structure, the greater the expectation that the administrator will be subject to court-like procedural constraints. If the legislature does not apply them, reviewing courts often will. Even apart from these constraints, adjudicatory procedure tends to be slow, cumbersome, and expensive. Case-by-case attention, direct citizen participation, and procedural protection come at a price.[60]

Another important decision is where to confer rule-making power. Rules[61] are a popular and economical way of dealing with large-scale, recurring situations, and maximize consistency and predictability. On the other hand, they can be rigid and arbitrary if not carefully designed and applied. Rule-making by the administrative process is not subject to the elaborate process of cabinet scrutiny, legal drafting, and legislative publicity applied to the making of statutes,[62] yet valid formal subordinate legislation has the same legal effect as statutes, and is far more numerous than statutes. If

controls are too cumbersome, though, they could destroy flexibility and discourage the use of administrative rules in the first place.

Policy makers will also have to decide how much discretion to confer on the new body, and where. Discretion, or choice, is the essence of flexibility, and it can enable administrators to take full advantage of their expertise. On the other hand, discretion can permit inconsistency or partiality, and is far less visible than adjudicatory decisions or rules.

The decision to use an adjudicatory procedure, a rule, or discretion is often left up to the administrator himself or herself. Sometimes the enabling legislation explicitly permits this choice; often, the choice is made informally by the administrator.[63] Discretion, especially, is an option that is almost always present; the administrator almost always has an implied option of failing to exercise a power, or of failing to do so fully or immediately.[64]

Compliance Options

Where policy makers resort to coercive action to achieve their goals, they must act through laws, and be concerned to ensure that these laws are obeyed. To do this, they have a great variety of potential sanctions at their disposal. These range from the drastic sanction of imprisonment to fines and negative publicity. Where licences are involved, the sanctions may include licence suspension or revocation. Where the law is not mandatory but permissive, or where government's objective is set out only in policy, policy makers may use less coercive measures, such as public education or inducements, to try to secure compliance.[65]

The appropriateness of the sanction will depend heavily on (i) the government's (and the public's) perception of the urgency of the policy goal; (ii) the potential harm of non-compliance; and (iii) the potential adverse consequences of the sanction on other parties. With pollution control regulation, for example, policy makers may be inhibited from using severe sanctions by fear that the company might lay off workers or re-locate, contributing to unemployment and economic decline. Conversely, a penalty that is too lenient could be regarded by industry as a licence to pollute.[66]

Where policy measures are implemented by the administrative process, administrators themselves will have a discretion in selecting compliance options.[67] Where there is no formal choice, there may still be an effective informal choice. For example, an administrator might choose to delay imposing a sanction in return for a commitment from the regulated party. Informal sanction-making provides flexibility, but risks closed-door arrangements that are not contemplated in the enabling legislation and cannot be properly contested by third parties.[68] As the *Westray* story[69] suggests, it may be necessary to sacrifice some flexibility for openness.

Notes

1. Most bodies with state responsibilities must act under mandates in statutes (or subordinate legislation pursuant to statute). This is partly because state responsibilities tend to involve varying degrees of coercive power affecting individual rights, and power of this kind must normally be authorized by statute: see, for example, *Entick* v. *Carrington* (1765) 19 St. Tr. 1030, 95 E.R. 807 (K.B.). A small number of administrative bodies, such as the Passport Office, are constituted under the royal prerogative power. Government can also create bodies with the capacity to contract, allocate property interests, and distribute public funds and benefits. However, subject to the Constitution, the royal prerogative power, contractual power, and all other non-statutory power is subject to restriction by legislation. Hence virtually all bodies with state responsibilities must act either under or subject to statute.

2. This definition is not exhaustive, as some aspects of administrative law can extend outside it, not only into the so-called "private" sphere, but well beyond the more apparent concerns of the state. For example, basic procedural requirements of administrative law may be extended to membership requirements of trade unions and religious organizations. In most of these situations, though, there is a special governmental or public aspect to the power in question, and an especially severe impact on those affected by it.

3. Chapter 1, above.

4. For some of these approaches, see Alan C. Hutchinson and Patrick Monahan, eds. *The Rule of Law: Ideal or Ideology?* (Toronto: Carswell, 1987); Keith Culver, ed., *Readings in the Philosophy of Law* (Peterborough, Ont.: Broadview Press, 2000); and articles in Alan Brudner, ed., and David Dyzenhaus, book review ed., *University of Toronto Law Journal Special Issue — Essays in Honour of John Willis, Administrative Law Today: Culture, Ideas, Institutions, Processes, Values* (2005) 55:3 U.T.L.J. 1 *et seq.*

5. See, for example, the extract from Harry Arthurs, "Mechanical Arts and Merchandise": Canadian Public Administration in the New Economy (1997) 42 McGill L.J. 29, in this chapter, and also H.W. Arthurs, "Public Law in a Neoliberal Globalized World: the Administrative State Goes to Market (And Cries Wee, Wee, Wee' All The Way Home)," (2005) 55 U.T.L.J. 797. Arthurs tends to oppose strong external controls on administrative bodies, especially those imposed by the courts. He suggests that controls of this kind may be even more inappropriate for what he regards as the weakened modern administrative process.

6. This is the definition adopted tentatively in D.W. Elliott, *Introduction to Public Law Sourcebook*, 6th ed. (Concord, Ont.: Captus Press Inc., 2003) at 2. The definition will be adopted here, in the same way, as a starting point for exploring aspects of public law.

7. For general discussions of modern legal positivism, see J.L. Coleman & B. Leiter, "Legal Positivism" in D. Patterson, ed., A Companion to Philosophy of Law and Legal Theory (Oxford: Blackwell, 1996) at 241–60; Robert P. George, *The Autonomy of Law: Essays on Legal Posi-*

tivism (Oxford: Clarendon Press, 1996); and Matthew Kramer, *In Defense of Legal Positivism: Law Without Trimmings* (Oxford: Clarendon Press, 1999).

8. Note that many leading positivists — such as John Austin, Jeremy Bentham, H.L.A. Hart, Neil MacCormick, and Joseph Raz — have been from the United Kingdom, which lacks a formal written constitution. In Canada, section 52 of the *Constitution Act, 1982* says that the Constitution of Canada includes a number of constitutional documents, and says that "[t]he Constitution of Canada is the supreme law of Canada, and any law that is inconsistent with the provisions of the Constitution is, to the extent of the inconsistency, of no force or effect": *Constitution Act, 1982*, being Schedule B to the *Canada Act 1982*(U.K.), 1982, c. 11, s. 52(1). Note, though, that section 52 says the Constitution of Canada "includes" certain documents, not that it is limited to documents.

9. See, for example, Robert P. George, "Natural Law and Positive Law," in Robert P. George, ed., *The Autonomy of Law: Essays on Legal Positivism* (Oxford: Clarendon Press, 1996); Jeffrey Goldsworthy, *The Sovereignty of Parliament: History and Philosophy* (Oxford: Clarendon Press, 1999). George says that the question is not whether there is a distinct natural law independent of the Constitution, but whether it gives judges a power to enforce it: *ibid.* See also W.J. Waluchow, "The Many Faces of Legal Positivism," (1998) 48 U.T.L.J. 387, stressing the variety of approaches that bear the positivist label. One contrast is between exclusive positivists, who say that legality cannot be determined on the basis of moral criteria, and inclusive positivists, who say that legality may or may not be determined on the basis of moral criteria, depending on the particular legal system: see Matthew Kramer, "How Moral Principles Can Enter Into the Law" (2000) 6 Legal Theory 8.

10. See, for example, John Finnis, *Natural Law and Natural Rights* (Oxford: Clarendon Press, 1993); Robert P. George, ed., *Natural Law Theory: Contemporary Essays* (Oxford: Oxford University Press, 1995); Keith Culver, ed., *Readings in the Philosophy of Law* (Peterborough, Ont.: Broadview Press, 2000) Ch. 1.

11. The "right reason" of the Roman Cicero was fixed, changeless, and "derived from the nature of the universe": see excerpts from *De Legibus*, quoted in J.M. Kelly, *A Short History of Western Thought* (Oxford: Clarendon Press, 1992) at 57–57. As Kelly illustrates, Thomas Aquinas portrayed the concept of natural reason as an aspect of the divine law of God: see excerpts from writings of St. Thomas, *ibid.* at 143–44.

12. See, for example, Kelly, *ibid.* esp. ch. 9 and 10; John Finnis, *Natural Law and Natural Rights* (Oxford: Clarendon Press, 1993); and David Braybrooke, *Natural Law Modernized* (Toronto: University of Toronto Press, 2001), considering the influence of natural law concepts on classical philosophers such as Hobbes, Locke, Hume, and Rousseau. Lon Fuller, a leading American natural law proponent, argued that there is an "inner morality" of eight practical requirements — such as generality, promulgation, non-retroactivity, and clarity — that are needed to make law possible: Lon L. Fuller, *The Morality of Law*, rev'd. ed. (New Haven and London: Yale University Press, 1971).

13. In contrast, positivists tend to maintain that when moral principles are kept separate from the question of the legality of written texts, the latter can be assessed more objectively: see Frederick Schauer, "Positivism as Pariah," in Robert P. George, ed., *Natural Law Theory: Contemporary Essays* (Oxford: Oxford University Press, 1995) Ch. 2. For some of the many debates between positivists and natural law supporters, see the works on positivism and natural law referred to above; H.L.A. Hart, "Positivism and the Separation of Law and Morals" (1958) in H.L.A. Hart, ed., *Essays in Jurisprudence and Philosophy* (Oxford: Oxford University Press, 1983); H.L.A.

Hart, *The Concept of Law* (Oxford: Oxford University Press, 1961); Lon L. Fuller, *The Morality of Law* (New Haven, CT: Yale University Press, 1969); Ronald Dworkin, *Taking Rights Seriously*, rev. ed. (London: Duckworth, 1977); Joseph Raz, *Ethics in the Public Domain: Essays in the Morality of Law and Politics* (Oxford: Clarendon Press, 1994); and Chief Justice Beverley McLachlin, *Remarks of the Right Honourable Beverley McLachlin, P.C. Given at the 2005 Lord Cooke Lecture in Wellington, New Zealand December 1st, 2005* <http://www.scc-csc.gc.ca/aboutcourt/judges/speeches/UnwrittenPrinciples_e.asp>.

14. See Keith Culver, ed., *Readings in the Philosophy of Law* (Peterborough, Ont.: Broadview Press, 2000) Ch. 4. The best-known Canadian administrative law philosopher in the realist tradition was John Willis, discussed below.

 The realist school originated with American writers such as Justice Oliver Wendell Holmes, Jr., Jerome Frank, Karl Llewellyn, and Roscoe Pound. For the critical legal studies branch of realism, see Roberto Unger, "The Critical Legal Studies Movement," (1983) 95 Harvard Law Rev. 561; Allan C. Hutchinson, "Crits and Cricket: A Deconstructive Spin (Or Was It a Googly?)" in *Canadian Perspectives on Legal Theory*, R. Devlin, ed. (Toronto: Emond Montgomery, 1991). Critical feminist legal theory also has links to legal realism. It tends to look at law and other institutions in light of the power realities that affect women and gender: see, for example, Catharine A. MacKinnon, *Toward A Feminist Theory of the State* (Cambridge, Mass.: Harvard University Press, 1989).

15. For a general discussion of the impact of this approach on the Supreme Court of Canada, see Shalin M. Sugunasiri, "Contextualism: The Supreme Court's New Standard of Judicial Analysis and Accountability," (1999) 22 Dal. L.J. 126. In administrative law, an influential contextualist (and functionalist and realist) work was H. Wade MacLauchlan, "Judicial Review of Administrative Action: How Much Formalism Can We Reasonably Bear?" (1986) 36 U.T.L.J. 343. For an examples of a contextualist approach to procedural and substantive judicial review, see *Baker v. Canada (Minister of Citizenship and Immigration)*, [1999] 2 S.C.R. 817, in Chapters 4 and 5, below.

16. Traditional procedural review also has strong positivist roots: it was — and remains — a matter of rebuttable statutory interpretation. However, it draws on a conceptually distinct set of presumptions known as the rules of natural justice. These impose on administrators a sliding scale of protection, depending on statutory wording and a variety of contextual factors. Because of their conceptual autonomy and their contextual aspect, the presumptions of natural justice are a unique blend of positivist, natural law and realist elements. See further Chapter 4, below.

17. Although certain well-established forms of defect — such as fraud, malice, and bad faith — were presumed not to be authorized, the focus was on the wording of the enabling statute: see further, Chapter 5, below.

18. For example, in *Dr. Q v. College of Physicians and Surgeons of British Columbia*, [2003] 1 S.C.R. 226 at para. 22, the Supreme Court said the modern contextual approach to substantive review "inquires into legislative intent, but does so against the backdrop of the courts' constitutional duty to protect the rule of law."

19. Again, see the examples in *Baker v. Canada (Minister of Citizenship and Immigration)*, [1999] 2 S.C.R. 817, in Chapter 5, below.

20. Like natural law, the unwritten legal constitutional principles are regarded as underlying norms that can affect the interpretation and validity of ordinary statutes: see, *Reference Re Secession of Quebec*, [1998] 2 S.C.R. 217 in Chapter 12, below; *Lalonde v. Ontario (Commission de restructuration des services de santé)* (2001), 56 O.R. (3d) 577 (C.A.); Mark D. Walters, "The Common Law Constitution in Canada: Return of *Lex Non Scripta* as Fundamen-

tal Law," (2001) 51 U.T.L.J. 91. For arguments favouring unwritten principles control, see Chief Justice Beverley McLachlin, *Remarks of the Right Honourable Beverley McLachlin, P.C. Given at the 2005 Lord Cooke Lecture in Wellington, New Zealand December 1st, 2005* <http://www.scc-csc.gc.ca/aboutcourt/judges/speeches/UnwrittenPrinciples_e.asp>.

21. For a high-profile study that stresses the need to strengthen the traditional controls of the legislature over the executive, see Canada, Commission of Inquiry into the Sponsorship Program and Advertising Activities, *Who is Responsible? Fact Finding Report* (Phase 1 Fact Finding Report) and *Restoring Accountability: Recommendations, Phase 2 Report*, by Justice John H. Gomery (Ottawa: November 1, 2005) <http://www.gomery.ca/en/phase1report/ffr/index.asp>. The Gomery recommendations are discussed in Chapter 3, below. For a text that emphasizes the importance of traditional judicial control, see David Phillip Jones and Anne S. De Villars, *Principles of Administrative Law*, 4th ed. (Scarborough, Ont.: Thomson Canada, 2004).

22. For a classic example, see Harry Arthurs, *Without the Law: Administrative Justice and Legal Pluralism in Nineteenth Century England* (Toronto: University of Toronto Press, 1985), and the extract from *Without the Law* in Chapter 6, below.

23. See, for example, Roderick A. Macdonald, "Metaphors of Multiplicity: Civil Society, Regimes and Legal Pluralism" (1998) 15 Arizona J. Int. and Comparative Law 69.

24. The classic functionalist work in administrative law. See Henry Hart Jr. and Albert Sacks, *The Legal Process, Basic Problems in the Making and Application of Law* (Westbury, N.Y.: Library Foundation Press, 1984 [original, unpublished, 1958]). See also Michael Trebilcock et al., *The Choice of Governing Instrument* (Ottawa: Economic Council of Canada, 1982). The best-known Canadian functionalist was John Willis, discussed below. This tradition remains a dominant strand in Canadian academic commentary. In the special form of judicial deference to administrative expertise, functionalism became an important theme in Canadian substantive review in the 1970s: see *Transition to Modern Substantive Review* in Chapter 5, below.

25. See Albert Venn Dicey, *An Introduction to the Study of The Law of The Constitution*, 10th ed. (London: MacMillan, 1959, first published in 1895), and the discussion of Dicey's linked parliamentary sovereignty and rule of law principles in Chapter 6, below. Dicey's approach was positivist in its emphasis on legal rules and on the absence of legal limits to Parliament. However, Dicey stressed that parliament's sovereign legal power was subject to the ultimate political power of the electorate (*ibid.* at 73) and to the practical requirement of interpretation by the judiciary (413–14). Morever, Dicey's rule of law and its interplay with parliamentary sovereignty suggest that he acknowledged a necessary institutional content to the British parliamentary system in which the law operated: legislative control of the executive (413), citizen control of the legislature (73), residual state liability to ordinary legal actions (193–94), and judicial protection of individual rights (203). Subject to the Constitution of Canada and some other significant modifications, these aspects of Dicey's parliamentary sovereignty principle and rule of law continue to play a role in Canadian constitutional and administrative law today: see Chapter 6.

 For some of the voluminous and largely critical Canadian academic commentary on Dicey, see H.W. Arthurs, "Rethinking Administrative Law: A Slightly Dicey Business" (1979) 17 Osgoode Hall L.J. 1; David Sugarman, "The Legal Boundaries of Liberty: Dicey, Liberalism and Legal Science" (1983) 46 Mod. L. Rev. 102; Judith Sklar, "Political Theory and the Rule of Law," in Alan C. Hutchinson and Patrick Monahan, eds. *The Rule of Law: Ideal or*

Ideology? (Toronto: Carswell, 1987) Robert Yalden, "Deference and Coherence in Administrative Law: Rethinking Statutory Interpretation" (1988) 46 U. T. Fac. Law Rev. 136. For some academic proposals to re-shape the content of Dicey's rule of law, see articles in Part IV of Alan Brudner, ed., and David Dyzenhaus, book review ed. *supra* 4, 691 *et seq.*

26. See John Willis, "Statute Interpretation in a Nutshell" (1938) 16 Can. Bar Rev. 1; John Willis, *The Parliamentary Powers of Government Departments* (Cambridge: Harvard University Press, 1933) [Parliamentary Powers]; John Willis, "Three Approaches to Administrative Law: The Judicial, the Conceptual and the Functional" (1935) 1 U.T.L.J. 53; John Willis, "The McRuer Report: Lawyers' Values and Civil Servants' Values" (1968) 18 U.T.L.J. 351.

    For some of the (largely positive) body of Canadian commentary on John Willis, see all articles in Alan Brudner, ed. and David Dyzenhaus, *supra* note 4; Michael Taggart, "Prolegomenon to an Intellectual History of Administrative Law in the Twentieth Century: the Case of John Willis and Canadian Administrative Law" (2005) 43 Osgoode Hall L. J. 223. As shown in the articles by Taggart and others, above, Willis' views had a major impact on subsequent administrative law writers and legal developments.

27. For example, the Privy Council Office, the Public Service Commission, the Treasury Board, and the Treasury Board Secretariat.

28. For example, the Department of Indian and Northern Affairs and the Department of Foreign Affairs, formerly External Affairs at the federal level. The traditional departments are hierarchical in structure, headed by a minister and — under the minister — by a career public servant called a deputy minister. Except at the highest levels, appointments to departments are governed by a merit system based on competitive examinations and monitored by the independent Public Service Commission. The provinces have similar structures. See René Dussault and Louis Borgeat, *Administrative Law: A Treatise*, 2d ed., trans. by Murray Rankin (Toronto: Carswell, 1985), 83–99; Kenneth Kernaghan and David Siegel, *Public Administration in Canada*, 4th ed. (Scarborough, Ont.: ITP Nelson, 1999) Ch. 8; Rand Dyck, *Canadian Politics: Critical Approaches*, 4th ed. (Scarborough, Ont.: Thomson Nelson, 2004) Ch. 21.

29. For example, regulatory agencies such as the Canadian Radio-Television and Communications Commission, the National Energy Board, the Canadian Transportation Agency, and the Canada Industrial Relations Board; funding and advisory councils or commissions, and specialized bodies such as the RCMP. The independent agencies generally have collegiate memberships supported by an administrative staff. Although they are free of day-to-day ministerial control, their members are generally appointed at the discretion of cabinet for fixed terms, often of five to 10 years. Some cabinet control may also be exercised by general policy directives or review procedures. The provinces have similar structures. See *Administrative Law: A Treatise, ibid.*, at 112–40; *Public Administration in Canada, ibid.*, Ch. 10; *Canadian Politics: Critical Approaches, ibid.*

30. For example, commercial or quasi-commercial bodies such as the Canada Post Corporation and Via Rail Canada Inc., and a variety of specialized bodies such as the National Museums of Canada. These have a corporate structure, with boards of directors and chief executives generally appointed for fixed terms at the discretion of cabinet. They are generally free of day-to-day ministerial control. Provincial Crown corporations, including the large provincial hydro-electric corporations, have similar structures. See *Administrative Law: A Treatise*, *supra* note 28 at 141–60; *Public Administration in Canada, ibid.*, Ch. 9; *Canadian Politics: Critical Approaches, ibid.*

31. These exist at the provincial and territorial levels. They generally comprise an elected mayor or reeve and elected councillors, supported by an administrative staff. They vary significantly in their size, complexity, and relative independence of provincial or territorial governments. Municipal by-laws are generally subject to approval by a provincial or territorial authority, such as a municipal board. Another important local entity is the school board, whose actions are normally directed by elected trustees or commissioners, subject to ultimate provincial control. See I.M. Rogers, *The Law of Canadian Municipal Corporations*, 2d ed. [looseleaf] (Toronto: Carswell, 1987), c. I (general features of municipal corporations); *Administrative Law: A Treatise*, *supra* note 28 at 169–88 (Quebec school boards), 188–208 (Quebec municipal and regional government structures), and 208–18 (Aboriginal governmental structures under the *James Bay and Northern Quebec Agreement*, 1975).

32. For example, universities, hospitals, statutory arbitrators, professional disciplinary bodies, mixed public-private agencies such as the Canada Wheat Board, non-profit "private" bodies with public responsibilities, such as Nav Canada, and Aboriginal self-government structures.

33. *Supra* note 1, and *Reference Re Anti-Inflation Act* (1976), 68 D.L.R. (3d) 452, 502 (S.C.C.).

34. See *Constitution Act, 1982*, being Schedule B to the *Canada Act, 1982*, c. 11, s. 52(1).

35. *Canadian Charter of Rights and Freedoms*, Part I of the *Constitution Act, 1982*, ibid.

36. See *Singh*, Chapter 4, below, and *B.C. Motor Vehicles Reference*, Chapter 8, below.

37. Chapter 4, below.

38. As in *Roncarelli*, Chapter 3, below.

39. Or, exceptionally, by the royal prerogative.

40. D.C. Holland and J.P. McGowan, *Delegated Legislation in Canada* (Toronto: Carswell, 1989), c. 2. See also two earlier reports: Parliament of Canada, Standing Joint Committee of the Senate and the House of Commons on Regulations and Other Statutory Instruments, *Second Report*, Second Session of Thirtieth Parliament, 1976–77, and *Third Report*, Second Session of the Thirty-second Parliament, 1984.

41. See "Structure," above.

42. Arguably, the legislatures are hardly a spent force. Although their formal legislative functions are normally controlled by majority governments, opposition members and backbenchers still have many opportunities to criticize, publicize, and refine policy, proposed legislation, estimates, and expenditures. In a minority government period, loss of confidence in elected legislators can topple the government.

43. See generally, G.M. Craig, ed., *Lord Durham's Report* (Toronto: McClelland & Stewart, 1963) at 66–67, 77, 82–83, 99–105, and 108–09; K.G. Crawford, *Canadian Municipal Government* (Toronto: University of Toronto Press, 1954) at 22–41; and J.E. Hodgetts, *Pioneer Public Service: An Administrative History of the United Canadas, 1841–1867* (Toronto: University of Toronto Press, 1955) Ch. 2. Lord Durham said of Lower Canada that "A people can hardly be congratulated on having had at little cost a rude and imperfect administration of justice, hardly the semblance of police, no public provision for education, no lighting, and bad pavements in its cities, and [extremely inadequate facilities for transporting articles to market]" (Craig: 77). Upper Canada had spent large sums on major public works such as canals, to the detriment of roads and local facilities such as post offices and schools (82–83, 99–104). Durham described the eastern colonies as peaceful but backward, with a "mortifying" lack of good roads and schools (108–09).

44. Canada: R.I. Cheffins and R.N. Tucker, *The Constitutional Process in Canada*, 2d ed. (Toronto: McGraw-Hill, 1976) at 51–56; Canada, Law Reform Commission of Canada,

Working Paper 25: Independent Administrative Agencies (Ottawa: Supply and Services Canada, 1980) Ch. 1; D. Olsen, *The State Elite* (Toronto: McClelland & Stewart, 1980) Ch. 1; Economic Council of Canada, *Reforming Regulation* (1981); T.L. Powrie, "The Growth of Government" in T.C. Pocklington, ed., *Liberal Democracy in Canada and the United States* (Toronto: Holt, 1985) Ch. 2; G. Fry, *The Growth of Government* (London, England: Cass, 1979).

45. Thomas Hobbes, *Leviathan* [1651], ed. M. Oakshott (Oxford: Blackwell, 1947) part II. See also extracts from Hobbes in Chapter 1, above.

46. *The Globe and Mail* (21 December 1994) A-12.

47. Figures are from John C. Strick, *The Public Sector in Canada: Programs, Finance and Policy* (Toronto: Thompson Educational Publishing, 1999), compiled from Statistics Canada tables. Strick notes that before 1948, the total expenditure was expressed as the gross national product.

48. Report of March 11, 2005 interview with Niels Veldhuis, Senior Research Economist, The Fraser Institute, in Frontier Centre for Public Policy, <http://www.fcpp.org/main/publication_detail_print.php?PubID=980>.

49. Organization for Economic Cooperation and Development, "Table on Government Sector 2004: Total Government Expenditure, % of GDP", in *OECD in Figures, 2005 Edition* (17 November 2005), <http://www.ocde.p4siteinternet.com/publications/doifiles/12005061T016.xls>. See also "Government finance: Revenue, expenditure and surplus" *The Daily* (16 June 2005), <http://www.statcan.ca/Daily/English/050616/d050616a.htm>.

50. In February 2003, for example, the federal government agreed to spend an additional $41 billion on health care funding for the provinces, over a 10-year period.

51. There were 2.7 million people employed in the Canadian public sector in 2004, approximately 16% of the total 2004 Canadian labour force of 17.1 million. Although the 2.7 million figure was lower than the 2.9 million record reached in 1992, Statistics Canada observed that "[g]overnment employment has been increasing steadily since hitting a low of just over 2.5 million in 1999": see Statistics Canada, "Labour force and participation rates by sex and age group: 2004": <http://www40.statcan.ca/l01/cst01/labor05.htm> and Statistics Canada, "The Daily, Wednesday, May 25, 2005. Public sector employment," <http://www.statcan.ca/Daily/English/050525/d050525e.htm>.

52. See, for example, John C. Strick, *The Public Sector in Canada: Programs, Finance and Policy* (Toronto: Thompson Educational Publishing, 1999) Ch. 1.

53. *The Legal Process*, *supra* note 24, especially 132–34 and 870–88. For similar approaches in the Canadian context, see M. Trebilcock et al., *The Choice of Governing Instrument* (1982); and Canada, Law Reform Commission of Canada, *Working Paper 51: Policy Implementation, Compliance, and Administrative Law* (Ottawa: Law Reform Commission of Canada, 1986).

54. For example, most of tort, property, contract and criminal law.

55. For example, rewards, contracts, and the many forms of direct government action, such as education, publicity, research services, public works, public insurance, loans, and government enterprises.

56. *The Legal Process*, *supra* note 24 at 873–77. See also Canada, *Working Paper 51, Policy Implementation, Compliance, and Administrative Law*, *supra* note 53 at 40–44.

57. The term "independent agency" is generic, referring to special purpose autonomous bodies called agencies, or such names as boards, commissions, tribunals, or inquiries. Adjudicative functions are usually predominant in a body that is called a tribunal; agencies with other names may or may not have adjudicative functions. The term

"Special Operating Agency" describes a unit that is located within a traditional government department but has greater autonomy than its surrounding departmental structure.

58. See generally, Government of Canada, Privy Council Office, "Ministers and their Departments" in *Responsibility in the Constitution*, Part VI, <http://www.pco-bcp.gc.ca/default.asp?Page=Publications&Language=E&doc=constitution/toc_e.htm>; Rand Dyck, *Canadian Politics: Critical Approaches*, 4th ed. (Scarborough, Ont: Thomson Nelson, 2004) Ch. 21.

59. On the historical growth of independent agencies in Canada, see *Working Paper 25: Independent Administrative Agencies*, *supra* note 44; Canada, Law Reform Commission of Canada, *Independent Administrative Agencies* (Ottawa: Supply and Services Canada, 1985). See also H.N. Janisch, "Independence of Administrative Tribunals: In Praise of Structural Heretics" (1987) 1 Can. J. Admin. L. and Practice 1.

60. On the functional costs and benefits of adjudication, legislation, and discretion, see J. Jowell, "The Legal Control of Administrative Discretion" (1973) *Public Law* 178, below.

61. Administrative rules expressly authorized by the legislature are generally referred to as subordinate legislation. Expressly permitted by statute, subordinate legislation must also stay within the scope of its enabling statute. It can be repealed at any time by any competent statute. Subject to these restrictions, though, subordinate legislation has the same legal status as statutes and is subject to the general judicial rules of statutory interpretation. See further, D.C. Holland and J.P. McGowan, *Delegated Legislation in Canada* (Toronto: Carswell, 1989).

62. See generally, E.A. Dreidger, *The Composition of Legislation*, 2d [rev.] ed. (Ottawa: Department of Justice, 1976); Department of Justice Canada, *The Federal Legislative Process in Canada* (Ottawa: Supply and Services Canada, 1987).

63. Note, however, that there are stringent constitutional limitations on non-statutory rule-making. Rules that can impose penalties on individuals must be authorized by statute: see "Constitutional Basics," above.

64. See generally, K.C. Davis, *Discretionary Justice: A Preliminary Inquiry* (Baton Rouge, Louisiana: Louisiana State University Press, 1969).

65. A field that involves an especially wide array of coercive and less coercive options is pollution control. In addition to the sources in the notes below, see G.B. Doern, ed., *Getting it Green: Case Studies in Canadian Environmental Regulation* (Toronto: C.D. Howe Institute, 1990); D. Estrin and J. Swaigen, *Environment on Trial: A Guide to Environmental Law and Policy*, 3d ed. (Toronto: Emond Montgomery, 1993); and B. Mitchell, *Environmental Change and Challenge: A Canadian Perspective* (Toronto: Oxford University Press, 1997).

66. J.H. Strick, *The Economics of Government Regulation: Theory and Canadian Practice*, 2d ed. (Toronto: Thompson Educational, 1994) Ch. 12.

67. See Law Reform Commission of Canada, *Pollution Control in Canada: The Regulatory Approach in the 1980s* (Ottawa: Law Reform Commission of Canada, 1988) Ch. 1, noting a legislative trend toward greater administrative discretion in the choice and application of pollution control sanctions.

68. Law Reform Commission of Canada, Working Paper 51, *Policy Implementation, Compliance and Administrative Law* (Ottawa: Law Reform Commission of Canada, 1986) Chs. 4, 5.

69. See *The Westray Story* extracts below.

(b) "Mechanical Arts and Merchandise": Canadian Public Administration in the New Economy†

H.W. Arthurs

NOTE

Here and in a 2005 article, Arthurs argues that winds of technological innovation, globalization, and ideological change are battering and re-shaping traditional concepts of the administrative process and administrative law, replacing older concepts of public interest and equity with the "invisible hand" of the market. (See also H.W. Arthurs, "Public Law in a Neoliberal Globalized World: the Administrative State Goes to Market (And Cries 'Wee, Wee, Wee' All The Way Home)" (2005) 55 Univ. of Toronto L.J. 797). Arthurs says these pressures have resulted in a new administrative process: smaller, weaker, hobbled by transnational and constitutional constraints, and expected to facilitate rather than to regulate most private activity. In Arthurs' view, this new situation calls for a rethinking of old concepts of administrative law control, with their focus on keeping the state in check.

Is Arthurs' suggestion that the Canadian administrative state is in its "declining age" a little premature? Despite deregulation, downsizing and privatization in the 1990s, the administrative state is arguably still a large and vital presence in modern Canadian life. On the other hand, few can dispute Arthurs' contention that winds of change are blowing. The key questions are, where are they blowing, and how should Canadians respond?

EXTRACT

INTRODUCTION

> In the youth of a state, arms do flourish; in the middle age of a state, learning; and then both of them together for a time; in the declining age of a state, mechanical arts and merchandise.[1]

Bacon, it seems, was a better philosopher and public administrator than he was a prophet. Canada is past the age of arms which helped to define our nationhood. We appear to have put behind us the age of learning, which laid the foundations of our modern economy and society in the post-war years. But alas, now that Canada edges towards its "declining age," our economy — our "mechanical arts and merchandise" — is not flourishing. Ironically, the Canadian state we have known since the war — the welfare state — is declining precisely because the economy is not flourishing. Without a vibrant economy, we cannot afford the state we deserve; and without a healthy state, we will not have the essentials of the economy we need. The challenge for Canada is to affirm what the harsh realities and heady slogans of the "New Economy" seem to deny: the need for a dynamic private sector working in tandem with a benign and effective government. We once thought that we could count on a strong public administration to meet that challenge. The ambition of this paper is to see whether there is any likelihood that we ever can again.

From the inception of modern industrial society, and especially for the past sixty years, governments in all industrialized democracies have been served by a large and powerful administration, organized as some variant or other of Weberian bureaucracy.[2] For much of this period in most democratic countries, the leitmotif of conventional political and economic debate was where to strike the balance of power between these public bureaucracies on the one hand, and private interests and market forces on the other. In more recent iterations, however, while bureaucracy has remained the central issue, the agenda of debate has shifted considerably. From the sixties onward, critics on the left began to ask which private interests actually did benefit from the support of public administrators. Fears of regulatory capture and failures of accountability and stewardship alienated various constituencies that had been aligned with the activist state and the bureaucracies that were its agents.

---

† (1997) 42 McGill L.J. 29 at 31–36, 39–41, 45–46, and 61. Reproduced with permission of the publisher and the author. [Commentary note by David W. Elliott.]

More recently, critics on the right have begun to ask not simply whether we can cure bureaucracy, nor even whether we can afford it, but whether indeed there is much need for public administration at all.

Public law has likewise been preoccupied with bureaucracy, especially with the allocation of power and responsibility within and amongst the administrative departments and agencies of the state, and as between the executive branch of government and the legislative and judicial branches. Even the theory and practice of the modern science of management in the private sector has been much influenced by the study of public bureaucracies, the first large-scale, complex secular organizations.[3]

In short, bureaucracy — and public administration, which is its paradigmatic form — has been a site of contestation for control of some of the most important concepts and institutions in our society. But these familiar institutions and concepts — democratic government and politics, public administration and public law, corporate management, bureaucracy itself — are constructs, shaped by time, place and circumstance. They are not immutable. All are being reshaped by the advent of the New Economy.

The New Economy, itself a construct, is a compendious reference to three intersecting trends: startling developments in technology — especially information technology — and resulting changes in the social organization of work; liberalization of the economies of most western democracies, accompanied by globalization of economic activity and the growth of regional economic integration; and shifts in the boundary between the state and civil society derived in part from the fiscal and economic crises engendered by the first two phenomena but also from long-term changes in political ideology, culture and institutions.

... Public administration and public law are not likely to continue unchanged in a political economy in which traditional forms of work organization are being revised, in which important actors — principally global corporations — can evade domestic regimes of regulation, and in which growing numbers of citizens are increasingly agnostic about the fundamental premise upon which democratic public administration is built — the desirability, legitimacy, necessity and efficacy of state intervention.

The two projects of this essay, then, are to explore the impact of the New Economy on public administration as we have known it, and to consider how various strategies said to be appropriate for the reform of public administration — law, professionalism, democracy and markets — are likely to play themselves out in the context of the New Economy.

I.   THE NEW ECONOMY AND ITS IMPACT ON PUBLIC ADMINISTRATION

. . . .

A.   Changes in Technology and the Social Organization of Work

While debate continues over the exact extent, consequences and significance of the shift from fordist to post-fordist modes of production, it is clear that the social organization of work in all industrialized countries has been altered largely to the benefit of employers and the prejudice of workers. The changes usually identified with this shift include: the introduction of computer-driven technologies; the adoption of flexible manufacturing and just-in-time supply strategies supported by corporate alliances and networks of suppliers and subcontractors; a dramatic reduction in the number of industrial workers and in the power of their unions; a corresponding rise in employment in the service sector, especially in casual and non-standard employment arrangements; the decline of traditional managerial hierarchies; the rise of a corporate "technostructure" comprising experts and professionals; and the proliferation of small consultancies. For present purposes, two important implications of these changes must be identified.

First, they have largely eviscerated the paradigmatic assumptions underlying not only our collective-labour laws, but many of the public policies that operated on similar assumptions about the nature and character of our industrial economy, about the workers, families and communities such an economy might be expected to sustain, and about the social-welfare system needed to maintain the viability of a society organized around the fordist mode of production.[4] The resulting disjunctures of policy have caused great dislocation in public finance and program design, and as a result, in public administration.

Second, the social organization of work in the public sector is itself undergoing important changes similar to those observed in the private sector. Indeed, one of the most striking changes is the increasing use by public-sector managers of private-sector rhetoric, analytical tools and employment strategies.[5] Such changes are motivated, no doubt, by efficiency concerns, but also by a wish to be aligned with the dominant anti-state tendency in political discourse.

The affinities between private- and public-sector developments are considerable. State fiscal crises are made to stand proxy for global competition, as justification for hiring and wage freezes, redundancies and rollbacks. Privatization of government functions is treated as analogous to corporate divestiture of unprofitable subsidiaries, in order to achieve a clear focus on activities deemed central to its primary "business"; this is a self-justifying argument for reducing the scope of government activity and the size of the government workforce without actually having to assess the social consequences. Emulating the "make-or-buy" decisions of private firms, governments are "out-sourcing" many functions. The result is the creation of hybrid agencies and networks involving horizontal and vertical links among government agencies and with private firms, relationships known in the private sector as "strategic alliances." The reduction of government research capability, coupled with the demand for more accountability for internal programs and the need for more monitoring of privatized functions, is spurring the growth of numerous consultancies — often employing former civil servants — which in effect serve as "just-in-time contractors" for government. The flattening of public-service management structures to produce "lean organizations" is eliminating familiar career paths. And so on.

. . . .

Further, apart from transforming the social organization of work in the public service, technology has also had some powerful transformative effects on the state's capacity for social control. In some respects, technology has enhanced government's powers. For the first time, democratic governments find themselves with the technical capacity to maintain close surveillance not only of citizens implicated in criminal or anti-social behaviour, but of virtually everyone. This has forced a whole series of issues onto the agenda of public administration — the protection of confidential data banks, the creation of registers of individuals at risk from contagious or degenerative diseases, the use of electronic bracelets to monitor paroled offenders, the surveillance of highways with photo radar to detect speeders.

In other respects, however, technology has imposed new limits on government's regulatory powers. Innovations in telecommunications technology have rendered governments virtually incapable of controlling commercial and cultural activities traditionally within the state's natural sphere of influence. Rail and air transportation and postal services, once considered quintessential public enterprises and policy instruments, must now compete with private-sector alternatives offering identical or substitute ser-

vices. Photocopiers, fax machines and electronic mail have made it so easy for private parties to disseminate or exchange funds, secrets, smut and hate propaganda that it is hard to see how government can ever reassert even minimally effective control. These developments, it seems, open up new chapters in the centuries-old debate over whether the state's regulatory reach can, should or does exceed its technological grasp.

Finally, technology not only shapes public employment, provides tools for regulators and defines the practical limits of government control, it is also a regulatory system. Technology demands a certain kind of behaviour from those who design, produce and use it. For example, the need to ensure that computers, television and telephones can interact requires that certain technical standards be internationally agreed; these agreed standards, in effect, then function as a form of legislation. Technology users, such as air-traffic controllers or tax examiners, must possess certain competencies, follow standard procedures and function with no more or less discretion than is compatible with the demands and possibilities of the technology itself. Hence technology, by determining the way in which public servants perform their jobs, also operates normatively to establish, in effect, standards of airline safety and the limits of tolerance for tax evasion.

In each of these examples, private decisions about the design or adoption of technology shape public policies....

. . . .

B. Globalization and Regional Economic Integration

Globalization has a private perspective and a public perspective. In the private perspective, globalization occurs as corporations reach across national borders to organize production and distribution, investors participate in international markets, and transnational institutions such as banks, brokers and law firms facilitate such activities. But this private perspective ultimately resides within the public perspective of globalization. For all of these activities to occur, states must abandon the familiar regulatory regimes of the post-war period, with which they protected their national economic space, in favour of domestic policies and international treaty commitments designed to liberalize trade. In so doing, states commit themselves not just to the free movement across national borders of goods, services and capital, but also to the increasing integration of their national economies and polities into larger systems, regional or global.

However, globalization can also be seen in quite different perspectives — the illicit traffic in drugs, guns and dirty money, the movement of immigrants and refugees, the ubiquitous preoccupation with "world-wide" news, entertainment, fashion and sport, or the emerging international human-rights and environmental movements — all of which both depend upon and challenge the capacity of states to define and protect national interests.

Even the most ardent supporters of globalization and free trade are not content to leave business activity entirely unregulated, either at home or abroad: trade marks must be protected, fraud must be punished, contracts must be enforced. Even the most highly principled humanitarians accept that movements of refugees and immigrants must be subject to some controls. And even the most cynical of governments — whatever their actual behaviour — will seldom confess to supporting the drug trade, terrorism or money laundering. However, since the ability of individual states to regulate international movements of all kinds has diminished, they have perforce begun to experiment with structures which might facilitate regulation and social control across national boundaries. Such arrangements include closer coordination and cooperation amongst national agencies concerned with fraud (Interpol), treaties or conventions whose signatory states agree to enact or enforce labour or environmental laws that meet specified standards (I.L.O., N.A.F.T.A. side-accords), the creation of regional trade blocs with regulatory powers (the E.U.), and regimes that define the terms of global trade (G.A.T.T./W.T.O.) or migration (the International Convention on Refugees). This globalization of the regulation not only of economic activity, but of crime and migration as well, considerably alters the dynamic of Canadian public administration.

. . . .

The diminished corporate presence of multinationals in Canada has potential repercussions for public administration. Much regulation becomes effective through moral suasion and, as noted, the socialization of corporate decision-makers. If corporate representatives are no longer present in Canada to be suased [*sic*] or socialized, governments will have to fall back on more formal techniques of enforcement, which are often slow, costly and undependable. Worse yet: to the extent that regulation does depend upon the state's use, or threatened use, of its coercive powers, we are left with diminished

capacity to coerce. Companies that serve the Canadian market from abroad, as part of a larger North American market, are essentially beyond the reach of Canadian law. And multinationals that retain a base in Canada can face down the state by making increasingly credible threats to reduce their Canadian operations, or even to leave Canada altogether.

. . . .

C. Shifting the Boundaries between State and Civil Society: The Ideology of the New Economy

In the liturgy of the New Economy, few hymns are so popular as the Nunc Dimittis, sung whenever the state appears in its interventionist role. The chorus joins many different voices in celebration of the retrenchment of the state....

. . . .

... [O]nly in the 1970s did governments begin serious retrenchment of their activities and personnel, and only in the 1980s was retrenchment accompanied by aggressive measures to limit the power of public-sector unions to resist it.[6] Now, in the 1990s, we are experiencing not merely cyclical qualms about state intervention, not merely modest rollbacks of public-service wages and staff complements, not merely modernization and reconfiguration of government, but a successful attack on the very idea both of interventionist government and of the need for committed public servants as its agents. The result is that, almost for the first time, governments are requiring that the public service participate in its own systematic denigration. Whether this is a "commonsense" revolution or not, it clearly presages a revolution of some sort in Canadian public administration.

. . . .

The ideology of the New Economy ... is not merely — perhaps not primarily — a belief in the virtue of markets. Changing attitudes towards individualism, communities, nations, states, politics, public institutions, law and civic participation have converged around a central conviction that the boundaries between the state and civil society should be redrawn — the realm of private action expanded, and the role of government reduced. This conviction, however, is shot through with ironies. First, the boundaries between state and civil society have always been shifting and permeable; the state has never had a total monopoly on legitimacy or coercion; it could never count on having its way with the market or with local communities; it has always shared with private institutions its putative authority over regulation and social control.[7] Second, in the early running at least, civil society — newly revivified — is demonstrating only a limited inclination and capacity to address the complex and urgent problems of our times; we may soon find ourselves reinventing the state. And third, those who move and shake the New Economy do not have a monopoly on disdain for government and public administration. As the next section of this essay suggests, they are joined by many who are nominally committed to the idea of an interventionist state. But three ironies do not a paradigm confute. The new anti-state ideological consensus has important, and possibly transformative, implications for public administration.

. . . .

... [T]he *Charter*'s greatest effect is not so much direct as indirect. It has helped to reshape the consciousness of Canadians, and thereby to reinforce the power of the New Economy paradigm. The *Charter* has legitimated — and arguably even launched — the growing tendency to see ourselves as rights-bearing individuals rather than as members of a community, as operating at odds with the state rather than as its beneficiaries, as seekers of personal redress through litigation rather than as agents of social improvement through political activity. These perceptions, for obvious reasons, are very pertinent to the ways in which we relate to the state and its administration.

. . . .

II. THE NEW ECONOMY AND ITS ADMINISTRATION: LAW, PROFESSIONALISM, DEMOCRACY AND MARKETS

In that innocent, far-off time — until, say, the 1990s — when resuscitation of the activist state remained a project with some plausibility, three main strategies were proposed for the reform of public administration: increased external accountability through legal controls; internal accountability through enhanced professionalism; and greater democratic participation. None of these was ever particularly promising, but in the event all have now acquired a faint whiff of anachronism. More recently, in the heyday of the New Economy, another strategy has come into prominence, the "reinvention" of public administration as its own antithesis — a market.

This strategy, by contrast, is promising indeed, but what it promises may not be to everyone's liking.

. . . .

[Arthurs sees little hope for the first three strategies above. He says that in the interests of efficiency the New Economy is turning from formal legal controls to "low visibility", high flexibility tools of government such as orders-in-council, ministerial directives and others. According to him, enhanced professionalism is unlikely, as it suffers from a general suspicion of expertise, and from the tendency of New Economy governments to impose their political agendas on bureaucracy. Arthurs suggests that greater democratization of public administration is anathema to New Economy neo-conservatives, and that others may be concerned about its practical costs. Finally, he concludes that continued application of market principles to government will likely further diminish public regulation and generate more regulation carried out solely in the interests of specific private groups.]

Michael Trebilcock, a strong believer in the efficacy of markets and one of the most thoughtful Canadian proponents of "reinventing government," is generally sympathetic to the proposition that the state should no longer row — it should steer.[8] At the risk of mixing metaphors, as Trebilcock himself acknowledges, this is a far cry from the proposition that the invisible hand, rather than the state's, should rest on the tiller. The fundamental question for public administration, then, is not "How will it get there?" but "Where is it going?" These two questions are closely related, however, in the sense that both must be answered in order to imagine what public administration and public law will look like in the New Economy, in the "declining age" of the Canadian state.

Notes

1. Sir Francis Bacon, "Of Vicissitude of Things" (Essay LVIII, ll. 177–180) in M. Kiernan, ed., *The Essayes or Counsels, Civill and Morall* (Oxford: Clarendon Press, 1985) 172 at 176 [modernized].
2. See M. Weber, *The Theory of Social and Economic Organization*, 1st American ed. by T. Parsons, trans. A.M. Henderson & T. Parsons (New York: Oxford University Press, 1947).
3. See ibid.; H. Fayol, *General and Industrial Management*, trans. C. Storrs (London: Pitman, 1949).
4. For a more extended account of this phenomenon, see H.W. Arthurs, "Labour Law Without the State?" (1996) 46 U.T.L.J. 1.

5. See e.g. D. Cameron, "The Discipline and the Profession of Public Administration: An Academic's Perspective" (1982) 25 Can. Pub. Admin. 496; H.L. LaFramboise, "The Future of Public Administration in Canada" (1982) 25 Can. Pub. Admin. 507; D. Savoie, "Studying Public Administration" (1990) 33 Can. Pub. Admin. 389. See also K. Kernaghan, "Reshaping Government: The Post-Bureaucratic Paradigm" (1993) 36 Can. Pub. Admin. 636, which reviews a number of influential American contributions and cites as meriting "special attention" D. Osborne & T. Gaebler, *Reinventing Government: How the Entrepreneurial Spirit is Transforming the Public Sector* (Reading, Mass.: Addison-Wesley, 1992).

6. See L. Panitch & D. Swartz, *The Assault on Trade Union Freedoms: From Wage Controls to Social Contract*, rev. ed.

(Toronto: Garamond Press, 1993); D. Drache & H. Glasbeek, *The Changing Workplace: Reshaping Canada's Industrial Relations System* (Toronto: James Lorimer and Company Publishers, 1992).

7. This, of course, has been the great insight of legal pluralist scholarship. See e.g. S.E. Merry, "Legal Pluralism" (1988) 22 Law & Soc'y Rev. 869 at 890: "The dialectical analysis of relations among normative orders provides a framework for understanding the dynamics of the imposition of law and of resistance to law...."

8. See M.J. Trebilcock, *The Prospects for Reinventing Government* (Toronto: C.D. Howe Institute, 1994). The metaphor is that of Osborne & Gaebler, *supra* note 5, whose work is the subject of Trebilcock's commentary.

(c)   The Economics of Government Regulation: Theory and Canadian Practice†

John C. Strick

NOTE

One of the most important of all activities of government and the administrative process is regulation — the control or direction of economic and social activity. (Regulation in this sense is thus different from a regulation, which is a rule enacted by the executive branch of government pursuant to statutory authority.)

Many writers have stressed that regulation, like most law, is a human process. For example, in a classic 1987 article, W.T. Stanbury argued that Canadian "economic" regulation has often been as much political as strictly economic in character: W.T. Stanbury, "Direct Regulation and its Reform: A Canadian Perspective" (1987) Brigham Young University L. Rev. 467. Some, like Liora Salter, argue that specific regulatory theories (such as the capture theory) fail to depict the full social context of regulation (which often requires significant cooperation between regulator and regulatee): L. Salter, "Capture or Co-Management: Democracy and Accountability in Regulatory Agencies", in G. Albo et al., eds., *A Different Kind of State? Popular Power and Democratic Administration* (London, Oxford University Press, 1993), 87.

During the 1990s, there was much focus on deregulation. There was significant shrinkage. However, much regulation remained, and in some cases deregulation really meant *re*-regulation, administered by someone else. This is hardly surprising. Despite its status as favoured scapegoat of the New Economy, effective regulation can be vital. Consider, for example, the 1992 Westray story recounted later in this chapter and the 2000 Walkerton, Ontario tainted water tragedy.

In the extract below, John Strick describes some of the leading theories of regulation. Some — like the market failure and public interest theory and the income redistribution and stability theory — focus on the apparent intent of regulation; others — like the capture, cartel, and political-bureaucratic theories — purport to describe how regulation works in practice. Strick concludes that no single theory can adequately describe all forms of regulation.

EXTRACT

The focus on failures of the market economy to serve the public interest is one of the earliest attempts to explain regulation and has been referred to as the public interest theory of regulation. It is based on the assumption that government seeks to maximize social welfare. When the freely-operating market system fails to achieve efficiency of resource

---

†   Excerpts from John C. Strick, *The Economics of Government Regulation: Theory and Canadian Practice*, 2d ed. (Toronto: Thompson Educational, 1994) at 20, 22–23, 28–29, 32, and 34. Reproduced with permission of the publisher. [Commentary note by David W. Elliott.]

use and welfare maximization, the government assumes an obligation to correct or compensate for market failures and inefficiencies. Regulation is one of a number of policy instruments at the disposal of government to achieve this objective.[1]

. . . .

The public interest theory can explain and justify a wide range of government regulatory devices. Regulation of monopoly industries, including prices, and promotion of competition is justified on the grounds that monopoly produces higher prices and smaller outputs than competition. The host of consumer protectionist policies — including standards for weights and measures, regulations on advertising, standards relating to food and drugs, and safety standards in the workplace — can all be justified in the public interest. On a more general level, it can certainly be argued that the control of industrial emissions, the use of chemicals, transportation of dangerous chemicals, regulation of nuclear energy, etc., is in the interests of society because of potential harmful externalities over which the market system provides inadequate and inefficient control.

Furthermore, the market system has a tendency to waste certain resources that fall into the category of "common property." These would include natural resources.... A case can be made for government regulating or managing the use of common property resources in the public interest to prevent waste and abuse....

. . . .

[Strick says that the public interest theory has been criticized as too general to describe the complexity of modern government and economies, overly concerned with control of monopolies, and unduly naive in assuming that government can always regulate market failures and effectively promote the public interest.]

In the capture theory [of regulation], regulatory agencies tend to weaken over time and gradually fall prey to the power of the firms or industry that they were originally established to regulate. The argument is made that regulatory agencies must frequently contend with large and powerful firms. These firms command large resources and expertise in their areas of operations. They frequently employ highly-organized and well-funded lobby and interest groups with a high degree of expertise and are in a position to wield considerable public and political influence.

Many regulatory agencies constantly complain about lack of adequate funding and insufficient staff to discharge their regulatory functions adequately. This makes them vulnerable to the expertise, evidence, and pressures that regulated firms can [marshal] in support of their requests and positions.

[Strick says that although capture may be quite possible where there are strong regulated industries, the theory fails to account for cases in which regulations go against the interests of the regulated bodies or are heavily shaped by consumer groups, and is not helpful in identifying captors in multi-service or multi-product industries.]

. . . .

A cartel is formed when a group of firms come together for the purpose of gaining control of prices and output in their industry. The objective is to reduce competition and increase profits.

. . . .

[The] theory of cartels forms the basis of the cartel theory of regulation.[2] It was argued that a cartel and regulation produce similar results in the form of control over entry, production, and prices. According to the theory, industries will seek regulation when they desire the benefits of cartels but find that forming a cartel is too costly or is illegal. A largely competitive industry with numerous producers, such as agriculture, may seek regulation to maintain price and income levels because it is too costly to form a cartel. On the other hand, monopoly or a tight oligopoly may seek regulation to protect their monopolistic positions.

. . . .

[Strick says this theory "does not explain many cases of regulation or non-regulation." He says that, although some oligopoly or monopoly industries, such as airlines and telecommunications, have traditionally been regulated, other oligopolistic industries, such as automobiles, textiles and food processing, are free from regulation of prices and output.]

. . . .

According to [political-bureaucratic behaviour theories of regulation], regulation stems from the coalition of various special interest groups which are manipulated by government to obtain their political support. Regulatory decisions are not unlike pork-barrel politics where government doles out special favours, concessions, and benefits to special groups and industries in return for their political support. Coalitions are consequently formed with these groups which are delicately balanced through favourable governmental regulations, as well as other policies and activities, to maximize support.

. . . .

[Strick says this approach assumes that regulators can make arbitrary decisions, free from judicial or other controls, that regulators can be readily manipulated by politicians, and that the costs and gains of alternative regulatory or political actions can be easily measured.]

. . . .

[The income redistribution and stability theory of regulation] attributes regulation to government's desire to replace freely-operating markets with institutions to promote fairness in the distribution of income and to maintain income stability. This approach has its origin in the generally accepted goal of society, and consequent function of government, to achieve an equitable distribution of income and wealth in society.[3]

. . . .

[Strick says that while this theory helps explain the general growth of government regulation, it does not account for the instability resulting from recent deregulation measures, and provides no criteria for measuring equity.]

. . . .

Each of the various theories of regulation possesses some degree of validity in that each can be applied to some particular constitutional regulatory activity under certain circumstances. But there is no one theory that can explain regulation in all areas where regulation is observed and the manner in which it is applied.... The usefulness of the [theories described above] lies in their contribution to a greater understanding of various aspects and issues of regulation and the rationale of regulation.[4]

Notes

1. Market failures and the need for government action to correct or compensate for these failures is discussed in most textbooks in public finance or public sector economics. See, for example, R.A. Musgrave, Peggy Musgrave and R.M. Bird, *Public Finance in Theory and Practice*, First Canadian Edition (Toronto: McGraw-Hill Ryerson Ltd., 1987), Ch. 1, 3, 4; or R.W. Broadway and D. Wildasin, *Public Sector Economics*, 2nd ed. (Toronto: Little, Brown and Co., 1984), Ch. 3.
2. George J. Stigler, "The Theory of Economic Regulation" (Spring 1971), 2:1 *The Bell Journal of Management Science*.
3. An explanation and analysis of the government function to achieve an equitable distribution of wealth, along with criteria for equity and government policies, is contained in most textbooks on public sector economics. See, for example, Musgrave, Musgrave and Bird, [*ibid.*, note 1], Ch. 5.
4. [For a discussion of regulation theories in an American context, see L.N. Gerston, C. Fraliegh and R. Schwarb, "Theories of Regulation and Deregulation" in The Regulated Society (Pacific Grove: Brooks/Cole Publishing, 1988), 66.]

(d) The Westray Story: A Predictable Path to Disaster†

Justice K. Peter Richard

NOTE

Consider the role played by government regulation in this tragic tale. Can bureaucratic neglect be as harmful as overzealous administrative action? Is there a greater need for regulation where restraints from within — such as labour unions — are absent? Is effective regulation possible in a political climate

---

† Excerpts from Justice K. Peter Richard, Commissioner, "Executive Summary", *The Westray Story: A Predictable Path to Disaster; Report of the Westray Mine Public Inquiry* (Halifax, Nova Scotia: Westray Mine Public Inquiry, November 1997) at i–ii, 1–13. © Province of Nova Scotia, 1997. [Commentary note by David W. Elliott.]

that relies desperately on private sector jobs? What does the Westray Story suggest about the way we should look at regulatory reform?

EXTRACT

In the early morning of 9 May 1992 a violent explosion rocked the tiny community of Plymouth, just east of Stellarton, in Pictou County, Nova Scotia. The explosion occurred in the depths of the Westray coal mine, instantly killing the 26 miners working there at the time. On 15 May 1992, I was appointed by Order in Council to inquire into and report on this disaster.

. . . .

The Order in Council that established this Inquiry gives me power to "inquire into ... whether the occurrence was or was not preventable." Of course it was. For this Report we have chosen the title *The Westray Story: A Predictable Path to Disaster* to convey that message. The message is that the Westray tragedy was predictable and, therefore, preventable. The Report contains recommendations and suggestions aimed at avoiding a similar occurrence in the future.

Anyone who hopes to find in this Report a simple and conclusive answer as to how this tragedy happened will be disappointed. Anyone who expects that this Report will single out one or two persons and assess total blame for the tragedy will be similarly disappointed. The Westray Story is a complex mosaic of actions, omissions, mistakes, incompetence, apathy, cynicism, stupidity, and neglect....

. . . .

Prelude to the Tragedy: History, Development, and Operation

The Westray mine is located at Plymouth, near Stellarton, in Pictou County, Nova Scotia. Westray was the only operating underground coal mine in Pictou County at the time of the explosion. The Pictou coalfield had been mined for some 200 years, and elements of the disaster rest in the nature of that coalfield with its thick and gassy seams. The Foord seam, which Westray was mining, has hosted at least eight mines. The Allan mine, the most productive and the one that lay just northwest of Westray's workings, finally closed in the 1950s, but during its 40-year lifetime, it experienced eight methane explosions.

The Westray project was controversial from the outset. Although various companies ... had been interested in the area with its low-sulphur coal, it was Curragh Resources Inc. that eventually put the pieces together, incorporated Westray Coal in November 1987, and some 16 months later began underground development.... On 9 September 1988, Westray finalized a deal for Suncor's coal interests in Pictou County and signed an agreement with Nova Scotia Power Corporation, which agreed to purchase Westray coal for its new coal-burning generating stations at nearby Trenton, Nova Scotia. A letter dated that same day was sent to Westray by Donald Cameron, provincial minister of industry, trade, and technology, which committed the province to a mining lease, a loan of $12 million, and a take-or-pay agreement for 275,000 tonnes of coal per year for 15 years. The cabinet did not approve the take-or-pay agreement until two years later.

The proposed mine developed amid opposition from the bureaucracy and unwavering support from the provincial government.... In the end, the strong and single-minded political backing for the project, by Donald Cameron in particular, prevailed. Westray received tremendous financial support from the public sector, which resulted in minimal equity investment by the company. In addition to the $12 million provincial loan and a most unusual take-or-pay agreement with the province, Curragh managed to secure a federal loan guarantee of approximately $85 million, a direct contribution against interest, and an $8 million interim loan.

Before all the financing was in place, the underground work began. Early in 1989, Curragh's subcontractor, Canadian Mining Development (CMD), began driving the main access slopes. The Department of Natural Resources had approved Curragh's application for the mining lease in 1988, and, in January 1989, the department discovered that the tunnel alignment had been changed from the approved layout.... The Department of the Environment had a number of concerns about the effect of the development on the area. The Department of Labour expressed concern about training and certification, equipment approvals, plans for emergencies, and delays in setting up a workplace safety committee. The Department of Natural Resources was concerned that the new tunnel alignment would intersect major geological faults at oblique angles, resulting in extensive tunnel development through bad ground. Poor roof conditions in the earliest days of tunnel development gave credence to that concern.

. . . .

... In the rush to reach saleable coal, workers without adequate coal mining experience were promoted to newly created supervisory positions. Workers were not trained by Westray in safe work methods or in recognizing dangerous roof conditions, despite a major roof collapse in August. Basic safety measures were ignored or performed inadequately. Stonedusting, for example, a critical and standard practice that renders coal dust non-explosive, was carried out sporadically by volunteers on overtime following their 12-hour shifts.

The official opening of the mine was on 11 September 1991. For that occasion, the mine was "spruced up" and stonedusted.

Four more roof falls were reported in September and October. The mine manager, Gerald Phillips, minimized the seriousness of roof problems, claiming that the falls were controlled and that they posed little threat to the miners or to production. To the contrary, realistic accounts of the miners' experiences revealed a series of near misses and increasing danger. There were approximately 160 employees at the site by October, a large majority of them working shifts underground. Management trivialized the concerns of workers, some of whom quit their jobs at the mine. Although the mine inspectors asked the company for roof support plans, as well as stonedusting plans, it repeatedly deferred supplying them. Westray is a stark example of an operation where production demands resulted in the violation of the basic and fundamental tenets of safe mining practice.

The first drive to unionize the workforce at Westray was officially begun on 2 October 1991 by local 26 of the United Mine Workers of America. The union was defeated by 20 votes in January 1992. In the spring of 1992, the United Steelworkers of America succeeded in its drive to unionize the workers, but certification was not granted until after the 9 May explosion.

The Southwest section was plagued with roof problems. The decision to drive into the Southwest section was proving a serious mistake. The levels of production and the quality of the coal were less than anticipated. Production remained behind schedule, and the company was not able to meet its commitments to supply coal. In late March 1992, the workforce was literally chased out of the Southwest 1 section by rapidly deteriorating ground conditions. In its determination to save equipment, the company put employees at extreme risk during the abandonment.

The Department of Natural Resources staff expressed concern about proximity to the old Allan mine workings, potential subsidence problems, and deviations from the approved mine plan. The depart-ment suggested that non-compliance could threaten the company's mining permit but inexplicably retreated from its position. Skeletal new plans submitted by the company were approved, and the department assisted the company in developing a surface mining operation to help meet its coal supply obligations. Federal and provincial money and expertise met most of the costs of technical studies for monitoring roof conditions and subsidence.

The regulatory framework in Nova Scotia requires that almost every person employed in underground coal mining hold a certificate of competency issued by an appointed provincial board of examiners. Section 11 of the *Coal Mines Regulation Act* (1989) sets out the education and work experience required for the various certificates. The administration of certification for mine rescue and for competency as a coal miner was delegated to the Department of Labour. In Nova Scotia, the company is responsible for training miners. The role of the Department of Labour is to ensure that the company complies with the *Coal Mines Regulation Act* and the *Occupational Health and Safety Act*.

It is clear that the company was derelict in carrying out its obligations for training. The testimony of the miners shows that training fell far short of need....

Quite simply, management did not instil a safety mentality in its workforce. Although it stressed safety in its employee handbook, the policy it laid out there was never promoted or enforced. Indeed, management ignored or encouraged a series of hazardous or illegal practices....

It was equally clear that the Department of Labour was derelict in its duty to enforce the requirements of the two acts.

The Explosion: An Analysis of Underground Conditions

Early in this Inquiry, I reached the conclusion that ventilation is the most crucial aspect of mine safety in an underground coal mine. Methane fires and explosions cannot happen if the gas is kept from accumulating in flammable and explosive concentrations. A coal mine can be quite "forgiving" with respect to other aspects of safety, as long as the ventilation system is properly planned, efficient, and conscientiously maintained. The other major requirement of coal mine safety is control of coal dust, through strict clean-up procedures and regular stonedusting.

... A mine ventilation system has to deal with both gaseous and particulate pollutants. Methane is a dangerous pollutant present in coal. Although non-toxic, it is hazardous because of its flammability. It will explode in concentrations of between 5 and about 15 per cent by volume in air, and it reaches maximum explosiveness at about 9.6 per cent.

Methane is a natural component of coal, a by-product of the decomposition of the plant matter from which coal is formed. Methane is released as the coal-cutting machines break coal away from the face.... One of the principal functions of a ventilation system is to clear the methane at the working face of the mine and to exhaust it from the mine in non-explosive concentrations. It is clear that the Westray ventilation system was grossly inadequate for this task. It is also clear that the conditions in the mine were conducive to a coal-dust explosion.

The miners, faced with management pressure for production, undoubtedly indulged in many dangerous and foolhardy practices in the days immediately preceding 9 May 1992....

... Had it not been for these unsafe practices attributed to the miners, would the explosion of 9 May have occurred? The answer must be yes, it would have. The consensus of the experts suggests strongly that Westray was an accident waiting to happen.

The Regulators: Departmental and Ministerial Responsibility

The Department of Natural Resources (the Department of Mines and Energy before September 1991) was charged with regulatory authority over the mine-planning approval process. As the testimony at the Inquiry unfolded, it became clear that the Department of Natural Resources had failed to carry out its statutory duties and responsibilities as they related to the Westray project. Natural Resources witnesses had mixed views on fundamental regulatory issues, such as whether the department was within its mandate to regulate for "safety," or whether its duty included monitoring Westray to ensure that it was operating in conformity with the approved mine plan.

The mandate of the department vis-à-vis the Department of Labour and the mine inspectorate was not formally defined in any way, and the changes affecting the departments over their history contributed to this lack of definition. Before 1986, both the mine engineering unit and the mine inspection unit were part of the Department of Mines and Energy, and their duties overlapped somewhat. When the inspectorate transferred to the occupational health and safety division of the Department of Labour in

1986, it lost its link to the engineering section. When the chief inspector left a short time later, the liaison between the two functions effectively ended. It is clear that the Department of Natural Resources, in spite of these changes, retained legislative responsibility to ensure, before permits are granted, that mining plans are not only efficient but safe.

In the view of the Department of Natural Resources, its responsibility for monitoring the Westray operation for compliance with the approved mine plan was limited to an annual review of plans submitted by the operator. Section 93 of the *Mineral Resources Act* (1990) is explicit: the permit holder "shall conduct mining operations in conformity with the approved mining plan." The Department of Natural Resources was ill-advised in approving the Westray mine proposal in the form submitted. The department did not insist that the company submit sufficient information to support its application. Furthermore, it did not insist that the company submit any changes to approved plans. Consequently, for a critical period, the department was not aware that Westray was working [in] an unapproved section of the mine. The department's explanation was that such day-to-day monitoring was the responsibility of the Department of Labour. What it did not explain was why the department failed to shut down a company that was undeniably in violation of the *Mineral Resources Act* — an action that fell squarely within its own mandate. The evidence of the public servants of the Department of Natural Resources is replete with examples of neglect of duties, submissiveness to Westray management, and just plain apathy.

The Department of Labour shares with the Department of Natural Resources the responsibility for failure to coordinate the several aspects of mine regulation. The Department of Labour was responsible for regulating occupational health and safety at the mine, and as such was the body most responsible for the exercise of regulatory authority respecting safe mining at Westray. What is clear from the testimony of Labour witnesses at the Inquiry is that the department did not discharge its duties with competence or diligence, and thereby failed to carry out its mandated responsibilities to the workers at Westray and to the people of Nova Scotia.

The Report enumerates in detail the many ways in which Westray Coal violated the regulations governing mine operations. The Department of Labour's mine inspectorate should have detected these violations and ensured compliance. To give just one example, despite the company's repeated violations of the *Coal Mines Regulation Act* in the matters of clearing coal dust from the working sections of the mine and applying stonedust to render the coal dust inert, the mine inspectorate did not use the means at its disposal to ensure compliance. It was not until 29 April 1992 that inspector Albert McLean gave oral orders, followed up by written orders, to Westray underground manager Roger Parry and mine manager Gerald Phillips to clean up and treat the coal dust immediately and to produce the stonedusting and dust sampling plans that had been promised in September 1991. McLean failed to follow up on his orders during his visit to the mine on 6 May 1992.

The Report also examines the involvement of politicians in the development of the Westray project and their very active support of a project that would mean jobs in Pictou County. The three provincial politicians most involved with the Westray project were John Buchanan, Donald Cameron, and Leroy Legere. Cameron had the most prominent and enduring role in the project, serving as minister of industry, trade, and technology from April 1988 until he succeeded Buchanan as premier in February 1991, a position he held until late spring 1993. Legere was appointed minister of labour in February 1991. It became clear in the course of the Inquiry that Buchanan, Cameron, and Legere had disparate understandings of their roles as ministers of the [C]rown. The fact that they had such an imperfect understanding of the nature of their responsibilities suggests that a formal clarification of constitutional responsibilities is required. In the Report, I recommend establishing a program offering guidelines to ministers on their responsibilities, perhaps modelled on the one used in the United Kingdom. At the same time, there appears to be some misunderstanding respecting the concept of ministerial responsibility, and for that reason I have devoted some attention to what it means in modern government.

As part of the preparation before the public hearings began, I undertook a general review of legislation pertaining to mining and safety in Nova Scotia and in other jurisdictions. Clearly, the aim of mining legislation should be the protection of the miner in the mining environment. Coal mining is inherently hazardous, and safety regulations must protect the miner in a way that is consistent with the economic viability of the undertaking. This goal has been expressed in terms of safe mine production. "Attitude," which may be the most significant single factor in attaining safe mine production, cannot of course be legislated. It must, however, be cultivated within an organization, whether it be a mining company, a union, or a government agency charged with enforcement of safety legislation.

The Aftermath: Rescue Efforts and the Inquiry

I would be remiss if I did not comment on the selfless bravery shown by the rescue teams in the days following the explosion.... We can only be thankful for this valiant display of concern for fellow workers. I also wish to recognize the entire community for its selfless work in those difficult days.

I must point out that Westray Coal was ill prepared for a disaster. I have made a number of recommendations pertaining to what a company can do in preparation, as well as what the regulator's role should be.

Finally, I describe my preparations for the public hearings of this Inquiry, which was established six days after the explosion amid grief, calls for recrimination, and confusion. I then record the factors that caused the delay in concluding the Inquiry.

In Conclusion

The conclusions below are additional to the observations and comments made throughout the Report.

Responsibility

As the evidence emerged during this Inquiry, it became clear that many persons and entities had defaulted in their legislative, business, statutory, and management responsibilities. There is always the danger that when so many are implicated and bear some degree of responsibility the principal focus may be somewhat diminished by the sheer multiplicity of defaults. In the case of Westray, there is a clear "hierarchy" of responsibility for the environment that set the stage for 9 May 1992 and we ought not to lose sight of this hierarchy.

The fundamental and basic responsibility for the safe operation of an underground coal mine, and indeed of any industrial undertaking, rests clearly with management. The internal responsibility system merely articulates this responsibility and places it in context. Westray management, starting with the chief executive officer, was required by law, by good business practice, and by good conscience to design and operate the Westray mine safely. Westray management failed in this primary responsibility, and the significance of that failure cannot be mitigated or diluted simply because others were derelict in their responsibility.

The Department of Labour through its mine inspectorate must bear a correlative responsibility for its continued failure in its duty to ensure compliance with the *Coal Mines Regulation Act* and the *Occupational Health and Safety Act*. Indeed, the many and varied faults of Westray management and its derelict attitude towards safety should have prompted the Department of Labour inspectorate to adopt a firm and uncompromising position on strict compliance. Instead, the evidence indicates that the demeanour of the inspectorate was one of apathy and complaisance.

With its "hands-off" attitude, its general indifference to the quality of mine planning, and its lassitude about any safety responsibility, the Department of Natural Resources failed to discharge its duties in a creditable manner. The general attitude of wilful blindness pervaded the department's dealings with Westray. Thus, the stage was set for Westray management to maintain an air of arrogance and cynicism, knowing that it was not going to be seriously challenged.

Compliance with the Coal Mines Regulation Act

Much has been said throughout this Inquiry about the inadequacy of the *Coal Mines Regulation Act*. As outdated and archaic as the present act is, it is painfully clear that this disaster would not have occurred if there had been compliance with the act.

- *If* the "floor, roof and sides of the road and the working places"[1] had been systematically cleared so as to prevent the accumulation of coal dust;
- *If* the "floor, road and sides of every road"[2] had been treated with stonedust so that the resulting mixture would contain no more than 35 per cent combustible matter (adjusted downward to allow for the presence of methane); and
- *If* the mine had been "thoroughly ventilated and furnished with an adequate supply of pure air to dilute and render harmless inflammable and noxious gases,"[3] then....

... the 9 May 1992 explosion could not have happened, and 26 miners would not have been killed.

Compliance with these sections of the *Coal Mines Regulation Act* was the clear duty of Westray management, from the chief executive officer to the first-line supervisor. To ensure that this duty was undertaken and fulfilled by management was the legislated duty of the inspectorate of the Department of Labour. Management failed, the inspectorate failed, and the mine blew up.

What If?

In the opening statement to this Report ... I [commented] that the Westray story is a "complex mosaic of actions, omissions, mistakes, incompetence, apathy, cynicism, stupidity, and neglect." It seems fitting that I ought now, in this conclusion to the Report, [to] revisit this comment and relate it to the extensive evidence that has been summarized in the preceding pages. The following questions are posed, in a somewhat rhetorical manner, to underscore the proposition that the Westray story is, indeed, a "complex mosaic."

What if — Clifford Frame, as Westray's chief executive officer, had acknowledged that the motivation for mine safety begins at the top? What if he had sent a clear message to Westray management that a safe working environment was paramount?

What if — Gerald Phillips, Roger Parry, Glyn Jones, and other Westray managers, with a clear directive from the chief executive officer, had conscientiously directed compliance with the Manager's Safe Working Procedures?

What if — the *Coal Mines Regulation Act* had been applied and enforced by the inspectorate of the Department of Labour? Would it have made a difference if the executive director of occupational health and safety had even read the act?

What if — the public servants at the Department of Natural Resources had fulfilled their legislative responsibilities and determined, before issuing mining permits, that the mine plans submitted by Westray assured "safe and efficient" use of the resources and then followed up to determine that Westray was mining in accordance with those plans?

What if — the Westray miners, at the certification vote on 5 and 6 January 1992, had voted in favour of the application of the United Mine Workers of America to represent them as the bargaining agent under the Nova Scotia *Trade Union Act*?

What if — Department of Labour inspector Albert McLean, while at Westray on 6 May 1992, had returned underground to evaluate the company's progress in complying with the several oral and written orders issued during the inspectors' visit of 29 April 1992?

Notes

1. Section 70(1).
2. Section 71(3).
3. Section 71(1).

(e) Lessons of Walkerton†

NOTE

In the 1990s, federal and provincial governments reduced their deficits by cutting back the public sector. Downsizing, privatization, contracting out, and regulation-chopping were paramount. These measures were especially dramatic in Ontario. There the government called them "the Common Sense Revolution".

In May 2000, in the Ontario town of Walkerton, seven people died and thousands became ill. Toxic E. coli bacteria had contaminated the drinking water supply. An inquiry tried to determine how this had happened, and to help ensure that it would never happen again. On January 18, 2002, after 95 days of hearings, Justice Dennis O'Connor released Part One of the *Report of the Walkerton Inquiry.* The 700 pages of Part One were concerned with the causes of the contamination; Part Two, released later, contained detailed proposals for reform.

Part One is summarized briefly in the following editorial from *The Globe and Mail.* Although the Report did not allocate specific blame, it noted the incompetence and dishonesty of two local waterworks managers. But as the editorial points out, the Report also stressed the role played by government policy. Provincial government cost-cutting had contributed to inadequate regulations, shoddy inspections, and poor communication. But for these factors, the tragedy might have been averted. A key problem, then, was not government action but government inaction. Are there echoes here of Westray?

EXTRACT

It was Stan Koebel's job, assisted by his brother Frank, to make sure the drinking water was safe in the farming community of Walkerton, Ont. Stan Koebel ... falsified reports for years. Besides that, he was untrained; Frank was no better. When, on May 17, 2000, Stan Koebel received laboratory reports that the water supply was contaminated, he kept silent. As people began falling ill in his community, he repeatedly assured public-health officials the water was fine.

Seven people died in Canada's worst-ever E. coli outbreak, and 2,300 out of 5,000 townsfolk fell sick. Some children and elderly people will experience kidney disease and other effects for the rest of their lives.

Yet, in spite of the Koebel brothers' astounding incompetence and lack of integrity, the Ontario government could have prevented the tragedy if it had carried out its duties properly. That is the conclusion of Mr. Justice Dennis O'Connor, who conducted an inquiry into the events and yesterday released a 700-page report on his findings.

Judge O'Connor does not say explicitly who is more to blame, but it is clear that both the Koebels and the government are culpable. In effect, an Ontario government hell-bent on simultaneously slashing its budget and lifting burdensome regulations was as weak a guardian of public health as ... [an] untrained, lying general manager of a small-town water-works. This is an indictment of a government that always had an ear for its Red Tape Commission, but turned its back on its public health responsibilities.

Judge O'Connor points out that, in cutting 750 employees (30 per cent of staff) and $200-million a year from the Environment Ministry's budget, the government did not bother first to assess whether the ministry could still fulfil its statutory responsibilities. Further, in private laboratory testing in 1996, it did not require — because of its fatal obsession with "red tape" — that those labs notify the Environment Ministry or the local health department when it found contaminated water. And it paid no heed to internal warnings of the risks.

The result was a tragedy of errors. When heavy rains washed manure into a well, proper monitoring equipment was not in use. If the ministry had been properly inspecting local waterworks, it would have known this. When a lab found contaminated water, an alarm could have been raised if proper reporting rules had been in place, and much sickness prevented.

---

† Excerpts from Editorial, "Lessons of Walkerton", *The Globe and Mail* (19 January 2002) A14. The Globe and Mail. All rights reserved. [Commentary note by David W. Elliott.]

Walkerton was an avoidable tragedy. It will forever stand for gross incompetence in public service. The experience should also give pause to those who

would, in restructuring government services, simply let the chips fall where they may....

(f) Rules vs. Adjudication†

J. Jowell

NOTE

As we noted at the beginning of this chapter, policy makers usually have a choice of structural options for addressing any given social problem. Here Jeffrey Jowell considers some of the characteristic advantages and disadvantages of two of the most common structural options or techniques employed in administrative law: (i) rules and (ii) adjudication.

EXTRACT

Administrative Advantages of Rules

. . . .

(I) PLANNING AND ROUTINISATION

... [B]usiness convenience is seen as being furthered by certain and predictable rules which will serve as guides to facilitate planning....

Rules will also aid in the dispatch of cases. Mass transactions almost always require routinised treatment. Decisions upon the merits of each case *de novo* would in many situations prove an insupportable burden upon administrative time. For example, it might theoretically be possible for the administrators of a welfare scheme to judge the need of every applicant for aid on a case-by-case basis. Realistically, however, the demands upon an administrator's time require him to make decisions by reference to a minimum of predetermined rules which would provide him with a checklist of objective criteria (such as age, number in family, and so on), which could be applied routinely to determine the eligibility of all his clients.

All announced rules will possess administrative benefits to the extent that they allow affected

persons to know them (subject to the major qualification that rules are frequently imperfectly communicated). Rules will therefore serve to help announce or clarify official policies to affected parties, thus facilitating obedience to them. At the same time they often serve the additional function of reducing the agency's workload by promoting the possibility of individual application of official policies, without the necessity of official intervention.

(II) RULES AS SHIELDS

For the conscientious administrator, the making of decisions that are not clearly guided by reference to defined standards or rules is a task that involves the expenditure of energy and anxiety that arises from the constant re-examination of basic premises in the light of new conditions. Of course, not all administrators pursue their task with the ideal degree of zeal. Some might be happy to take the line of least resistance, to follow the argument where the strongest pressures lead, and to repeat past decisions or actions without bothering to distinguish facts or to reappraise premises. But if most administrators tend to fall into fixed decision-making patterns it is in part because they, like all people, possess limited energy, limited intellectual resources, and a limited capacity to engage daily the pressures thrust upon them. Rules to guide decisions will often be welcomed as a device to conserve official resources of energy and intellect, and to protect officials from undue tensions and pressures.

It takes constant mental energy to assess afresh the "needs" of every welfare claimant, or the "substandardness" of every house examined (assuming that these concepts can be appropriately assessed at all). It is relatively easy to have a checklist against which to measure objective characteristics (such as date of last grant of a winter coat, age, number of

---

† Excerpts from J. Jowell, "The Legal Control of Administrative Discretion" (1973) Public Law 178 at 189–92, 194, and 196–200. Reproduced with permission of Sweet & Maxwell Limited. [Commentary note by David W. Elliott.]

children). The adjectives used to describe the application of rules include "impersonal," "mechanical," "disinterested," "objective" — all of which suggest the exclusion of human or affective considerations. Max Weber's portrayal of the ideal-typical bureaucratic official applying rules *"sine ira et studio* — without hatred or passion, and hence without affection or enthusiasm," alludes to the low anxiety factor involved in rule-application. To the decision-maker, a rule might therefore "reduce headaches" and provide relief from the tension of having to decide each case anew without the benefit of authoritative guidance.

In addition to providing protection from the psychic pressures of continuing discretionary decision, rules also tend to insulate that decision-maker from political pressures to which he is subject. Clearly, the greater the freedom of a decision-maker's choice, the greater will be the opportunity to affected parties to influence the choice. A rule, however, will provide the decision-maker with an authoritative excuse to stand firm. Where the rule has been enacted after a process of participatory consultation, its legitimacy is likely to be enhanced.

Subject to the fact that announced rules may, in the course of their exposure of administrative policies, open an agency to more rigorous accountability, rules will provide an effective political shield behind which officials may hide, safe in the knowledge that in response to pressures they have a foolproof reply: "I'd like to help you, but I'm bound by this rule."

The Defects of Rules

Much of what we have just considered to be advantages of rules will be contradicted by what follows. The two positions are not reconcilable. They are not meant to be. Rules possess merits and demerits — in the abstract. It is argued here that the debate about legalisation should not be pursued in the abstract, but in the light of the particular task to be performed, and in the knowledge that the perspective of the actor (official or public) often determines the perception of rules as a merit or defect.

Rigidity and Legalism
The relative certainty of rules may, at times, prove a hindrance both to the administrator and client. The administrator who wishes to avoid committing himself to a course of action might regard a rule as a fetter upon his future options and a hindrance upon his freedom to change his mind. Interference with interests who have built a reliance upon the rule may be considered unfair, and resistance or

procedural technicalities may make change difficult. Announcing policy through case-by-case determinations (or through flexible advisory circulars) may be seen as a strategy better suited to its gradual elaboration.

When administration is charged with the application of rules, organisational routines may be set in motion whenever a set of categorised facts occur. We have seen that certain problems must be solved by a minimum of routine handling through the categorization of data. The effect of this is to reduce the personality both of the official and of the affected client who is seen as a "carrier of data" relevant to the task at hand. He is thus a "complainant of discrimination," a "welfare claimant," a "speeder." Weber's "objective" discharge of business "without regard to persons" thus occurs.

On the other hand, all persons who come into contact with rules will have noted that, as categorising general directions, rules may easily catch within their ambit technical violators whose actions could not be said to have contravened the objectives of the enforcing administration.

. . . .

To the client, therefore, the official refuge behind rules might be seen as an excuse to ignore valid claims. The obligation of a reasoned decision *de novo*, while not guaranteeing the absence of official ignorance or prejudice, constitutes at least some protection against the mechanical application of rules in situations that do not further rational objectives; at best it provides an assurance of personal attention and "individualised justice." The administrator might also prefer to look at each case anew, and to preserve the flexibility that a rule may preclude.

THE MERITS AND DEFECTS OF ADJUDICATION

. . . .

Adjudication will ... refer here to the technique of decision-making that guarantees participation to parties affected, through a number of procedural devices. The more procedural devices used, the more "judicialised" the process will be. The technique may be the sole forum for the elaboration of policies (as for example in many licence-applications, or determinations of fair rents by rent assessment committees) or it may be a forum where previous administrative determinations are challenged (as for example in the Supplementary Benefit Appeals Tribunals). We shall be comparing adjudication as case-by-case elaboration of legislative policy both with administrative decision-making by rules determined in advance of specific dispute-situations and with case-by-case discretionary determination that is not controlled by predetermined rules, nor by the adjudicative format.

The Merits of Adjudication

Perhaps the most obvious merit of adjudication, from the perspective of the litigant, arises from the definition we have adopted: adjudication guarantees participation to affected parties. This participation, and the challenge involved in adversary proceedings, will provide an incentive to administrative integrity for the following reasons: First, it allows the parties to the dispute also to be involved in the decision-making process. Although they do not make the final decision, they are nevertheless permitted to suggest the justification for a decision in their favour and to challenge each other's proofs and arguments. Being immediately involved, they will have knowledge of the "particular facts" of a situation, and thus be well placed to advance the strongest case for their proposition.

Secondly, the decision-maker is normally under a duty to articulate a reasoned basis for his decision. Rules, as we have seen, are in a sense nonrational. Whatever the reasoning behind the passage of legislation, the rule appears to an affected party as a plain injunction, for example, not to exceed thirty miles per hour, or not to park fifteen feet from the corner. The adjudicator's obligation to reason will provide a check against the use of criteria that are improper, arbitrary, legalistic or that fail to achieve congruence between the effect of the decision and official objectives. Adjudication contains a desire to give "formal and institutional expression to the influence of reasoned argument in human affairs." The requirement of a written and published reasoned justification of a decision implies that the justification is open to public criticism on similar rational grounds. Thus adjudication will, especially when accompanied by a public reasoned decision, provide an opportunity for scrutiny and thus for the accountability of the decision-makers to their clientele and to the public.

A related reason for the tendency of adjudication to promote administrative integrity arises from the fact that the judicial decision must be justified by a rule, standard or principle. The relevance of ascriptive or particularistic criteria will by implication be reduced. The litigants will make their claims as members of a legally defined class, as particular instances of a generalised category. In consequence,

an appeal to power, private interests, or political expediency will be inappropriate. The adjudicator will in turn be bound to evaluate the relative merits of claims in the light of accepted techniques for determining their importance and weight, and by reference to authoritative guides, irrespective of his personal view of the result.

We have seen that a rule might provide administrators with a welcome refuge from the obligation of reasoned decision and from political and personal pressures. Adjudication does not excuse the obligation of decision; when reasoned decisions are required, the obligation is only increased. However, the claimant's appeal to a rule, principle or standard reduces the possibility of litigants appealing to political or private interests. In this sense, therefore, the decision-maker will be insulated from such pressures.

Administrators might also derive benefits from the fact that a reasoned decision was made and was openly arrived at with equal participation. The process of adjudication, irrespective of the substance of a decision, might therefore itself provide administrative action with the gloss of legitimacy.

A final administrative advantage of adjudication over rule-governed decision is the fact that it allows incremental elaboration of laws on the basis of a case-by-case treatment of issues. Although an organisation might feel itself bound by its own decisions, adjudication deals with a specific fact-situation, and later cases can be "distinguished" from earlier ones on the basis of the facts. Thus, despite pressures for consistency and the gradual reduction of discretion (features that students of the common law know too well [lead] often to the ossification of a developing principle) the case-by-case approach of adjudication tends to allow an administrative body to deal with specific classes of cases as they arise, to change its mind, and to build its commitments gradually.

The Defects of Adjudication

. . . .

The adversary structure of adjudication ... might contain costs. In welfare cases, as Titmuss has pointed out, the continuing relationship between the recipient and the Commission might make a recipient reluctant to challenge the Commission in an adversary situation that could damage the relationship. Similarly, tenants might be afraid that to challenge their landlords legally would provoke retaliatory measures.

The adversary adjudicative situation also places the participants in what game theorists call a "zero-sum" situation. One side must win and the other must lose; the defendant is liable or not liable, guilty or not guilty. Except for the possibility of a flexible settlement out of court, the matter is placed in a clear yes-no, either-or, more-or-less setting. Matters that are suited to compromise, mediation, and [accommodation] are not best pursued in the structured adversary setting of adjudication.

Rules, as we have seen, may be of benefit to officials as a means of announcing policies to affected parties. Individual application of laws is thus possible without the necessity of administrative intervention. Adjudicative decisions, however, are less possible of communication, since they arise in the context of specific dispute-situations, which may be distinguished from others. In addition, the adjudicative decision is less available to the lay public. Even lawyers may have difficulty in extrapolating the *ratio* from a decision, and the precise content of a rule.

The specific dispute-orientation of adjudication highlights another defect from the administrative perspective, as compared with rules. The adjudicative decision concerns individual rights, and may thus bear little or no relation to the primary administrative function, which involves the performance of a particular task. A particular case, for example, may raise questions wider than the questions at issue. The adjudicator may deal with the wider questions, but he is not required to do so for the purpose of the decision in hand, and remarks that are made on the wider issue are strictly considered *obiter dicta*, and thus not binding on future cases. Furthermore, although the specific decision may affect parties similarly situated to the direct participants in the litigation, the decision-maker is not required to consult or to notify these wider interests. For example, a welfare claimant may complain to a tribunal that she was refused a winter coat. The grant of the coat is of interest to other recipients and to welfare rights organisations wanting to advise their members about the conditions concerning new coats, and other winter clothing. The tribunal would not normally however consult or notify the organisation or other recipients, and would confine their decision to the particular claimant at hand.

These defects of adjudication point up its limitations as a planning device. In fact, decision-makers in the adjudicative context may lay their own complaints, announce their rules clearly, deal with issues that are wider than the question at issue, consult interests that are wider than those directly represented by the litigants, and even allow these interests to be represented as parties to the litigation. Planning officials, for example, often inform amenity groups and others of a pending application for development permission; "interested parties" may appear at planning inquiries. Normally, however, adjudication is deficient to achieve wide-ranging planning, since it is geared to the resolution of individual disputes, rather than to the managerial tasks required to "get the work of society done."

[Jowell says that there are some situations for which rules and adjudication are inappropriate. Some issues, for example, are better handled by broad standards or principles than by precise rules. Can you think of some examples here? Jowell adds that adjudication is poorly suited to complex "polycentric" problems in which the answer to one aspect may affect the answers to others. Jowell concludes that neither rules, adjudication, nor any other specific technique is inherently superior to the others, and that each can only be assessed in relation to the needs of a specific, concrete situation.]

(g) The Mandarins Acquiesce†

François Perreault

NOTE

In February 2004, Prime Minister Paul Martin appointed Mr. Justice John Gomery to head the Commission of Inquiry into the Sponsorship Program and Advertising Activities (Gomery Commission). The federal Sponsorship Program (more fully described in Chapter 3) was a venture that spent

---

† Excerpts from F. Perreault, *Inside Gomery*, translated by Carl Angers (Vancouver: Douglas & McIntyre, 2006) at 28–31. Reproduced with permission from the publisher.

approximately $50 million a year for eight years, at various cultural events in Quebec, attempting to increase the visibility of Canada's contribution to that province. Allegations of abuse and fraud connected to the administration of that program, and its unwieldy spending, had been published in the media and by the Auditor General of Canada. The Gomery Commission's mandate was presumably to get straight to the "heart of the matter", but that was not apparent from the initial terms of reference presented to the Commissioner by the federal government. As you read the excerpt below, ask yourself: why would a government that initiates a broad public investigation of its activities attempt to simultaneously narrow the scope of those same proceedings? Are there political and bureaucratic interests afoot in government that might conflict with the public interests to fully understand a matter whenever a Commission of Inquiry is appointed to investigate a question? What implications, if any, does that present for ensuring peace, order and good (administrative) government for Canadians?

EXTRACT

Gomery was not comfortable with the unknown. He needed an interpreter to fully understand the federal realm and to learn survival tactics. He arranged to meet with Sheila-Marie Cook, who came highly recommended, as she had already been involved in several commissions of inquiry. "I've taken a look at your c.v.," Gomery said. "I was impressed. You're hired as executive director and secretary of the commission. This will therefore be your fourteenth commission of inquiry, not counting the one I am told you declined to work on. As for your authority, I intend to delegate to you all administrative powers according to Section 34 of the Public Administration Act. We will be meeting on Monday. Now, if you could just tell me how to get to the Treasury Board — I'm expected there in fifteen minutes."

Sheila-Marie Cook was in a spin. "I am flattered," she said. "You know, a commissioner cannot entirely back away from all administrative duties. We have to divide them up..."

"Listen," he said, "a long time ago, I had to choose between law and administration. I opted for law at the time, and I therefore intend to assume this task once again for the commission."

Cook knew all the internal workings of the federal government administration. Even better, she knew the people who made it work. In four decades,

she had seen them rise in rank, mingle with the powerful elite and sometimes drop out or be dropped. Sheila-Marie Cook had made her first inroads as a legislative assistant, working for Pierre Elliott Trudeau. That was in 1968. The years that followed marked the beginning of profound changes in our society and, by extension, in the organization of government.

"If I may, what meeting are you going to now?" she asked Gomery.

"Some deputy ministers are going to give me the terms of reference of my mandate."

"Allow me to give you a first bit of advice. Don't sign anything! Take the document they hand to you and leave, then read over all the fine print. Believe me, this isn't their first commission of inquiry."

Never again, she thought, will he go to this type of meeting alone.

That day though, he was in fact alone as he faced a panel of five men who were intent on observing a judge they had not personally recruited, for a commission [whose] existence they did not necessarily want. Gomery felt they were annoyed by his take-charge attitude. They must have realized quickly that the agenda of the meeting would soon be in the commissioner's hands. Gomery was tall and calm, and his voice had an assurance that was typical of a high-court judge. He spoke smoothly, but his remarks were so precise and authoritative that they precluded any misunderstanding.

In fact, after the bureaucrats had met Gomery, it was clear that they might eventually have to testify before him. Until that meeting, the question of having one day to account for what they actually knew, what they saw or what they pretended not to have seen, had not been raised. Imagine — senior public servants dragged into this humiliating process!

Judd, Marshall, Rozenberg, Rawling ... and the other. They were the highest ranking non-elected personnel, the field marshals of the federal administration. They derived their immense power from the duties and functions delegated to them by their respective ministers or the prime minister himself. Before Gomery, they appeared busy but courteous.

"It's a pleasure to meet you, Mr. Justice," said one.

"We're glad you accepted our offer," said another, more cheekily.

It was no doubt at this meeting that Gomery noticed for the first time how senior public servants from Ottawa use the "we" when referring to their departments.

That private observation later became an irritation that he voiced publicly on many occasions, as government officials, in their testimonies, instinctively tried to recount conversations or written exchanges without revealing the identity of anyone involved. They would admit having met with, e-mailed, obtained authorization from or given instructions to the Treasury Board, Public Works, the Privy Council or the Prime Minister's Office, rather than to Jacques, Paul, Irene or John. Each time, the commissioner would reply, "But with whom, exactly? I'm conducting an inquiry here. Give me some names, please!"

After the deputy ministers had made their presentations, Gomery immersed himself in reading the terms of reference of his mandate, as if he were alone in the room. One of the senior civil servants attempted to break the silence: "As you can see, it's all there, in keeping with the prime minister's announcement. The powers conferred on you are unprecedented for a commission of inquiry."

Absorbed in his reading, Gomery deliberately avoided all the required clauses establishing the legal framework, those endless and unavoidable paragraphs. He went quickly to the heart of his concerns — briefly, the authority given him by the urgency of the situation, independence in his choice of staff and freedom to establish a work schedule. It was all there, except for one essential prerogative. This can't be an oversight, he thought; it's impossible. Did they really think I wouldn't notice?

The silence lay heavy in the room. The bureaucrats must have wondered what he was thinking about. If he wanted more, how far would he go?

This time, Gomery's commanding voice had a clear target. "Gentlemen," he said, "correct me if I'm wrong, but it seems to me that the prime minister insisted that this inquiry would get to the bottom of things, without omitting any fact, any document pertaining to the circumstance of this sponsorship affair. Am I not right?

"That is true, Mr. Commissioner. You have, as we say, carte blanche."

"Not quite," replied Gomery. "I see no reference in this text to documents coming out of the Prime Minister's Office, nor to minutes of Cabinet meetings, nor to internal memos prepared by the Privy Council. Did Mr. Martin not insist that we uncover the political interference in this scandal? You absolutely must lift this classified status."

An awkward silence ensued. "I'm afraid that will be impossible," answered the boldest deputy sitting at the table. "By their very nature, these documents must remain out of the public eye. The management

of state affairs is at stake. To open that door would be reckless."

Gomery lost his composure, throwing his audience off track for a moment. "Well, as far as I'm concerned, the danger is elsewhere. I don't see myself accepting a mandate that I can only half fulfill. In my mind, *that* is what is impossible. Incidentally, the prime minister did not appear to me to have made only a halfway commitment when he announced the creation of my commission."

Whether it is the tone of his voice, the look in his eyes or the expression on his face, Gomery's annoyance always makes an impression on those he confronts. Or maybe it's the combination of all three signals that causes immediate, deep-seated discomfort. Whatever the case, reaction from the bureaucrats was immediate. Nobody in the room dared to consider returning to the prime minister to report that his commissioner, [whose] nomination had already made the headlines, had been forced to decline the offer on the spot because he lacked the authority he needed to conduct the inquiry.

And yet, one of the senior civil servants excused himself from the room, claiming that he needed authorization from his superiors before he could accept the judge's terms. When he returned, his colleagues reluctantly swallowed the pill: the confidentiality requirement on all documents whose contents might be useful to the inquiry had been lifted.

After the meeting, the bureaucrats must have wondered whether anything at all would remain absolute in their world, much less their own power.

From that point forward, all documents requested by the commission were examined with a fine-tooth comb before being submitted. In certain cases, excessive censoring led to fierce debates and battles as legal staff demanded more complete versions. One such episode concerned the minutes of a special Cabinet meeting held on February 1 and 2, 1996. It was at this meeting that the decision was made to improve federal visibility in Quebec, by the government and, by extension, according to the participants, the Liberal Party. In these minutes it was apparent that the two entities had not always been differentiated during Cabinet discussions. The commission had to spend a great deal of time and produce many arguments before finally getting responses to its requests. For example, in a letter to Gomery, Alex Himelfarb, clerk of the Privy Council, stated that in his opinion some of the information contained in the documents requested by the commission was irrelevant, and therefore he had censored certain passages. By wielding his authority in this way, Himelfarb, the highest-ranking public servant in the country, must have thought he had finished with John Gomery. If so, he underestimated the commissioner, who became more and more frustrated and certainly was not deceived by the bluff. Moreover, through his actions, the clerk had exposed the government to the possibility of a court order to hand over the documents. For some items, the negotiations resulted in three different versions of documents being submitted to the counsel, each one with slightly fewer amputations than the last.

The Opposition parties jumped on the bandwagon at this point. The Conservative leader, Stephan Harper, decried Liberal secrecy; Bloc leader Gilles Duceppe compared the blocked-out texts to a game of Mystery Word.

At the meeting with the senior bureaucrats, Gomery was satisfied that he had gained access to restricted documents. He probably did not foresee what at high price he would have to pay for demanding access from people who rarely make such concessions when their personal power is at stake.

3   Non-Judicial and Judicial Control

(a)   Control

David W. Elliott

A CASE FOR CONTROL

Increased size and powers help government get things done, but we expect more of government than this. We expect it to do what we, the electors, ask it to do, and to do this fairly and according to law. Of administrators, we ask that they obey their statutory and constitutional mandates, and show reasonable respect for those affected by their actions.

To obtain this compliance and respect, we must rely in large part on administrators' good sense and good will. Our administrative process, like our governmental process, would simply break down without some trust and shared values between governors and governed. But since administrators are human and wield power, they have the potential to abuse it. To help ensure that administrators *do* obey mandates and respect those affected, some control[1] is necessary. We might go further and say that effective control is as necessary for administrative action as its effective exercise in the first place.

The sheer size of government increases the need for control. A typical exchange between an administrator and an ordinary citizen is an uneven match, with power and resources on the side of the administrator. The larger the administrative process, the more frequent this kind of exchange, and the greater the chances of unintentional — and even intentional — abuse of power, with resulting harm to the citizen affected. When the new powers are discretionary, quasi-legislative, or quasi-judicial, further problems are generated for those seeking to maintain effective control.

At the same time, not all objects of government control are weak or defenceless. Some are large corporations or other private organizations with vast power of their own. Government has no monopoly on power, and much of the administrative process is concerned with controlling abuses of private power.[2] Excessive controls on the administrative process could leave these abuses unchecked. Ideologies traditionally associated with control, such as the rule of law, may be used for purposes beyond checking abuse of power, to favour some social groups over others. Moreover, the staffs of institutions of control are no less fallible than administrators, and each specific form of control has its own characteristic drawbacks.

None of these potential problems removes the need to check abuse of administrative power. What they do suggest is that control is a double-edged sword, to be wielded with caution. A balance must be sought between inadequate and excessive control, and one should consider the strengths and weaknesses of forms of control as well as of forms of administration.

Mechanisms for controlling the executive can be divided into those that are non-judicial and those that are judicial. Non-judicial controls are administered primarily outside the courts of law. Judicial control is administered directly through the courts of law.

NON-JUDICIAL CONTROL

Internal Controls

Internal controls operate within the executive branch of government itself. On request, for example, an official may be prepared informally to reconsider his or her decision. Some regulatory authorities, such as the Canadian Industrial Relations Board, have specific statutory provisions that provide for internal review. In the hierarchical structure of departments or ministries, an official's decision is usually subject to some kind of check or review by an immediate superior. Most of the quasi-judicial and regulatory authorities and Crown corporations lack direct hierarchical control over their decisions, but are subject to "collegial" checks[3] that require officers to make decisions jointly with colleagues. In some cases, a decision of one authority may be subject to a statutory appeal to a second authority within the executive branch.

Internal controls offer a number of distinctive strengths.[4] They can be informal, in the case of a reconsideration. They have a wide potential scope. They can address positive concerns, such as meeting deadlines and filling quotas, as well as more negative concerns, such as preventing or remedying mistakes. Those who administer them likely have special expertise. Few will know more about the subject matter of a decision than the official who made it and his or her other colleagues or superiors. On the other hand, the very proximity that helps ensure expertise in making a decision militates against independence in controlling it. Wholly independent controls are more easily imposed from outside the administrative process.

Political executive control of independent administrative agencies is a special form of internal review. This kind of control is exercised either through cabinet or ministerial regulations or directives[5] that fill in gaps in an agency's statutory mandate, or through direct *ex post facto* cabinet or ministerial review of specific agency decisions.[6] *Ex post facto* political review is exceptional and controversial, justified by some because it permits elected leaders to correct decisions at odds with major government policy, and criticized by others because of its capacity to undermine the independence and credibility of agencies supposedly removed from partisan influences.

Parliamentary and Electoral Controls

A second important group of controls is connected with the parliamentary and electoral process. At the heart of our system of parliamentary democracy is the notion that our government is directed by those who represent the general wishes of the public at large and are accountable to them through the electoral process.[7] Controls that are part of this system include the requirement of federal, provincial, and territorial elections at least every five years; the party system, and the critical role expected of opposition parties; the requirement that a session of the federal, provincial, or territorial legislative assembly be convened at least once a year; the want of confidence motion; the daily question period; the doctrine of ministerial responsibility, by which a minister is answerable for the policies and actions of executive departments and units under his or her control; the requirement that administrative agencies, Crown corporations, and other semi-independent institutions, such as the Auditor-General, submit annual reports to Parliament; scrutiny by legislative committees; the good offices of the M.P. or M.L.A. (or elected municipal politician) for relevant electoral districts.

Controls through the parliamentary and electoral process can result in major changes through legislation. The effectiveness of publicity in Parliament or the good offices of an individual elected politician should not be underestimated.[8]

On the other hand, the electoral process is a periodic phenomenon. When they do occur, elections under the traditional first-past-the-post system of representation can yield wide discrepancies between party seats and the popular vote. Opposition parties have far less information and expertise at their disposal than those in power.[9] Want of confidence motions are generally ineffective during periods of majority government because of strict party discipline. Except where there has been personal fault on their part, ministers tend not to resign because of governmental problems. Legislative committees are usually dominated by members of the party in power, who rarely criticize major government policy. Elected officials, however well intentioned, may lack influence if they are backbenchers or opposition members. Two of the greatest defects of legislatures as effective controls on the executive are (a) their domination by the political parties forming the government of the time (which are dominated, in turn, by a cabinet and prime minister or premier) and (b) their crowded agendas, which tend to squeeze out issues without nation-wide or province-wide concern. My dispute with a public authority seeking to expropriate a corner of my garden may be all-important to me, but it is unlikely to become a national election issue.

The Media

The media serve as a control on executive and other government action in two ways. First, by making information about the decisions and actions of the executive more widely available, the media contribute to the effectiveness of other forms of control, such as the parliamentary and electoral process and public opinion. Second, through editorial campaigns and ombudsman-type columnists, the media may serve as a more direct agent of control.

The key strengths of the media are their special facilities for extracting information and their access to publicity. Moreover, Canada is fortunate that its media are relatively independent, if not (at least by American standards) highly aggressive. On the negative side, the media are a selective form of control, favouring the colourful and newsworthy, and tending to ignore less dramatic concerns. They are sporadic in their application. Often they fail to follow up on the long-term results of a concern. They lack certainty of enforcement.

Public and Private Interest Controls

Public and private interest controls are a diverse form of control whose strength lies in numbers, persistence, and publicity. They include general interest groups — such as the Consumers Association of Canada — and specific interest groups, such as a neighbourhood seeking to obtain a local bus route. They include public interest representative techniques, wherein a representative of a public or private interest is appointed to serve that interest on a public authority. One of the most powerful — and unpredictable — of public and private interest controls is the poll, which purports to represent public opinion at a particular time.

To the extent that they can claim to speak on behalf of wide segments of public opinion, public and private interest controls can often be very effective. On the other hand, they lack certainty of enforcement and are limited to concerns shared by groups, especially very large groups.

Miscellaneous Controls

Apart from the ultimate constraints of the *Charter* and other parts of the Constitution, the executive may be subject to a variety of miscellaneous controls, such as ombudsmen,[10] auditors-general, the Privacy Commissioner, the Commissioner for Official Languages, and access to information legislation. Some — such as task forces, royal commissions, and public inquiries — are temporary in nature. The ombudsman and the auditors-general have the widest scope of these bodies, but even they have limits.[11] Most of these miscellaneous controls rely on publicity. On the other hand, many can do no more than recommend: their determinations cannot be enforced.

JUDICIAL CONTROL

Aim and Functions

The general aim of judicial control is to help ensure that administrative action is carried out fairly, without interfering unduly with administrative efficiency.[12] Judicial review, the main traditional form of judicial control, has the additional aim of enforcing the intent of Parliament and the general mandate of the electorate.

Judicial control of administrative action is based on the principle that the state should act only pursuant to law,[13] and on the further notion that it is the courts' responsibility to interpret this law.[14]

For the first principle, the all-important source of state power is the statute.[15] The principle assumes that all law is either formally enacted by elected legislators, or can be changed by them. It is intended to ensure that administrative and other government action is sanctioned by elected representatives accountable to the public, and, conversely, that ordinary citizens' interests are not restricted without the sanction of these elected representatives.

The second principle, that courts are responsible for interpreting the law, is intended to provide a relatively independent, authoritative means of determining what the law means in individual cases, on an ongoing basis. By virtue of parliamentary sovereignty and the supremacy of the Constitution, the court's role is auxiliary in the sense that it must be based on the legislative or constitutional text. On the other hand, the courts feel free to evolve their own principles for construing the written texts. In constitutional interpretation, at least, it is their construction that usually prevails.

The courts exercise judicial control by examining an administrator's decision to determine if it is consistent with the relevant (i) legislation or subordinate legislation; (ii) constitutional provisions; and (iii) presumptions of common law. Inconsistent administrative decisions or actions are invalid and may give rise to claims for compensation; those which are consistent are valid.

At the heart of judicial control is a series of balancing acts. Courts must try to balance the needs of government efficiency with the need to ensure fair and non-arbitrary treatment to specific groups. Excessive judicial intervention could prejudice the principle that — subject to the Constitution — the will of elected legislators should prevail. It could duplicate, slow down, and even paralyze government action. Courts must adapt the law to new circumstances, but their law-making powers are restricted by the doctrine of sovereignty of Parliament,[16] by the notion that justice requires that like cases should be treated alike, and by the functional drawbacks of judicial law-making powers in comparison with those of the executive and legislative branches.[17] Similarly, although courts cannot disregard policy considerations outside the text of the relevant legislation, their own structural limitations and the risk of undermining the responsibility of elected representatives suggest that they should also avoid elevating policy considerations over the written text.

Subject Matter

The immediate subject matter of judicial control of administrative action is the decisions, actions, and omissions of the members of the administrative process. In the last chapter we saw that the administrative process includes the executive branch of government together with certain private or semi-private bodies that also exercise public statutory powers. Within the executive, there is a central administrative process, which is under the direct responsibility of a cabinet minister.[18] There is also an outlying administrative process, which is the part of the executive that lies outside the direct responsibility of a cabinet minister.[19] Outside the executive branch lies the quasi-administrative process, an assorted collection of institutions that exercise significant statutory powers even though they are predominantly private in character. Examples of the quasi-administrative process include universities and trade unions.

This variety is complicated by the fact that even a single public authority may discharge widely varying functions in different situations. We saw in the last chapter that these may include court-like functions, rule-making functions, and discretionary power. It should be remembered, too, that the administrative process consists, ultimately, of individual human beings, with widely varying backgrounds, temperaments, and expertise.

This extraordinary diversity and complexity militates against detailed judicial reconsideration of administrative decisions, and suggests that judicial control must be limited control.

Main Forms

There are four basic forms of judicial control: judicial review, constitutional control, judicial appeal, and the action for damages.

Judicial review is an examination of a decision of a public authority to determine if it was authorized by statute. It will be considered in more detail later.[20]

Constitutional control is an examination of a decision of a public authority and its governing statute to see if they were authorized by the Constitution. Normally, constitutional control assesses administrative action in relation to the written portion of the Constitution. Unlike other judicial control, it assesses the validity of enabling statutes as well as action under them. While non-constitutional control can be restricted by ordinary statutes, constitutional control can be limited — if at all — only pursuant to the provisions of the *Constitution Act, 1982*.

Before 1982, constitutional control was exercised only indirectly in regard to administrative action. Usually it resulted from a finding that a legislature was acting outside the areas of exclusive legislative jurisdiction prescribed in sections 91 and 92 and similar provisions of the *Constitution Act, 1867*.[21] Sometimes it resulted from a finding that the requirements of section 96 of this Act had been violated.[22]

Constitutional control has become much more important since 1982. Administrative decisions may now be controlled by traditional or entrenched criteria, depending on the situation. If courts give a wide scope to *Charter* provisions such as sections 1, 2, 7, and 15, constitutional control could eventually eclipse judicial review in importance. Constitutional control pursuant to the *Charter* will be discussed in more detail later.[23]

Judicial appeal, the third main form of judicial control, is a reconsideration of a decision of a public authority. Unlike judicial review, statutory appeal is a "creature of statute". Its scope depends on what the legislature has provided, and without an appeal statute there can be no judicial appeal. Theoretically, an unqualified appeal provision could permit an unrestricted reconsideration of an administrative decision. In practice, appeal provisions tend to be limited to specific aspects, such as questions of law. Moreover, courts tend to apply the same general criteria for deciding on the level of appeal that they apply to deciding on a standard of judicial review.

An action for damages is the fourth basic kind of judicial control. It can be defined as a proceeding for monetary compensation for an unauthorized common law or civil law wrong. Like judicial review, actions for damages are based on the common law. Note, however, should be made of the situation in Quebec, where the equivalent of an action for damages is based on article 1457 of the *Civil Code of Quebec* (formerly article 1053). Except for proceedings under section 24(1) of the *Charter*, actions for damages and article 1457 of the *Civil Code* are the only kind of judicial control that can provide relief by way of monetary compensation.

Normally, the action for damages is only available where it is shown that the public authority lacks statutory power to perform the action complained of.[24] Similarly, a proceeding under article 1457 can be excluded or restricted by a specific statute expressly permitting the action in question.

The action for damages and article 1457 of the *Civil Code* are regarded as essentially private proceedings, affecting an officer or corporate or other legal entity in his, her, or its private capacity. Nevertheless, they are relevant to public law to the extent that the officers or other entities are also public authorities.

Main Elements

Cross-cutting these four main kinds of judicial control are the main elements of virtually any judicial control proceeding — relief, grounds of control, and remedies. Relief is the redress a complainant desires from judicial control, from quashing to prohibiting to enjoining to receiving monetary compensation. To obtain relief, though, a complainant must prove more than harm. He or she must normally show that the harm resulted from a recognized form of defect, or "ground" of judicial control.

This might be a breach of natural justice in the case of judicial review, a violation of a *Charter* right or freedom in the case of constitutional control, or a trespass in the case of an action for damages. Only in an unrestricted judicial appeal can one obtain relief without pointing to a specific ground, and most appeals *are* limited by statute to various grounds, such as error of law and jurisdiction.

Remedies — the individual forms of proceeding for obtaining judicial control — comprise the third main element of judicial control.[25] The action for damages[26] is both a distinct form of judicial control and a remedy in its own right. Judicial review has many different remedies. A first group includes the common law prerogative remedies[27] of *certiorari*,[28] prohibition,[29] *mandamus*[30] and *habeas corpus*.[31] A second group comprises the common law private law remedies[32] of declaration[33] and injunction.[34] Yet a third group includes the statutory remedies, from the section Federal Court of Appeal's application to quash and — in Ontario and British Columbia — the statutory application for judicial review.[35] The variety of the common law remedies is extraordinary; so, unfortunately, is their diversity.

Notes

1. The term "control" is used here in the sense of a "check" or "restraint."
2. For example, economic monopolies and other examples of "market failure," pollution, industrial and safety hazards, and other harm to individuals or groups. The need to control these general and economic problems has given rise to the "public interest" and "economic" theories of regulation: see John C. Strick, *The Economics of Government Regulation: Theory and Canadian Practice*, 2d ed. (Toronto: Thompson Educational, 1994) Ch. 2; and L.N. Gerston et al., "Theories of Regulation and Deregulation" in *The Regulated Society* (Pacific Grove: Brooks/Cole, 1988) at 66–79. The fact that regulation does not necessarily achieve these objectives is stressed in the "capture" and "bureaucratic" (or "political bureaucratic behaviour") theories of regulation. They claim, respectively, that regulators are, or over time become, captured by the interests they are supposed to regulate, and that regulators are heavily influenced by their own goals, such as bureaucratic survival: *ibid.*
3. See the classic account in A. Abel, "The Dramatis Personae of Administrative Law" (1972), 10 *Osgoode Hall L.J.* 61, 90.
4. *Ibid.* at 89–91.
5. For example, s. 26 of *Broadcasting Act, 1991*, c. 11.
6. For example, s. 28 of the *Broadcasting Act*, S.C. 1991, c. 11.
7. Chapter 2, above.
8. R.J. Van Loon and M.S. Whittington, *The Canadian Political System: Environment, Structure, and Process*, 4th ed. (Toronto: McGraw-Hill Ryerson, 1987) at 604 (re "general audit function" of Parliament) and 608–609 (re "ombudsman function" of individual M.P.); Rand Dyck, *Canadian Politics: Critical Approaches*, 4th ed. (Scarborough, Ont.: Thomson Nelson, 2004) Ch. 22.
9. A point stressed in *The Canadian Political System*, *ibid.* at 598–99.
10. See extract below.
11. *Ibid.*
12. Fairness and efficiency are themselves means of achieving the goals set out in administrative mandates. On the dangers of treating efficiency as an end in itself rather than as a means, see Janice G. Stein, *The Cult of Efficiency* (Toronto: Anansi, 2001).
13. See, for example, *Roncarelli v. Duplessis*, [1959] S.C.R. 121 at 184; *Re Anti-Inflation Act*, [1976] 2 S.C.R. 373 at 433; and *Canada v. Newfoundland Telephone Company Ltd.*, [1987] 2 S.C.R. 466 at 478.

14. See, for example, *Fraser v. Public Staff Labour Relations Board*, [1985] 2 S.C.R. 455 at 469–70.

15. "Everything that a public officer, whose office has been created and defined by statute, does in his official capacity must find its ultimate legal foundation in statutory authority": *Canada v. Newfoundland Telephone Company Ltd.*, [1987] 2 S.C.R. 466 at 478. Another potential source of power, the royal prerogative, is severely curtailed by convention and by common law principles such as the requirement that action penalizing or prejudicing individuals must be authorized by statute. The common law is a more indirect and elusive source: subordinate to contrary statutes, generally limited to discerning statutory meaning, but applied by independent institutions with ultimate responsibility for interpreting superlegislative constitutional norms.

16. In Canada, the principle of sovereignty of Parliament holds that, subject to the Constitution, statutes enacted by Canadian legislatures prevail over other forms of law, such as the common law and the royal prerogative.

17. E.g., the *ex post facto* and party-oriented focus of most judicial decisions, and the limited evidentiary, research, and planning resources of courts.

18. For example, the ordinary government departments and ministries, and coordinating bodies such as the Finance Department and Treasury Board Secretariat, the Prime Minister's Office, the Privy Council Office, and their provincial counterparts. See, further: *The Canadian Political System: Environment, Structure, and Process*, *supra* note 8 at 492–94 (central coordinating bodies) and 540–56 (bureaucracy as a whole); Kenneth Kernaghan and David Siegel, *Public Administration in Canada: A Text*, 4th ed. (Scarborough, Ont.: ITP Nelson, 1999) Ch. 8 (departments and central agencies), c. 9 (public enterprise and privatization), c. 10 (regulatory agencies and deregulation) and c. 11 (alternative service delivery); and Statistics Canada, *Labour Force Information: June, 2001* (Ottawa: Statistics Canada, 2001), Table 2: Catalogue No. 71-001-PIB (labour force in various parts of government).

19. For example, regulatory agencies, such as the National Energy Board, at the federal level, and the provincial municipal boards, and Crown corporations, such as Canada Post, at the federal level, and the hydro authorities in the provinces. See also *supra* note 15.

20. Chapter 4, below.

21. For an early example, see *Re Board of Commerce and Combines and Fair Prices Act*, [1922] 1 A.C. 191 (J.C.P.C.).

22. For example, *Re Residential Tenancies Act*, [1981] 1 S.C.R. 714. Section 96 gives the federal government the exclusive power to appoint superior and county court judges. It has been interpreted as preventing provincial governments from creating tribunals whose features resemble too closely those of superior or county courts. One feature of superior courts is their own absolute freedom from judicial review. When provincial legislatures go too far in seeking to protect their tribunals from judicial review, they may find the tribunals declared unconstitutional for violation of s. 96. At first glance, the wording of this section does not impose restrictions on the federal

government. However, if s. 96 is construed more broadly as reflecting a general guarantee of superior court review, it might apply to both the provincial and federal governments. See Peter W. Hogg, *Constitutional Law of Canada*, 2005 student ed. (Scarborough, Ont.: Carswell, 2005) under heading 7.3.

23. Chapters 7 to 11, below.

24. In some cases, the question as to whether there is statutory protection against damages compensation is established in the course of the damages action itself. For example, for the common law tort of negligence, courts look first to see if under the circumstances it would be reasonable to impose a *prima facie* (rebuttable) duty of care on a public body. If so, they then look to see if there are any policy considerations that would make it unwise to impose this duty. Among these considerations is the question as to whether the legislature intended to exclude damages in this particular case. This might be done by use of express wording to this effect, or impliedly, by making the action in question part of a broad planning or "policy" decision or of an adjudicatory quasi-judicial decision: for the latter two situations, see *Cooper v. Hobart*, [2001] 3 S.C.R. 537 at para. 38.

25. See generally David Phillip Jones and Anne S. de Villars, *Principles of Administrative Law*, 4th ed. (Toronto: Carswell, 2004), Part IV; David J. Mullan, *Administrative Law* (Toronto: Irwin Law, 2001) Part IV.

26. A proceeding for relief by way of monetary compensation. This is a private law remedy, but unlike the private law review remedies of the declaration and injunction, it is available *only* in regard to private law defects.

27. These are remedies that originated from the royal prerogative power to supervise the administration of justice; are limited to judicial review proceedings; can be issued only by the superior courts, and only in regard to the jurisdiction or legality of a decision of a public authority; have a distinct style of cause, the Crown proceeding against the public authority, on behalf of (*ex parte*) the applicant.

28. The prerogative remedy with the effect of quashing a public authority's decision.

29. The prerogative remedy that requires a public authority to discontinue proceedings.

30. The prerogative remedy that orders a public authority to perform a statutory duty.

31. The prerogative remedy that can declare invalid a decision to hold a person in physical detention.

32. These remedies did not originate from the royal prerogative power; are not limited to judicial review (the declaration and injunction issuing for private law defects such as torts as well as public law grounds); and can be granted by inferior courts. Their style of cause involves a plaintiff proceeding against a defendant.

33. The private law remedy that provides a formal judicial statement respecting the legal validity or invalidity of a decision.

34. The private law remedy that orders proceedings to be discontinued or a public or private duty be performed.

35. See "Note" and "Postscript" to extracts from *Statutory Powers Procedure Act*, Chapter 6, below.

(b) Tribunals and Control at the IRB†

Peter Showler

NOTE

As we saw in Chapter 2, when an adjudicatory body is created, we generally expect that it will have enough independence make impartial decisions, and that we will be able to contribute to these decisions if they affect us directly. Of course, the institutions with the greatest decision-making independence and the most extensive procedures for procedural participation are the ordinary courts of law. But courts tend to be slow, formal, rigid, and expensive.

To avoid these problems and make use of specialized expertise, policy makers may give adjudicatory duties to administrative agencies rather than to courts. These agencies come in many shapes, sizes, and functions. They may be called tribunals, boards, commissions, inquiries, authorities, or agencies, sometimes to reflect special functions and sometimes not. Although these agencies adjudicate, most must carry out policy mandates as well. Conversely, although these agencies are within the executive branch of government, they generally work at some distance from ministerial and other centralized controls.

The number and variety of these agencies attest to their great popularity and flexibility. Nevertheless, their hybrid nature poses complex challenges for control. What independence safeguards are needed to protect impartiality? What ministerial and other central controls should be retained? Where central controls have been loosened, what controls should take their place? Although the answers may vary greatly with the individual context, the questions persist.

In this extract, the chairperson of the largest federal administrative tribunal comments on some of the features and challenges of tribunals, and about the response to these challenges at his tribunal. Note his reference to the goals of efficiency, fairness, and quality (presumably "high quality"?) decision-making. Another way to look at these goals is to regard efficiency and fairness as the two main goals for the administrative *process*, and high quality decisions as a key goal for the *outcome* of this process. What processes and controls have been put in place to address these goals at the Immigration and Refugee Board? Can you think of any possible alternatives?

Note that the chairperson is speaking mainly of kinds of internal controls. What kinds of external (judicial and other) controls apply to the IRB?

EXTRACT

INTRODUCTION

Tribunals are often described by what they are not. They are not courts nor are they government departments.[1] Many tribunals, particularly those quasi-judicial in nature and prone to judicialization, are often perceived as courts. Yet courts and tribunals are by conception different creatures. In fact, tribunals were originally conceived of as alternatives to courts, offering the speedy adjudication of claims by specialised, expert decision-makers.[2] "Like the courts, administrative agencies are expected to be impartial and fair. As an alternative to the courts, they are also expected to be more accessible, less costly and more able to reach a decision in a timely and effective manner."[3]

In its recent *Ocean Port* decision the Supreme Court underlined the fundamental distinction between administrative tribunals and courts. [Administrative tribunals] are, in fact, created precisely for the purpose of implementing government policy. Implementation of that policy may require them to make quasi-judicial decisions. They thus may be seen as spanning the constitutional divide between the executive and the judicial branches of government.[4] [See *Ocean Port Hotel Ltd. v. British Columbia (General Manager, Liquor Control and Licensing Branch)* (2001), S.C.C. 52, at para. 24.]

---

† Peter Showler, former Chairperson, Immigration and Refugee Board, and Lori Disenhouse, Legal Advisor, Immigration and Refugee Board, "Tribunal Management: In Search of Nimbleness" (Presentation at the Council of Canadian Administrative Tribunals, Ottawa, Ontario, 3 June 2002), online: <http://www.ccat-ctac.org/en/conferences/2002_conf.php>. [Endnotes omitted.] Reproduced with permission. [Commentary note by David W. Elliott.]

Administrative tribunals are meant to embody the core values of fairness and rationality.[5] More specifically, adjudicative agencies and tribunals should strive to attain or respect three fundamental principles:

1. Efficiency — participants in an adjudication system have a right to timely decisions and a process that is neither cumbersome nor unduly costly;
2. Fairness — the adjudicative process must respect natural justice;
3. Quality decision-making — the process must produce accurate decisions that reflect correct findings of fact and accurate application of the law.

The first quality, efficiency, is one of the primary elements distinguishing administrative tribunals from courts. The expectation of tribunals is that they can adjudicate more efficiently while still rendering well-reasoned and fair decisions in a transparent manner.

The challenge facing tribunal managers is the co-ordination of the efficiency imperative while guaranteeing the fair and quality components. One must not be compromised for the other.

If it is to fulfil its original promise, administrative justice should be nimble and dynamic. This means that tribunal processes should be fast, fair, accessible, and responsive to the needs of the parties, and that tribunal jurisprudence should be original, vigorous and continually evolving.[6]

At the Immigration and Refugee Board (IRB), which adjudicates questions that affect a person's right to life, liberty and security, the challenge is even greater to find the balance between delivering accurate, consistent decisions of high quality and the responsibility to the Canadian public to operate an efficient and cost effective system. Refugee claimants, applicants and detainees have a Charter right to fundamental justice and fair and just decisions must be made in each individual case while producing overall results that at all times maintain the integrity and credibility of the system. The IRB has a duty to the constituency it serves to make decisions reasonably, efficiently, fairly and in accordance with the law. The Board has undertaken to deal simply, quickly and fairly with everyone.[7]

. . . .

EFFICIENCY, FAIRNESS AND QUALITY DECISION-MAKING

There is a common perception that efficiency, fairness and quality decisions are at odds with one another and that tribunals constantly struggle to observe inherently conflicting principles. At best this perception is a half-truth. It is possible to adopt policies and procedures where efficiency, fairness and quality decision-making reinforce one another in a balanced, symbiotic manner. The overall standard of excellence of a tribunal, and of its decision-makers, are decisions that embody all three core principles. Each of the three principles articulated in the introduction is incorporated into the policies and procedures of the IRB. As a result, these policies do not easily lend themselves to the simplistic categorisations of efficiency, fairness and quality decision-making — as noted previously, they frequently span all three principles....

. . . .

THE IMMIGRATION AND REFUGEE BOARD: PROCESSES, POLICIES AND PROCEDURES

Before examining specific IRB policies and procedures, some background on the Immigration and Refugee Board may be helpful. The IRB is the largest federal administrative tribunal in Canada. It has three divisions: the Convention Refugee Determination Division (CRDD), the Immigration Appeal Division (IAD) and the Adjudication Division. The three divisions have more than 1,000 employees. The CRDD and IAD have a complement of some 230 independent decision-makers who are appointed by the Governor–in–Council for terms of approximately two to five years. The CRDD makes determinations on refugee claims while the IAD deals with appeals from refusals by Citizenship and Immigration Canada to allow sponsored relatives of permanent residents. The IAD also deals with appeals by permanent residents who face removal from Canada. The Adjudication Division has approximately thirty decision-makers who are public servants and conduct detention reviews and immigration inquiries for certain categories of people believed to be inadmissible to or removable from Canada.

The size of the IRB is significant in terms of its development as a highly specialised tribunal with a culture of efficiency and fairness. Not only does it have three separate divisions with diverse functions, but it is also spread across Canada in five regional locations. Further underscoring this diversity, the CRDD hearing process is inquisitorial while the IAD and the Adjudication Division are adversarial in nature. The tribunal deals with a high volume caseload, with most cases requiring an oral hearing. The pressures on the IRB are particularly magnified at the CRDD. In 2001 the CRDD received more than 44,000 claims. The claims it hears are complex and the stakes could not be higher.

Refugee status determination is among the most difficult forms of adjudication, involving as it does fact-finding in regard to foreign conditions, cross-cultural and interpreted examination of witnesses, everpresent evidentiary voids, and a duty to prognosticate potential risks rather than simply to declare the more plausible account of events.[23]

In this environment the task of maintaining consistent and high quality decisions while remaining timely and accountable to the public is daunting.

The IRB stands in contrast to many smaller, single-mandate, centralised tribunals. Some of the challenges we face may be somewhat unique. While the same principles apply to all tribunals, each must find its own way to fulfil its statutory mandate and create its own culture of decision-making. The inherent flexibility and dynamism of administrative tribunals allows each tribunal to adapt its practices and processes to best suit the nature of the issues adjudicated.

The following section provides a brief exposition of some of the IRB's policies that exemplify the basic theme of this paper, namely that policies can symbiotically promote fairness, efficiency and quality decisions.

1. Expedited Process

... Full hearings take time to complete and, with a burgeoning caseload, many tribunals cannot accommodate the number of full hearings required without incurring a serious backlog. Of course, fairness cannot be compromised in the race to productivity. One initiative developed to address this situation is expedited interviews at the CRDD. Countries identified as having high positive determination rates are earmarked for the expedited process. A profile is developed to screen into the process those claimants who are likely to have a positive outcome to their claim. Those individuals are then informally interviewed by a Refugee Claims Officer (RCO) in the presence of counsel. At the conclusion of the interview the RCO may either recommend that a member render a positive decision or refer the matter to a full hearing. The final decision rests with the member. The Expe-

dited Policy requires that RCO interviews be recorded and that RCOs provide brief written reasons for their recommendation....

2. Streamlining

... The central element of the streamlining initiative is to assign dedicated resources to triage claims into four different streams, according to the nature and characteristics of the case. Building on current IRB processes, an increased number of suitable claims that may be allowed without a hearing will be directed to an interview (instead of a full hearing), which will help finalise such cases more quickly. Straightforward cases with only one or two issues will quickly be sent to short hearings.

Regular cases will proceed to a full hearing. Cases involving security or complex issues will be identified early to ensure necessary case preparation and prompt scheduling of the hearing....

3. Alternate Dispute Resolution

The IAD has also developed an alternative to full hearings on the merits. The highly successful Alternate Dispute Resolution (ADR) program permits that certain cases be earmarked for mediation. ADR was set up to deal with sponsorship appeals, which account for 80% of the IAD's caseload, without a formal hearing. It has resulted in the resolution of some 52% of cases without requiring a hearing, thus removing a significant proportion of appeals from the formal hearing process. An ADR session averages less than one hour, as compared to 2 or 3 hours for non-ADR cases.

4. Single-Member Panels

One of the most successful productivity initiatives was to have decision-makers sit as single members. The IAD used its statutory authority to establish single member panels as the norm for most of its cases. The CRDD followed suit. The Act requires a two-member panel unless the claimant consents to a single member hearing.... At the moment, more than half of all refugee claims are heard by a single member. The new legislation grants the IRB the authority to designate single member panels in all Divisions....

5. Oral Reasons

Because of the very serious consequences of a negative decision for a refugee claimant, written reasons were required by legislation for all negative decisions of the CRDD. However, this led to lengthy delays between the conclusion of the hearing and the rendering of a final decision with reasons. A management decision was taken to encourage oral reasons at the conclusion of a claim, whether positive or negative. The delivery of oral reasons had already become normative at the IAD with great success. The oral reasons policy asked members to render oral reasons for straightforward negative decisions where complex factual or legal issues did not arise. At the same time, the policy required that members provide reasons for all of their decisions, positive or negative, in the expectation that the great majority of positive reasons could be rendered orally. Many members were concerned that the quality of their reasons might suffer, however, that has proven not to be the case....

6. New Member Training and Customised Training

Although all new IRB members pass a candidate selection process before appointment to the Board, many do not have legal training, nor, for the CRDD, do they necessarily have expertise in international refugee protection matters.[24] Consequently, there is a steep learning curve involved in developing the legal skills and knowledge necessary to hear cases. New members are offered an intensive three-week course in law and procedure which is then followed by a six-month training program. In that six-month period, new members are teamed with a member mentor, legal advisor and professional development advisor. It is the responsibility of the team to help the new member achieve full competency and a full caseload within the six months. A similar mentor program is also available for experienced members who require extra training to reach their full potential as productive members....

... While the primary purpose of the training program is to deliver fair, well-reasoned decisions, more highly skilled members can make faster decisions, with less wasted motion and with fewer decisions being returned by the Federal Court for re-hearing.

7. Member Performance Appraisals

... Members of each Division of the IRB receive a formal appraisal annually. Targets are set for them both in terms of their professional skills development and their productivity. In this way, managers and decision-makers work together to set reasonable goals and to make sure the goals are met. If there are significant deficiencies in the member's performance, the member may be referred to a mentor for customised training....

8. Code of Conduct

... To encourage an atmosphere of professionalism, a Code of Conduct governs members of the IRB. The public may institute a complaint against a member on the grounds that he or she has breached the code of conduct through an established public complaint mechanism. This increases the public accountability and transparency of the tribunal and ultimately it results in a tribunal in which fairness permeates, not only the hearing process, but the comportment and professionalism of its decision-makers. Compliance with the Code of Conduct is an element in the member performance appraisal....

9. Reasons Review

The law that tribunal members are to apply can often be complex and the Federal Court jurisprudence interpreting the law is sometimes conflicting. Given that the majority of tribunal members are not legally trained, staff lawyers are available to assist members with advice and with a legal review of their draft reasons if requested.... The voluntary nature of such reviews and the discretion as to whether or not to accept legal advice put these services on the side of administrative consistency and quality without crossing the line of undue influence. Legal advisors are scrupulously careful not to influence the member's findings of fact or law.

10. Geographic Teams

One of the most far-reaching consistency initiatives is the development of the team model. At the CRDD, decision-makers, RCOs, support staff and managers are grouped together in geographic teams. The teams are assigned specific countries for which they can develop a highly specialised knowledge of country conditions. At the team level, members are encouraged to discuss inconsistencies in documentation and share individual assessments of legal and factual issues pertaining to claims from their countries....

... Where significant discrepancies in acceptance rates arise between regions, the Board employs a more focussed strategy to ensure consistency.... Where regional variations in legal analyses are identified, the issues are raised at team meetings and made the subject of *Consolidated-[Bathurst]*[31] discussions [i.e., informal, voluntary policy discussions].

Where appropriate, continuing education sessions will present new country information, or updated analyses of Federal Court jurisprudence. The primary goal of the strategy is to ensure a coherent distribution of the objective country information and to provide a full and thoughtful analysis of the relevant legal principles. The objective is never to impose a pre-determined conclusion....

11. Chairperson's Guidelines and Lead Cases

Under section 65(3) and (4) of the *Immigration Act* the Chairperson may issue Guidelines to assist members in areas where the law is subject to significant divergence or there is an issue of importance over which members require some guidance. They represent the accumulated experience and expertise of the tribunal on a specific subject matter and are issued following extensive research and consultation. Guidelines are one of the areas where the IRB has been very successful in promoting consistency while respecting the independence of decision-makers.[32] The Guidelines set out the law in a particular area and suggest a preferred approach.

. . . .

... [M]embers know that guidelines do not replace their obligation to fully consider the case before them on its merits and there is no erosion of their independence as decision-makers. The public also benefits from guidelines and policies because they help reassure those affected by tribunal decisions that they are being treated impartially, in the sense of consistently with others in similar circumstances.[33]

. . . .

12. Security of Tenure

IRB members enjoy a clear measure of security of tenure. They are appointed by the Governor in Council for a fixed term of up to seven years and there are very limited circumstances under which a member may be removed during his of her term.[38] However, first appointments have typically been for a period of two years with the possibility of re-appointment for a lengthier term of five years. The majority of members seek re-appointment after their first and even second terms. Member performance is evaluated annually by member managers primarily for the purposes of skills development and goal setting but also, secondarily, for providing advice to the Minister of Citizenship and Immigration on the merits of the member's performance prior to re-appointment.

. . . .

CONCLUSION

Good tribunal managers know that while efficiency, fairness and quality are ends unto themselves, they are not sufficient unless all other elements crucial to the proper functioning of a tribunal are met. Finding the balance is a subtle but not impossible task, for once a manager understands the culture of the tribunal, efficiency, fairness and quality are not competing values. Every initiative undertaken by an administrative tribunal should bring it closer to the goal of meeting the needs of its constituency. In this context efficiency, fairness and quality decision-making are indivisibly wound up in the management of an efficient administrative tribunal. And each tribunal, working within its own statutory, institutional and social context, will have to evolve its own version of "nimble justice."[40]

(c) *British Columbia Development Corp. v. British Columbia (Ombudsman)*†

NOTE

The British Columbia Development Corporation (B.C.D.C.) was a wholly owned B.C. Crown corporation created in 1973 to encourage industrial development in B.C. The corporation had a subsidiary, First Capital Development, which was formed in 1977 to manage a waterfront development in the

---

† [1984] 2 S.C.R. 447, aff'g. (1982) 139 D.L.R. (3d) 307 (B.C.C.A.), rev'g. a judgment of the British Columbia Supreme Court. [Commentary note by David W. Elliott.]

area in which the King Neptune Restaurant was located. B.C.D.C. and First Capital wanted to have a hotel built on the land where King Neptune stood after the restaurant's lease expired. However, they were willing to permit King Neptune to locate elsewhere in the proposed development. After negotiations between them broke down, King Neptune complained to the B.C. Ombudsman, Karl Friedmann, that B.C.D.C. and First City had bargained in bad faith.

The Ombudsman started to investigate, but B.C.D.C. and First City obtained an interlocutory injunction to halt the Ombudsman's proceedings. Section 10 (1) of the *Ombudsman Act*, R.S.B.C. 1979, c. 306, said that "[t]he Ombudsman, with respect to a matter of administration, on a complaint or on his own initiative, may investigate (a) a decision or recommendation made; (b) an act done or omitted; or (c) a procedure used by an authority that aggrieves or may aggrieve a person." The British Columbia Supreme Court held that a decision by a Crown corporation was not a "matter of administration", so the Ombudsman had no power to investigate. When the British Columbia Court of Appeal affirmed this decision, King Neptune appealed to the Supreme Court of Canada. The result was the leading case on the powers of Canadian ombudsmen.

EXTRACT

[DICKSON C.J. for the COURT:]

The Ombudsman's Jurisdiction

General

As I have noted, the Ombudsman is a creature of statute. As such, his power to investigate complaints depends upon the meaning to be given the language the Legislature has used to define the ambit of his jurisdiction. Section 8 of the *Interpretation Act*, R.S.B.C. 1979, c. 206, provides a guideline for the interpretation of provincial legislation like the *Ombudsman Act*. It states:

> **8.** Every enactment shall be construed as being remedial, and shall be given such fair, large and liberal construction and interpretation as best ensures the attainment of its objects.

I do not think the remedial nature of the *Ombudsman Act* could fairly be doubted. The objects of the legislation and the degree to which it should receive a large and liberal interpretation can best be under-

stood by examining the scheme of the statute as well as the factors that have motivated the creation of the Ombudsman's office.

Historical Development

The need for some means of control over the machinery of government is nearly as old as government itself. The Romans, as long ago as 200 B.C., established a tribune — an official appointed to protect the interests and rights of the plebeians from the patricians. They also had two censors — magistrates elected approximately every five years to review the performance of officials and entertain complaints from the citizenry. And the dynastic Chinese had the Control *Yuan*, an official who supervised other officials and handled complaints about maladministration.

The office of the Ombudsman and the concept of a grievance procedure which would be neither legal nor political in a strict sense are of Swedish origin, *circa* 1809. The constitution which established Sweden as a democratic monarchy, and created the Swedish Parliament, also provided for parliamentary oversight of the bureaucratic machinery through a new official called the *Justitieombudsman*.

As originally conceived, the Swedish Ombudsman was to be Parliament's overseer of the administration, but over time the character of the institution gradually changed. Eventually, the Ombudsman's main function came to be the investigation of complaints of maladministration on behalf of aggrieved citizens and the recommendation of corrective action to the governmental official or department involved.

The institution of Ombudsman has grown since its creation. It has been adopted in many jurisdictions around the world in response to what R. Gregory and P. Hutchesson in *The Parliamentary Ombudsman* (1975) refer to (at 15) as "one of the dilemmas of our times" namely, that "[i]n the modern state ... democratic action is possible only through the instrumentality of bureaucratic organization; yet bureaucratic power — if it is not properly controlled — is itself destructive of democracy and its values."

The factors which have led to the rise of the institution of Ombudsman are well-known. Within the last generation or two the size and complexity of government has increased immeasurably, in both qualitative and quantitative terms. Since the emergence of the modern welfare state the intrusion of government into the lives and livelihood of individuals has increased exponentially. Government now provides services and benefits, intervenes actively in the marketplace, and engages in proprietary functions that 50 years ago would have been unthinkable.

As a side effect of these changes, and the pro-fusion of boards, agencies and public corporations necessary to achieve them, has come the increased exposure to maladministration, abuse of authority and official insensitivity. And the growth of a distant, impersonal, professionalized structure of government has tended to dehumanize interaction between citizens and those who serve them. See L. Hill, *The Model Ombudsman* (1976) at 4–8.

The traditional controls over the implementation and administration of governmental policies and programs — namely, the legislature, the executive and the courts — are neither completely suited nor entirely capable of providing the supervision a burgeoning bureaucracy demands. The inadequacy of legislative response to complaints arising from the day-to-day operation of government is not seriously disputed. The demands on members of legislative bodies is such that they are naturally unable to give careful attention to the workings of the entire bureaucracy. Moreover, they often lack the investigative resources necessary to follow up properly any matter they do elect to pursue. See Powles, "Aspects of the Search for Administrative Justice" (1966), 9 *Can. Pub. Admin.* 133 at 142–3.

The limitations of courts are also well-known. Litigation can be costly and slow. Only the most serious cases of administrative abuse are therefore likely to find their way into the courts. More importantly, there is simply no remedy at law available in a great many cases.

H.W.R. Wade describes this problem and the special role the Ombudsman has come to fill:

> But there is a large residue of grievances which fit into none of the regular legal moulds, but are none the less real. A humane system of government must provide some way of assuaging them, both for the sake of justice and because accumulating discontent is a serious clog on administrative efficiency in a democratic country.

> . . . . .

> The vital necessity is that the impartial investigation of complaints.... What every form of government needs is some regular and smooth-running mechanism for feeding back the reactions of its disgruntled customers, after impartial assessment, and for correcting whatever may have gone wrong. Nothing of this kind existed in our system before 1968, except in very limited spheres. Yet it is a fundamental need in every system. It was because it filled that need that the device of the ombudsman suddenly attained immense popularity, sweeping round the democratic world and taking root in Britain and in many other countries, as well as inspiring a vast

literature. (See Wade, *Administrative Law*, 5th ed., 73–74.)

This problem is also addressed by Professor Donald C. Rowat, in an article entitled "An Ombudsman Scheme for Canada" (1962), 28 *Can. J. Econ. & Poli. Sc.* 543 at 543:

> It is quite possible nowadays for a citizen's right to be accidentally crushed by the vast juggernaut of the government's administrative machine. In this age of the welfare state, thousands of administrative decisions are made each year by governments or their agencies, many of them by lowly officials; and if some of these decisions are arbitrary or unjustified, there is no easy way for the ordinary citizen to gain redress.

The Ombudsman represents society's response to these problems of potential abuse and of supervision. His unique characteristics render him capable of addressing many of the concerns left untouched by the traditional bureaucratic control devices. He is impartial. His services are free, and available to all. Because he often operates informally, his investigations do not impede the normal processes of government. Most importantly, his powers of investigation can bring to light cases of bureaucratic maladministration that would otherwise pass unnoticed. The Ombudsman "can bring the lamp of scrutiny to otherwise dark places, even over the resistance of those who would draw the blinds": *Re Ombudsman Act* (1970), 72 W.W.R. 176 (Alta. S.C.) *per* Milvain C.J. at 192–193. On the other hand, he may find the complaint groundless, not a rare occurrence, in which event his impartial and independent report, absolving the public authority, may well serve to enhance the morale and restore the self-confidence of the public employees impugned.

In short, the powers granted to the Ombudsman allow him to address administrative problems that the courts, the legislature and the executive cannot effectively resolve.

The Legislative Scheme

The Ombudsman is an "officer of the Legislature," *Ombudsman Act*, subs. 2(1), and responsible solely to the Legislative Assembly, to which he must report annually, (subs. 30(1)). His term of office is six years (subs. 3(1)). He receives the salary of a Supreme Court Judge (subs. 4(1)). His duties, simply put, consist of investigating suspected shortcomings in the administration of government, at the request of the Legislature (subs. 10(3)), on his own initiative or on the basis of complaints made by members of the public (subs. 10(1)).

In order to facilitate his investigative role, the Ombudsman is granted wide powers. Pursuant to s. 15, he may, *inter alia* enter and inspect premises; require anyone to produce documents or furnish information; summon and examine under oath anyone possessed of relevant information; and conduct hearings. Teeth are given to the Ombudsman's powers by s. 31, which prohibits, upon pain of penal sanction, any conduct intended to interfere with an investigation.

The Act does ensure that all sides of any issue are properly aired by affording any affected party the opportunity to be heard. The Ombudsman must give notice of his investigation to any governmental authority he is investigating and to any other appropriate person and he must consult with the authority upon request (s. 14). He must give the authority and any other person who may be adversely affected the chance to make either oral or written representations before rendering any report or recommendation (s. 16).

It is important to note that the Ombudsman has no power directly to force any governmental authority to remedy a wrong he uncovers. The Act does, however, create a variety of mechanisms whereby the Ombudsman may move the government to implement any decision he reaches after an investigation. He may recommend corrective action to an authority who must then notify him of what action will be taken, if any, and where no action is planned the reasons why (s. 23). If the Ombudsman remains unsatisfied, he may report the matter to the Lieutenant-Governor-in-Council and to the Legislative Assembly (s. 24). And he may comment publicly on any case where he deems it appropriate (s. 30).

It is these sections that ultimately give persuasive force to the Ombudsman's conclusions: they create the possibility of dialogue between governmental authorities and the Ombudsman; they facilitate legislative oversight of the workings of various government departments and other subordinate bodies; and they allow the Ombudsman to marshal public opinion behind appropriate causes.

Read as a whole, the *Ombudsman Act* of British Columbia provides an efficient procedure through which complaints may be investigated, bureaucratic errors and abuses brought to light and corrective action initiated. It represents the paradigm of remedial legislation. It should therefore receive a broad, purposive interpretation consistent with the unique role the Ombudsman is intended to fulfil. There is an abundance of authority to this effect. See, particularly, *Re Ombudsman Act, supra*; *Re Ont. Ombudsman and Ont. Health Disciplines Bd. of Ont.* (1979), 26 O.R. (2d) 105, 104 D.L.R. (3d) 597 (Ont. C.A.); also see *Re Ont. Ombudsman and Ont. Min. of Housing* (1979), 26 O.R. (2d) 434, 103 D.L.R. (3d) 117 (Ont. H.C.) [affirmed (sub nom. *Re Ombudsman of Ont. and R.*) 30 O.R. (2d) 768, 117 D.L.R. (3d) 613 (Ont. C.A.)]; *Re Ombudsman Act*, [1974] 5 W.W.R. 176, 46 D.L.R. (3d) 452 (sub nom. *Re Ombudsman Act* (Sask.)) (Sask. Q.B.); *Police Comm. Bd.* v. *Tickell*, [1979] 2 W.W.R. 361, 95 D.L.R. (3d) 473 (sub nom. *Re Sask. Police Commrs. Bd. and Tickell*) (Sask. Q.B.).

. . . .

In my view, the phrase "a matter of administration" [the subject matter of the Ombudsman's jurisdiction] encompasses everything done by governmental authorities in the implementation of government policy. I would exclude only the activities of the Legislature and the courts from the Ombudsman's scrutiny.

(d)　Caught in the Act†

André Marin

NOTE

In 2008, the federal government announced that Canada would host the 2010 G8 Summit (G8), a gathering of eight important world leaders, to discuss issues of global concern: A. Marin, *Caught in the Act* at 14. A year later, Prime Minister Stephen Harper indicated that the City of Toronto would

† Excerpts from Ombudsman Report: Investigation into The Ministry of Community Safety and Correctional Services' conduct in relation to Ontario Regulation 233/10 under the Public Works Protection Act, *Caught in the Act*, by A. Marin (Toronto: Ombudsman of Ontario, December 2010) at 6–13. Reproduced with permission of Ombudsman of Ontario. [Photos, footnotes, and paragraph numbering omitted.]

serve as the host for Canada for the 2010 G20 Summit (G20). The G20 meeting would discuss international economic issues and attract world leaders from 19 countries and the European Union, as well as representatives of the International Monetary Fund and World Bank: *ibid*. The G20 summit meeting saw the largest mass arrest in Canadian history, with approximately 1,105 people arrested: *ibid*. at 25. Many people were picked up for breach of the peace; others faced a variety of *Criminal Code* offences, and at least two found themselves in violation of the *Public Works Protection Act*. Of those initially detained, about 700 were eventually released without charge. Many of the charges in connection with the G20 summit have been stayed or withdrawn. The cost for hosting the events was estimated at more than $1 billion: *ibid*.

The Ombudsman investigated the events surrounding these meetings and came to several stark conclusions. (See generally *"Caught in the Act"* at 7, where a summary of the Ombudsman's conclusions and verbatim quotations have been sourced that are relied upon herein.) Among other things, he found that Regulation 233/10, passed to enhance security during the G20 summit, should never have been enacted. The effect of Regulation 233/10, now expired, infringed the freedom of expression in a way that does not seem justifiable in a free and democratic society. Moreover, the passage of the regulation "triggered the extravagant police authority found in the *Public Works Protection Act*, including the power to arbitrarily arrest and detain people and to engage in unreasonable searches and seizures": *ibid*. The *Public Works Protection Act* authorized regulations to be created to protect infrastructure, not to provide security to people during events. Regulation 233/10 was therefore likely illegal as it exceeded the lawful authority of the statute under which it was passed. The decision of the Ministry of Community Safety and Correctional Services to sponsor the regulation was, the Ombudsman found, itself unreasonable. The provincial government should have handled its passage better. The Ombudsman suggested that the passage of the regulation should have been "aggressively publicized" and accompanied by training on its use for the Toronto Police Service. The Ombudsman added that "[p]erversely, by changing the rules of the game without real notice, Regulation 233/10 acted as a trap for the responsible — those who took the time to educate themselves about police powers before setting out to express legitimate political dissent."

Notably, the federal and provincial governments responsible for establishing and administering the G8 and G20 meetings were both re-elected at the next general election. Moreover, one might legitimately ask what high-ranking public officials involved in providing security to both summits were reprimanded for their part in what the Ombudsman himself termed "a fiasco": *ibid*. at 80. To date, one police officer has been convicted of assaulting a protester during the G20 summit and sentenced to 45 days in jail, but was granted bail pending an appeal: Canadian Press, "G20 assault: Babak Andalib-Goortani gets 45-day sentence", *CBC News* (9 December 2013), online: CBC News, <http://www.cbc.ca/news/canada/toronto/g20-assault-babak-andalib-goortani-gets-45-day-sentence-1.2456893>. As you read the Ontario Ombudsman's report, ask yourself what value such a report has when it speaks "truth to power" in this way. When few, if any, individuals are publicly punished for their part in large scale misconduct, can reports like this one truly have any positive effect on the future administration of government?

EXTRACT

Dave Vasey, a York University master's student, had never heard of the *Public Works Protection Act* before 4 p.m. on Thursday, June 24, 2010. In fact, it may have been the best-kept secret in Ontario's legislative history, although it wasn't a secret at all. The *Public Works Protection Act* had sat largely dormant on Ontario's statute books for more than 70 years, a hoary relic of World War II and veritable civil rights land mine waiting to be tripped. And Mr. Vasey certainly didn't know about Regulation 233/10 passed under that Act, to provide additional legal support for the security perimeter constructed for the G20 summit. Like the *Public Works Protection Act*, Regulation 233/10 was hidden in plain sight. It was announced not in newspapers, public service messages, or on ministry or police websites, but in the government's seldom-read and little-known electronic legislative database and then in the *Ontario Gazette*, a publication of interest only to civil servants, pundits and the occasional lawyer. Soon, however, Mr. Vasey would gain up close and personal knowledge of the *Public Works Protection Act* and Regulation 233/10.

Mr. Vasey and a friend, like many Torontonians, were simply curious about the massive steel grey security fence that wound its way through downtown streets. When they wandered near the fence to take a look that day, after taking part in a peaceful march, they were stopped by police and questioned. Standing on what he understood to be his rights, Mr. Vasey declined to provide identification. Soon after, he found himself under arrest by authority of the *Public Works Protection Act*. At least one other person was detained and charged under the Act in connection with G20 summit security, and numerous others were questioned and searched using the sweeping powers conferred by the Act, and activated by Regulation 233/10.

While many of those stopped and questioned by police under the *Public Works Protection Act* in the week leading up to and during the G20 summit were involved in demonstrations, many others were simply Torontonians going about the activities of their daily lives. Rob Kittredge practiced law just outside the secure perimeter zone. When he went to take photographs of the zone one evening before the summit meeting, police searched him, examined his photographs, and purported to "ban" him under the Act. Nancy Ryan was on her way home from grocery shopping, outside of the security fence, when police approached her and required that she submit her bags to a search.

It wasn't that the Ministry of Community Safety and Correctional Services didn't mean well in promoting the use of the Act through Regulation 233/10 to assist Toronto police in maintaining security during the summit. Typically, international summits attract protests, and protests can turn violent and even deadly. The world's leaders have also been subject to terrorist threats. But the security needs associated with protecting foreign dignitaries and the public from harm must be weighed against constitutionally entrenched rights. Protest is a democratic right. Ontario's citizens were entitled to the freedom to express themselves as well as from unreasonable search and arbitrary arrest during the G20 summit. Unfortunately, when it came to Regulation 233/10, the Ministry got the balance wrong.

Regulation 233/10's enactment triggered the *Public Works Protection Act*, a statute containing unusual, even extravagant police powers that could be — and in fact were — used to intimidate and arrest people who had done no harm. By designating gaps in the security perimeter as "public works" and reconfirming the authority to use the full powers of the Act within the exterior security zone, remarkable legal obligations were imposed on citizens seeking entry. A new landscape was created in which people were compelled to identify themselves and explain why they wanted to enter, sometimes even in writing, and they were required to submit to warrantless searches. And even if they were refused entry, changed their mind and wished to walk away, they were still required to identify themselves, answer questions and submit to a search. Those who declined could be arrested. Those who declined could even be prosecuted and jailed.

The only way to understand why the Legislature of Ontario would create a statute conferring police powers of this kind is to hearken to history. The *Public Works Protection Act* is a war measure. It was enacted in 1939 during an emergency session of the Legislature in the days following the declaration of war against Germany to deal with the threat posed by saboteurs against Ontario's infrastructure. Guards and peace officers were given the kind of authority one might expect in a time of war or emergency circumstance — the kind of authority that stretches, if not transgresses, constitutional rights. Yet here, in 2010, was the province of Ontario conferring wartime powers on police officers in peacetime. That is a decision that should not have been taken lightly, particularly not in the era of the *Canadian Charter of Rights and Freedoms*.

In fact, Regulation 233/10 was of doubtful constitutional validity. By creating security zones to bar entry and by authorizing arrest, it imposed definite limits on freedom of expression. It was therefore in prima facie violation of the *Charter* as a matter of law, likely in ways that are not constitutionally justifiable. Regulation 233/10 worked to trip the powers of the *Public Works Protection Act*, thereby enabling the arrest and muting of protesters and others who had done nothing wrong. The impact of Regulation 233/10 on freedom of expression was therefore almost certainly disproportionate. The government should have been wary of relying on a statute of doubtful constitutional validity in preference to dealing openly with the matter in the Legislature.

Even leaving the *Charter* aside, there is every reason to believe that the regulation was illegal. It was also almost certainly beyond the authority of the government to enact. The *Public Works Protection Act*, by its name and by its terms, was enacted to protect public property. Nowhere does the *Public Works Protection Act* authorize the government to enact a regulation to protect people rather than places. Nowhere does it grant authority to the government to confer additional police powers in order to protect internationally protected persons. There may be room for a law that does so, and this Act may have been used with the best of intentions, but it was used instrumentally and unnecessarily. The security perimeter it provided for would have been legal without it, and the existing common law and statutory authority of peace officers would have been ample to screen and prevent entry to those who might pose a threat to G20 participants. Simply put, Regulation 233/10 was of dubious legality and of no utility. It was unreasonable for the Ministry of Community Safety and Correctional Services to have promoted its passage.

The problems with the Ministry's handling of Regulation 233/10 are not confined to its passage. Both the follow-up to and the publication of the regulation were inadequate.

When the regulation was passed, the Ministry of Community Safety and Correctional Services had simply intended to restrict the Act's application to the area within the exterior security fence around the restricted zones housing foreign dignitaries. However, once the sleeping giant had been awakened, it could not be controlled. The Ministry was caught short when the Toronto Police Service misapprehended the boundaries of the security area designated under Regulation 233/10, and used the authority of the *Public Works Protection Act* to arrest people who were simply in the vicinity of the security fence. Moreover, throughout the weekend of the G20 summit, police exercised their powers under the Act well beyond the limits of the security perimeter, even after the misinterpretation on the part of the Chief of the Toronto Police Service had been corrected.

To be sure, the government of Ontario is not responsible for misunderstandings on the part of police officials. Yet even the power that was properly conferred by Regulation 233/10 was inordinate, and went well beyond the normal understanding of Ontario's citizens as to their obligations when dealing with police. The Ministry, who had sponsored the regulation, should have satisfied itself that Toronto Police Service officers understood it and had been properly trained. This was not done. The Ministry simply handed over to the Toronto Police Service inordinate powers, without any efforts made to ensure those powers would not be misunderstood.

More importantly, it was grossly unreasonable and unfair for the Ministry of Community Safety and Correctional Services to let Regulation 233/10 fly under the radar the way it did. No one knew about the regulation until after the news of Mr. Vasey's arrest under the Act went viral. Not the public, not the press, not the administrators of the very city in which it was to be implemented. As our investigation revealed, quite remarkably, not even the Integrated Security Unit Steering Committee lead or key members of the Integrated Security Unit's G20 Public

Affairs Communications Team knew of the regulation. While municipal authorities in Toronto did a fine job of ensuring that the public was aware of the traffic plan for the G20, nowhere was it announced that police officers would have extraordinary powers of compulsion and arrest. Municipal officials didn't inform citizens for the same reason that Mr. Vasey didn't comply with police requests on June 24, 2010: They simply didn't know about it. And the Ministry of Community Safety and Correctional Services did nothing to ensure that people would be aware of these powers so that they could govern themselves accordingly. Apart from insiders in the government of Ontario, only members of the Toronto Police Service knew that the rules of the game had changed, and they were the ones holding the deck of "go directly to jail" cards.

By any measure, a regulation conferring temporary police powers and imposing unusual obligations on citizens was unexpected. What was not unexpected was that, in the incendiary protest atmosphere of an international political event, individuals would question and even test the limits of police authority. Prudence alone would have required that the regulation be aggressively publicized in order to reduce the risk of unnecessary confrontation. Yet it was not.

By changing the legal landscape without fanfare in this way, Regulation 233/10 operated as a trap for those who relied on their ordinary legal rights. Reasonably, protesters were trained by advocacy groups in "know your rights" sessions and advised through websites and brochures that they would not have to identify themselves or submit to search unless they were otherwise arrested. In fact, the inconspicuous Regulation 233/10 made it an offence for protesters to fail to identify themselves when approaching the secured area. Ensuring that protesters know their rights and the limit on those rights is something to be encouraged. Those who attempted to do so set themselves up. They and those they counseled were caught up in the Act's all but invisible web.

Given questions about its constitutional validity and legality, Regulation 233/10 deserved to be tested in the courts — not after it expired and had served its purpose, but before it was implemented. It is an infamous problem in protest situations that police tactics that control protesters cannot be challenged until those tactics have served their purpose — after it is too late. In the interests of ensuring a proper balance between civil rights and security, the Ministry of Community Safety and Correctional Services should have ensured that anyone intent on challenging security plans would have the opportunity to do so. The Ministry promoted the regulation. It should have stood up and ensured that those affected by it would be aware of it.

It is therefore my view that the Ministry of Community Safety and Correctional Services promoted a regulation that was of questionable legality and that conferred unnecessary police powers of questionable constitutionality. It was unreasonable to have done so. Moreover, the Ministry unreasonably and unjustly failed to ensure that the citizens of this province would be aware of the highly exceptional police authority that had been conferred.

The government has announced that the *Public Works Protection Act* will be reviewed in consultation with stakeholder groups. This is a step in the right direction. I have recommended that in the context of this review, the Ministry should take steps to revise or replace the Act. If it wants to claim the authority to designate security areas to protect persons, it should give consideration to creating an integrated statute that could be used not only to protect public works but that would clearly provide direct authority for ensuring the security of persons during public events when required. The range of police powers conferred by the Act should also be considered, including whether it is appropriate to give police the authority to arrest those who have already been excluded entry to secured areas, and the authority of guards and peace officers to offer conclusive testimony, whether right or wrong, about the location of security boundaries.

I have also recommended that the Ministry of Community Safety and Correctional Services develop a protocol that would call for public information campaigns when police powers are modified by subordinate legislation, particularly in protest situations.

On November 1, 2010, the Minister confirmed on behalf of the government his unequivocal commitment to act on my recommendations in a timely manner. I am satisfied with the Minister's response to my recommendations and will monitor the Ministry's progress in implementing them.

(e) *Roncarelli v. Duplessis*†

NOTE

Mr. Roncarelli owned a fashionable Montreal restaurant. He was also a member of a religious group called the Witnesses of Jehovah. During the 1940s, the Witnesses were engaged in an all-out campaign against the Roman Catholic Church. When fellow Witnesses were arrested by Montreal police for distributing allegedly seditious pamphlets, Mr. Roncarelli had helped them by providing security to ensure their release on bail. None of the Witnesses he had helped had defaulted on bail.

Mr. Archambault, Chairman of the Quebec Liquor Commission, advised Premier Duplessis, who was also Attorney-General, that the Roncarelli who was providing bond security was also the holder of a liquor permit provided by the province. The Premier advised Mr. Archambault to confirm this. Mr. Archambault did so, and telephoned the Premier a second time. In the second telephone call it was decided that Mr. Roncarelli's liquor licence should be cancelled. This was done, without prior notice to Mr. Roncarelli, on December 4, 1946.

Without the liquor licence, Mr. Roncarelli's restaurant business collapsed. He sued the Premier for the financial damage caused to him as a result of the cancellation. Could Mr. Roncarelli recover compensation? Should he?

This case is one of the most dramatic in all Canadian administrative law. An individual citizen sued the Premier of a province, and won. The Supreme Court's decision seemed to illustrate all three tenets of Dicey's "rule of law". The state was not permitted to harm a citizen without specific statutory authorization. The state, including one of its highest officers, was subject, ultimately, to the ordinary law as to compensation for damages. And in this pre-*Charter* era, an individual's rights were vindicated by concrete legal remedies rather than general constitutional guarantees.

† [1959] S.C.R. 121, (1959), 16 D.L.R. (2d) 689, rev'g. [1956] Que. Q.B. 447 (Q.B.), rev'g. [1952] 1 D.L.R. 680 (S.C.).

It should not be forgotten, though, that there were strong arguments on the other side. As Premier and Attorney-General, Mr. Duplessis had responsibility for the administration of justice. The Witnesses' attacks on the religion of a majority of Quebecers were congesting the courts, and — arguably — upsetting public order. Legislation gave the Commission a broad discretion to cancel permits "at its discretion", and a statutory privative clause purported to protect public officers from actions in damages. If the award of damages depended on the common law, there was a problem in finding a common law tort to cover what had happened. Moreover, there was a controversy as to whether it was the Chairman of the Liquor Commission or the Premier who had caused the licence to be cancelled. Although Mr. Roncarelli finally won a 6–3 majority in the Supreme Court, eight of the total of 15 judges who had heard the case at three levels of courts had decided in favour of Mr. Duplessis.

Roncarelli's "victory" won him less than half the compensation he had sought, over 12 years after he had first gone to the courts. On the other hand, what non-judicial alternatives did he have?

Extracts from the majority reasons of Martland J. are reproduced below. Kerwin and Locke JJ. agreed with Martland J. Abbott and Rand JJ. also agreed generally with Martland J., except that they did not find that the Commission had abdicated its discretion, and Rand J. thought there might be liability at common law as well as civil law. Fauteux, Taschereau, and Cartwright JJ. dissented. Fauteux J. felt that the Commission had abdicated its discretion and that Mr. Duplessis had caused the cancellation, but held that Mr. Duplessis was protected by the privative clause. Taschereau J. held simply that Mr. Duplessis was protected by the privative clause. Cartwright J. thought that because of the Commission's discretion it was not "quasi-judicial" and thus not subject to natural justice. He added that if the decision really *were* quasi-judicial, there could be still be no damages because quasi-judicial officers are protected from damages when they act without malice!

EXTRACT

[MARTLAND J.:]

This is an appeal from a judgment of the Court of Queen's Bench, Appeal Side, for the Province of

Quebec, District of Montreal, rendered on April 12, 1956 [[1956] Que. K.B. 447], over-ruling the judgment of the Superior Court rendered on May 2, 1951 [1952] 1 D.L.R. 680], under the terms of which the appellant had been awarded damages in the sum of $8,123.53 and costs.

The appellant had appealed from the judgment of the Superior Court in respect of the amount of damages awarded. This appeal was dismissed.

. . . .

The appellant commenced action against the respondent on June 3, 1947, claiming damages in the total sum of $118,741. He alleged that the respondent, without legal or statutory authority, had caused the cancellation of his liquor permit as an act of reprisal because of his having acted as surety or bondsman for the Witnesses of Jehovah in connection with the charges above mentioned. He alleged that the permit had been arbitrarily and unlawfully cancelled and that, as a result, he had sustained the damages claimed.

[In his defence Mr. Duplessis said that Mr. Roncarelli had encouraged the Jehovah's Witnesses pamphlet campaign by acting as surety for many of those who had been arrested, permitting them to repeat their offences and continue their campaign. Mr. Duplessis said he concluded that it would be contrary to public order to permit the appellant to continue to enjoy the privileges of the liquor permit, and that he, Mr. Duplessis, had recommended the cancellation.]

... He alleged that in the matter he had acted in his quality of Prime Minister and Attorney-General of the Province of Quebec and, accordingly, could not incur any personal responsibility. He further pleaded the provisions of art. 88 of the *Code of Civil Procedure* and alleged that he had not received notice of the action as required by the provisions of that article.

. . . .

... [A]fter reviewing the evidence, I am satisfied that there was ample evidence to sustain the finding of the trial Judge that the cancellation of the appellant's permit was the result of instructions given by the respondent to the Manager of the Commission.

. . . .

[Martland J. quoted from some of the evidence regarding the two telephone calls. After Mr. Archambault called back to confirm that Roncarelli, the Jehovah's Witnesses supporter and Roncarelli, the Quebec liquor permit holder were one and the same person, Mr. Duplessis related what he replied:]

> ... j'ai cru que c'était mon devoir, en conscience, de dire au Juge que ce permis-là, le Gouvernement de Québec ne pouvait pas accorder un privilège à un individu comme Roncarelli qui tenait l'attitude qu'il tenait.

The respondent further says that he told Mr. Archambault: "Vous avez raison, ôtez le permis, ôtez le privilège."

. . . .

[Martland J. noted that Mr. Duplessis had later told the press that the permit had been cancelled on his orders.]

I, therefore, agree with the learned trial Judge that the cancellation of the appellant's permit was the result of an order given by the respondent.

The second point for consideration is as to whether the respondent's acts were justifiable as having been done in good faith in the exercise of his official functions as Attorney-General and Prime Minister of the Province of Quebec.

In support of his contention that the respondent had so acted, we were referred by his counsel to the following statutory provisions:

[Martland J. referred to *The Attorney-General's Department Act*, R.S.Q. 1941, c. 46, which entrusted the Attorney-General with superintending "all matters connected with the administration of justice in the Province", and "advising department heads regarding law and the administration of justice"; *The Executive Power Act*, R.S.Q. 1941, c. 7, which referred to the office of Prime Minister; and to *The Alcoholic Liquor Act*, R.S.Q. 1941, c. 255, s. 148, which entrusted the Attorney-General with enforcing observance of that Act.]

. . . .

I do not find, in any of these provisions, authority to enable the respondent, either as Attorney-General or Prime Minister, to direct the cancellation of a permit under the *Alcoholic Liquor Act*. On the contrary, the intent and purpose of that Act appears to be to place the complete control over the liquor traffic in Quebec in the hands of an independent Commission. The only function of the Attorney-General under that statute is in relation to the assuring of the observance of its provisions. There is no evidence of any breach of that Act by the appellant.

. . . .

In my view, the respondent was not acting in the exercise of any official powers which he possessed in doing what he did in this matter.

The third point to be considered is as to whether the appellant's permit was lawfully cancelled by the Commission under the provisions of the *Alcoholic Liquor Act*. Section 35 of that Act makes provision for the cancellation of a permit in the following terms:

> 35.(1) Whatever be the date of issue of any permit granted by the Commission, such permit shall expire on the 30th of April following, unless it be cancelled by the Commission before such date, or unless the date at which it must expire be prior to the 30th of April following.
>
> The Commission may cancel any permit at its discretion.

. . . .

With respect to [the allegation that there was a breach of the rules of natural justice], it would appear to be somewhat doubtful whether the appellant had a right to a personal hearing, in view of the judgment of Lord Radcliffe in *Nakkuda Ali* v. *M.F. De S. Jayaratne*, [1951] A.C. 66. However, regardless of this, it is my view that the discretionary power to cancel a permit given to the Commission by the *Alcoholic Liquor Act* must be related to the administration and enforcement of that statute. It is not proper to exercise the power of cancellation for reasons which are unrelated to the carrying into effect of the intent and purpose of the Act. The association of the appellant with the Witnesses of Jehovah and his furnishing of bail for members of that sect, which were admitted to be the reasons for the cancellation of his permit and which were entirely lawful, had no relationship to the intent and purpose of the *Alcoholic Liquor Act*.

Furthermore, it should be borne in mind that the right of cancellation of a permit under the Act is a substantial power conferred upon what the statute contemplated as an independent Commission. That power must be exercised solely by that corporation. It must not and cannot be exercised by any one else....

. . . .

In the present case it is my view, for the reasons already given, that the power was not, in fact, exercised by the Commission, but was exercised by the respondent, acting through the Manager of the Commission. Cancellation of a permit by the Commission at the request or upon the direction of a third party, whoever he may be, is not a proper and valid exercise of the power conferred upon the Commission by s. 35 of the Act. The Commission cannot abdicate its own functions and powers and act upon such direction.

Finally, there is the question as to the giving of notice of the action by the appellant to the respondent pursuant of art. 88 of the *Code of Civil Procedure*, which reads as follows:

Actions Against Public Officers

88. No public officer or other person fulfilling any public function or duty can be sued for damages by reason of any act done by him in the exercise of his functions, nor can any verdict or judgment be rendered against him, unless notice of such action has been given him at least one month before the issue of the writ of summons.

Such notice must be in writing; it must state the grounds of the action, and the name of the plaintiff's attorney or agent, and indicate his office; and must be served upon him personally or at his domicile.

. . . .

[However] I do not think that it was a function either of the Prime Minister or of the Attorney-General to interfere with the administration of the Commission by causing the cancellation of a liquor permit. That was something entirely outside his legal functions. It involved the exercise of powers which, in law, he did not possess at all.

. . . .

... [H]ere there was nothing on which the respondent could found that he was entitled to deprive the appellant of his liquor permit.

On the issue of liability ... the respondent, by acts not justifiable in law, wrongfully caused the cancellation of the appellant's permit and thus caused damage to the appellant. The respondent intentionally inflicted damage upon the appellant and, therefore in the absence of lawful justification, which I do not find, he is liable to the appellant for the commission of a fault under art. 1053 of the *Civil Code*. [Article 1053 of the Civil Code had said that "everyone ... is responsible for the injury caused by his fault to another." See now article 1457 of the Civil Code of Quebec, S.Q. 1992, c. 57, which says that "[every person] is responsible for the injury he causes to another person."]

I now turn to the matter of damages.

. . . .

... in all the circumstances, the amount of these damages must be determined in a somewhat arbitrary fashion. I consider that $25,000 should be allowed as damages for the diminution of the value of the goodwill and for the loss of future profits.

I would allow both appeals, with costs here and below, and order the respondent to pay to the appellant damages in the total amount of $33,123.53, with interest from the date of the judgment in the Superior Court, and costs.

Appeals allowed.

(f) The Sponsorship Scandal and the Accountability Act: A Cautionary Tale of Control

David W. Elliott

The federal sponsorship program of the late 1990s provided a dramatic illustration of the need for effective controls on a crucial and controversial activity of the executive branch of government — the expenditure of public funds. The scandal over this misguided advertising program put a spotlight on the relationship between the elected and appointed components of the executive. What began as a naive attempt to buy national unity through government spending cascaded into a major scandal that helped topple a government and launch a major new accountability initiative.

The sponsorship program was a pro-federalism advertising campaign intended to convince Quebeckers to stay in Canada. As a key part of the program, the Department of Public Works and Government Services Canada was to contract with advertising agencies who would arrange for federal government sponsorship and advertising at sporting and cultural events. Although the assumption that this kind of publicity would promote national unity was questionable enough, the program went badly awry.[36] An official in the Department's Communications Coordination Services Branch was allowed to hand out advertising contracts quite independently of his own deputy minister. He reported directly to Prime Minister Chrétien's Chief of Staff, and later to the Minister. There was no effort to hold the private advertising companies to account for their contracts. Some companies collected vast sums[37] of public money, and provided little or nothing in return. Some may have used sponsorship funding to make illegal contributions to the federal Liberal party. None of these activities was known to the public or to most senior government officials.

From one perspective, then, the sponsorship scandal is a story about controls, with bleak early chapters about bypassed, ignored, or missing preventive controls,[38] long intermediate chapters involving investigatory controls that finally detected and identified the problems, and inconclusive later chapters about remedial controls to resolve the problems.

As the Gomery Commission later reported, the sponsorship program bypassed the usual preventive controls of ministerial responsibility.[39] Ministerial responsibility holds a minister accountable to Parliament for what happens in his or her department, to help ensure that the vast administrative apparatus of government is subject, ultimately, to the political process. In the view of the Commission, a Cabinet minister had failed to discharge his ministerial duty to ensure that the sponsorship policy was properly administered. By taking over much of the direction of the program and then failing to oversee its administration, the Prime Minister had made a similar error. Ministerial responsibility relies on a chain of administrative accountability, running through the deputy minister to the lower reaches of government. This chain was broken when an intermediate government official was allowed to make sponsorship arrangements outside the supervision of the deputy minister, and a political aide in the Prime Minister's office gave orders to public servants. For government spending, ministerial responsibility controls are supposed to be supplemented by special financial controls. These, too, were violated by the sponsorship program. Government funds were paid to private contractors without proper certification that the contract terms had been met that government had received reasonable value for the money paid, contrary to the *Financial Administration Act*. One of the ultimate preventive controls is the principle of openness, reinforced in some respects by certification and record requirements and by access legislation. But because of the secrecy surrounding the sponsorship program, its mismanagement went unnoticed by parliamentary control bodies such as the Public Accounts Committee.

As the normal preventive controls had failed to stop the sponsorship problems, there was a pressing need for investigatory controls to detect the problems and identify their causes. The first investigatory control, an internal government audit in August 1999, produced inconclusive results. Instead, it fell to two more independent investigatory controls to bring the sponsorship problems to the attention of the public. One of these was the media, acting through the *Access to Information Act*[40]; the other was a special parliamentary control, the Auditor General. In 1999, acting on the results of access to information requests, Globe and Mail reporter Daniel Leblanc published the first of a series of reports that pointed to questionable and, possibly, even fraudulent spending practices. Then, in reports issued on May 2002 and November 2003, the Auditor General, Ms. Sheila Fraser, found that federal officials had failed to follow *Financial Administration Act*[41] and Treasury Board rules for tendering and monitoring contracts, and had spent hundreds of millions of dollars on advertising, with little return.[42] Under increasing public pressure, the government asked the RCMP to investigate the advertising firms' actions, and on December 13, 2004 Paul Martin cancelled the sponsorship program.

In February 2004, the government appointed a commission of inquiry under Quebec Superior Court Justice John Gomery to determine just what had happened, what had led to the problems, and what could be done to prevent similar mismanagement in future.[43] As this mandate suggests, a commission of inquiry can be a hybrid form of control, part investigatory and part remedial in nature. During his inquiry, Justice Gomery made some comments allegedly disparaging one of the subjects of the inquiry, former Prime Minister Jean Chrétien.[44] When Mr. Chrétien started legal proceedings on the ground of bias, Canadians witnessed an attempt to submit one form of control to yet another. In April 2005, Prime Minister Martin agreed to submit the sponsorship scandal to the ultimate control, an election, to be held within 30 days of the release of the final Gomery report. In fact, the Liberal federal government was defeated after the first Gomery report, but before the last.

The sponsorship scandal led Justice Gomery to propose a set of remedial controls. However, the new Conservative government had its own ideas as to the best solution, and implemented a quite different set in its 2006 *Federal Accountability Act*.[45]

The main thrust of the Gomery recommendations was "to enable the House of Commons to hold the Government, individual Ministers and their departments to account and to review more effectively the Government's proposed spending plans."[46] To do this, Justice Gomery stressed the importance of clarifying who should be accountable, and for what subject matter. He said that parliamentary committees, especially the Public Accounts Committee, should be better funded; deputy ministers should be appointed by an open and competitive process, should have greater security of tenure for at least up to three years, and should be accountable before the Public Accounts Committee for areas under their responsibility; controversies between ministers and deputy ministers should be resolved by the Treasury Board; special financial reserves should be managed by the Treasury Board or the Department of Finance; ministerial political aids should not be able to direct public servants or to enter the public service outside the standard competition process; the Registrar of Lobbyists should report directly to Parliament; there should be enforceable legislation requiring public servants to record decisions and recommendations; public servants should be dismissed without compensation for violating the *Financial Administration Act*'s requirement that contract money must not be paid without first certifying that the contract terms had been met and that government had received reasonable value for the money paid;[47] and chief executive officers of Crown corporations should be appointed and dismissible by the corporation's board of directors.

Compare the Gomery recommendations with the controls that have been actually put in place in the 2006 *Federal Accountability Act*.[48] This 317-section omnibus bill was intended to implement the federal Conservative platform for enhancing accountability, minimizing conflict of interest, and promoting financial responsibility and transparency in the federal government. In regard to conflict of interest, the legislation tightens conflict of interest rules regarding jobs and contracts of present or former government employees or former employees and creates a Conflict of Interest and Ethics Commissioner; limits political donations to amounts of $1000 or less from individuals; strengthens the *Lobbyists Registration Act*[49] and creates a Commissioner of Lobbying; and subjects former political assistants to competitive exams if they seek employment in the public service.

For greater financial responsibility and transparency, the legislation creates a Parliamentary Budget Officer to provide an independent analysis of government finances; attempts to improve security of tenure by increasing the maximum terms for certain order in council appointments to Crown corporations; creates a Procurement Auditor and a more open process for awarding government contracts; provides for rewards and protection for whistleblowers who disclose government wrongdoing; expands the scope of access to information legislation to certain Crown corporations, federal foundations, and parliamentary agents such as the Auditor-General; requires deputy heads to establish internal audit committees and makes them accountable before the relevant parliamentary committee; requires controversies between ministers and deputy heads regarding Treasury Board policies to be resolved by the Treasury Board; and expands the powers of the Auditor-General.

In a few cases, provisions of the legislation closely resemble specific Gomery recommendations. Examples are the provision that makes deputy heads accountable before parliamentary committees in regard to departmental audit matters, and the provision that requires former minister's assistants to take part in normal competitions before appointment to the public service. However, the legislation does relatively little to strengthen parliamentary committees, in particular the Public Accounts Committee. Instead, it concentrates on appointing new or enhanced parliamentary watchdogs: for example, a new Conflict of Interest and Ethics Commissioner, a Commissioner of Lobbying, Parliamentary Budget Officer, and a Procurement Auditor. The legislation makes no attempt to limit

Cabinet's discretion in appointing deputy heads; on the other hand, it increases the maximum tenure of many non-chief directors of Crown corporations. The legislation approaches Gomery's proposed duty to keep records by offering rewards for whistleblowers and by proposing a slight expansion in the scope of the *Access to Information Act*. The legislation goes beyond the Gomery recommendations in the areas of conflict of interest, lobbying, and campaign donations.

How do the new controls compare with those proposed by Justice Gomery? The federal legislation is much more detailed that the Gomery recommendations, and goes well beyond these recommendations in some respects. Beyond this obvious difference, there is a subtler contrast in emphasis. While the Gomery approach would have strengthened financial control of government by the House of Commons and its committees, the 2006 legislation strengthens financial control of government by officers of Parliament appointed by Cabinet. The new legislative broom may sweep a broad path, but government is keeping a firm grip on the handle.

Notes

1. The details are recounted in Canada, Commission of Inquiry into the Sponsorship Program and Advertising Activities, *Who is Responsible? Phase 1 Report*, by Justice John H. Gomery (Ottawa: November 1, 2005), <http://www.gomery.ca/en/phase1report/ffr/index.asp>.
2. Of the total of $332 million spent by the Sponsorship Program between 1994 and 2003, $147 million were spent on money paid to advertising and communications companies: *ibid.* at 14. Justice Gomery described this as "a depressing story of multiple failures to plan a government program appropriately and to control waste — a story of greed, venality and misconduct both in government and advertising and communications agencies, all of which contributed to the loss and misuse of huge amounts of money at the expense of Canadian taxpayers": *ibid.* at xix of *Preface.*
3. See generally, *Who is Responsible? Phase 1 Report, ibid.* Note, however, that Justice Gomery made the following comment *(ibid. at xx to xxi)*:

   ... Without diminishing the importance of the findings of impropriety and wrongdoing in the *Report*, the evidence presented reveals that, in

general, the administration of government programs by the federal bureaucracy is competent and praiseworthy, a conclusion that has been emphasized by the Auditor General herself. Let me also suggest that a system of government that would impose upon itself a searching inquiry by an independent commissioner, armed with the authority to compel the production of incriminating documentation from the public administration and able to subpoena witnesses from every level of society, with a far-reaching mandate to investigate and report on matters that could prove to be embarrassing to the Government itself, is proof that our democratic institutions are functioning well and objectively.

4. See generally Canada, Commission of Inquiry into the Sponsorship Program and Advertising Activities, *Who is Responsible? Phase 1 Report*, by Justice John H. Gomery (Ottawa: November 1, 2005), c. 5-16 <http://www.gomery.ca/en/phase1report/ffr/index.asp>.
5. R.S.C. 1985, c. A-1.
6. R.S.C. 1985, c. F-11.
7. See Office of the Auditor General, *Report to the Minister of Public Works and Government Services on Three Contracts Awarded to Groupaction* (Ottawa: Office of the Auditor General, May 8, 2002); Office of the Auditor General of Canada, *Report of the Auditor General to the House of Commons: Government-Wide Audit of Sponsorship, Advertising, and Public Opinion Research* (Ottawa: Minister of Public Works and Government Services Canada, November 2003) Ch. 3 — *The Sponsorship Program* <http://www.cbc.ca/news/background/auditor general/report2004.html>. In her second report, the Auditor General concluded that Parliament had not been properly informed of the sponsorship program's objectives, the program had a weak control environment, there was a lack of transparent decision-making, the sources of the funding were hidden to the Crown agencies concerned, and government had obtained questionable value for its money.
8. Order in Council P.C. 2004-110, promulgated on 19 February 2004 pursuant to Part I of the *Inquiries Act*. For the Inquiry's mandate, see Commission of Inquiry into the Sponsorship Program and Advertising Activities, *Terms of Reference*, <http://www.gomery.ca/en/termsofreference/>.
9. For these, see CBC News Indepth: Sponsorship Scandal: Timeline <http://www.cbc.ca/news/background/groupaction/timeline.html>
10. Bill C-2, *An Act providing for conflict of interest rules, restrictions on election financing and measures respecting administrative transparency, oversight and accountability*, first reading in the House of Commons, April 11, 2006.
11. "Rebalancing the Relationship Between Parliament and Government", from *Restoring Accountability: Recommendations, Phase 2 Report*, c. XI at 199.
12. *Supra* note 5, s. 33.
13. *Supra* note 9.
14. R.S.C. 1985, c. 44 (4th Supp.).

Judicial Review and Procedural Control

(a) Judicial Review and Procedural Control

David W. Elliott

JUDICIAL REVIEW

Judicial review is an examination of an administrator's decision to see if it was authorized by statutory or other governmental power. Even after the *Charter*, judicial review remains the most common form of judicial control of administrative action.

Judicial review is available only from the higher "superior" courts. It is administered by the common law superior courts in each province[1] (for example, the British Columbia Supreme Court) and by the Federal Court and the Federal Court of Appeal.[2] On the other hand, judicial review decisions can be appealed to higher appellate courts.

Judicial review is a form of interpretation, primarily statutory interpretation. In theory, review cannot amount to an all-out appeal of an administrator's decision, because this would go beyond interpretation. However, statutory intent is often not explicit. Hence reviewing courts have evolved many presumptions as to what they feel Parliament must have intended — or must not have intended — in its legislation. Subject to constitutional constraints, though, the fact that review is based on interpretation gives Parliament the last word if it expresses itself explicitly. Subject to the Constitution, Parliament can restrict judicial review, or modify, or even reverse, its effects. A classic example of this followed the 1969 *Metropolitan Life* case. Here the Ontario legislature amended the law to permit a board to do precisely what the Supreme Court had said it could not do.[3]

There are two main forms of judicial review. The first is procedural review, which is concerned with the process by which an administrator's decision is made. The second is substantive review,[4] which deals more with the content of an administrator's decision. However, not all aspects of an administrator's decision are reviewable. Over the centuries, the courts have tended to identify a number of defects or situations that they consider to justify review. Since judicial review is generally concerned with statutory authority,[5] courts hold that defects or situations of this kind cannot have been intended to be authorized by statute. Accordingly, decisions in which they occur are considered to be *ultra vires* the administrator's statutory power or jurisdiction.

PROCEDURAL CONTROL

Procedural review is also one of two main forms of judicial control of administrative procedure. The other, constitutional control, will be discussed below.[6] Procedural review[7] is judicial review of the procedure by which a decision is made.[8]

Not surprisingly, procedural judicial review can issue where a public authority has contravened express procedural requirements in its enabling statute, in subordinate legislation, or in a procedural code such as Ontario's *Statutory Powers Procedure Act*.[9] Where there are no express requirements, procedural review may still be available if there has been a breach of one of the two "rules of natural justice" (or "procedural fairness" or the "duty to act fairly").[10] Because often there are no express requirements, these "rules" are important.

Natural Justice

The first main rule of natural justice is the *audi alteram partem* rule. This presumes that a person adversely affected by an administrative decision will be given an opportunity to be heard on his or her own behalf. The second is the rule against bias. It presumes that no administrator will or can be a judge in his or her own cause. These "rules" are really presumptions of judicial interpretation, subject to statutory modification.

Two of the most important questions about the rules of natural justice are (i) where do they apply? and (ii) what do they require when they do apply?

Scope of Natural Justice

Statutory Exclusion

Because the rules of natural justice are interpretive presumptions, they can be excluded by very explicit privative clauses in a constitutionally competent statute.[11] They may also be excluded as a matter of interpretation where the court finds that their application would defeat the purpose of the governing statute.[12]

Statutory Inclusion

Procedural safeguards are often provided for expressly in individual enabling acts, and sometimes in general statutory codes. In this situation the legislature can design the procedural régime it considers best suited to the administrator and to the administrator's responsibilities. Violation of these safeguards can be enforced in courts as a breach of statutory duty or a simple excess of power.[13]

Cooper Principle

There is a general presumption in favour of natural justice, even in the absence of express statutory procedural requirements. This was the principle affirmed in the classic 19th century case of *Cooper v. Wandsworth Board of Works*.[14] Here the Board had failed to give Cooper notice or an opportunity to be heard before tearing down his house. The Board claimed that it was subject to no procedural requirements because there were none in its governing statute. The reviewing court disagreed. One judge said that:

> ... although there are no positive words in a statute requiring that the party shall be heard, yet the justice of the common law will supply the omission of the legislature.[15]

Natural Justice Scope Criteria

In the absence of statutory procedural provisions, courts normally[16] apply the rules of natural justice to all *public*[17] statutory[18] or prerogative[19] decisions of administrators that seriously affect the rights or other interests[20] of an individual.[21] These criteria tend to comprise the general threshold for the scope of common law natural justice.

For many years, it was thought that natural justice required not only these conditions (which are only court-like in the most general sense), but also some *additional* especially court-like feature in the functions of the public authority in question.[22] As a result of case law in the latter part of the 20th century, this special court-like element is no longer required unless a statute especially requires it.[23] As we will see later, though, the court-like character of a decision may still be relevant to the level of procedural protection required in a particular situation.

In the criteria that normally *are* required, notice the subjective nature of notions such as "seriously", "rights" and "interests". Procedural review, like other forms of judicial control, protects the interests that *courts* consider important. Not surprisingly, considering the backgrounds of most judges and of most parties able to afford judicial proceedings, the rules of natural justice have traditionally centred on the protection of property and public employment interests. More recently, however, there has been some tendency to open the doors to other interests, such as those of prisoners[24] and people who depend on low-income housing.[25] Beyond these conceptual questions, though, remain grave practical questions of accessibility. What use is an open door to those who cannot afford the admission fee?[26]

Content of Natural Justice[27]

Contextual Factors

What factors govern the content of natural justice, and just what is its content? Natural justice includes a range of possible procedural requirements, most of which relate either to the *audi alteram partem* presumption or to the presumption against bias described above. For both of these presumptions, the precise level and shape of safeguard to be applied will depend on a number of contextual factors. The following list is derived from a summary in the Supreme Court's decision in *Baker*,[28] below:

(i) *the wording and context of the statute*[29] (for example, higher-level protection may be required where there are no alternative means of procedural redress or where the administrator has been given no special discretion in relation to procedure)

(ii) *the court-like nature of the decision*[30] (a more court-like decision may attract a higher level of protection)

(iii) *the actions of the administrator*[31] (for example, safeguards may be affected by administrative actions creating legitimate expectations and by the administrator's particular choice of procedures)

(iv) *the importance of the decision to those affected by it*[32] (the more important the decision, the higher the level of protection).

The *Baker* list is not exhaustive.[33] For example, in some cases a higher level of protection may be imposed because the alternatives are considered inadequate for an effective presentation of a case.[34] In virtually all cases, the benefits of requiring a particular level of protection (or any protection at all) must be weighed against any corresponding costs to the efficiency of the administrator's process for achieving its statutory mandate.[35]

Content of Audi Alteram Partem Rule

Depending on a court's analysis of the contextual factors it considers most important, the general *audi* requirement of a fair opportunity to be heard may require minimal safeguards or more rigorous procedural safeguards.

Under the *audi* rule, the requirement most likely to be required is that notice of the decision or action contemplated be given to the person affected. You can't make yourself heard very effectively if you don't know where and when the decision or action — or a prior hearing — is to occur.

As well as notice, the courts usually require that the person affected be able to make some kind of representation on his or her own behalf. To do this effectively, the person affected must normally be informed of at least the essence of the case against him or her.

The safeguards above are relatively minimal and do not usually make extensive demands on administrative efficiency. Reviewing courts do not normally impose standards higher than these when they differentiate between fairness and conventional natural justice, and find that only the requirements of the former concept must be met.

In some cases, reviewing courts may find that more stringent procedural protections are necessary to allow an effective opportunity to be heard. They may find that the contextual factors require an oral hearing. Especially where there is a subsequent right of appeal, they may require some form of reasons for the administrative decision. In an oral hearing, courts may afford parties a right to cross-examination and representation by legal counsel. They may require a hearing before a legally trained decision maker, and may even require the public authority to adhere to strict court-type rules of evidence.

Overall, the content of natural justice tends to resemble a sliding scale on a continuum, ranging from the most minimal of protections to virtually all the procedural protections of an ordinary court of law.[36] Assigning a standard in an individual case is an exercise of discretion by the reviewing court.

Although the discretion is guided by a relatively well known set of potential procedural protections and contextual factors, it is often very difficult to predict whether a given form of protection will be required in a particular context. In *Consolidated-Bathurst*,[37] for example, the Ontario Labour Relations Board's hearing panel consulted with the full Board on a policy matter before reaching a final decision. Because the consultation occurred in the absence of the parties, there were allegations of a breach of the *audi* rule.[38] A majority of the Supreme Court held that the parties had no right to be present during the consultations, because existing policy — not new policy arguments or fact — had been discussed.[39] However, three judges dissented strongly on the ground that there was no evidence that a policy new to the parties had not been discussed.[40] Eleven years later, a Supreme Court majority again rejected an *audi* challenge to the Board's consultation process. They did so on the ground that the consultation involved law rather than fact.[41] Again there was a dissent, this time on the basis that the consultation really did involve matters of fact.

Uncertainty as to where an oral hearing will be required can make it difficult for administrators to resist litigants' demands for oral hearings. Oral hearings offer an incomparable opportunity for assessing personal credibility (see *Singh* case, below) and for assessing contested matters of fact, but tend to be long, expensive, and — once started — difficult to limit or stop. Oral hearings before some regulatory boards can exceed a hundred days in length, and can involve elaborate court-like procedures and armies of highly paid legal counsel.

Content of Rule Against Bias[42]

At least as subjective as the *audi* rule is the rule against bias or partiality. Bias or lack of impartiality certainly includes cases of actual bias, as where the decision maker has a direct monetary interest in the outcome of the decision he or she is adjudicating. However, courts also require that "justice should not only be done, but should manifestly and undoubtedly be seen to be done."[43] Thus an appearance of bias may result from non-monetary interest in the outcome of a decision because of a special connection to one of the parties or issues, or from comments by the decision maker that suggest a closed mind or stereotyping in regard to a party or issue in question. The usual test is whether a reasonable person, aware of the facts, would have had a reasonable apprehension that the decision maker was biased. Behind this test, a key question is often the degree of connection between the decision maker and the party or issue that allegedly prejudices the result.

Whether there were grounds for this reasonable apprehension is often a very difficult question of fact, leading to diverging conclusions. In the *Marshall Crowe* case,[44] the issue was whether the chairman of the National Energy Board should be disqualified from participating in a pipeline application before the Board. Two years before the scheduled hearing, Mr. Crowe had participated in a study group that led to the formation of the two rival applications before the Board. There were differing views as to how actively he had participated, and how closely the earlier proposals resembled those now before the Board. Had Mr. Crowe's earlier connection with these applications and their subject matter been so great that there could be a reasonable apprehension of bias? Five judges[45] thought so; three judges[46] thought not. As a result, the majority of the Supreme Court of Canada held that Mr. Crowe should be disqualified.

Although the rule against bias lacks the many different levels of protection possible under *audi alteram partem*, contextual factors can affect its application too. For example, where a statute contemplates policy decisions, or where it confers power on elected politicians who must take fixed stands on public issues, reviewing courts may refuse to intervene for prejudgment unless the official had a completely "closed mind".[47] Conversely, where an individual's interests are very seriously affected, courts may be willing to find bias even in the absence of clear evidence as to the precise reasons of the decision makers.[48]

In recent years, bias has been accompanied by the related ground of lack of independence.[49] The notion of independence, which addresses the status of the decision maker in relation to other institutions and parties, supports the idea of impartiality, which is concerned more specifically with the mind of the decision maker.

Procedural Control Under the Canadian Bill of Rights

Subsection 2(e) of the *Canadian Bill of Rights*[50] provides, *inter alia*, that except in the case of an explicit statutory exemption, all federal laws shall be construed and applied so as not to:

> ... deprive a person of the right to a fair hearing in accordance with the principles of fundamental justice for the determination of his rights or obligations....[51]

The *Canadian Bill of Rights* has now fallen under the shadow of the *Charter*. However, in the *Singh* case,[52] one-half of the sitting members of the Supreme Court[53] treated "fundamental justice" in section 2(e) as analogous to natural justice. They held that an *Immigration Act* provision that denied an oral hearing to applicants for "Convention refugee status" was inoperative because it contravened section 2(e) of the *Bill*. They felt the quasi-constitutional status of the *Bill* rendered defences such as necessary or statutory bias unavailable.

Reviewing courts have accorded basic statutory charters such as the *Canadian Bill of Rights* and the Quebec *Charter of Rights and Freedoms*[54] a quasi-constitutional status. Except where they are specifically amended, they can prevail over past or subsequent legislation of the enacting jurisdiction.

Procedural Control Under the *Charter*

One of the most important provisions of the *Canadian Charter of Rights and Freedoms* for administrative law procedure is section 7.[55] Here courts require a deprivation of one or more of life, liberty, or security of the person, as well as a breach of fundamental justice.[56] They have said that fundamental justice includes at least the content of the common law rules of natural justice,[57] but includes substantive matters as well.[58]

While common law natural justice applies to economic as well as physical harm, it is not clear how far section 7 extends into the economic and regulatory spheres that are important to administrative law.[59] So far, the Supreme Court appears to be limiting section 7 mainly to criminal and quasi-criminal contexts, while allowing it some scope beyond this for cases of state interference with bodily freedom and integrity, or serious state-imposed psychological stress.[60]

While common law natural justice includes all government bodies and some non-governmental bodies with public functions,[61] *Charter* protection applies to the legislative branch, to governmental bodies within the executive branch or under its direct control; to non-governmental bodies carrying out specific government policies or implementing coercive statutory powers; to situations where a litigant relies on a statute,[62] and to the common law rules that involve executive and legislative action or are issued for a public purpose.[63]

It is the *status*, more than the content or scope of section 7, that distinguishes s. 7 *Charter* control from ordinary procedural review. As long as no special constitutional constraints are present, procedural review can be limited or even excluded by statute, and the results of a review decision can be reversed at any time by an ordinary statute. With s. 7 control, this is not so. The only prospect short of constitutional amendment is a special override, a rarely used option that has never been invoked for section 7 alone.[64]

Other *Charter* provisions that can affect administrative law procedure include section 8, prohibiting unreasonable searches and seizures,[65] and section 11(c), guaranteeing a person charged with an offence the right to a fair hearing before an "independent and impartial" tribunal.[66]

Notes

1. The superior common law courts have an "inherent" review power that derives from provisions in their constituent statutes that conferred on them all the authorities and powers of the Court of King's (or Queen's) Bench in England. This court had the common law-shaped power to issue the prerogative writs to determine the legality of the proceedings of public authorities created by statute. At first these writs were issued mainly to lower or "inferior" courts of law. However, as more and more government administration was delegated to specialized public authorities outside the judicial hierarchy, the Court of King's Bench extended its review function over them. In turn, this function has been inherited by the common law superior courts.
2. These two federal courts have been given common law-type review powers by their constituent statutes.
3. See Chapter 5, below.
4. *Ibid.*
5. There is one main exception to this proposition. First, judicial review is also available in regard to prerogative power: see, for example, *Volker Stevin N.W.T. ('29) Ltd. v. Northwest Territories (Commissioner)* (1994), 113 D.L.R. (4th) 639 at para. 19, referring to the leading English decisions *R. v. Criminal Injuries Compensation Board, Ex*

Parte Lain, [1967] 2 Q.B. 864 (U.K.C.A.) and *Council of Civil Service Unions v. Minister for the Civil Service*, [1985] A.C. 374 (H.L.). The royal prerogative is based on the remaining rights and privileges of the Crown. The issuing of passports and the creation of non-statutory commissions of inquiry are examples this power. See generally, P. Lordon, *Crown Law* (Markham: Butterworths, 1991). Since all coercive government action requires statutory authorization, administrative law challenges to prerogative power alone are rare.

A former exception, now virtually obsolete, was the historic ground of error of law on the face of the record. Its concern was not with statutory authorization, but with statutory or common law legality: see David Phillip Jones and Anne S. de Villars, *Principles of Administrative Law*, 4y ed. (Toronto: Carswell, 2004) Ch. 11; David J. Mullan, *Administrative Law* (Toronto: Irwin Law, 2001) Ch. 5.
6. See "Procedural Control Under the *Charter*," below.
7. See generally, W.W. Pue, *Natural Justice in Canada* (Vancouver: Butterworths, 1981); D.J. Baum, *Cases and Materials on Administrative Law* (Toronto: Butterworths, 1987) Chs. 3–8; David J. Mullan, ed., *Administrative Law: Cases, Text, and Materials*, 5th ed. (Toronto: Emond Montgomery, 2003) Part II; H.W.R. Wade and C.F. Forsyth, *Administrative Law*, 9th ed. (Oxford: Oxford University Press, 2004) Part VI; P.P. Craig, *Administrative Law*, 5h ed. (London, England: Sweet & Maxwell, 2003) Chs. 13 and 14; *De Smith's Judicial Review of Administrative Action*, abridged ed. (London: Sweet & Maxwell, 1999); *Principles of Administrative Law*, *supra* note 5, Chs. 8–10; and David J. Mullan, *Administrative Law* (Toronto: Irwin Law, 2001) Part Three.
8. It can be contrasted with substantive review, the other main form of judicial review, which is considered in the next chapter. The distinction is simply one of convenience, not an impermeable boundary. We will focus here mainly on procedural and substantive judicial review, but will refer to other forms of control as well.
9. Chapter 6, below.
10. In *Re Therrien*, [2001] 2 S.C.R. 3 at para. 81, said the phrase "duty to act fairly" refers to rules of natural justice as they apply to administrative bodies acting under statutory authority. It is too soon to know if this statement marks a change in the Court's general approach, which has been to use the terms interchangeably unless a statutory provision requires otherwise. Where a statute differentiates distinctly between higher and lower levels of procedural review, the term "duty to act fairly" tends to be reserved for the latter situation.
11. A dramatic example of this occurred in *Woodward Estate v. Minister of Finance*, [1973] S.C.R. 120 (S.C.C.). Here the Supreme Court of Canada found that a provincial cabinet minister had failed to allow an affected party an opportunity to be heard, and thus breached the rules of natural justice. However, the relevant statute contained a sweeping privative clause that even purported to ratify otherwise valid decisions. The Court concluded that the statute had effectively barred judicial review.
12. In *Bishop v. Ontario Securities Commission*, [1964] 1 O.R. 17 (O.C.A.) (involving the Ontario Securities Commission), for example, the Ontario Court of Appeal held that to insist on the full application of the protections of the rules of natural justice would defeat the statute's objective of protecting investors. A more sophisticated exclusion occurred in *I.W.A. v. Consolidated-Bathurst Packaging Ltd.*, [1990] 1 S.C.R. 282 (S.C.C.), where a majority of the Supreme Court felt a board should be able to consult internally between its members (including members who had not heard the parties themselves), as long as the consultation is limited to matters of policy. The need to formulate consistent policy under the Act outweighed the full application of the *audi* rule.

13. However, where the statute has only made partial provision for procedural safeguards, the effect is more uncertain. In this situation, do the rules of natural justice apply where there are no express statutory provisions? Will the partial provision be construed as an indication of a general legislative intent that protections should be imposed? Either result is possible!

14. (1863), 14 C.B.(N.S.) 180, 143 E.R. 414 (C.P.). For a recent affirmation of the principle, see *Supermarches Jean Labrecque Inc. v. Labour Court et al.*, [1987] 2 S.C.R. 219 at 234.

15. *Ibid.* at 194.

16. See generally, *Minister of National Revenue v. Coopers and Lybrand*, [1979] S.C.R. 495; *Martineau v. Matsqui Institution Disciplinary Board (No. 2)*, [1980] S.C.R. 602; *Knight v. Indian Head School Division No. 19*, [1990] S.C.R. 653 (repudiating the old exception for dismissals from positions held at pleasure); *Baker v. Canada (Minister of Citizenship and Immigration)*, [1999] 2 S.C.R. 817, below. In *Baker*, the Court said that "[t]he fact that a decision is administrative and affects 'the rights, privileges or interests of an individual' is sufficient to trigger the application of the duty of fairness": para. 20.

17. Decisions of purely private individuals are normally excluded: see *R. v. Electricity Commissioners, Ex p. London Electricity Joint Committee Co.*, [1924] 1 K.B. 171 (U.K.C.A.) at 205, cited in *Vander Zalm v. British Columbia (Commissioner of Conflict of Interest)* (1991), 80 D.L.R. (4th) 291, 295 (B.C.S.C.). However, disciplinary proceedings of private organizations open to the public, such as clubs, professional associations, and churches, may be subject to natural justice. In regard to church disciplinary proceedings, see *Lakeside Colony of Hutterite Brethren v. Hofer*, [1992] 3 S.C.R. 165.

18. Decisions based more on contractual rather than statutory power are normally excluded: see *Knight v. Indian Head School Division 19*, [1990] 1 S.C.R. 653 at 672 (holding that the situation there was sufficiently statutory to attract procedural fairness requirements).

19. *Supra* note 5.

20. *Baker v. Canada (Minister of Citizenship and Immigration)*, [1999] 2 S.C.R. 817 at para. 20. Decisions which are considered — by judges — too trivial, too remote, or too tentative to affect individuals seriously enough to be said to affect their interests or rights are excluded.

21. This normally excludes policy decisions or legislation affecting the general public as a whole: see *Canada (A.G.) v. Inuit Tapirisat of Canada*, [1980] 2 S.C.R. 735; *Knight v. Indian Head School Division 19*, [1990] 1 S.C.R. 653 at 670.

22. This requirement was arbitrary and uncertain. There was little agreement as to precisely what additional feature or features these quasi-judicial functions required. One view was that there should be a *lis inter partes*, or dispute between two contesting parties before an administrator in the position of a neutral judge. Another view was that quasi-judicial functions required specific rules in the relevant governing statute, as opposed to a broad discretionary power. For example, in *Roncarelli v. Duplessis*, [1959] S.C.R. 121, four judges appeared to feel that the Commission's wide discretionary power to cancel any licence negated a finding that its functions were quasi-judicial and prevented the application of the rules of natural justice (Martland, Kerwin, Locke, and Cartwright JJ.).

23. See, for example, *Ridge v. Baldwin*, [1964] A.C. 40 (H.L.); *Nicholson v. Haldimand-Norfolk Regional Board of Commissioners of Police*, [1979] 1 S.C.R. 311, below; and *Martineau v. Matsqui Institution Disciplinary Board (No. 2)*, [1980] 2 S.C.R. 602 (S.C.C.). In his judgment in the English *Ridge* decision, Lord Reid showed how the suggestion that more was needed, such as a dispute between two parties or an absence of discretion, had been based on a misunderstanding of earlier case law. In *Nicholson*,

the Supreme Court of Canada recognized that the narrow approach to natural justice needed relaxing. In *Matsqui*, the Supreme Court took an approach quite similar to that in *Ridge*, stressing that the key threshold question was whether the administrative decision affected the rights of an individual.

24. For example, *Cardinal and Oswald v. Director of Kent Institution*, [1985] 2 S.C.R. 643.

25. For example, *Re Webb and Ontario Housing Corporation* (1978), 93 D.L.R. (3d) 187 (Ante. C.A.).

26. A 1995 report on civil justice in Ontario estimated that the average cost of civil litigation was $38,000 per case: R. Blair, *Civil Justice Review, First Report* (Toronto: Ontario Civil Justice Review, 1995) at 143–45. Although legal aid may provide help in some cases, it is selective, its availability varies from province to province, and it has been subject to extensive cutbacks: see S.T. Easton et al., *Legal Aid: Efficiency, Cost and Competitiveness* (Kingston: Queen's University School of Policy Studies, 1994); H.W. Arthurs and R. Kreklewich, "Law, Legal Institutions, and the Legal Profession in the New Economy" (1996) 34 Osgoode Hall L.J. 1 at para. 99 (on cutbacks); A. Currie, "Legal Aid Delivery Models in Canada: Past Experience and Future Developments" (2000) 33 U.B.C. L. Rev. 285 (on varieties of delivery structure); S. Mertl, "B.C. Legal-aid Cutbacks Mean People Cut Off from Justice, Says Study" *Canadian Press Newstext* (3 October 2001); Statistics Canada, *Legal Aid in Canada: Resource and Caseload Data Tables* <http://dsp-psd.pwgsc.gc.ca/dsp-psd/Pilot/Statcan/index-e.html>.

27. See generally, *Principles of Administrative Law*, *supra* note 5, Chs. 8–10; David J. Mullan, *Administrative Law* (Toronto: Irwin Law, 2001) Ch. 8E(1).

28. *Baker v. Canada (Minister of Citizenship and Immigration)*, [1999] 2 S.C.R. 817 at paras. 23–27.

29. *Ibid.* at para. 24.

30. *Ibid.*, paras. 26 and 27, referring respectively to actions creating legitimate expectations and the administrator's own choice of procedures.

31. *Ibid.* at para. 23.

32. *Ibid.* at para. 25.

33. *Ibid.* at para. 28.

34. E.g., *Toronto Newspaper Guild v. Globe Printing Co.*, [1953] 2 S.C.R. 18.

35. For illustrations of this point, consider the effect that administrative efficiency had on the majority and dissenting judgments in *Committee for Justice and Liberty v. National Energy Board*, [1978] 1 S.C.R. 369 (S.C.C.) and *I.W.A. v. Consolidated-Bathurst Packaging Ltd.*, [1990] 1 S.C.R. 282 (S.C.C.).

36. See *Minister of National Revenue v. Coopers and Lybrand*, [1979] S.C.R. 495. However, some procedural protections may have no direct basis in the court model. One example is the doctrine of legitimate expectations, discussed but not applied in *Mount Sinai Hospital Center v. Quebec (Minister of Health and Social Services)*, [2001] 2 S.C.R. 281.

37. *I.W.A. Local 2-69 v. Consolidated-Bathurst Packaging Ltd.*, [1990] 1 S.C.R 282.

38. There was also an allegation of lack of independence, which was rejected in this case by all the judges. However, in *Tremblay v. Québec (Commission affaires sociales)*, [1992] S.C.R. 952, defects in the consultation process were held to be fatal to the independence of a panel.

39. *Ibid.* The majority said that while policy goes beyond the parties, fact directly affects the parties and requires their constant input. They felt the line would have been crossed if *new* policy arguments had been introduced.

40. *Ibid.* These judges also stressed the difficulty of distinguishing between policy and fact.

41. *Ellis-Don Ltd. v. Ontario (Labour Relations Board)*, [2001] 1 S.C.R. 221. The majority said the issue appeared to turn on the legal consequences to be derived from facts,

not the facts themselves, so it could not conclude that there was a breach of natural justice.

42. See generally, *Principles of Administrative Law, supra* note 5, Ch. 10; David J. Mullan, *Administrative Law* (Toronto: Irwin Law, 2001) Ch. 14. Note that there is also a special concept of institutional bias. It exists where the facts would raise a reasonable apprehension of bias over a period of time.

43. *R. v. Sussex Justices Ex Parte McCarthy*, [1924] 1 K.B. 256 at 259 (Q.B.).

44. *Committee for Justice and Liberty v. National Energy Board*, [1978] 1 S.C.R. 369 (S.C.C.).

45. Laskin C.J.C. and Ritchie, Spence, Pigeon, and Dickson JJ.

46. de Grandpré, Martland, and Judson JJ.

47. See, for example, *Old St. Boniface Residents Association Inc. v. Winnipeg (City of)*, [1990] 3 S.C.R. 1170 (municipal councillor); *Newfoundland Telephone Co. v. Newfoundland (Board of Commissioners of Public Utilities)*, [1992] 1 S.C.R. 623 at 636–39 (administrator with policy functions).

48. In *Baker v. Canada (Minister of Citizenship and Immigration)*, [1999] 2 S.C.R. 817, the trial judge's appraisal of the hearing officer's field notes was quite different from that of the Supreme Court. The trial judge concluded that the first officer's negative recommendation could have derived legitimately from (i) the negative aspects of the report of the medical officer and (ii) a valid concern about Ms. Baker's capacity to care for her children. The trial judge also thought that the recommendation need not have been affected by the officer's expressed frustration with the "system": [1995] F.C.J. No. 1444 (F.C.T.D.). Looking at the same notes, the Supreme Court inferred negative stereotyping on the part of the first officer, and refused to accept that any defect in his recommendation may have been cured by the review by his superior.

49. The main criteria for assessing independence are security of tenure, pay, or administrative freedom at the general institutional level, and decision-making freedom at the individual structural level. See *I.W.A. v. Consolidated-Bathurst Packaging Ltd.*, [1990] 1 S.C.R. 282; *Tremblay v. Québec (Commission affaires sociales)*, [1992] S.C.R. 952; *Canadian Pacific Ltd. v. Matsqui Indian Band*, [1995] 1 S.C.R. 3; *Ellis-Don Ltd. v. Ontario (Labour Relations Board)*, [2001] 1 S.C.R. 221; *Ocean Port Hotel v. British Columbia (General Manager Liquor Control)*, [2001] 2 S.C.R. 781.

50. R.S.C. 1970, App. III.

51. *Ibid.*

52. *Singh v. Minister of Employment and Immigration*, [1985] 1 S.C.R. 177.

53. Beetz J., Estey, and McIntyre JJ.

54. S.Q. 1986. c. C-12.

55. Section 7 of *Constitution Act, 1982*, Appendix II to *Canada Act, 1982* U.K., c. 11. For an early assessment, see A.W. MacKay, "Fairness After the Charter: A Rose By Any Other Name?" (1985) 10 *Queen's L.J.* 263. See also *Principles of Administrative Law, supra* note 5, Ch. 2(5)(d); David J. Mullan, *Administrative Law* (Toronto: Irwin Law, 2001) Ch. 10(B)(3).

56. See, for example, *Re Singh and Minister of Employment and Immigration*, [1985] 1 S.C.R. 177.

57. Or fairness: *Singh, ibid.*

58. *Re section 94(2) of the Motor Vehicle Act*, [1985] 2 S.C.R. 486.

59. See, for example, *Irwin Toy Ltd. v. Quebec (Attorney General)*, [1989] 1 S.C.R. 927 (Chapter 9, below); *Reference re ss. 193 and 195(1)(c) of the Criminal Code*, [1990] 1 S.C.R. 1123.

60. See *Blencoe v. British Columbia (Human Rights Commission)*, [2000] 2 S.C.R. 307 at paras. 81–86.

61. For example, disciplinary committees of clubs and professional associations. See, for example, *Lakeside Colony of Hutterite Brethren v. Hofer*, [1992] 3 S.C.R. 165. Natural justice has also been applied to appeal bodies created by Indian bands under the *Indian Act*: *Canadian Pacific Ltd. v. Matsqui Indian Band*, [1995] 1 S.C.R. 3.

62. Chapter 8, below.

63. See, for example, *British Columbia Government Employees' Union v. British Columbia*, [1988] 2 S.C.R. 214 at 244, where a court jurisdiction to prohibit picketing in front of a courthouse was held to be "entirely 'public'" in nature and within the scope of the *Charter*.

64. The override has been used on fewer than 20 occasions since 1982: most notably, by the Parti Québécois in Quebec between 1982 and 1989; by the Saskatchewan government in 1986 in regard to freedom of association; by the Quebec Liberal government in 1988 (after *Ford*, Chapter 79, below) in regard to freedom of expression; and by the Alberta government in 1999 in regard to equality before the law.

65. The leading case is *Hunter v. Southam*, [1984] 2 S.C.R. 145. See generally, N. Finkelstein and M.A. Finkelstein, *Constitutional Rights in the Investigative Process* (Markham: Butterworths, 1991); J.A. Fontana, *The Law of Search and Seizure*, 5th ed. (Markham, Ont.: LexisNexis Butterworths, 2002).

66. However, the requirement of an "offence" has been held to limit this *Charter* provision to criminal or penal proceedings: see *R. v. Wigglesworth*, [1987] 2 S.C.R. 541, 559. The main contribution of s. 11 to administrative law has been more indirect: it has helped encourage the development of a requirement of independence as an aspect of the common law rules of natural justice.

(b) *Re Nicholson and Haldimand-Norfolk Regional Board of Commissioners of Police†*

NOTE

A board of commissioners of police dismissed a probationary constable without providing notice or basic information about the case against him. Although the *Police Regulations* entitled a full constable to a hearing before dismissal, they said this provision did not apply to a probationary constable. The majority of the Supreme Court assumed that (i) the board's functions in dismissing a probationary constable were administrative rather than quasi-judicial in nature, and (ii) therefore the protections of "traditional" natural justice were unavailable. The majority then endorsed an emerging notion of "fairness", or "a duty to act fairly", which they said involved "something less than the procedural protection of traditional natural justice." They concluded that although the board was not required to give the probationary constable a full oral hearing, it should at least have informed him of the charges against him and given him either an oral or written opportunity to reply.

EXTRACT

[LASKIN C.J. for himself and for RITCHIE, SPENCE, DICKSON, and ESTEY JJ.:]

The issue in this appeal arises out of a letter of June 10, 1974, written to the appellant by the Deputy Chief of Police of the regional Municipality of Haldimand-Norfolk advising him that "the Board of Commissioners of Police have approved the termination of your services effective June 4, 1974." The appellant, then a second class constable of the regional municipality, had been in its service since April 1, 1974, but he carried over his service as a police constable with the Town of Caledonia, which had been amalgamated with the Town of Haldimand on that date as an area municipality within the Regional Municipality of Haldimand-Norfolk.

The appellant was engaged as a constable, third class, by the Town of Caledonia on March 1, 1973, under an oral hiring of which a term was that he would serve a probationary period of 12 months. On March 1, 1974, he was promoted to constable second class, and pursuant to the *Regional Municipality of Haldimand-Norfolk Amendment Act*, 1973 (Ont), c. 155, s. 75, he became a member of the regional police force, carrying over his previous service to the same extent as if appointed by the Haldimand-Norfolk Police Board.

Subject to some observations to be made later in these reasons on the question whether the appellant knew why his services had been terminated, the formal record indicates that he was not told why he was dismissed nor was he given any notice, prior to dismissal, of the likelihood thereof or of the reason therefor, nor any opportunity to make representations before his services were terminated. Counsel for the appellant does not assert any right on his behalf to an adjudication of the existence of proper cause but rests primarily on the contention that, however fragile was the appellant's security of position, he was in law entitled to be treated fairly and there was a corresponding duty on the respondent to act fairly toward the appellant. This, it is said, the respondent did not do.

The fragility of the appellant's tenure, the allegation that in law he had no security of position and was [dismissible] at pleasure, is at the foundation of the respondent's case; and from this base it was contended that there was no obligation to give any notice or to assign any reason or to hear any representations from the appellant before dispensing with his services.

It is common ground that the relevant legislation within which the respective contentions of the parties are to be assessed is the *Police Act*, R.S.O. 1970, c. 351, and, particularly, s. 26(b) [am. O. reg.296/73, s. 1] of R.R.O. 1970, Reg 680, made pursuant thereto. Section 27 of the Regulation is as follows:

† *Nicholson v. Haldimand Norfolk (Regional) Police Commissioners*, [1979] 1 S.C.R. 311, rev'g. (1976), 12 O.R. (2d) 337 (O.C.A.), rev'g. (1975), 9 O.R. (2d) 481 (O.H.C.-D.C.), quashing a decision of the Board of Commissioners of Police to dismiss Arthur G. Nicholson. (Martland, Pigeon, Beetz and Pratte JJ. dissenting). [Commentary note by David W. Elliott.]

27. No chief of police, constable or other police officer is subject to any penalty under this Part except after a hearing and final disposition of a charge on appeal as provided by this Part, or after the time for appeal has expired, but nothing herein affects the authority of a board or council,

(a) subject to the consent of the Commission, to dispense with the services of any member of a police force for the purpose of reducing the size of or abolishing the police force, where the reduction or abolition is not a contravention of the Act;

(b) to dispense with the services of any constable within eighteen months of his becoming a constable....

. . . .

Following his dismissal the appellant instituted proceedings to quash the decision of June 4, 1974, made by Haldimand-Norfolk Board of Police Commissioners. They came before the Ontario Divisional Court under the *Judicial Review Procedure Act, 1971*, (Ont.), c. 48....

. . . .

... [The central question was whether] in the case of a constable who has served less than the eighteen months specified in s. 27(b), the Board may dismiss peremptorily without obligation to give previous notice or assign a reason or give any opportunity to contest the proposed dismissal. Hughes J. [for the Divisional Court, in 61 D.L.R. (3d) 36, 9 O.R. (2d) 481], put the point in terms of whether a hearing was required as well as notice of the complaint against a constable. Arnup J.A., speaking for the Court of Appeal, which reversed the Divisional Court, took a like view of the issue, putting it as follows at the very front of his reasons [69 D.L.R. (3d) 13 at 14, 12 O.R. (2d) 337]:

Can the services of a police constable be dispensed with within eighteen months of his becoming a constable, without observance by the authority discharging him of the requirements of natural justice, including a hearing?

Counsel for the appellant did not, in his main submission here, put his case that high, as I have already noted.

. . . .

... Hughes J., [in the Divisional Court,] was of the view that *Ridge* v. *Baldwin*, [1964] A.C. 40, was in point in obliterating the distinction between those who perform ministerial acts and those who perform judicial acts, and in proclaiming a duty to act fairly applicable to the former as to the latter. He posed and answered the issue in the following passage of his reasons [61 D.L.R. (3d) at 44–45]:

Can it be that the disclaimer in s. 27(b) of reg. 680, which otherwise enshrines the principles of natural justice as they affect the dismissal or suspension of a police officer, confers an immunity from the application of those principles on members of a board when dealing with a police officer, who has taken the oath of office and upon whom has been conferred the province-wide powers prescribed in the *Police Act*, but who has not yet completed 18 months of service? I do not believe that it can. It may relieve them from complying with the Regulations and preclude the officer's appeal to the Ontario Police Commission, but it cannot relieve them of the duty to act judicially with all which that implies.

He concluded his reasons by stating that a duty to act fairly rested squarely upon the Board of Police Commissioners of Haldimand-Norfolk, adding this:

Their deliberations may be untrammelled by regulations made under the *Police Act*, but this Court should not allow them to proceed as if the principles of natural justice did not exist.

Hughes J. did not spell out the elements of the duty to act fairly but, in the course of his reasons, and adverting to s. 27(b), he stated that [at 40]: "What this Court has to decide is whether s. 27(b) by 'not specifically requiring a hearing,' confers upon the Haldimand-Norfolk board power to dismiss a constable, not having served for 18 months, without one." In a later part of his reasons, he said the crucial question was whether the dismissal could be made without any notice of the complaint against the appellant and without a hearing. It can be taken from his reasons that he was asserting a duty of compliance with the rules of natural justice in their traditional sense of notice and hearing, with an opportunity to make representations, and with reviewability of the decision as much as a less onerous duty of acting fairly.

. . . .

For Arnup J.A., [in the Ontario Court of Appeal] the consequence of the appellant being short of eighteen months' service when he was separated from his position was that (to use his words [69 D.L.R. (3d) at 22]) "the Board may act as it was entitled to act at common law, i.e., without the necessity of prior notice of allegations or of a hearing, and *a fortiori* with no right of appeal by the constable." He also relied on the *expressio unius* rule of construction by noting that "the Legislature has expressly required notice and hearing for certain purposes and has by necessary implication excluded them for other purposes." There is no recognition in his reasons, as there was in those of Hughes J., that there may be a common law duty to act fairly falling short of a requirement of a hearing or, indeed, falling short of a duty to act judicially. Counsel for the appellant asserted that there is an emerging line of authority in this distinction which this Court should approve, and that although it may be regarded as an aspect of natural justice it has a procedural content of its own. It does not, however, rise to the level of what is required to satisfy natural justice where judicial or *quasi*-judicial powers are being exercised. I shall come to this line of authority later in these reasons.

. . . .

The effect of the judgment below is that a constable who has served eighteen months or more is afforded protection against arbitrary discipline or discharge through the requirement of notice and hearing and appellate review, but there is no protection at all, no half-way house, between the observance of natural justice aforesaid and arbitrary removal in the case of a constable who has held office for less than eighteen months. In so far as the Ontario Court of Appeal based its conclusion on the *expressio unius* rule of construction, it has carried the maxim much too far.... [It was said in] *Colquhoun* v. *Brooks* (1888), 21 Q.B.C. 52, [65] ... that "the maxim ought not to be applied, when its application, having regard to the subject-matter to which it is applied, leads to inconsistency or injustice." This statement commends itself to me and I think it relevant to the present case where we are dealing with the holder of a public office, engaged in duties connected with the maintenance of public order and preservation of the peace, important values in any society.

. . . .

This case does not ... fall to be determined on the ground that the appellant was [dismissible] at pleasure. The dropping of the phrase "at pleasure" from the statutory provision for engagement of constables, and its replacement by a regime under which regulations fix the temporal point at which full procedural protection is given to a constable, indicates to me a turning away from the old common law rule even in cases where the full period of time has not fully run....

. . . .

In short, I am of the opinion that although the appellant clearly cannot claim the procedural protections afforded to a constable with more than eighteen months' service, he cannot be denied any protection. He should be treated "fairly" not arbitrarily. I accept, therefore, for present purposes and as a common law principle what Megarry J., accepted in *Bates* v. *Lord Hailsham of St. Marylbone*, [1972] 1 W.L.R. 1373 at 1378, "that in the sphere of the so-called quasi-judicial the rules of natural justice run, and that in the administrative or executive field there is a general duty of fairness."

The emergence of a notion of fairness involving something less than the procedural protection of traditional natural justice has been commented on in de Smith, *Judicial Review of Administrative Action, supra*, at 208–09....

. . . .

What rightly lies behind this emergence is the realization that the classification of statutory functions as judicial, *quasi*-judicial or administrative is often very difficult, to say the least; and to endow some with procedural protection while denying others any at all would work injustice when the results of statutory decisions raise the same serious consequences for those adversely affected, regardless of the classification of the function in question: see, generally, Mullan, "Fairness: The New Natural Justice," 25 Univ. of Tor. L.J. 281 (1975).

. . . .

Not long after [the distinction was drawn in *Pearlberg* v. *Varty (Inspector of Taxes)*, [1972] 1 W.L.R. 534 (H.L.), Lord Morris of Borth-Y-Guest said in *Furnell* v. *Whangarei High School Board*, [1973] A.C. 660, 679 (J.C.P.C.) that "natural justice is but fairness writ large and juridically. It has been described as 'fair play in action.' Nor is it a leaven to be associated only with judicial or quasi-judicial occasions. But as was pointed out by Tucker L.J. in *Russel* v. *Duke of Norfolk*, [1949] 1 All E.R. 109, 118, the requirements of natural justice must depend on the circumstances of each particular case and the subject matter under consideration." The majority concluded in that case that "the scheme of the procedure gives no scope for action which can properly be described as unfair and there are no grounds for thinking that the sub-committee acted unfairly" (at 682). The two dissenting Judges were of a different view. The importance of the case lies in the respect paid by both the majority and the dissenting Judges to a duty to act fairly.

. . . .

The present case is one where the consequences to the appellant are serious indeed in respect of his wish to continue in a public office, and yet the respondent Board has thought it fit and has asserted a legal right to dispense with his services without any indication to him of why he was deemed unsuitable to continue to hold it.

In my opinion, the appellant should have been told why his services were no longer required and given an opportunity, whether orally or in writing as the Board might determine, to respond. The Board itself, I would think, would wish to be certain that it had not made a mistake in some fact or circumstance which it deemed relevant to its determination. Once it had the appellant's response, it would be for the Board to decide on what action to take, without its decision being reviewable elsewhere, always premising good faith. Such a course provides fairness to the appellant, and it is fair as well to the Board's right, as a public authority to decide, once it had the appellant's response, whether a person in his position should be allowed to continue in office to the point where his right to procedural protection was enlarged. Status in office deserves this minimal protection, however brief the period for which the office is held.

It remains to consider whether the appellant should not be heard to complain of want of fairness because he was aware of the reason for his dismissal. The only evidence in the record that goes to this point, is his cross-examination on his affidavit in support of his application for judicial review. Questions were put to him respecting the performance of various of his duties, and among them was a reference to a telephone call made by Nicholson to police headquarters in Simcoe, asking for instructions for obtaining and completing an overtime slip. It apparently angered his superior, one Sergeant Burger, that the appellant "was going over his head" in making the call (which Nicholson charged to himself and not to the police department). He was told by Burger that this was disobedience to direct order (Nicholson said he was unaware of any relevant order) and that he was being suspended indefinitely. The cross-examination shows that Nicholson asked if any charges would be laid and the answer he got was "there won't be any charges." All of this happened on May 29, 1974, some six days before the dismissal by the Board. An inspector, whom Nicholson went to see the same day, had been told by

Burger of his suspension of Nicholson, and the inspector said he supported what Burger had done and that Nicholson had no future in the department.

The cross-examination also revealed that the inspector invited or offered to let Nicholson resign. Nicholson denied that he was told by the inspector that "subject to the confirmation of the Board, [he was] no longer a policeman," these words being put to him by counsel for the Board on his cross-examination. When asked what he thought his position was when he left the inspector's office, Nicholson said this:

> I thought that if they felt I was dispensed with, I thought it was illegal. There were no charges, there was no lawful suspension, there was no lawful firings and I was in a quandary. I knew that I was off probation, so I decided to go and see a lawyer, and retain a lawyer.

If the making of the telephone call of which Burger disapproved (and which he said was disobedience of a direct order, Nicholson saying he was unaware of any relevant order) was the basis of the proposed dismissal, it would have been simple enough to say so. I can hardly credit that in itself it could be a reason for dismissing a constable who had served for 15 months. If it was an allegedly culminating event this too could be easily stated, or if there was another ground Nicholson could have been told of it prior to dismissal. I do not regard it as giving a reason for dismissal to tell Nicholson that he had no future in the department. Moreover, there is nothing in the record to show that an inspector, the particular inspector, had the power to dismiss a constable with less than 18 months' service.

I would allow the appeal, set aside the judgment of the Ontario Court of Appeal and restore the order of the Division Court, with costs to the appellant throughout.

[MARTLAND, PIGEON, BEETZ, and PRATTE JJ. dissented. In the dissenting judgment, delivered by Martland J., the dissenting judges felt that the office in this case was held "at pleasure", a category recognized as an exception to the normal *audi alteram partem* requirement in *Ridge v. Baldwin*. As well, they felt that the intent of the probationary scheme was to confer on the Board an unrestricted discretion to dispense with a probationary constable's services. That being so, the Board's functions were "administrative" and (in their view) not subject to natural justice.]

Appeal allowed.

(c) *Re Singh and Minister of Employment and Immigration and Six Other Appeals*†

NOTE

Mr. Singh and six other refugees were either refused admission to Canada or denied permission to remain here. They all claimed protection under a United Nations convention that gives certain refugee claimants a right to not be returned to a country where their life or freedom would be threatened.

After their claims were rejected by the Minister of Employment and Immigration, they applied for a redetermination of their claims before the former Immigration Appeal Board. This redetermination would involve a full oral hearing, but first the Board was required to make a preliminary decision whether or not to hold the redetermination. At the preliminary decision stage, no oral hearing was available, and Mr. Singh and the others had no way of knowing and responding to the full case against them.

They claimed that the statutory provisions that created the preliminary decision stage were contrary to the procedural guarantees in the *Canadian Bill of Rights* and the *Canadian Charter of Rights and Freedoms*, and three Supreme Court judges agreed with each of these claims.

As well as representing an eleventh-hour revival of the *Canadian Bill of Rights*, this was the first major Supreme Court decision to apply the *Charter* to a key area of administrative law procedure. A new era was starting in Canadian administrative law, an era whose full implications still remain to be seen.

EXTRACT

[BEETZ J. for himself and for ESTEY and McINTYRE JJ.:]

Like my colleague Madame Justice Wilson, whose reasons for judgment I have had the advantage of reading, I conclude that these appeals ought to be allowed. But I do so on the basis of the *Canadian Bill of Rights*. I refrain from expressing any views on the question whether the *Canadian Charter of Rights and Freedoms* is applicable at all to the circumstances of these cases and more particularly, on the important question whether the *Charter* affords any protection against a deprivation or the threat of a deprivation of the right to life, liberty or security of the person by foreign governments.

. . . .

As I said earlier, the relevant provision of the *Canadian Bill of Rights* is s. 2(e) but it will also be convenient to quote s. 1:

1. It is hereby recognized and declared that in Canada there have existed and shall continue to exist without discrimination by reason of race, national origin, colour, religion or sex, the following human rights and fundamental freedoms, namely,

(a) the right of the individual to life, liberty, security of the person and enjoyment of property, and the right not to be deprived thereof except by due process of law;

(b) the right of the individual to equality before the law and the protection of the law;

(c) freedom of religion;

(d) freedom of speech;

(e) freedom of assembly and association; and

(f) freedom of the press.

2. Every law of Canada shall, unless it is expressly declared by an Act of the Parliament of Canada that it shall operate notwithstanding the *Canadian Bill of Rights*, be so construed and applied as not to abrogate, abridge or infringe or to authorize the abrogation, abridgment or infringement of any of the rights or freedoms herein recognized and declared, and in particular, no law of Canada shall be construed or applied so as to

...

(e) deprive a person of the right to a fair hearing in accordance with the principles of fundamental justice for the determination of his rights and obligations.

---

† *Singh v. Canada (Minister of Employment and Immigration)*, [1985] 1 S.C.R. 177, rev'g. decisions of the Federal Court of Appeal dismissing applications for judicial review of decisions of the Immigration Appeal Board dismissing applications for redetermination of refugee claims. [Commentary note by David W. Elliott.]

. . . .

... It is true that the first part of s. 2 refers to "the rights or freedoms herein recognized and declared," but s. 2(e) does protect a right which is fundamental, namely "the right to a fair hearing in accordance with the principles of fundamental justice" for the determination of one's rights and obligations, fundamental or not....

. . . .

Accordingly, the process of determining and redetermining appellants' refugee claims involves the determination of rights and obligations for which the appellants have, under s. 2(e) of the *Canadian Bill of Rights*, the right to a fair hearing in accordance with the principles of fundamental justice. It follows also that this case is distinguishable from cases where a mere privilege was refused or revoked....

. . . .

What the appellants are mainly justified of complaining about in my view is that their claims to refugee status have been finally denied without their having been afforded a full oral hearing at a single stage of the proceedings before any of the bodies or officials empowered to adjudicate upon their claim on the merits. They have actually been heard by the one official who has nothing to say in the matter, a senior immigration officer. But they have been heard neither by the Refugee Status Advisory Committee who could advise the Minister, neither by the Minister, who had the power to decide and who dismissed their claim, nor by the Immigration Appeal Board which did not allow their application to proceed and which determined, finally, that they are not Convention refugees.

. . . .

Again, I express no views as to the applicability of the *Canadian Charter of Rights and Freedoms*, but I otherwise agree with these submissions: threats to life or liberty by a foreign power are relevant, not with respect to the applicability of the *Canadian Bill of Rights*, but with respect to the type of hearing which is warranted in the circumstances. In my opinion, nothing will pass muster short of at least one full oral hearing before adjudication on the merits.

There are additional reasons why the appellants ought to have been given an oral hearing. They are

mentioned in the following submission with which I agree:

> The appellants submit that although "fundamental justice" will not require an oral hearing in every case, where life or liberty may depend on findings of fact and credibility, and it may in these cases, the opportunity to make written submissions, even if coupled with an opportunity to reply in writing to allegations of fact and law against interest, would be insufficient.

. . . .

The appeals are allowed, the decisions of the Federal Court of Appeal and of the Immigration Appeal Board are set aside. The applications of the appellants for redetermination of their refugee claims are remanded to the Immigration Appeal Board which is directed to adjudicate upon them on the merits after a full oral hearing in each case, in accordance with the directions contained in these reasons.

For the purposes of these seven cases, I would declare inoperative all the words of s. 71(1) of the *Immigration Act, 1976*, following the words:

> Where the Board receives an application referred to in subsection 70(2), it shall forthwith consider the application.

. . . .

[WILSON J., for herself and for DICKSON C.J. and LAMER J.:]

. . . .

The Immigration Appeal Board's duties in considering an application for redetermination of a refugee status claim are set out in s. 71 which reads as follows:

> **71.** (1) Where the Board receives an application referred to in subsection 70(2), it shall forthwith consider the application and if, on the basis of such consideration, it is of the opinion that there are reasonable grounds to believe that a claim could, upon the hearing of the application, be established, it shall allow the application to proceed, and in any other case it shall refuse to allow the application to proceed and shall thereupon determine that the person is not a Convention refugee.
>
> (2) Where pursuant to subsection (1) the Board allows an application to proceed, it shall notify the Minister of the time and place where

the application is to be heard and afford the Minister a reasonable opportunity to be heard.

(3) Where the Board has made its determination as to whether or not a person is a Convention refugee, it shall, in writing, inform the Minister and the applicant of its decision.

(4) The Board may, and at the request of the applicant or the Minister shall, give reasons for its determination.

If the Board were to determine pursuant to s. 71(1) that the application should be allowed to proceed, the parties are all agreed that the hearing which would take place pursuant to s. 71(2) would be a quasi-judicial one to which full natural justice would apply. The Board is not, however, empowered by the terms of the statute to allow a redetermination hearing to proceed in every case. It may only do so if "it is of the opinion that there are reasonable grounds to believe that a claim could, upon the hearing of the application, be established...."

. . . .

... The issue directly before this Court in *Kwiatkowsky* was not whether there had been a denial of natural justice but whether the Immigration Appeal Board had applied the wrong test in exercising its power under s. 71(1). It is implicit in the Court's decision, however, that the Act imposes limitations on the scope of the hearing afforded to refugee claimants which it is difficult to reconcile with the principles of natural justice....

. . . .

... In the present instance, however, it seems to me that s. 71(1) is precisely the type of express provision which prevents the courts from reading the principles of natural justice into a statutory scheme for the adjudication of the rights of individuals.

The substance of the appellants' case, as I understand it, is that they did not have a fair opportunity to present their refugee status claims or to know the case they had to meet. I do not think there is any basis for suggesting that the procedures set out in the *Immigration Act, 1976* were not followed correctly in the adjudication of these individuals' claims. Nor do I believe that there is any basis for interpreting the relevant provisions of the *Immigration Act* in a way that provides a significantly greater degree of procedural fairness or natural justice than I have set out in the preceding discussion.

The Act by its terms seems to preclude this. Accordingly, if the appellants are to succeed, I believe that it must be on the basis that the *Charter* requires the Court to override Parliament's decision to exclude the kind of procedural fairness sought by the appellants.

. . . .

... [I]t seems to me that it is incumbent upon the Court to give meaning to each of the elements, life, liberty and security of the person, which make up the "right" contained in s. 7.

To return to the facts before the Court, it will be recalled that a Convention refugee is by definition a person who has a well-founded fear of persecution in the country from which he is fleeing. In my view, to deprive him of the avenues open to him under the Act to escape from that fear of persecution must, at the least, impair his right to life, liberty and security of the person in the narrow sense advanced by counsel for the Minister. The question, however, is whether such an impairment constitutes a "deprivation" under s. 7.

. . . .

... It seems to me that even if one adopts the narrow approach advocated by counsel for the Minister, "security of the person" must encompass freedom from the threat of physical punishment or suffering as well as freedom from such punishment itself. I note particularly that a Convention refugee has the right under s. 55 of the Act not to "... be removed from Canada to a country where his life or freedom would be threatened...." In my view, the denial of such a right must amount to a deprivation of security of the person within the meaning of s. 7.

. . . .

I should note, however, that even if hearings based on written submissions are consistent with the principles of fundamental justice for some purposes, they will not be satisfactory for all purposes. In particular, I am of the view that where a serious issue of credibility is involved, fundamental justice requires that credibility be determined on the basis of an oral hearing. Appellate courts are well aware of the inherent weakness of written transcripts where questions of credibility are at stake and thus are extremely loath to review the findings of tribunals which have had the benefit of hearing the testimony of witnesses in person.... I find it difficult to conceive of a situation in which compliance with fundamental justice could be achieved by a tribunal making significant findings of credibility solely on the basis of written submissions.

.   .   .   .

It seems to me that the basic flaw in Mr. Bowie's characterization of the procedure under ss. 70 and 71 is his description of the procedure as non-adversarial. It is in fact highly adversarial but the adversary, the Minister, is waiting in the wings. What the Board has before it is a determination by the Minister based in part on information and policies to which the applicant has no means of access that the applicant for redetermination is not a Convention refugee. The applicant is entitled to submit whatever relevant material he wishes to the Board but he still faces the hurdle of having to establish to the Board that on the balance of probabilities the Minister was wrong. Moreover, he must do this without any knowledge of the Minister's case beyond the rudimentary reasons which the Minister has decided to give him in rejecting his claim. It is this aspect of the procedures set out in the Act which I find impossible to reconcile with the requirements of "fundamental justice" as set out in s. 7 of the *Charter*.

.   .   .   .

Under the Act as it presently stands ... a refugee claimant may never have the opportunity to make an effective challenge to the information or policies which underlie the Minister's decision to reject his claim. Because s. 71(1) requires the Immigration Appeal Board to reject an application for redetermination unless it is of the view that it is more likely than not that the applicant will be able to succeed, it is apparent that an application will usually be rejected before the refugee claimant has had an opportunity to discover the Minister's case against him in the context of a hearing. Indeed, given the fact that s. 71(1) resolves any doubt as to whether or not there should be a hearing against the refugee claimant, I find it difficult to see how a successful challenge to the accuracy of the undisclosed information upon which the Minister's decision is based could ever be launched.

I am accordingly of the view that the procedures for determination of refugee status claims as set out in the *Immigration Act, 1976* do not accord refugee claimants fundamental justice in the adjudication of those claims and are thus incompatible with s. 7 of the *Charter*....

.   .   .   .

... Certainly the guarantees of the *Charter* would be illusory if they could be ignored because it was administratively convenient to do so. No doubt considerable time and money can be saved by adopting administrative procedures which ignore the principles of fundamental justice but such an argument, in my view, misses the point of the exercise under s. 1. The principles of natural justice and procedural fairness which have long been espoused by our courts, and the constitutional entrenchment of the principles of fundamental justice in s. 7 implicitly recognize that a balance of administrative convenience does not override the need to adhere to these principles....

.   .   .   .

Even if the cost of compliance with fundamental justice is a factor to which the courts would give considerable weight, I am not satisfied that the Minister has demonstrated that this cost would be so prohibitive as to constitute a justification within the meaning of s. 1....

.   .   .   .

Confining myself to the decisions of the Immigration Appeal Board which are under review, I would allow the appeals, set aside the decisions of the Federal Court of Appeal and of the Immigration Appeal Board and remand all seven cases for a hearing on the merits by the Board in accordance with the principles of fundamental justice articulated above. Since s. 71(1) of the *Immigration Act, 1976* which restricts the Board's power to allow hearings to proceed to cases in which it is of the opinion that the applicant for redetermination is more likely than not to succeed upon a hearing of his claim, is inconsistent with the principles of fundamental justice set out in s. 7 of the *Charter*, the appellants are also entitled to a declaration that s. 71(1) is of no force and effect to the extent of the inconsistency.

(d) *Baker v. Canada (Minister of Citizenship and Immigration)*†

NOTE

Ms. Baker was ordered to leave Canada for over-staying a visitor's permit by 11 years. She applied for a humanitarian and compassionate considerations exemption from the deportation order. She claimed that deportation would separate her four Canadian-born children from her and would deprive her of proper facilities for her medical condition. The Immigration Department dismissed Ms. Baker's application without reasons. However, on Ms. Baker's request, the Department provided her with the notes made by the investigating immigration officer (Officer Lorenz) and used by the senior officer (Officer Caden) in making his decision. The notes stressed the number of Ms. Baker's children (eight altogether) and the ongoing nature of her medical condition, expressed concern that the immigration system could permit her to remain so long, and suggested that she would be a strain on the welfare system.

Ms. Baker claimed that:

   (i)   she was entitled to procedural rights, including an oral interview before the decision maker;
   (ii) she was entitled to reasons;
   (iii) the investigating officer's notes gave rise to a reasonable apprehension of bias; and
   (iv) the decision was incorrect in law because the decision maker failed to exercise his discretion in accordance with a U.N. Convention requirement that the best interests of the child be a primary consideration in humanitarian and compassionate considerations decisions.

The extracts here deal with procedural fairness and bias.

EXTRACT

[L'HEUREUX-DUBÉ for herself and GONTHIER, McLACHLIN C.J., BASTARACHE J., and BINNIE J.:]

[20] Both parties agree that a duty of procedural fairness applies to H & C decisions. The fact that a decision is administrative and affects "the rights, privileges or interests of an individual" is sufficient to trigger the application of the duty of fairness....

. . . .

[22] ... [T]he purpose of the participatory rights contained within the duty of procedural fairness is to ensure that administrative decisions are made using a fair and open procedure, appropriate to the decision being made and its statutory, institutional, and social context, with an opportunity for those affected by the decision to put forward their views and evidence fully and have them considered by the decision-maker.

[23] Several factors have been recognized in the jurisprudence as relevant to determining what is required by the common law duty of procedural fairness in a given set of circumstances. [L'Heureux-Dubé J. said these factors include (i) the resemblance of the administrative process in question to the judicial process, (ii) the wording of the statute, for example where it allows no appeal or further proceedings, (iii) the importance of the decision to the individual affected, (iv) the legitimate expectations of the person challenging the decision, and (v) the agency's own procedural choices, especially where it has discretion or expertise regarding the procedures. L'Heureux-Dubé J. said there could be no legitimate expectation of higher than usual procedural protections here, and continued:]

[30] The next issue is whether, taking into account the other factors related to the determination of the content of the duty of fairness, the failure to accord an oral hearing and give notice to Ms. Baker or her children was inconsistent with the participatory rights required by the duty of fairness in these circumstances....

---

† [1999] 2 S.C.R. 817, rev'g, [1997] 2 F.C. 127 (F.C.A.), answering a question certified by Simpson J. in [1995] F.C.J. No. 1441 (F.C.T.D.). [Commentary note by David W. Elliott.]

[31] ... First, an H & C decision is very different from a judicial decision, since it involves the exercise of considerable discretion and requires the consideration of multiple factors. Second, its role is ... an exception to the general principles of Canadian immigration law. These factors militate in favour of more relaxed requirements under the duty of fairness. On the other hand, there is no appeal procedure.... In addition, considering the third factor, this is a decision that in practice has exceptional importance to the lives of those with an interest in its result — the claimant and his or her close family members — and this leads to the content of the duty of fairness being more extensive. Finally, applying the fifth factor described above, the statute accords considerable flexibility to the Minister to decide on the proper procedure, and immigration officers, as a matter of practice, do not conduct interviews in all cases.... Thus, it can be seen that although some of the factors suggest stricter requirements under the duty of fairness, others suggest more relaxed requirements further from the judicial model.

[32] Balancing these factors, I ... [feel that] the circumstances require a full and fair consideration of the issues....

. . . .

[34] I agree that an oral hearing is not a general requirement for H & C decisions.... In this case, the appellant had the opportunity to put forward, in written form through her lawyer, information about her situation, her children and their emotional dependence on her, and documentation in support of her application from a social worker at the Children's Aid Society and from her psychiatrist. These documents were before the decision-makers, and they contained the information relevant to making this decision.... [T]he lack of an oral hearing or notice of such a hearing did not, in my opinion, constitute a violation of the requirements of procedural fairness to which Ms. Baker was entitled in the circumstances, particularly given the fact that several of the factors point toward a more relaxed standard....

. . . .

[43] ... [I]n certain circumstances, the duty of procedural fairness will require the provision of a written explanation for a decision. ... [I]n cases such as this where the decision has important significance for the individual, when there is a statutory right of appeal, or in other circumstances, some form of reasons should be required. This requirement has been

developing in the common law elsewhere. The circumstances of the case at bar, in my opinion, constitute one of the situations where reasons are necessary....

[44] In my view, however, the reasons requirement was fulfilled in this case, since the appellant was provided with the notes of Officer Lorenz. The notes were given to Ms. Baker when her counsel asked for reasons....

[45] Procedural fairness also requires that decisions be made free from a reasonable apprehension of bias, by an impartial decision-maker. The respondent argues that Simpson J. was correct to find that the notes of Officer Lorenz cannot be considered to give rise to a reasonable apprehension of bias because it was Officer Caden who was the actual decision-maker, who was simply reviewing the recommendation prepared by his subordinate. In my opinion, the duty to act fairly and therefore in a manner that does not give rise to a reasonable apprehension of bias applies to all immigration officers who play a significant role in the making of decisions, whether they are subordinate reviewing officers, or those who make the final decision....

. . . .

[48] In my opinion, the well-informed member of the community would perceive bias when reading Officer Lorenz's comments. His notes, and the manner in which they are written, do not disclose the existence of an open mind or a weighing of the particular circumstances of the case free from stereotypes. Most unfortunate is the fact that they seem to make a link between Ms. Baker's mental illness, her training as a domestic worker, the fact that she has several children, and the conclusion that she would therefore be a strain on our social welfare system for the rest of her life. In addition, the conclusion drawn was contrary to the psychiatrist's letter, which stated that, with treatment, Ms. Baker could remain well and return to being a productive member of society. Whether they were intended in this manner or not, these statements give the impression that Officer Lorenz may have been drawing conclusions based not on the evidence before him, but on the fact that Ms. Baker was a single mother with several children, and had been diagnosed with a psychiatric illness. His use of capitals to highlight the number of Ms. Baker's children may also suggest to a reader that this was a reason to deny her status. Reading his comments, I do not believe that a reasonable and well-informed member of the community would con-

clude that he had approached this case with the impartiality appropriate to a decision made by an immigration officer. It would appear to a reasonable observer that his own frustration with the "system" interfered with his duty to consider impartially whether the appellant's admission should be facilitated owing to humanitarian or compassionate considerations. I conclude that the notes of Officer

Lorenz demonstrate a reasonable apprehension of bias.

. . . .

[IACOBUCCI J. gave separate reasons for himself and CORY J. They agreed with the comments above.]

(e)   *Congrégation des témoins de Jéhovah de St-Jérôme-Lafontaine v. Lafontaine (Village)*†

NOTE

In the Village of Lafontaine, houses of worship could be constructed only in P-3 community zones. For land for a proposed Kingdom Hall, the Jehovah's Witnesses tried to buy a main road lot owned by a Ms. Jolicoeur. Ms. Jolicoeur told them that the main road lot was not for sale. Although she had another lot available off the main road, she did not mention it. Concluding that there was no P-3 land available, the Jehovah's Witnesses bought a lot in a residential area and applied to the municipality to re-zone it to P-3 status. The municipality refused. It said that this would place too high a tax burden on residential ratepayers, as churches don't pay tax. The Jehovah's Witnesses then found a lot in a commercial zone and applied to the municipality to re-zone it to P-3 status. The municipality refused again. It said that there was land available in the P-3 zones, but provided no details. The Jehovah's Witnesses obtained written evidence that there was no land available in the P-3 zones and applied again to have the commercial lot re-zoned to P-3 status. The municipality refused again, this time with no reasons at all. It said that "[t]he municipal council of Lafontaine is not required to provide you with a justification and we therefore have no intention of giving reasons for the council's decision."

The Jehovah's Witnesses argued that the municipality's refusal was an unjustifiable breach of their *Charter* right of freedom of religion. In the lower courts, the judges all focused on this *Charter*

issue. The trial judge found that P-3 was available. He concluded that Mrs. Jolicoeur had failed to mention the lot off the main road because she had mistakenly thought that the Jehovah's Witnesses were interested only in her main road lot. As a result, there was no absolute prohibition on acquiring P-3 land for a house of worship, and no breach of freedom of religion. A majority of the Quebec Court of Appeal held that although there was no P-3 land available, there was no breach of freedom of religion because (a) the unavailability of land had been caused by the unwillingness of private owners to sell, not by the action of the municipality, and (b) there is no positive obligation on government to preserve freedom of religion.

When reading the judgments in the Supreme Court, consider the following questions:

1. Did a majority of the Supreme Court decide this decision on the basis of (a) whether there was a breach of a non-*Charter* procedural fairness right to reasons or (b) the *Charter* issue of freedom of religion?

2. Given the Jehovah's Witnesses had based their arguments on the question of freedom of religion under the *Charter*, why did some of the judges base their decision on the non-*Charter* procedural fairness issue? Should they have done so?

3. Were there any points of agreement between the two main Supreme Court judgments on the procedural issue?

---

† [2004] 2 S.C.R. 650, rev'g. [2002] R.J.Q. 3015, [2002] Q.J. No. 4728 (QL), aff'g. a judgment of the Superior Court, J.E. 99-333. [Commentary note by David W. Elliott.]

4. Suppose that the municipality had accompanied its last refusal with the statement that there were lots available. Would that have affected any of the judgments in the Supreme Court?

5. How did the questions as to (a) whether land was available and (b) whether any lack of availability of land was caused by government or private parties affect the *Charter* issue of freedom of religion?

EXTRACT

[McLACHLIN C.J. for herself and IACOBUCCI, BINNIE, ARBOUR and FISH JJ.:]

I.   SUMMARY

1 The issue in this case is whether the municipality of the village of Lafontaine (the "Municipality") lawfully denied an application for rezoning to permit the Congrégation des témoins de Jéhovah de St-Jérôme-Lafontaine (the "Congregation") to build a place of worship. Unlike my colleague Justice LeBel, I conclude the Municipality did not. Although the Municipality's first denial of permission to rezone complied with the law, the second and third did not, in my view, because the Municipality gave no reasons for its denial, instead taking the position that it enjoyed absolute discretion to refuse the zoning variance with no explanation to the Congregation.

2 In weighing the merits of the Congregation's rezoning requests, the Municipality was discharging a duty delegated to it by the Legislature. It was bound to exercise the powers conferred upon it fairly, in good faith and with a view to the public interest. Here, on the facts as found by the trial judge, the Municipality failed to do so. Accordingly, I would remit the matter to the Municipality for reconsideration.

II.   THE DUTY ON
THE MUNICIPALITY

3 A public body like a municipality is bound by a duty of procedural fairness when it makes an administrative decision affecting individual rights, privileges or interests: *Cardinal v. Director of Kent Institution*, [1985] 2 S.C.R. 643; *Attorney General of Canada v. Inuit Tapirisat of Canada*, [1980] 2 S.C.R. 735; *Martineau v. Matsqui Institution Disciplinary Board*, [1980] 1 S.C.R. 602; *Nicholson v. Haldimand-Norfolk Regional Board of Commissioners of Police*, [1979] 1 S.C.R. 311. The decision to deny the application for rezoning affected the Congregation's rights and interests.

There can thus be no question that the Municipality owed the Congregation a duty of fairness.

4 At issue in this case is the content of this duty. More particularly and on the facts as found, does the duty require the Municipality to give the Congregation reasons for refusing the rezoning application? Or does it clothe the Municipality with absolute discretion to refuse the Congregation's application?

5 The content of the duty of fairness on a public body varies according to five factors: (1) the nature of the decision and the decision-making process employed by the public organ; (2) the nature of the statutory scheme and the precise statutory provisions pursuant to which the public body operates; (3) the importance of the decision to the individuals affected; (4) the legitimate expectations of the party challenging the decision; and (5) the nature of the deference accorded to the body: *Baker v. Canada (Minister of Citizenship and Immigration)*, [1999] 2 S.C.R. 817. In my view and having regard to the facts and legislation in this appeal, these considerations require the Municipality to articulate reasons for refusing the Congregation's second and third rezoning applications.

6 The first factor — the nature of the decision and the process by which it is reached — merges administrative and political concerns. The decision to propose a draft by-law rezoning municipal territory is made by an elected council accountable to its constituents in a manner analogous to that in which Parliament and the provincial legislatures are accountable to their own: *Godbout v. Longueuil (City)*, [1997] 3 S.C.R. 844, at para. 51. This decision is moreover tempered by the municipality's charge to act in the public interest: *Toronto (City) v. Trustees of the Roman Catholic Separate Schools of Toronto*, [1926] A.C. 81 (P.C.), at p. 86. What is in the public interest is a matter of discretion to be determined solely by the municipality. Provided the municipality acts honestly and within the limits of its statutory powers, the reviewing court is not to interfere with the municipal decision unless "good and sufficient reason be established"....

7 However, the elected councillors cannot deny a rezoning application in an arbitrary manner. Where the municipal council acts in an arbitrary fashion in

the discharge of its public function, "good and sufficient reason" exists to warrant intervention from the reviewing court in order to remedy the proven misconduct. The need for judicial oversight of arbitrary municipal decision making is only heightened by the aggravated potential for abuse of discretionary statutory authority. As Rand J. has made clear in *Roncarelli v. Duplessis*, [1959] S.C.R. 121, at p. 140, no discretion casts a net wide enough to shield an arbitrary or capricious municipal decision from judicial review:

> In public regulation of this sort there is no such thing as absolute and untrammelled "discretion", that is that action can be taken on any ground or for any reason that can be suggested to the mind of the administrator; no legislative Act can, without express language, be taken to contemplate an unlimited arbitrary power exercisable for any purpose, however capricious or irrelevant, regardless of the nature or purpose of the statute.

8 The second factor is the statutory scheme and its provisions, in this case the *Act respecting land use planning and development*, R.S.Q., c. A-19.1, which grants the Municipality authority to consider a rezoning application. Even so, the absence of an appeal provision demands greater municipal solicitude for fairness. Enhanced procedural protections "will be required when no appeal procedure is provided within the statute, or when the decision is determinative of the issue and further requests cannot be submitted": *Baker, supra*, at para. 24, per L'Heureux-Dubé J.

9 The third factor requires us to consider the importance of the decision to the Congregation. The stringency of procedural protection is directly proportional to the importance of the decision to the lives of those affected and the nature of its impact on them: *Baker, supra*, at para. 25; see also *Kane v. Board of Governors of the University of British Columbia*, [1980] 1 S.C.R. 1105, at p. 1113. Here, it becomes important that the municipal decision affects the Congregation's practice of its religion. The right to freely adhere to a faith and to congregate with others in doing so is of primary importance, as attested to by its protection in the *Canadian Charter of Rights and Freedoms* and the *Quebec Charter of human rights and freedoms*, R.S.Q., c. C-12.

10 The fourth factor — the legitimate expectations of the Congregation — also militates in favour of heightened procedural protection. Where prior conduct creates for the claimant a legitimate expectation that certain procedures will be followed as a matter of course, fairness may require consistency: *Baker, supra*, at para. 26; see also *Bendahmane v. Canada (Minister of Employment and Immigration)*, [1989] 3 F.C. 16 (C.A.); *Qi v. Canada (Minister of Citizenship and Immigration)* (1995), 33 Imm. L.R. (2d) 57 (F.C.T.D.); *Mercier-Néron v. Canada (Minister of National Health and Welfare)* (1995), 98 F.T.R. 36. Here, the Municipality followed an involved process in responding to the Congregation's first rezoning application, in so doing giving rise to the Congregation's legitimate expectation that future applications would be thoroughly vetted and carefully considered.

11 The fifth factor — the nature of the deference due to the decision maker — calls upon the reviewing court to acknowledge that the public body may be better positioned than the judiciary in certain matters to render a decision, and to examine whether the decision in question falls within this realm. Municipal decisions on rezoning fall within the sphere in which municipalities have expertise beyond the capacity of the judiciary, thus warranting deference from reviewing courts. However, this factor may not carry much weight where, as here on the second and third applications for rezoning, there is no record to indicate that the Municipality has actually engaged its expertise in evaluating the applications.

12 The five *Baker* factors suggest that the Municipality's duty of procedural fairness to the Congregation required the Municipality to carefully evaluate the applications for a zoning variance and to give reasons for refusing them. This conclusion is consistent with the Court's recent decision in *Prud'homme v. Prud'homme*, [2002] 4 S.C.R. 663, 2002 SCC 85, at para. 23, holding that municipal councillors must always explain and be prepared to defend their decisions. It is also consistent with *Baker*, where it was held, at para. 43 dealing with a ministerial decision, that if an organ of the state has a duty to give reasons and refuses to articulate reasons for exercising its discretionary authority in a particular fashion, the public body may be deemed to have acted arbitrarily and violated its duty of procedural fairness.

13 Giving reasons for refusing to rezone in a case such as this serves the values of fair and transparent decision making, reduces the chance of arbitrary or capricious decisions, and cultivates the confidence of citizens in public officials. Sustained by both law and policy, I conclude that the Municipality was bound to give reasons for refusing the Congregation's second and third applications for rezoning. This duty applied to the first application, and was complied with. If anything, the duty was stronger on the Congregation's second and third applications, where legitimate expectations of fair process had been established by the Municipality itself.

III.   APPLYING THE DUTY OF FAIRNESS TO THE FACTS

14 Before considering the rezoning applications, it is necessary to deal with a preliminary question: does the trial judge's finding that Mrs. Jolicoeur was willing to sell a P-3 property to the Congregation resolve the matter and make it unnecessary to consider the Municipality's treatment of the Congregation's application for rezoning, as LeBel J. concludes?

15 Like LeBel J., I accept the finding of fact that land was available in Zone P-3. However, this does not resolve the issue, in my view, because the Municipality's duty of procedural fairness to the Congregation is not contingent upon the interactions of the Congregation with third parties, namely Mrs. Jolicoeur. The Municipality's duty exists independent of the Congregation's own conduct.

16 I therefore find it necessary to consider whether the Municipality fulfilled its duty of procedural fairness in responding to the rezoning applications brought by the Congregation. In my view, the answer is no.

17 The Congregation requested a zoning variance from the Municipality on three separate occasions. On each occasion, the Municipality refused the request. The process by which the Municipality refused the first request withstands judicial scrutiny. But the process followed to respond to the second and third requests does not.

[McLachlin C.J. described the three requests from the Jehovah's Witnesses and the three responses from the municipality].

28 Where, one asks, is the recognition that the Municipality must exercise its legislatively conferred discretion in the public interest? Where is the recognition that the Municipality owed a duty of fairness to the Congregation? The Congregation in making its second and third applications was acting in good faith on the advice it had received from the municipal inspector following the rejection of its first application.

The Congregation offered evidence of good faith searches for land in P-3 to no avail — evidence the Municipality did not bother to comment on, much less rebut.

29 The Municipality's attitude was clear. The Congregation was welcome to find land in P-3 on its own. If it was unable to do so, the Municipality was prepared to neither accept an application for rezoning nor justify its refusal. The letter effectively foreclosed any possibility that the Municipality would assist the Congregation in its quest for land upon which to build its place of worship. Not surprisingly, the Congregation concluded further applications would be fruitless and commenced this litigation.

30 In refusing to justify its decision to deny the second and third applications for zoning variances, the Municipality breached the duty of procedural fairness it owed to the Congregation — a duty heightened by the expectations established by the Municipality's own conduct and the importance of the decision to the Congregation, impacting as it did on the right of the Congregation to practise the religion of its choice. The Municipality acted in a manner that was arbitrary and straddled the boundary separating good from bad faith. It follows that the second and third refusals do not comply with the law and must be set aside.

IV.   REMEDY

31 I would allow the appeal, set aside the second and third rezoning refusals, and remit the matter to the Municipality for reconsideration of the Congregation's rezoning application.

32 The Congregation argues that this remedy is inadequate because it fears that the Municipality will once again refuse its application, this time with proper reasons. Accordingly, it asks this Court to order the Municipality to grant its rezoning application. But such an order presupposes that the Congregation is entitled to a favourable decision by the Municipality in the proper exercise of its discretion. Having already discussed the broad scope of the municipal power to pursue its urban planning program with fairness, in good faith and with a view to the public interest, I take no position on this matter.

33 It may be that in appropriate cases, high-handed or outrageous conduct as that of the Municipality in this appeal might support an order for solicitor-and-client costs or punitive damages: *Whiten v. Pilot*

Insurance Co., [2002] 1 S.C.R. 595, 2002 SCC 18; *Young v. Young*, [1993] 4 S.C.R. 3. Although the Congregation has made no such request to this Court, we nevertheless retain the right to issue an order for solicitor-and-client costs where circumstances so warrant: *Supreme Court Act*, R.S.C. 1985, c. S-26, s. 47. However, in light of our inability to conclude on the facts whether the Municipality acted in bad faith in denying the Congregation's second and third rezoning applications, I would decline to award solicitor-and-client costs in this appeal.

34 It is also unnecessary to consider the constitutionality of the impugned provisions of the Act respecting land use planning and development and to answer the constitutional questions.

V.   CONCLUSION

35 I would allow the appeal with costs to the Congregation and remit the Congregation's rezoning application for the property located at 2373 Labelle Boulevard to the Municipality, to be considered in accordance with these reasons and in observance of the lawful exercise of discretionary authority.

36 MAJOR J., dissenting: I agree with the result in the judgment of LeBel J. but restrict my reasons to his conclusions on the findings of fact of the trial judge and the absence of any infringement to freedom of religion.

[LEBEL J. for himself, BASTARACHE J., and DESCHAMPS J., dissenting:]

.   .   .   .

70 I concluded above that the trial judge's findings of fact regarding the availability of certain lots in Zone P-3 and, more specifically, of the one belonging to Ms. Jolicoeur, should be restored in this case. As this lot should have been considered available, the appellants cannot complain that the zoning by-law, by making it impossible for them to establish a place of worship in the municipality, violates their freedom of religion. The appellants could in fact have built a Kingdom Hall, on Ms. Jolicoeur's lot at least, had they come to an agreement with her.

71 As the municipality is required to be neutral in matters of religion, its by-laws must be structured in such a way as to avoid placing unnecessary obstacles in the way of the exercise of religious freedoms.

However, it does not have to provide assistance of any kind to religious groups or actively help them resolve any difficulties they might encounter in their negotiations with third parties in relation to plans to establish a place of worship. In the case at bar, the municipality did not have to provide the appellants with access to a lot that corresponded better to their selection criteria. Such assistance would be incompatible with the municipality's duty of neutrality in that the municipality would be manipulating its regulatory standards in favour of a particular religion. Such support for a religious group could jeopardize the neutrality the municipality must adopt toward all such groups. Moreover, as this Court stated in *Edwards Books*, "[s]ection 2(a) does not require the legislatures to eliminate every minuscule state-imposed cost associated with the practice of religion" (p. 759). Although the very nature of the zoning by-law means that the appellants do not have absolute freedom to choose the location of their place of worship, this limit is necessary to protect safety and order, and ensure proper land use, in the municipality and does not constitute a violation of freedom of religion. Neither the purpose nor the effect of this by-law has been to infringe the appellants' freedom of religion.

72 Since at least one lot remains available in Zone P-3 for the construction of their place of worship, the appellants must comply with the municipality's zoning by-law and build their place of worship in that zone, where such a use is authorized. Their religious beliefs and practices do not exempt them from complying with municipal by-laws. For this reason, I would dismiss the appeal. Having reached this conclusion, I could end my analysis here. However, for the sake of discussion only, and because of the nature of the debate that has taken place in the Quebec courts and in this Court and the importance of the constitutional issues raised, I propose to go on to review the parties' positions based on a different, fictitious premise. I will now consider what the legal consequences would have been had the evidence shown that no land was available in Zone P-3 for the appellants to establish a place of worship.

.   .   .   .

74 In the case at bar, the appellants have shown that their Kingdom Hall, a place of prayer and contemplation that serves as a venue for weddings and funerals, is necessary to the manifestation of their religious faith. They should therefore be free to

establish such a facility within the boundaries of the municipality. If no land were available in Zone P-3, they would be prevented from doing so, in which case they would be unable to practise their religion, and their freedom guaranteed by s. 2(a) of the *Charter* would be infringed accordingly.

. . . .

85 In addition to the constitutional questions discussed so far, this appeal has administrative law implications. However, the appellants declined to base their case on the principles of administrative law, preferring to focus on their arguments based on freedom of religion. As a result, the questions of administrative law cannot form the basis of this Court's decision, although some comments are in order due to the importance of these questions.

. . . .

89 When applied to the case at bar, [the *Baker*] factors would, at the least, place the municipality under an obligation to give reasons for its repeated refusals to amend its zoning by-law. The municipality's decision regarding the application to amend the zoning by-law, which was not subject to a specific decision-making process, could not be appealed by the appellants even though it had a direct effect on their right to freedom of religion guaranteed by s. 2(a) of the *Charter*. Normally, the appellants could expect to

receive reasons from the municipality for its decision. The importance of a negative decision to the appellants, who as a result found it impossible to build the place of worship they needed to practice their religion, in itself placed the municipality under an obligation to give reasons for its decision.

90 The municipality did not give sufficient reasons for its decisions....

. . . .

92 More detailed reasons would have given the appellants a better understanding of the municipality's decision and, above all, demonstrated to them that there were in fact lots available in Zone P-3. As a result, they would not have been left with the impression that the municipality's decision was arbitrary or that the municipality had acted in bad faith. A more precise and rigorous justification would therefore have given the municipality's decision-making process the required transparency and the appearance of procedural fairness.

VIII. CONCLUSION

93 For the reasons set out here, I would answer the constitutional questions in the negative and dismiss the appeal with costs.

Substantive Review

(a) Substantive Review†

David W. Elliott

INTRODUCTION

Substantive review[1] is judicial review of the non-procedural aspects of an administrative decision.[2] It is concerned more with what was decided than with how a decision was made. For example, while procedural review is concerned with impartiality, independence, and allowing a fair opportunity to be heard, substantive review is concerned more with whether the content of the decision was what the statute intended.

Although substantive judicial review is always in flux, we can identify three main review periods in Canada. The approach that prevailed until the early 1970s might be called classical substantive review. The approach that has evolved since that time until about 2007 will be called modern substantive review, and the one in the current period, from 2008, will be referred to as post-modern substantive review. There is no precise dividing line between these periods, and there is still much overlap. Nevertheless, the modern approach and the post-modern approach have quite a different appearance from that of the judicial review that existed four decades ago.

CLASSICAL SUBSTANTIVE REVIEW

Classical review was based on a general theoretical distinction between judicial review and judicial appeal on the merits. Although an unlimited judicial appeal can permit reconsideration of the merits —

of the overall "rightness" or "wrongness" — of an administrative decision,[3] judicial review was considered to be limited to judicial interpretation of questions of jurisdiction and legality. Although judicial review does not require express statutory authorization, judicial appeal cannot exist unless a statute expressly creates it. Hence classical review held that common law substantive review cannot extend to a complete judicial reconsideration of the merits of an administrator's decision. That would amount to a full appeal, which must be expressly created by statute.

Classical substantive review was also based heavily on the wording of the relevant statutory text. The emphasis was on express statutory interpretation rather than on consideration of broad policy. Of course, it was the courts who interpreted the statutory text, and they made use of their own common law presumptions in doing so.

Under classical review, courts purported to limit their supervision to situations where administrators exceeded their statutory authority (jurisdiction) or made obvious mistakes of law. Jurisdictional (originally called "collateral") provisions were statutory provisions that constituted limits to the administrator's power.[4] Courts held that these limits had to be interpreted correctly before the administrator could exercise the content of the special power conferred by the enabling statute. Otherwise the administrative decision lacked jurisdiction and was *ultra vires*.

Even while addressing questions within these limits, an administrator could still *lose* jurisdiction

---

† Revised and updated by Nick E. Milanovic.

because of a jurisdictional defect such as fraud, improper purpose, or irrelevant considerations. Courts considered jurisdictional defects to be too serious to have been intended by statute. Finally, in rare cases administrative tribunals acting within jurisdiction could still commit an illegality if they made an error of law that appeared in the official record of their proceedings.

The classical approach was complex. It favoured formal interpretation techniques and abstract concepts over policy. Moreover, it was often unclear which statutory provisions were intended to be "jurisdictional". On the other hand, when it was cautiously applied, classical substantive review could yield relatively restrained results.[5] In the 1960s and early 1970s, though, some very wide Supreme Court interpretations of jurisdictional provisions and defects raised concerns about judicial interventionism.[6] At the same time, Canadian legislators became increasingly anxious to block or curb substantive review in areas such as labour law.

STATUTORY EXCLUSION

Why this concern? If judicial control provides a means of checking abuse of power by the administrative process, and — in the case of judicial review — a means of reinforcing parliamentary mandates, why exclude or limit it? There are two main reasons for excluding or limiting judicial control — the institutional weaknesses of judges and courts, and the availability of non-judicial control alternatives. Like everything else, judicial control comes at a price. It can involve a partial or total replacement of an administrator's decision by that of a court. In areas such as labour law, administrators were created originally in the interests of special expertise, increased speed, informality and finality, and lower cost. Typically, courts are slow, formal, and expensive, and judges lack special non-legal expertise. The more wide-ranging the judicial control, the greater the risk that its costs will outweigh its benefits. Similarly, the broader the scope of judicial control, the greater the risk of neglect to effective *non*-judicial controls.

Legislators have two means of trying to exclude or limit judicial control. First, they may try to do this directly by enacting a privative clause, a legislative provision that purports to exclude or limit judicial control. Privative clauses may bar remedies (e.g., "no *certiorari*"); bar review (e.g., "the decision shall not be questioned or reviewed in any court",

etc.); or give the administrator exclusive power to decide (e.g., "the Board shall have exclusive jurisdiction"). Alternatively, legislators may resort to more indirect means of restraining judicial control. For example, they may confer a broad discretion on an administrator; require a consent as a prerequisite to legal proceedings; or simply enact restrictive wording that is less forceful than full privative clauses (e.g., "shall be final").

Traditionally, Canadian courts reacted negatively to privative clauses. True, the principle of sovereignty of Parliament requires that — subject to the Constitution — courts must give effect to a clearly expressed statute. However, courts could and sometimes did conclude that a privative clause was *not* sufficiently clear to exclude judicial control in the circumstances at hand. In substantive review, they held that although a clause could exclude a non-jurisdictional ground of review, it was generally not sufficient to exclude a jurisdictional ground. However, privative clauses often *were* highly explicit, and the distinction between jurisdictional and non-jurisdictional issues seemed highly subjective. Thus, when the jurisdictional grounds were construed very broadly, as in the *Metropolitan Life* case,[7] it looked as if parliamentary sovereignty and administrative needs were taking a back seat to judicial discretion, and that review and appeal were being collapsed into one.

MODERN SUBSTANTIVE REVIEW

After *Metropolitan Life*, the Supreme Court adopted a deliberately deferential approach to review.[8] It narrowed the scope of review for jurisdictional error, and later preferred to call it "correctness" review instead. It reduced the previous emphasis on jurisdictional defects. Where there were privative clauses or other reasons for restraint, the Court replaced the old ground of error of law on the face of the record and qualified the old jurisdictional defects with a more restrictive standard of review known as patent unreasonableness. Eventually the Court added a third standard, review for unreasonableness.

Modern substantive review[9] is based on these changes. The Supreme Court says that there is a general presumption of deference, especially in areas such as labour relations.[10] The Court has arranged the modern standards of substantive review along a spectrum of levels of intensity.[11] There are three main standards — an intensive review for incorrectness,[12] a restrained review for patent unreasonableness,[13] and a middle standard of review for unreasonableness.[14] Incorrectness review applies where the relevant question is "jurisdictional" in the sense that the statute requires a correct answer as a basis for jurisdiction or power to proceed.[15] Under correctness review, reviewing courts ask if the administrator was wrong. Under patent unreasonableness, they ask if the interpretation or decision is one that no reasonable administrator could have made. Reasonableness, which catches unreasonable decisions, requires something less than patent unreasonableness but something more than correctness.

The move to three-standard review has been accompanied by a shift in emphasis from statutory wording to the contextual factors that surround the wording. Specific enabling provisions and privative clauses are still relevant, but they have lost their preeminent position, and can be outweighed by other factors the court considers relevant. To determine the standard of review the legislator intended in a given situation, courts tend to focus on three main factors:[16]

(i) the purpose and wording of the relevant statute;[17]

(ii) the expertise of the administrator;[18] and

(iii) the nature of the administrator's decision.[19]

Finally, although there was still a distinction between simple review and judicial appeal,[20] the spectrum above includes both review and appeal.[21] Here the presence of a judicial appeal provision is just one possible indicator that a higher, rather than a lower, standard should be used.[22]

The modern approach had several positive features. It looks nuanced, open, and streamlined. It gave privative clauses some weight without capitulating to them. On the other hand, the new approach was highly discretionary. The review standard depended on the relative weight the court assigns to the contextual factors and their constituent elements. Expertise — a complex and often subjective concept — plays a prominent role.[23] The lines between correctness, reasonableness, and patent unreasonableness tend to run into each other. Moreover, the Court has yet to clarify just how the three-standard approach relates to the older grounds.[24]

Note that the modern approach seemed to put relatively less emphasis on specific statutory signals such as privative clauses, wording restricting power, and language conferring administrative discretion. It seems to put relatively more emphasis on broad context-related factors.

As we will see later in this chapter, the Supreme Court of Canada recently revised the modern approach — set out above and in *Baker*, which was partially described in Chapter 4 — in an effort to address some of the concerns it posed. For now, it is important to note that the postmodern approach employed by the courts today attempts to significantly clarify substantive judicial review and represents a continuing evolution in the judiciary's approach to review.

SUBSTANTIVE REVIEW AND CONSTITUTIONAL CONTROL

In judicial review and common law actions for damages, as long as there are no relevant constitutional restrictions, the legislature still has the last word. If it wishes, it can often intervene — as it did in the *Metropolitan Life* case — to reverse the effects of judicial review.

Where there are constitutional constraints, however, the court has the last word. Constitutional control enables a court to examine an administrator's decision and the enabling statute to see if they were both authorized by the Constitution of Canada. Thus, this kind of control can prevail over the enabling legislation as well as the administrative decision itself. Although privative clauses may be able to limit sub-constitutional control,[25] they cannot block constitutional control. For these reasons, constitutional control is generally more powerful than ordinary judicial review, actions for damages, or judicial appeal. In the last few decades, though, the courts have narrowed this distinction a little. They have held that provinces, and perhaps even Parliament, are constitutionally barred from excluding judicial review of administrative action on jurisdictional grounds.[26]

One of the main foundations of direct constitutional control of administrative decisions is section 7 of the *Canadian Charter of Rights and Freedoms*.[27] Section 7 protects against a deprivation of the right to life, liberty, or security of the person, where this deprivation is not in accordance with fundamental justice. The deprivation and denial of fundamental justice must be carried out by the government or pursuant to government legislation, and the relevant legislature must not have acted to override this guarantee. If these requirements are met, section 7 is available regardless of privative clauses or any other restrictive provisions in the statute. This can be seen clearly in the s. 7 *Singh* decision in Chapter 4.[28] Other *Constitution Act,*

1982 provisions of special importance to administrative law include sections 1 (the justification section), 2, 8–15, 32 (scope of the *Charter*), and 35 (for Aboriginal and treaty rights administration).

Notes

1. See generally David J. Mullan, *Administrative Law* (Toronto: Irwin Law, 2001) Part Two.
2. Procedural judicial review and constitutional procedural control are discussed in Chapter 4, above.
3. In practice, judicial review is often limited to specific issues, such as questions of law. A statutory appeal without these specific statutory limits permits reconsideration of merits. To complicate things further, even where there was a statutory appeal unencumbered by specific statutory limits, courts might still limit their appellate control to something short of merits in the presence of a factor such as administrative discretion.
4. This is a simplified description, based on the later description of "jurisdictional provision" in *Re Syndicat des Employés de Production du Quebec et de l'Acadie and Canada Labour Relations Board* (1985), 14 D.L.R. (4th) 457 (S.C.C.), describing a "jurisdictional provision." *Syndicat* contrasted errors on jurisdictional provisions with "mere errors of law." (Now that courts have adopted the three-part incorrectness/reasonableness/patent unreasonableness approach, errors of law may be treated as jurisdictional).
5. See D.J. Mullan, "The Supreme Court of Canada and Tribunals — Deference to the Administrative Process: A Recent Phenomenon or a Return to Basics?" (2000) 80 Can. Bar. Rev. 399 (a preliminary survey of Supreme Court administrative law cases from 1867 to 1949) and P.W. Hogg, "The Supreme Court of Canada and Administrative Law, 1949–71" (1973) 11 Osgoode Hall L.J. 187 at 221 (a survey of over 100 Supreme Court administrative law cases from 1949 to 1971). In the latter study, in an otherwise critical assessment, Hogg noted that "[b]y and large, it seems to me that the Supreme Court of Canada has been restrained in the exercise of its review function. The overall figures show that the agency wins more than half the time."
6. *Jarvis v. Associated Medical Service Inc.*, [1964] S.C.R. 497; *Metropolitan Life Insurance Co. v. International Union of Operating Engineers, Local 796*, [1970] S.C.R. 425; *Bell v. Ontario (Human Rights Commission)*, [1971] S.C.R. 756. Note, though, that the *overall* record from 1949 to 1971 was not highly interventionist: *ibid.*
7. *Metropolitan Life Insurance Co. v. International Union of Operating Engineers, Local 796*, [1970] S.C.R. 425.
8. One of the foundation decisions of the deferential approach was *Canadian Union of Public Employees, Local 963 v. New Brunswick Liquor Corporation*, [1979] 2 S.C.R. 227.
9. And judicial appeal, although appeal is potentially a more intensive form of control than review: see Chapter 4(a), above.
10. *Ivanhoe Inc. v. United Food and Commercial Workers, Local 500*, [2001] 2 S.C.R. 565 at para. 31.
11. See *Pezim v. British Columbia (Superintendent of Brokers)*, [1994] 2 S.C.R. 557, 589–90, articulating the "spectrum" approach.
12. Or "correctness." Cf. the broader correctness approaches in cases such as *Metropolitan Life Insurance Co. v. International Union of Operating Engineers, Local 796*, [1970] S.C.R. 425 and *Bell v. Ontario (Human Rights Commission)*, [1971] S.C.R. 756.
13. Pioneered especially in *Canadian Union of Public Employees, Local 963 v. New Brunswick Liquor Corp.*, [1979] 2 S.C.R. 227.

14. *Canada (Director of Investigation and Research, Competition Act) v. Southam Inc.*, [1997] 1 S.C.R. 748.
15. See *Southam, ibid. (statutory appeal); and Pushpanathan v. Canada (Minister of Citizenship and Immigration)*, [1998] 1 S.C.R. 982 (judicial review).
16. E.g., *Syndicat national des employés de la Commission scolaire régionale de l'Outaouis v. Bibeault*, [1988] 2 S.C.R. 1048, 1086; *Pushpanathan v. Canada (Minister of Citizenship and Immigration)*, [1998] 1 S.C.R. 982, paras. 29–38; and *Baker v. Canada (Minister of Citizenship and Immigration)*, [1999] 2 S.C.R. 817, paras. 57–62.
17. Under this factor, elements pointing to a lower standard include a statutory purpose that would be thwarted by judicial intervention; lack of a statutory appeal provision; the presence of a full privative clause; and specific statutory wording that commits the relevant matter to the discretion, expertise, or final decision of the administrator.
18. Under this factor, the greater the administrator's expertise, the likelier that a lower standard will be adopted. In this context, expertise is not just an area delineated by specific statutory wording. Rather, it is a relative quality — relative to the expertise of other administrative bodies, relative to that of the reviewing court, and relative to the kind of administrative decision in question.
19. Under this factor, the more the relevant decision relates to an issue of fact rather than law, or to an issue that is specific to the circumstances of the case at hand, the likelier it is that a lower standard will be adopted.
20. *Kourtessis v. M.N.R.*, [1993] 2 S.C.R. 53, 69–70; *R. v. Meltzer*, [1989] 1 S.C.R. 1764, 1773; *Regina v. Rhingo* (1997), 33 O.R. (3d) 202 (C.A.), apps. for leave to appeal to the Supreme Court of Canada dismissed 18 September 1997 (S.C.C. Bulletin, 1997, p. 1544). In *Saskatchewan Medical Assn. v. Saskatchewan (Medical Compensation Review Board)* (1988), 54 D.L.R. (4th) 752 (C.A.), the Court said: "The proceeding before the judge was not an appeal from the review board's decision. It was not the judge's function, nor is it this court's function, to adjudicate upon the merits of the review board's decision. Rather, the judge's function, and ultimately this court's function, was to adjudicate upon the legality of the review board's decision. Put another way, the question before the courts was not whether the review board was right or wrong to rule as it did but whether it had the legal power to rule as it did." See also *Leung v. Cheng*, [1996] B.C.J. No. 1447 (B.C.S.C.), para. 9.
21. See, for example, *Canada (Deputy Minister of National Revenue — M.N.R.) v. Mattel Canada Inc.*, [2001] 2 S.C.R. 100. Although *Mattel* involved a statutory appeal provision, the Supreme Court applied the three-part review standard analysis to it, referring to it (at para. 26) as "appellate review."
22. See *Mattel, ibid.* at 27.
23. The Supreme Court has called expertise the most important of the contextual factors relevant to determining the standard of review: *Canada (Deputy Minister of National Revenue — M.N.R.) v. Mattel Canada Inc.*, [2001] 2 S.C.R. 100 at para. 28.
24. In extreme cases of "obvious" jurisdictional issues, can the Court still approach correctness review through the old ground of jurisdictional error? David J. Mullan argues, persuasively, that it can: *Administrative Law* (Toronto: Irwin Law, 2001) Ch. 3. Mullan suggests that cases of obvious jurisdictional questions could include constitutional issues and competing claims between different administrative regimes. A court might also recognize a jurisdictional issue where its presence is agreed by all parties: See *Trinity Western University v. British Columbia College of Teachers*, [2001] 1 S.C.R. 772 at para. 14. On the other hand, there seems to be little place left in the modern approach for error of law on the face of the record, except where this form of review is expressly required by statute.

Another question related to the role of the old juris-dictional defects. Will they continue to be used, but as indicators of patent unreasonableness or unreasonable-ness? There is early precedent for this in *W.W. Lester (1978) Ltd. v. United Association of Journeymen and Apprentices of the Plumbing and Pipefitting Industry, Local 740*, [1990] 3 S.C.R. 644, where lack of evidence was taken as an indication of patent unreasonableness.

The Supreme Court's more recent decisions in *Toronto Board of Education v. Ontario Secondary School Teachers' Federation, District 15*, [1997] 1 S.C.R. 487 at paras. 44–46 and *Suresh v. Canada (Minister of Citizen-ship and Immigration)*, [2002] S.C.J. No. 3 at paras. 29 and 41 suggest that lack of evidence and the traditional defects relating to discretion (e.g., bad faith and failure to consider a relevant factor) will be treated as examples of patent unreasonableness or of unreasonableness, depending on the relevant standard.

25. Note, though, the constitutional restriction on privative clauses purporting to prevent judicial review on jurisdic-tion grounds: infra note 26.

26. This line of reasoning has been built on s. 96 and related sections of the *Constitution Act, 1867*. The Supreme Court interprets s. 96 to mean that provinces cannot confer on provincial tribunals judicial functions that were mainly or exclusively exercised by s. 96 common law supe-rior courts at the time of Confederation, unless these functions are an integral part of a provincial legislative scheme: see *Reference Nova Scotia Residential Tenancies Act*, [1996] 1 S.C.R. 186. However, in *Crevier v. Quebec (A.G.)*, [1981] 2 S.C.R. 220 the Court seemed to suggest not only that (i) provinces cannot create "s. 96" courts, but also that (ii) provinces cannot prevent common law superior courts from reviewing decisions of provincial tri-bunals on jurisdictional grounds. In *MacMillan Bloedel v. Simpson*, [1995] 4 S.C.R. 725, it was suggested, *obiter*, that this latter restriction also applies to federal legislation and tribunals.

27. Section 7 of *Constitution Act, 1982* being Appendix II to *Canada Act, 1982* U.K., 1982, c. 11, s. 7.

28. *Singh v. Canada (Minister of Employment and Immigra-tion)*, [1985] 1 S.C.R. 177.

(b)   Transition to Post-Modern Substantive Review†

David W. Elliott

Metropolitan Life was decided at a time of social upheaval in North America and other Western countries. During the 1960s and 70s, people were questioning orthodox values. Youth unrest, rights movements, Quebec separatism, and alienation in western Canada were all signs of growing distrust of authority.[1] In the legal field, commentators con-demned judges for excessive interventionism and for concealing their value judgments under tradi-tional formal doctrines.[2] The theory of jurisdiction, invoked in such a cursory way in *Metropolitan Life*, was seen as one of these suspect doctrines.[3]

In response to these pressures, the Supreme Court made some major changes to substantive review. Today, more than four decades after *Metro-politan Life*, the classical approach has been superseded by post-modern substantive review.

The evolution from classical to modern sub-stantive review took place in several stages. First, the *CUPE*[4] decision in 1979 introduced a stan-dard of review called patent unreasonableness and stated an explicit court policy of deference toward administrative bodies. Second, during an intermedi-ate phase in the 1980s, Supreme Court judges such as Beetz. J. articulated a factor-weighing approach for determining the new standard of review and tried to reconcile this approach with the jurisdiction concept of classical review.[5] Third, in the decisions such as *Southam*[6] in 1997 and *Pushpanathan*[7] in 1998, the Supreme Court refined the factor-weighing approach and applied it to judi-cial appeals as well as judicial review.

The 1999 *Baker*[8] decision and the decisions that followed it marked the fourth phase. *Baker* extended the new standard-oriented, factor-weighing approach to the field of discretionary power. Cases such as *Dr. Q*,[9] in 2003, continued the pattern of de-emphasizing the role of statutory wording and even of statutory intent. Meanwhile, there appeared to be less emphasis on a general policy of curial deference to administrative bodies.

However, throughout this period, courts said relatively little as to what remained of the theory and concepts of classical review. How, if at all, did ideas such as jurisdiction and the old grounds of review relate to the new criteria? As well, there were lingering questions about the nature and rela-tive importance of the factors for determining review standards, and about the nature of the stan-dards themselves. After four decades of major

† Revised and updated by Nick E. Milanovic.

change, there was still more work to be done, and that task was adopted in *Dunsmuir v. New Brunswick*.[10] The present period of review is referred to as post-modern substantive review here because the Supreme Court's approach to clarifying the former approach atttempts to provide an evolved, practical approach to judicial review. In this connection, the method of review employed in *Dunsmuir* relies on concrete experience with judicial review to reform itself and de-emphasizes universal legal principles as a means to rectifying the weaknesses found in the former modern approach. In this respect, there is a movement from a modern to a post-modern approach of substantive judicial review.

Notes

1. See, for example, Barbara L. Tischler, *Sights on the Sixties (Perspectives on the Sixties)* (New Brunswick, N.J.: Rutgers, 1992) (for the American situation); Michael Ignatieff, *The Rights Revolution* (Toronto: Anansi, 2000); J.L. Finlay and D.N. Sprague, *The Structure of Canadian History*, 5th ed. (Scarborough, Ont.: Prentice Hall Allyn and Bacon, 1997) Chs. 26–28.

2. See, for example, Alan Hutchinson and Patrick Monahan, "Law, Politics and the Critical Legal Scholars: The Unfolding Drama of American Legal Thought" (1984) 36 Stan. L. Rev. 199; H. Wade MacLauchlan, "Judicial Review of Administrative Interpretations of Law: How Much Formalism Can We Reasonably Bear?" (1986), 36 *U.T.L.J.* 343; and Jamie Cassels and Maureen Maloney, "Critical Legal Education: Paralysis With a Purpose" (1989) 4 C.J.L.S. 99. On the critical legal studies movement generally, see J.D. Leonard, *Legal Studies as Cultural Studies: A Reader in (Post)modern Critical Theory* (Albany, N.Y.: State University of New York, 1995).

3. See, for example, P.W. Hogg, "The Jurisdictional Fact Doctrine in the Supreme Court of Canada" (1971) 9 Osgoode Hall L. J. 203; P.C. Weiler, *In The Last Resort: A Critical Study of the Supreme Court of Canada* (Toronto: Carswell, 1974) Ch. 5; MacLauchlan, "How Much Formalism Can We Reasonably Bear?", *ibid*.

4. *Canadian Union of Public Employees, Local 963 v. New Brunswick Liquor Corp.*, [1979] 2 S.C.R. 227.

5. See, for example, *Re Syndicat des Employés de Production du Quebec et de l'Acadie and Canada Labour Relations Board*, [1984] 2 S.C.R. 41; *U.E.S., Local 298 v. Bibeault*, [1988] 2 S.C.R. 1048.

6. *Canada (Director of Investigation and Research) v. Southam Inc.*, [1997] 1 S.C.R. 748.

7. *Pushpanathan v. Canada (Minister of Citizenship and Immigration)*, [1998] 1 S.C.R. 982.

8. *Baker v. Canada (Minister of Citizenship and Immigration)*, [1999] 2 S.C.R. 817.

9. The factor-weighing approach put less weight on statutory wording, which became just one consideration among others for determining the appropriate level of review. *Dr. Q.* de-emphasized not only statutory wording, but statutory intent: see *Dr. Q. v. College of Physicians and Surgeons of British Columbia*, [2003] 1 S.C.R. 226 at para. 21.

10. [2008] 1 S.C.R. 190.

(c)   *Dunsmuir v. New Brunswick*†

NOTE

David Dunsmuir was appointed by cabinet to the offices of the Clerk of the Court of Queen's Bench, and Clerk of the Probate Court of New Brunswick, for the Judicial District of Fredericton. He had some difficulty in these roles and was reprimanded on three different occasions, including a warning that his employment was in jeopardy if his performance did not improve. In the midst of a performance review, he was informed that he did not meet the needs of his employer and was eventually discharged from his employment, and his cabinet appointments were revoked: paras. 2–8. Mr. Dunsmuir launched a grievance under the *Public Service Labour Relations Act* arguing, among other things, that his employer had not given him an opportunity to respond to its concerns and violated his procedural fairness guarantees. The Province responded that its only obligation was to provide him with reasonable notice. The adjudicator found, in part, that Dunsmuir was denied procedural fairness when his employment was terminated, and he was therefore reinstated: paras. 9–16.

The Supreme Court of Canada reviewed the decision and indicated a significant reform of the law was underway when it noted it would "address first and foremost the structure and characteristics of the system of judicial review as a whole": para. 33. Among other things, the Supreme Court redefined the standards courts must apply in deciding whether to judicially review a decision of an arbitrator or administrative tribunal. Courts are now to choose between two standards for reviewing such

---

† 2008 SCC 9, [2008] 1 S.C.R. 190. [In-text references omitted.]

decisions — correctness or unreasonableness — and that the third standard of patent unreasonableness found in modern substantive review has been abolished: para. 34. As well, the ruling truncated the "due process" rights of public office holders, ruling that those who occupy their positions on a contractual basis (and not just "at pleasure") have no greater entitlement to procedural fairness in matters of dismissal than the typical employee: paras. 102–103.

As you read the excerpt below, ask yourself: does the new unified standard of reasonable simplify the approach of the courts taken in these matters? Is the focus on context similar to, or uniquely different from, the "pragmatic and functional approach" used during the modern era of substantive review? Will judges now easily be able to inquire into the qualities that make a decision reasonable when they scrutinize the basis of justification, transparency, and intelligibility found in the decision making process? Is this approach less discretionary than the former approach found in the classical or modern approaches to substantive judicial review?

EXTRACT

[McLACHLIN C.J. and BASTARACHE, LEBEL, FISH and ABELLA JJ:]

[32] Despite the clear, stable constitutional foundations of the system of judicial review, the operation of judicial review in Canada has been in a constant state of evolution over the years, as courts have attempted to devise approaches to judicial review that are both theoretically sound and effective in practice. Despite efforts to refine and clarify it, the present system has proven to be difficult to implement. The time has arrived to re-examine the Canadian approach to judicial review of administrative decisions and develop a principled framework that is more coherent and workable.

. . . .

[34] The current approach to judicial review involves three standards of review, which range from correctness, where no deference is shown, to patent unreasonableness, which is most deferential to the decision maker, the standard of reasonableness *simpliciter* lying, theoretically, in the middle. In our view, it is necessary to reconsider both the number and definitions of the various standards of review, and the

analytical process employed to determine which standard applies in a given situation. We conclude that there ought to be two standards of review — correctness and reasonableness.

. . . .

[41] As discussed by LeBel J. at length in *Toronto (City) v. C.U.P.E.*, notwithstanding the increased clarity that *Ryan* brought to the issue and the theoretical differences between the standards of patent unreasonableness and reasonableness *simpliciter*, a review of the cases reveals that any actual difference between them in terms of their operation appears to be illusory.... Indeed, even this Court divided when attempting to determine whether a particular decision was "patently unreasonable", although this should have been self-evident under the existing test.... This result is explained by the fact that both standards are based on the idea that there might be multiple valid interpretations of a statutory provision or answers to a legal dispute and that courts ought not to interfere where the tribunal's decision is rationally supported. Looking to either the magnitude or the immediacy of the defect in the tribunal's decision provides no meaningful way in practice of distinguishing between a patently unreasonable and an unreasonable decision. As [Professor] Mullan has explained:

> [T]o maintain a position that it is only the "clearly irrational" that will cross the threshold of patent unreasonableness while irrationality simpliciter will not is to make a nonsense of the law. Attaching the adjective "clearly" to irrational is surely a tautology. Like "uniqueness", irrationality either exists or it does not. There cannot be shades of irrationality. ...

. . . .

[47] Reasonableness is a deferential standard animated by the principle that underlies the development of the two previous standards of reasonableness: certain questions that come before administrative tribunals do not lend themselves to one specific, particular result. Instead, they may give rise to a number of possible, reasonable conclusions. Tribunals have a margin of appreciation within the range of acceptable and rational solutions. A court conducting a review for reasonableness inquires into the qualities that make a decision reasonable, referring both to the process of articulating the reasons and to outcomes. In judicial review, reasonableness is concerned mostly with the existence of justification, transparency and intelligibility within the decision-

making process. But it is also concerned with whether the decision falls within a range of possible, acceptable outcomes which are defensible in respect of the facts and law.

[48] The move towards a single reasonableness standard does not pave the way for a more intrusive review by courts and does not represent a return to pre-*Southam* formalism. In this respect, the concept of deference, so central to judicial review in administrative law, has perhaps been insufficiently explored in the case law. What does deference mean in this context? Deference is both an attitude of the court and a requirement of the law of judicial review. It does not mean that courts are subservient to the determinations of decision makers, or that courts must show blind reverence to their interpretations, or that they may be content to pay lip service to the concept of reasonableness review while in fact imposing their own view. Rather, deference imports respect for the decision-making process of adjudicative bodies with regard to both the facts and the law. The notion of deference "is rooted in part in a respect for governmental decisions to create administrative bodies with delegated powers".... We agree with David Dyzenhaus where he states that the concept of "deference as respect" requires of the courts "not submission but a respectful attention to the reasons offered or which could be offered in support of a decision"....

[49] Deference in the context of the reasonableness standard therefore implies that courts will give due consideration to the determinations of decision makers. As Mullan explains, a policy of deference "recognizes the reality that, in many instances, those working day to day in the implementation of frequently complex administrative schemes have or will develop a considerable degree of expertise or field sensitivity to the imperatives and nuances of the legislative regime".... In short, deference requires respect for the legislative choices to leave some matters in the hands of administrative decision makers, for the processes and determinations that draw on particular expertise and experiences, and for the different roles of the courts and administrative bodies within the Canadian constitutional system.

[50] As important as it is that courts have a proper understanding of reasonableness review as a deferential standard, it is also without question that the standard of correctness must be maintained in respect of jurisdictional and some other questions of law. This promotes just decisions and avoids inconsistent and unauthorized application of law. When applying the correctness standard, a reviewing court will not show deference to the decision maker's reasoning process; it will rather undertake its own analysis of the question. The analysis will bring the court to decide whether it agrees with the determination of the decision maker; if not, the court will substitute its own view and provide the correct answer. From the outset, the court must ask whether the tribunal's decision was correct.

.   .   .   .

[52] The existence of a privative or preclusive clause gives rise to a strong indication of review pursuant to the reasonableness standard. This conclusion is appropriate because a privative clause is evidence of Parliament or a legislature's intent that an administrative decision maker be given greater deference and that interference by reviewing courts be minimized. This does not mean, however, that the presence of a privative clause is determinative. The rule of law requires that the constitutional role of superior courts be preserved and, as indicated above, neither Parliament nor any legislature can completely remove the courts' power to review the actions and decisions of administrative bodies. This power is constitutionally protected. Judicial review is necessary to ensure that the privative clause is read in its appropriate statutory context and that administrative bodies do not exceed their jurisdiction.

[53] Where the question is one of fact, discretion or policy, deference will usually apply automatically.... We believe that the same standard must apply to the review of questions where the legal and factual issues are intertwined ... and cannot be readily separated.

[54] Guidance with regard to the questions that will be reviewed on a reasonableness standard can be found in the existing case law. Deference will usually result where a tribunal is interpreting its own statute or statutes closely connected to its function, with which it will have particular familiarity.... Deference may also be warranted where an administrative tribunal has developed particular expertise in the application of a general common law or civil law rule in relation to a specific statutory context.... Adjudication in labour law remains a good example of the relevance of this approach. The case law has moved away considerably from the strict position evidenced in *McLeod v. Egan*, [1975] 1 S.C.R. 517, where it was held that an administrative decision maker will always risk having its interpretation of an external statute set aside upon judicial review.

[55] A consideration of the following factors will lead to the conclusion that the decision maker should be given deference and a reasonableness test applied:

- A privative clause: this is a statutory direction from Parliament or a legislature indicating the need for deference.

  A discrete and special administrative regime in which the decision maker has special expertise (labour relations for instance).
- The nature of the question of law. A question of law that is of "central importance to the legal system ... and outside the ... specialized area of expertise" of the administrative decision maker will always attract a correctness standard (*Toronto (City) v. C.U.P.E.*, at para. 62). On the other hand, a question of law that does not rise to this level may be compatible with a reasonableness standard where the two above factors so indicate.

[56] If these factors, considered together, point to a standard of reasonableness, the decision maker's decision must be approached with deference in the sense of respect discussed earlier in these reasons. There is nothing unprincipled in the fact that some questions of law will be decided on the basis of reasonableness. It simply means giving the adjudicator's decision appropriate deference in deciding whether a decision should be upheld, bearing in mind the factors indicated.

[57] An exhaustive review is not required in every case to determine the proper standard of review. Here again, existing jurisprudence may be helpful in identifying some of the questions that generally fall to be determined according to the correctness standard.... This simply means that the analysis required is already deemed to have been performed and need not be repeated.

[58] For example, correctness review has been found to apply to constitutional questions regarding the division of powers between Parliament and the provinces in the *Constitution Act, 1867*: *Westcoast Energy Inc. v. Canada (National Energy Board)*, [1998] 1 S.C.R. 322. Such questions, as well as other constitutional issues, are necessarily subject to correctness review because of the unique role of s. 96 courts as interpreters of the Constitution....

[59] Administrative bodies must also be correct in their determinations of true questions of jurisdiction or *vires*. We mention true questions of vires to distance ourselves from the extended definitions adopted before *CUPE*. It is important here to take a robust view of jurisdiction. We neither wish nor intend to return to the jurisdiction/preliminary question doctrine that plagued the jurisprudence in this area for many years. "Jurisdiction" is intended in the narrow sense of whether or not the tribunal had the authority to make the inquiry. In other words, true jurisdiction questions arise where the tribunal must explicitly determine whether its statutory grant of power gives it the authority to decide a particular matter. The tribunal must interpret the grant of authority correctly or its action will be found to be *ultra vires* or to constitute a wrongful decline of jurisdiction ... We reiterate the caution of Dickson J. in *CUPE* that reviewing judges must not brand as jurisdictional issues that are doubtfully so.

[60] As mentioned earlier, courts must also continue to substitute their own view of the correct answer where the question at issue is one of general law "that is both of central importance to the legal system as a whole and outside the adjudicator's specialized area of expertise" (*Toronto (City) v. C.U.P.E.*, at para. 62, *per* LeBel J.). Because of their impact on the administration of justice as a whole, such questions require uniform and consistent answers. Such was the case in *Toronto (City) v. C.U.P.E.*, which dealt with complex common law rules and conflicting jurisprudence on the doctrines of *res judicata* and abuse of process — issues that are at the heart of the administration of justice (see para. 15, *per* Arbour J.).

[61] Questions regarding the jurisdictional lines between two or more competing specialized tribunals have also been subject to review on a correctness basis....

[62] In summary, the process of judicial review involves two steps. First, courts ascertain whether the jurisprudence has already determined in a satisfactory manner the degree of deference to be accorded with regard to a particular category of question. Second, where the first inquiry proves unfruitful, courts must proceed to an analysis of the factors making it possible to identify the proper standard of review.

6 — Theory, Problems, and Reform

(a) Reform Challenges

David W. Elliott

STATE GOALS AND REFORM PRIORITIES

Effective law reform requires agreement as to existing problems and social and financial support for proposed solutions. For administrative law, it also requires some consensus on the proper role of the state and law, and on the allocation of power between the institutions of government. As suggested in Chapter 2, though, these are partly questions of personal judgment and value.[1] Different views of state goals may have a big influence on administrative law policy-makers and commentators.

For example, those who see collective action as a paramount state goal will support measures to enhance administrative law efficiency. Those whose priorities are control and accountability will seek restraints. So will those who are concerned to protect private interests, although their preferred restraints may be different. Citizen participation and accountability may be sought through direct participation and the electoral process, while private interests are typically enforced though the courts. The goal of equality is best furthered by either efficiency or control mechanisms, depending on whether the administrative process is viewed as an instrument for achieving equality or a threat to it. Other social goals, such as demands for Aboriginal self-government, favour greater pluralism in administrative structures.

As suggested in Chapter 2,[2] similar value-based differences are likely between those who take positivist, realist, or functionalist approaches to the role of law, and between those who take more traditional or less traditional approaches to the question of the proper allocation of governmental authority. At a particular time, one or more of these views may predominate, depending on their perceived appropriateness to prevailing social conditions, and — often a challenge in administrative law! — on their ability to engage broad public support.

JUDICIAL FEATURES AND REFORM

Another important requirement of administrative law reform is some consensus on the role courts should play in it. This is a controversial question for a number of reasons. First, the courts have been important historically as vehicles for controlling the administrative process, and they have been traditionally associated with private interests that conflict with it. Moreover, these have often been the property and commercial interests of those with large stakes in the *status quo*. It would be reasonable to expect greater support for an expanded judicial role from these groups than others, and *vice versa*.

Second, the courts have a number of distinctive institutional strengths and weaknesses to attract both supporters and opponents. On the positive side, courts have a reputation for procedural fairness and impartiality. They can provide an authoritative resolution of disputes. They are required to decide cases with reference to rules, and to aim for consistency in similar situations. On the negative side, they are usually slow, expensive, and not very accessible to the public at large. Their procedure is rigid, and their investigative and information resources are limited. They tend to be backward-looking, remedying past problems and tied to precedents. They produce winner-loser results, with limited opportunity for negotiation and compromise, especially between large social groups. Finally, judges are appointed, not elected, and operate beyond the normal reach of electoral controls. In any proposed reform, the courts' role may hinge heavily on the reformers' assessment of these strengths and weaknesses, and on the prospects for maximizing the former.

Third, the courts' impact has been greatly expanded by the advent of the *Charter*, providing extra ground for supporters' hopes and opponents' fears. When *Charter* control imposes procedural constraints, these constraints can affect statutes as well as administrative decisions pursuant to statutes, and they cannot be avoided by ordinary statutory amendments. Thus *Charter* control is both more powerful and more removed from traditional democratic checks than is subconstitutional judicial control.

TRADITIONAL APPROACH TO CONTROL AND CRITICISMS

Complicating the lack of consensus on the role of state and courts is a continuing controversy as to whether it is better to repair weaknesses in our traditional control system or to jettison it in favour of largely or entirely new approaches.

Traditional Approach

The traditional approach to control of the administrative process is based on the interlocking principles of parliamentary power, parliamentary accountability, and judicial interpretation. After the 17th century, it was established that normally all administrators must act pursuant to statutory power. The only exception was for government action under the royal prerogative, and even the prerogative was subject to statutory restriction and could not permit government action that affected individuals adversely. This meant that administrative action was subject to public oversight, at first by a relatively small privileged electorate and then by larger and larger numbers as the franchise was slowly broadened. By the mid-20th century, it meant that administrative action, like all government action, is subject to the ultimate control of the general adult public.

A requirement of statutory authorization is only effective if there is a mechanism available to enforce it on individual occasions. The mechanism that has been used for this purpose is the judiciary, an institution that emerged from the 17th century with both prestige and relative independence. Courts enforce the requirement of statutory authorization and can provide relief to victims of unauthorized or illegal administrative action.

However, since the statutory authorization requirement applies to courts too, they have had to disclaim any independent power in carrying out this monitoring and relief role. They maintain that judicial review — a major means of control — is simply an aspect of the normal judicial function of interpreting statutes.

The traditional approach is grounded on the assumption that the government is essentially a chain of mandates.[3] The theory is that the electorate start the process by giving a mandate to the government of the day. The government then acts through Parliament to give more precise mandates, in the form of statutes, to administrators. The administrators then carry out these mandates, through action that affects the general public. Ultimately, and ideally, then, the public is in control of the government and the administrative process that affects it. The courts' role is essentially to ensure that the administrators keep within the terms of their statutory mandates, and to provide relief where unauthorized or illegal action causes harm.

Within this conceptual framework, the courts have enhanced their subservient role by intervening on the basis of implicit as well as explicit statutory conditions. Where legislators fail to make their intention clear, courts often *infer* a legislative intent to attach implied restrictions to mandates. All the while, courts insist that their own review goes no further than interpretation. In procedural matters, implied restrictions tend to be limited to statutes involving functions that are, in a loose sense,[4] "court-like" in nature.

Judicial review may be supplemented by actions for damages, where administrative action without statutory authorization amounts to a common law or civil law tort. Another possibility is judicial appeal, which can extend to reconsideration of the merits of a decision but is only available where a statute expressly provides for it. Since 1982, these traditional controls have been supplemented by constitutional control under the *Charter*. In effect, a new set of "negative" mandates based on *Charter* requirements has been added to the chain. Courts must also determine if statutes and administrative action are consistent with them.

Some Criticisms of
the Traditional Approach

Decline of Traditional Accountability

Some critics feel that judicial review needs re-thinking because the traditional approach to the role of government, Parliament, and control is obsolete and inaccurate. For example, it is argued that ministerial responsibility, the power of opposition parties, the influence of backbench legislators, and the collective law-making and monitoring capacity of Parliament as a whole are too weak to ensure that elected legislators and those whom they represent can have any significant control over the administrative process. Thus, even if judicial review succeeds in enforcing statutory limits, statutory limits themselves provide no guarantee of accountability.[5]

Formalism

A related criticism is that review based on the notion of limits to statutory power is excessively "formalistic". This criticism has been levied against the notion of jurisdiction, and against the judicial practice of applying a catalogue of forms of defect capable of removing jurisdiction and permitting judicial review. Anti-formalists have urged more judicial consideration of the social context of the administrative decision, its potential impact, and the relative expertise of the administrator and the reviewing court.[6] The force of this kind of "functional" criticism has diminished somewhat as courts have moved away from strict categories and have done more to identify specific factors influencing their standards of review.

A more radical strand of anti-formalist criticism sees the rules applied by courts as masks to disguise the fact that they are protecting vested interests and power imbalances. This approach, typified by Critical Legal Studies supporters, urges that the mask of rules and conceptual categories be removed to reveal the subjective value preferences beneath them.[7] Presumably, in this stark new light, decision makers would be shamed into providing more help for the disadvantaged.

Intrusiveness

Until recently, a key criticism of the traditional approach has been that it permits excessive judicial intervention. Statutory intention is difficult to ascertain at the best of times, and the judicial practice of finding implied restrictions in mute or ambiguous statutes was felt by many critics to have gone too far.

The criticism was strongest in the area of labour relations, where courts tended to impose judicial review even where legislative privative clauses seemed to require exactly the reverse. The controversy reached a peak after a dramatic interventionist decision in 1970.[8] Since that time, Canadian courts have adopted a general policy of judicial restraint,[9] especially with regard to privative clauses, labour relations issues, and non-procedural defects.

Narrow Scope

Another set of criticisms has been directed specifically at judicial review. It has been argued that judicial review and other traditional forms of control have protected too narrow a range of interests — mainly property and commercial interests — to the detriment of less privileged groups, such as welfare recipients and immigrants.[10] Another argument is that because its scope is limited mainly to government, judicial review also fails to take into account the presence of power — and the abuse of power — *outside* government, and can disable government from effectively controlling abuse of power by private entities.[11]

Functional Limits of Courts and Judges

Many criticisms of traditional judicial review are based on the functional limits of courts. Critics tend to emphasize the courts' negative institutional features,[12] just as supporters accent the positive. Some critics suggest other forms of control, ranging from administrative law appeal tribunals to specialist monitoring bodies, to statutory constraints, to controls within the legislative process itself.[13] Another approach would be to consider which *forms* of judicial control attract the more negative attributes of courts, and to concentrate on reforming them. For example, what is the advantage of subjecting a decision by a (presumably) expert administrator to an almost complete re-decision by an inexpert judge? That can happen under some forms of appeal. Should it?

Cost

The high cost of judicial control, like that of virtually all judicial proceedings, is a special concern because it limits the protections of judicial control to the wealthy or those with outside financial assistance. The cost of an average case exceeds $600,[14] while a lengthy *Charter* case in the Supreme Court of Canada may cost over a million dollars.[15] Legal aid is limited and selective, and varies greatly in scope from province to province.[16]

This leaves a large segment of the population for whom judicial control is a practical impossibility. Should legal aid be expanded further, at greater public expense? If so, should standing be restricted, to offset costs and eliminate all but very serious cases? How can "seriousness" be measured?

NON-JUDICIAL CHALLENGES

Although we have focused mainly on administrative law issues involving the judiciary, there are many *non*-judicial fields that have attracted criticisms as well.

Appointments

In most traditional public service departments, appointments below the political executive and deputy minister level follow advertised competitive examinations or similar requirements based on merit, supervised by an independent commission.[17] In contrast, most appointments of members of the independent regulatory agencies and Crown corporations are by orders in council, without competitive examinations based on merit. Appointments to these positions are open to charges of patronage and favouritism.[18] This seems a paradoxical, even astounding, situation when it is recalled that a major motive for creating structures independent from the central executive was to remove them from undue political control.

Public Spending

The federal government sponsorship scandal and the Gomery Commission reports of 2005 and 2006[19] highlighted serious defects in government mechanisms for controlling public spending by the administrative process. Public spending is normally regulated on an ongoing basis by controls such as the annual parliamentary supply process, the requirements of the *Financial Administration Act*,[20] the policies and oversight of central coordinating bodies such as the Treasury Board, hierarchical bureaucratic supervision, and — at the highest levels — the doctrine of ministerial responsibility. But in the sponsorship program, large sums of public money eluded these and other controls, and were either wasted or directed to questionable purposes. It wasn't until the media and the Auditor General alerted the public that a full investigation was made. The Gomery Commission focused on recommendations to strengthen oversight of spend-

ing by parliamentary committees; the federal government's statutory reforms focused on the creation of new supervisory officers of Parliament.[21] It remains to be seen if the statutory reforms succeed.

Independent Bodies and Political Controls

Should a decision be considered at great length by an independent regulatory agency, with extensive hearings and procedural safeguards, only to have it overturned by a Cabinet decision? Conversely, in important policy areas such as energy, should regulatory decisions be in the hands of an "independent" agency in the first place, or should they be made by people directly subject to ministerial responsibility?

Clearly, the answers to these questions may vary with the importance the observer attaches to the principles of responsible government.[22] On the other hand, what of the indirect political influence that may result where (as is typically the case) an agency member is appointed for a three-year term, of which renewal depends solely on the political discretion? Is *this* kind of political control desirable?

Independence and Regulatees

To what extent do regulatory agencies become "captive" to those they are supposed to regulate? Are there some situations, such as the granting of short terms of administrative tenure, the technical nature of the subject matter, and the prevalence of informal regulatory contacts, that may be particularly receptive to capture?[23]

Making of Rules and Other Subordinate Legislation

Should agencies spend vast amounts of time "re-inventing the wheel" with elaborate adjudicatory hearings (perhaps only to attract judicial review at the end of the day), when rule-making may often be a more efficient, economical, and predicable way of communicating decisions?[24] If so, though, what constraints are appropriate to rule-making?[25] Should subordinate rules and other legislation be subject to advance notice procedures similar to those required for ordinary administrative decisions by the rules of natural justice? To what extent should the nature of the control vary with the nature of the subordinate legislation?

Administrative Implementation Mechanisms

Can administrators be given a greater range of mechanisms to ensure that their decisions are properly enforced? Many regulatory statutes, for example, are enforceable by fines. In some areas, would it be preferable to permit administrators to impose other measures, such as performance bonds or adverse publicity? Should administrators be free to negotiate compromise arrangements with those subject to their regulation, or would this approach be open to allegations of abuse, third-party prejudice, and inconsistency?[26]

Simplification

In most Canadian jurisdictions, each administrative body operates in a statutory world that is distinct, unique, and often very complex. This proliferation of different administrative jurisdictions generates extraordinary complexity. Would greater standardization and simplification be possible without sacrificing desirable pluralism? For example, should there be greater use of minimum codes of fair procedure?

Access to Information

The federal government and most provinces have enacted access to information legislation, with complementary measures to protect individual privacy.[27] Could existing statutes be streamlined to remove some of the many current exceptions and make government information sources better known? Should there be a general right to independent appeal tribunals?

Access legislation is part of a larger issue about a citizen's right to know about government.[28] Why is there so little consistency about the publication of reasons for decisions by members of the administrative process? Should government be required to provide advance notice of proposed subordinate legislation? What are the possibilities and constraints of special information-gathering agencies, such as ombudsmen, auditors general, human rights commissions, special inquiries, and elected legislators? What are the possible negative side-effects of information-gathering? Finally, in light of the vital importance to democracy of access to information, should courts recognize a general implied constitutional right of access to information as an aspect of the principle of democracy?[29]

Ombudsmen

There are ombudsmen in all provinces. Why is there still no federal ombudsman? Should the offices of existing provincial ombudsmen be consolidated with those of other complaint-oriented bodies, such as human rights commissions?

Parliamentary Process

Could technology be used to enhance the relevance of the parliamentary process? What are the possibilities of "open-line" question periods, where voters could telephone questions to members of Parliament sitting in televised sessions? Of telephones replacing ballot boxes for elections? Of citizen "telephone votes" (or "Internet votes"?) on matters of general and non-partisan importance? Could statutory preambles be used more regularly to help clarify legislative intent? Can't statutes be more simply worded? Shouldn't subordinate legislation be more accessible and more clearly indexed?

Empirical Research

There will be no attempt here to resolve the challenges and questions above; some may never be resolved. On the other hand, in many cases reformers can raise the level of debate by greater use of empirical research. What, for example, *is* the average cost of proceedings before an administrative authority in a given area? What is the average cost of judicial proceedings in a comparable area? Just how effective are existing enforcement mechanisms, and when are they used? What proportion of order-in-council agency or Crown corporation appointees are former fundraisers or candidates for the political party in power? As long as we bear in mind that even empirical research has its drawbacks — the framing of a question will help shape the answer, for example[30] — it is an essential supplement to discussions of social values and goals.[31]

Notes

1. See, for example, "Social Goals" in Chapter 1, above, and "Theory", in Chapter 2, above.
2. See "Theory" in Chapter 2, above.
3. See "Government and Administration as a Process," Chapter 2, above.
4. However, the rigid administrative/judicial dichotomy of the early 20th century has been firmly rejected.
5. This argument is summarized in P.P. Craig, *Administrative Law*, 5th ed. (London: Sweet & Maxwell, 2003) Ch. 1. The traditional system has also been altered by the *Charter* and intergovernmental conferences and consultations: M.D. Priest, "Structure and Accountability of Administrative

112

Agencies," in Spec. Lect. L.S.U.C., *Administrative Law* (Toronto: Carswell, 1992) at 11, 49–50.

6. H.W. MacLauchlan, "Judicial Review of Administrative Interpretations of Law: How Much Formalism Can We Reasonably Bear?" (1986) 36 U.T.L.J. 343; H.W. MacLauchlan, "Reconciling Curial Deference with a Functional Approach in Substantive and Procedural Judicial Review" (1994) 7 C.J.A.L.P. 1; H.W. MacLauchlan, "Transforming Administrative Law: The Didactic Role of the Supreme Court of Canada" (2001) 80 Can. Bar Rev. (vol. 2) 281. (MacLauchlan is more satisfied with the general direction of the Court in the 2001 article.) A leading administrative law sourcebook also tends to take an anti-formalist approach: David J. Mullan, ed., *Administrative Law: Cases, Texts, and Materials*, 5th ed. (Toronto: Emond Montgomery, 2003).

7. For example, A.C. Hutchinson, "The Rise and the Ruse of Administrative Law and Scholarship" (1985), 48 Modern L. Rev. 293 at 299, note 22.

8. The *Metropolitan Life* decision, Chapter 5, above. For one of the most trenchant criticisms of *Metropolitan Life*, see P. Weiler, *In the Last Resort: A Critical Study of the Supreme Court of Canada* (Toronto: Carswell, 1974) Ch. 5.

9. At least in regard to non-constitutional control.

10. See M. Jackman, "The Protection of Welfare Rights Under the Charter" (1988) Ottawa L. Rev. 257; P.P. Craig, *Administrative Law*, 5th ed. (London: Sweet & Maxwell, 2003) Ch. 1.

11. A.A. Hutchinson, "Of Kings and Dirty Rascals: The Struggle for Democracy" (1984), 9 Queen's L.J. 273; W.W. Pue, "The Law Reform Commission of Canada and Lawyers' Approaches to Public Administration" (1987) 2 Can. J.L. & Society 165.

12. Some of these features are described in "Judicial Features and Reform," paragraphs 2–4, above. See the criticisms in H. Arthurs, "Rethinking Administrative Law: A Slightly Dicey Business" (1979) 17 Osgoode Hall L.J. 1; *'Without the Law': Administrative Justice and Legal Pluralism in Nineteenth-Century England* (Toronto: University of Toronto Press, 1985) at 1–7.

13. *Ibid.* at 210–11 (administrative law appeal tribunal); R. Macaulay, *Directions: Review of Ontario's Regulatory Agencies* (Toronto: Ontario Queen's Printer, 1989) (a monitoring body to supervise tribunals); A. Abel, "The *Dramatis Personae* of Administrative Law" (1972) 10 Osgoode Hall L.J. 61.

14. See, for example, S.T. Easton et al., *Legal Aid: Efficiency, Cost and Competitiveness* (Kingston: Queen's University School of Policy Studies, 1994) at 65, Table 10, referring to staff/judicare costs per case in 11 provinces in 1990.

15. David M. Beatty, *Talking Heads and the Supremes: The Canadian Production Constitutional Review* (Toronto: Carswell, 1990) at 253–54.

16. *Ibid.* at Ch. 3.

17. See, for example, René Dussault and Louis Borgeat, *Administrative Law: A Treatise*, vol. 2, trans. by Murray Rankin (Toronto: Carswell, 1998) Ch. 1, s. 3.

18. See, for example, R. Dussault and R. Borgeat, *ibid.* at Ch. 2, s. 1; M.D. Priest, "Structure and Accountability of Administrative Agencies" in Spec. Lect. L.S.U.C., *Administrative Law* (Toronto: Carswell, 1992) at 11, 50–52.

19. See "Sponsorship and Aftermath: A Cautionary Tale of Control" in Chapter 3, above.

20. R.S.C. 1985, c. F-11.

21. *Ibid.*

22. See the thoughtful discussions in Canada, Law Reform Commission of Canada, *Report [26] on Independent Agencies: A Framework for Decision Making* (Ottawa: Law Reform Commission of Canada, 1985).

23. S. Scott, "The Continuing Debate over the Independence of Regulatory Tribunals" in Spec. Lect. L.S.U.C., *Administrative Law* (Toronto: Carswell, 1992) at 79, 86–88 (focusing on informal contacts).

24. H.N. Janisch, "The Choice of Decision-making Method: Adjudication, Policies and Rulemaking" in Spec. Lect. L.S.U.C., *Administrative Law* (Toronto: Carswell, 1992) at 259.

25. For the existing constraints, see D.C. Holland, J.P. McGowan, *Delegated Legislation in Canada* (Toronto: Carswell, 1989); J.M. Keyes, *Executive Legislation: Delegated Law Making by the Executive Branch* (Toronto: Butterworths, 1992). For a recent initiative designed to streamline the making and control of federal regulations, see Bill C–84, *Regulations Act*, 1st Sess., 35th Parl., 1994 (1st reading 26 April 1995).

26. See Canada, Law Reform Commission of Canada, *Policy Implementation, Compliance and Administrative Law, Working Paper 51* (Ottawa: Law Reform Commission of Canada, 1986).

27. See generally, C.H.H. McNairn and C.D. Woodbury, *Government Information: Access and Privacy* (Don Mills, Ont.: De Boo, 1989) [looseleaf].

28. The scope and content of the rules of natural justice and other court-enforced access measures are another aspect of this issue: see "Traditional Approach to Control and Criticisms," above.

29. My thanks to my colleague Professor Vincent Kasmierski for this thought. The principle of democracy was recognized as an unwritten legal constitutional principle in the *Reference Re Secession of Quebec*, [1998] 2 S.C.R. 217.

30. See Karl Popper's critique of the empirical inductive approach, in *Conjectures and Refutations* (London: Routledge & Kegan Paul, 1972).

31. For some of the general challenges of social science research, see T.B. Dawson, "Legal Research in a Social Science Setting: The Problem of Method" (1991–92), Dalhousie L.J. 445; H. Blaikie, *Approaches to Social Enquiry* (Cambridge: Polity Press, 1993); and G. King et al., *Designing Social Inquiry: Scientific Inference in Qualitative Research* (Princeton N.J.: Princeton University Press, 1994).

(b) Four Views on the Role and Rule of Law

David W. Elliott

While administrative law reform raises general questions about the role of the state, it also raises more specific — but no less controversial — questions about the role of law. A key ideological justification for law is the notion of the rule of law. The Supreme Court has called the rule of law "a fundamental principle of the Canadian Constitution".[32] The preamble to the *Canadian Charter of Rights and Freedoms* says that Canada is founded "upon principles that recognize the supremacy of God and the rule of law."[33]

On the other hand, the formal written part of the Canadian Constitution provides no definition of the rule of law. For a starting point, it may be helpful to go back to the 19th century constitutional lawyer Albert Venn Dicey. The first item below summarizes A.V. Dicey's formulation of the rule of law and of the linked principle of the sovereignty of Parliament.

The second item summarizes quite a different approach to the rule of law, by a contemporary socialist historian. E.P. Thompson sees the rule of law as a paradoxical refuge in the midst of a class-dominated social structure. In the third item, Harry Arthurs, one of Dicey's strongest critics, offers a pluralist alternative to what he regards as an obsession with the rule of law and judicial review. The fourth item contains a description of the rule of law by the Supreme Court of Canada in the *Reference Re Secession of Quebec*.

DICEY'S VIEW

A.V. Dicey's view has had a profound influence on British and Canadian constitutional law. Dicey formulated two principles: the rule of law, and the sovereignty of Parliament. Both endure in various forms to this day.

In Dicey's view, the rule of law has at least three distinct but related meanings:

1. Government action must be expressly authorized by law; it cannot result simply from the exercise of wide or arbitrary discretionary power.[34]
2. Every person — regardless of power, position, or governmental authority — should be subject to the ordinary law, administered in the ordinary courts.[35]
3. Peoples' rights should depend not on general constitutional declarations but on specific, concrete judicial remedies.[36]

According to Dicey, the rule of law is closely related to another fundamental principle, the principle of sovereignty or supremacy of Parliament. Under this principle, Parliament can make or unmake any law, and all laws properly made by Parliament must be obeyed by the courts.[37] Dicey saw sovereignty of Parliament as a form of legal supremacy, subject to the even more ultimate *political* sovereignty of the electorate.[38]

In the Canadian context, Dicey's two concepts must be qualified in several ways. First, parliamentary sovereignty is shared by the federal Parliament and 10 different provincial legislatures. Second, parliamentary legal supremacy here is subject to the provisions of the formal part of the Constitution, the Constitution of Canada. This, of course, includes the *Canadian Charter of Rights and Freedoms*. Third, in Canada the last tenet of the rule of law must include both specific concrete judicial remedies *and* general constitutional provisions. Beyond this, in both Britain and Canada, the discretionary and specialized public powers of modern administration probably go well beyond what Dicey had in mind when he formulated the first two tenets of his rule of law.

Many modern commentators, especially opponents of extensive judicial review, have condemned Dicey's rule of law as formalistic, unrealistic, and skewed in favour of courts.[39] On the other hand, Dicey's rule of law has been cited in the Supreme Court of Canada.[40] Examples in the case law suggest that the ideas behind it are still very much alive.[41] Certainly, the view that harmful government action should have legislative sanction, and the notion that government officials should be as accountable as anyone else if they act outside their statutory power, are both vital to modern Canadian constitutional and administrative law.

THOMPSON'S VIEW[42]

In *Whigs and Hunters: The Origins of the Black Act*,[43] socialist historian E.P. Thompson made some provocative observations about the rule of law and social and economic inequality. Thompson's view contrasts with that of traditional Marxists. These people have tended to see state and law as mechanisms to maintain or disguise the dominance of the ruling class over oppressed groups in society.[44] Thompson's view also contrasts with the perspectives of other modern socialist writers. Many of these see legal forums and the rule of law itself in largely negative terms.[45]

Thompson studied the "Black Act".[46] This repressive statute penalized poachers on the large forest and estate preserves of the 18th century English Whig aristocracy. Thompson acknowledged that the Act was an instrument of the ruling class. It served and legitimated class power.[47] However, Thompson argued that the legal processes for enforcing this Act did offer *some* protection to the accused, and helped curb the exercise of power by the ruling class. They were part of a developing ideology that emphasized fairness, natural justice, and the idea that disputes should be resolved by known rules rather than sheer force. Paradoxically, then, the Act helped generate a tradition of respect for justice. This, in turn, contributed to the important reforms achieved by the English working class in later centuries.[48] Thus, although the Black Act was undeniably an instrument of repression and a disguise for inequality, in a broader sense it contributed to the rule of law. This rule, said Thompson, is "an unqualified human good".[49]

WITHOUT THE LAW: ADMINISTRATIVE JUSTICE AND LEGAL PLURALISM IN 19TH CENTURY ENGLAND†

One need not dwell upon the extent to which Dicey's critics have demolished his logic and falsified his evidence; one need not trace the development of more sophisticated versions of his thesis by successive generations of legal scholars. It is sufficient ... to remind ourselves of the grip his version of the rule of law continues to have upon judges and lawyers....

. . . .

... For most lawyers, administrative law is not the law *of* the administration; it is the law directed *against* the administration, the law by which reviewing judges ensure that the administration does not overreach....

. . . .

Judges, even today's judges, have often displayed antipathy or insensitivity toward regulatory and social welfare schemes. The delays and technicalities involved in adversary hearings, appeals, and other legal proceedings become a new factor in the calculus of "rights," a factor that tends to favour those with time and money and access to the best lawyers. Nor, as it turns out, do judicial review or appeal always operate effectively *in terrorem* to ensure

administrative compliance with legislative policy or fair procedures. The doctrine is too incoherent, the outcomes too random, the very object of review too elusive and ill-defined to support any credible assessment of the net results of judicial intervention.

But most important, ordinary legal attitudes, procedures, and remedies seldom address the defects they are meant to correct. The Appeal to ordinary law does not add a penny to the total welfare budget, but it may divert some part of that limited budget to administration and litigation. A constitutional or statutory requirement of notice prior to regulation-making will not alter the attitude of a regulator who has been captured, but it may speed his capitulation in the face of a well-financed frontal assault by the big battalions of industry. On the other hand, the requirement of trial-type hearings and full-scale appeals may well have, from the point of view of a regulated industry, the desired effect of discouraging all but the most determined administrator by forcing him to focus his scarce resources on a relatively small number of cases so clear that they are likely to survive even judicial scrutiny. The public's interest in attaining regulatory objectives is, in the end, not likely to be served by appeals to ordinary law.

... [The system of ordinary law is] designed and administered by a relatively homogeneous group of lawyers, whose expertise seldom extends beyond legal doctrine, whose ideology tends toward conservatism, and whose experience largely consists in dealing with isolated cases in an adversarial context....

. . . .

If ordinary law will not do the job, what will? In truth, there are two kinds of jobs to be done, and each requires a different approach.

First, there are the political jobs. If, as has been suggested, regulatory capture results from a collapse of political will, then governments must be forced to confront their responsibility for appointing administrators who are not resolute, or for failing to revive their flagging morale. If welfare budgets are insufficient to meet the need, governments should acknowledge this fact by overt policy statements which the voters can judge. If regulation is thought to cost society more than it is worth, let government deregulate, if it dares to. These are not tasks for either administrators or judges.

---

† Excerpts from H.W. Arthurs, *Without the Law: Administrative Justice and Legal Pluralism in Nineteenth Century England* (Toronto: University of Toronto Press, 1985) at 5–6, and 200–201. [Notes omitted.] Reproduced with permission of the author.

Second, there are the more limited jobs of ensuring the effectiveness and integrity of administration in each specific instance where it is mandated by the political process. Quality control ... is more than a matter of careful inspection after the fact; it must be "engineered in" from the beginning and accepted as a cardinal commitment by everyone involved in the production process. So too with administration. Accepting the need to check administrative behaviour from time to time (although not necessarily by means of conventional judicial review), the best prospects for improving the quality of administration reside in the initial design of structures and procedures and in the genuine commitment of administrators to high standards of performance.

REFERENCE RE SECESSION OF QUEBEC†

This important decision is discussed in more detail in Chapter 12.[50] The federal government initiated it by asking, *inter alia*, if, under the Canadian Constitution, Quebec could secede from Canada unilaterally. The Court said the answer to this question was affected not only by the text of the Canadian constitution, but by important constitutional principles.

The Court (Lamer C.J. and L'Heureux-Dubé, Gonthier, Cory, McLachlin, Iacobucci, Major, Bastarache and Binnie JJ.):[51]

[49] ... Our Constitution is primarily a written one, the product of 131 years of evolution. Behind the written word is an historical lineage stretching back through the ages, which aids in the consideration of the underlying constitutional principles. These principles inform and sustain the constitutional text: they are the vital unstated assumptions upon which the text is based. The following discussion addresses the four foundational constitutional principles that are most germane for resolution of this Reference: federalism, democracy, constitutionalism and the rule of law, and respect for minority rights. These defining principles function in symbiosis. No single principle can be defined in isolation from the others, nor does any one principle trump or exclude the operation of any other.

...

[para70] The principles of constitutionalism and the rule of law lie at the root of our system of government. The rule of law, as observed in *Roncarelli* v. *Duplessis*, [1959] S.C.R. 121, at p. 142, is "a fundamental postulate of our constitutional structure." As we noted in the *Patriation Reference*, [1981] 1 S.C.R. 753 at pp. 805–6, "[t]he 'rule of law' is a highly textured expression, importing many things which are beyond the need of these reasons to explore but conveying, for example, a sense of orderliness, of subjection to known legal rules and of executive accountability to legal authority." At its most basic level, the rule of law vouchsafes to the citizens and residents of the country a stable, predictable and ordered society in which to conduct their affairs. It provides a shield for individuals from arbitrary state action.

[71] In the *Manitoba Language Rights Reference*, [1985] 1 S.C.R. 721 at pp. 747–52, this Court outlined the elements of the rule of law. We emphasized, first, that the rule of law provides that the law is supreme over the acts of both government and private persons. There is, in short, one law for all. Second, we explained, at p. 749, that "the rule of law requires the creation and maintenance of an actual order of positive laws which preserves and embodies the more general principle of normative order." ... A third aspect of the rule of law is, as recently confirmed in the *Provincial Judges Reference*, [1997] 3 S.C.R. 3 at para. 10, that "the exercise of all public power must find its ultimate source in a legal rule." Put another way, the relationship between the state and the individual must be regulated by law....

The Court said that underlying constitutional principles (such as the rule of law) "may in certain circumstances give rise to substantive legal obligations."[52] The Court went on to hold, *inter alia*, that Quebec cannot secede from Canada unilaterally. Unilateral secession would push aside the principles of federalism, the rule of law, the rights of individuals and minorities, and the operation of democracy in the other provinces or in Canada as a whole.[53] However, the Court also said that a clear expression of the will of Quebecers to secede would be an expression of the principle of democracy in Quebec. As such, it would require the rest

---

† *Reference Re Secession of Quebec* (IN THE MATTER OF Section 53 of the Supreme Court Act, R.S.C., 1985, c. S-26; AND IN THE MATTER OF a Reference by the Governor in Council concerning certain questions relating to the secession of Quebec from Canada, as set out in Order in Council P.C. 1996-1947, dated the 30th day of September, 1996, [1998] 2 S.C.R. 217 (argument: 16, 17, 18, and 19 February 1998; decision: 20 August 1998) para. 49.

of Canada to negotiate with Quebec on the subject of secession.[54]

Thus the rule of law and similar constitutional principles can have enforceable legal status in some situations. What are the implications of this for administrative law?

Notes

1. *Reference Re Remuneration of Judges*, [1997] S.C.R. 3 at para. 99. See also *Reference Re Manitoba Language Rights*, [1985] 1 S.C.R. 271 at 749 and *Reference Re Secession of Quebec*, [1998] 2 S.C.R. 217 at para. 49.
2. *Constitution Act, 1982*, Schedule B to the *Canada Act 1982*, (U.K.), 1982, c. 11.
3. This is a rough summary: for the original formulation, see Albert Venn Dicey, *An Introduction to the Study of The Law of The Constitution*, 10th ed. (London: MacMillan, 1959, first published in 1895) at 188.
4. *Ibid.* at 193.
5. *Ibid.* at 195–96.
6. *Ibid.* at 39–40.
7. *Ibid.* at 83.
8. See, for example, H. Arthurs, "Rethinking Administrative Law: A Slightly Dicey Business" (1979) 17 Osgoode Hall L.J. 1 at 7; the Arthurs extract below; R. Yalden, Deference and Coherence in "Administrative Law: Rethinking Statutory Interpretation" (1988) U.T.L.J. 137 at 154; and A.C. Hutchinson, "The Rise and Ruse of Administrative Law and Scholarship" (1990) 48 Mod. L. Rev. 293 at 322. Not all Dicey's critics favour a narrow role for courts. In *The Rule of Law, Justice, and Interpretation* (Montreal & Kingston: McGill University Press, 1997), Luc Tremblay's concern is that Dicey's approach is based on a notion of legal positivism that fails to explain the importance of value judgments in legal decision-making. Tremblay feels that the rule of rule of law should be associated with a broad concept of "justice," incorporating notions such as consistency, moral acceptability, and equity.
9. See, for example, *Immeubles Port Louis Ltée. v. Lafontaine (Village)*, [1991] 1 S.C.R. 326 at 360 (re-formulating Dicey's tenets slightly). For a more critical view, see Wilson J., dissenting in *National Corn Growers' Assn. v. Canada (Canadian Import Tribunal)*, [1990] 2 S.C.R. 1324 at 1332–36. For a reference to Dicey's concept of the sovereignty of Parliament, see *Reference Re Remuneration of Judges*, [1997] S.C.R. 3 at para. 308.

   Note, though, that in at least one respect the Court has gone beyond Dicey's formulation of the rule of law. For example, in *Re Language Rights under s. 23 of Manitoba Act, 1870 and s. 133 of Constitution Act, 1867*, [1985] 1 S.C.R. 721 at 748–49, it said that the rule of law requires (i) that law is supreme over officials as well as private individuals, thus precluding arbitrary power, and (ii) *"the creation and maintenance of an actual order of positive laws which preserves and embodies the more general principle of normative order."* [Emphasis added.] See also *Reference Re Secession of Quebec*, [1998] 2 S.C.R. 217, extracts below.
10. See, for example, *Roncarelli v. Duplessis*, [1959] 1 S.C.R. 121 at 184 (reproduced in part in Chapter 3, above); *Re Anti-Inflation Act*, [1976] 2 S.C.R. 373 at 504 and *Shell*

Canada Products Ltd. v. Vancouver (City), [1994] 1 S.C.R. 231. For an interesting discussion of the rule of law in the lower courts, see *Vanguard Coatings and Chemicals Ltd. v. M.N.R.*, [1987] 1 F.C. 367 at 390–93 (F.C.T.D), varied in *R. v. Vanguard Coatings & Chemicals Ltd.* (1988), 30 Admin. L.R. 121 (F.C.A.). See also I. Holloway, "A Sacred Right: Judicial Review of Administrative Action as a Cultural Phenomenon" (1993) 22 Manitoba L. Rev. 28 at 33 *et seq.*
11. E.P. Thompson, *Whigs and Hunters: The Origins of the Black Act* (London: Penguin, 1977 [first published 1975, by Allen Lane]).
12. *Whigs and Hunters: The Origins of the Black Act, ibid.*
13. For example, Karl Marx referred to the state as "the form in which the individuals of a ruling class assert their common interests": K. Marx, "German Ideology" in T.B. Bottomore, ed. and trans., *Selected Writings in Sociology and Social Philosophy* (New York: McGraw-Hill, 1964, 223), reproduced in Chapter 1, above. P.I. Stuchta, an early 20th century Marxist, described law as "a system ... of social relationships which corresponds to the interests of the dominant class and is safeguarded by the organized force of that class": "The Revolutionary Part Played by Law and the State — A General Doctrine of Law" in H.W. Baba and J.N. Hazard, eds., *Soviet Legal Philosophy* (Cambridge, Mass.: Harvard University Press, 1951) at 20. E.B. Pashukanis, another leading Soviet Marxist, had a similar negative view of law, *ibid.* at 139. He felt that in a true communist society the need for law and the state itself would eventually wither away: *ibid.* at 123–24.
14. For example, Glasbeek and Mandel argue in Chapter 7, below that the *Canadian Charter of Rights and Freedoms* is a mask that diverts attention from great economic inequalities. In the same chapter, Hutchinson and Monahan take aim at the notion of the rule of law itself. They see it as a set of élitist, often reactionary, law and court-oriented norms that distract from more genuinely democratic measures. For a modern view that law and the state are, in capitalist and post-capitalist societies, a necessary evil — or at best a very qualified "good" — and should eventually "wither away" in a true communist society, see O. Taiwo, *Legal Naturalism: A Marxist Theory of Law* (Ithaca and London: Cornell University Press, 1996) Ch. 6. For a more positive modern view — from a socialist perspective — see A. Hunt, *Explorations in Law and Society: Towards a Constitutive Theory of Law* (New York: Routledge, 1993).
15. 9 George I c. 22 (1723). The "Blacks" were hunters who blacked their faces and wore disguises while poaching deer and other game in the private forests and estates of the rich. The Act was subsequently extended to cover many different forms of poaching. Over 50 offences in the Act were punishable by capital punishment. See Thompson, *supra* note 11, "Introduction" and Chapter 1, above.
16. *Supra* note 1 at 260 and 262.
17. *Ibid.* at 269.
18. *Ibid.* at 266. Note how Thompson sees the rule of law as both a concrete process and an ideology.
19. See especially Chapter 12, below.
20. *Reference Re Secession of Quebec*, [1998] 2 S.C.R. 217.
21. *Ibid.* at para. 54.
22. *Ibid.* at paras. 91 and 151.
23. Paras. 88 and 151.

(c) *Statutory Powers Procedure Act*†

NOTE

The most extensive set of administrative law reforms in Canada to date were implemented in Ontario in the early 1970s. In response to the recommendations of the Royal Commission Inquiry into Civil Rights (the McRuer Commission), the Ontario government enacted (i) the *Statutory Powers Procedure Act* to provide a code of minimum rules of fair procedure and create a body to oversee tribunals' procedural rule-making on an ongoing basis; (ii) the *Judicial Review Procedure Act*[1] to streamline the remedies used in judicial review; and (iii) the *Judicature Amendment Act*[2] to create a separate branch of the Ontario High Court with jurisdiction to review decisions of Ontario tribunals.

The *Statutory Powers Procedure Act* (*S.P.P.A.*), reproduced in part below, has some similarity with the American *Administrative Procedure Act* and the *Administrative Procedures Act* in Alberta. The *S.P.P.A.* is really a code of "medium" rules of fair procedure, with minimum rules left to the common law and maximum rules in individual statutes. In this regard, it is important to look at the scope as well as the content of the *S.P.P.A.*, especially section 3. Note, too, that the individual procedural safeguards reproduced here are balanced to some extent by "efficiency" provisions, such as a tribunal's right to have its decisions enforced by a court order (s. 19).

An important part of the original *S.P.P.A.* was the Statutory Powers Procedure Rules Committee, intended to supervise the making of procedural rules by tribunals. Unlike its English counterpart the Council on Tribunals, the Statutory Powers Procedure Rules Committee met only rarely, issued few reports, and generally did little.

After a quarter of a century, the *S.P.P.A.* and other McRuer legislation was ready for re-appraisal.

The Rules Committee was finally abolished in 1995, and numerous additional technical changes were made at that time.[3] Generally, though, many of the possible reform issues, discussed in the "Reform Challenges" above, have not been resolved in Ontario or elsewhere in Canada. Despite countless commissions of inquiry and recommendations, administrative law reform is usually kept on the back burner. It is time now to break the inertia, to develop areas of consensus and priority, and to bring constructive reform to the front.

EXTRACT

Application of Act

3.(1) Subject to subsection (2), this Act applies to a proceeding by a tribunal in the exercise of a statutory power of decision conferred by or under an Act of the Legislature, where the tribunal is required by or under such Act or otherwise by law to hold or to afford to the parties to the proceeding an opportunity for a hearing before making a decision.

Where Act does not apply

(2) This Act does not apply to a proceeding,

(a) before the Assembly or any committee of the Assembly;

(b) in or before [ordinary courts of law];

(c) to which the Rules of Civil Procedure apply;

(d) before an arbitrator to which the *Arbitrations Act* or the *Labour Relations Act* applies;

(e) at a coroner's inquest;

(f) of a commission appointed under the *Public Inquiries Act, 2009*;

(g) of one or more persons required to make an investigation and to make a report, with or without recommendations, where the report is

---

† R.S.O. 1990, c. S. 22 (first enacted as S.O. 1971, c. 47, assented to on 23 July 1971), as am. by S.O. 2009, c. 33, Sched. 6, s. 87. For administrative law reforms outside Ontario, see "Postscript" following the extracts below. [Commentary note by David W. Elliott.]

[1] *Judicial Review Procedure Act*, R.S.O. 1990, c. J.1 (first enacted as S.O. 1971, c. 48) (streamlining judicial review remedies).

[2] See *Courts of Justice Act*, R.S.O. 1990, c. C.43, ss. 18–21 (first enacted as *Judicature Act Amendment*, S.O. 1971, c. 97 and *Judicature Amendment Act (No. 4)*, S.O. 1970, c. 97) (creating a separate division of the Ontario High Court, the General Division of the Ontario Court of Justice called the Divisional Court).

[3] *Statutory Amendment Act*, S.O. 1994, c. 27, in effect on 1 April 1995. See M.D. Priest and Burton, "Amendments to the Statutory Powers Procedure Act (Ontario); Analysis and Comments," *Law Society of Upper Canada Continuing Legal Education Program: Recent Developments in Administrative Law* (Toronto: L.S.U.C., 17 January 1995).

for the information or advice of the person to whom it is made and does not in any way legally bind or limit that person in any decision he or she may have power to make; or

(h) of a tribunal empowered to make regulations, rules or by-laws in so far as its power to make regulations, rules or by-laws is concerned.

. . . .

Waiver of procedural requirement

4.(1) Any procedural requirement of this Act, or of another Act or a regulation that applies to a proceeding, may be waived with the consent of the parties and the tribunal.

Same, rules

(2) Any provision of a tribunal's rules made under section 25.1 may be waived in accordance with the rules.

Disposition without hearing

4.1 If the parties consent, a proceeding may be disposed of by a decision of the tribunal given without a hearing, unless another Act or a regulation that applies to the proceeding provides otherwise.

Panels, certain matters

4.2(1) [tribunals assigned to decide interlocutory matters in panels]

. . . .

Written hearings

5.1(1) A tribunal whose rules made under section 25.1 deal with written hearings may hold a written hearing in a proceeding.

Exception

(2) The tribunal shall not hold a written hearing if a party satisfies the tribunal that there is good reason for not doing so.

Same

(2.1) Subsection (2) does not apply if the only purpose of the hearing is to deal with procedural matters.

Documents

(3) In a written hearing, all the parties are entitled to receive every document that the tribunal receives in the proceeding.

Electronic hearings

5.2(1) A tribunal whose rules made under section 25.1 deal with electronic hearings may hold an electronic hearing in a proceeding.

Exception

(2) The tribunal shall not hold an electronic hearing if a party satisfies the tribunal that holding an electronic rather than an oral hearing is likely to cause the party significant prejudice.

Same

(3) Subsection (2) does not apply if the only purpose of the hearing is to deal with procedural matters.

Participants to be able to hear one another

(4) In an electronic hearing, all the parties and the members of the tribunal participating in the hearing must be able to hear one another and any witnesses throughout the hearing.

. . . .

Notice of hearing

6.(1) The parties to a proceeding shall be given reasonable notice of the hearing by the tribunal.

Statutory authority

(2) A notice of a hearing shall include a reference to the statutory authority under which the hearing will be held.

Oral hearing

(3) A notice of an oral hearing shall include,

(a) a statement of the time, place and purpose of the hearing; and

(b) a statement that if the party notified does not attend at the hearing, the tribunal may proceed in the party's absence and the party will not be entitled to any further notice in the proceeding.

Written hearing

(4) A notice of a written hearing shall include,

(a) a statement of the date and purpose of the hearing, and details about the manner in which the hearing will be held;

(b) a statement that the hearing shall not be held as a written hearing if the party satisfies the tribunal that there is good reason for not holding a written hearing (in which case the tribunal is required to hold it as an electronic or oral hearing) and an indication of the procedure to be followed for that purpose;

(c) a statement that if the party notified neither acts under clause (b) nor participates in the hearing in accordance with the notice, the tribunal may proceed without the party's participation and the party will not be entitled to any further notice in the proceeding.

Electronic hearing

(5) A notice of an electronic hearing shall include,

(a) a statement of the time and purpose of the hearing, and details about the manner in which the hearing will be held;

(b) a statement that the only purpose of the hearing is to deal with procedural matters, if that is the case;

(c) if clause (b) does not apply, a statement that the party notified may, by satisfying the tribunal that holding the hearing as an electronic hearing is likely to cause the party significant prejudice, require the tribunal to hold the hearing as an oral hearing, and an indication of the procedure to be followed for that purpose; and

(d) [a statement regarding non-participation similar to the preceding section]

Effect of non-attendance at hearing after due notice

7.(1) Where notice of an oral hearing has been given to a party to a proceeding in accordance with this Act and the party does not attend at the hearing, the tribunal may proceed in the absence of the party and the party is not entitled to any further notice in the proceeding.

[Subsection 2 and 3 contain similar statements for written and electronic hearings]

Where character, etc., of a party is in issue

8. Where the good character, propriety of conduct or competence of a party is an issue in a proceeding, the party is entitled to be furnished prior to the hearing with reasonable information of any allegations with respect thereto.

Hearings to be public, exceptions

9.(1) An oral hearing shall be open to the public except where the tribunal is of the opinion that,

(a) matters involving public security may be disclosed; or

(b) intimate financial or personal matters or other matters may be disclosed at the hearing of such a nature, having regard to the circumstances, that the desirability of avoiding disclosure thereof in the interests of any person affected or in the public interest outweighs the desirability of adhering to the principle that hearings be open to the public,

in which case the tribunal may hold the hearing in the absence of the public.

Written hearings

(1.1) In a written hearing, members of the public are entitled to reasonable access to the documents submitted, unless the tribunal is of the opinion that clause (1) (a) or (b) applies.

Electronic hearings

(1.2) An electronic hearing shall be open to the public unless the tribunal is of the opinion that,

(a) it is not practical to hold the hearing in a manner that is open to the public; or

(b) clause (1) (a) or (b) applies.

Maintenance of order at hearings

(2) A tribunal may make such orders or give such directions at an oral or electronic hearing as it considers necessary for the maintenance of order at the hearing, and, if any person disobeys or fails to comply with any such order or direction, the tribunal or a member thereof may call for the assistance of any peace officer to enforce the order or direction, and every peace officer so called upon shall take such action as is necessary to enforce the order or direction and may use such force as is reasonably required for that purpose.

9.1 [consolidation of Proceedings involving similar questions]

Right to representation

10. A party to a proceeding may be represented by a representative.

Examination of witnesses

10.1 A party to a proceeding may, at an oral or electronic hearing,

(a) call and examine witnesses and present evidence and submissions; and

(b) conduct cross-examinations of witnesses at the hearing reasonably required for a full and fair disclosure of all matters relevant to the issues in the proceeding.

Rights of witnesses to representation

11.(1) A witness at an oral or electronic hearing is entitled to be advised by a representative as to his or her rights, but such representative may take no other part in the hearing without leave of the tribunal.

Idem

(2) Where an oral hearing is closed to the public, the witness's representative is not entitled to be present except when that witness is giving evidence.

Summonses

12.(1) A tribunal may require any person, including a party, by summons,

(a) to give evidence on oath or affirmation at an oral or electronic hearing; and

(b) to produce in evidence at an oral or electronic hearing documents and things specified by the tribunal,

relevant to the subject-matter of the proceeding and admissible at a hearing.

. . . . .

Interim decisions and orders

16.1(1) A tribunal may make interim decisions and orders.

Conditions

(2) A tribunal may impose conditions on an interim decision or order.

Reasons

(3) An interim decision or order need not be accompanied by reasons.

Time frames

16.2 A tribunal shall establish guidelines setting out the usual time frame for completing proceedings that come before the tribunal and for completing the procedural steps within those proceedings.

Decision

17.(1) A tribunal shall give its final decision and order, if any, in any proceeding in writing and shall give reasons in writing therefor if requested by a party.

Interest

(2) A tribunal that makes an order for the payment of money shall set out in the order the principal sum, and if interest is payable, the rate of interest and the date from which it is to be calculated.

Notice of decision

18.(1) The tribunal shall send each party who participated in the proceeding, or the party's representative, a copy of its final decision or order, including the reasons if any have been given ...

. . . . .

Record of proceeding

20. A tribunal shall compile a record of any proceeding in which a hearing has been held which shall include,

(a) any application, complaint, reference or other document, if any, by which the proceeding was commenced;

(b) the notice of any hearing;

(c) any interlocutory orders made by the tribunal;

(d) all documentary evidence filed with the tribunal, subject to any limitation expressly imposed by any other Act on the extent to or the purposes for which any such documents may be used in evidence in any proceeding;

(e) the transcript, if any, of the oral evidence given at the hearing; and

(f) the decision of the tribunal and the reasons therefor, where reasons have been given.

Adjournments

21. A hearing may be adjourned from time to time by a tribunal of its own motion or where it is shown to the satisfaction of the tribunal that the adjournment is required to permit an adequate hearing to be held.

Correction of errors

21.1 A tribunal may at any time correct a typographical error, error of calculation or similar error made in its decision or order.

Power to review

21.2(1) A tribunal may, if it considers it advisable and if its rules made under section 25.1 deal with the matter, review all or part of its own decision or order, and may confirm, vary, suspend or cancel the decision or order.

Time for review

(2) The review shall take place within a reasonable time after the decision or order is made.

Conflict

(3) In the event of a conflict between this section and any other Act, the other Act prevails.

Administration of oaths

22. A member of a tribunal has power to administer oaths and affirmations for the purpose of any of its proceedings and the tribunal may require evidence before it to be given under oath or affirmation.

Abuse of processes

23.(1) A tribunal may make such orders or give such directions in proceedings before it as it considers proper to prevent abuse of its processes.

Limitation on examination

(2) A tribunal may reasonably limit further examination or cross-examination of a witness where it is satisfied that the examination or cross-examination has been sufficient to disclose fully and fairly all matters relevant to the issues in the proceeding.

Exclusion of representatives

(3) A tribunal may exclude from a hearing anyone, other than a person licensed under the *Law Society Act*, appearing on behalf of a party or as an adviser to a witness if it finds that such person is not competent properly to represent or to advise the party or witness, or does not understand and comply at the hearing with the duties and responsibilities of an advocate or adviser.

Notice, etc.

24.(1) Where a tribunal is of the opinion that because the parties to any proceeding before it are so numerous or for any other reason, it is impracticable,

  (a) to give notice of the hearing; or

  (b) to send its decision and the material mentioned in section 18,

to all or any of the parties individually, the tribunal may, instead of doing so, cause reasonable notice of the hearing or of its decision to be given to such parties by public advertisement or otherwise as the tribunal may direct.

Contents of notice

(2) A notice of a decision given by a tribunal under clause (1) (b) shall inform the parties of the place where copies of the decision and the reasons therefor, if reasons were given, may be obtained.

Appeal operates as stay, exception

25.(1) An appeal from a decision of a tribunal to a court or other appellate body operates as a stay in the matter unless,

  (a) another Act or a regulation that applies to the proceeding expressly provides to the contrary; or

  (b) the tribunal or the court or other appellate body orders otherwise.

Idem

(2) An application for judicial review under the *Judicial Review Procedure Act*, or the bringing of proceedings specified in subsection 2 (1) of that Act is not an appeal within the meaning of subsection (1).

Control of process

25.0.1 A tribunal has the power to determine its own procedures and practices and may for that purpose,

  (a) make orders with respect to the procedures and practices that apply in any particular proceeding; and

  (b) establish rules under section 25.1.

Rules

25.1(1) A tribunal may make rules governing the practice and procedure before it.

Application

(2) The rules may be of general or particular application.

Consistency with Acts

(3) The rules shall be consistent with this Act and with the other Acts to which they relate.

Public access

(4) The tribunal shall make the rules available to the public in English and in French.

Legislation Act, 2006, Part III

(5) Rules adopted under this section are not regulations as defined in Part III (Regulations) of the *Legislation Act, 2006*.

Additional power

(6) The power conferred by this section is in addition to any power to adopt rules that the tribunal may have under another Act.

Regulations

26. The Lieutenant Governor in Council may make regulations prescribing forms for the purpose of section 12.

. . . .

Conflict

32. Unless it is expressly provided in any other Act that its provisions and regulations, rules or by-laws made under it apply despite anything in this Act, the provisions of this Act prevail over the provisions of such other Act and over regulations, rules or by-laws made under such other Act which conflict therewith.

[Former sections 29 to 31 and 33 and 34 as well as Forms 1 and 2 were repealed.]

(d)   Unjust by Design†

Ron Ellis

NOTE

The administrative system of justice flourished with the growth of the State into many spheres of life that were formerly considered beyond the grasp of government. As time passed, the executive branch set up quasi-judicial bodies to decide a myriad of important disputes without replicating the institutional guarantees of the judiciary. The administrative justice system is far from perfect, with the executive branch generally providing competent decision-making; yet, as the piece below argues, without observing constitutional guarantees of independent and/or impartial adjudication. As you read the critique below, ask yourself what incentive the executive or legislative branches have in guaranteeing a truly independent and impartial adjudicative framework that might constrain the State's legal authority to act in the future. If reform is possible in this area of law, what might such transformation look like, and how might that improve the efficiency and quality of administrative action?

EXTRACT

When I had been the chair of Ontario's Workers' Compensation Appeals Tribunal for a few years, a letter arrived on my desk from a mother living in a small Ontario town. The mother's young adult son had been seeking workers' compensation benefits for a major, disabling injury — benefits that would provide the income he could no longer earn for himself. Notwithstanding the seriousness of her son's injury, the Ontario Workers' Compensation Board had decided that the circumstances under which it had occurred did not bring the injury within the coverage of the Workers' Compensation Act; it had rejected his application. The Board's decision had been appealed to my Appeals Tribunal. A panel that I had assigned to hear the appeal had agreed with the

---

† Reproduced with permission of the Publisher from *Unjust by Design* by Ron Ellis © University of British Columbia Press 2013 at 1–28. All rights reserved by the Publisher. [Original endnotes and formatting omitted.]

Board. Her son's appeal had been rejected. "Dear Mr. Ellis," the mother wrote, "I thought that as Chair of this so-called Tribunal you might want to see the enclosed." The "enclosed" was the last page of my Tribunal's decision in her son's appeal. The last line on that page read: "Appeal denied." Her son, the mother explained in her letter, had read the decision, gone out to the back shed, taken down the family shotgun, and killed himself. On the last page of the decision, below the words "Appeal denied," he had scrawled the words "Life denied." His mother had sent it to me in the blood-spattered condition in which she had found it.

THE ADMINISTRATIVE JUSTICE SYSTEM IN CONTEXT

The "so-called Tribunal" the grieving mother held responsible for her son's death is just one of hundreds of executive branch "administrative tribunals" to which Canadian legislatures have assigned the judicial branch function of making judicial decisions, decisions that are frequently of a life-altering nature. Currently, these tribunals are mainly referred to as "adjudicative tribunals" or "quasi-judicial tribunals," but for reasons to be explained later I choose to call them "judicial tribunals." Taken together, they add up to a surrogate system of justice — the Canadian administrative justice system — the system of justice that is the subject of this book.

This administrative justice system is the system to which Canadians are required to turn for the enforcement or vindication of their rights in a broad range of everyday matters. These matters currently include retirement pensions, disability pensions, veteran's pensions, compensation for personal injuries arising from automobile accidents, compensation for workplace injuries, enforcement of human rights laws, involuntary incarceration of individuals in psychiatric institutions, enforced medical treatment and withdrawal of medical treatment, mental competence issues, parole eligibility, social welfare benefits, residential landlord and tenant issues, labour relations issues, employment standards, the conduct or competence of medical practitioners, the validity of doctors' billings, access to assisted living accommodations, access to programs of special education, child and family services, compensation for victims of crime, immigration, asylum for refugees, employment insurance, cruelty to animals, compliance with building codes, and so on and so forth.

In any Canadian province, on any particular day, one will typically find over thirty executive branch judicial tribunals conducting hearings and exercising their specialized judicial functions. The total number of judicial decisions made by these tribunals across the country in the course of a year is unknown but is clearly very large indeed. In Ontario alone, for instance, one estimate puts the number of rights-related decisions by administrative tribunals at over a million each year. In 2010, the Ontario Workplace Safety and Insurance Board dealt with a quarter of a million applications for the adjudication of new compensation claims, and the Landlord and Tenant Board dealt with 78,000 applications for the judicial determination of rights disputes between residential landlords and their tenants, a large proportion of which involved landlords applying for eviction orders.

Although the administrative justice system is the part of our justice system to which Canadians must now look for the recognition or vindication of a majority of their everyday legal rights — the only justice system that most people are ever likely to encounter — it is, as a system, largely unknown. Lawyers, law professors, and judges know it, but even to them it presents an uncertain topography. It is an ad hoc system that has emerged over the past several decades as an unplanned consequence of the inexorable parade of new statutes creating important everyday rights and obligations in which the judicial function of adjudicating those rights and obligations has been routinely assigned not to the courts but to executive branch tribunals.

This uncertainty — even in the minds of academics, lawyers, and judges — about what the system consists of stems from the fact that Canada's administrative law landscape is awash with bodies that are authorized by statute to exercise rights-determining functions, only some of which are judicial functions. Thus, the judicial tribunals that constitute the administrative justice system are to be found mixed in with an array of rights-determining bodies that may structurally resemble judicial tribunals, may exercise functions that are rather like those of judicial tribunals, and, most confusingly, are often called by the same names — tribunals, boards, commissions, committees, and so on. It is always a puzzle to distinguish one from the other and it has not helped that in the administrative law conversation in Canada — in our literature and jurisprudence — it has rarely been thought necessary to do so.

... I divide the myriad of statutory, rights-determining bodies found in the modern Canadian polity into four groups: (1) executive branch administrative justice bodies, (2) executive branch regulatory bodies, (3) non-government regulatory bodies, and (4) non-government adjudicative bodies.

Administrative justice bodies are the executive branch, non-court judicial tribunals whose principal statutory assignment is the exercise of judicial functions. They are the core constituents of the administrative justice system and are the principal focus of this book. They are typically the judicial arms of the executive branch's statutory rights enterprises. They have been known in the past as government "agencies," but are now more commonly referred to as "tribunals." As indicated above, in this book they will be called "judicial tribunals." This group, of course, includes the adjudicator members of judicial tribunals. The prototypical examples of judicial tribunals are the workers' compensation appeals tribunals.

Within this first group I also include the individuals appointed to government offices that exercise rights-determining functions that are in fact properly judicial functions. Here I am thinking principally of public servants employed in a government department or ministry (including, perhaps in some instances, ministers themselves) to whose office a statutory provision may have assigned a rights-determining function that meets the definition of a judicial function. (As we will see, this definition includes, in part, the requirement that the rights-determining decision be a final decision — "final" in the sense that its conclusions concerning both facts and law cannot be appealed, as of right, to another judicial tribunal.)

In my view, the exercise of judicial functions of such final nature by public servants or cabinet ministers is neither compatible with the rule of law nor constitutionally permissible; where this has occurred, reforming the system will require these functions to be restructured. Fortunately, most of these in-house ministerial rights-determining functions are not judicial but only interim decision-making functions or administrative functions. The latter may often be of a "quasi-judicial" nature and so governed by the principles of procedural fairness (see below), but, as I will demonstrate in due course, a rights-determining function that is properly characterized as "quasi-judicial" is not a judicial function. (The differentiation of "quasi-judicial" administrative functions from "judicial" functions has in recent years been muted in the Supreme Court of Canada's jurisprudence, but it is a difference that in my view is constitutionally essential....

It is in the interest of completeness that I have noted the fact that in-house, ministerial rights-determining judicial functions are necessarily part of the administrative justice system, but in fact the exercise of such functions by public servants or ministers is rare.

The second of my four groups includes all government organizations that have been assigned regulatory functions. These functions are principally rights-determining functions of an administrative nature. Even when they are seen to be of a quasi-judicial nature, they remain fundamentally administrative in nature and are not part of the administrative justice system — not as that system is rationally conceived. These organizations are commonly referred to as "regulatory agencies" — a practice that I will follow — and prototypical examples are energy boards, securities commissions, the Canadian Radio-television and Telecommunications Commission (CRTC), and the like. In this group of regulatory bodies, I also include the individuals appointed to government offices who have been assigned rights-determining functions that are in fact properly regulatory functions. Here, as before, I have in mind public servants employed in a government ministry (including, in some instances, ministers themselves), to whose office a statutory provision may have assigned a rights-determining function of a regulatory nature. These functions may also often be of a quasi-judicial nature but they are not judicial functions and the individuals exercising them are not part of the administrative justice system.

Associated with this group of regulatory bodies is the important sub-category of functions often assigned to regulatory agencies that are in fact judicial functions, properly so called. In my view, these functions are, by definition, part of the administrative justice system and they present especially difficult issues that I will deal with later. I will refer to these functions as "adjunct" judicial functions.

My third group, the non-government rights-determining bodies, are bodies that are not executive branch organizations and whose statutory rights-determining functions are principally regulatory in nature. Examples are law society disciplinary tribunals, or bodies dealing with disciplinary issues or academic rights within the college and university communities. I will refer to the bodies in this group as non-government regulatory agencies. As with the executive branch regulatory agencies, one will find many of these agencies exercising adjunct judicial functions but I do not include these functions as part of the administrative justice system for the purposes of this book. To them, different arguments apply.

The fourth and final group, the non-government adjudicators, I also leave out of the frame as far as this book is concerned. Examples of these decision makers are grievance arbitrators appointed under collective bargaining agreements, and commercial arbitrators appointed pursuant to an arbitration act by the parties to a business dispute. In these cases, because the decision maker is chosen by agreement of the parties, the usual constitutional concerns about independence and impartiality of bodies exercising judicial functions are by and large answered.

This categorizing of bodies exercising statutory, rights-determining functions into four separate groups is, of course, anything but a scientific exercise. At the margins, it will often not be clear into which group a particular function or tribunal properly falls. Eventually, the lines of demarcation will have to be drawn through a case-by-case consideration of the fit of the applicable principles in the marginal cases; meanwhile, my analysis of those principles and their application will be focused on that core of tribunals that are beyond question judicial tribunals — executive branch tribunals whose principal rights-determining function is obviously a judicial function.

To sum up, this book is about the executive branch's judicial tribunals and the administrative justice system of which they are the core components. This justice system looms over everyone's everyday life, waiting to be summoned to invasive action by the arrival of some exigent but everyday circumstance. Nevertheless, if one asks anyone who is not a lawyer about "judicial tribunals" and the "administrative justice system" one may expect only a blank stare. This is not surprising, since each judicial tribunal has a different appearance and a unique name, and none of them is actually called a "judicial tribunal." They are also easily confused with regulatory agencies; moreover, they are located in the executive branch of government, where no one should expect to find a judicial tribunal, much less a justice system. The variability in the appearance and structure of judicial tribunals reflects the fact that there is no central design-coordination or any standard design principles or criteria, and the choice of names is purely arbitrary. Each tribunal is typically a one-off structure designed by the staff of the responsible portfolio ministry to reflect the particular political circumstances out of which the felt need for a judicial tribunal emerged in the first place. In these designs, the structural rule-of-law implications of the tribunal's role as an instrument of justice — as the surrogate for a court — have almost always been ignored. That the design of each Canadian judicial tribunal is idiosyncratic and that their structures are, as we will see, typically unprincipled from a rule-of-law perspective is surprising enough, but even more remarkable is the fact that although their justice-system role is obvious as a matter of fact, as a matter of law their place in Canada's constitutional arrange-

ments has yet to be determined. Finally ... it is important to remind ourselves at the outset what the rule of law means. In its Imperial Tobacco decision in 2005, the Supreme Court defined the role of the rule of law in Canada's Constitution:

> The rule of law is "a fundamental postulate of our constitutional structure" that lies "at the root of our system of government." It is expressly acknowledged by the preamble to the Constitution Act, 1982, and implicitly recognized in the preamble to the Constitution Act, 1867 ...
>
> This Court has described the rule of law as embracing three principles. The first recognizes that "the law is supreme over officials of the government as well as private individuals, and thereby preclusive of the influence of arbitrary power" ... The second "requires the creation and maintenance of an actual order of positive laws which preserves and embodies the more general principle of normative order" ... The third requires that "the relationship between the state and the individual ... be regulated by law."

MY OWN EXPERIENCE OF THE ADMINISTRATIVE JUSTICE SYSTEM

. . . .

But, but — I can hear the question — what about the letter from the grieving mother to the "so-called Tribunal"? Good question. I did not, however, tell that story to point to a tribunal gone wrong. The son's appeal had been given a fair hearing by a tribunal that was, as we shall see, as independent and impartial — as rule-of-law-compliant — as one could hope for, and, although no one can ever be satisfied that any adjudicative decision is right in any absolute sense, I was, and am, confident that this decision was, at least in law, correct. Certainly, it was a decision that would have withstood court scrutiny on judicial review. I told the story to make the point that what judicial tribunals do truly matters — as much as what courts do — and I wanted to make that point as clearly as possible at the outset.

. . . .

WHAT EXPERIENCE TEACHES

My experience with the administrative justice system recounted ... has led me to firm convictions on three fundamental points.

1. *What judicial tribunals do really matters — often desperately.* It was to drive this point home that I told the story about the blood-spattered missive from the grieving mother. What judicial tribunal members do is too important for them to be pursuing their own political or ideological goals, or dabbling in public service, or wending their way to a comfortable retirement; just like judges, they are engaged in serious business where the consequence of getting things wrong may be the infliction on the parties who appear before them, and on their families, of injustices and hardships of the gravest kind.

2. *Canadian administrative judicial tribunals and their members are not independent, do not meet the rule-of-law criteria for impartiality, and cannot be counted on for competence.* The evidence for this will be found throughout this book.

3. *Hardly anyone cares — on the evidence, certainly not the politicians or the bureaucrats.* In the spring of 2003, Auditor General of Canada Sheila Fraser blew the whistle on the federal Liberals' sponsorship scandal. At or about the same time, Peter Showler blew the whistle on patronage abuse at the Immigration and Refugee Board. Showler knew whereof he spoke. He was the outgoing chair of the IRB and had been a member of that Board for nine years. Here are some of the remarkable things he said to a reporter:

> Political patronage is a devastating blight on the Immigration and Refugee Board ... [It] undermines the Board's work, the morale of its staff and the implementation of Canada's immigration and refugee policy ... Political influence ... is pervasive and pernicious ... [The Board's] real problem is ... mediocrity and incompetence among some of its members [caused by political patronage] ... The Board is hobbled by patronage ... [P]olitical infighting within the [federal] Liberal Party and caucus over who should get the patronage plums has often resulted in lengthy delays in filling vacancies, despite unprecedented pressure on the Board to perform ... Members who get mediocre or even bad [performance] ratings can find themselves appointed to a second term because of political connections, while members who have excelled are sometimes denied a second term ... The Board's internal process for evaluating the work of its members can also become tainted by political influence, with managers coming under political pressure to give positive evaluations to members who have more powerful political friends than they do.

Federal government officials and politicians know that the competent implementation of Canada's troubled immigration and refugee policy depends on the quality of the people appointed to the IRB. They also know that these appointees are entrusted with adjudication of the immigrant or refugee status of individuals — frightened individuals, often in desperate straits, whose future and the future of their families, and sometimes their very lives, depend on a fair, competent, and timely adjudication of their rights. In light of these facts, it seems to me that it should be plain for all to see that the patronage abuse of IRB appointments described by Showler is on moral and ethical grounds far more shameful than the mere misappropriation of public funds. Yet, unlike Sheila Fraser's revelations, Peter Showler's equally public and authoritative exposé appears to have startled no one; it certainly sparked no outrage, led to no inquiry, threatened no one's job, and brought down no government. Nor, of course, was Showler the first to highlight the problem of patronage in appointments to administrative judicial tribunals; indeed, there had been a long history of known patronage abuse at the IRB itself. I cite this one instance as a particularly compelling demonstration of a general problem: except for its victims, no one seems to be concerned about our shameful administrative justice system.

．　．　．　．

WHAT THIS BOOK IS ABOUT

Given that administrative judicial tribunals are the only embodiment of our justice system that most Canadians will ever personally face, and that the decisions of those tribunals are often life-altering for the parties involved, casual admirers of Canadian justice would presumably expect to find in these tribunals what they expect to find in Canadian courts: a strong tradition of independence, impartiality, and competence. Instead, however, we have an executive branch system of judicial tribunals where the reality is typically an intransigent culture of government dominance and control, a system that ignores the rule of law and the Constitution, and a system that is, at a minimum, careless of competence. The executive branch proclaims its administrative judicial tribunals to be independent in their decision making, but requires that they operate in the ordinary course under the influence of pervasive conflicts of interest that are irredeemably toxic to any reasonable perception of independence or impartiality, conflicts that would not be tolerated in any other setting.

.   .   .   .

The judicial functions that comprise this system are all deployed, controlled, and administered by the executive branch of government. From the beginning, the executive branch has understood that permitting these judicial functions to be protected by the structures required of a rule-of-law-compliant justice system — structures designed to ensure the independence and impartiality of the bodies exercising the judicial functions — would be inimical to its interests, and has simply chosen not to permit it. Thus, everywhere in Canada (with the exception of Quebec) we have a state-sponsored justice system to which the majority of our rights disputes have been assigned for final adjudication but where the rule of law has been willfully disrespected and actively resisted — by the government. As I say, a scandal.

7 | Basic Values and Their Protection

(a) Basic Values and Their Protection

David W. Elliott

DEFINITION

Basic values are values that societies consider to be especially important. For example, many Western democracies claim to prize individual worth and dignity; more socialist countries stress the notions of community and equality. Non-dictatorial societies value public control of government. Often, these individual and general values are supplemented by the special values of specific groups.

FORMS OF STATE SUPPORT

One of the most important phenomena of our time is the tendency to protect basic values by recognizing them as legal rights. Supporters argue that some basic values are not just desirable benefits, but moral rights to which individuals or groups should be entitled. Governments may respond by enshrining these values in legislation or constitutional enactments, for enforcement by courts or court-like constitutional tribunals. Canada, with its human rights codes, bills of rights, and *Charter*, illustrates this tendency.

Recognizing basic legal rights is not the only possible means of supporting basic values. For example, the state can support these values through conventions of self-restraint. By staying out of certain areas, it can carve zones of freedom for individuals and groups. Alternatively, the state can intervene positively through its legislative and executive branches to protect or promote general values, such as law and order and economic equality.

CHARACTERISTICS

Although recognizing basic values as legal rights changes their status, it may not transform their underlying character. Basic values are subjective, often controversial, relative rather than absolute, and can conflict with each other. Legal status doesn't automatically end these features. It makes the values enforceable, and subjects them to definition by judges and legislators. Entrenched constitutional status raises their impact one rung higher. It makes them enforceable even against legislators, and subject only to courts.

KINDS[1]

Basic values may focus mainly on individuals, groups, or society as a whole. Individual values include freedom of speech and conscience, and religion; group values include collective bargaining interests; and more general social values include law and order, security, education, and social welfare.[2] Individual and group values are normally thought to require protection against harmful action by the state or private actors; general social values are normally thought to require promotion by the state or private actors.

INDIVIDUAL AND GROUP RIGHTS: PROTECTION PHASES

The Canadian state has passed through three distinct phases in protecting individual and group values, phases that correspond to shifts in emphasis

129

from convention to statute to constitution. Throughout this time, the state has also undergone a gradual evolution in promoting general social values.[3] We will look first at the protection of individual and group values.

In phase one,[4] from 1867 to the Second World War, individual values were protected mainly by self-restraint. The politician had a negative "enforcement" role here, bound by tradition to respect the rule of law and the conventions of responsible government. The courts' role was marginal. Much depended on a sense of decency and community among individual citizens. Some group rights — such as denominational school rights and certain language rights — had constitutional protection, but this was exceptional.

From the Second World War to 1982, there was an increasing tendency to regard some important individual or group values as moral rights, and a tendency by Canadian governments to recognize and protect the claimed moral rights in law. The focus was on statutory protections, such as human rights codes and bills of rights. These were directed mainly against potential abuses in the private sector, but the bills of rights were directed against abuse by the state. None of these statutes had entrenched constitutional status.

In phase three, after April 17, 1982, Canadians supplemented self-restraint and statutory safeguards with constitutional guarantees.

These marked the latest step in general movement not only toward greater state protection, but also toward greater judicial protection, of basic individual and group values.

Some might regard this movement as one of increasing enlightenment and progress, with the *Charter* standing near the pinnacle.[5] Certainly things were far from perfect during the traditional phase in Canada. Self-restraint assumes a high level of tolerance and shared interests, features that are sometimes lacking, and may do little to remove discrimination against the disadvantaged. Consider, for example, *Christie v. York Corporation*,[6] where a black man had been refused a drink at a city-operated tavern because of his colour. The Supreme Court refused to help because they were unwilling to restrict the principle of freedom of commerce! Another example of unfairness was the Canadian government's internment of Japanese Canadians during the Second World War. Even basic democratic rights weren't shared equally. Women — one-half the population — were denied the right to vote in federal elections until 1918, and in Quebec provincial elections until 1940. Registered Indians on reserves could not vote in federal elections until 1960, and later in some provincial elections. Clearly, changes of some kind were imperative.

Nor were things anywhere near perfect under the régime of human rights codes and bills of rights between the Second World War and April 17, 1982. The codes did provide statutory penalties and administrative sanctions for combatting discrimination, and soon spread to every jurisdiction. But these are specialized tools, limited to discrimination by private individuals, groups, and government in regard to such areas as employment, public accommodation, and public communications. As well, three provinces and the federal government enacted bills of rights during this period. Unlike the codes, the bills of rights are intended to provide individuals with rights against the state. These range from the right to equality before the law to criminal procedural rights in the federal bill, and even educational rights in the Quebec statute. The other remaining provincial bill, in Alberta, is rarely invoked.

The federal bill, the *Canadian Bill of Rights*, was rarely invoked successfully, and left behind a trail of conflicting case law. The first and last time the Supreme Court applied the equality guarantee to render a federal statute inoperative was in the 1970 *Drybones* case.[7] Four years later, an Indian lady named Mrs. Lavell complained that the eligibility provisions of the *Indian Act* discriminated against her on the basis of sex. Under the Act, an Indian woman lost her Indian status when she married a non-Indian man, but when an Indian man married a non-Indian woman, he retained his Indian status. The majority of the Supreme Court refused to invalidate the eligibility provisions.[8] They said that since eligibility is a necessary part of federal constitutional power regarding Indians, the Bill would have to be more explicit than it was in order to invalidate the provisions. They added that equality means equality in the administration of the law by the law enforcement authorities and the ordinary courts. Mrs. Lavell, unlike Mr. Drybones, had not suffered inequality in this special sense.

The *Lavell* decision was followed by further refusals to enforce equality, and by further shifts in the definition of the concept. As a result of cases like these, the *Canadian Bill of Rights* was regarded by many as a failure. Indeed, the perceived weaknesses of the *Canadian Bill of Rights* contributed to the strong public support in the 1970s and the 1980s for a constitutional charter of rights.

However, the perception of continuous progress in protecting basic individual and group values is not beyond question. First, although Canada has had some dismal failures (e.g., the long-delayed enfranchisement of women), in many areas (such as freedom of speech) its traditional record was more passable. Although the early human rights codes were marginal and weak, legislatures have broadened their scope and have created human rights commissions to oversee them. Although the *Canadian Bill of Rights* failed to strike down the sexual discrimination provisions of the *Indian Act*, it led to legislative changes to the Act that were more complicated and sophisticated than anything that could have been achieved by a judicial fiat.

Second, some of the supposed failure of the *Canadian Bill of Rights* may be attributable not to its unentrenched status but to the nature of the values it sought to protect. Basic values tend to be less than absolute, uncertain in scope, and often in conflict with other values.[9] The legal status of the *Bill of Rights* was only part of the problem in cases like *Lavell*. As well as saying the *Bill* had not been sufficiently explicit, four of the majority judges also redefined equality in terms that were hardly recognizable from *Drybones*. Some of this inconsistency may be understandable. Like most basic values, equality is an extraordinarily complex, relative, and policy-laden concept.[10] It can't be applied without subjective comparisons between different social groups, and trade-offs between conflicting social interests. In *Lavell*, for example, the Court not only had to compare the situation of Indian men and women, and that of Indian and non-Indian women, but it also had to balance the individual rights of Indian women against the group rights of Indians to an eligibility scheme. More generally, the Court had to balance the principle of equality against the principle of special status for Canadian Indian people.

The complex, contingent, and relative nature of many basic values can be seen from other examples. Economic freedoms are of limited use to those without property to protect. Freedom of speech for one citizen may be slander for another. Procedural safeguards for some may threaten law and order for others. Individual workers' rights can clash with collective bargaining interests. Group cultural interests, such as Quebec society's interest in preserving the French language and culture, may conflict with non-French group values and the individual value of freedom of expression.

Third, the modern legal and constitutional protections for basic values come in a "package deal". They are enforced in courts, which have a strong reputation for procedural fairness and impartiality, but are slow, expensive, inexpert, limited by constraints of precedent, evidence, and procedure, and unelected.

They are enforced by law, which is backed by force. The drama, costs, and adversarial format of litigation are poorly suited to compromise and accommodation. Judicial enforcement can overshadow other priorities such as education, ethics, and development of a greater sense of social involvement and responsibility among individual citizens.

This is not to suggest that movement to stronger legal and judicial protections is necessarily misguided. It would be folly to try to turn back the clock to a traditional golden era of rights protection that never existed. But when we assess the relationship between the *Charter* and individual and group values, it is helpful to consider all sides of the ledger.

PROMOTION OF GENERAL SOCIAL VALUES

In discussions about basic values, general social values tend to be overlooked, or subsumed in discussions about rights. However, while most basic individual and group values have acquired the status of moral or legal rights, most general social values have not. Their emphasis is on public responsibility, not private entitlement. For general social values, state intervention tends to take the form of schools, police forces, workers' compensation programs, rent control, environmental regulation, and state health insurance, rather than legislative codes, bills of rights or constitutional charters. Change here has usually been a gradual process, rather than a series of observable shifts in protection mechanisms.

The main feature of this change has been increasing state involvement in promoting general social values.[11] Before Confederation, the state's role was relatively modest, limited mainly to defence, law and order, and assisting with transportation facilities and colonial settlement.[12] Most social help was left to religious or local charitable organizations.

Toward the end of the century, the state expanded its involvement in providing education. The First World War brought a number of state pension and other social welfare schemes, and the inauguration of a national income tax. Although

131

some of these schemes ended with the war, social disruption from the Depression of the 1930s and the Second World War led to the key elements of the modern welfare state — unemployment insurance, state medical insurance, an expanded government pension plan, and a national social assistance plan.[13] As well, provincial governments became more and more involved in education and other social programs. These programs were accompanied by increased state regulation of industry to promote public interests such as fairness to consumers, health, safety, and environmental concerns.

For advancing most general social values, law is used more as a facilitator than as an enforcement mechanism. During the 20th century, state involvement here has been significant. Nevertheless, verdicts of "progress" must be qualified. First, the modern Canadian welfare state remains a place of great economic disparity where many thousands lack jobs, adequate shelter, and adequate food.[14] Second, there can be great controversy about the general social values to support. During the 1990s, for example, there was a heated debate between proponents of deficit reduction and those who insisted on maintaining the integrity of existing social programs. Both fiscal responsibility and the benefits of the welfare state were represented as social values that are basic to the whole community. The proponents of fiscal responsibility gained the upper hand, and the "progress" of the welfare state went into reverse. By the beginning of the next century, the debt situation had improved, and some money flowed back into social programs. It was hard to predict what would happen to the welfare state in the new century.

Finally, it should be noted that some state efforts in support of general social values can threaten other values. This is a special risk with public security measures. As seen later in this chapter, in 2001, the Canadian government responded to the alarming September 11 terrorist attacks in the United States with a package of security measures that sharply limited personal civil liberties.[15] The provisions of the *Anti-Terrorism Act*[16] imposed raised serious concerns about citizens' access to fair trials, to privacy, and to freedom of association and speech. Responding to some of these concerns, the federal government submitted the preventive and warrantless arrest powers and the investigative hearing provisions to a five-year sunset provision. But during the pre-sunset period, and for the many provisions outside the sunset provision, the concerns remain.

Notes

1. Cf. the civil/political/social rights classification of T.H. Marshall, "Citizenship and Social Class" in David Held et al., eds., *States and Societies* (Oxford: Basil Blackwell, 1985) at 248–60, *infra* note 4.
2. These are distinctions of degree, not of kind. For example, some individual values have significant collective or general aspects to them. Equality can include the notion of absence of discrimination against an individual on the basis of his or her membership in a group, and political involvement (through voting or running for election, etc.) is an individual value directed at participation in the community as a whole. Note that Marshall, *ibid.*, and *infra* note 5, distinguishes between political rights and other individual "civil" rights.
3. Cf. Marshall, note 5, *infra*.
4. For phases one and two, see W.S. Tarnopolsky, *The Canadian Bill of Rights*, 2d ed. (Toronto: McClelland & Stewart, 1975) (up to 1975); D. Gibson, *The Law of the Charter: General Principles* (Toronto: Carswell, 1986) Ch. 1.
5. For example, the relatively optimistic historical account in *The Law of the Charter: General Principles*, *supra* note 4. For quite a different "progressivist" approach to rights, in an English context, see T.H. Marshall, "Citizenship and Social Class" in David Held et al., eds., *States and Societies* (Oxford: Basil Blackwell, 1985) at 248–60. Marshall says citizenship or full membership in a community can give rise potentially to three different kinds of rights — civil rights, such as freedom of speech and the right to property and justice; political rights, such as the right to vote and participate in political institutions; and social rights, such as the right to education and basic economic welfare. He argues that the first kind of rights to be attached to citizenship were civil rights. These were followed by political rights, and more recently by some social rights. Marshall thinks this latter development will limit the scope for economic inequalities. Note that in Canada, at least, Marshall's "social rights" are generally moral rights or expectations, rather than legally enforceable rights. They would correspond roughly to the general social values discussed below. Compare Marshall's view with that in Isaiah Berlin, *Two Concepts of Liberty: An Inaugural Lecture Delivered Before the University of Oxford on 31 October 1958* (Oxford, England: Clarendon Press, 1958); and in H. Glasbeek and M. Mandel, "The Legalization of Politics in Advanced Capitalism" in R. Martin, [guest] ed. *Critical Perspectives on the Constitution* [Socialist Studies Series] (Winnipeg, Man.: Society for Socialist Studies, 1984) 84 at 93–108.
6. [1941] S.C.R. 139.
7. *R. v. Drybones*, [1970] S.C.R. 282. Mr. Drybones, a Northwest Territories Indian, was charged with being drunk off a reserve, contrary to a provision of the *Indian Act*. However, the corresponding territorial ordinance only penalized drunkenness in a public place, and imposed lower penalties. Mr. Drybones argued that this contravened the equality guarantee in the *Canadian Bill of Rights*, and won his case. A majority of the Supreme Court said equality before the law is violated when government makes it an offence, punishable on account of race, to do what others can do freely. It said the *Bill of Rights* is more than a mere canon of construction, and renders inconsistent legislation inoperative.
8. *Canada (A.G.) v. Lavell*, [1974] S.C.R. 1349.
9. See, however, R. Dworkin's arguments that controversies about rights can be adjudicated in a relatively objective manner: *Taking Rights Seriously* (Cambridge, Mass.: Harvard University Press, 1977) Chs. 4 and 13.
10. See also Chapter 10, below.
11. See generally, R.I. Cheffins and R.N. Tucker, *The Constitutional Process in Canada*, 2d ed. (Toronto: McGraw-Hill, 1976) at 49–57; C.D. Baggaley, *The Emergence of the*

Regulatory State in Canada 1867–1939, Economic Council of Canada Technical Report No. 15 (Ottawa: Economic Council of Canada, 1981) at 70; T.L. Powrie, "The Growth of Government" in T.C. Pocklington, ed., *Liberal Democracy in Canada and the United States* (Toronto: Harcourt Brace & Co. 1985) Ch. 2; W.T. Stanbury, *Business-Government Relations in Canada* (Toronto: Methuen, 1986); W.T. Stanbury, "Direct Regulation and Its Reform: A Canadian Perspective" (1987) *Brigham Young University L. Rev.* 467; A. Moscovitch, "The 'Benevolent' State" in A. Moscovitch and J. Albert, eds., *The "Benevolent" State* (Toronto: Garamond Press, 1987) Ch. 1; A.C. Cairns, "The Past and Future of the Canadian Administrative State" (1990) 40 *U.T.L.J.* 319; A. Moscovitch, "Welfare State" in J.H. Marsh, ed., *The Canadian Encyclopedia*, Year 2000 ed. (Toronto: McClelland & Stewart, 1999), at 2493–96.

12. See "Historical Development", Chapter 2, above.
13. See generally, A. Moscovitch, "Welfare State" in J.H. Marsh, ed., *The Canadian Encyclopedia*, supra note 11.
14. See, for example, J. Porter, *The Vertical Mosaic* (1965); *Report of the Royal Commission on Taxation* (1966); D. Olsen, *The State Elite* (1980); and L. McQuaig, *Behind Closed Doors* (1987).
15. Other Western governments enacted broadly similar measures. In the United States, see the *USA Patriot Act*, Pub. L. 107–56, 26 October 2001. In Britain, see the *Terrorism Act 2000*, 2000, c. 11 and the *Anti-terrorism, Crime and Security Act 2001*, 2001, c. 24.
16. S.C. 2001, c. 41.

(b)   A Democratic Approach to Civil Liberties†

Peter H. Russell

[Russell wrote this article in 1969. How relevant is it in the era of the *Charter*?]

In our society the phrase 'civil liberties' is apt to conjure up the image of the great popular majority, the demos, crushing the sacred rights of the individual or the small minority. For, traditionally 'The Tyranny of the Majority' has been the great peril which has inspired our active civil libertarians to seek safeguards for the fundamental rights and freedoms of the individual. For this tradition of civil liberty the most attractive panacea has been the instrument of a bill of rights — a fundamental code of basic rights enforced by a group of wise and independent judges against the illiberal demands of legislative majorities and their executives. In Canada it has been the common mission of a whole generation of civil libertarians to press for a bill of rights which would effectively guarantee that neither national nor provincial majorities could ride roughshod over minority rights.[1] ...

Those of us who are concerned about the quality of liberty in our civil society should step back for a moment and take a good long look at the approach to civil liberty which the bill of rights proposal represents. How realistic is it as a diagnosis of the main threat to our liberty? How plausible is its prescription for our emancipation? Do you feel menaced by the prospect of the great Canadian majority, acting through its elected representatives in Ottawa, steam-rolling over your basic rights and liberties in pursuit of its own interests? ...

When we confront the realities of democratic life in the modern state, we recognize at once the fantasy quality of the paradigm of majority tyranny and minority rights. In no significant way does the majority conduct the government of a large modern democracy. Certainly governments in democracies govern in the name of the people, or of the majority; also in a vague sort of way the exigencies of periodic elections, legislative debates, public discussion, and pressure-group activity make it incumbent on our democratic governments to be sensitive to a larger range of claims and interests than they might otherwise consider. But the majority of citizens themselves do not, and indeed cannot, deliberately rise up and seize the power formally granted to them by democratic constitutions to realize their ends at the expense of severe deprivations of the minority's freedom. It has been a central preoccupation of western political science for more than half a century to explain that this is so. One suspects that even civil libertarians of the classical mould have heard that message, in at least one of their ears, and yet they continue to fulminate about the need to check the will of the majority by a judicially enforced code of basic rights.

---

† (1969), 19 U.T.L.J. 109 at 109–11, 114–15, 117–20, 122–23, and 128–31. Reproduced with permission from University of Toronto Press (www.utpjournals.com).

. . . .

... In the history of political ideas it was the guiding instinct of democratic theory to seek a design for power which by virtue of popular participation would make government less coercive. From the Renaissance until the emergence of 'mature liberal democracies' in relatively modern times, this was the path along which the main core of western political thought sought to provide for a maximum of liberty in an ordered society. But in our century and in our society it has very nearly become an abandoned path. This is because we have lost the thread of democratic theory as our guide to the enlargement of our civil liberty. For the most part we have become either disillusioned or complacent about the democratic character of our system of government. We no longer are armed with a theory of democracy which we can use as a critical device for liberalizing the exercise of public authority.

. . . .

... [W]e should return to the original inspiration of democratic philosophy to find effective ways of enlarging the citizen's liberty or preventing its diminution. Such a course means seriously examining the possibility of overcoming or at least reducing the barriers to fulfilling the underlying aspiration of democracy — the ideal of diminishing coercion and expanding freedom by making government responsive to the interests of the governed.

To explore thoroughly the various avenues towards a more thorough democratization of our public life would be an enormous task, far exceeding the scope of this paper. Much of the idealism of the 'New Left' is already directed along this path. The principal point which I wish to urge here is that this orientation rather than the conventional advocacy of judicial checks on popular power is the correct approach to civil liberty. The fundamental libertarian problem is not too much democracy but too little democracy.

Still it is worth while suggesting some of the more promising means for increasing the democratic character of our system of public authority. Within the context of our large modern governments, there are two factors of crucial importance to our democratic possibilities — the scale and the scope of governmental activity.

The scale of government is likely to have a decisive influence on the degree to which government policy coincides with the preferences of the governed. Where individuals have different preferences concerning policy issues, the larger the group to be governed the more likely it is that some dissenting portion of the group will be subject to a governmental decision contrary to its members' interests.[7] Or, to put the same point another way, smaller units of government have a better chance of coinciding with groups of people that are more nearly homogeneous in their policy preferences. This, of course, is the essential justification for federal systems of government, and for the decentralization of authoritative decision-making generally.

. . . .

... [I]f as liberals we are genuinely committed to maximizing the individual's capacity for self-development, we should recognize that in our day and age it is as essential to be critical of unnecessary exercises of governmental coercion, as it is to attack avoidable sources of private coercion. Indeed one of the liberal's key areas of concern should be precisely those forms of government intervention in the broad fields of social welfare and education, where the objective is to provide individuals with vital economic or cultural opportunities which they would not otherwise enjoy. All too often the regulatory side of governmental activity in these fields has been extended far beyond the point required to redress the mal-distribution of opportunity in society....

. . . .

... Now it should become the goal of the committed democrat to overcome the grossest sources of social and economic inequality in order to give some real content to the constitutional guarantee of political equality. Even in terms of merely voting in elections, the evidence suggests that the distinction between voter and non-voter corresponds with basic social differences. As E.E. Schattschneider pointed out in his classic analysis of the limits of organized politics in the United States, 'Every study of the subject supports the conclusion that non-voting is a characteristic of the poorest, least well-established, least educated stratum of the community.'[10] Or again, as Robert Dahl wrote in acknowledging the prime social barriers to the effective realization of political equality, 'By their propensity for political passivity the poor and uneducated disenfranchise themselves.'[11]

The focal point of any programme aimed at raising the political efficacy of the socially disenfranchised must be the educational opportunities in an essential step in removing the most severe social and economic disabilities of the disenfranchised; in a more fundamental way, the content of education must direct people towards the effective exercise of their political rights. Universally accessible public education up to any level will do little to improve the democratic quality of our system if that education is conducted in an authoritarian way.

. . . .

... I wish to advocate ... a much larger and more systematic use of public opinion polls.

. . . .

The classical solution to the inter-election problem was the practice of representative government: it was the function of the elected representatives to sensitize government to public opinion. More recent political science has included the activity of organized pressure groups and lobbies as an essential component in the process of exposing government to the demands and interest of the governed. But neither the elected legislature nor the network of organized interests is able to provide a fair indication of the range of opinion on many policy issues. Parliamentary parties and members of parliament are often notoriously out of touch with large segments of the community; all too often they are overly sensitive to the interest of some special group in the community. Pressure groups tend to be highly elitist within their own structures; anyone who has belonged to a trade union or a professional organization should realize how frequently there is little correspondence between the views of the organization's officials and those of its rank and file members. And then there are a host of interests and preferences which, for a variety of reasons, never become well enough organized to enter into the so-called 'bargaining' process of modern pluralistic government at all.

In advocating frequent and systematic consultation of public opinion polls by government, I am not calling for a system of government by plebiscite. I am not suggesting that government automatically adjust its policy to follow the results of the latest gallup poll. The use of opinion polls which I favour is as a counter-weight to the unbalanced character of the influences to which government is subject through parliamentary and pressure-group activity. Well-conducted polling is the only way to give public representation to that body of opinion which, because of the mal-distribution of political efficacy in our society, does not gain access to the established channels of political communication.

. . . .

Any assessment of the bill of rights idea must begin by recognizing that a really effective bill of rights would entail a transfer of power from the legislative branch of government to the judiciary....

. . . .

... [I]t is essential to recognize the kind of decision-making which is involved here. The process of applying the general ideals inscribed in a bill of rights involves a delicate balancing of social priorities. As anyone who has given this question a little thought must acknowledge, 'fundamental rights and freedoms' cannot be treated as ethical absolutes. Those who subscribe in a general way to these values will invariably insist that in practice they must be circumscribed; exponents of freedom of speech will make an exception of laws against slander and libel or obscenity; advocates of religious freedom will endorse the prohibition of the 'religious experience' associated with LSD; opponents of racial discrimination will support laws restricting the distribution of liquor to Indians; adherents of fair trial procedures do not usually insist that all administrative agencies affecting the rights of the citizen follow all the 'fair hearing' requirements of normal courtroom procedure; and so on. Reasonable, liberal persons will certainly disagree on which exceptions to allow, but the question raised here is who should resolve these issues — the court or the legislature?

A simple majority-rule democrat might conclude that the answer is obvious — the legislature which represents the majority must settle these issues as it should settle all others, for otherwise we would have a system of minority rule. As it stands, this is not a very convincing answer, even for the democrat. For it assumes that the majority's views are expressed through the decisions of the elected legislature — a most dubious assumption in the light of hard-headed political science which has shown us how unlikely it is that the host of decisions made by elected officials in the modern democratic state will always reflect the views of a majority of its citizens. Besides, some of the rights and freedoms asserted in bills of rights, especially the communicative freedoms, refer to social practices which are essential if a genuine majority will is to be articulated in the political process.

But the majority-rule democrat is on the right track. For a society that aspires to be democratic should formally resolve the most important questions of public policy through its elected legislature. And

135

the delicate balancing of social priorities involved in adopting the fundamental concepts of political freedom and civil rights to the other goals of public policy is certainly among the most important issues of government. Granted that the representative legislature may not always be truly representative, it is still the branch of government whose deliberations are most thoroughly exposed to public purview and whose decisions enter most immediately into political debate and discussion. The concrete determination of the degree to which the state should permit its citizens to enjoy the kinds of rights and freedoms listed in a bill of rights is among the most significant of a community's policy-making tasks. It is far too important an exercise in social ethics to be left to appointed judges in the cloistered sanctuaries of judicial tribunals.

. . . .

The bill of rights approach assumes that the legislative majority is the most serious threat to civil liberty and that traditional courts of law provide the most effective vehicle for overcoming the illiberal acts of the aggressive majority. This approach is wrong on both counts. It is the executive side of government, the ever-expanding bureaucratic labyrinth, public or semi-public, whose members make those day-to-day decisions which have a vital and immediate effect on what the citizen can or cannot do — it is this side of government, not the legislature, which is most likely to deprive the individual citizen of some fundamental right or encroach unfairly on his liberty. It is true that, according to the legal doctrine of parliamentary supremacy which our country is suppose to follow, everything this bureaucracy does must ultimately find some authorization in a formal legislative act. It might therefore seem sufficient protection for the citizen to be able to ask a court to determine whether the government official who allegedly mistreated him exceeded the powers given him by the legislature. Unquestionably the citizen has such a legal right which occasionally is effectively asserted in our system. But he might have to spend many years and risk thousands of dollars in legal costs in the process of exercising this right. Besides, our legislatures bestow on the executive vast areas of discretionary power which are beyond review by even the most aggressive of courts.

The legal profession's limited social vision has, I suspect, been the prime factor in blinding many of its members, including so many of those who would describe themselves as civil libertarians, to the inadequacy of traditional judicial techniques for correcting abuses of executive power....

Such realistic complacency is completely blind to how seldom in fact the traditional legal remedies are relevant or available to the individual who finds himself confronted by what he regards as an unfair or incompetent act by a government official or bureau. In such situations what the individual usually requires, most urgently, is a quick, impartial, and inexpensive investigation of his complaint. A less legalistic, more realistic perspective would surely acknowledge that it is of little avail to inform the individual caught in such a situation that for several hundred dollars he can consult a lawyer to find out whether it is worth going to court and that, in any case, his particular grievance is likely not a 'legal' issue but deals with some question of administrative neglect or oversight beyond the courts' ken.

It is the great merit of the ombudsmen movement to recognize the short-comings of existing legal devices for reviewing citizens' complaints of abusive administrative acts....

. . . .

The ombudsman-like institutions advocated for Canada are, unlike courts, not decision-making institutions — they are primarily investigatory agencies. Their principal function is to investigate the citizen's complaint of maladministration and to initiate legal action or recommend administrative or legislative reform where remedial action seems to be required. In practice, Scandinavian experience suggests that only a small percentage of grievances, probably under ten per cent, would warrant any corrective action, after initial investigation. But this does not detract from the merits of the scheme, for fundamentally the ombudsman should be regarded as a technique for improving our system of public communication. Above all, he should help to plug that yawning gap in our communications system between the individual citizen affected by a particular governmental act and the elected representatives finally responsible for the acts of all public authorities. It would also do something to counteract the worst consequences of a system which enables the members of a privately run guild, the legal profession, to enjoy a monopoly in the distribution of legal knowledge.

. . . .

But the Ombudsman is only one example of the more direct ways of achieving many of the values which a bill of rights is designed to secure. To take another example, racial equality, if we learn anything from the American experience it is that a bill of rights like that of the USA does very little to alleviate racial discrimination in the private sector where, in a 'free-enterprise' society, it is most serious. For this task an agency such as Ontario's Human Rights Commission which can take the initiative in enforcing egalitarian norms directly on private employers and landlords will be a much more useful instrument than a bill of rights.[29]

What we must recognize is that just as on the input side of collective decision-making our political technology must evolve novel methods for organizing and gauging public demand and interest, so also on the output side we require new institutional techniques for identifying and correcting abuses of public authority. In the future, government, no matter how sensitively and democratically we adjust its range and scale, will penetrate the lives of ordinary citizens so deeply that it would be folly to continue to rely on the thin and sticky trickle of formal court-room litigation as the prime defence of our rights. Today we should be no more inclined to accept the established judicial procedures as adequate for the purpose of mediating between the citizen and the state, than the

leading English lawyers of several centuries ago were willing to acquiesce in a system which left the monarch's personal discretion as the final repository of justice between citizens.

Notes

1. See, for example, F.R. Scott, *Civil Liberties and Canadian Federalism* (Toronto: University of Toronto Press, 1959); D.A. Schmeiser, *Civil Liberties in Canada* (London: Oxford University Press, 1964); Bora Laskin, "The Supreme Court and Civil Liberties" (1955), 41 *Queen's Quarterly* at 455; W.F. Bowker, "Basic Rights and Freedoms: What Are They?" (1959), 37 *Can. Bar Rev.* at 43; Mark R. MacGuigan, "Civil Liberties in Canada" (1965), 72 *Queen's Quarterly* at 270.

...

7. For an exposition of the logic of this proposition see Roland Pennock, "Federal and Unitary Government-Disharmony and Frustration" (1959), 4 *Behavioural Sciences* at 147–57.

...

10. E.E. Schattschneider, *The Semisovereign People* (New York: Holt, Rinehart and Winston, 1960), at 105.
11. Robert A. Dahl, [*Who Governs?: Democracy and Community Power in an American City* (New Haven, CT: Yale University, Press, 1961)], at 81.

...

29. Mr. Trudeau, in stating the case for including egalitarian rights in his proposed charter of human rights, acknowledges the importance of provincial and federal legislation aimed at enforcing such rights in the private sector. See his *A Canadian Charter of Human Rights* (Ottawa: The Queen's Printer, 1968), at 25.

(c) Democracy and Rule of Law[†]

A.C. Hutchinson and P. Monahan

NOTE

What is meant here by the "thick" and "thin" versions of the rule of law? What are Hutchinson and Monahan's main criticisms of the rule of law approach they ascribe to the legal philosopher Ronald Dworkin? How valid are the criticisms? How viable is the alternative approach suggested here? Does it provide a satisfactory resolution of the apparent tension between judicial rights enforcement and traditional processes of democracy? Why, or why not?

EXTRACT

The Thick and the Thin

If not non-democratic in aspiration and orientation, the Rule of Law is democratically indifferent in character and scope. The enduring concerns of the Rule of Law are the limitation of state power, the maintenance of a broad sphere of private liberty and the preservation of a market-exchange economy. In its many academic manifestations, it has been connected, to greater and lesser extents, to an individualistic theory of political justice and jurisprudence.

---

† Excerpts from A.C. Hutchinson and P. Monahan, eds., *The Rule of Law: Ideal or Ideology* (Toronto: Carswell, 1987) 96 at 100–102, 106–108, 111, 112, 114–116, and 117–23. [Notes omitted.] Reproduced with permission of the authors. [Commentary note by David W. Elliott.]

Ostensibly, there have been two versions of the Rule of Law, but they both represent a commitment to liberalism; it is simply that one tends to be more explicit and marked than the other.

The "thin" version of the Rule of Law amounts to a constitutional principle of legality. It demands that government be conducted in accordance with established and performable norms; its voice remains silent or, at best, whispered on the issue of substantive policies. Rule must be by law and not discretion. Also, and especially, the lawmaker itself must be under the law, at least until it changes the law. In this "thin" form, the Rule of Law is targeted against arbitrary government and palm-tree justice....

Although far from explicit or necessarily so, its substantive tendency is clearly toward a liberal society in which the best government is the one which governs least. However, unless such a constitutional requirement of official legality is supplemented by a "thicker" theory of political justice, the Rule of Law will be a weak restraint on an ambitiously unjust regime. It might even tend to legitimate its substantive excesses under a patina of formal justice. Unrepresentative government and the Rule of Law are not mutually exclusive; democracy is an entirely dispensable feature of this form of the Rule of Law. As Herbert Hart has observed, "however great the aura of majesty or authority which the official system may have, its demands in the end must be submitted to moral scrutiny." Accordingly, a full and proper defence and understanding of the Rule of Law must be based on its foundational and substantive political connections.

The "thick" version of the Rule of Law incorporates the thinner one as merely one dimension of a liberal theory of justice. This conception of the Rule of Law goes back to the Greeks and Romans, but finds its modern roots in the Enlightenment. Indeed, there is an almost direct line of descent from the theory and practice of 17th century England to that of late 20th century Anglo-America. The intellectual lineage runs almost unbroken from John Locke and Thomas Hobbes to John Rawls and Ronald Dworkin, through Thomas Paine, John Stuart Mill, A.V. Dicey and Friedrich Hayek. The modern defence of this "thick" version posits the necessary connection between procedural and substantive justice. The Rule of Law demands that positive law embody a particular vision of social justice, structured around the moral rights and duties which citizens have against each other and the state as a whole.

. . . .

The Contemporary Debate:
Democratizing the Rule of Law

The work of Ronald Dworkin, temporarily at least, dominates the animated contemporary debate over the judicial role under the Rule of Law. Adjudication is claimed to satisfy the Rule of Law by meeting the democratic demand for judicial objectivity and the popular need for political equity. While some rail that an activist judiciary is antithetical to democratic governance, Dworkin argues that, if judges are to fulfil their democratic responsibilities under the Rule of Law, they must make political decisions, albeit not personal or partisan ones. His claim is bold and brilliant. The traditional formalistic, rule-book conception of the Rule of Law requires judges in hard cases to be unconstrainedly creative or to dissemble. Dworkin's rights conception of the Rule of Law incorporates a dimension of substantive fairness and thereby appropriately constrains and guides the judge in the resolution of hard cases. In defending such a version of the Rule of Law, Dworkin keeps himself firmly within the tradition of Locke and the constitutional priority of liberty; "the idea of individual rights ... is the zodiac sign under which America was born."

For Dworkin, judges are political actors whose power is limited by a legal system's history and its liberal character. The state does not give them a blank check on which to write in the political currency of their choice; they must interpret the regnant legal materials in their best light as a theory of political morality. The judge breathes political vitality into the lifeless words of legal texts by applying the twin tests of "formal fit" and "substantive justice." Any interpretation must be able to demonstrate some plausible connection with society's legal history. However, the better theory is not necessarily the one that accounts for the most decisions or statutes; "formal fit" is only a heuristic device or rule-of-thumb. This requirement acts as a threshold and combines with the test of "substantive justice." This obliges the judge to develop a scheme of rights which a just state would establish and enforce. While this task can only be provisionally and partially performed, the conscious striving for such a perfected theory is the hallmark of adjudication under the Dworkinian conception of the Rule of Law. Accordingly, judicial power is legitimated by this commitment to uphold the existing political order of rights and only to extend it in a consistent and principled manner. In this way, law is and remains rational, just and objective.

It is to Dworkin's credit that he does not disguise his individualistic revitalization of the Rule of Law. He openly concedes that his conception might well exact a price in the development of a communitarian spirit. Yet, anxious to deflect charges of being insufficiently democratic, he reminds us that his conception of the Rule of Law "enriches democracy by adding an independent forum of principle ... [where] justice is in the end a matter of individual right, and not independently a matter of the public good." He casts the Supreme Court as the central constitutional institution through which the citizenry can debate, articulate and implement its collective standards for social justice. Dworkin is not alone in elevating legal conversation to a privileged form of democratic discourse. Joined by other writers, like Owen Fiss and Laurence Tribe, Bruce Ackerman has gone so far as to suggest that:

> Not that a vigorous and constructive legal dialogue can ever hope to compensate for an apathetic and muddled political debate. Yet the reverse is also true: political commitment is no substitute for legal deliberation. While the future of America depends on the American people, the future of American law depends, in a special way, on the way American lawyers interpret their calling.

DEMOCRATIC INDIVIDUALISM AND THE RULE OF LAW

. . . .

These claims that the Rule of Law can serve as an indispensable means of popular control are profoundly mistaken. The Rule of Law sustains elitist politics, with its impoverished sense of community. It does so in at least two related, but distinct ways. First, the Rule of Law's language of rights reinforces the assumption that communities are nothing more than aggregations of private interests. Rightholders are defined in contradistinction to the community rather than as integral components of it. Second, and more significantly, a politics dominated by the Rule of Law is a politics with limited scope for popular participation and control. It cramps and compresses the ability of individuals to debate and define the conditions of their communal life. In attempting to avoid the tyranny of the majority, it mistakenly embraces a doctrine of expertise and dependency which carries with it a subtle, yet despotic dominion of its own.

Citizens as Rightholders

. . . .

... [For rights theorists, i]ndividuals are entitled to be treated as ends in themselves, rather than as a means to someone else's ends. In order to give effect to this background political ideal, it is necessary to specify the conditions under which each individual's qualities of moral agency and personality are recognized. These political conditions form a coherent whole. They can be expressed in the form of a series of entitlements or rights which must be respected by the community if it is to be true to the notion of individual autonomy. A community cannot be said to be just or rightly ordered until and unless it recognizes and guarantees these individual rights. Such a schema represents the fixed fulcrum around which democratic politics must swing.

Although this rights theory purports to leave basic democratic principles intact, it frustrates and paralyzes them. This results as much from what is excluded as included in the theory. Significantly, a rights-based conception of the Rule of Law has an impoverished or non-existent conception of communal politics....

. . . .

The difficulty with this individualistic ideology is that it ignores and suppresses actual human experience. Individuals are located in history, within a context of allegiances. They are not abstract or bloodless, but are in part constituted by their social context. To divorce individuals from this structure of allegiances is to rob them of the "railings to which [individuals] can cling as they walk into the mist of their social lives." It stunts the possibility of developing a set of shared ends and values, a precondition to the emergence of a genuine populist democratic practice. By developing a moral sense and practical experience of community, individuals will be better able to contribute to the growth of a shared set of values and institutions in accordance with which social life could be organized. Persons might come to be respected as themselves and not as simply rightholders. In this way, society could develop a modus vivendi that encourages caring and sharing and actualizes the possibility for meaningful connection with others.

Adjudication and Social Change

Notwithstanding the corrosive implications of rights-based theories for communal aspirations, the

Rule of Law might still be characterized as the ally of democracy. Democratic politics is usually thought to involve a utilitarian calculus of the general welfare. There is no guarantee that this calculus will be conducted in a principled manner. Individual claims to autonomy and personhood might be ignored or bypassed simply in order to further the ephemeral interests of the community as a whole. On this view, the Rule of Law is required in order to ensure that considerations of principle and individual right enter into the societal calculus. The institution of judicial review is an attempt to transform a jungle of deals into a world of rights. As Ronald Dworkin urges, judicial review promises that "the deepest, most fundamental conflicts between individual and society will once, someplace, finally, become questions of justice."

. . . .

The Rule of Law is premised on a set of beliefs about the relation between adjudication and social behaviour. It assumes that judicial decisions are a significant and positive instrument for shaping popular attitudes and social action. As an explanation of social change, the account is simplistic and lacks any empirical foundation. Indeed, the gathering of social data to ground their instrumental assumptions forms no part of the agenda of traditional jurisprudence. The limited available evidence suggests that the public is only vaguely aware of judicial activity and that there is little correlation between judicial pronouncements and societal life. For instance, numerous opinion surveys confirm that the public has only marginal awareness of legal institutions and decisions....

. . . .

Of Vitamins and Virtues

... The meaningful issue is why an elite judiciary should have responsibility for making such decisions in the first place. Reliance on the Supreme Court undermines popular control and participation in the policy-making process. Although the Supreme Court receives extensive attention in the media and the law reviews, publicity is no substitute for participation and does not overcome the exclusion of citizens from such debate. The media is dominated by much the same elite voices and institutional actors as litigation. For citizens, Supreme Court judges seem to resemble inscrutable Platonic figures who make decisions in which they have no part and of which they are largely ignorant. When a decision does come to

their attention, they are likely to disagree with it. This further decreases the extent to which individuals have control over their own lives.

The citizens' role as distant spectators is exacerbated by the arcane and stylized language of constitutional litigation. As disputes move into the magnetic field of law, they are translated into the received argot. To partake of the law's special privileges and prizes, citizens must become proficient in its idioms and nuances. In this way, legal discourse enforces its own canons of relevance, rationality and reasonableness. The lawyerly sentinels of power ensure that citizens comport to the rules of constitutional grammar; those who do not are deprived of a voice and are rendered powerless. The courts' historical function has not been to express popular justice, but rather "to ensnare it, control it and to strangle it, by re-inscribing it within institutions which are typical of a state apparatus."

. . . .

... [A]dvances in social justice have been achieved through legislative rather than judicial action. Both Canadian and American courts have been as much a source of reaction and chauvinism as of edification and enlightenment. Much of the social welfare legislation enacted by the federal government in the 1930s was ruled unconstitutional by the courts as an intrusion on provincial jurisdiction. The practical effect of these decisions, such as the *Unemployment Insurance Reference* of 1937, was to make the enactment of such legislation impossible since the provinces lacked the fiscal resources to undertake such costly programs. The judicial decision in this particular instance was overcome only after the political branches of government secured a constitutional amendment which specifically empowered the federal government to put in place an unemployment insurance scheme.

. . . .

Even in the so-called "progressive" constitutional decisions, the difficult question is whether the elimination of popular control in favour of an elite institution like the Supreme Court will actually promote the long-term cause of justice and equality. At the institutional level, there may be a marked negative effect. Because judicial decisions tend to persuade people that things are being done, reformative energy may be frustrated and other governmental institutions may feel relieved of the pressure and responsibility to initiate and facilitate social change.

Moreover, the assumption seems to be that values such as justice and freedom can be defined in some external forum, like the Supreme Court, and then simply foisted on a recalcitrant public. But the reality is precisely the opposite. Public values cannot be abstractly manufactured in some antiseptic political laboratory and administered, like vitamin tablets, to a malnourished and lethargic mass.

Values such as justice and equality are the products of politics, not its antecedents. They take root in a public that engages in debate and argument and that is given the opportunity to nurture notions of reasonableness and commonality. Deprived of such empowerment, public values corrode and civic energy dissipates. Deferring to "specialists," citizens lose the capacity to define their own values and traditions. Public morality will atrophy rather than be energized. The appointment of the judicial philosopher king exacerbates the problem it was intended to remedy.

Democracy means the greatest possible engagement by people in the greatest possible range of communal tasks and public action. As people reclaim control over their own lives, they will develop an appetite and a talent for more. This rejects the prevailing pessimism about the competence of ordinary citizens; their present apathy and disaffection is a product of their current powerlessness rather than any natural infirmity. This insight is easily forgotten in a setting in which the opportunities for meaningful popular participation are few. The central importance of participation and debate in the shaping of public morality can only be grasped by focussing on an institution which rejects values of expertise and elitism in favour of participatory self-government.

Such an institution is the jury system. To suggest that the jury system represents a paradigm of democratic practice may seem anachronistic or naïve. Critics on both the right and the left have condemned the jury as a device to legitimate bigotry, ignorance or racism. These criticisms of the jury parallel those issued against democracy in general; the basic complaints are that these institutions produce decisions that are oppressive and that individual citizens are incapable of making such decisions.

Yet, whatever the failings of individual juries, the jury system as a whole embodies to a remarkable degree values of self-government. The jury system rejects rule by experts; people assume the responsibility for making important civic decisions on a rotating basis. Discussions and argument are central to the success of the institution. The jurors do not simply observe the trial and then cast their votes individually in the privacy of a polling booth. They are expected to arrive at a common verdict, through persuasion and argument. Without such debate, "the jury system as a whole would be devalued, and ... individual jurors would value their own roles less." The jury system represents a commitment to the principle that the ordinary citizen is competent to debate and decide important issues in the community. As E.P. Thompson states,

> I can imagine better laws and I can imagine better jurors, but I cannot imagine a better system. I would like to think of the jury system as a lingering paradigm of an alternative mode of participatory self-government, a nucleus around which analogous modes might grow in our town halls, factories and streets.

With its emphasis on persuasion, argument and consensus, it is democratic rule writ small. True, the jury often acts as a rubber stamp for state values, but it can also act as a lamp of liberty which might illuminate the potential and power of ordinary people.

There is no quick fix for bigotry or prejudice. Certainly, it would be naïve to suppose that such deplorable attitudes would simply disappear with the dawn of a genuine democratic community. Democracy does not guarantee civic enlightenment. But if communal morality is to become more informed and developed, this will be achieved through more rather than less democracy. It is only through public talk that small minded or superficial attitudes might be exposed and attacked. The ambition is not to attain some romantic or utopian harmony, but a political order which facilitates individual participation in the continuing social deliberation over political ends.

Judicial musing, enforced by fiat, is no substitute for civic deliberation. Rule by judiciary supposes that the only way to deter oppression is to impose external restraints on the political process. But because such restraints deny the moral competence of citizens, they undermine the very process of reflection and self-criticism which might lead to a more mature collective morality. Elitist politics breed only a mob; the nurturing of citizens demands democratic culture.

CONSTRUCTION AND CONSTRAINT

The Rule of Law democrat lives in a society bereft of community. Given its historical obsession with abstract individual rights and liberties, liberal legalism stymies the establishment of a truly communal modus vivendi in which people can satisfy their collective and personal aspirations. Within a legalistic ethic, communal ambitions are destined to remain etiolated. We have tried to free democracy from its bondage to the Rule of Law. Emancipated, it might serve rather than stifle the flourishing of communal life and fulfilled citizens.

. . . .

A commitment to democracy does not mean that constraints on popular decision making must always and everywhere by condemned. It is important that the basic institutions and practices of democracy — free elections, debate and assembly — be guaranteed and extended. Further, democracy implies the necessity for general laws which do not single out particular groups or individuals for special treatment and which are applied in nondiscriminatory fashion across the whole community. But there is a distinction between constitutional safeguards which constrain democratic activity in the name of democracy and those which constrain democratic activity in the name of "right answers." The latter type of constraints seek to substitute the judgments of philosophy for those of the people simply because

the popular judgments are regarded as tainted. As Michael Walzer observes,

> ... any extensive incorporation of philosophical principles into the law ... is ... to take them out of the political arena where they properly belong. The interventions of philosophers should be limited to the gifts they bring. Else they are like Greeks bringing gifts, of whom the people should beware, for what they have in mind is the capture of the city.

Democrats should always be wary of constraints that seek to substitute the cold hand of philosophy for popular judgment, no matter how presently plausible or attractive they might appear. Of course, instances will arise in which public sentiments appear so wrong-headed that they demand instant repudiation. Even a committed democrat would likely be tempted by the siren song of the Rule of Law. But to tie oneself to the post of "principle" is to court seduction rather than salvation. Far from purifying public morality, it would merely ensure its continued debasement.

(d) The Legalization of Politics in Advanced Capitalism†

H. Glasbeek and M. Mandel

NOTE

Compare the views expressed in the extracts earlier in this chapter with those of the English writer T.H. Marshall in "Citizenship and Social Class" in David Held et al. (eds.), *States and Societies* (Oxford: Basil Blackwell, 1985), 248–60 (and see "Basic Values and Their Protection", in this chapter). Now consider the approach taken by Glasbeek and Mandel. Early in their article, Glasbeek and Mandel argue that the *Charter* was originally less a response to popular demand than a way of helping sell the idea of entrenched language rights. They claim that judicial enforcement of guaranteed rights tends to be reactionary, ignores class differences, and deflects energy from political participation. See also M. Mandel, *The*

Charter of Rights and the Legalization of Politics in Canada (Toronto: Thompson Educational Publishing, 1992).]

EXTRACT

In his influential *Legitimation Crisis*, Habermas has noticed [that extensive state involvement in the economy breaks down the illusion that the economy is a "private" matter, whose ownership in the hands of a few is a matter beyond the concern of the general public]:

> Genuine participation of citizens in the processes of political will-formation ... that is, substantive democracy, would bring to consciousness the contradiction between administratively socialized

† Excerpts from R. Martin, [guest] ed., *Critical Perspectives on the Constitution*, vol. 2 (Winnipeg, Man.: Society for Socialist Studies, 1984) 84 at 93–108. Reproduced with permission of the publisher. [Commentary note by David W. Elliott.]

production and continued private appropriation and use of surplus value.[136]

The solution for capitalism, Habermas suggests, is "a system of formal democracy" which among other things involves "a legitimation process that elicits generalized motives — that is, diffuse loyalty — but avoids participation. This structural alteration of the bourgeois public realm provides for application of institutions and procedures that are democratic in form, while the citizenry ... enjoy the status of passive citizens." Successful depoliticisation of the public realm entails two "residual requirements" for Habermas. One is "civic privatism — that is, political abstinence combined with an orientation to career, leisure and consumption." The other is a *justification* of the structural depoliticisation itself, which is supplied "either by democratic élite theories ... or by technocratic systems theories.[137]

For [Habermas and another author], the heavy involvement of the state in the private sphere requires that the state be somehow de-democratized, that some way be found to ward off real popular participation, when demands for it are likely to be stepped up. One of the arguments in support of the *Charter of Rights* is a dissatisfaction with the possibility of real popular participation in the modern capitalist state. We suggested [earlier] that, as a solution to the failings of democracy, the *Charter of Rights and Freedoms* seemed a strange instrument compared to the more obvious solution of democratising popular institutions. This peculiarity disappears, however, when we see that the problem is not to *enhance* real democracy but rather to *avoid* that enhancement by offering some formal substitute.... [T]he legalization of politics does not mean that fundamentally different results will obtain just because courts become more prominent in decision-making, but that a different form of legitimation for the retention of the same non-democratic relations of power has come to the fore.

. . . .

... The crisis of late capitalism, at least in advanced capitalist countries such as Canada, is fundamentally an economic one of severely declining living standards for workers.... This cannot be legitimated by the kind of "civil privatism" envisaged by Habermas, premised as it is on consumerism. And it cuts the ground out from under "technocratic systems theories" types of justifications for a lack of

democracy, since these depend on the "goods" being delivered by the expert technocrats. Consequently, according to O'Connor, "new legitimations ... have to be essentially political in nature" ...

. . . .

... The legalization of Canadian politics represented by the *Charter of Rights and Freedoms* promotes a false unity, that is, one not built on class lines, in an attempt to maintain in the public sphere at least, this distinction between economic and political issues.

No doubt, some of the concrete rights that might be comprehended by the abstract formulations in the *Charter of Rights and Freedoms* are rights that socialists would fight for. Others, however, are rights that we should fight against. As we noted earlier, given that the interest, points of view and strategic judgments of courts sometimes diverge from those of legislators, and even from those of the bourgeoisie, victory in the courts is sometimes possible. But history tells us that there will be many more losses than victories.... We should not be seduced or forced to do our fighting in courts according to the rules devised for capitalism's maintenance and survival.... We should not do our fighting by denying the existence of class. On the contrary; it is at this moment that we should be doing our fighting on the basis of class. Collaboration in the legalization of politics will prevent us from doing this.[145]

Notes

136. J. Habermas, *Legitimation Crisis* (Boston: Beacon Press, 1975). [For Habermas the preferable response to legitimation and motivation crises is a more genuine democratization of society based on respect for equality and pluralism: S. Seidman, *Jürgen Habermas on Society and Politics: A Reader* (Boston: Beacon Press, 1989) at 295. For Habermas' more recent thoughts on democratic theory, see J. Bohman, "Complexity, Pluralism, and the Constitutional State: On Habermas' *Faktizität und Geltung*" (1994) 28 *Law & Society Review* 897.]

137. *Ibid.* at 36–37.

...

145. It is not for us to pontificate on the forms the struggle must take. From our point of view, however, the object of struggle must be the widest and deepest democratisation of both the so-called "private" and "public" spheres. Among other things [such as proportional representation, real popular or lay participation in government agencies, more frequent use of referenda, deprofessionalisation of the legal profession, and increased democratic participatory rights in the private sphere] this must include a restriction of judicial power to the narrow confines which enable the attainment of the ideal of the rule of law.

(e) *Canada (Citizenship and Immigration) v. Harkat*†

NOTE

After the terrorist attack in the United States of America on September 11, 2001, governments around the world took measures to improve their national security. In the Canadian context, some of the actions taken by the federal government were challenged in court in an attempt to declare these measures as unconstitutional. In *Charkaoui v. Canada (Citizenship and Immigration)*, [2007] 1 S.C.R. 350, the Supreme Court of Canada reviewed the security certificate system used to detain and deport non-citizens found in the *Immigration and Refugee Protection Act* (*IRPA*). Initially, the security certificate system was found to be overly secretive because it denied the person named in the certificate the opportunity to know the case put against him or her and to contest the government's action under this regime (para. 65). In turn, the lack of information impaired the Court's ability to decide the matter on all the relevant facts and law as any decision would necessarily be based on a part of the relevant evidence. In this connection, the Court found if the affected individual's right to life, liberty, and the security of the person was to be satisfied, either the person must be given the necessary information, or a substantial substitute for that information must be found (paras. 50–52). As there were less intrusive ways to protect the individual, namely using special counsel to act on behalf of the affected person, the judicial approval of certificates was found to be inconsistent with the *Charter*. However, the declaration that the law was of no force or effect was suspended for a year in order to permit Parliament an opportunity to bring the *IRPA* into conformity with the *Charter* (paras. 139–141).

In 2008, Parliament responded to the *Charkaoui* decision and made several amendments to the *IRPA*, including crafting a role for special advocates, who were used to protect the interests of affected persons in closed hearings after having received disclosure of the record: *Canada (Citizenship and Immigration) v. Harkat*, 2014 SCC 37 at para. 10. Mohamed Harkat was alleged to have come to Canada for the purposes of terrorism. A security certificate declaring him inadmissible to Canada on national security grounds was issued against him under the former legislation. The new security certificate scheme permitted a second security certificate to be issued against Harkat. The second certificate was referred to the Federal Court to determine its reasonableness. Among other things, this case decided that the security certificate scheme under the revised *IRPA* was constitutional, and it was eventually appealed to the Supreme Court of Canada.

In *Harkat*, the revised *IRPA* was found to be constitutional. After an unprecedented secret hearing (para. 23), the Supreme Court of Canada ruled on a number of issues, declaring that the *IRPA* was constitutional, given the broad discretion given to judges to consider the fairness of the government's action and the place of the special advocates to act as substitutes for the named person in the process (para. 77).

When reviewing the excerpt of the case below, ask yourself the following questions. Would you want to be subject to this legislative process if you were suspected of being involved in terrorist activities? If not, why not? Would this scheme pass constitutional scrutiny under section 7 if it applied to Canadian citizens as well as to permanent residents and foreign nationals? If your answer to these questions is in the negative, what implications does this decision have for the notion that section 7 guarantees that "[e]veryone has the right to life, liberty and security of the person and the right not to be deprived thereof except in accordance with the principles of fundamental justice"? Is it merely hyperbole to suggest that the war on terror has amounted to a proxy war on our Constitution, given the fact that the government has justified a significant erosion of the *Charter* rights of non-citizens in Canada based on its national security interests? Finally, ask yourself whether the collective security interests of the state ever justify the restriction on rights that we see in *Harkat*. In light of the decision of the Supreme Court of Canada in *Harkat*, should this security cer-

---

† 2014 SCC 37.

tificate system be reformed? If so, how would you accomplish such a task? If not, why not?

EXTRACT

[McLACHLIN C.J. (LeBel, Rothstein, Moldaver, Karakatsanis and Wagner JJ. concurring):]

. . . .

Overview of the IRPA Scheme
COMMENCEMENT OF PROCEEDINGS

[30] A security certificate may be issued by the ministers for the removal from Canada of a non-citizen (whether a permanent resident or a foreign national) who is inadmissible on security grounds. The grounds for inadmissibility include engaging in terrorism, being a danger to the security of Canada, engaging in acts of violence that would or might endanger the lives or safety of persons in Canada, or being a member of an organization that engages in terrorism: s. 34, *IRPA*. The ministers must have reasonable grounds to believe that the facts giving rise to inadmissibility have occurred, are occurring, or may occur: s. 33, *IRPA*.

[31] As a practical matter, the process commences when CSIS presents a Security Intelligence Report ("SIR") to the ministers. The SIR sets out in detail the allegations and evidence grounding inadmissibility. If the ministers conclude that the allegations in the SIR are reasonably grounded, they issue a security certificate.

[32] Once the certificate is issued, the ministers must refer it to the Federal Court: s. 77(1), *IRPA*. The Federal Court judge who is designated to hear the case "shall determine whether the certificate is reasonable and shall quash the certificate if he or she determines that it is not": s. 78, *IRPA*. If the designated judge deems the certificate to be reasonable, the named person is inadmissible and the certificate becomes a removal order in force: s. 80, *IRPA*. The named person may be arrested and detained for the duration of the proceedings before the Federal Court: s. 81, *IRPA*.

THE DISCLOSURE OF SUMMARIES TO THE NAMED PERSON

[33] The named person must be given summaries of the information and evidence which allow him to be reasonably informed of the case against him: ss. 77(2) and 83(1)(e), *IRPA*. The summaries must "not include anything that, in the judge's opinion, would be injurious to national security or endanger the safety of any person if disclosed": s. 83(1)(e), *IRPA*.

SPECIAL ADVOCATES

[34] The judge must appoint one or more special advocates to protect the interests of the named person in closed hearings: s. 83(1)(b), *IRPA*. These hearings are held *in camera* and *ex parte*, in order to permit the Minister to present information and evidence the public disclosure of which could be injurious to national security or endanger the safety of a person: s. 83(1)(c), *IRPA*.

[35] Special advocates are security-cleared lawyers whose role is to protect the interests of the named person and "to make up so far as possible for the [named person's] own exclusion from the evidentiary process": S. Sedley, "Terrorism and Security: Back to the Future?", in D. Cole, F. Fabbrini and A. Vedaschi, eds., *Secrecy, National Security and the Vindication of Constitutional Law* (2013), 13, at p. 16. During the closed hearings, they perform the functions that the named person's counsel (the "public counsel") performs in the open hearings. They do so by challenging the Minister's claims that information or evidence should not be disclosed, and by testing the relevance, reliability, and sufficiency of the secret evidence: s. 85.1(1) and (2), *IRPA*. They are active participants in the closed hearings. They may make submissions and cross-examine witnesses who appear in those hearings: s. 85.2(a) and (b), *IRPA*. The *IRPA* scheme also provides that the special advocates may "exercise, with the judge's authorization, any other powers that are necessary to protect the interests" of the named person: s. 85.2(c), *IRPA*.

[36] No solicitor–client relationship exists between the special advocates and the named person: s. 85.1(3), *IRPA*. However, solicitor–client privilege is deemed to apply to exchanges between the special advocates and the named person, provided that those exchanges would attract solicitor–client privilege at common law: s. 85.1(4), *IRPA*. As Lutfy C.J. put it, "[a]s between special advocates and named persons, Division 9 protects information and not relationships.... The information that passes between them, absent the solicitor and client relationship, is deemed to be protected": *Almrei (Re)*, 2008 FC 1216, [2009] 3 F.C.R. 497, at paras. 56–57.

[37] Strict communication rules apply to special advocates, in order to prevent the inadvertent disclosure of sensitive information. After the special advocates are provided with the confidential information

and evidence, they "may, during the remainder of the proceeding, communicate with another person about the proceeding only with the judge's authorization and subject to any conditions that the judge considers appropriate": s. 85.4(2), *IRPA*. Read plainly, "this prohibition covers all information about the proceeding from both public and private sessions, including any testimony given in the absence of the public and the named person and their counsel": *Almrei*, at para. 16. By contrast, any other person — such as the ministers' counsel or the court personnel in attendance at closed hearings — is subject to significantly fewer restrictions on communication. Other persons must refrain from communicating about the proceedings only (i) if that person has had a court-authorized communication with the special advocates and the judge has specifically prohibited that person from communicating with anyone else about the proceeding, or (ii) if the communication would disclose the content of a closed hearing: ss. 85.4(3), 85.5(a) and (b), *IRPA*.

ADMISSIBILITY OF EVIDENCE

[38] The usual rules of evidence do not apply to the proceedings. Instead, "the judge may receive into evidence anything that, in the judge's opinion, is reliable and appropriate, even if it is inadmissible in a court of law, and may base a decision on that evidence": s. 83(1)(h), *IRPA*.

[39] The *IRPA* scheme provides that the judge's decision can be based on information or evidence that is not disclosed in summary form to the named person: s. 83(1)(i). It does not specify expressly whether a decision can be based in whole, or only in part, on information and evidence that is not disclosed to the named person.

The Section 7 Charter Right to a Fair Process

[40] In *Charkaoui I*, this Court found that the *IRPA* scheme engages significant life, liberty, and security of the person interests: paras. 12–16. Laws that interfere with these interests must conform to the principles of fundamental justice. If they fail to do so, they breach s. 7 of the *Charter* and fall to be justified under s. 1 of the *Charter*.

[41] Pursuant to the principles of fundamental justice, a named person must be provided with a fair process: *Charkaoui I*, at paras. 19–20. At issue in the present appeal are two interrelated aspects of the right to a fair process: the right to know and meet the case, and the right to have a decision made by

the judge on the facts and the law. The named person must "be informed of the case against him or her, and be permitted to respond to that case": *Charkaoui I*, at para. 53. Correlatively, the named person's knowledge of the case and participation in the process must be sufficient to result in the designated judge being "exposed to the whole factual picture" of the case and having the ability to apply the relevant law to those facts: *ibid.*, at para. 51.

[42] This said, the assessment of whether a process is fair must take into account the legitimate need to protect information and evidence that is critical to national security. As I wrote in *Charkaoui I*, "[i]nformation may be obtained from other countries or from informers on condition that it not be disclosed. Or it may simply be so critical that it cannot be disclosed without risking public security": para. 61.

[43] Full disclosure of information and evidence to the named person may be impossible. However, the basic requirements of procedural justice must be met "in an alternative fashion appropriate to the context, having regard to the government's objective and the interests of the person affected": *Charkaoui I*, at para. 63. The alternative proceedings must constitute a substantial substitute to full disclosure. Procedural fairness does not require a perfect process — there is necessarily some give and take inherent in fashioning a process that accommodates national security concerns: *Ruby v. Canada (Solicitor General)*, 2002 SCC 75, [2002] 4 S.C.R. 3, at para. 46.

[44] The overarching question, therefore, is whether the amended *IRPA* scheme provides a named person with a fair process, taking into account the imperative of protecting confidential national security information.

The Guiding Principles of the IRPA Scheme

[45] The alleged defects in the *IRPA* scheme must be assessed in light of the scheme's overall design. Two central principles guide the scheme.

[46] First, the designated judge is intended to play a gatekeeper role. The judge is vested with broad discretion and must ensure not only that the record supports the reasonableness of the ministers' finding of inadmissibility, but also that the overall process is fair: "[I]n a special advocate system, an unusual burden will continue to fall on judges to respond to the absence of the named person by pressing the government side more vigorously than might otherwise be the case": C. Forcese and L. Waldman, "Seeking

Justice in an Unfair Process: Lessons from Canada, the United Kingdom, and New Zealand on the Use of "Special Advocates" in National Security Proceedings" (2007) (online), at p. 60. Indeed, the *IRPA* scheme expressly requires the judge to take into account "considerations of fairness and natural justice" when conducting the proceedings: s. 83(1)(a), *IRPA*. The designated judge must take an interventionist approach, while stopping short of assuming an inquisitorial role.

[47] Second, participation of the special advocates in closed hearings is intended to be a substantial substitute for personal participation by the named person in those hearings. With respect to the confidential portion of the case against the named person, the special advocates must be in a position to act as vigorously and effectively as the named person himself would act in a public proceeding. Indeed, Parliament added special advocates as a feature of the *IRPA* scheme in order to bring it into compliance with the substantive requirements of s. 7 of the *Charter*, as articulated in *Charkaoui I*. Whether the scheme allows for this intention to become a reality is the central constitutional issue in this appeal, to which I now turn.

The Alleged Shortfalls of the IRPA Scheme

[48] In essence, Mr. Harkat alleges that the disclosure of public summaries and the representation of the interests of the named person by special advocates do not suffice to bring the *IRPA* scheme into compliance with the requirements of s. 7 of the *Charter*. I will address each of the alleged defects of the scheme in turn.

DOES THE SCHEME PROVIDE THE NAMED PERSON WITH SUFFICIENT DISCLOSURE?

[49] Mr. Harkat contends that the public summaries of the closed record are too vague and general. In his view, they do not allow a named person to know and meet the case against him or her. He argues that the essence of the right to know and meet a case is the ability to meet detail with detail. He also contends that the *IRPA* scheme takes too categorical an approach to disclosure: a named person will *never* obtain disclosure of information which would be injurious to national security or to the safety of any person, regardless of the importance of disclosure to the named person's case. A less rights-impairing alternative would be a balancing approach such as the one found in s. 38.06(2) of the *Canada Evidence Act*, R.S.C. 1985, c. C-5 ("*CEA*"), which permits the public interest in non-disclosure to be balanced against the public interest in disclosure.

[50] In my view, the *IRPA* scheme provides sufficient disclosure to the named person to be constitutionally compliant. I base this conclusion on the designated judge's statutory duty to ensure that the named person is reasonably informed of the Minister's case throughout the proceedings.

· · · ·

Concluding Remarks on the Constitutionality of the IRPA Scheme

[77] I have concluded that the impugned provisions of the *IRPA* scheme are constitutional. They do not violate the named person's right to know and meet the case against him, or the right to have a decision made on the facts and the law. However, it must be acknowledged that these provisions remain an imperfect substitute for full disclosure in an open court. There may be cases where the nature of the allegations and of the evidence relied upon exacerbate the limitations inherent to the scheme, resulting in an unfair process. In light of this reality, the designated judge has an ongoing responsibility to assess the overall fairness of the process and to grant remedies under s. 24(1) of the *Charter* where appropriate — including, if necessary, a stay of proceedings.

(a)   Scope and Interpretation of the *Charter*, and Judicial Activism†1

David W. Elliott

KEY ISSUES AND DIMENSIONS

Canada is now more than three decades into the *Charter* age. Entrenched protection of basic rights is a major part of contemporary constitutional reality. Canadian courts no longer play supporting roles in the constitutional drama: they are at the centre. Bound up with this new prominence and power is a basic question: how actively should our courts interpret the *Charter*? To help with this question, it is necessary to look at the most important elements of the *Charter*, to explore what we mean by activism, and then to examine some of the *Charter* decisions themselves.

We approached the first of these questions in a general way in the last chapter. Now it is time to look at the provisions of the *Charter* and see what the courts have done so far.

Like many documents, the *Charter* has several main dimensions. The first dimension, which will be addressed in this chapter, is its general scope. A second and related dimension is the scope and content of its individual rights, which will be examined in detail in later chapters. Throughout these readings, it will be helpful to keep in mind the first of our two basic questions: how expansively *should* our courts interpret the *Charter*?

SCOPE QUESTIONS

What subject matter is bound by the *Charter*? Who can benefit from it? When can its guarantees be overridden or restricted? How far can it be enforced? How broadly are rights violations and the rights themselves interpreted? These issues are aspects of the wider question: how actively do the courts construe the *Charter*?

WHO AND WHAT IS BOUND?

What subject matter is bound by the *Charter*? The *Charter* provision most relevant to this question is section 32, whose key words are "Parliament", "legislatures", and "government". Generally speaking, the meaning of section 32 has been construed as follows:

1. No subject matter, such as policy or foreign policy affairs, is automatically excluded from the application of the *Charter*.[2]
2. The *Charter* applies to the executive branch of government, including the administration,[3] as long as the institution is directly controlled by Cabinet or the central government agencies.[4]
3. The *Charter* applies to bodies implementing specific government policies.[5]

---

†   Revised and updated by Nick E. Milanovic.

4. The *Charter* applies to (a) legislation, including legislation regulating private activity,[6] (b) those functions of legislative assemblies that are not excluded by parliamentary privilege,[7] and (c) bodies exercising coercive statutory powers.[8]

5. The *Charter* applies to the courts (a) when they issue public orders on their own initiative,[9] and (b) when their decisions involve the executive branch, including prerogative power,[10] or the legislative branch.

6. The *Charter* does not apply to private activity,[11] except to the extent that one of the four situations immediately above is involved.

Note that this is an evolving picture. When the private activity exclusion was articulated in the 1986 *Dolphin Delivery* decision,[12] the *Charter* seemed to be restricted to quite a narrow legislative and governmental sphere. The main "non-governmental" application of the *Charter* appeared to be the situation in *Blainey*, where one of two private litigants launched a *Charter* challenge against legislation relied on by the other.[13] In the 1990 *McKinney* decision, it seemed that "government" would be strictly construed.[14] Since then, though, a growing number of otherwise "private" situations have been regarded as affected by legislative and governmental functions.[15]

WHO CAN BENEFIT?

Who can benefit from the *Charter*? This depends on the wording of individual *Charter* rights provisions, which vary in generality. However, where these provisions have wide subjects — such as "everyone" — the courts may have to provide some definition themselves. For example, to what extent can economic, corporate, and labour union interests invoke *Charter* help? This question arises especially in regard to the guarantee against deprivation of life, liberty, and security of the person without fundamental justice in section 7, and to the guarantees of freedom of expression and association in section 2. Note how the Court has attempted a precarious balancing act between commercial and corporate interests (e.g., *Big M*,[16] *Irwin Toy*,[17] *Ford*,[18] and *B.C. Motor Vehicles Reference*[19]) and those of labour and trade unions. How successful has this been? What are the implications for administrative law if section 7 is given broad economic content? For the *Charter* as an instrument of social reform or protection of the *status quo*? Does the Court's 2000

decision in *Blencoe* signal an effort to limit section 7 to criminal law and exceptional non-criminal law situations?[20]

WHEN CAN THE RIGHTS BE OVERRIDDEN?

The key override provision is section 33, which applies to section 2 and sections 7 to 15 of the *Charter*, and the key decision on section 33 is *Ford*.[21] As seen in *Ford*, the courts take a liberal approach to the legislature's powers to invoke the override. Despite this, it has been used on very few occasions. The Parti Québécois used the notwithstanding provision in the early 1980s to protest against the *Charter*, adding the clause to every provincial statute in the province.[22] After the defeat of the Partis Québécois in 1985, the provincial Liberal government ended the blanket override, but the clause continued to be used in the province, on over a dozen occasions.[23] It was used in 1986 in Saskatchewan to protect provincial back-to-work legislation from an apprehended *Charter* challenge, but was withdrawn when the legislation was held to be valid on its own.[24] In December 1988, the Supreme Court struck down a Quebec law that restricted the use of English on signs, on the ground that the law was an unjustified violation of *Charter* freedom of expression.[25] Almost immediately, Premier Bourrassa used the clause to protect a new law that restricted the use of English on outdoor signs. This move generated much concern outside Quebec. Many people regarded the action as a direct attack on *Charter* rights, made possible by the notwithstanding clause.[26] Since 1988, the notwithstanding clause has been used on a handful of occasions by the Quebec government. Outside Quebec, the only[27] use of the override was a 2000 Alberta statute on opposite-sex marriage, based on a private member's bill.[28] At least outside Quebec, then, there may be emerging a convention against use of the clause.

WHEN IS RIGHTS RESTRICTION JUSTIFIED?

The question of justification for *Charter* restriction relates mainly to section 1 of the *Charter*. Once a claimant has shown that the *Charter* applies to the situation at hand (by virtue of ss. 32 and 33), and that a *Charter* right has been breached, the onus shifts to government or the other parties relying on the restriction to show that the *Charter* right violation is justified under s. 1.[29] The more stringent the justification required under s. 1, the greater the force of the *Charter* guarantees. Section 1 provides that

> [t]he *Canadian Charter of Rights and Freedoms* guarantees the rights and freedoms set out in it subject only to such reasonable limits prescribed by law as can be demonstrably justified in a free and democratic society.

The key judicial requirements for section 1 have been stated in the *"Oakes"* test, named after the test articulated in *R. v. Oakes*, [1986] 1 S.C.R. 103. Note, however, that section 1 requires that a s. 1 limit be prescribed by "law" and that courts also require that a s. 1 limit be within the legislative authority of the legislature in question.

The *Oakes* test has two general components. The first general component is a requirement that the objective of the legislative provision breaching the *Charter* rights must be sufficiently important to justify breaching the right. This requirement is met if it can be shown that the provision's objective is "pressing and substantial".

The second general component is a three-part "proportionality" test. The first tenet of this test requires that the means the legislator has chosen to implement its objective must be rationally connected to this objective. The second tenet requires that the means used to implement the objective must infringe the *Charter* right as little as reasonably possible.[30] The third tenet requires that the benefits of the objective outweigh the costs of the harm caused by the *Charter* breach.[31]

Although the *Oakes* test looks objective, it leaves courts with a lot of discretion as to how they apply it. For example, the more widely the legislative objective is described, the easier it will be to find that the legislative objective is rationally connected to it. For the first tenet, there is room for many different criteria to determine what is "rational" and what constitutes a "connection". For minimal impairment, the Supreme Court has moved from requiring that the means infringe the *Charter* right as little as possible in a literal sense, to as little as *reasonably* possible.[32] The third tenet asks courts to quantify different degrees of importance when they look at the legislative objective. Underlying all these questions is the standard of proof to be used in measuring "harm". It appears that courts will require a lower standard for an activity that is more marginal to the purpose of a rights guarantee, and a higher standard for those that are more central.[33]

How closely does the *Oakes* test follow the literal wording of section 1? Has the *Oakes* test been applied more or less rigorously since its formulation in 1986? Which is the most important of the three proportionality tests? How objective are these tests? Should the rigour of section 1 vary with the subject matter of the litigation?

Section 1 has become the central forum for addressing conflicts between protected rights and general community concerns. Its interpretation in future cases will be crucial to the scope and the impact of the *Charter*.

HOW ARE RIGHTS AND RIGHTS VIOLATIONS CONSTRUED?

The question of the Court's interpretation of individual *Charter* rights relates more to the content than the scope of the *Charter*, and will be explored in subsequent chapters. At this point, though, it is relevant to note the Court's general approach to both scope and content. The Court set the stage for a liberal interpretation of the *Charter* in the early 1980s. At that time, it said that *Charter* interpretation should be generous rather than legalistic,[34] flexible rather than rigid,[35] and "purposive" rather than literal.[36] The Court said that the Constitution must be "capable of growth and development over time to meet new social, political and historical realities often unimagined by its framers"[37] and that it should be given a "generous interpretation ... to give individuals the full measure of the fundamental rights and freedoms referred to."[38] It said that the restrictive attitude to the *Canadian Bill of Rights* ought to be re-examined;[39] and that "[a]djudication under the *Charter* must be approached free of any lingering doubts as to its legitimacy."[40] On the other hand, the Supreme Court cautioned that the legislature should be left some discretion to carry out its "high duties".[41] It also said that courts should be careful "not to overshoot the actual purpose of the right or freedom in question"[42] or to question "the wisdom of enactments".[43] With these general cautions, the purposive approach continues as a key paradigm of *Charter* interpretation. In a recent decision, for example, the Court said:

> It is well accepted that the *Charter* should be given a generous and expansive interpretation and not a narrow, technical, or legalistic one.... The need for a generous interpretation flows from the principle that the *Charter* ought to be interpreted purposively. While courts must be

careful not to overshoot the actual purposes of the *Charter*'s guarantees, they must avoid a narrow, technical approach to *Charter* interpretation which could subvert the goal of ensuring that right holders enjoy the full benefit and protection of the *Charter*.[44]

Another general way of assessing the scope given to the *Charter* is to look at the relationship between the activity claiming *Charter* protection and legislation that allegedly restricts this activity. The Supreme Court said in *Big M* that the effects as well as the purpose of legislation are relevant in considering whether there has been compliance with the *Charter*, and that unconstitutional effects will render a law invalid even if its purpose was constitutional.[45] This is a more aggressive approach than under the *Constitution Act, 1867*, where unconstitutional effects will not affect the validity of a law with a valid constitutional purpose.[46] It has an especially important effect in equality jurisprudence, where laws can offend section 15 because of a discriminatory effect as well as a discriminatory purpose.[47]

HOW ARE REMEDIES ENFORCED?

Another scope frontier lies in the question of how and how far courts should enforce *Charter* rights. The first question, normally, is whether or not a legislative provision should be declared unconstitutional. Where the provision is ambiguous, a court may find that it can give it an interpretation that is consistent with the *Charter*.[48] This, in turn, may have the effect of invalidating some administrative action taken pursuant to the affected provision.[49]

If the court decides that a provision is inconsistent with the *Charter* and cannot be given an interpretation that is consistent with it, the court may be able to choose from potential alternatives such as the following:

1. Declaring the provision to be invalid (s. 52(1) of the *Constitution Act, 1982* says that any law that is inconsistent with the Constitution of Canada is of no force and effect to the extent of the inconsistency).[50]
2. Declaring the provision to be invalid and suspending the declaration of invalidity for a specified period of time.[51]
3. Severing the unconstitutional portion of the provision from the constitutional portion, and declaring the severed portion to be invalid.[52]

4. Reading in a portion of a provision that was unconstitutionally omitted.[53]
5. Declaring a constitutional exemption (a declaration that a provision is unconstitutional in regard to specified parties only).[54]
6. Awarding other remedies, in cases where section 24(1) of the *Charter* is invoked.[55]
7. Withholding a remedy.[56]

Each of the alternatives above raises its own set of questions, which in turn requires more guidance from the Supreme Court. For example, how willing should courts be to construe an ambiguous provision to make it consistent with the *Charter*?[57] In a case of unconstitutionality, how much of a provision should courts declare invalid? To put this another way, how broadly should courts define the extent of the inconsistency with the *Charter*?[58] What factors should govern the suspension of invalidity and the period of suspension?[59] Where should courts resort to severance or reading in?[60] When is a constitutional exemption appropriate?[61] Where are section 24(1) remedies appropriate?[62] To the extent that section 24(1) permits individual remedies such as damages, can they be combined with a declaratory remedy under section 52(1)?[63] What other remedies are possible under section 24(1), and when should they be awarded?[64] When should a court withhold a *Charter* remedy?[65]

Charter remedial action cannot be classed as activist or restrained simply in terms of the extent to which courts invalidate legislative provisions or administrative action. For example, a delayed declaration of invalidity can have a significant effect on a government legislative agenda. Severance, reading in, and constitutional exemptions can have the effect of substantially rewriting legislation. Positive remedies, such as reading in, can compel significant new government action and expenditures. *Charter* remedies, then, are as complex in their effects as they are discretionary in their use.

HOW BROADLY ARE THE RIGHTS CONSTRUED?

Although we cannot explore this question in detail until we look at individual *Charter* rights, we can note tentatively some apparent general interpretation trends. Throughout most of the 1980s, the Supreme Court took an enthusiastic, expansive approach to the *Charter*. It said judicial interpretation of the *Charter* should be generous rather than legalistic,[66] flexible rather than rigid,[67] and "purposive" rather than literal.[68] It said that the Constitution must be "capable of growth and development over time to meet new social, political and historical realities often unimagined by its framers";[69] that it should be given a "generous interpretation ... to give individuals the full measure of the fundamental rights and freedoms referred to";[70] that the restrictive attitude to the *Canadian Bill of Rights* ought to be re-examined;[71] and that "[a]djudication under the *Charter* must be approached free of any lingering doubts as to its legitimacy."[72]

Words of restraint were less frequent in the early years. The Court did concede that the legislature should be left some discretion to carry out its "high duties".[73] It did say it should be careful "not to overshoot the actual purpose of the right or freedom in question"[74], or to question "the wisdom of enactments".[75] McIntyre J. warned that "the *Charter* was not intended to turn the Canadian legal system upside down"[76] and that "[i]t is not for the Court to substitute its own views on the merits of a given question for those of Parliament."[77] McIntyre J. also said that "while a liberal and not overly legalistic approach should be taken to constitutional interpretation, the *Charter* should not be regarded as an empty vessel to be filled with whatever meaning we might wish from time to time."[78] But this caution was exceptional. McIntyre J.'s comments were in dissenting or separate majority opinions. During this early period, the Court's dominant tone was activist and positive.

By the mid-1990s, commentators noted that the Court was taking a significantly less interventionist approach to checking governmental power.[79] At least in some areas, there was a new tone of restraint.[80]

Is this still the case? Or has this pattern changed again in recent years? How *should* the courts approach the *Charter*? Compare the views expressed in the extracts in Chapter 7 with the nature and effect of the *Charter* cases in this volume. What is your view?

Notes

1. For additional reading on the *Charter*, see Select Bibliography below, Part III.B.
2. *Operation Dismantle v. The Queen*, [1985] 1 S.C.R. 441 at 472 and 479. Note, however, that the presence of wide-ranging legislative policy questions may have an impact on s. 1 analysis: see, for example, La Forest J. in *R. v. Edwards Books & Art Ltd.*, [1986] 2 S.C.R. 713 at 794: "I am of the view that the nature of the choices and compromises that must be made in relation to Sunday closing are essentially legislative in nature. In the absence of unreasonableness or discrimination, courts are simply not in a position to substitute their judgment for that of the legislature." See also *P.S.A.C. v. Canada*

(*Attorney-General*), [1987] 1 S.C.R. 424 at 442; *R. v. Morgentaler*, [1988] 1 S.C.R. 30 at 46, and 136–41; *Irwin Toy Ltd. v. Quebec (Attorney General)*, [1989] 1 S.C.R. 924 at 990; *McKinney v. University of Guelph*, [1990] 3 S.C.R. 229 at 304–305; *Re Canada Assistance Plan*, [1991] 2 S.C.R. 525 at 545–46 (in the context of a reference); *Lavigne v. O.P.S.E.U.*, [1991] 2 S.C.R. 211 at 338–39. Note the comment in *Symes v. Canada (Attorney General)*, [1993] 4 S.C.R. 695 at 753, saying that deference to legislative judgment on economic policy should be limited to analysis under s. 1 of the *Charter*.
3. *R.W.D.S.U. v. Dolphin Delivery Ltd.*, [1986] 2 S.C.R. 573 at 598 and 602.
4. *McKinney v. University of Guelph*, [1990] 3 S.C.R. 229 at 262; *Stoffman v. Vancouver General Hospital*, [1990] 3 S.C.R. 483; *Douglas/Kwantlen Faculty Association v. Douglas College*, [1990] 3 S.C.R. 570.
5. *Eldridge v. British Columbia (A.G.)*, [1997] 3 S.C.R. 624 at para. 43.
6. *Vriend v. Alberta*, [1998] 1 S.C.R. 493 at para. 65.
7. *New Brunswick Broadcasting Co. v. Nova Scotia*, [1993] 1 S.C.R. 319 at 373.
8. *Blencoe v. British Columbia (Human Rights Commission)*, [2000] 2 S.C.R. 307 at paras. 38 and 39.
9. *British Columbia Government Employees' Union v. British Columbia*, [1988] 2 S.C.R. 214 at 244.
10. *R.W.D.S.U. v. Dolphin Delivery Ltd.*, [1986] 2 S.C.R. 573 at 598–600.
11. *R.W.D.S.U. v. Dolphin Delivery Ltd.*, [1986] 2 S.C.R. 573 at 598–99. The Court's exclusion of private law activity raises the question of the viability of the general public/private matters distinction.
12. *R.W.D.S.U. v. Dolphin Delivery Ltd.*, [1986] 2 S.C.R. 573.
13. *Re Blainey and Ontario Hockey Association* (1986), 26 D.L.R. (4th) 728 (O.C.A.) at 735.
14. *McKinney v. University of Guelph*, [1990] 3 S.C.R. 229.
15. See, for example, propositions 4 to 6, above, and the following decisions: *Eldridge v. British Columbia (A.G.)*, [1997] 3 S.C.R. 624; *Vriend v. Alberta*, [1998] 1 S.C.R. 493, in *Blencoe v. British Columbia (Human Rights Commission)*, [2000] 2 S.C.R. 307.
16. *R. v. Big M Drug Mart Ltd.*, [1985] 1 S.C.R. 295.
17. *Irwin Toy v. Quebec (A.G.)*, [1989] 1 S.C.R. 927.
18. *Ford v. Quebec (A.G.)*, [1988] 2 S.C.R. 712.
19. *Reference re Section 94(2) of Motor Vehicle Act (British Columbia)*, [1985] 2 S.C.R. 486.
20. See *Blencoe v. British Columbia (Human Rights Commission)*, [2000] 2 S.C.R. 307.
21. *Ford v. Quebec (A.G.)*, [1988] 2 S.C.R. 712.
22. On the blanket override in Quebec and the Supreme Court's approach to it in 1988, see L. Weinrib, 'Learning to Live with the Override' (1990) 35 McGill L.J. 541. For a history of use of the override in Canada, see T. Kahana, "The Notwithstanding Mechanism and Public Discussions: Lessons from the Ignored Practice of Section 33" (2001) 43 Can. J. of Public Admin. 255; Peter W. Hogg, *Constitutional Law of Canada*, 2005 student ed. (Scarborough, Ont.: Carswell, 2005), section 36.2.
23. *Ibid.*
24. *Saskatchewan v. Retail, Wholesale and Department Store Union*, [1987] 1 S.C.R. 424.
25. See *Ford v. Quebec*, [1988] 2 S.C.R. 712, discussed in Chapter 9.
26. See generally Russell, Peter H., *Constitutional Odyssey: Can Canadians Become a Sovereign People?*, 2d ed. (Toronto: University of Toronto Press, 1993) Ch. 9.
27. Hogg notes that the clause was included in a provision in a 1982 statute of the Yukon Territory that was never brought into force: Hogg, *Constitutional Law of Canada*, *supra* note 22.
28. *Marriage Amendment Act*, S.A. 2002, c. 3, s. 5.
29. The general order of approach (after a decision that the activity is sufficiently governmental) was described in *Ford*

v. Quebec (A.G.), [1988] 2 S.C.R. 712, 166 as follows: "First, consideration will be given to the interests and purposes that are meant to be protected by the particular right or freedom in order to determine whether the right or freedom has been infringed in the context presented to the court. If the particular right or freedom is found to have been infringed, the second step is to determine whether the infringement can be justified by the state within the constraints of s. 1. It is within the perimeters of s. 1 that courts will in most instances weigh competing values in order to determine which should prevail."

30. See *R. v. Sharpe*, [2001] 1 S.C.R. 45 at para. 96, stressing that "it is not necessary to show that Parliament has adopted the least restrictive means of achieving its end. It suffices if the means adopted fall within a range of reasonable solutions to the problem confronted. The law must be reasonably tailored to its objectives; it must impair the right no more than reasonably necessary, having regard to the practical difficulties and conflicting tensions that must be taken into account...."

31. "The final proportionality assessment takes all the elements identified and measured under the heads of Parliament's objective, rational connection and minimal impairment, and balances them to determine whether the state has proven on a balance of probabilities that its restriction on a fundamental *Charter* right is demonstrably justifiable in a free and democratic society: *Sharpe, ibid.* at para. 102.

32. Compare the early statement in *R. v. Oakes*, [1986] 1 S.C.R. 103 at 138–42 with *R. v. Edwards Books & Art Ltd.*, [1986] 2 S.C.R. 713 at 794; *Law Society of British Columbia v. Andrews*, [1989] 1 S.C.R. 143 at 184–85; *Irwin Toy v. Quebec (Attorney General)*, [1989] 1 S.C.R. 927 at 993–94; *Vancouver General Hospital v. Stoffman*, [1990] 3 S.C.R. 483 at 527–28; *R. v. Chaulk*, [1990] 3 S.C.R. 1303 at 1341; and *R. v. Sharpe*, [2001] 1 S.C.R. 45 at para. 96.

33. *Sharpe, ibid.* at para. 85: "This raises a question pivotal to this appeal: what standard of proof must the Crown achieve in demonstrating harm — scientific proof based on concrete evidence or a reasoned apprehension of harm? The trial judge insisted on scientific proof based on concrete evidence. With respect, this sets the bar too high. In *Butler, supra*, considering the obscenity prohibition of the *Criminal Code*, this Court rejected the need for concrete evidence and held that a 'reasoned apprehension of harm' sufficed (at p. 504). A similar standard must be employed in this case."

34. *Hunter v. Southam Inc.*, [1984] 2 S.C.R. 145, 156.

35. *Law Society of Upper Canada v. Skapinker*, [1984] 2 S.C.R. 145 at 156.

36. *Hunter v. Southam Inc.*, [1984] 2 S.C.R. 145 at 156.

37. *Ibid.* at 155.

38. *Ibid.* at 156, quoting from *Minister of Home Affairs v. Fisher*, [1980] A.C. 319 at 328 (J.C.P.C.). See also *R. v. Big M Drug Mart Ltd.*, [1985] 1 S.C.R. 295 at 344, below.

39. Wilson J. in *Singh v. Minister of Employment and Immigration*, [1985] 1 S.C.R. 178 at 209.

40. *Re Section 94(2) of B.C. Motor Vehicle Act*, [1985] 2 S.C.R. 486 at 496, below.

41. *Law Society of Upper Canada v. Skapinker*, [1984] 1 S.C.R. 359 at 368, quoting from Chief Justice Marshall in *M'Cullough v. State of Maryland* (1819), 17 U.S. 316 at 407.

42. *R. v. Big M Drug Mart Ltd.*, [1985] 1 S.C.R. 295 at 344.

43. Lamer J. in *Re Section 94(2) of B.C. Motor Vehicles Act*, [1985] 2 S.C.R. 486 at 498. Some of the more emphatic early warnings were issued by McIntyre J., often in dissenting judgments. He cautioned that "the *Charter* was not intended to turn the Canadian legal system upside down" (*Mills v. The Queen*, [1986] 1 S.C.R. 863 at 953); that "[i]t is not for the Court to substitute its own views on the merits of a given question for those of Parliament": *R. v. Morgentaler*, [1988] 1 S.C.R. 30 at 138; and

that "while a liberal and not overly legalistic approach should be taken to constitutional interpretation, the *Charter* should not be regarded as an empty vessel to be filled with whatever meaning we might wish from time to time": *Re Public Service Employees Relations Act*, [1987] 1 S.C.R. 313 at 394.

44. *Doucet-Boudreau v. Nova Scotia (Minister of Education)*, [2003] 3 S.C.R. 3 at para. 23.

45. *R. v. Big M Drug Mart Ltd.*, [1985] 1 S.C.R. 295 at 331.

46. See Hogg, *Constitutional Law of Canada, supra* note 22 at heading 33.1.

47. *R. v. Andrews*, [1989] 1 S.C.R. 143.

48. As in *Slaight Communications Inc. v. Davidson*, [1989] 1 S.C.R. 1038.

49. See, for example, *Slaight Communications Inc. v. Davidson*, [1989] 1 S.C.R. 1038.

50. As in *R. v. Big M Drug Mart*, [1985] 1 S.C.R. 295.

51. As in *Eldridge v. British Columbia (Attorney-General)*, [1997] 3 S.C.R. 624.

52. As in *R v. Sharpe*, [2001] 1 S.C.R. 452 at para. 114.

53. As in *Vriend v. Alberta*, [1998] 1 S.C.R. 493.

54. The Supreme Court does not appear to have applied this remedy to date. However, it has affirmed that it might be available in very special situations: see *Corbiere v. Canada*, [1999] 2 S.C.R 203.

55. The usual remedy under s. 24(1), as under s. 52(1), is a declaration: see, for example, *Eldridge v. British Columbia (Attorney-General)*, [1997] 3 S.C.R 624 at 96.

56. As in *Schachter v. Canada*, [1992] 2 S.C.R. 679.

57. The Supreme Court has said that : "[A]lthough this Court must not add anything to legislation or delete anything from it in order to make it consistent with the *Charter*, there is no doubt in my mind that it should also not interpret legislation that is open to more than one interpretation so as to make it inconsistent with the *Charter* and hence of no force or effect": *Slaight Communications Inc. v. Davidson*, [1989] 1 S.C.R. 1038, 1078, cited in *R. v. G. (B.)*, [1999] 2 S.C.R. 475 at para. 42. (The caution at the opening of this passage is directed to a court's initial interpretation of a legislative provision, not to the question of remedies for constitutional invalidity.)

58. See *Schachter v. Canada*, [1992] 2 S.C.R. 679, 717–18, where the Supreme Court said that the inconsistency should be construed (a) broadly where the objective of the legislation is not pressing and substantial, (b) narrowly where the purpose is pressing and substantial but the means for achieving it are not rationally connected to it, and (c) flexibly where there is no problem with the objective or the rational connection, but the means are unduly intrusive or have an effect that is disproportionate to the importance of the legislative objective.

59. In *Schachter, ibid.* at 719, the Court said that a temporary suspension of a declaration is appropriate where striking down a provision without any replacement would cause public danger or threaten the rule of law, or where legislation in question was underinclusive, so that striking it down would prejudice legitimate beneficiaries without benefiting those who were left out.

60. In *Schachter, ibid.* at 718, the Supreme Court said that severance or reading in should be limited to situations where the legislative objective is obvious, the legislative means are flexible, and these remedies would have a limited budgetary impact.

61. Probably because they require a selective application of the law, applications for constitutional exemptions are generally refused. In *Corbiere v. Canada (Minister of Indian and Northern Affairs)*, [1999] 2 S.C.R. 203 at para. 22, the Supreme Court said that where there has been suspension of invalidity a constitutional exemption might be used to protect the interests of the claimant. However, the Court concluded that a constitutional exemption was not appropriate in regard to the delayed declaration of invalidity in this particular case.

62. The Supreme Court has said that s. 24(1) proceedings are appropriate where the claimant is not challenging the validity of legislation: *Schachter* at p. 719.
63. The answer appears to be "normally, no": see *Guimond v. Quebec (Attorney-General)*, [1996] 3 S.C.R. 347 at para. 19.
64. The wording of s. 24(1) is open-ended, permitting "such remedy as the court considers appropriate and just in the circumstances". Possibilities other than damages include injunctions and costs, but s. 24(1) remedies other than declarations are rare. In *R. v. 974649*, [2001] 3 S.C.R. 575 at para. 87, the Supreme Court awarded costs, but cautioned that this s. 24(1) remedy should be limited to "exceptional circumstances".
65. In *Schachter v. Canada*, [1992] 2 S.C.R. 679, the Supreme Court withheld a remedy because the legislation in question had been repealed by the time of its judgment.
66. *Hunter v. Southam Inc.*, [1984] 2 S.C.R. 145, 156.
67. *Law Society of Upper Canada v. Skapinker*, [1984] 2 S.C.R. 145 at 156.
68. *Hunter v. Southam Inc.*, [1984] 2 S.C.R. 145 at 156.
69. *Ibid.* at 155.
70. *Ibid.* at 156, quoting from *Minister of Home Affairs v. Fisher*, [1980] A.C. 319 at 328 (J.C.P.C.). See also *R. v. Big M Drug Mart Ltd.*, [1985] 1 S.C.R. 295 at 344, below.
71. Wilson J. in *Singh v. Minister of Employment and Immigration*, [1985] 1 S.C.R. 178 at 209.
72. *Re Section 94(2) of B.C. Motor Vehicle Act*, [1985] 2 S.C.R. 486 at 496, below.

73. *Law Society of Upper Canada v. Skapinker*, [1984] 1 S.C.R. 359 at 368, quoting from Chief Justice Marshall in *M'Cullough v. State of Maryland* (1819), 17 U.S. 316 at 407.
74. *R. v. Big M Drug Mart Ltd.*, [1985] 1 S.C.R. 295 at 344.
75. Lamer J. in *Re Section 94(2) of B.C. Motor Vehicles Act*, [1985] 2 S.C.R. 486 at 498.
76. McIntyre J. in *Mills v. The Queen*, [1986] 1 S.C.R. 863 at 953.
77. *R. v. Morgentaler*, [1988] 1 S.C.R. 30 at 138.
78. *Re Public Service Employees Relations Act*, [1987] 1 S.C.R. 313 at 394.
79. See, for example, R. Elliott, "The Supreme Court's Rethinking of the Charter's Fundamental Questions (Or Why the Charter Keeps Getting More Interesting)" in P. Bryden et al., *Protecting Rights and Freedoms* (Toronto: University of Toronto Press, 1994) 129 at 132, noting that in 1989–90 the overall success rate for parties invoking the *Charter* had dropped to 17.5% from a rate of 60% for the period 1983–1986; and James B. Kelly, "The *Charter of Rights and Freedoms* and the Rebalancing of Liberal Constitutionalism in Canada, 1982–1997" (1999) 37 Osgoode Hall L.J. 625–95, extracts below.
80. Elliott, *ibid.* at 136–42, argued that the Court was taking a more restrained approach to state power, promoting the interests of vulnerable groups, while continuing to intervene actively where the state represented community interests against those of individuals. Where did Kelly, *ibid.*, see the main areas of restraint?

(b) Canadian Charter of Rights and Freedoms†

WHEREAS Canada is founded upon principles that recognize the supremacy of God and the rule of law:

GUARANTEE OF RIGHTS AND FREEDOMS

Rights and freedoms in Canada

1. The Canadian Charter of Rights and Freedoms guarantees the rights and freedoms set out in it subject only to such reasonable limits prescribed by law as can be demonstrably justified in a free and democratic society.

Fundamental Freedoms

2. Everyone has the following fundamental freedoms:

(a) freedom of conscience and religion;
(b) freedom of thought, belief, opinion and expression, including freedom of the press and other media of communication;

(c) freedom of peaceful assembly; and
(d) freedom of association.

Democratic rights of citizens

3. Every citizen of Canada has the right to vote in an election of members of the House of Commons or of a legislative assembly and to be qualified for membership therein.

Maximum duration of legislative bodies

4.(1) No House of Commons and no legislative assembly shall continue for longer than five years from the date fixed for the return of the writs at a general election of its members.

(2) In time of real or apprehended war, invasion or insurrection, a House of Commons may be continued by Parliament and a legislative assembly may be continued by the legislature beyond five years if such continuation is not opposed by the

---

† *Constitution Act, 1982* (Part 1), being Schedule B of *Canada Act, 1982* (U.K.), 1982, c. 11.

votes of more than one-third of the members of the House of Commons or the legislative assembly, as the case may be.

Annual sitting of legislative bodies

5. There shall be a sitting of Parliament and of each legislature at least once every twelve months.

Mobility of citizens; Rights to move and gain livelihood

6.(1) Every citizen of Canada has the right to enter, remain in and leave Canada.

(2) Every citizen of Canada and every person who has the status of a permanent resident of Canada has the right

(a) to move to and take up residence in any province; and

(b) to pursue the gaining of a livelihood in any province.

. . . .

Limitation

(3) The rights specified in subsection (2) are subject to

(a) any laws or practices of general application in force in a province other than those that discriminate among persons primarily on the basis of province of present or previous residence; and

(b) any laws providing for reasonable residency requirements as qualification for the receipt of publicly provided social services.

(4) Subsections (2) and (3) do not preclude any law, program or activity that has as its object the amelioration in a province of conditions of individuals in that province who are socially or economically disadvantaged if the rate of employment in that province is below the rate of employment in Canada.

Life, liberty and security of person

7. Everyone has the right to life, liberty and security of the person and the right not to be deprived thereof except in accordance with the principles of fundamental justice.

Search or seizure

8. Everyone has the right to be secure against unreasonable search or seizure.

Detention or imprisonment

9. Everyone has the right not to be arbitrarily detained or imprisoned.

Arrest or detention

10. Everyone has the right on arrest or detention

(a) to be informed promptly of the reasons therefor;

(b) to retain and instruct counsel without delay and to be informed of that right; and

(c) to have the validity of the detention determined by way of habeas corpus and to be released if the detention is not lawful.

Proceedings in criminal and penal matters

11. Any person charged with an offence has the right

(a) to be informed without unreasonable delay of the specific offence;

(b) to be tried within a reasonable time;

(c) not to be compelled to be a witness in proceedings against that person in respect of the offence;

(d) to be presumed innocent until proven guilty according to law in a fair and public hearing by an independent and impartial tribunal;

(e) not to be denied reasonable bail without just cause;

(f) except in the case of an offence under military law tried before a military tribunal, to the benefit of trial by jury where the maximum punishment for the offence is imprisonment for five years or a more severe punishment;

(g) not to be found guilty on account of any act or omission unless, at the time of the act or omission, it constituted an offence under Canadian or international law or was criminal according to the general principles of law recognized by the community of nations;

(h) if finally acquitted of the offence, not to be tried for it again and, if finally found guilty and punished for the offence, not to be tried or punished for it again; and

(i) if found guilty of the offence and if the punishment for the offence has been varied between the time of commission and the time of sentencing, to the benefit of the lesser punishment.

Treatment or punishment

12. Everyone has the right not to be subjected to any cruel and unusual treatment or punishment.

Self-crimination

13. A witness who testifies in any proceedings has the right not to have any incriminating evidence so given used to incriminate that witness in any other proceedings, except in a prosecution for perjury or for the giving of contradictory evidence.

Interpreter

14. A party or witness in any proceedings who does not understand or speak the language in which the proceedings are conducted or who is deaf has the right to the assistance of an interpreter.

Equality before and under law and equal protection and benefit of law

15.(1) Every individual is equal before and under the law and has the right to the equal protection and equal benefit of the law without discrimination and, in particular, without discrimination based on race, national or ethnic origin, colour, religion, sex, age or mental or physical disability.

(2) Subsection (1) does not preclude any law, program or activity that has as its object the amelioration of conditions of disadvantaged individuals or groups including those that are disadvantaged because of race, national or ethnic origin, colour, religion, sex, age or mental or physical disability.

Official languages of Canada

16.(1) English and French are the official languages of Canada and have equality of status and equal rights and privileges as to their use in all institutions of the Parliament and government of Canada.

(2) English and French are the official languages of New Brunswick and have equality of status and equal rights and privileges as to their use in all institutions of the legislature and government of New Brunswick.

(3) Nothing in this Charter limits the authority of Parliament or a legislature to advance the equality of status or use of English and French.

Proceedings of Parliament

17.(1) Everyone has the right to use English or French in any debates and other proceedings of Parliament.

(2) Everyone has the right to use English or French in any debates and other proceedings of the legislature of New Brunswick.

Parliamentary statutes and records

18.(1) The statutes, records and journals of Parliament shall be printed and published in English and French and both language versions are equally authoritative.

(2) The statutes, records and journals of the legislature of New Brunswick shall be printed and published in English and French and both language versions are equally authoritative.

Proceedings in courts established by Parliament

19.(1) Either English or French may be used by any person in, or in any pleading in or process issuing from, any court established by Parliament.

(2) Either English or French may be used by any person in, or in any pleading in or process issuing from, any court of New Brunswick.

Communications by public with federal institutions

20.(1) Any member of the public in Canada has the right to communicate with, and to receive available services from, any head or central office of an institution of the Parliament or government of Canada in English or French, and has the same right with respect to any other office of any such institution where

(a) there is a significant demand for communications with and services from that office in such language; or
(b) due to the nature of the office, it is reasonable that communications with and services from that office be available in both English and French.

(2) Any member of the public in New Brunswick has the right to communicate with, and to receive available services from, any office of an institution of the legislature or government of New Brunswick in English or French.

Continuation of existing constitutional provisions

21. Nothing in sections 16 to 20 abrogates or derogates from any right, privilege or obligation with respect to the English and French languages, or either of them, that exists or is continued by virtue of any other provision of the Constitution of Canada.

Rights and privileges preserved

22. Nothing in sections 16 to 20 abrogates or derogates from any legal or customary right or privilege acquired or enjoyed either before or after the coming into force of this Charter with respect to any language that is not English or French.

Minority Language Educational Rights

23.(1) Citizens of Canada

(a) whose first language learned and still understood is that of the English or French linguistic minority population of the province in which they reside, or

(b) who have received their primary school instruction in Canada in English or French and reside in a province where the language in which they received that instruction is the language of the English or French linguistic minority population of the province,

have the right to have their children receive primary and secondary school instruction in that language in that province.

(2) Citizens of Canada of whom any child has received or is receiving primary or secondary school instruction in English or French in Canada, have the right to have all their children receive primary and secondary school instruction in the same language.

(3) The right of citizens of Canada under subsections (1) and (2) to have their children receive primary and secondary school instruction in the language of the English or French linguistic minority population of a province

(a) applies wherever in the province the number of children of citizens who have such a right is sufficient to warrant the provision to them out of public funds of minority language instruction; and

(b) includes, where the number of those children so warrants, the right to have them receive that instruction in minority language educational facilities provided out of public funds.

Enforcement of guaranteed rights and freedoms

24.(1) Anyone whose rights or freedoms, as guaranteed by this Charter, have been infringed or denied may apply to a court of competent jurisdiction to obtain such remedy as the court considers appropriate and just in the circumstances.

(2) Where, in proceedings under subsection (1), a court concludes that evidence was obtained in a manner that infringed or denied any rights or freedoms guaranteed by this Charter, the evidence shall be excluded if it is established that, having regard to all the circumstances, the admission of it in the proceedings would bring the administration of justice into disrepute.

Aboriginal rights and freedoms not affected by Charter

25. The guarantee in this Charter of certain rights and freedoms shall not be construed so as to abrogate or derogate from any aboriginal, treaty or other rights or freedoms that pertain to the aboriginal peoples of Canada including

(a) any rights or freedoms that have been recognized by the Royal Proclamation of October 7, 1763; and

(b) any rights or freedoms that now exist by way of land claims agreements or may be so acquired. [*Constitution Amendment Proclamation, 1983*, s. 1]

Other rights and freedoms not affected by Charter

26. The guarantee in this Charter of certain rights and freedoms shall not be construed as denying the existence of any other rights or freedoms that exist in Canada.

Multicultural heritage

27. This Charter shall be interpreted in a manner consistent with the preservation and enhancement of the multicultural heritage of Canadians.

Rights guaranteed equally to both sexes

28. Notwithstanding anything in this Charter, the rights and freedoms referred to in it are guaranteed equally to male and female persons.

Rights respecting certain schools preserved

29. Nothing in this Charter abrogates or derogates from any rights or privileges guaranteed by or under the Constitution of Canada in respect of denominational, separate or dissentient schools.

Application to territories and territorial authorities

30. A reference in this Charter to a province or to the legislative assembly or legislature of a province shall be deemed to include a reference to the Yukon Territory and the Northwest Territories, or to the appropriate legislative authority thereof, as the case may be.

Legislative powers not extended

31. Nothing in this Charter extends the legislative powers of any body or authority.

Application of Charter

32.(1) This Charter applies

(a) to the Parliament and government of Canada in respect of all matters within the authority of Parliament including all matters relating to the Yukon Territory and Northwest Territories; and

(b) to the legislature and government of each province in respect of all matters within the authority of the legislature of each province.

(2) Notwithstanding subsection (1), section 15 shall not have effect until three years after this section comes into force.

Exception where express declaration

33.(1) Parliament or the legislature of a province may expressly declare in an Act of Parliament or of the legislature, as the case may be, that the Act or a provision thereof shall operate notwithstanding a provision included in section 2 or sections 7 to 15 of this Charter.

(2) An Act or a provision of an Act in respect of which a declaration made under this section is in effect shall have such operation as it would have but for the provision of this Charter referred to in the declaration.

(3) A declaration made under subsection (1) shall cease to have effect five years after it comes into force or on such earlier date as may be specified in the declaration.

(4) Parliament or the legislature of a province may re-enact a declaration made under subsection (1).

(5) Subsection (3) applies in respect of a re-enactment made under subsection (4).

Citation

34. This Part may be cited as the Canadian Charter of Rights and Freedoms.

. . . .

[The following section is not part of the *Charter*, but affects its application.]

Primacy of Constitution of Canada

52.(1) The Constitution of Canada is the supreme law of Canada, and any law that is inconsistent with the provisions of the Constitution is, to the extent of the inconsistency, of no force or effect.

(2) The Constitution of Canada includes

(a) the *Canada Act 1982*, including this Act;

(b) the Acts and orders referred to in the schedule; and (c) any amendment to any Act or order referred to in paragraph (a) or (b).

(3) Amendments to the Constitution of Canada shall be made only in accordance with the authority contained in the Constitution of Canada.

(c) B.C. Motor Vehicles Reference†

NOTE

Section 94 of the British Columbia *Motor Vehicles Act* provided that a person driving while subject to a licence suspension or driving prohibition was liable to a fine and mandatory imprisonment, whether or not he or she knew about the suspension or imprisonment. In effect, it attached mandatory

---

† *Reference re Motor Vehicles Act (British Columbia) s. 94(2)*, [1985] 2 S.C.R. 486, aff'g. (1983), 147 D.L.R. (3d) 539 (B.C.C.A), in a reference concerning the constitutional validity of s. 94(2) of the *Motor Vehicle Act of British Columbia*. [Commentary note by David W. Elliott.]

imprisonment to an "absolute liability" offence that dispensed with the usual criminal law presumption of innocence. After some questions were raised about its constitutionality, the Government of British Columbia referred the provision to the British Columbia Court of Appeal.

Although the penalties in section 94 were drastic, they were not strictly procedural in nature. Thus a central question was whether fundamental justice in section 7 of the *Charter* goes beyond procedural matters. The British Columbia Court of Appeal and the Supreme Court held that it does. Before arriving at this conclusion, the Supreme Court made one of the strongest statements yet in favour of judicial activism in interpreting the *Charter*.

EXTRACT

[LAMER J. for himself and for DICKSON C.J. and BEETZ, CHOUINARD, LAMER, and LE DAIN JJ.:]

A law that has the potential to convict a person who has not really done anything wrong offends the principles of fundamental justice and, if imprisonment is available as a penalty, such a law then violates a person's right to liberty under s. 7 of the *Charter of Rights and Freedoms* (*Constitution Act, 1982*, as enacted by the *Canada Act 1982* (U.K.), c. 11).

In other words, absolute liability and imprisonment cannot be combined.

. . . .

Introduction

The issue in this case raises fundamental questions of constitutional theory, including the nature and the very legitimacy of constitutional adjudication under the *Charter* as well as the appropriateness of various techniques of constitutional interpretation. I shall deal first with these questions of a more general and theoretical nature as they underlie and have shaped much of the discussion surrounding s. 7.

The Nature and Legitimacy of Constitutional Adjudication under the *Charter*

The British Columbia Court of Appeal has written in the present case that the *Constitution Act, 1982* has added a new dimension to the role of the courts in that the courts have now been empowered by s. 52 to consider not only the vires of legislation

but also to measure the content of legislation against the constitutional requirements of the *Charter*.

The novel feature of the *Constitution Act, 1982*, however, is not that it has suddenly empowered courts to consider the content of legislation. This the courts have done for a good many years when adjudicating upon the vires of legislation.... This process has of necessity involved a measurement of the content of legislation against the requirements of the Constitution, albeit within the more limited sphere of values related to the distribution of powers.

The truly novel features of the *Constitution Act, 1982* are that it has sanctioned the process of constitutional adjudication and has extended its scope so as to encompass a broader range of values. Content of legislation has always been considered in constitutional adjudication. Content is now to be equally considered as regards new constitutional issues. Indeed, the values subject to constitutional adjudication now pertain to the rights of individuals as well as the distribution of governmental powers. In short, it is the scope of constitutional adjudication which has been altered rather than its nature, at least, as regards the right to consider the content of legislation.

In neither case, be it before or after the *Charter*, have the courts been enabled to decide upon the appropriateness of policies underlying legislative enactments. In both instances, however, the courts are empowered, indeed required, to measure the content of legislation against the guarantees of the Constitution....

. . . .

Yet, in the context of s. 7, and in particular of the interpretation of "principles of fundamental justice" there has prevailed in certain quarters an assumption that all but a narrow construction of s. 7 will inexorably lead the courts to "question the wisdom of enactments," to adjudicate upon the merits of public policy.

From this have sprung warnings of the dangers of a judicial "super-legislature" beyond the reach of Parliament, the provincial legislatures and the electorate. The Attorney General for Ontario, in his written argument, stated that

> ... the judiciary is neither representative of, nor responsive to the electorate on whose behalf, and under whose authority policies are selected and given effect in the laws of the land.

This is an argument which was heard countless times prior to the entrenchment of the *Charter* but which has in truth, for better or for worse, been settled by the very coming into force of the *Constitution Act, 1982*. It ought not to be forgotten that the historic decision to entrench the *Charter* in our Constitution was taken not by the courts but by the elected representatives of the people of Canada. It was those representatives who extended the scope of constitutional adjudication and entrusted the courts with this new and onerous responsibility. Adjudication under the *Charter* must be approached free of any lingering doubts as to its legitimacy.

The concerns with the bounds of constitutional adjudication explain the characterization of the issue in a narrow and restrictive fashion, i.e., whether the term "principles of fundamental justice" has a substantive or merely procedural content. In my view, the characterization of the issue in such fashion preempts an open-minded approach to determining the meaning of "principles of fundamental justice."

The substantive/procedural dichotomy narrows the issue almost to an all-or-nothing proposition. Moreover, it is largely bound up in the American experience with substantive and procedural due process. It imports into the Canadian context American concepts, terminology and jurisprudence, all of which are inextricably linked to problems concerning the nature and legitimacy of adjudication under the U.S. Constitution. That Constitution, it must be remembered, has no s. 52 nor has it the internal checks and balances of ss. 1 and 33. We would, in my view, do our own Constitution a disservice to simply allow the American debate to define the issue for us, all the while ignoring the truly fundamental structural differences between the two constitutions. Finally, the dichotomy creates its own set of difficulties by the attempt to distinguish between two concepts whose outer boundaries are not always clear and often tend to overlap. Such difficulties can and should, when possible, be avoided.

The overriding and legitimate concern that courts ought not to question the wisdom of enactments, and the presumption that the legislator could not have intended same, have to some extent distorted the discussion surrounding the meaning of "principles of fundamental justice." This has led to the spectre of a judicial "super-Legislature" without a full consideration of the process of constitutional adjudication and the significance of ss. 1 and 33 [of the *Charter*] and s. 52 of the *Constitution Act, 1982*. This in turn has also led to a narrow characterization of the issue and to the assumption that only a procedural content to "principles of fundamental justice" can prevent the courts from adjudicating upon the merits or wisdom of enactments. If this assump-

tion is accepted, the inevitable corollary, with which I would have to then agree, is that the legislator intended that the words "principles of fundamental justice" refer to procedure only.

But I do not share that assumption. Since way back in time and even recently the courts have developed the common law beyond procedural safeguards without interfering with the "merits or wisdom" of enactments (e.g., *Kienapple* v. *The Queen*, [1975] 1 S.C.R. 729, entrapment, non-retrospectivity of offences, presumptions against relaxing the burden of proof and persuasion, to give a few examples).

The task of the court is not to choose between substantive or procedural content *per se* but to secure for persons "the full benefit of the *Charter*'s protection" (Dickson J. (as he then was) in *R.* v. *Big M Drug Mart Ltd.*, [1985] 1 S.C.R. 295, at p. 344), under s. 7, while avoiding adjudication of the merits of public policy. This can only be accomplished by a purposive analysis and the articulation (to use the words in *Curr* v. *The Queen*, [1972] S.C.R. 889, at p. 899) of "objective and manageable standards" for the operation of the section within such a framework.

I propose therefore to approach the interpretation of s. 7 in the manner set forth [earlier decisions of the court that called for "a generous rather than a legalistic" interpretation for the *Charter*]....

. . . .

[Here Lamer J. made a detailed analysis of the wording, context, and legislative history of section 7.]

Conclusion

I have, in this judgment, undertaken a purposive analysis of the term "principles of fundamental justice" in s. 7 of the *Charter* in accordance with the method established by this Court in *R.* v. *Big M Drug Mart Ltd., supra*. Accordingly, the point of departure for the analysis has been a consideration of the general objectives of the *Charter* in the light of the general principles of *Charter* interpretation set forth in *Law Society of Upper Canada* v. *Skapinker, supra*, and *Hunter* v. *Southam Inc., supra*. This was followed by a detailed analysis of the language and structure of the section as well as its immediate context within the *Charter*.

The main sources of support for the argument that "fundamental justice" is simply synonymous with natural justice have been the Minutes of the Proceedings and Evidence of the Special Joint Committee on the Constitution and the *Canadian Bill of Rights* jurisprudence. In my view, neither the Minutes nor the *Canadian Bill of Rights* jurisprudence are persuasive or of any great force. The historical usage of the term "fundamental justice" is, on the other hand, shrouded in ambiguity. Moreover, not any one of these arguments, taken singly or as a whole, manages to overcome in my respectful view the textual and contextual analyses.

Consequently, my conclusion may be summarized as follows:

The term "principles of fundamental justice" is not a right, but a qualifier of the right not to be deprived of life, liberty and security of the person; its function is to set the parameters of that right.

Sections 8 to 14 address specific deprivations of the "right" to life, liberty and security of the person in breach of the principles of fundamental justice, and as such, violations of s. 7. They are therefore illustrative of the meaning, in criminal or penal law, of "principles of fundamental justice"; they represent principles which have been recognized by the common law, the international conventions and by the very fact of entrenchment in the *Charter*, as essential elements of a system for the administration of justice which is founded upon a belief in the dignity and worth of the human person and the rule of law.

Consequently, the principles of fundamental justice are to be found in the basic tenets and principles, not only of our judicial process, but also of the other components of our legal system.

We should not be surprised to find that many of the principles of fundamental justice are procedural in nature. Our common law has largely been a law of remedies and procedures.... This is not to say, however, that the principles of fundamental justice are limited solely to procedural guarantees....

.   .   .   .

Absolute Liability and Fundamental Justice in Penal Law

It has from time immemorial been part of our system of laws that the innocent not be punished. This principle has long been recognized as an essential element of a system for the administration of justice which is founded upon a belief in the dignity and worth of the human person and on the rule of law. It is so old that its first enunciation was in Latin *actus non facit reum nisi mens sit rea*.

.   .   .   .

In my view it is because absolute liability offends the principles of fundamental justice that this Court created presumptions against legislatures having intended to enact offences of a regulatory nature falling within that category. This is not to say, however, and to that extent I am in agreement with the Court of Appeal, that, as a result, absolute liability per se offends s. 7 of the *Charter*.

A law enacting an absolute liability offence will violate s. 7 of the *Charter* only if and to the extent that it has the potential of depriving of life, liberty, or security of the person.

Obviously, imprisonment (including probation orders) deprives persons of their liberty. An offence has that potential as of the moment it is open to the judge to impose imprisonment. There is no need that imprisonment, as in s. 94(2), be made mandatory.

I am therefore of the view that the combination of imprisonment and of absolute liability violates s. 7 of the *Charter* and can only be salvaged if the authorities demonstrate under s. 1 that such a deprivation of liberty in breach of those principles of fundamental justice is, in a free and democratic society, under the circumstances, a justified reasonable limit to one's rights under s. 7.

.   .   .   .

... [I]n penal law, absolute liability always offends the principles of fundamental justice irrespective of the nature of the offence; it offends s. 7 of the *Charter* if as a result, anyone is deprived of his life, liberty or security of the person, irrespective of the requirement of public interest. In such cases it might only be salvaged for reasons of public interest under s. 1.

.   .   .   .

... Section 1 may, for reasons of administrative expediency, successfully come to the rescue of an otherwise violation of s. 7, but only in cases arising out of exceptional conditions, such as natural disasters, the outbreak of war, epidemics, and the like.

.   .   .   .

In the final analysis, it seems that both the appellant and the respondent agree that s. 94 will impact upon the right to liberty of a limited number of morally innocent persons. It creates an absolute liability offence which effects a deprivation of liberty for a limited number of persons. To me, that is sufficient for it to be in violation of s. 7.

Section 1

Having found that s. 94(2) offends s. 7 of the *Charter* there remains the question as to whether the appellants have demonstrated that the section is salvaged by the operation of s. 1 of the *Charter*....

. . . .

I do not take issue with the fact [stressed by the provincial government] that it is highly desirable that "bad drivers" be kept off the road. I do not take issue either with the desirability of punishing severely bad drivers who are in contempt of prohibitions against driving. The bottom line of the question to be addressed here is: whether the Government of British Columbia has demonstrated as justifiable that the risk of imprisonment of a few innocent is, given the desirability of ridding the roads of British Columbia of bad drivers, a reasonable limit in a free and democratic society. That result is to be measured against the offence being one of strict liability open to a defence of due diligence, the success of which does nothing more than let those few who did nothing wrong remain free.

As did the Court of Appeal, I find that this demonstration has not been satisfied, indeed, not in the least.

In the result, I would dismiss the appeal and answer the question in the negative, as did the Court of Appeal, albeit for somewhat different reasons, and declare s. 94(2) of the *Motor Vehicle Act*, R.S.B.C. 1979, as amended by the *Motor Vehicle Amendment Act, 1982*, inconsistent with s. 7 of the *Canadian Charter of Rights and Freedoms*.

Having come to this conclusion, I choose, as did the Court of Appeal, not to address whether the section violates the rights guaranteed under ss. 11(d) and 12 of the *Charter*.

. . . .

[McINTYRE J.:]

... I agree with Lamer J. that s. 94(2) of the *Motor Vehicle Act*, R.S.B.C. 1979, c. 288, as amended by the *Motor Vehicle Amendment Act*, 1982, 1982 (B.C.), c. 36, s. 19, is inconsistent with s. 7 of the *Canadian Charter of Rights and Freedoms*. I agree that "fundamental justice," as the term is used in the *Charter*, involves more than natural justice (which is largely procedural) and includes as well a substantive element. I am also of the view that on any definition of the term "fundamental justice" the imposition of minimum imprisonment for an offence in respect of

which no defence can be made, and which may be committed unknowingly and with no wrongful intent, deprives or may deprive of liberty and it offends the principles of fundamental justice.

I would accordingly dismiss the appeal and answer the constitutional question in the negative.

. . . .

[WILSON J.:]

. . . .

I approach the interpretive problem raised by the phrase "the principles of fundamental justice" on the assumption that the legislature was very familiar with the concepts of "natural justice" and "due process" and the way in which those phrases had been judicially construed and applied. Yet they chose neither. Instead they chose the phrase "the principles of fundamental justice." What is "fundamental justice"? ... I would conclude ... that if the citizen is to be guaranteed his right to life, liberty and security of the person — surely one of the most basic rights in a free and democratic society — then he certainly should not be deprived of it by means of a violation of a fundamental tenet of our justice system.

It has been argued very forcefully that s. 7 is concerned only with procedural injustice but I have difficulty with that proposition. There is absolutely nothing in the section to support such a limited construction....

. . . .

... It will be for the courts to determine the principles which fall under the rubric "the principles of fundamental justice." Obviously not all principles of law are covered by the phrase; only those which are basic to our system of justice.

. . . .

It is basic to any theory of punishment that the sentence imposed bear some relationship to the offence; it must be a "fit" sentence proportionate to the seriousness of the offence....

. . . .

I believe that a mandatory term of imprisonment for an offence committed unknowingly and unwittingly and after the exercise of due diligence is grossly excessive and inhumane. It is not required to reduce the incidence of the offence. It is beyond anything required to satisfy the need for "atonement." And society, in my opinion, would not [abhor] an unintentional and unknowing violation of the section. I believe, therefore, that such a sanction offends the principles of fundamental justice embodied in our penal system. Section 94(2) is accordingly inconsistent with s. 7 of the *Charter* and must, to the extent of the inconsistency, be declared of no force and effect under s. 52. I express no view as to whether a mandatory term of imprisonment for such an offence represents an arbitrary imprisonment

within the meaning of s. 9 of the *Charter* or "cruel and unusual treatment or punishment" within the meaning of s. 12 because it is not necessary to decide those issues in order to answer the constitutional question posed.

I would dismiss the appeal and answer the constitutional question in the negative.

Appeal dismissed.
The constitutional question is
answered in the negative.

(d) *Retail, Wholesale and Department Store Union, Local 580 v. Dolphin Delivery Ltd.*†

NOTE

Embroiled in a bitter labour dispute with its employees, Purolator Courier Incorporated locked them out and continued its deliveries through an arrangement with another courier called Dolphin Delivery. The employees' union responded by threatening to picket Dolphin Delivery. Dolphin Delivery obtained a temporary injunction to prevent the picketing. The judge agreed that this would constitute "secondary picketing", going beyond the immediate parties to the labour dispute. He based the injunction on the common law tort of inducing a breach of contract. The union appealed the injunction, arguing that it violated the *Charter* guarantee of freedom of expression, but they were unsuccessful before the British Columbia Court of Appeal and the Supreme Court of Canada.

The Supreme Court grappled with three main legal issues: (i) does the *Charter* apply to judicial actions that are based on the common law (here a common law tort)? (ii) does the *Charter*'s guarantee of freedom of expression protect secondary picketing? and, if so, (iii) was the injunction's restriction on secondary picketing justified under section 1 of the *Charter*?

Beyond the legal issues were wider questions. For example, should the Court limit the *Charter*'s reach to government, restricting constitutional protections to the boundaries of the old distinction between public and private matters? How should it define "government" for the purposes of the *Charter*? Should the Court extend the fundamental freedoms into the economic sphere? If it did not, would it be refusing to protect a right regarded by many as crucial to effective collective bargaining?

Dolphin Delivery was one of a group of decisions that denied *Charter* protection to collective bargaining interests. See also *Re Public Service Employee Relations Act*, [1987] 1 S.C.R. 313; (1987), 38 D.L.R. (4th) 161 (S.C.C.); *Public Service Alliance of Canada v. The Queen in Right of Canada*, [1987] 1 S.C.R. 424 (S.C.C.); and *Government of Saskatchewan v. Retail, Wholesale and Department Store Union*, [1987] 1 S.C.R. 460 (S.C.C.). On the question of secondary picketing, compare *Dolphin Delivery* with *Retail, Wholesale and Department Store Union, Local 558 v. Pepsi-Cola Canada Beverages (West) Ltd.*, [2002] S.C.J. No. 7, January 24, 2002.

---

† *Retail, Wholesale and Department Store Union, Local 580 [R.W.D.S.U.] v. Dolphin Delivery Ltd.*, [1986] 2 S.C.R. 573, aff'g. [1984] 3 W.W.R. 481 (B.C.C.A.), aff'g. [1983] B.C.W.L.D. 100 (B.C.S.C.), granting an interlocutory injunction. [Commentary note by David W. Elliott.]

EXTRACT

[McINTYRE J. for himself and for DICKSON C.J., and ESTEY, CHOUINARD, and LE DAIN JJ.:]

... I would accept as a fact that the respondent was found by the Chambers judge to be a third party to the dispute. In addition, the Chambers judge found that the purpose of the picketing was tortious and that the dominant purpose was to injure the plaintiff rather than the dissemination of information and protection of the defendant's interest.

Hutcheon J.A., in the Court of Appeal also seems to have recognized the difficulty regarding the factual underpinning. He said [at p. 484]:

> The interim injunction was granted before any picketing took place. The proper assumptions to be made are that the picketing would be peaceful, that some employees of Dolphin Delivery and other trade union members of customers would not cross the picket line, and that the daily business of Dolphin Delivery would be disrupted to a considerable extent.

These assumptions are reasonable and I adopt them. In summary then, it has been found that the respondent was a third party, that the anticipated picketing would be tortious, that the purpose was to injure the plaintiff. It was assumed that the picketing would be peaceful, that some employees of the respondent and other trade union members of customers would decline to cross the picket lines, and that the business of the respondent would be disrupted to a considerable extent.

The following questions arise:

1. Does the injunction complained of in this case restrict the freedom of expression secured under s. 2(b) of the *Canadian Charter of Rights and Freedoms*?
2. Does the *Charter* apply to the common law?
3. Does the *Charter* apply in private litigation?
4. If it is found that the injunction does restrict freedom of information, is the limit imposed by the injunction a reasonable limit in accordance with s. 1 of the *Charter*?

Freedom of Expression

As has been noted above, the only basis on which the picketing in question was defended by the appellants was under the provisions of s. 2(b) of the *Charter* which guarantees the freedom of expression as a fundamental freedom. Freedom of expression is not, however, a creature of the *Charter*. It is one of the fundamental concepts that has formed the basis for the historical development of the political, social and educational institutions of western society. Representative democracy, as we know it today, which is in great part the product of free expression and discussion of varying ideas, depends upon its maintenance and protection.

. . . .

The importance of freedom of expression has been recognized since early times: see John Milton, *Areopagitica; A Speech for the Liberty of Unlicenc'd Printing, to the Parliament of England* (1664), and as well John Stuart Mill, "On Liberty" in *On Liberty and Considerations on Representative Government* (Oxford 1946)....

. . . .

... [A]fter stating that "All silencing of discussion is an assumption of infallibility," [Mill] said, at p. 16:

> Yet it is as evident in itself, as any amount of argument can make it, that ages are no more infallible than individuals; every age having held many opinions which subsequent ages have deemed not only false but absurd; and it is as certain that many opinions now general will be rejected by future ages, as it is that many, once general, are rejected by the present.

Nothing in the vast literature on this subject reduces the importance of Mill's words. The principle of freedom of speech and expression has been firmly accepted as a necessary feature of modern democracy....

. . . .

The question now arises: Is freedom of expression involved in this case? In seeking an answer to this question, it must be observed at once that in any form of picketing there is involved at least some element of expression. The picketers would be conveying a message which at a very minimum would be classed as persuasion, aimed at deterring customers and prospective customers from doing business with the respondent. The question then arises. Does this expression in the circumstances of this case have *Charter* protection under the provisions of s. 2(b), and if it does, then does the injunction abridge or infringe such freedom?

The appellants argue strongly that picketing is a form of expression fully entitled to *Charter* protection....

. . . .

The respondent contends for a narrower approach to the concept of freedom of expression. The position is summarized in the respondent's factum:

> **4.** We submit that constitutional protection under section 2(b) should only be given to those forms of expression that warrant such protection. To do otherwise would trivialize freedom of expression generally and lead to a downgrading or dilution of this freedom.

. . . .

On the basis of the findings of fact that I have referred to above, it is evident that the purpose of the picketing in this case was to induce a breach of contract between the respondent and Supercourier and thus to exert economic pressure to force it to cease doing business with Supercourier. It is equally evident that, if successful, the picketing would have done serious injury to the respondent. There is nothing remarkable about this, however, because all picketing is designed to bring economic pressure on the person picketed and to cause economic loss for so long as the object of the picketing remains unfulfilled. There is, as I have earlier said, always some element of expression in picketing. The union is making a statement to the general public that it is involved in a dispute, that it is seeking to impose its will on the object of the picketing, and that it solicits the assistance of the public in honouring the picket line. Action on the part of the picketers will, of course, always accompany the expression, but not every action on the part of the picketers will be such as to alter the nature of the whole transaction and remove it from *Charter* protection for freedom of expression. That freedom, of course, would not extend to protect threats of violence or acts of violence. It would not protect the destruction of property, or assaults, or other clearly unlawful conduct. We need not, however, be concerned with such matters here because the picketing would have been peaceful. I am therefore of the view that the picketing sought to be restrained would have involved the exercise of the right of freedom of expression.

Section 1 of the *Charter*

It is not necessary, in view of the disposition of this appeal that I propose, to deal with the application of s. 1 of the *Charter*. It was, however, referred

to in the Court of Appeal and I will deal with it here....

. . . .

The question then is: Can an injunction based on the common law tort of inducing a breach of contract, which has the effect of limiting the *Charter* right to freedom of expression, be sustained as a reasonable limit imposed by law in the peculiar facts of this case?

. . . .

From the evidence, it may well be said that the concern of the respondent is pressing and substantial. It will suffer economically in the absence of an injunction to restrain picketing. On the other hand, the injunction has imposed a limitation upon a *Charter* freedom. A balance between the two competing concerns must be found. It may be argued that the concern of the respondent regarding economic loss would not be sufficient to constitute a reasonable limitation on the right of freedom of expression, but there is another basis upon which the respondent's position may be supported. This case involves secondary picketing — picketing of a third party not concerned in the dispute which underlies the picketing. The basis of our system of collective bargaining is the proposition that the parties themselves should, wherever possible, work out their own agreement.

. . . .

When the parties do exercise the right to disagree, picketing and other forms of industrial conflict are likely to follow. The social cost is great, man-hours and wages are lost, production and services will be disrupted, and general tensions within the community may be heightened. Such industrial conflict may be tolerated by society but only as an inevitable corollary to the collective bargaining process. It is therefore necessary in the general social interest that picketing be regulated and sometimes limited. It is reasonable to restrain picketing so that the conflict will not escalate beyond the actual parties. While picketing is, no doubt, a legislative weapon to be employed in a labour dispute by the employees against their employer, it should not be permitted to harm others....

. . . .

It should be noted here that in the Province of British Columbia, secondary picketing of the nature involved in this case, save for the picketing of allies of the employer, has been made unlawful by the combined effect of ss. 85(3) and 88 of the *British Columbia Labour Code*, R.S.B.C. 1979, c. 212, as amended. This statute, of course, does not apply in this case, but it is indicative of the legislative policy, in respect of the regulation of picketing in that Province. It shows that the application of s. 1 of the *Charter* to sustain the limitation imposed by the common law would be consistent with legislative policy in British Columbia. I would say that the requirement of proportionality is also met, particularly when it is recalled that this is an interim injunction effective only until trial when the issues may be more fully canvassed on fuller evidence. It is my opinion then that a limitation on secondary picketing against a third party, that is, a non-ally, would be a reasonable limit in the facts of this case. I would therefore conclude that the injunction is "a reasonable limit prescribed by law which can be demonstrably justified in a free and democratic society."

Does the *Charter* Apply to the Common Law?

In my view, there can be no doubt that it does apply....

. . . .

The English text [of section 52(1) of the *Constitution Act, 1982*] provides that "any law that is inconsistent with the provisions of the Constitution is, to the extent of the inconsistency, of no force or effect." If this language is not broad enough to include the common law, it should be observed as well that the French text adds strong support to this conclusion in its employment of the words "elle rend inoperantes les dispositions incompatibles *de tout autre règle de droit.*" (Emphasis added.) To adopt a construction of s. 52(1) which would exclude from *Charter* application the whole body of the common law which in great part governs the rights and obligations of the individuals in society, would be wholly unrealistic and contrary to the clear language employed in s. 52(1) of the Act.

Does the *Charter* Apply to Private Litigation?

This question involves consideration of whether or not an individual may found a cause of action or defence against another individual on the basis of a breach of a *Charter* right. In other words, does the *Charter* apply to private litigation divorced completely from any connection with Government? ...

. . . .

... [I]n considering whether the *Charter* should be directly applicable, the courts should bear in mind its drawbacks as a method of dealing with private action and the advantages of leaving the regulation of such conduct to human rights legislation or other legal controls. Legislation can be tailored to deal with the tension between privacy rights and equality or that between freedom of expression and prohibition of hate literature. It can expressly limit the applicability of equality guarantees to services or to areas open to the public, or specify the right to set bona fide job qualifications. The *Charter* is not so refined, and provides no guidelines for its application. These would have to be judicially determined.

As well, statutes such as particular human rights and equal pay laws contain an administrative structure designed to promote mediated settlements of disputes, rather than resort to litigation....

. . . .

I am in agreement with the view that the *Charter* does not apply to private litigation. It is evident from the authorities and articles cited above that that approach has been adopted by most judges and commentators who have dealt with this question. In my view, s. 32 of the *Charter*, specifically dealing with the question of *Charter* application, is conclusive on this issue.

. . . .

... In [section 32(1)] it may be seen that Parliament and the legislatures are treated as separate or specific branches of government, distinct from the executive branch of government, and therefore where the word 'government' is used in s. 32 it refers not to government in its generic sense — meaning the whole of the governmental apparatus of the state — but to a branch of government. The word "government," following as it does the words "Parliament" and "legislature," must then, it would seem, refer to the executive or administrative branch of government. This is the sense in which one generally speaks of the Government of Canada or of a province. I am of the opinion that the word "government" is used in s. 32 of the *Charter* in the sense of the executive government of Canada and the provinces. This is the sense in which the words

"Government of Canada" are ordinarily employed in other sections of the *Constitution Act*, 1867. Sections 12, 16 and 132 all refer to the Parliament and the Government of Canada as separate entities. The words "Government of Canada," particularly where they follow a reference to the word "Parliament," almost always refer to the executive government.

It is my view that s. 32 of the *Charter* specifies the actors to whom the *Charter* will apply. They are the legislative, executive and administrative branches of government. It will apply to those branches of government whether or not their action is invoked in public or private litigation. It would seem that legislation is the only way in which a legislature may infringe a guaranteed right or freedom. Action by the executive or administrative branches of government will generally depend upon legislation, that is, statutory authority. Such action may also depend, however, on the common law, as in the case of the prerogative. To the extent that it relies on statutory authority which constitutes or results in an infringement of a guaranteed right or freedom, the *Charter* will apply and it will be unconstitutional. The action will also be unconstitutional to the extent that it relies for authority or justification on a rule of the common law which constitutes or creates an infringement of a *Charter* right or freedom. In this way the *Charter* will apply to the common law, whether in public or private litigation. It will apply to the common law, however, only in so far as the common law is the basis of some governmental action which, it is alleged, infringes a guaranteed right or freedom.

The element of governmental intervention necessary to make the *Charter* applicable in an otherwise private action is difficult to define. We have concluded that the *Charter* applies to the common law but not between private parties. The problem here is that this is an action between private parties in which the appellant resists the common law claim of the respondent on the basis of a *Charter* infringement. The argument is made that the common law, which is itself subject to the *Charter*, creates the tort of civil conspiracy and that of inducing a breach of contract. The respondent has sued and has procured the injunction which has enjoined the picketing on the basis of the commission of these torts. The appellants say the injunction infringes their *Charter* right of freedom of expression under s. 2(b)....

. . . .

... While in political science terms it is probably acceptable to treat the courts as one of the three fundamental branches of Government, that is, legisla-

tive, executive, and judicial, I cannot equate for the purposes of *Charter* application the order of a court with an element of governmental action. This is not to say that the courts are not bound by the *Charter*. The courts are, of course, bound by the *Charter* as they are bound by all law. It is their duty to apply the law, but in doing so they act as neutral arbiters, not as contending parties involved in a dispute. To regard a court order as an element of governmental intervention necessary to invoke the *Charter* would, it seems to me, widen the scope of *Charter* application to virtually all private litigation. All cases must end, if carried to completion, with an enforcement order and if the *Charter* precludes the making of the order, where a *Charter* right would be infringed, it would seem that all private litigation would be subject to the *Charter*. In my view, this approach will not provide the answer to the question. A more direct and a more precisely-defined connection between the element of government action and the claim advanced must be present before the *Charter* applies.

An example of such a direct and close connection is to be found in *Re Blainey and Ontario Hockey Association*....

. . . .

... In the *Blainey* case, a law suit between private parties, the *Charter* was applied because one of the parties acted on the authority of a statute, i.e., s. 19(2) of the *Ontario Human Rights Code*, which infringed the *Charter* rights of another. *Blainey* then affords an illustration of the manner in which *Charter* rights of private individuals may be enforced and protected by the courts, that is, by measuring legislation — government action — against the *Charter*.

. . . .

It would also seem that the *Charter* would apply to many forms of delegated legislation, regulations, orders in council, possibly municipal by-laws, and by-laws and regulations of other creatures of Parliament and the Legislatures. It is not suggested that this list is exhaustive. Where such exercise of, or reliance upon, governmental action is present and where one private party invokes or relies upon it to produce an infringement of the *Charter* rights of another, the *Charter* will be applicable. Where, however, private party "A" sues private party "B" relying on the common law and where no act of government is relied upon to support the action, the *Charter* will not apply. I should make it clear, however, that this is a distinct issue from the question whether the judiciary ought to apply and develop the principles of the common law in a manner consistent with the fundamental values enshrined in the Constitution. The answer to this question must be in the affirmative. In this sense, then, the *Charter* is far from irrelevant to private litigants whose disputes fall to be decided at common law. But this is different from the proposition that one private party owes a constitutional duty to another, which proposition underlies the purported assertion of *Charter* causes of action or *Charter* defences between individuals.

Can it be said in the case at bar that the required element of government intervention or intrusion may be found? In *Blainey*, s. 19(2) of the Ontario *Human Rights Code*, an Act of a legislature, was the factor which removed the case from the private sphere. If in our case one could point to a statutory provision specifically outlawing secondary picketing of the nature contemplated by the appellants, the case — assuming for the moment an infringement of the *Charter* — would be on all fours with *Blainey* and, subject to s. 1 of the *Charter*, the statutory provision could be struck down. In neither case, would it be, as Professor Hogg would have it, the order of a court which would remove the case from the private sphere. It would be the result of one party's reliance on a statutory provision violative of the *Charter*.

In the case at bar however we have no offending statute. We have a rule of the common law which renders secondary picketing tortious and subject to injunctive restraint, on the basis that it induces a breach of contract. While, as we have found, the *Charter* applies to the common law, we do not have in this litigation between purely private parties any exercise of or reliance upon governmental action which would invoke the *Charter*. It follows then that the appeal must fail. The appeal is dismissed. The respondent is entitled to its costs. In the circumstances of this case, it becomes unnecessary to answer the constitutional question framed by the Chief Justice on September 5, 1984.

.   .   .   .

[Wilson J. gave separate reasons concurring in the result.]

[BEETZ J.:]

I agree with the reasons of the majority in the British Columbia Court of Appeal for holding that in the circumstances and on the evidence of this case, the picketing which has been enjoined would not have been a form of expression and that no question of infringement of s. 2(b) of the *Canadian Charter of Rights and Freedoms* could accordingly arise. This reason suffices for the dismissal of the appeal with costs.

(e) *Eldridge v. British Columbia (A.G.) and Medical Services Commission*†

NOTE

Ms. Robin Eldridge was deaf. She preferred to communicate by sign language. Because of her medical conditions, Ms. Eldridge had to pay numerous visits to doctors and a hospital. Ms. Eldridge's doctors did not know sign language, and the hospital had no interpreters. Although Ms. Eldridge hired an interpreter for surgery in the hospital, she could not afford to hire one for every medical visit. Without an interpreter, she felt she could not communicate adequately with the doctors.

Ms. Eldridge and two others claimed that the failure to provide interpreters as an insured benefit under provincial health care legislation violated their s. 15 right to equality under the *Canadian Charter of Rights and Freedoms*. The Supreme Court of Canada agreed, and said the violation was not justified under section 1. It held that the legislation must be administered so as to provide free sign language interpreters for deaf persons.

A preliminary issue in *Eldridge* was whether the *Charter* applies to provincial hospitals and to bodies such as the Medical Services Commission,

---

† [1997] 3 S.C.R. 624; rev'g. (1995), 125 D.L.R. (4th) 323 (B.C.C.A.); aff'g. (1992), 75 B.C.L.R. (2d) 6, [1992] B.C.J. No. 2229 (QL) (B.C.S.C.). [Commentary by David W. Elliott.]

a nine-member panel of government and private representatives established to administer benefits under provincial health care legislation. Earlier, the Supreme Court had appeared to hold that — at least for some purposes — hospitals are not sufficiently "governmental" in nature to come under the *Charter*. How did the Court distinguish this precedent? Consider the possible implications of *Eldridge* for privatization. After *Eldridge*, privatizing *structures* may not be enough to escape *Charter* obligations.

Eldridge also raised questions about the scope of judicial remedies under the *Charter*. Earlier cases contained suggestions that courts should give government a wide latitude in distributing financial resources.[†] As will be seen in Chapter 10, Ms. Eldridge was claiming "adverse effects" discrimination. In this situation, the discrimination, results not from an express government distinction but the adverse impact of legislation or other government action on people with a particular disadvantage. As well, Ms. Eldridge's concern related not to a state burden, but to a state benefit. In *Symes*,[1] the majority had said:

> We must take care to distinguish between effects which are wholly caused, or are contributed to, by an impugned provision, and those social circumstances which exist independently of such a provision.

Assuming that the Court should provide a remedy for the discrimination claimed by Ms. Eldridge, as addressed in Chapter 10, what remedy should it impose? If courts prescribe more of the content of government expenditures, how will this affect government accountability to the electorate?

EXTRACT

[LA FOREST J. for himself, LAMER C.J., and L'HEUREUX-DUBÉ, SOPINKA, GONTHIER, CORY, McLACHLIN, IACOBUCCI and MAJOR JJ.:

La Forest J. said that since neither the *Hospital Insurance Act* nor the *Medical and Health Care Services Act* prohibited the provision of sign language services as insured services, any violation of the *Charter* lay with the hospitals and the Medical Services Commission.]

[35] Having identified the sources of the alleged s. 15(1) violations, it remains to be considered whether the *Charter* actually applies to them. At first blush, this may seem to be a curious question. As I have discussed, it is a basic principle of constitutional theory that since legislatures may not enact laws that infringe the *Charter*, they cannot authorize or empower another person or entity to do so; *Slaight Communications Inc.* v. *Davidson*, [1989] 1 S.C.R. 1038. It is possible, however, for a legislature to give authority to a body that is not subject to the *Charter*. Perhaps the clearest example of this is the power of incorporation. Private corporations are entirely creatures of statute; they have no power or authority that does not derive from the legislation that created them. The *Charter* does not apply to them, however, because legislatures have not entrusted them to implement specific governmental policies. Of course, governments may desire corporations to serve certain social and economic purposes, and may adjust the terms of their existence to accord with those goals. Once brought into being, however, they are completely autonomous from government; they are empowered to exercise only the same contractual and proprietary powers as are possessed by natural persons. As a result, while the legislation creating corporations is subject to the *Charter*, corporations themselves are not part of "government" for the purposes of s. 32 of the *Charter*.

[36] Legislatures have created many other statutory entities, however, that are not as clearly autonomous from government. There are myriad public or quasi-public institutions that may be independent from government in some respects, but in other respects may exercise delegated governmental powers or be otherwise responsible for the implementation of government policy. When it is alleged that an action of one of these bodies, and not the legislation that regulates them, violates the *Charter*, it must be established that the entity, in performing that particular action, is part of "government" within the meaning of s. 32 of the *Charter*.

[37] Perhaps the fullest discussion of the meaning of "government" in s. 32 is found in *McKinney* v. *University of Guelph*, [1990] 3 S.C.R. 229, and its companion cases, *Harrison* v. *University of British Columbia*, [1990] 3 S.C.R. 451, *Stoffman* v. *Vancouver General Hospital*, [1990] 3 S.C.R. 483, and

---

† For example, *McKinney v. University of Guelph*, [1990] 3 S.C.R. 229.
1 *Symes v. Canada*, [1993] 4 S.C.R. 695, 764–65.

Douglas/Kwantlen Faculty Assn. v. *Douglas College*, [1990] 3 S.C.R. 570....

. . . .

[41] While it is well established that the *Charter* applies to all the activities of government, whether or not those activities may be otherwise characterized as "private," this Court has also recognized that the *Charter* may apply to non-governmental entities in certain circumstances; see generally Robin Elliot, "Scope of the *Charter*'s Application" (1993), 15 Adv. Q. 204, at pp. 208–209. It has been suggested, for example, that the *Charter* will apply to a private entity when engaged in activities that can in some way be attributed to government....

. . . .

The idea that certain activities of non-governmental entities may be viewed as the responsibility of government was further elucidated in my reasons in *Lavigne* where, after discussing *McKinney*, *Harrison*, *Douglas* and *Stoffman*, I stated as follows, at p. 312:

> The majority in the above cases relied solely on the element of control in determining what fell within the apparatus of government, *although it made clear that government may, in some circumstances, be subject to Charter scrutiny in respect of activities in the private sector where the government could be said to have some responsibility for that activity.* [Emphasis added.]

[42] It seems clear, then, that a private entity may be subject to the *Charter* in respect of certain inherently governmental actions. The factors that might serve to ground a finding that an activity engaged in by a private entity is "governmental" in nature do not readily admit of any *a priori* elucidation. *McKinney* makes it clear, however, that the *Charter* applies to private entities in so far as they act in furtherance of a specific governmental program or policy. In these circumstances, while it is a private actor that actually implements the program, it is government that retains responsibility for it. The rationale for this principle is readily apparent. Just as governments are not permitted to escape *Charter* scrutiny by entering into commercial contracts or other "private" arrangements, they should not be allowed to evade their constitutional responsibilities by delegating the implementation of their policies and programs to private entities. In *McKinney*, *supra*, I pointed to *Slaight*, *supra*, as an example of a situation where action taken in furtherance of a government policy was held to fall within the ambit of the *Charter*. I noted, at p. 265, that the arbitrator in that case was "part of the governmental administrative machinery for effecting the specific purpose of the statute." "It would be strange," I wrote, "if the legislature and the government could evade their *Charter* responsibility by appointing a person to carry out the purposes of the statute"; see *idem*. Although the arbitrator in *Slaight* was entirely a creature of statute and performed functions that were exclusively governmental, the same rationale applies to any entity charged with performing a governmental activity, even if that entity operates in other respects as a private actor; see A. Anne McLellan and Bruce P. Elman, "To Whom Does the *Charter* Apply? Some Recent Cases on Section 32" (1986), 24 Alta. L. Rev. 361, at p. 371.

[43] Two important points must be made with respect to this principle. First, the mere fact that an entity performs what may loosely be termed a "public function," or the fact that a particular activity may be described as "public" in nature, will not be sufficient to bring it within the purview of "government" for the purposes of s. 32 of the *Charter*. Thus, with specific reference to the distinction between the applicability of the *Charter*, on the one hand, and the susceptibility of public bodies to judicial review, on the other, I stated as follows, at p. 268 of *McKinney*:

> It was not disputed that the universities are statutory bodies performing a public service. As such, they may be subjected to the judicial review of certain decisions, *but this does not in itself make them part of government within the meaning of s. 32 of the Charter.*... In a word, the basis of the exercise of supervisory jurisdiction by the courts is not that the universities are government, but that they are public decision-makers. [Emphasis added.]

In order for the *Charter* to apply to a private entity, it must be found to be implementing a specific governmental policy or program. As I stated further on in *McKinney*, at p. 269, "[a] public purpose test is simply inadequate" and "... is simply not the test mandated by s. 32."

[44] The second important point concerns the precise manner in which the *Charter* may be held to apply to a private entity. As the case law discussed above makes clear, the *Charter* may be found to apply to an entity on one of two bases. First, it may be determined that the entity is itself "government" for the purposes of s. 32. This involves an inquiry into whether the entity whose actions have given rise to

the alleged *Charter* breach can, either by its very nature or in virtue of the degree of governmental control exercised over it, properly be characterized as "government" within the meaning of s. 32(1). In such cases, all of the activities of the entity will be subject to the *Charter*, regardless of whether the activity in which it is engaged could, if performed by a non-governmental actor, correctly be described as "private." Second, an entity may be found to attract *Charter* scrutiny with respect to a particular activity that can be ascribed to government. This demands an investigation not into the nature of the entity whose activity is impugned but rather into the nature of the activity itself. In such cases, in other words, one must scrutinize the quality of the act at issue, rather than the quality of the actor. If the act is truly "governmental" in nature — for example, the implementation of a specific statutory scheme or a government program — the entity performing it will be subject to review under the *Charter* only in respect of that act, and not its other, private activities.

[45] In the present case, the controversy over the *Charter*'s application centres on the question of hospitals. The respondents argue that if the failure to provide sign language interpreters does not flow from the Act but rather from the discretion of individual hospitals, then s. 15(1) is not engaged because the *Charter* does not apply to hospitals. Hospitals, they say, are not "government" for the purposes of s. 32 of the *Charter*. In their view, this result flows from a straightforward application of this Court's decision in *Stoffman, supra*.

[46] The foregoing analysis, however, establishes that it is not enough for the respondents to say that hospitals are not "government" for the purposes of s. 32 of the *Charter*. In *Stoffman*, the Court found that the Vancouver General Hospital was not part of the apparatus of government and that its adoption of a mandatory retirement policy did not implement a government policy. *Stoffman* made it clear that, as presently constituted, hospitals in British Columbia are non-governmental entities whose private activities are not subject to the *Charter*. It remains to be seen, however, whether hospitals effectively implement governmental policy in providing medical services under the *Hospital Insurance Act*.

. . . .

[48] ... [In *Stoffman*], the hospital's mandatory retirement policy, which was embodied in *Medical Staff Regulation* 5.04, was a matter of internal hospital management. Notwithstanding the requirement of

ministerial approval, the Regulation was developed, written and adopted by hospital officials. It was not instigated by the government and did not reflect its mandatory retirement policy. Hospitals in British Columbia, moreover, exhibited great variety in their approaches to retirement. That each of these policies obtained ministerial approval reflected the large measure of managerial autonomy accorded to hospitals in this area.

[49] The situation in the present appeal is very different. The purpose of the *Hospital Insurance Act* is to provide particular services to the public. Although the benefits of that service are delivered and administered through private institutions — hospitals — it is the government, and not [the] hospitals, that is responsible for defining both the content of the service to be delivered and the persons entitled to receive it. As previously noted, s. 3(1) states that every person eligible to receive benefits is "entitled to receive the general hospital services provided under this Act." Section 5(1) defines "general hospital services" to include various services normally available in hospitals. As the definition of "hospital" in s. 1 makes clear, moreover, hospitals are required to furnish the general hospital services specified in the Act. While no single hospital makes all of these services available, the net effect of the Act is to entitle every qualified person to receive, and to require hospitals to supply, a complete range of medically required hospital services. Indeed, if the legislation did not assure this, it would run afoul of the *Canada Health Act*. It is also apparent that while hospitals are funded on a "lump sum" and not a "fee-for-service" basis, they are not entirely free to spend this money as they choose. This is apparent from s. 10(1) of the Act, which mandates the annual payment of a sum "determined by the minister to reimburse the hospital ... for the cost of rendering to beneficiaries those general hospital services authorized by this Act the hospital is required by the minister to provide for beneficiaries," as well as from s. 15(3)(c), which authorizes the minister to make "payments to hospitals for the service provided for under this Act" and s. 13(1), which provides that payments to a hospital "for services rendered by it ... shall be deemed to be payment in full for the services...."

[50] The structure of the *Hospital Insurance Act* reveals, therefore, that in providing medically necessary services, hospitals carry out a specific governmental objective. The Act is not, as the respondents contend, simply a mechanism to prevent hospitals from charging for their services. Rather, it provides for the delivery of a comprehensive social program....

[51.] Unlike *Stoffman*, then, in the present case there is a "direct and ... precisely-defined connection" between a specific government policy and the hospital's impugned conduct. The alleged discrimination — the failure to provide sign language interpretation — is intimately connected to the medical service delivery system instituted by the legislation. The provision of these services is not simply a matter of internal hospital management; it is an expression of government policy. Thus, while hospitals may be autonomous in their day-to-day operations, they act as agents for the government in providing the specific medical services set out in the Act. The Legislature, upon defining its objective as guaranteeing access to a range of medical services, cannot evade its obligations under s. 15(1) of the *Charter* to provide those services without discrimination by appointing hospitals to carry out that objective. In so far as they do so, hospitals must conform with the *Charter*.

[52] The case of the Medical Services Commission is more straightforward. It was not contested that the *Charter* applies to the Commission in exercising its power to determine whether a service is a benefit pursuant to s. 4(1) of the *Medical and Health Care Services Act*. It is plain that in so doing, the Commission implements a government policy, namely, to ensure that all residents receive medically required services without charge. In lieu of setting out a comprehensive list of insured services in legislation, the government has delegated to the Commission the power to determine what constitutes a "medically required" service. There is no doubt, therefore, that in exercising this discretion the Commission acts in governmental capacity and is thus subject to the *Charter*. As there is no need to do so, I refrain from commenting on whether the Commission might be considered part of government for other purposes.

. . . .

[La Forest J. held that the failure to provide for sign language interpreters was an unjustified denial of *Charter* equality and directed the provincial government to administer the legislation in a manner consistent with the requirements of *Charter* s. 15(1). La Forest J. rejected arguments that this approach interfered excessively with the government's discretion to allocate benefits or with the government's financial responsibilities.]

. . . .

[73] ... It has been suggested that s. 15(1) of the *Charter* does not oblige the state to take positive actions, such as provide services to ameliorate the symptoms of systemic or general inequality; see *Thibaudeau*, *supra*, at para. 37 (*per* L'Heureux-Dubé J.). Whether or not this is true in all cases, and I do not purport to decide the matter here, the question raised in the present case is of a wholly different order....

. . . .

[77] This Court has consistently held ... that discrimination can arise both from the adverse effects of rules of general application as well as from express distinctions flowing from the distribution of benefits. Given this state of affairs, I can think of no principled reason why it should not be possible to establish a claim of discrimination based on the adverse effects of a facially neutral benefit scheme....

. . . .

[87] ... [T]he estimated cost of providing sign language interpretation for the whole of British Columbia was only $150,000, or approximately 0.0025 per cent of the provincial health care budget at the time.... In these circumstances, the refusal to expend such a relatively insignificant sum to continue and extend the service cannot possibly constitute a minimum impairment of the appellants' constitutional rights.

. . . .

[91] The respondents also contend that recognition of the appellants' claim will have a ripple effect throughout the health care field, forcing governments to spend precious health care dollars accommodating the needs of myriad disadvantaged persons. "Virtually everyone in the health care system who is denied a service," they submit, "will either be medically disadvantaged or could argue that a medical disadvantage will arise from the lack of service." Similarly, in his concurring opinion in the Court of Appeal, Lambert J.A. observed that many of the medical services and products required by the disabled are not publicly funded. In these circumstances, he asserted, governments must have the freedom to allocate scarce health care dollars among various disadvantaged groups.

[92] ... The respondents have presented no evidence that this type of accommodation, if extended to other government services, will unduly strain the fiscal resources of the state. To deny the appellants' claim on such conjectural grounds, in my view, would denude s. 15(1) of its egalitarian promise and render the disabled's goal of a barrier-free society distressingly remote.

[95] I have found that where sign language interpreters are necessary for effective communication in the delivery of medical services, the failure to provide them constitutes a denial of s. 15(1) of the *Charter* and is not a reasonable limit under s. 1. Section 24(1) of the *Charter* provides that anyone whose rights under the *Charter* have been infringed or denied may obtain "such remedy as the court considers appropriate and just in the circumstances." In the present case, the appropriate and just remedy is to grant a declaration that this failure is unconstitutional and to direct the government of British Columbia to administer the *Medical and Health Care Services Act* [now the *Medicare Protection Act*] and the *Hospital Insurance Act* in a manner consistent with the requirements of s. 15(1) as I have described them.

[96] A declaration, as opposed to some kind of injunctive relief, is the appropriate remedy in this case because there are myriad options available to the government that may rectify the unconstitutionality of the current system. It is not this Court's role to dictate how this is to be accomplished. Although it is to be assumed that the government will move swiftly to correct the unconstitutionality of the present scheme and comply with this Court's directive, it is appropriate to suspend the effectiveness of the declaration for six months to enable the government to explore its options and formulate an appropriate response. In fashioning its response, the government should ensure that, after the expiration of six months or any other period of suspension granted by this Court, sign language interpreters will be provided where necessary for effective communication in the delivery of medical services. Moreover, it is presumed that the government will act in good faith by considering not only the role of hospitals in the delivery of medical services but also the involvement of the Medical Services Commission and the Ministry of Health.

(f)   Policy-Making Trends on the Supreme Court†

Donald R. Songer

NOTE

How actively has the Supreme Court been interpreting the *Canadian Charter of Rights and Freedoms*? Is a strong *Charter* and constitutional role by the Court consistent with parliamentary democracy?

In a 1994 study of 195 Supreme Court *Charter* decisions between 1982 and 1992, F.L. Morton, Peter Russell, and Troy Riddell suggested that although the Supreme Court's intervention rate had declined from an initial period of extreme activism, the Court's application of the *Charter* posed a challenge for both federalism and democracy.

Conducting a statistical analysis of 157 Supreme Court *Charter* decisions between 1993 and 1997, James Kelly in "The *Charter of Rights* and *Freedoms* and the Rebalancing of Liberal Constitutionalism in Canada 1982–1997" (1997) 37 Osgoode Hall L.J. 625 came to quite different conclusions. For example, in the extract below, Kelly found that where the Court did invalidate government action, this tended to be administrative action rather than legislation. In a 2000 public lecture, the Chief Justice of the Supreme Court made a similar point. She also argued that democracy itself requires not only elected legislatures but basic constitutional rights, vigorously enforced by independent courts of law: B. McLachlin, C.J.C., Ruth and Dick Bell Lecture, "Parliament, the Supreme Court and the *Charter*", Carleton University, October 18, 2000, and cf. Jürgen Habermas in *Between Facts and Norms* (Cambridge, Mass.: MIT Press, 1999) in Chapter 7.

† Excerpt from Donald R. Songer, *The Transformation of the Supreme Court of Canada: An Empirical Examination* (Toronto: University of Toronto Press, 2008) at 168–172. Reproduced with permission of the publisher. [Notes and in-text references omitted.] [Commentary note by David W. Elliott, revised and updated by N.E. Milanovic.]

For their part, writers such as Christopher P. Manfredi in *Judicial Power and the Charter: Canada and the Paradox of Liberal Constitutionalism*, 2d ed. (Don Mills, Ont.: Oxford University Press, 2001) and F.L. Morton and Rainer Knopff in *The Charter Revolution and the Court Party* (Peterborough: Broadview Press, 2000) have argued that *Charter* judicial activism is a serious threat to parliamentary democracy. In the extract below, Donald Songer sets out more recent data concerning the Supreme Court's *Charter* decisions. Does the record of the Supreme Court of Canada indicate a judicially active high court or a restrained body when it renders *Charter* judgements?

What is your view?

EXTRACT

The Charter of Rights has thirty-four sections, and both the frequency of litigation and the success of Charter claimants have varied dramatically according to which sections of the Charter are being 'called out.' Also, appellants sometimes raise issues relating to multiple provisions of the Charter and scholars disagree over which of the several provisions litigated is really the 'most important' issue in the case at hand. Usually there is no completely objective way to determine which of the Charter issues raised in the case is the most important. The analysis below of the success of Charter claimants relies on the judg-

ment of the Court's professional staff. For each case, those people prepare a series of 'tag lines' — which appear at the top of each opinion — that abstract the key legal issues from their perspective. These tag lines are widely used by lawyers and legal scholars to search for cases of interest. For the analysis below, the first two Charter provisions that were mentioned in the tag lines were used and the case outcome was coded as to whether the opinion supported or opposed the position of the Charter claimant on each of these two Charter issues.

The tag lines for the cases indicate that ... just eleven Charter sections have accounted for the bulk of claims resolved by the Supreme Court. Table 6.9 displays the results for all sections of the Charter with decisions by the Court in at least ten cases. Overall, through the end of 2003, Charter claimants have been successful in just under 40 percent of the challenges that have reached the Court. Whether one takes this as evidence that the Court is 'liberal' or 'conservative' depends on one's frame of reference. By a conventional calculus, one could say that the Court has made a conservative decision in a substantial proportion of its decisions; thus the Court is 'conservative' and the Charter has advanced a conservative rather than a liberal agenda. Alternatively, one might take the pre-Charter status quo as the point of reference. From that reference point, one would conclude that on 240 occasions, litigants have challenged the status quo, been able to take their rights claim all the way to the Supreme Court, and

---

TABLE 6.9
Support for Charter Claimants by the Supreme Court of Canada for Selected Sections of the Charter of Rights

Charter section	Pro-rights claimant (%)	N
1 Reasonable limits to rights	62.5	164
2 Fundamental freedoms	35.5	62
6 Enter and leave Canada	38.5	13
7 Life, liberty, and security of person	35.1	151
8 Search and seizure	37.7	69
9 No arbitrary detention	42.9	14
10 Right to counsel and habeas corpus	57.5	40
11 Criminal procedure rights	33.3	81
12 No cruel and unusual punishment	27.3	11
15 Equality rights	28.6	42
24 Exclusion of evidence	50.8	65
Other rights	46.5	43
Total	39.5	607

achieved the validation of a right previously not recognized.

Moreover, the Charter's impact has been much greater than the simple success rate might suggest, because presumably there has been a ripple effect, with both the lower courts and the executive taking account of each successive rights decision of the Court and altering their subsequent behaviour accordingly. There is, then, a multiplier effect from each rights decision by the Supreme Court that affects many more people than the litigants in the Court. The nature of the ripple effect can be guessed by noting the pattern over time. As noted above (see Morton, Russell, and Withey 1992), in its first two years of Charter litigation, close to two-thirds of Charter rights claimants were successful, but subsequently the success of rights claimants dropped significantly. Table 6.9 indicates that the success of those claimants continued at near these lower rates through 2003. One might interpret these findings as indicating that there was an initial period in which challenges were brought to practices and laws whose origin was prior to the Charter and that the Court sought to bring these prior practices into conformity with the Charter's new requirements. In these initial challenges, rights claimants were often successful. These early Charter decisions were presumably watched carefully both by lower-court judges and by government administrators, who then tried to adjust their own behaviour to conform to the Supreme Court's initial interpretations of the Charter. Subsequently, interest groups and other rights claimants sought to expand their initial gains by bringing 'second generation' rights claims, which sought to push the interpretation of the Charter towards even greater protection of rights. It is likely that the second- and third-generation issues brought to the Court typically asked either that the Court extend the protection of the Charter into new areas or that the Court give a more expansive reading of the rights guarantees than had been provided in earlier cases. As Justice J noted in an interview with the author, litigants (especially those supported by organized groups) tend to 'flex their muscles' after being encouraged by a previous pro-rights decision with the result that the '*Charter* is pled in everything' that comes to the Court over the following few years. In such a scenario, it would be likely that the proportion of cases in which rights claimants were successful would be relatively modest even if the Court was steadily expanding rights (i.e., moving policy in a liberal direction) at the margins.

For example, in *R v. Brydges* a unanimous court ruled that the Charter required police to notify sus-pects of their right to retain counsel and that police must refrain from eliciting information from the detainee until he or she had had a reasonable opportunity to exercise that right. This was an easy win for rights claimants because the result seemed mandated in a fairly straightforward manner by the words of the Charter itself. Then, four years later, in *R v. Prosper*, the courts faced a more difficult 'second generation' question: Did the Charter require the government to provide free and immediate counsel to indigent detainees? Here it was possible to make a reasoned argument in favour of the position advocated by the rights claimants, but a pro-claimant outcome was certainly not mandated in an unambiguous manner by the Charter's text (see Kelly 2005, 116).

Similarly, a recent analysis indicates that most of the statutes struck down before 1990 had been passed before the Charter's adoption. In the 1990s and the twenty-first century, however, most statutes challenged on Charter grounds have been passed *since* the Charter, and these statutes have undergone extensive Charter screening by Cabinet before passage (and thus the rights protected in these 1990s decisions have been more expansive than many of the rights in the decisions in the 1980s). The pre-1982 legislation 'was designed in a policy context that placed less emphasis on protected rights' (ibid., 144). Thus, though the percentage of pro-rights decisions made by the Supreme Court in the late 1990s and the early part of the twenty-first century is lower than the analogous percentage of decisions in the period immediately after the Charter, it is plausible that the Court may now be supporting an even more expansive interpretation of rights because the recent laws struck down have been the ones that have undergone extensive vetting by Cabinet to ensure that they protect Charter rights. This vetting process includes consideration of past Charter decisions by the appellate courts.

Table 6.9 also indicates that rights claimants have had different degrees of success litigating different provisions of the Charter. The lowest rates of success for rights claimants have come in cases raising a series of criminal procedure rights listed in Sections 11 and 12, which include a prohibition of unreasonable delay in being brought to trial, protection against self-incrimination, prohibition of unreasonable bail, and prohibitions against double jeopardy and cruel and unusual punishment. Rights claimants have also had low success rates litigating under Section 7, which is similar to the 'due process' clause of the U.S. Bill of Rights. Section 7 states: 'Everyone has a right to life, liberty and security of the person and the right not to be deprived thereof except in accordance with the principles of fundamental justice.' The relatively broad and vague language of this section perhaps invites rights claimants to challenge a wide variety of well-established practices, with the low success rate indicating that these claims often ask the Court to depart from the status quo to a greater extent than the justices are willing to permit. Finally, given the nature of the criticism of Charter politics offered by critics such as Morton and Knopff, one might expect that claimants under the equality rights provisions of Section 15 would have a high rate of success. Instead, table 6.9 indicates that claims of denial of equal rights succeeded less than one-third of the time.

Conclusions

While the proportion of the Supreme Court's docket devoted to criminal appeals and civil liber-

ties claims has increased substantially over the past third of a century, the success of criminal defendants and rights claimants remains relatively low. Yet there appears to be little support for Epp's controversial claim that bills of rights do not have any appreciable impact on the policy outcomes of high courts. Since the Charter, in percentage terms, there has been a substantial increase in constitutional challenges — an increase driven by rights claims. Moreover, while the overall success rate of rights claimants remains below 50 per cent, that rate has increased substantially since the Charter. It may also be inferred that changes in policy brought about by litigation under the Charter have been quite substantial in the aggregate if one focuses not on the percentage of successful appeals but rather on the number of changes in the status quo that have been brought about both directly and indirectly by the Charter of Rights.

Fundamental Freedoms and Fundamental Justice

(a) Fundamental Freedoms and Fundamental Justice

David W. Elliott

FUNDAMENTAL FREEDOMS

Freedom of speech, freedom of conscience, freedom of association. . . . In ordinary times, these are as commonplace to Canadians as fresh air and clean water, and may seem little more remarkable. We often tend to take them for granted.

A good corrective is to read William Shirer's long, grim chronicle, *The Rise and Fall of the Third Reich*.[1] Follow it up with the *Diary of a Young Girl*,[2] the short, tragic story of Ann Frank. Consider, too, the repression and brutality that plague so many corners of the globe today. Even Western democracies aren't immune to problems. For example, when crime and terrorism threaten personal property and safety, governments are under pressure to respond with control measures that can threaten personal liberty. Like fresh air and clean water, the fundamental freedoms are fragile.

Why preserve them? First, if human beings have value as individuals, not just as social building blocks, then there is merit in letting them make their own decisions, as free as possible from external constraints.[3] Second, as Mill suggested, sound opinions and proposals are likelier to emerge in contexts where ideas are freely debated than where they are restricted or controlled.[4] Third, free access to information, and the ability to associate freely with others, exchange ideas, criticize, and express opinions is vital to citizens' ability to maintain effective control of government.[5]

The entrenchment of many of these freedoms in the *Charter* raises their profile, and encourages a re-exploration of their rationales. Dickson J. linked the freedoms of conscience and religion to our democratic traditions in his eloquent judgment in *Big M*. But *Big M* also shows that the fundamental freedoms are no more precisely defined than any other basic rights. Among other things, the Court had to determine if freedom of religion includes freedom *from* religion, and if freedom of religion can benefit corporations as well as individuals.

The fundamental freedoms cases share another feature with other basic rights. As Peter Russell noted, the further we move from basic rights' usual "core" areas of application, the less agreement there is about them.[6] *Ford*, *Irwin Toy*, and *Keegstra* all involve situations at some distance from the normal application of a fundamental freedom. Is choice of language protected by freedom of speech? Commercial speech? Is speech protected even when its content is hate propaganda? Similarly, in *Dolphin Delivery*[7] the Court had to determine if freedom of speech includes secondary picketing.

Equally important, like other basic rights, the fundamental freedoms must be limited.[8] We *do* live in social units, and civilized life would be impossible without them.[9] Constraints are needed to achieve common goals, ensure public safety, prevent exploitation, allocate common resources, and assist the more vulnerable and deprived.

Since the *Charter* addresses rights and justification separately, a finding that a fundamental freedom was violated must be followed by a decision as to whether it was validly restricted. As suggested in the last chapter, section 1 of the *Charter*, the justification section, is a crucial provision.

FUNDAMENTAL JUSTICE AND SECTION 7

"Fundamental justice" in section 7 of the *Charter* was even less defined than the fundamental freedoms. Fundamental justice was a relatively untested term in 1982. It occurred in the *Canadian Bill of Rights*, where it had attracted little attention, and had appeared only rarely in the common law. If fundamental justice had a core, it was probably natural justice or procedural fairness, an assumption confirmed by the court in *Singh*. But how about *non*-procedural injustice? Was it caught by section 7 as well? In the *Motor Vehicles Reference*, one of the most activist of all *Charter* decisions, the Supreme Court's answer was as definite as its definition of fundamental justice was indefinite. In *Suresh*,[10] the Supreme Court has held that fundamental justice can include some norms of international law. What other norms will qualify? *Suresh* has also said that fundamental justice requires a "balancing" approach by courts. How will this affect section 1?

In the other limb of section 7, one important question is how far "liberty" or "security of the person" will protect economic interests. The answer to this question could do much to shape the general thrust of the *Charter*. Section 7 is a *"status quo"* provision, offering protection to those with interests to protect. In the economic area, wealthy individuals, corporations, and other organizations have more to protect than the rest of us. An expansive interpretation of section 7 in the economic sphere, combined with an expansive interpretation of funda-

mental justice, could tilt the direction of the *Charter* more toward preservation of the economic *status quo*. Alternatively, it could prompt courts to try to balance this with a more expansive interpretation of "reformist" provisions such as section 15. As with the fundamental freedoms, what happens will be determined almost exclusively by one institution — the courts.

Notes

1. W.L. Shirer, *The Rise and Fall of the Third Reich: A History of Nazi Germany* (New York: Simon, 1960).
2. Ann Frank, *Diary of a Young Girl [1939–43]*, trans. of *Net. Achterhuis* (Garden City, N.Y.: Doubleday, 1952). See also N. Mandela, *Long Walk to Freedom: The Autobiography of Nelson Mandela* (New York: Little, Brown and Co., 1994), describing Mr. Mandela's painful, life-long struggle against the brutality of apartheid in South Africa.
3. *Cf.* N.M. MacCormick, *Legal Right and Social Democracy* (Oxford: Oxford University Press, 1982) at 11–12. In many cases the result of this freedom may be a decision to band together to achieve in groups what individuals might be unable or unlikely to accomplish separately. The collective bargaining process is an example of this.
4. J.S. Mill, "On Liberty [1859]" in *On Liberty; Representative Government; The Subjection of Women: Three Essays*, intro. by M.G. Fawcett, London, Oxford University Press, 1966) at 17–18 and 92–94. See extracts from Mill in Chapter 1, above.
5. See Peter W. Hogg, *Constitutional Law of Canada*, 4th ed. (Scarborough, Ont.: Carswell, 1997) at heading 40.4, referring to this and the other two main rationales in the context of freedom of expression.
6. P.H. Russell, "The Political Purposes of the Canadian Charter of Rights and Freedoms" (1983) 61 Canadian Bar Rev. 30.
7. Chapter 8, above.
8. Or perhaps extended in some cases to groups.
9. See Michael Mac Neil, "Courts and Liberal Ideology: An Analysis of the Application of the *Charter* to Some Labour Law Issues" (1989) 34 McGill L.J. 86.
10. *Suresh v. Canada (Minister of Citizenship and Immigration)*, [2002] 1 S.C.R. 3.

(b) *R. v. Big M Drug Mart Ltd. et al.*†

NOTE

Big M was an Alberta drug store that was charged with unlawfully carrying on the sale of goods on a Sunday, contrary to the federal *Lord's Day Act*. Big M challenged the constitutionality of the Act, arguing that it was beyond the powers conferred

on Parliament by the *Constitution Act, 1867*, and that it violated the *Charter*'s guarantee of freedom of religion. The Supreme Court of Canada held that although the Act fell under federal jurisdiction in the *Constitution Act, 1867*, it did violate the *Charter* guarantee of freedom of religion, and was not justified under section 1 of the *Charter*.

---

† [1985] 1 S.C.R. 295, aff'g. (1983) 5 D.L.R. (4th) 121 (A.C.A), aff'g. a judgment of Stevenson Prov. Ct. J. [Commentary note by David W. Elliott.]

In this early case, the Supreme Court gave every indication that it would take an activist approach to the *Charter*. Dickson J.'s eloquent judgment re-affirmed the Court's intention to give the *Charter* "a generous rather than a legalistic" interpretation; gave the benefit of a *Charter* defence to a corporation; rejected the "frozen rights" approach to freedom of religion under the *Canadian Bill of Rights*; defined freedom *of* religion to include freedom *from* religion; and drew a link between the basic freedoms in section 2(d) of the *Charter* and Canada's democratic political tradition.

EXTRACT

[DICKSON J. for himself and for BEETZ, McINTYRE, CHOUINARD, and LAMER JJ.:]

The Facts and the Legislation

On Sunday, May 30, 1982, police officers of the City of Calgary attended at premises owned by Big M and open to the public. They witnessed several transactions including the sale of groceries, plastic cups and a bicycle lock. Big M was charged with a violation of s. 4 of the *Lord's Day Act*.

The Lord's Day Act

An understanding of the scheme of that Act and its basic purpose and effect is integral to any analysis of its constitutional validity. Section 2 defines, *inter alia*, the Lord's Day:

> "Lord's Day" means the period of time that begins at midnight on Saturday night and ends at midnight on the following night;

Section 4 contains the basic prohibition against any work or commercial activity upon the Lord's Day:

> **4.** It is not lawful for any person on the Lord's Day, except as provided herein, or in any provincial Act or law in force on or after the 1st day of March 1907, to sell or offer for sale or purchase any goods, chattels, or other personal property, or any real estate, or to carry on or transact any business of his ordinary calling, or in connection with such calling, or for gain to do, or employ any other person to do, on that day, any work, business, or labour.

. . . .

The Act makes it an offence punishable on summary conviction for: any person to violate the Act (s. 12); any employer to direct any violation of the Act (s. 13); any corporation to authorize, direct or permit any violation of the Act (s. 14).

. . . .

... In my view, both purpose and effect are relevant in determining constitutionality; either an unconstitutional purpose or an unconstitutional effect can invalidate legislation. All legislation is animated by an object the legislature intends to achieve. This object is realized through the impact produced by the operation and application of the legislation. Purpose and effect respectively, in the sense of the legislation's object and its ultimate impact, are clearly linked, if not indivisible. Intended and actual effects have often been looked to for guidance in assessing the legislation's object and thus, its validity.

. . . .

If the acknowledged purpose of the *Lord's Day Act*, namely, the compulsion of sabbatical observance, offends freedom of religion, it is then unnecessary to consider the actual impact of Sunday closing upon religious freedom. Even if such effects were found inoffensive, as the Attorney General of Alberta urges, this could not save legislation whose purpose has been found to violate the *Charter*'s guarantees. In any event, I would find it difficult to conceive of legislation with an unconstitutional purpose, where the effects would not also be unconstitutional.

. . . .

... [T]he legislation's purpose is the initial test of constitutional validity and its effects are to be considered when the law under review has passed or, at least, has purportedly passed the purpose test. If the legislation fails the purpose test, there is no need to consider further its effects, since it has already been demonstrated to be invalid. Thus, if a law with a valid purpose interferes by its impact, with rights or freedoms, a litigant could still argue the effects of the legislation as a means to defeat its applicability and possibly its validity. In short, the effects test will only be necessary to defeat legislation with a valid purpose; effects can never be relied upon to save legislation with an invalid purpose.

... [In a second related submission by the Attorney General of Saskatchewan, i]t is urged that courts, in ignoring the religious motivation for the legislation as well as its religious terminology are implicitly assessing the legislation's effects rather than the purposes which originally underlay its enactment. (See, for example, Frankfurter J. in *McGowan* v. *Maryland, supra*, at 466.) A number of objections can be advanced to this "shifting purpose" argument.

First, there are the practical difficulties. No legislation would be safe from a revised judicial assessment of purpose.... Not only would this encourage uncertainty in the law, but it would encourage re-litigation of the same issues....

.   .   .   .

Furthermore, the theory of a shifting purpose stands in stark contrast to fundamental notions developed in our law concerning the nature of "Parliamentary intention." Purpose is a function of the intent of those who drafted and enacted the legislation at the time, and not of any shifting variable.

.   .   .   .

... In result, therefore, the *Lord's Day Act* must be characterized as it has always been, a law the primary purpose of which is the compulsion of sabbatical observance.

Freedom of Religion

A truly free society is one which can accommodate a wide variety of beliefs, diversity of tastes and pursuits, customs and codes of conduct. A free society is one which aims at equality with respect to the enjoyment of fundamental freedoms and I say this without any reliance upon s. 15 of the *Charter*. Freedom must surely be founded in respect for the inherent dignity and the inviolable rights of the human person. The essence of the concept of freedom of religion is the right to entertain such religious beliefs as a person chooses, the right to declare religious beliefs openly and without fear of hindrance or reprisal, and the right to manifest religious belief by worship and practice or by teaching and dissemination. But the concept means more than that.

Freedom can primarily be characterized by the absence of coercion or constraint. If a person is compelled by the state or the will of another to a course of action or inaction which he would not otherwise have chosen, he is not acting of his own volition and he cannot be said to be truly free. One of the major purposes of the *Charter* is to protect, within reason, from compulsion or restraint. Coercion includes not only such blatant forms of compulsion as direct commands to act or refrain from

acting on pain of sanction, coercion includes indirect forms of control which determine or limit alternative courses of conduct available to others. Freedom in a broad sense embraces both the absence of coercion and constraint, and the right to manifest beliefs and practices. Freedom means that, subject to such limitations as are necessary to protect public safety, order, health, or morals or the fundamental rights and freedoms of others, no one is to be forced to act in a way contrary to his beliefs or his conscience.

What may appear good and true to a majoritarian religious group, or to the state acting at their behest, may not, for religious reasons, be imposed upon citizens who take a contrary view. The *Charter* safeguards religious minorities from the threat of "the tyranny of the majority."

To the extent that it binds all to a sectarian Christian ideal, the *Lord's Day Act* works a form of coercion inimical to the spirit of the *Charter* and the dignity of all non-Christians. In proclaiming the standards of the Christian faith, the Act creates a climate hostile to, and gives the appearance of discrimination against, non-Christian Canadians. It takes religious values rooted in Christian morality and, using the force of the state, translates them into a positive law binding on believers and non-believers alike. The theological content of the legislation remains as a subtle and constant reminder to religious minorities within the country of their differences with, and alienation from, the dominant religious culture.

Non-Christians are prohibited for religious reasons from carrying out activities which are otherwise lawful, moral and normal. The arm of the state requires all to remember the Lord's day of the Christians and to keep it holy. The protection of one religion and the concomitant non-protection of others imports disparate impact destructive of the religious freedom of the collectivity.

I agree with the submission of the respondent that to accept that Parliament retains the right to compel universal observance of the day of rest preferred by one religion is not consistent with the preservation and enhancement of the multicultural heritage of Canadians. To do so is contrary to the expressed provisions of s. 27....

.   .   .   .

This Court has already, in some measure, set out the basic approach to be taken in interpreting the *Charter*. In *Hunter* v. *Southam Inc.*, [1984] 2 S.C.R. 145, this Court expressed the view that the proper approach to the definition of the rights and freedoms guaranteed by the *Charter* was a purposive one. The meaning of a right or freedom guaranteed by the *Charter* was to be ascertained by an analysis of the purpose of such a guarantee; it was to be understood, in other words, in the light of the interests it was meant to protect.

In my view this analysis is to be undertaken, and the purpose of the right or freedom in question is to be sought by reference to the character and the larger objects of the *Charter* itself, to the language chosen to articulate the specific right or freedom, to the historical origins of the concepts enshrined, and where applicable, to the meaning and purpose of the other specific rights and freedoms with which it is associated within the text of the *Charter*. The interpretation should be, as the judgment in *Southam* emphasizes, a generous rather than a legalistic one, aimed at fulfilling the purpose of the guarantee and securing for individuals the full benefit of the *Charter*'s protection. At the same time it is important not to overshoot the actual purpose of the right or freedom in question, but to recall that the *Charter* was not enacted in a vacuum, and must therefore, as this Court's decision in *Law Society of Upper Canada* v. *Skapinker*, [1984] 1 S.C.R. 357, illustrates, be placed in its proper linguistic, philosophic and historical contexts.

With regard to freedom of conscience and religion, the historical context is clear. As they are relevant to the *Charter*, the origins of the demand for such freedom are to be found in the religious struggles in post-Reformation Europe. The spread of new beliefs, the changing religious allegiance of kings and princes, the shifting military fortunes of their armies and the consequent repeated redrawing of national and imperial frontiers led to situations in which large numbers of people — sometimes even the majority in a given territory — found themselves living under rulers who professed faiths different from, and often hostile to, their own and subject to laws aimed at enforcing conformity to religious beliefs and practices they did not share.

English examples of such laws, passed during the Tudor and Stuart periods, have been alluded to in the discussion above of the criminal law character of Sunday observance legislation. Opposition to such laws was confined at first to those who upheld the prohibited faiths and practices, and was designed primarily to avoid the disabilities and penalties to which these specific adherents were subject. As a consequence, when history or geography put power into the hands of these erstwhile victims of religious oppression the persecuted all too often became the persecutors.

Beginning, however, with the Independent faction within the Parliamentary party during the Commonwealth or Interregnum, many, even among those who shared the basic beliefs of the ascendant religion, came to voice opposition to the use of the State's coercive power to secure obedience to religious precepts and to extirpate non-conforming beliefs. The basis of this opposition was no longer simply a conviction that the State was enforcing the wrong set of beliefs and practices but rather the perception that belief itself was not amenable to compulsion. Attempts to compel belief or practice denied the reality of individual conscience and dishonoured the God that had planted it in His creatures. It is from these antecedents that the concepts of freedom of religion and freedom of conscience became associated, to form, as they do in s. 2(a) of our *Charter*, the single integrated concept of "freedom of conscience and religion."

What unites enunciated freedoms in the American First Amendment, s. 2(a) of the *Charter*, and in the provisions of other human rights documents in which they are associated is the notion of the centrality of individual conscience and the inappropriateness of governmental intervention to compel or to constrain its manifestation. In *Hunter* v. *Southam Inc.*, *supra*, the purpose of the *Charter* was identified, at p. 155, as "the unremitting protection of individual rights and liberties." It is easy to see the relationship between respect for individual conscience and the valuation of human dignity that motivates such unremitting protection.

It should also be noted, however, that an emphasis on individual conscience and individual judgment also lies at the heart of our democratic political tradition. The ability of each citizen to make free and informed decisions is the absolute prerequisite for the legitimacy, acceptability, and efficacy of our system of self-government. It is because of the centrality of the rights associated with freedom of individual conscience both to basic beliefs about human worth and dignity and to a free and democratic political system that American jurisprudence has emphasized the primacy or "firstness" of the First Amendment. It is this same centrality that in my view underlies their designation in the Canadian *Charter of Rights and Freedoms* as "fundamental." They are the *sine qua non* of the political tradition underlying the *Charter*.

Viewed in this context, the purpose of freedom of conscience and religion becomes clear. The values that underlie our political and philosophic traditions demand that every individual be free to hold and to manifest whatever beliefs and opinions his or her conscience dictates, provided *inter alia* only that such manifestations do not injure his or her neighbours or their parallel rights to hold and manifest beliefs and opinions of their own. Religious belief and practice are historically prototypical and, in many ways, paradigmatic of conscientiously-held beliefs and manifestations and are therefore protected by the *Charter*. Equally protected, and for the same reasons, are expressions and manifestations of religious non-belief and refusals to participate in religious practice.... [W]hatever else freedom of conscience and religion may mean, it must at the very least mean this: government may not coerce individuals to affirm a specific religious belief or to manifest a specific religious practice for a sectarian purpose....

. . . .

Two bases for restricting the scope of s. 2(a) have been suggested by the appellant and his supporting intervenors. First was the approach ... which maintained that there is no compulsion of religion. Abstention from work on Sunday does not, in itself, have any religious significance. Its effect is, therefore, merely secular.

This argument cannot be accepted for reasons already outlined. Once the purpose has been classified as offensive, then the legislation cannot be saved by permissible effect....

. . . .

A second basis for urging a more restricted reading of freedom of conscience and religion was the position of the American courts on Sunday observance legislation. Such legislation has been sustained by the United States Supreme Court, though it has been recognized that such legislation might offend the non-establishment clause of the First Amendment. The absence of such a clause in the *Charter*, it was submitted, indicated that this Court should sustain the *Lord's Day Act*.

Such a finding is not possible, in light of the earlier discussion in these reasons on the relevance of the absence of an anti-establishment provision in s. 2(a) of the *Charter*.

In my view, the guarantee of freedom of conscience and religion prevents the government from compelling individuals to perform or abstain from performing otherwise harmless acts because of the religious significance of those acts to others. The element of religious compulsion is perhaps somewhat

more difficult to perceive (especially for those whose beliefs are being enforced) when, as here, it is non-action rather than action that is being decreed, but in my view compulsion is nevertheless what it amounts to.

. . . .

On the authorities and for the reasons outlined, the true purpose of the *Lord's Day Act* is to compel the observance of the Christian Sabbath and I find the Act, and especially s. 4 thereof, infringes upon the freedom of conscience and religion guaranteed in s. 2(a) of the *Charter*. The answer to the first constitutional question will be in the affirmative.

Section 1 of the *Charter*

Is the *Lord's Day Act*, and especially s. 4 thereof, justified on the basis of s. 1 of the *Canadian Charter of Rights and Freedoms*? That is the second question posed.

The appellant submits that even if the *Lord's Day Act* does involve a violation of freedom of conscience and religion as guaranteed by s. 2(a) of the *Charter*, the provisions of the Act constitute a reasonable limit, demonstrably justifiable in a free and democratic society, on that right and that therefore the Act can be saved pursuant to s. 1 of the *Charter*....

. . . .

[Dickson J. said that the breach of section 2(a) could not be justified under section 1 for religious reasons because these were the very reasons the provision violated section 2(b). Nor could it be justified under section 1 for secular reasons, since the purpose of the statute was not secular, but religious.]

. . . .

If a court or tribunal finds any statute to be inconsistent with the Constitution, the overriding effect of the *Constitution Act, 1982*, s. 52(1), is to give the Court not only the power, but the duty, to regard the inconsistent statute, to the extent of the inconsistency, as being no longer "of force or effect." That, in my view, is the position in respect of the *Lord's Day Act*. The answer to the second question will be in the negative.

Classification

The third question put in issue by this Court is this:

> Is the *Lord's Day Act*, R.S.C. 1970, c. L-13, and especially s. 4 thereof enacted pursuant to the criminal law power under s. 91(27) of the *Constitution Act, 1867*.

All members of the Alberta Court of Appeal agreed that settled authority compelled the conclusion that the *Lord's Day Act* was competent to Parliament pursuant to its power to legislate in relation to criminal law under s. 91(27). The appellant and his supporting interveners submit that the Court of Appeal was correct in their conclusion and the respondent concedes the point.

The *Lord's Day Act* has been held "early, regularly and recently" to be in relation to a criminal law matter because, at risk of penalty, it compels the observance of a religious obligation, specifically the preservation of the sanctity of the Christian Sabbath. The *Lord's Day Act* is legislation in relation to a matter which falls within s. 91(27), one of the classes of subjects reserved to the exclusive authority of Parliament, because it is directed towards the maintenance of public order and public morals....

. . . .

It should be noted, however, that this conclusion as to the federal Parliament's legislative competence to enact the *Lord's Day Act* depends on the identification of the purpose of the Act as compelling observance of Sunday by virtue of its religious significance. Were its purpose not religious but rather the secular goal of enforcing a uniform day of rest from labour, the Act would come under s. 92(13), property and civil rights in the province and, hence, fall under provincial rather than federal competence: *In the Matter of Legislative Jurisdiction Over Hours of Labour*, [1925] S.C.R. 505; *Attorney-General for Canada* v. *Attorney-General for Ontario*, [1937] A.C. 326 (P.C.). The answer to the third question will be in the affirmative.

Conclusion

In my view the majority in the Alberta Court of Appeal was correct in its disposition of the issues in this appeal. The *Lord's Day Act* is enacted pursuant to the criminal law power under s. 91(27) of the *Constitution Act, 1867*. In providing for the compulsory observance of the religious institution of the Sabbath (Sunday), the Act and especially s. 4 thereof does infringe on the guarantee of freedom of conscience and religion in s. 2(a) of the *Canadian Charter of Rights and Freedoms* and this infringement cannot be justified on the basis of s. 1 of the *Charter*. I would declare the *Lord's Day Act* to be of no force or effect, by reason of s. 52(1) of the *Constitution Act, 1982*.

. . . .

[Wilson J. agreed with the conclusions of Dickson J.]

Appeal dismissed with costs.

POSTSCRIPT

Compare *Big M* with the Supreme Court's more recent freedom of religion decision in *Multani v. Commission scolaire Marguerite-Bourgeoys*, 2006 SCC 6. There a majority of the Court held that school authorities' decisions to prohibit a Sikh student from wearing a ceremonial kirpan to school were an unjustified violation of freedom of religion. Note that *Multani* involved a claim to freedom of religion, not freedom *from* religion. In the later case, the judges had little doubt that the Sikh student's freedom of religion had been violated or disregarded. However, the government action in *Multani* involved administrative decisions rather than laws or regulations. In such a case, should courts use an ordinary judicial review approach and consider if the decisions were unreasonable, patently unreasonable, or incorrect, and therefore outside the authority of their enabling legislation? Two Supreme Court judges thought so. Alternatively, should judges take a constitutional approach, and determine if there was an unjustified violation of a guaranteed *Charter* right or freedom? This was the approach favoured by the majority in *Multani*. A court's decision to apply the *Charter* rather than non-constitutional criteria, or *vice versa*, is not a mere technical or academic matter, as it can have significant legal consequences. For example, it is normally easier for a legislature to reverse the effects of an ordinary judicial review decision, than it is to reverse the effects of a *Charter* decision. Why is this so?

(c) *Ford v. Quebec (A.G.)*†

NOTE

Ms. Ford, operator of a Pointe-Claire wool shop, and two other Quebec business concerns were warned that they were contravening the *Charter of the French Language* (also known as Bill 101). Two other Quebec businesses were formally charged with violating it. The *Quebec Language Charter* allowed only French on signs and advertising (s. 58) and permitted only the French version of firm names (s. 69). Although Ms. Ford's firm name was all in French, the sign outside her wool shop contained in the words "LAINE" and "WOOL", side by side. In 1982, the Parti Québécois government had applied a standard override provision to exempt all of Bill 101 from sections 2 and 7 to 15 of the *Canadian Charter of Rights and Freedoms*. The standard override had expired for section 69, but it had been re-applied to section 58.

The businesses argued that sections 58 and 69 violated the freedom of expression guarantees in the federal *Charter* and in the Quebec *Charter of Human Rights and Freedoms*, and were not saved by sections 1 and 9.1, in the federal and provincial charters, respectively. They also argued that the override provision must be more explicit in order to have effect.

Ford drew the Court into three questions of major significance. First, how much scope should courts give to the will of elected representatives, as expressed in the federal *Charter*'s override provision? Second, what protection — if any — should courts give to an economic interest such as freedom of commercial expression? Third, how much scope should courts give to the Quebec government's attempts to preserve a French "visage linguistique" in the province, at the expense of the anglophone and allophone minorities?

Within days of the Supreme Court's decision, the Quebec government introduced legislation to limit the use of English to the interior of most Quebec business premises. In response to that action, the Manitoba government announced that it would not be ratifying the Meech Lake Accord. The Court's decision had gone to the very centre of Canadian constitutional politics. But whatever its decision, could it have done otherwise?

EXTRACT

[The COURT:]

With great respect for the contrary view, this Court is of the opinion that a s. 33 declaration is sufficiently express if it refers to the number of the section, subsection or paragraph of the *Charter* which contains the provision or provisions to be overridden. Of course, if it is intended to override only a part of the provision or provisions contained in a section, subsection or paragraph then there would have to be a sufficient reference in words to the part to be overridden. In so far as requirements of the democratic process are relevant, this is the form of reference used in legislative drafting with respect to legislative provisions to be amended or repealed. There is no reason why more should be required under s. 33....

. . . .

Therefore, s. 52 of An Act to amend the *Charter of the French Language* is a valid and subsisting exercise of the override authority conferred by s. 33 of the *Canadian Charter of Rights and Freedoms* that protects s. 58 of the *Charter of the French Language* from the application of s. 2(b) of the Canadian *Charter*. Section 69 of the *Charter of the French Language* is not so protected since it was not affected by an Act to amend the *Charter of the French Language*. In the result, as indicated in the following Part VI of these reasons, s. 58 is subject to s. 3 of the Quebec *Charter of Human Rights and Freedoms* while s. 69 is subject to both s. 2(b) of the Canadian *Charter* and s. 3 of the Quebec *Charter*.

. . . .

... Language is so intimately related to the form and content of expression that there cannot be true freedom of expression by means of language if

---

† [1988] 2 S.C.R. 712, aff'g. (1987) 36 D.L.R. (4th) 374 (Q.C.A.), aff'g. (1985) 18 D.L.R. (4th) 711 (Q.C.A.), aff'g. in part an application for a declaration that certain sections of the *Charter of the French Language* were inoperative. [Commentary note by David W. Elliott.]

one is prohibited from using the language of one's choice. Language is not merely a means or medium of expression; it colours the content and meaning of expression. It is, as the preamble of the *Charter of the French Language* itself indicates, a means by which a people may express its cultural identity. It is also the means by which the individual expresses his or her personal identity and sense of individuality. That the concept of "expression" in s. 2(b) of the Canadian *Charter* and s. 3 of the Quebec *Charter* goes beyond mere content is indicated by the specific protection accorded to "freedom of thought, belief [and] opinion" in s. 2 and to "freedom of conscience" and "freedom of opinion" in s. 3. That suggests that "freedom of expression" is intended to extend to more than the content of expression in its narrow sense.

. . . .

... Given the earlier pronouncements of this Court to the effect that the rights and freedoms guaranteed in the Canadian *Charter* should be given a large and liberal interpretation, there is no sound basis on which commercial expression can be excluded from the protection of s. 2(b) of the *Charter*. It is worth noting that the courts below applied a similar generous and broad interpretation to include commercial expression within the protection of freedom of expression contained in s. 3 of the Quebec *Charter*. Over and above its intrinsic value as expression, commercial expression which, as has been pointed out, protects listeners as well as speakers, plays a significant role in enabling individuals to make informed economic choices, an important aspect of individual self-fulfilment and personal autonomy. The Court accordingly rejects the view that commercial expression serves no individual or societal value in a free and democratic society and for this reason is undeserving of any constitutional protection.

Rather, the expression contemplated by s. 58 and 69 of the *Charter of the French Language* is expression within the meaning of both s. 2(b) of the Canadian *Charter* and s. 3 of the Quebec *Charter*. This leads to the conclusion that s. 58 infringes the freedom of expression guaranteed by s. 3 of the Quebec *Charter* and s. 69 infringes the guaranteed freedom of expression under both s. 2(b) of the Canadian *Charter* and s. 3 of the Quebec *Charter*. Although the expression in this case has a commercial element, it should be noted that the focus here is on choice of language and on a law which prohibits the use of a language. We are not asked in this case to deal with the distinct issue of the permissi-ble scope of regulation of advertising (for example to protect consumers) where different governmental interests come into play, particularly when assessing the reasonableness of limits on such commercial expression pursuant to s. 1 of the Canadian *Charter* or to s. 9.1 of the Quebec *Charter*. It remains to be considered whether the limit imposed on freedom of expression by ss. 58 and 69 is justified under either s. 1 of the Canadian *Charter* or s. 9.1 of the Quebec *Charter*, as the case may be.

. . . .

The qualifications of the requirement of the exclusive use of French in other provisions of the *Charter of the French Language* and the regulations do not make ss. 58 and 69 any less prohibitions of the use of any language other than French as applied to the respondents. The issue is whether any such prohibition is justified. In the opinion of this Court it has not been demonstrated that the prohibition of the use of any language other than French in ss. 58 and 69 of the *Charter of the French Language* is necessary to the defence and enhancement of the status of the French language in Quebec or that it is proportionate to that legislative purpose. Since the evidence put to us by the government showed that the predominance of the French language was not reflected in the "visage linguistique" of Quebec, the governmental response could well have been tailored to meet that specific problem and to impair freedom of expression minimally. Thus, whereas requiring the predominant display of the French language, even its marked predominance, would be proportional to the goal of promoting and maintaining a French "visage linguistique" in Quebec and therefore justified under the Quebec *Charter* and the Canadian *Charter*, requiring the exclusive use of French has not been so justified. French could be required in addition to any other language or it could be required to have greater visibility than that accorded to other languages. Such measures would ensure that the "visage linguistique" reflected the demography of Quebec: the predominant language is French. This reality should be communicated to all citizens and non-citizens alike, irrespective of their mother tongue. But exclusivity for the French language has not survived the scrutiny of a proportionality test and does not reflect the reality of Quebec society. Accordingly, we are of the view that the limit imposed on freedom of expression by s. 58 of the *Charter of the French Language* respecting the exclusive use of French on public signs and posters and in commercial advertising is not justified under s. 9.1 of the Quebec *Charter*.

In like measure, the limit imposed on freedom of expression by s. 69 of the *Charter of the French Language* respecting the exclusive use of the French version of a firm name is not justified under either s. 9.1 of the Quebec *Charter* or s. 1 of the Canadian *Charter*.

. . . .

... In this case, the limit imposed on that right was not a justifiable one under s. 9.1 of the Quebec *Charter*. The distinction based on language of use

created by s. 58 of the *Charter of the French Language* thus has the effect of nullifying the right to full and equal recognition and exercise of this freedom. Section 58 is therefore also of no force or effect as infringing s. 10 of the Quebec *Charter*. The same conclusion must apply to s. 69 of the *Charter of the French Language*....

. . . .

Appeal dismissed with costs.

(d) *Irwin Toy Ltd. v. Quebec (A.G.)*†

NOTE

Irwin Toy Ltd. challenged the validity of provisions in a Quebec law that prohibited advertising aimed at children under the age of 13. The toy company argued that the provisions infringed on exclusive federal legislative jurisdiction over broadcasting, and contravened sections 2(b) and 7 of the *Charter*.

The Supreme Court held that the law did not infringe the federal broadcasting power, and fell under provincial jurisdiction over property and civil rights. It re-affirmed that "expression" in section 2(b) of the *Charter* can include commercial expression. (Note the Court's tests for determining (a) if an activity constitutes expression and (b) if a legislative provision restricts expression). The Court held that freedom of expression was breached here. However, the majority held that the breach was justified under section 1 of the *Charter*.

Irwin Toy also argued that the provisions deprived them of their economic liberty and were so vague as to deny them fundamental justice, so that they breached section 7 of the *Charter*. The Court said that corporations cannot invoke section 7, except as a defence in criminal proceedings. It stressed that section 7 does not protect "property", and suggested that it would not apply to corporate-commercial economic interests.

Parts of the Court's discussion of freedom of expression are reproduced below.

EXTRACT

[DICKSON C.J. and LAMER and WILSON JJ.:]

Does advertising aimed at children fall within the scope of freedom of expression? This question must be put even before deciding whether there has been a limitation of the guarantee. Clearly, not all activity is protected by freedom of expression, and governmental action restricting this form of advertising only limits the guarantee if the activity in issue was protected in the first place. Thus, for example, in *Reference Re Public Service Employee Relations Act (Alta.)*, [1987] 1 S.C.R. 313; *PSAC v. Canada*, [1987] 1 S.C.R. 424; and *RWDSU v. Saskatchewan*, [1987] 1 S.C.R. 460, the majority of the Court found that freedom of association did not include the right to strike. The activity itself was not within the sphere protected by s. 2(d); therefore the government action in restricting it was not contrary to the *Charter*. The same procedure must be followed with respect to an analysis of freedom of expression; the first step to be taken in an inquiry of this kind is to discover whether the activity which the plaintiff wishes to pursue may properly be characterized as falling within "freedom of expression." If the activity is not within s. 2(b), the government action obviously cannot be challenged under that section.

. . . .

---

† [1989] 1 S.C.R. 927, rev'g. (1986), 32 D.L.R. (4th) 641 (Q.C.A.), rev'g. [1982] C.S. 96 (Q.S.C.). [Commentary note by David W. Elliott.]

"Expression" has both a content and a form, and the two can be inextricably connected. Activity is expressive if it attempts to convey meaning. That meaning is its content. Freedom of expression was entrenched in our Constitution and is guaranteed in the Quebec *Charter* so as to ensure that everyone can manifest their thoughts, opinions, beliefs, indeed all expressions of the heart and mind, however unpopular, distasteful or contrary to the mainstream. Such protection is, in the words of both the Canadian and Quebec *Charter*s, "fundamental" because in a free, pluralistic and democratic society we prize a diversity of ideas and opinions for their inherent value both to the community and to the individual....

. . . .

We cannot ... exclude human activity from the scope of guaranteed free expression on the basis of the content or meaning being conveyed. Indeed, if the activity conveys or attempts to convey a meaning, it has expressive content and *prima facie* falls within the scope of the guarantee. Of course, while most human activity combines expressive and physical elements, some human activity is purely physical and does not convey or attempt to convey meaning. It might be difficult to characterize certain day-to-day tasks, like parking a car, as having expressive content. To bring such activity within the protected sphere, the plaintiff would have to show that it was performed to convey a meaning. For example, an unmarried person might, as part of a public protest, park in a zone reserved for spouses of government employees in order to express dissatisfaction or outrage at the chosen method of allocating a limited resource. If that person could demonstrate that his activity did in fact have expressive content, he would, at this stage, be within the protected sphere and the s. 2(b) challenge would proceed.

The content of expression can be conveyed through an infinite variety of forms of expression: for example, the written or spoken word, the arts, and even physical gestures or acts. While the guarantee of free expression protects all content of expression, certainly violence as a form of expression receives no such protection....

. . . .

The broad, inclusive approach to the protected sphere of free expression here outlined is consonant with that suggested by some leading theorists. Thomas Emerson, in his article entitled "Toward a

General Theory of the First Amendment" (1963), 72 *Yale L.J.* 877, notes (at 886) that:

> ... the theory of freedom of expression involves more than a technique for arriving at better social judgments through democratic procedures. It comprehends a vision of society, a faith and a whole way of life. The theory grew out of an age that was awakened and invigorated by the idea of a new society in which man's mind was free, his fate determined by his own powers of reason, and his prospects of creating a rational and enlightened civilization virtually unlimited. It is put forward as a prescription for attaining a creative, progressive, exciting and intellectually robust community. It contemplates a mode of life that, through encouraging toleration, skepticism, reason and initiative, will allow man to realize his full potentialities. It spurns the alternative of a society that is tyrannical, conformist, irrational and stagnant.

. . . .

Thus, the first question remains: Does the advertising aimed at children fall within the scope of freedom of expression? Surely it aims to convey a meaning, and cannot be excluded as having no expressive content. Nor is there any basis for excluding the form of expression chosen from the sphere of protected activity....

. . . .

In sum, the characterization of government purpose must proceed from the standpoint of the guarantee in issue. With regard to freedom of expression, if the government has aimed to control attempts to convey a meaning either by directly restricting the content of expression or by restricting a form of expression tied to content, its purpose trenches upon the guarantee. Where, on the other hand, it aims only to control the physical consequences of particular conduct, its purpose does not trench upon the guarantee. In determining whether the government's purpose aims simply at harmful physical consequences, the question becomes: does the mischief consist in the meaning of the activity or the purported influence that meaning has on the behaviour of others, or does it consist, rather, only in the direct physical result of the activity.

Effects

Even if the government's purpose was not to control or restrict attempts to convey a meaning, the Court must still decide whether the effect of the government action was to restrict the plaintiff's free expression. Here, the burden is on the plaintiff to demonstrate that such an effect occurred. In order so to demonstrate, a plaintiff must state her claim with reference to the principles and values underlying the freedom.

We have already discussed the nature of the principles and values underlying the vigilant protection of free expression in a society such as ours. They were also discussed by the Court in *Ford* (at 765–67), and can be summarized as follows: (1) seeking and attaining the truth is an inherently good activity; (2) participation in social and political decision-making is to be fostered and encouraged; and (3) the diversity in forms of individual self-fulfillment and human flourishing ought to be cultivated in an essentially tolerant, indeed welcoming, environment not only for the sake of those who convey a meaning, but also for the sake of those to whom it is conveyed. In showing that the effect of the government's action was to restrict her free expression, a plaintiff must demonstrate that her activity promotes at least one of these principles. It is not enough that shouting, for example, has an expressive element. If the plaintiff challenges the effect of government action to control noise, presuming that action to have a purpose neutral as to expression, she must show that her aim was to convey a meaning reflective of the principles underlying freedom of expression. The precise and complete articulation of what kinds of activity promote these principles is, of course, a matter for judicial appreciation to be developed on a case by case basis. But the plaintiff must at least identify the meaning being conveyed and how it relates to the pursuit of truth, participation in the community, or individual self-fulfillment and human flourishing.

In the instant case, the plaintiff's activity is not excluded from the sphere of conduct protected by freedom of expression. The government's purpose in enacting ss. 248 and 249 of the *Consumer Protection Act* and in promulgating ss. 87 to 91 of the Regulation respecting the application of the *Consumer Protection Act* was to prohibit particular content of expression in the name of protecting children. These provisions therefore constitute limitations to s. 2(b) of the Canadian *Charter* and s. 3 of the Quebec *Charter*. They fail to be justified under s. 1 of the Canadian *Charter* and s. 9.1 of the Quebec *Charter*.

. . . .

... Broadly speaking, the concerns which have motivated both legislative and voluntary regulation in this area are the particular susceptibility of young children to media manipulation, their inability to differentiate between reality and fiction and to grasp the persuasive intention behind the message, and the secondary effects of exterior influences on the family and parental authority. Responses to the perceived problems are as varied as the agencies and governments which have promulgated them. However the consensus of concern is high.

. . . .

The s. 1 and s. 9.1 materials demonstrate, on the balance of probabilities, that children up to the age of thirteen are manipulated by commercial advertising and that the objective of protecting all children in this age group is predicated on a pressing and substantial concern. We thus conclude that the Attorney General has discharged the onus under the first part of the *Oakes* test.

. . . .

[The majority judges held that the ban on advertising directed at children was rationally connected to the goal of protecting children from advertising. They ruled that *non*-commercial advertising *was* permitted.]

. . . .

In sum, the evidence sustains the reasonableness of the legislature's conclusion that a ban on commercial advertising directed to children was the minimal impairment of free expression consistent with the pressing and substantial goal of protecting children against manipulation through such advertising. While evidence exists that other less intrusive options reflecting more modest objectives were available to the government, there is evidence establishing the necessity of a ban to meet the objectives the government had reasonably set. This Court will not, in the name of minimal impairment, take a restrictive approach to social science evidence and require legislatures to choose the least ambitious means to protect vulnerable groups. There must nevertheless be a sound evidentiary basis for the government's conclusions. In *Ford*, there was no evidence of any kind introduced to show that the exclusion of all languages other than French was necessary to achieve the objective of protecting the French language and reflecting the reality of Quebec society. What evidence was introduced established, at most, that a marked preponderance for the French language in the "visage linguistique" was proportional to that objective. The Court was prepared to allow a margin of appreciation to the government despite the fact that less intrusive measures, such as requiring equal prominence for the French language, were available. But there still had to be an evidentiary basis for concluding that the means chosen were proportional to the ends and impaired freedom of expression as little as possible. In *Ford*, that evidentiary basis did not exist.

. . . .

There is no suggestion here that the effects of the ban are so severe as to outweigh the government's pressing and substantial objective. Advertisers are always free to direct their message at parents and other adults. They are also free to participate in educational advertising. The real concern animating the challenge to the legislation is that revenues are in some degree affected. This only implies that advertisers will have to develop new marketing strategies for children's products. Thus, there is no prospect that "because of the severity of the deleterious effects of [the] measure on individuals or groups, the measure will not be justified by the purposes it is intended to serve" (*Oakes*, at 140). The final component of the proportionality test is easily satisfied. In *Ford*, by contrast, the Attorney General of Quebec underscored the importance of the "visage linguistique" for francophone identity and culture and yet the effect of the measure taken was to prohibit the public manifestation of the identity and culture of non-francophones.

. . . .

[McINTYRE J. for himself and BEETZ J., dissenting:]

Can it be said that the welfare of children is at risk because of advertising directed at them? I am not satisfied that any case has been shown that it is. There was evidence that small children are incapable of distinguishing fact from fiction in advertising. This is hardly surprising: many adults have the same problem. Children, however, do not remain children. They grow up and, while advertising directed at children may well be a source of irritation to parents, no case has been shown here that children suffer harm. Children live in a world of fiction, imagination and make believe. Children's literature is based upon these concepts. As they mature, they make adjustments and can be expected to pass beyond the range of any ill which might be caused by advertising. In

my view, no case has been made that children are at risk. Furthermore, even if I could reach another conclusion, I would be of the view that the restriction fails on the issue of proportionality. A total prohibition of advertising aimed at children below an arbitrarily fixed age makes no attempt at the achievement of proportionality.

In conclusion, I would say that freedom of expression is too important to be lightly cast aside or limited. It is ironic that most attempts to limit freedom of expression and hence freedom of knowledge and information are justified on the basis that the limitation is for the benefit of those whose rights will be limited. It was this proposition that motivated the early church in restricting access to information, even to prohibiting the promulgation and reading of the scriptures in a language understood by the people. The argument that freedom of expression was dangerous was used to oppose and restrict public education in earlier times. The education of women was greatly retarded on the basis that wider knowledge would only make them dissatisfied with their role in society. I do not suggest that the limitations imposed by ss. 248 and 249 are so earth shaking or that if sustained they will cause irremediable damage. I do say, however, that these limitations represent a small abandonment of a principle of vital importance in a free and democratic society and, therefore, even if it could be shown that some child or children have been adversely affected by advertising of the kind prohibited, I would still be of the opinion that the restriction should not be sustained. Our concern should be to recognize that in this century we have seen whole societies utterly corrupted by the suppression of free expression. We should not lightly take a step in that direction, even a small one.

It must be recognized that freedom of expression despite its singular importance is, like all rights, subject to limitations. It is not absolute. We have all heard the familiar statement that nobody has a right to shout "fire" in a crowded theatre. It illustrates the extreme and obvious case, but there will, of course, be other cases where limitations on the right may well be necessary and therefore justifiable. This, however, in my view, is not such a case. Freedom of expression, whether political, religious, artistic or commercial, should not be suppressed except in cases where urgent and compelling reasons exist and then only to the extent and for the time necessary for the protection of the community.

In my view, no justification can be found under s. 1 of the *Charter* for these sections, and I would dismiss the appeal and answer constitutional Question No. 2 as follows:

2. If question 1 is answered in the affirmative, do ss. 248 and 249 of the *Consumer Protection Act* infringe the rights, freedoms and guarantees contained in ss. 2(b) and 7 of the *Canadian Charter of Rights and Freedoms*, and if so, can those sections be justified under s. 1 of the *Canadian Charter of Rights and Freedoms*?

Answer: Sections 248 and 249 of the *Consumer Protection Act* infringe s. 2(b) of the Canadian *Charter* and s. 3 of the Quebec *Charter* and are not justified under s. 1 of the of the Canadian *Charter* and s. 9.1 of the Quebec *Charter*....

(e) Freedom of Expression after *Irwin Toy*

David W. Elliott

Irwin Toy left judges with a three-part test for assessing claimed breaches of freedom of expression under section 2(b) of the *Charter*: (1) Does the activity in question constitute a non-violent attempt to convey meaning? (2) Does the relevant legislation have the purpose of restricting the content — not just the physical consequences — of the expression? (3) If the answer to (2) is no, does the legislation have the effect of restricting expression that promotes (i) a search for truth, (ii) democracy, or (iii) individual self-fulfillment? The breadth of this test ensures that many allegations of breach of freedom of expression fulfill the requirements of section 2(b). Often, the subject matter of these allegations comprises expression that many people consider annoying, distasteful, or even harmful, expression such as commercial advertising, pornography, or hate propaganda. As a result, freedom of expression cases are often determined in the context of section 1, where the question is often whether the government is justified in restricting more questionable forms of a very fundamental right.

Not surprisingly, this has generated some contentious decisions involving section 1 of the *Charter*. As seen, there was a strong dissent in *Irwin Toy* itself as to whether the advertising restriction was justified. Four years later, in *RJR-MacDonald Inc. v. Canada (Attorney General)*, [1995] 3 S.C.R. 199, a majority of the Court held that a total ban on tobacco advertising was not the least intrusive means possible of reducing tobacco consumption. Hate propaganda, a much more reprehensible form of expression, was successfully restricted in *R. v. Keegstra*, [1990] 3 S.C.R. 697 but not in *R. v.*

Zundel, [1992] 2 S.C.R. 731, where another *Criminal Code* provision was used. Both were narrow majority decisions, where the crucial question was whether the restrictions were wider than necessary to deter their targets, and whether their chilling effect on innocent expression outweighed the importance of the deterrence. Obscenity, another controversial area of borderline expression, has also tended to centre on section 1. This was so in *R. v. Butler*, [1992] 1 S.C.R. 452, where the Supreme Court concluded that the general anti-pornography provision of the *Criminal Code* was a justified breach of freedom of expression; and in *R. v. Sharpe*, [2001] S.C.R. 45, where the Supreme Court held that most, although not all, the sections of a *Criminal Code* prohibition of possession of child pornography were a justified breach of this freedom.

In these cases, the Supreme Court has tended to impose less demanding requirements for section 1 justification for forms of freedom of expression that it considers to have a "discounted" value in comparison with more important forms: see *Keegstra*, above at para. 132. The Court said in *Butler* that:

> ... the kind of expression which is sought to be advanced does not stand on equal footing with other kinds of expression which directly engage the "core" of freedom of expression values. (para. 97)

Is this a general tendency that applies to other *Charter* rights as well? Where the Court relaxes the s. 1 justification test, how does it do this?

(f) Re Singh and Minister of Employment and Immigration†

David W. Elliott

Singh was one of the Supreme Court's first major decisions on section 7 of the *Charter*. Wilson J.'s reasons suggested that the content of fundamental justice can include that of common law natural justice or fairness. See the NOTE and EXTRACT for *Singh* in Chapter 4, and "Fundamental Justice and Section 7" in this chapter. Just how does fundamental justice differ from natural justice (a) in scope and (b) in content?

(g) B.C. Motor Vehicles Reference‡

David W. Elliott

Does section 7 of the *Charter* include non-procedural fundamental justice? What is fundamental justice? How active an approach should courts take to *Charter* issues in general? These were three of the main questions addressed in one of the most activist of early *Charter* decisions, the *B.C. Motor Vehicles Reference*. See the NOTE and EXTRACT for this reference in Chapter 8 and "Fundamental Freedoms and Fundamental Justice" in this chapter.

More recently, in *Suresh v. Canada (Minister of Citizenship and Immigration)*, [2002] S.C.J. No. 3 (QL), the Supreme Court said that fundamental justice can incorporate general international law norms, such as the prohibition against torture. As well, the Court seems to be taking a balancing approach to non-procedural fundamental justice, weighing fundamental justice interests against other concerns such as collective security. (Note, though, that the balance can be tilted in favour of the individual in situations that courts feel would "shock the conscience" of Canadians.) This approach bears some resemblance to that of procedural fundamental justice, where both collective efficiency and individual fairness are relevant to determining the appropriate procedural standard.

(h) Canada (Attorney General) v. PHS Community Services Society*

NOTE

In *Chaoulli v. Quebec (Attorney General)*, [2005] 1 S.C.R. 791, the Supreme Court of Canada ruled that the prohibition on private health insurance was a violation of the Quebec *Charter of Human Rights and Freedoms*, R.S.Q., c. C-12. A majority of the Court used the broad criterion of "arbitrariness" to

---

† *Singh v. Canada (Minister of Employment and Immigration)*, [1985] 1 S.C.R. 177, rev'g. decisions of the Federal Court of Appeal dismissing applications for judicial review of decisions of the Immigration Appeal Board dismissing applications for redetermination of refugee claims.

‡ *Reference re Motor Vehicle Act (British Columbia) s. 94(2)*, [1985] 2 S.C.R. 486, aff'g (1983), 147 D.L.R. (3d) 539 (B.C.C.A), in a reference concerning the constitutional validity of s. 94(2) of the *Motor Vehicle Act of British Columbia*.

* 2011 SCC 44, [2011] 3 S.C.R. 134.

determine whether the province's prohibition on purchasing private health services breached the provision of fundamental justice found in section 7 of the *Canadian Charter of Rights and Freedoms*: paras. 129–131. With billions of dollars expended on public health care in Canada every year, the judgement was much anticipated when it was rendered about a decade ago. Interestingly, the Supreme Court had little difficulty ruling on the kind of major economic and social policy question that is normally contested and decided by way of an electoral campaign. The decision in *Chaoulli* may have heralded the rise of "arbitrariness" as a new, far-reaching s. 7 criterion to limit the state's powers when a provision of the criminal law significantly threatens the life or security of persons that the law would otherwise punish.

In *Canada (Attorney General) v. PHS Community Services Society*, [2011] 3 S.C.R. 134, the Supreme Court again delved into a controversial area of social policy. As a result of widespread injection drug use in the downtown eastside of Vancouver, proliferating diseases such as HIV/AIDS and hepatitis C, local governments promoted a supervised safe injection site (Insite) to help care for drug users in the midst of their drug addiction: paras. 1–2. In 2003, Insite received a temporary exemption from provisions barring possession and trafficking under section 56 of the *Controlled Drugs and Substances Act* (*CDSA*). Among other things, Insite provides its clients with health care information and a detox centre, and it also closely monitors individuals during drug use: para. 100. Insite has been credited with preventing the death of injection drug users and improved health outcomes for its clients without also increasing crime or drug use. In 2008, after receiving two temporary extensions of its exemption, Insite was denied a renewed exemption by the federal Minister of Health: para. 123. This decision led to litigation to keep Insite open despite the Minister's decision not to provide a further exemption. The Supreme Court found that the Minister's decision threatened the health and lives of Insite's clients and that the denial was an arbitrary exercise of Ministerial discretion, given that it undermined the purpose of the *CDSA*, which was to protect health and public safety: paras. 129–132 and 148. Among other things, there was no s. 1 justification that could preserve the Minister's decision as it ran contrary to the very objects of the *CDSA*: paras. 137–40. The Supreme Court of Canada ordered the Minister of Health to grant Insite the exemption it requested: para. 150. When you review the follow-

ing excerpt, ask yourself: does the Court need to incorporate the broad "arbitrariness" criterion into its s. 7 analysis when it has the option of analysing this factor under section 1? Ultimately, does it matter where in the *Charter* courts use the criterion of arbitrariness? If so, why does it matter? More importantly, should the Court shelter what would otherwise be criminal behaviour for Insite's clients when many other drug users engaging in exactly the same behaviour are subject to arrest and imprisonment because they were not actively supervised by workers at a safe injection site? Doesn't the extension of *Charter* protection from criminal prosecution to Insite's clients seem almost arbitrary when considered against the reality that the vast majority of drug addicts will never have access to the safety provided to drug users at the Insite facility? In light of these circumstances, does section 7 require governments to set up similar safe injection sites across the country with exemptions similar to Insite's to promote the health of injection drug users? If not, why? Are these questions best answered by Parliament alone without the interference of the Supreme Court?

EXTRACT

[McLACHLIN C.J. (for the Court):]

VI.   *CHARTER* CLAIMS

.   .   .   .

C.   Has the Minister's Decision Violated the Claimants' Section 7 Rights?

[116] The main issue, as the appeal was argued, was the constitutionality of the *CDSA* itself. I have concluded that, properly interpreted, the statute is valid. This leaves the question of the Minister's decision to refuse an exemption. A preliminary issue arises whether the Court should consider this issue. In the special circumstances of this case, I conclude that it should. The claimants pleaded in the alternative that, if the *CDSA* were valid, the Minister's decision violated their *Charter* rights. The issue was raised at the hearing and the parties afforded an opportunity to address it. It is therefore properly before us and the Attorney General of Canada cannot complain that it would be unfair to deal with it. Most importantly, justice requires us to consider this issue. The claimants have established that their s. 7 rights are at

stake. They should not be denied a remedy and sent back for another trial on this point simply because it is the Minister's decision and not the statute that causes the breach when the matter has been pleaded and no unfairness arises.

[117] The discretion vested in the Minister of Health is not absolute: as with all exercises of discretion, the Minister's decisions must conform to the *Charter*: *Suresh v. Canada (Minister of Citizenship and Immigration)*, 2002 SCC 1, [2002] 1 S.C.R. 3. If the Minister's decision results in an application of the *CDSA* that limits the s. 7 rights of individuals in a manner that is not in accordance with the *Charter*, then the Minister's discretion has been exercised unconstitutionally.

[118] I note that this case is different from *Parker*, where the Ontario Court of Appeal held that the general prohibition on possession of marihuana was not saved by the availability of an exemption for possession for medical purposes under s. 56. No decision of the Minister was at stake in *Parker*, and the Court's conclusion rested on findings of the trial judge that, at that time, "the availability of the exemption was illusory" (para. 174).

(1) Has the Minister Made a Decision?

[119] The Attorney General of Canada argues that the Minister has not violated s. 7 because the Minister has not yet made a decision whether to grant a s. 56 exemption to Insite. He also submits that the decision of the British Columbia Courts that ss. 4(1) and 5(1) of the *CDSA* are unconstitutional prevents the Minister from exercising his powers to grant an exemption under s. 56. Although the declaration of unconstitutionality has been suspended and a temporary constitutional exemption granted to Insite by judicial order, the Minister says it would be improper for him to exercise his s. 56 discretion until the constitutionality of the *CDSA* has been finally resolved by this Court.

[120] In my view, the record establishes that the Minister *has* made a decision on the request for an exemption for Insite, and that that decision was to refuse the exemption.

[121] The essential facts are as follows. The first exemption for Insite, which lasted three years, was effective as of September 12, 2003. The Minister granted a temporary extension on September 11, 2006, to expire December 31, 2007. On October 2, 2007, the exemption was extended for another six months to June 30, 2008. In his letters to the VCHA

granting the exemption, the Minister stated that the extensions were to be for the purpose of allowing time for additional research on the impact of Insite on prevention, treatment and crime. In the course of the summary trial, on May 2, 2008, the VCHA sent an application to Health Canada formally requesting an extension of the exemption for another three years. The application was supported by the provincial Minister of Health. Health Canada responded on December 19, 2008, after the trial judge had rendered his judgment. It stated that, in view of the result at trial, an exemption was not required at that time.

[122] However, before December 2008, the Minister indicated that he had decided not to grant the exemption. The then federal Minister of Health, Tony Clement, spoke to the Standing Committee on Health on May 29, 2008. He had at that point received the report of the Expert Advisory Committee, a formal application for a continued exemption, and a statement of support for Insite from the provincial Minister of Health. The federal Minister's comments can be summarized briefly: he approved of the other services Insite was providing, but not supervised injection. He felt that the scientific evidence with respect to its effectiveness was mixed, but that the "public policy is clear", and that "the site itself represents a failure of public policy" (12: 40 (online)). He disagreed with the experts who saw Insite as a public health success, and stated he intended to appeal the trial judge's decision. These comments, coupled with the failure to accord an exemption, amount to an effective refusal of the application.

[123] The Attorney General of Canada draws our attention to this statement by the Minister near the end of his presentation to the Committee:

> Indeed, I want to state for the record, if I might, that should another exemption application come forward, I have a duty to once again look at all the evidence and once again turn my mind to it in a way that gives due process. So I'm not resigning from that obligation that I have as health minister. [13: 20 (online)]

This statement can be interpreted only in one way. The Minister was rejecting the formal application that was then before him, while asserting he would consider any new application "in a way that gives due process".

[124] To recap, the Minister had before him a formal application dated May 2, 2008. He was obliged, as he conceded, to consider all applications. The

Minister treated the application before him as denied; it was spent, and a duty to reconsider could only be triggered by a new application. The only rational conclusion is that the Minister had considered the application for an exemption that was then before him, and had decided not to grant it.

[125] More broadly, Canada's submission that there has been no decision to refuse the s. 56 application is in tension with its argument that this case is essentially about conflicting policy choices. Implicit in this is the concession that the federal government, through the Minister of Health, has made a policy choice to deny exemption under s. 56 of the *CDSA*.

(2) Are the Claimants' Section 7 Rights Engaged by the Minister's Decision?

[126] The last ministerial exemption expired on June 30, 2008. Absent the judicial exemption granted by Pitfield J. and extended by the Court of Appeal, the prohibition contained in s. 4(1) of the *CDSA* would apply to Insite. For the reasons discussed above, the application of s. 4(1) to the staff engages the staff's liberty interests, and engages the security of the person and life interests of the clients of Insite. I conclude that the Minister's rejection of the application for a s. 56 exemption likewise engages the s. 7 rights of the claimants. The only reason Insite users have continued to receive its health services is because of a temporary remedial order made by the trial judge, pending completion of these proceedings. A judicial order directed at preserving the *status quo* pending resolution of a dispute does not prevent the claimants from asserting their s. 7 rights.

(3) Does the Minister's Refusal to Grant an Exemption to Insite Accord With the Principles of Fundamental Justice?

[127] The next question is whether the Minister's decision that the *CDSA* applies to Insite is in accordance with the principles of fundamental justice. On the basis of the facts established at trial, which are consistent with the evidence available to the Minister at the relevant time, I conclude that the Minister's refusal to grant Insite a s. 56 exemption was arbitrary and grossly disproportionate in its effects, and hence not in accordance with the principles of fundamental justice.

[128] As noted above, the Minister, when exercising his discretion under s. 56, must respect the rights guaranteed by the *Charter*. This means that, where s. 7 rights are at stake, any limitations imposed by min-

isterial decision must be in accordance with the principles of fundamental justice. The Minister cannot simply deny an application for a s. 56 exemption on the basis of policy *simpliciter*; insofar as it affects *Charter* rights, his decision must accord with the principles of fundamental justice.

(A) ARBITRARINESS

[129] When considering whether a law's application is arbitrary, the first step is to identify the law's objectives. Decisions of the Minister under s. 56 of the *CDSA* must target the purpose of the Act. The legitimate state objectives of the *CDSA* (then the *Narcotic Control Act*, R.S.C. 1986, c. N-1) were identified by this Court in *Malmo-Levine* as the protection of health and public safety.

[130] The second step is to identify the relationship between the state interest and the impugned law, or, in this case, the impugned decision of the Minister. The relationship between the general prohibition on possession in the *CDSA* and the state objective was recognized in *Malmo-Levine* with respect to marihuana:

> The criminalization of possession is a statement of society's collective disapproval of the use of a psychoactive drug such as marihuana ..., and, through Parliament, the continuing view that its use should be deterred. The prohibition is not arbitrary but is rationally connected to a reasonable apprehension of harm. In particular, criminalization seeks to take marihuana out of the hands of users and potential users, so as to prevent the associated harm and to eliminate the market for traffickers. [para. 136]

The question is whether the decision that the *CDSA* applies to the activities at Insite bears the same relationship to the state objective. As noted above, the burden is on the claimants to establish that the limit imposed by the law is not in accordance with the principles of fundamental justice.

[131] The trial judge's key findings in this regard are consistent with the information available to the Minister, and are those on which successive federal Ministers have relied in granting exemption orders over almost five years, including the facts that: (1) traditional criminal law prohibitions have done little to reduce drug use in the DTES; (2) the risk to injection drug users of death and disease is reduced when they inject under the supervision of a health professional; and (3) the presence of Insite did not contribute to increased crime rates, increased incidents of public injection, or relapse rates in injection drug users. On the contrary, Insite was perceived

favourably or neutrally by the public; a local business association reported a reduction in crime during the period Insite was operating; the facility encouraged clients to seek counselling, detoxification and treatment. Most importantly, the staff of Insite had intervened in 336 overdoses since 2006, and no overdose deaths had occurred at the facility. (See trial judgment, at paras. 85 and 87–88.) These findings suggest not only that exempting Insite from the application of the possession prohibition does not undermine the objectives of public health and safety, but furthers them.

[132] The jurisprudence on arbitrariness is not entirely settled. In *Chaoulli*, three justices (*per* McLachlin C.J. and Major J.) preferred an approach that asked whether a limit was "necessary" to further the state objective (paras. 131–32). Conversely, three other justices (*per* Binnie and LeBel JJ.), preferred to avoid the language of necessity and instead approved of the prior articulation of arbitrariness as where "[a] deprivation of a right ... bears no relation to, or is inconsistent with, the state interest that lies behind the legislation" (para. 232). It is unnecessary to determine which approach should prevail, because the government action at issue in this case qualifies as arbitrary under both definitions.

(B) GROSS DISPROPORTIONALITY

[133] The application of the possession prohibition to Insite is also grossly disproportionate in its effects. Gross disproportionality describes state actions or legislative responses to a problem that are so extreme as to be disproportionate to any legitimate government interest: *Malmo-Levine*, at para. 143. Insite saves lives. Its benefits have been proven. There has been no discernable negative impact on the public safety and health objectives of Canada during its eight years of operation. The effect of denying the services of Insite to the population it serves is grossly disproportionate to any benefit that Canada might derive from presenting a uniform stance on the possession of narcotics.

(C) OVERBREADTH

[134] Having found the Minister's decision arbitrary and its effects grossly disproportionate, I need not consider this aspect of the argument.

[135] I conclude that, on the basis of the factual findings of the trial judge, the claimants have met the evidentiary burden of showing that the failure of the Minister to grant a s. 56 exemption to Insite is not in accordance with the principles of fundamental justice.

(4) Conclusion on the Challenge to Minister's Decision

[136] The Minister made a decision not to extend the exemption from the application of the federal drug laws to Insite. The effect of that decision, but for the trial judge's interim order, would have been to prevent injection drug users from accessing the health services offered by Insite, threatening the health and indeed the lives of the potential clients. The Minister's decision thus engages the claimants' s. 7 interests and constitutes a limit on their s. 7 rights. Based on the information available to the Minister, this limit is not in accordance with the principles of fundamental justice. It is arbitrary, undermining the very purposes of the *CDSA*, which include public health and safety. It is also grossly disproportionate: the potential denial of health services and the correlative increase in the risk of death and disease to injection drug users outweigh any benefit that might be derived from maintaining an absolute prohibition on possession of illegal drugs on Insite's premises.

D. Section 1

[137] If a s. 1 analysis were required, a point not argued, no s. 1 justification could succeed. The goals of the *CDSA*, as I have stated, are the maintenance and promotion of public health and safety. The Minister's decision to refuse the exemption bears no relation to these objectives; therefore they cannot justify the infringement of the complainants' s. 7 rights. However one views the matter, the Minister's decision was arbitrary and unsustainable. See *Chaoulli*, at para. 155, *per* McLachlin C.J. and Major J.

[138] Before leaving s. 1, I turn to the Minister's argument that granting a s. 56 exemption to Insite would undermine the rule of law and that denying an exemption is therefore justified.

[139] Canada submits that exempting Insite from the prohibitions in the *CDSA* "would effectively turn the rule of law on its head by dictating that where a particular individual breaks the law with such frequency and persistence that he or she becomes unable to comply with it, it is unconstitutional to apply the law to that person" (A.F., at para. 101). Canada raises the spectre of a host of exempt sites, where the country's drug laws would be flouted with impunity.

[140] The conclusion that the Minister has not exercised his discretion in accordance with the *Charter* in this case is not a licence for injection drug users to

possess drugs wherever and whenever they wish. Nor is it an invitation for anyone who so chooses to open a facility for drug use under the banner of a "safe injection facility". The result in this case rests on the trial judge's conclusions that Insite is effective in reducing the risk of death and disease and has had no negative impact on the legitimate criminal law objectives of the federal government. Neither s. 56 of the *CDSA* nor s. 7 of the *Charter* require condonation of crime. They demand only that, in administering the criminal law, the state not deprive individuals of their s. 7 rights to life, liberty and security of the person in a manner that violates the principles of fundamental justice.

VII. REMEDY

. . . .

[150] In the special circumstances of this case, an order in the nature of mandamus is warranted. I would therefore order the Minister to grant an exemption to Insite under s. 56 of the CDSA forthwith. (This of course would not affect the Minister's power to withdraw the exemption should the operation of Insite change such that the exemption would no longer be appropriate.) On the trial judge's findings of fact, the only constitutional response to the application for a s. 56 exemption was to grant it. The Minister is bound to exercise his discretion under s. 56 in accordance with the *Charter*. On the facts as found here, there can be only one response: to grant the exemption. There is therefore nothing to be gained (and much to be risked) in sending the matter back to the Minister for reconsideration.

[151] This does not fetter the Minister's discretion with respect to future applications for exemptions, whether for other premises, or for Insite. As always, the Minister must exercise that discretion within the constraints imposed by the law and the *Charter*.

[152] The dual purposes of the CDSA — public health and public safety — provide some guidance for the Minister. Where the Minister is considering an application for an exemption for a supervised injection facility, he or she will aim to strike the appropriate balance between achieving the public health and public safety goals. Where, as here, the evidence indicates that a supervised injection site will decrease the risk of death and disease, and there is little or no evidence that it will have a negative impact on public safety, the Minister should generally grant an exemption.

[153] The CDSA grants the Minister discretion in determining whether to grant exemptions. That discretion must be exercised in accordance with the *Charter*. This requires the Minister to consider whether denying an exemption would cause deprivations of life and security of the person that are not in accordance with the principles of fundamental justice. The factors considered in making the decision on an exemption must include evidence, if any, on the impact of such a facility on crime rates, the local conditions indicating a need for such a supervised injection site, the regulatory structure in place to support the facility, the resources available to support its maintenance, and expressions of community support or opposition.

(i) *Canada (Attorney General) v. Bedford*†

NOTE

In this case, three women involved in prostitution, Terri-Jean Bedford, Amy Lebovitch, and Valerie Scott, challenged the constitutionality of various provisions of the *Criminal Code*, R.S.C. 1985, c. C-46, which prohibited activities connected to prosti-

tution. Among other things, they argued that section 210 (creating an offence to keep or be in a bawdy-house), section 212(1)(j) (making it an offence to live off the avails of prostitution), and section 213(1)(c) (the prohibition on communicating in public for the purposes of prostitution) of the *Criminal Code* violated their right under section 7

---

† 2013 SCC 72, [2013] 3 S.C.R. 1101.

of the *Charter* to life, liberty, and security of the person: *Canada (Attorney General) v. Bedford*, 2013 SCC 72 at para. 4. These criminal law provisions were passed in order to prevent both the public nuisance associated with sex work and the exploitation of prostitutes. However, the women argued that the provision prevented sex workers from minimizing the risk associated with prostitution by preventing them from taking measures — such as hiring security guards and other staff — to reduce the potential for violence historically connected with this activity: *ibid.* at para. 6. As a result, the criminal law put the safety and lives of prostitutes at risk and could not be saved by section 1 of the *Charter*.

With respect to the s. 7 *Charter* arguments, the Supreme Court of Canada found that the three *Criminal Code* provisions imposed dangerous conditions on prostitutes by preventing people engaged in a hazardous — but legal — business from minimizing the risks associated with sex work: *ibid.* at para. 60. The reality that third parties (like "johns" and "pimps") cause much of the immediate violence faced by persons engaged in sex work did not diminish the state's role in making prostitutes more vulnerable to that violence: *ibid.* at para. 89. The three impugned provisions, noted above, were declared to be inconsistent with the *Charter*, and that declaration was suspended for a year to allow Parliament to amend the *Criminal Code* so that it could comply with the *Charter*: *ibid.* at para. 169. In striking down the impugned sections of the criminal law, the Supreme Court engaged the broad criteria of arbitrariness, overbreadth, and gross disproportionality as means to rationalize and justify its judgement. When reviewing the excerpt from *Bedford*, below, discussing these concepts, ask yourself: what are the limits by which these doctrines operate, and how far can courts now use these doctrines to strike down other *Criminal Code* provisions?

EXTRACT

[McLACHLIN C.J. (for the Court):]

. . . .

(3) Principles of Fundamental Justice
(A) THE APPLICABLE NORMS

[93] I have concluded that the impugned laws deprive prostitutes of security of the person, engaging s. 7. The remaining step in the s. 7 analysis is to determine whether this deprivation is in accordance with the principles of fundamental justice. If so, s. 7 is not breached.

[94] The principles of fundamental justice set out the minimum requirements that a law that negatively impacts on a person's life, liberty, or security of the person must meet. As Lamer J. put it, "[t]he term 'principles of fundamental justice' is not a right, but a qualifier of the right not to be deprived of life, liberty and security of the person; its function is to set the parameters of that right" (*Re B.C. Motor Vehicle Act*, [1985] 2 S.C.R. 486 ("Motor Vehicle Reference"), at p. 512).

[95] The principles of fundamental justice have significantly evolved since the birth of the *Charter*. Initially, the principles of fundamental justice were thought to refer narrowly to principles of natural justice that define procedural fairness. In the Motor Vehicle Reference, this Court held otherwise:

> ... it would be wrong to interpret the term "fundamental justice" as being synonymous with natural justice.... To do so would strip the protected interests of much, if not most, of their content and leave the "right" to life, liberty and security of the person in a sorely emaciated state. Such a result would be inconsistent with the broad, affirmative language in which those rights are expressed and equally inconsistent with the approach adopted by this Court toward the interpretation of *Charter* rights in *Law Society of Upper Canada v. Skapinker*, [1984] 1 S.C.R. 357, per Estey J., and Hunter v. Southam Inc., supra. [pp. 501–2]

[96] The Motor Vehicle Reference recognized that the principles of fundamental justice are about the basic values underpinning our constitutional order. The s. 7 analysis is concerned with capturing inherently bad laws: that is, laws that take away life, liberty, or security of the person in a way that runs afoul of our basic values. The principles of fundamental justice are an attempt to capture those values. Over the years, the jurisprudence has given shape to the content of these basic values. In this case, we are concerned with the basic values against arbitrariness, overbreadth, and gross disproportionality.

[97] The concepts of arbitrariness, overbreadth, and gross disproportionality evolved organically as courts were faced with novel *Charter* claims.

[98] Arbitrariness was used to describe the situation where there is no connection between the effect and the object of the law. In *Morgentaler*, the accused

challenged provisions of the Criminal Code that required abortions to be approved by a therapeutic abortion committee of an accredited or approved hospital. The purpose of the law was to protect women's health. The majority found that the requirement that all therapeutic abortions take place in accredited hospitals did not contribute to the objective of protecting women's health and, in fact, caused delays that were detrimental to women's health. Thus, the law violated basic values because the effect of the law actually contravened the objective of the law. Beetz J. called this "manifest unfairness" (*Morgentaler*, at p. 120), but later cases interpreted this as an "arbitrariness" analysis (see *Chaoulli v. Quebec (Attorney General)*, 2005 SCC 35, [2005] 1 S.C.R. 791, at para. 133, per McLachlin C.J. and Major J.).

[99] In *Chaoulli*, the applicant challenged a Quebec law that prohibited private health insurance for services that were available in the public sector. The purpose of the provision was to protect the public health care system and prevent the diversion of resources from the public system. The majority found, on the basis of international evidence, that private health insurance and a public health system could co-exist. Three of the four-judge majority found that the prohibition was "arbitrary" because there was no real connection on the facts between the effect and the objective of the law.

[100] Most recently, in *PHS*, this Court found that the Minister's decision not to extend a safe injection site's exemption from drug possession laws was arbitrary. The purpose of drug possession laws was the protection of health and public safety, and the services provided by the safe injection site actually contributed to these objectives. Thus, the effect of not extending the exemption — that is, prohibiting the safe injection site from operating — was contrary to the objectives of the drug possession laws.

[101] Another way in which laws may violate our basic values is through what the cases have called "overbreadth": the law goes too far and interferes with some conduct that bears no connection to its objective. In *R. v. Heywood*, [1994] 3 S.C.R. 761, the accused challenged a vagrancy law that prohibited offenders convicted of listed offences from "loitering" in public parks. The majority of the Court found that the law, which aimed to protect children from sexual predators, was overbroad; insofar as the law applied to offenders who did not constitute a danger to children, and insofar as it applied to parks where children were unlikely to be present, it was unrelated to its objective.

[102] In *R. v. Demers*, 2004 SCC 46, [2004] 2 S.C.R. 489, the challenged provisions of the Criminal Code prevented an accused who was found unfit to stand trial from receiving an absolute discharge, and subjected the accused to indefinite appearances before a review board. The purpose of the provisions was "to allow for the ongoing treatment or assessment of the accused in order for him or her to become fit for an eventual trial" (para. 41). The Court found that insofar as the law applied to permanently unfit accused, who would never become fit to stand trial, the objective did "not apply" and therefore the law was overbroad (paras. 42–43).

[103] Laws are also in violation of our basic values when the effect of the law is grossly disproportionate to the state's objective. In *Malmo-Levine*, the accused challenged the prohibition on the possession of marijuana on the basis that its effects were grossly disproportionate to its objective. Although the Court agreed that a law with grossly disproportionate effects would violate our basic norms, the Court found that this was not such a case: "... the effects on accused persons of the present law, including the potential of imprisonment, fall within the broad latitude within which the Constitution permits legislative action" (para. 175).

[104] In *PHS*, this Court found that the Minister's refusal to exempt the safe injection site from drug possession laws was not in accordance with the principles of fundamental justice because the effect of denying health services and increasing the risk of death and disease of injection drug users was grossly disproportionate to the objectives of the drug possession laws, namely public health and safety.

[105] The overarching lesson that emerges from the case law is that laws run afoul of our basic values when the means by which the state seeks to attain its objective is fundamentally flawed, in the sense of being arbitrary, overbroad, or having effects that are grossly disproportionate to the legislative goal. To deprive citizens of life, liberty, or security of the person by laws that violate these norms is not in accordance with the principles of fundamental justice.

[106] As these principles have developed in the jurisprudence, they have not always been applied consistently. The Court of Appeal below pointed to the confusion that has been caused by the "commingling" of arbitrariness, overbreadth, and gross disproportionality (paras. 143–51). This Court itself

recently noted the conflation of the principles of overbreadth and gross disproportionality (*R. v. Khawaja*, 2012 SCC 69, [2012] 3 S.C.R. 555, at paras. 38–40; see also R. v. S.S.C., 2008 BCCA 262, 257 B.C.A.C. 57, at para. 72). In short, courts have explored different ways in which laws run afoul of our basic values, using the same words — arbitrariness, overbreadth, and gross disproportionality — in slightly different ways.

[107] Although there is significant overlap between these three principles, and one law may properly be characterized by more than one of them, arbitrariness, overbreadth, and gross disproportionality remain three distinct principles that stem from what Hamish Stewart calls "failures of instrumental rationality" — the situation where the law is "inadequately connected to its objective or in some sense goes too far in seeking to attain it" (*Fundamental Justice: Section 7 of the Canadian Charter of Rights and Freedoms* (2012), at p. 151). As Peter Hogg has explained:

> The doctrines of overbreadth, disproportionality and arbitrariness are all at bottom intended to address what Hamish Stewart calls "failures of instrumental rationality", by which he means that the Court accepts the legislative objective, but scrutinizes the policy instrument enacted as the means to achieve the objective. If the policy instrument is not a rational means to achieve the objective, then the law is dysfunctional in terms of its own objective. ("The Brilliant Career of Section 7 of the *Charter*" (2012), 58 S.C.L.R. (2d) 195, at p. 209 (citation omitted))

[108] The case law on arbitrariness, overbreadth and gross disproportionality is directed against two different evils. The first evil is the absence of a connection between the infringement of rights and what the law seeks to achieve — the situation where the law's deprivation of an individual's life, liberty, or security of the person is not connected to the purpose of the law. The first evil is addressed by the norms against arbitrariness and overbreadth, which target the absence of connection between the law's purpose and the s. 7 deprivation.

[109] The second evil lies in depriving a person of life, liberty or security of the person in a manner that is grossly disproportionate to the law's objective. The law's impact on the s. 7 interest is connected to the purpose, but the impact is so severe that it violates our fundamental norms.

[110] Against this background, it may be useful to elaborate on arbitrariness, overbreadth and gross disproportionality.

[111] Arbitrariness asks whether there is a direct connection between the purpose of the law and the impugned effect on the individual, in the sense that the effect on the individual bears some relation to the law's purpose. There must be a rational connection between the object of the measure that causes the s. 7 deprivation, and the limits it imposes on life, liberty, or security of the person (Stewart, at p. 136). A law that imposes limits on these interests in a way that bears no connection to its objective arbitrarily impinges on those interests. Thus, in Chaoulli, the law was arbitrary because the prohibition of private health insurance was held to be unrelated to the objective of protecting the public health system.

[112] Overbreadth deals with a law that is so broad in scope that it includes some conduct that bears no relation to its purpose. In this sense, the law is arbitrary in part. At its core, overbreadth addresses the situation where there is no rational connection between the purposes of the law and some, but not all, of its impacts. For instance, the law at issue in Demers required unfit accused to attend repeated review board hearings. The law was only disconnected from its purpose insofar as it applied to permanently unfit accused; for temporarily unfit accused, the effects were related to the purpose.

[113] Overbreadth allows courts to recognize that the law is rational in some cases, but that it overreaches in its effect in others. Despite this recognition of the scope of the law as a whole, the focus remains on the individual and whether the effect on the individual is rationally connected to the law's purpose. For example, where a law is drawn broadly and targets some conduct that bears no relation to its purpose in order to make enforcement more practical, there is still no connection between the purpose of the law and its effect on the specific individual. Enforcement practicality may be a justification for an overbroad law, to be analyzed under s. 1 of the *Charter*.

[114] It has been suggested that overbreadth is not truly a distinct principle of fundamental justice. The case law has sometimes said that overbreadth straddles both arbitrariness and gross disproportionality. Thus, in *Heywood*, Cory J. stated: "The effect of overbreadth is that in some applications the law is arbitrary or disproportionate" (p. 793).

[115] And in *R. v. Clay*, 2003 SCC 75, [2003] 3 S.C.R. 735, the companion case to *Malmo-Levine*, Gonthier and Binnie JJ. explained:

> Overbreadth in that respect addresses the potential infringement of fundamental justice where the adverse effect of a legislative measure on the individuals subject to its strictures is grossly disproportionate to the state interest the legislation seeks to protect. Overbreadth in this aspect is, as Cory J. pointed out [in *Heywood*], related to arbitrariness. [Emphasis deleted; para. 38.]

[116 In part this debate is semantic. The law has not developed by strict labels, but on a case-by-case basis, as courts identified laws that were inherently bad because they violated our basic values.

[117] Moving forward, however, it may be helpful to think of overbreadth as a distinct principle of fundamental justice related to arbitrariness, in that the question for both is whether there is no connection between the effects of a law and its objective. Overbreadth simply allows the court to recognize that the lack of connection arises in a law that goes too far by sweeping conduct into its ambit that bears no relation to its objective.

[118] An ancillary question, which applies to both arbitrariness and overbreadth, concerns how significant the lack of correspondence between the objective of the infringing provision and its effects must be. Questions have arisen as to whether a law is arbitrary or overbroad when its effects are inconsistent with its objective, or whether, more broadly, a law is arbitrary or overbroad whenever its effects are unnecessary for its objective (see, e.g., *Chaoulli*, at paras. 233–34).

[119] As noted above, the root question is whether the law is inherently bad because there is no connection, in whole or in part, between its effects and its purpose. This standard is not easily met. The evidence may, as in *Morgentaler*, show that the effect actually undermines the objective and is therefore "inconsistent" with the objective. Or the evidence may, as in *Chaoulli*, show that there is simply no connection on the facts between the effect and the objective, and the effect is therefore "unnecessary". Regardless of how the judge describes this lack of connection, the ultimate question remains whether the evidence establishes that the law violates basic norms because there is no connection between its effect and its purpose. This is a matter to be determined on a case-by-case basis, in light of the evidence.

[120] Gross disproportionality asks a different question from arbitrariness and overbreadth. It targets the second fundamental evil: the law's effects on life, liberty or security of the person are so grossly disproportionate to its purposes that they cannot rationally be supported. The rule against gross disproportionality only applies in extreme cases where the seriousness of the deprivation is totally out of sync with the objective of the measure. This idea is captured by the hypothetical of a law with the purpose of keeping the streets clean that imposes a sentence of life imprisonment for spitting on the sidewalk. The connection between the draconian impact of the law and its object must be entirely outside the norms accepted in our free and democratic society.

[121] Gross disproportionality under s. 7 of the *Charter* does not consider the beneficial effects of the law for society. It balances the negative effect on the individual against the purpose of the law, not against societal benefit that might flow from the law. As this Court said in *Malmo-Levine*:

> In effect, the exercise undertaken by Braidwood J.A. was to balance the law's salutary and deleterious effects. In our view, with respect, that is a function that is more properly reserved for s. 1. These are the types of social and economic harms that generally have no place in s. 7. [para. 181]

[122] Thus, gross disproportionality is not concerned with the number of people who experience grossly disproportionate effects; a grossly disproportionate effect on one person is sufficient to violate the norm.

[123] All three principles — arbitrariness, overbreadth, and gross disproportionality — compare the rights infringement caused by the law with the objective of the law, not with the law's effectiveness. That is, they do not look to how well the law achieves its object, or to how much of the population the law benefits. They do not consider ancillary benefits to the general population. Furthermore, none of the principles measure the percentage of the population that is negatively impacted. The analysis is qualitative, not quantitative. The question under s. 7 is whether anyone's life, liberty or security of the person has been denied by a law that is inherently bad; a grossly disproportionate, overbroad, or arbitrary effect on one person is sufficient to establish a breach of s. 7.

POSTSCRIPT

Less than six months after the decision in *Bedford*, the federal government introduced Bill C-36, the *Protection Of Communities And Exploited Persons Act*. The proposed statute has several provisions, which would amend the *Criminal Code* to, among other things, create an offence that prohibits purchasing sexual services or communicating in any place for that purpose and forbids the advertisement of sexual services offered for sale, and to authorize the courts to order the seizure of materials containing such advertisements and their removal from the Internet.[1] In other words, this Bill focused on criminally punishing the purchase, but not the sale, of sexual activity and provided certain restrictions on the advertisement of prostitution. Its critics claim that sex workers, without the ability to advertise online or in print, will be unable to screen clients and will therefore make unsafe decisions.[2] Jean McDonald, executive director of Maggie's Toronto Sex Work Action Project, has pointed out that with advertising prostitutes can "speak to and email clients and negotiate a rate, discuss safer sex practices and sometimes get references." McDonald also claimed that "[o]ften clients will even give you work information, but they will not do that if they're worried about being arrested." "If sex work can't take place in public or online," McDonald says, "they're criminalizing the industry." Although the Minister of Justice believes it is "likely" to survive a constitutional challenge[3] if passed, Bill C-36 will almost certainly face such a challenge in an attempt to have the Bill deemed unconstitutional if passed into law. In addition, only about a third of Canadians support the proposed law, compared to almost half who say they oppose it, and about a fifth who say they aren't sure.[4] Can Parliament ever have a rational and informed debate on the topic of sex work that sees the passage of a *Charter* complaint statute that reflects the will of the people, given the division of the public on this matter? In light of the continued controversy surrounding the proposed enactment and the division of Canadians on this topic, should the Supreme Court have simply re-drafted the present law itself in *Bedford* so that it complied with the *Charter*? If so, would such a decision be decried as a judicially active decision that overstepped the proper bounds of the Court? Did the remedy that the Supreme Court gave in *Bedford* actually guarantee the life, liberty, and security of the person of prostitutes if Parliament simply passes a new *Criminal Code* that similarly heightens the risk associated with sex work, albeit with different criminal law provisions? In other words, is Parliament or the Supreme Court in the best position to determine what the law should be in this matter?

Notes

1. See Summary to Bill C-36, *An Act to amend the Criminal Code in response to the Supreme Court of Canada decision in Attorney General of Canada v. Bedford and to make consequential amendments to other Acts*, 2nd Sess., 41st Parl., 2014 (as passed by the House of Commons 4 June 2014).
2. Cynthia McQueen, "Kicking the can on near prostitution ban: Libs say Tories intentionally created laws that will not withstand court challenge to better position themselves for election", *NOW* 33:41 (12–19 June 2014), online: NOW <http://www.nowtoronto.com/news/story.cfm?content=198432>.
3. Josh Wingrove, "Prostitution bill 'likely' to pass constitutionality test, MacKay says", *The Globe and Mail* (9 September 2014) online: The Globe and Mail <http://www.theglobeandmail.com/news/politics/battle-over-canadas-controversial-prostitution-bill-spilling-into-the-senate/article20490536/>.
4. Angus Reid Global, "Gender split reveals deep divide between men, women on issues surrounding the sex trade" (11 June 2014), online: Angus Reid Global <http://www.angusreidglobal.com/polls/gender-split-reveals-deep-divide-between-men-women-on-issues-surrounding-the-sex-trade/>

10 Equality

(a) Equality and the *Charter*[†]

David W. Elliott

EQUALITY

Equality is one of the most central and most elusive of all human values. It is important to law, justice, philosophy, and modern notions of democracy. It is enshrined in national and international charters of rights[1] as a paramount human right.

It may seem surprising, then, that there has been so little consensus on the exact meaning of equality.[2] Aristotle linked equality to justice, and drew a distinction between distributive justice, involving a form of proportionate equality for allocating resources according to merit, and retributive justice, for equalizing the situations of parties to a wrong by restoring the *status quo*.[3] Rousseau distinguished between natural inequalities that result from such factors as health and social inequalities that result from property,[4] and urged the abolition of the latter. Karl Marx focused on economic class inequality and predicted a proletariat revolution that would end bourgeois capitalist domination.[5]

For A.V. Dicey, the second tenet of the rule of law meant "the equal subjection of all classes [including government officials] to the ordinary law of the land administered by the ordinary law courts."[6] John Rawls formulated a concept of justice whose first priority was equality of basic rights, such as freedom of speech and the right to vote, and whose second priority included the principle that inequalities of social and economic benefits should result in compensating benefits for the least advantaged members of society.[7] Anne Bayefsky and others distinguish between equality of opportunity and equality of results, and criticize the first as inadequate.[8] Feminist writers such as Kathleen Lahey urge that any notion of equality must take into account a wide variety of features unique to women.[9]

While all these formulations and proposals were being drafted, apparent inequalities abounded in the world outside. Women and slaves were shut out of ancient Greek notions of equality. Rousseau wrote during the last years of the intensely stratified French *ancien régime*. Marx and Friedrich Engels' *Communist Manifesto* was first published in 1848, the year of European revolutions against established hierarchies of authority. While Dicey was writing about the rule of law, English women were battling unsuccessfully for the right to vote.[10] Today, Canadian women still suffer from myriad social and economic disadvantages,[11] as do Aboriginal peoples[12] and others. Indeed, some of the greatest discrepancies in Canada are economic: a country in which pensioners and unemployed young people line up in soup kitchens is also home to several hundred millionaires.

What has the state done to further equality in Canada? During most of the 20th century, two key egalitarian measures were the development of the progressive income tax and the creation of

---

† See also A.F. Bayefsky and M. Eberts, eds., *Equality Rights and the Canadian Charter of Rights and Freedoms* (Toronto: Carswell, 1985); I. Greene, *The Charter of Rights* (Toronto: James Lorimer and Company Publishers, 1989) c. 6; Peter W. Hogg, *Constitutional Law of Canada*, 4th ed. (Scarborough, Ont.: Carswell, 1997) c. 52; Christopher P. Manfredi, *Judicial Power and the Charter and the Paradox of Liberal Constitutionalism* (Don Mills, Ont.: Oxford University Press, 2001) c. 5.

the programs of the welfare state. In the non-economic — or less economic — sphere, the state turned increasingly to legal and constitutional mechanisms for combatting discrimination. It moved away from the traditional reliance on conventions of tolerance and restraint to legislative codes or bills and to an entrenched *Charter*.[13]

EQUALITY AND THE *CHARTER*

The key equality provision of the *Canadian Charter of Rights and Freedoms* is section 15. Section 15(1) guarantees a number of equality rights "without discrimination", and, in particular, without discrimination based on a number of specified grounds. Section 15(2) provides that the first section does not preclude affirmative action laws, programs, or activities that are intended to ameliorate conditions of disadvantaged individuals or groups. This generates a complex procedural format. A typical equality case could commence with section 32 to determine if an entity is sufficiently governmental to attract the *Charter*, move to section 15(1) to determine if there has been prohibited discrimination, determine if any violation of section 15(1) is permitted by subsection (2), and then move to section 1 to see if a violation of section 15 was justified.

Section 15 does not define equality. Moreover, although it lists nine forbidden grounds of discrimination, it does not define discrimination, or any of the grounds themselves. Also, as seen in Chapter 8, section 1 of the *Charter* is a general provision, and does not indicate what equality restrictions are justified.

Conceptually, then, the *Charter* equality challenge facing the courts is two-fold. First, amid a mass of possibilities, they must formulate a workable concept of equality or inequality and discrimination. Second, they must determine how this concept is affected by the wording of sections 32, 15, and 1 of the *Charter*.

Behind this conceptual challenge is a social question: how far should courts go in attempting to redress inequality under the *Charter*? We live in the midst of profound differences, many of which generate indignity, suffering, and dissension. On the other hand, some differences may be justified, and some may be dealt with more effectively by repealable laws or ongoing administrative structures. Should equality be defined by accountable officials, or by dispassionate judges? Should it be encouraged for the long term by education, or implemented now through affirmative action and

litigation? As with other *Charter* questions, how the courts will respond will depend on the courts themselves.

When looking at *Charter* equality cases, it may be helpful to consider some of the following questions:

1. Is the effect of section 15 more to reform than to preserve the *status quo*? Do the other *Charter* provisions correspond more to Aristotle's notion of corrective justice? If so, is there a relationship between section 15 and the rest of the *Charter*? In your view, would an activist judicial approach to section 15 serve as little more than a legitimation device, giving people the illusion of justice while deflecting their attention from economic and class inequalities,[14] or could it produce major positive change?

2. Should there be any relationship between the scope of section 32 of the *Charter* and the scope that courts give to section 15?

3. Where section 15 conflicts with other constitutional provisions, which should prevail?[15]

4. Should the justification standard in section 1 of the *Charter* be the same for equality as for other basic rights? Should it vary with the kind of inequality involved?

5. To what extent should courts enforce section 15 where a law is neutral on its face, but affects one group more adversely than another?

6. Where discrimination does not fall within one of the "enumerated" categories of section 15, should courts look to see if the discrimination is based on a characteristic that is irrelevant to the individual's circumstances, or that is beyond his or her power to change, or if it attaches to a group that constitutes a "discrete and insular minority"?

7. To what extent should section 15 protect against economic inequality? (Suppose that a government announces a plan to reduce its deficit by cutting the money it spends annually on social welfare payments by a third. Could a welfare recipient challenge this action under section 15 of the *Charter*? Why, or why not?)

8. How far should courts go in requiring the state to take positive action to redress inequality?

Notes

1. For example, in Canadian provincial and federal human rights codes, the *Canadian Bill of Rights* (1960); *Canadian*

Charter of Rights and Freedoms (1982); United States *Bill of Rights* (1789, ratified in 1791); *[European] Convention for the Protection of Human Rights and Fundamental Freedoms* (1950, in force in 1953); *Charter* of the United Nations (1945); *Universal Declaration of Human Rights* (1948); *ILO Convention Concerning Discrimination in Respect of Employment and Occupation* (in force for Canada in 1965); *International Convention on the Elimination of All Forms of Racial Discrimination* (1965, in force for Canada in 1970); *International Covenant on Civil and Political Rights* (1966, adopted for Canada, 1976); *International Covenant on Economic, Social and Cultural Rights* (1966, in force for Canada, 1976); and *International Convention on the Elimination of All Forms of Discrimination Against Women* (1979, in force for Canada in 1982).

2. For a comparison of the views of Marx, Weber, Durkheim, and more recent theorists on equality (or inequality), see W.G. Grabb, *Social Inequality: Classical and Contemporary Theorists* (Toronto: Holt, Rinehart & Winston, 1984).

3. E. Barker, trans., *The Politics of Aristotle [330 B.C.?]* (Oxford: Oxford University Press, 1946), Book III at xii, 12-2b, Book V at i, 1301a; and "Commentary" in C.J. Friedrich, *The Philosophy of Law in Historical Perspective*, 2d ed. (Chicago: University of Chicago Press, 1963) at 21–22.

4. J-J. Rousseau, *Discours sur l'origin et des fondaments de l'inégalité parmi les hommes [1755]*, ed. by J-F. Braunstein (Paris: Integrales do Philo, 1981) at 45.

5. Karl Marx and Friedrich Engels, English trans., *The Communist Manifesto [1848]* (New York: Norton., 1988); Karl Marx, "Preface to Contribution to Critique of Political Economy [1859]" in T.B. Bottomore, ed. and trans., *Selected Writings in Sociology and Social Philosophy* (New York: McGraw-Hill, 1964) at 51–53, 223, 225; W.G. Grabb, *Social Inequality: Classical and Contemporary Theorists* (Toronto: Holt, Rinehart & Winston, 1984) Ch. 2. Grabb contrasts Marx's emphasis on inequalities of economic power with the more pluralistic approach of Max Weber, who felt that social power differences could derive from a combination of economic class, social status, and membership in voluntary parties: *ibid.* at c. 3.

6. Albert Venn Dicey, *An Introduction to the Study of the Law of the Constitution [1885]*, 10th ed. (London: MacMillan, 1959) Ch. IV.

7. J. Rawls, *A Theory of Justice* (Oxford: Oxford University Press, 1972) at 302–303.

8. A.F. Bayefsky, "Defining Equality Rights," in A.F. Bayefsky and M. Eberts, eds., *Equality Rights and the Canadian Charter of Rights and Freedoms* (Toronto: Carswell, 1985) at 1.

9. K.A. Lahey, "On Silences, Screams and Scholarship: An Introduction to Feminist Legal Theory" in R.F. Devlin, ed., *Canadian Perspectives on Legal Theory* (Toronto: Emond Montgomery, 1991) 319 at 325–28; K.A. Lahey, *Are We 'Persons' Yet? Law and Sexuality in Canada* (Toronto: University of Toronto Press, 1999).

10. Women over 30 years of age finally gained the right to vote in 1918, in the *Representation of the People Act* of that year: D. Thomson, *England in the Nineteenth Century* (Harmondsworth, England: Penguin, 1950) at 188.

11. *Supra* note 9, "On Silences", at 325–28. There have been some legal advances, as in *Brooks v. Canada Safeway Ltd.*, [1989] 1 S.C.R. 1219, holding that discrimination on the basis of pregnancy amounts to discrimination on the basis of sex; *R. v. Butler*, [1990] 1 S.C.R. 452, invoking the sexual equality principle to support a definition of pornography intended to protect women; and *Moge v. Moge*, [1992] 3 S.C.R. 813, recognizing the value of household work for spousal support purposes. Despite these, women continue to suffer from major social, occupational, and economic inequalities.

12. See G. York, *The Dispossessed: Life and Death in Native Canada* (Toronto: Lester, 1989); P. Comeau and A. Santin, *The First Canadians: A Profile of Canada's Native People Today* (Toronto: James Lorimer & Company, 1990); L. Krotz, *Indian Country: Inside Another Canada* (Toronto: McClelland & Stewart, 1992); J. Sawchuk, "Native People, Social Conditions" in J.H. Marsh, ed., *The Canadian Encyclopedia*, Year 2000 ed. (Toronto: McClelland & Stewart, 1999), at 1594–96; H. McCue, "Native People, Education," *ibid.* at 1581–82; J.A. Price, rev'd. F. Trovato and M. Mills, "Native People, Economic Conditions," *ibid.* at 1580–81; T.K. Young, "Native People, Health," *ibid.* at 1584–85.

13. See "Basic Values and Their Protection" in Chapter 7, above.

14. See H. Glasbeek and M. Mandel, "The Legalization of Politics in Advanced Capitalism" in [guest] ed. R. Martin, *Critical Perspectives on the Constitution* [Socialist Studies Series] (Winnipeg, Man.: Society for Socialist Studies, 1984) 84 at 93B108 (extracts in Chapter 7, above).

15. See *Re Bill 30 (Ontario Separate School Funding)*, [1987] S.C.R. 1148.

(b)   *Andrews v. Law Society of British Columbia*†

NOTE

Mr. Mark Andrews was a British subject who did not yet have his Canadian citizenship, but resided permanently in Canada. Mr. Andrews was refused admission to the British Columbia bar because of a provision in the provincial *Barristers and Solicitors Act* that required Canadian citizenship as a condition for admission. Andrews argued that the citizenship requirement violated section 15(1) of the *Charter*. His application for a declaration was dismissed at trial but allowed on appeal.

Although this was the Supreme Court's first major *Charter* equality case, the judges focused

---

† [1989] 1 S.C.R. 143 aff'g. (1986), 27 D.L.R. (4th) 600 (B.C.C.A.), rev'g. (1985), 66 22 D.L.R. (4th) 9 (B.C.S.C.), McIntyre and Lamer JJ. dissenting. [Commentary note by David W. Elliott.]

more on discrimination prohibited by section 15(1) than on the general notion of equality. On this section (but not on s. 1) the Court gave general support to the reasons of McIntyre J. Justice McIntyre described s. 15(1) discrimination as a government distinction with the force of law that (i) denies equal treatment to the complainant or has a differential impact on him or her; (ii) is based on grounds of discrimination that are either mentioned expressly in section 15(1) or are analogous to these (because they are based on irrelevant personal characteristics or involve a socially disadvantaged group); and (iii) imposes a relative disadvantage on the complainant. McIntyre J. concluded that the citizenship requirement did discriminate contrary to section 15(1). For himself and Lamer J., McIntyre J. went on to find that the requirement was nevertheless saved under section 1 because the government's objective was desirable and its means were reasonable. Using a similar test, La Forest J. concluded that the requirement was not justified. Using a somewhat more rigorous *Oakes* test, Wilson J. for herself, Dickson C.J. and L'Heureux-Dubé came to the same conclusion as La Forest J.

EXTRACT

[McINTYRE J. for himself and LAMER JJ. (dissenting in part):]

The Concept of Equality

Section 15(1) of the Charter provides for every individual a guarantee of equality before and under the law, as well as the equal protection and equal benefit of the law without discrimination. This is not a general guarantee of equality; it does not provide for equality between individuals or groups within society in a general or abstract sense, nor does it impose on individuals or groups an obligation to accord equal treatment to others. It is concerned with the application of the law. No problem regarding the scope of the word "law," as employed in s. 15(1), can arise in this case because it is an Act of the Legislature which is under attack. Whether other governmental or quasi-governmental regulations, rules, or requirements may be termed laws under s. 15(1) should be left for cases in which the issue arises.

The concept of equality has long been a feature of Western thought. As embodied in s. 15(1) of the Charter, it is an elusive concept and, more than any of the other rights and freedoms guaranteed in the

Charter, it lacks precise definition. As has been stated by John H. Schaar, "Equality of Opportunity and Beyond," in ed. J. Roland Pennock and John W. Chapman *Nomos IX: Equality,* (1967), at p. 228:

> Equality is a protean word. It is one of those political symbols — liberty and fraternity are others — into which men have poured the deepest urgings of their heart. Every strongly held theory or conception of equality is at once a psychology, an ethic, a theory of social relations, and a vision of the good society.

It is a comparative concept, the condition of which may only be attained or discerned by comparison with the condition of others in the social and political setting in which the question arises. It must be recognized at once, however, that every difference in treatment between individuals under the law will not necessarily result in inequality and, as well, that identical treatment may frequently produce serious inequality. This proposition has found frequent expression in the literature on the subject but, as I have noted on a previous occasion, nowhere more aptly than in the well-known words of Frankfurter J. in *Dennis* v. *United States*, 339 U.S. 162, at p. 184:

> It was a wise man who said that there is no greater inequality than the equal treatment of unequals.

. . . .

... [T]he admittedly unattainable ideal [of equality before the law in s. 15] should be that a law expressed to bind all should not because of irrelevant personal differences have a more burdensome or less beneficial impact on one than another.

. . . .

It is clear that the purpose of s. 15 is to ensure equality in the formulation and application of the law. The promotion of equality entails the promotion of a society in which all are secure in the knowledge that they are recognized at law as human beings equally deserving of concern, respect and consideration. It has a large remedial component....

. . . .

It must be recognized, however, as well that the promotion of equality under s. 15 has a much more specific goal than the mere elimination of distinctions. If the Charter was intended to eliminate all distinctions, then there would be no place for sections such as 27 (multicultural heritage); 2(a) (free-

205

dom of conscience and religion); 25 (aboriginal rights and freedoms); and other such provisions designed to safeguard certain distinctions. Moreover, the fact that identical treatment may frequently produce serious inequality is recognized in s. 15(2), which states that the equality rights in s. 15(1) do "not preclude any law, program or activity that has as its object the amelioration of conditions of disadvantaged individuals or groups...."

Discrimination

The right to equality before and under the law, and the rights to the equal protection and benefit of the law contained in s. 15, are granted with the direction contained in s. 15 itself that they be without discrimination. Discrimination is unacceptable in a democratic society because it epitomizes the worst effects of the denial of equality, and discrimination reinforced by law is particularly repugnant. The worst oppression will result from discriminatory measures having the force of law. It is against this evil that s. 15 provides a guarantee.

. . . .

... I would say then that discrimination may be described as a distinction, whether intentional or not but based on grounds relating to personal characteristics of the individual or group, which has the effect of imposing burdens, obligations, or disadvantages on such individual or group not imposed upon others, or which withholds or limits access to opportunities, benefits, and advantages available to other members of society. Distinctions based on personal characteristics attributed to an individual solely on the basis of association with a group will rarely escape the charge of discrimination, while those based on an individual's merits and capacities will rarely be so classed.

. . . .

The distinguishing feature of the Charter, unlike the other enactments, is that consideration of such limiting factors is made under s. 1. This Court has described the analytical approach to the Charter in *R. v. Oakes*, [1986] 1 S.C.R. 103; *R. v. Edwards Books and Art Ltd.*, [1986] 2 S.C.R. 713, and other cases, the essential feature of which is that the right guaranteeing sections be kept analytically separate from s. 1. In other words, when confronted with a problem under the Charter, the first question which must be answered will be whether or not an infringement of a guaranteed right has occurred. Any justification of an infringement which is found to have occurred must be made, if at all, under the broad provisions of s. 1. It must be admitted at once that the relationship between these two sections may well be difficult to determine on a wholly satisfactory basis. It is, however, important to keep them analytically distinct if for no other reason than the different attribution of the burden of proof. It is for the citizen to establish that his or her Charter right has been infringed and for the state to justify the infringement.

[McIntyre J. outlined three main alternative approaches that courts might take to interpreting the relationship between section 15(1) and section 1. The first was to treat all distinctions as violating section 15(1). The second was to limit section 15(1) to distinctions that are unfair or unreasonable. McIntyre J. said the first approach would catch even trivial distinctions, while the second approach would leave no role for section 1.]

A third approach, sometimes described as an "enumerated or analogous grounds" approach, adopts the concept that discrimination is generally expressed by the enumerated grounds. Section 15(1) is designed to prevent discrimination based on these and analogous grounds. The approach is similar to that found in human rights and civil rights statutes which have been enacted throughout Canada in recent times. The following excerpts from the judgment of Hugessen J.A. in *Smith, Kline & French Laboratories* v. *Canada (Attorney General)*, *supra*, for Canada, [1987] 2 F.C., at pp. 368–69, illustrate this approach:

> The rights which it [s. 15] guarantees are not based on any concept of strict, numerical equality amongst all human beings. If they were, virtually all legislation, whose function it is, after all, to define, distinguish and make categories, would be in *prima facie* breach of s. 15 and would require justification under s. 1. This would be to turn the exception into the rule. Since courts would be obliged to look for and find s. 1 justification for most legislation, the alternative being anarchy, there is a real risk of paradox: the broader the reach given to s. 15 the more likely it is that it will be deprived of any real content. The answer, in my view, is that the text of the section itself contains its own limitations. It only proscribes discrimination amongst the members of categories which are themselves similar. Thus the issue, for each case, will be to know which categories are permissible in determining similar-

ity of situation and which are not. It is only in those cases where the categories themselves are not permissible, where equals are not treated equally, that there will be a breach of equality rights.

...

As far as the text of s. 15 itself is concerned, one may look to whether or not there is "discrimination," in the pejorative sense of that word, and as to whether the categories are based upon the grounds enumerated or grounds analogous to them. The inquiry, in effect, concentrates upon the personal characteristics of those who claim to have been unequally treated. Questions of stereotyping, of historical disadvantagement, in a word, of prejudice, are the focus and there may even be a recognition that for some people equality has a different meaning than for others.

...

The analysis of discrimination in this approach must take place within the context of the enumerated grounds and those analogous to them. The words "without discrimination" require more than a mere finding of distinction between the treatment of groups or individuals. Those words are a form of qualifier built into s. 15 itself and limit those distinctions which are forbidden by the section to those which involve prejudice or disadvantage.

. . . .

The third or "enumerated and analogous grounds" approach most closely accords with the purposes of s. 15 and the definition of discrimination outlined above and leaves questions of justification to s. 1. However, in assessing whether a complainant's rights have been infringed under s. 15(1), it is not enough to focus only on the alleged ground of discrimination and decide whether or not it is an enumerated or analogous ground. The effect of the impugned distinction or classification on the complainant must be considered. Once it is accepted that not all distinctions and differentiations created by law are discriminatory, then a role must be assigned to s. 15(1) which goes beyond the mere recognition of a legal distinction. A complainant under s. 15(1) must show not only that he or she is not receiving equal treatment before and under the law or that the law has a differential impact on him or her in the protection or benefit accorded by law but, in addition, must show that the legislative impact of the law is discriminatory.

Where discrimination is found a breach of s. 15(1) has occurred and — where s. 15(2) is not applicable — any justification, any consideration of

the reasonableness of the enactment, indeed, any consideration of factors which could justify the discrimination and support the constitutionality of the impugned enactment would take place under s. 1. This approach would conform with the directions of this Court in earlier decisions concerning the application of s. 1 and at the same time would allow for the screening out of the obviously trivial and vexatious claim. In this, it would provide a workable approach to the problem.

It would seem to me apparent that a legislative distinction has been made by s. 42 of the *Barristers and Solicitors Act* between citizens and non-citizens with respect to the practice of law. The distinction would deny admission to the practice of law to non-citizens who in all other respects are qualified. Have the respondents because of s. 42 of the Act been denied equality before and under the law or the equal protection of the law? In practical terms it should be noted that the citizenship requirement affects only those non-citizens who are permanent residents. The permanent resident must wait for a minimum of three years from the date of establishing permanent residence status before citizenship may be acquired. The distinction therefore imposes a burden in the form of some delay on permanent residents who have acquired all or some of their legal training abroad and is, therefore, discriminatory.

The rights guaranteed in s. 15(1) apply to all persons whether citizens or not. A rule which bars an entire class of persons from certain forms of employment, solely on the grounds of a lack of citizenship status and without consideration of educational and professional qualifications or the other attributes or merits of individuals in the group, would, in my view, infringe s. 15 equality rights. Non-citizens, lawfully permanent residents of Canada, are — in the words of the U.S. Supreme Court in *United States* v. *Carolene Products Co.*, 304 U.S. 144 (1938), at pp. 152–53, n. 4, subsequently affirmed in *Graham* v. *Richardson*, 403 U.S. 365 (1971), at p. 372 — a good example of a "discrete and insular minority" who come within the protection of s. 15.

Section 1

Having accepted the proposition that s. 42 has infringed the right to equality guaranteed in s. 15, it remains to consider whether, under the provisions of s. 1 of the Charter, the citizenship requirement which is clearly prescribed by law is a reasonable limit which can be "demonstrably justified in a free and democratic society."

The onus of justifying the infringement of a guaranteed Charter right must, of course, rest upon the parties seeking to uphold the limitation, in this case, the Attorney General of British Columbia and the Law Society of British Columbia. As is evident from the decisions of this Court, there are two steps involved in the s. 1 inquiry. First, the importance of the objective underlying the impugned law must be assessed. In *Oakes*, it was held that to override a Charter guaranteed right the objective must relate to concerns which are "pressing and substantial" in a free and democratic society. However, given the broad ambit of legislation which must be enacted to cover various aspects of the civil law dealing largely with administrative and regulatory matters and the necessity for the Legislature to make many distinctions between individuals and groups for such purposes, the standard of "pressing and substantial" may be too stringent for application in all cases. To hold otherwise would frequently deny the community-at-large the benefits associated with sound social and economic legislation. In my opinion, in approaching a case such as the one before us, the first question the Court should ask must relate to the nature and the purpose of the enactment, with a view to deciding whether the limitation represents a legitimate exercise of the legislative power for the attainment of a desirable social objective which would warrant overriding constitutionally protected rights. The second step in a s. 1 inquiry involves a proportionality test whereby the Court must attempt to balance a number of factors. The Court must examine the nature of the right, the extent of its infringement, and the degree to which the limitation furthers the attainment of the desirable goal embodied in the legislation. Also involved in the inquiry will be the importance of the right to the individual or group concerned, and the broader social impact of both the impugned law and its alternatives....

. . . .

... There is no single test under s. 1; rather, the Court must carefully engage in the balancing of many factors in determining whether an infringement is reasonable and demonstrably justified. The section 15(1) guarantee is the broadest of all guarantees. It applies to and supports all other rights guaranteed by the Charter. However, it must be recognized that Parliament and the Legislatures have a right and a duty to make laws for the whole community: in this process, they must make innumerable legisla-

tive distinctions and categorizations in the pursuit of the role of government. When making distinctions between groups and individuals to achieve desirable social goals, it will rarely be possible to say of any legislative distinction that it is clearly the right legislative choice or that it is clearly a wrong one. As stated by the Chief Justice in *R.* v. *Edwards Books and Art Ltd.*, at pp. 781–82: A "reasonable limit" is one which, having regard to the principles enunciated in *Oakes*, it was reasonable for the legislature to impose. The Courts are not called upon to substitute judicial opinions for legislative ones as to the place at which to draw a precise line.

. . . .

[McIntyre J. concluded that ensuring that prospective lawyers are familiar with Canadian institutions was a desirable goal, and that requiring citizenship was a reasonable means of achieving this goal.]

[WILSON J. for herself and for DICKSON C.J. and L'HEUREUX-DUBÉ J.:]

. . . .

[Wilson J. said that the requirement of citizenship did *not* ensure familiarity with Canadian institutions, and was not rationally connected to this goal or to the goals of ensuring an attachment to Canada or the performance of public duties.]

. . . .

I have had the benefit of the reasons of my colleague, Justice McIntyre, and I am in complete agreement with him as to the way in which s. 15(1) of the *Canadian Charter of Rights and Freedoms* should be interpreted and applied. I also agree with my colleague as to the way in which s. 15(1) and s. 1 of the Charter interact. I differ from him, however, on the application of s. 1 to this particular case.

. . . .

I agree with my colleague that a rule which bars an entire class of persons from certain forms of employment solely on the ground that they are not Canadian citizens violates the equality rights of that class. I agree with him also that it discriminates against them on the ground of their personal characteristics i.e., their non-citizen status. I believe, therefore, that they are entitled to the protection of s. 15. Before turning to s. 1 I would like to add a brief comment to what my colleague has said concerning non-citizens permanently resident in Canada forming the kind of "discrete and insular minority" to which the Supreme Court of the United States referred in *United States* v. *Carolene Products Co.*, 304 U.S. 144 (1938), at pp. 152–53, n. 4. Relative to citizens, non-citizens are a group lacking in political power and as such vulnerable to having their interests overlooked and their rights to equal concern and respect violated. They are among "those groups in society to whose needs and wishes elected officials have no apparent interest in attending": see J.H. Ely, *Democracy and Distrust* (1980), at p. 151. Non-citizens, to take only the most obvious example, do not have the right to vote. Their vulnerability to becoming a disadvantaged group in our society is captured by John Stuart Mill's observation in Book III of *Considerations of Representative Government* that "in the absence of its natural defenders, the interests of the excluded [are] always in danger of being overlooked...." I would conclude therefore that non-citizens fall into an analogous category to those specifically enumerated in s. 15....

    . . . .

The first hurdle to be crossed in order to override a right guaranteed in the Charter is that the objective sought to be achieved by the impugned law must relate to concerns which are "pressing and substantial" in a free and democratic society....

    . . . .

[The *Oakes* test], in my view, remains an appropriate standard when it is recognized that not every distinction between individuals and groups will violate s. 15. If every distinction between individuals and groups gave rise to a violation of s. 15, then this standard might well be too stringent for application in all cases and might deny the community at large the benefits associated with sound and desirable social and economic legislation. This is not a concern, however, once the position that every distinction drawn by law constitutes discrimination is rejected as indeed it is in the judgment of my colleague, McIntyre J. Given that s. 15 is designed to protect those groups who suffer social, political and legal disadvantage in our society, the burden resting on government to justify the type of discrimination against such groups is appropriately an onerous one. The second step in a s. 1 inquiry involves the application of a proportionality test which requires the

Court to balance a number of factors. The Court must consider the nature of the right, the extent of its infringement, and the degree to which the limitation furthers the attainment of the legitimate goal reflected in the legislation....

    . . . .

In my view, the reasoning advanced in support of the citizenship requirement simply does not meet the tests in *Oakes* for overriding a constitutional right particularly, as in this case, a right designed to protect "discrete and insular minorities" in our society. I would respectfully concur in the view expressed by McLachlin J.A. at p. 617 that the citizenship requirement does not "appear to relate closely to those ends, much less to have been carefully designed to achieve them with minimum impairment of individual rights."

Disposition

I would dismiss the appeal with costs. I would answer the constitutional questions as follows:

[Q.1] Does the Canadian citizenship requirement to be a lawyer in the Province of British Columbia as set out in s. 42 of the *Barristers and Solicitors Act*, R.S.B.C. 1979, c. 26 infringe or deny the rights guaranteed by s. 15(1) of the *Canadian Charter of Rights and Freedoms*?

[A.] Yes.

[Q.2] If the Canadian citizenship requirement to be a lawyer in the Province of British Columbia as set out in s. 42 of the *Barristers and Solicitors Act*, R.S.B.C. 1979, c. 26 infringes or denies the rights guaranteed by s. 15(1) of the *Canadian Charter of Rights and Freedoms*, is it justified by s. 1 of the *Canadian Charter of Rights and Freedoms*?

[A.] No.

[LA FOREST J.:]

    . . . .

My colleague, Justice McIntyre, has set forth the facts and the judicial history of this appeal and it is unnecessary for me to repeat them. Nor need I enter into an extensive examination of the law regarding the meaning of s. 15(1), because insofar as it is relevant to this appeal I am in substantial agreement with the views of my colleague. I hasten to add that the relevant question as I see it is restricted to whether the impugned provision amounts to discrimination in the sense in which my colleague has defined it, i.e., on the basis of "irrelevant personal differences" such as those listed in s. 15 and, traditionally, in human rights legislation.

I am not prepared to accept at this point that the only significance to be attached to the opening words that refer more generally to equality is that the protection afforded by the section is restricted to discrimination through the application of law....

. . . .

Assuming there is room under s. 15 for judicial intervention beyond the traditionally established and analogous policies against discrimination discussed by my colleague, it bears repeating that considerations of institutional functions and resources should make courts extremely wary about questioning legislative and governmental choices in such areas.

. . . .

... Citizenship is, at least temporarily, a characteristic of personhood not alterable by conscious action and in some cases not alterable except on the basis of unacceptable costs.

Moreover, non-citizens are an example without parallel of a group of persons who are relatively powerless politically, and whose interests are likely to be compromised by legislative decisions....

. . . .

I would conclude that although the governmental objectives, as stated, may be defensible, [they are] simply misplaced *vis-à-vis* the legal profession as a whole. However, even accepting the legitimacy and importance of the legislative objectives, the legislation exacts too high a price on persons wishing to practice law in that it may deprive them, albeit perhaps temporarily, of the "right" to pursue their calling. I would, therefore, dismiss the appeal with costs. I would answer the first constitutional question in the affirmative and the second in the negative.

(c) *Andrews* Legacy

David W. Elliott

Andrews was clearly a landmark decision. It laid down a three-part test for interpreting section 15. It asked courts to look for differential treatment between groups, for differential treatment by way of personal characteristics based on enumerated or analogous grounds, and for consequential disadvantage. It also signalled a new liberal approach to section 15's equality guarantee. Henceforth, the concern was not only equality of opportunity, with its emphasis on express distinctions, but also substantive equality, with its emphasis on results. While it cleared new ground, though, *Andrews* left behind it a trail of new or unanswered questions.

The new, broad approach to equality was apparent in the step of *Andrews*' three-part test for discrimination. Here the Court went beyond simply looking for express distinctions. It focused instead on differential treatment — differential effect regardless of whether there was a formal distinction. This approach greatly expanded the potential reach of

section 15. Government action could now be invalidated for discriminating by *failing* to draw distinctions, a longstanding concern of groups representing women, disabled persons, and many others.

By looking beyond express distinctions, substantive equality analysis also raised the potential for difficult questions of causation and proof. In *Symes*,[1] for example, an income tax provision allowed a lower deduction for child care expenses than for business expenses. A majority of the Court[2] held that the provision did not discriminate against married businesswomen. They said that because of the nature of the provision, Ms. Symes must demonstrate that married businesswomen bear a disproportionate share of the *financial* cost of raising a child. Since she had shown only that married businesswomen bear the main burden of the *social* cost, she had failed to prove prejudice that resulted directly from the low child care tax deduction. In contrast, the dissenting judges[3] felt that both a social burden and a financial burden had been demonstrated.

Eldridge,[4] considered below, showed that the causation hurdle was not fatal in all substantive equality cases. A lower court judge had concluded that it was her own medical condition, not government discrimination, that caused the problem she faced.[5] How did the Court respond to this argument in *Eldridge*?

Andrews recognized that equality is "a comparative concept". Certainly, the notion of differential treatment suggests a comparison — between the claimant's group and some other group. The parameters for comparison can help shape a conclusion about discrimination, in much the same way as a polling question can help shape the results of the poll. In *Andrews*, the Supreme Court rejected a suggestion that the comparison should be drawn between those who are "similarly situated". It thought this test could permit serious discrimination. However, the Court failed to provide an alternative test, and the question remains a weak spot in equality analysis. In the later *Hodge* case, the Court tried to resolve this question by saying that:

> [T]he appropriate comparator group is the one which mirrors the characteristics of the claimant (or claimant group) relevant to the benefit or advantage sought except that the statutory definition includes a personal characteristic that is offensive to the Charter or omits a personal characteristic in a way that is offensive to the Charter.[6]

This formula clarifies that it is ultimately for courts, rather than claimants or legislatures, to determine the appropriate comparator group. However, it does little to clarify how much weight courts should place on legislative intent, how broadly they should characterize the claimant group, or how they should determine what is and is not relevant to the advantage sought.

The analogous grounds part of the *Andrews* test was an attempt to relate the general notion of discrimination to its legislative context in sections 15 and 1 of the *Charter*. Discrimination often suggests differential treatment that is irrelevant or otherwise unjust, but if courts assess justification in the context of section 15 discrimination, they risk leaving nothing to be considered under section 1, the traditional place for *Charter* justification analysis. Conversely, if courts construe section 15 to apply to all differential treatment, they face the alternative of significantly relaxing their test for

section 1, or significantly slowing the processes of government. As seen, in *Andrews* the Court sought a middle route between these extremes by limiting the scope of section 15 to discrimination based on the personal characteristics or grounds that were listed ("enumerated") in section 15 and on grounds that were analogous to the enumerated ones.

This raised questions as to the appropriate criterion for determining if a ground is "analogous". Here *Andrews'* three judgments offered three very different potential criteria for determining whether a ground was analogous — its irrelevance to the purpose of the legislation, its immutability, and the socially disadvantaged nature of the group claiming prejudice. In some post-*Andrews* decisions, some judges suggested that there was no discrimination if a ground was relevant to the legislative purpose.[7] Another view was that whether a ground was analogous depended on weighing up a number of factors at a given time. It was not until *Corbiere*[8] in 1999 that a majority of the court said clearly that the test for an analogous ground is whether or not it is immutable, and that the results of this test do not vary over time.[9]

The third part of the *Andrews* test seemed to require that the differential treatment had imposed a relative disadvantage on the group of which the claimant was a member. This generated causation problems, especially for substantive inequality claims, as seen above. It also raised a question as to how disadvantage should be assessed, and whether any kind of prejudice other than disadvantage should be considered. As we will see, the Court attempted an answer to these questions in its 1999 decision in *Law*.[10]

Finally, by taking an activist approach to equality, the Court in *Andrews* increased the chances that it would be asked to "rewrite" legislation by compelling legislatures to take positive steps to correct discriminatory omissions, and sometimes by prescribing the precise legislative language to be used. Not surprisingly, then, it is in the post-*Andrews* equality case of *Vriend*[11] that we will see one of the Supreme Court's most explicit defences of judicial activism under the *Charter*. *Vriend*, in turn, was part of the same-sex judicial equality revolution that culminated in the 2004 *Reference re Same-Sex Marriage*.[12]

Notes

1. *Symes v. Canada*, [1993] 4 S.C.R. 695.
2. Comprising all the male judges in the Court.
3. Comprising the Court's two female judges.
4. *Eldridge v. British Columbia (A.G.) And Medical Services Commission*, [1997] 3 S.C.R. 624.

5. See the discussion of this argument in *Eldridge, ibid.* at paras. 68–69.
6. *Hodge v. Canada*, [2004] 3 S.C.R. 357 at para. 18.
7. See *Miron v. Trudel*, [1995] 2 S.C.R. 418 at para. 37 and *Egan v. Canada*, 1995] 2 S.C.R. 513 at para. 27.
8. *Corbiere v. Canada*, [1999] 2 S.C.R. 203.
9. *Ibid.*, paras. 8–13.
10. *Law v. Canada (Minister of Employment and Immigration)*, [1999] 1 S.C.R. 497.

11. *Vriend v. Alberta*, [1998] 1 S.C.R. 493.
12. *Reference re Same-Sex Marriage (IN THE MATTER OF Section 53 of the Supreme Court Act, R.S.C. 1985, c. S-26, AND IN THE MATTER OF a Reference by the Governor in Council concerning the Proposal for an Act respecting certain aspects of legal capacity for marriage for civil purposes, as set out in Order in Council P.C. 2003-1055, dated July 16, 2003)*, [2004] 3 S.C.R. 698.

(d) *Eldridge v. British Columbia (A.G.) and Medical Services Commission*†

NOTE

The facts in *Eldridge* were recounted in Chapter 8. Ms. Eldridge was deaf, and thus belonged to a group specifically enumerated in section 15 of the *Charter*. As seen, the Supreme Court's interpretation of section 15 has been marked by differences between individual judges. For example, there has been disagreement as to whether the presence of an irrelevant personal characteristic is essential to a finding of discrimination, or is just one pertinent consideration. Moreover, Ms. Eldridge's own s. 15 claim was complicated by several special factors. In this case the alleged discrimination resulted not directly from legislation, nor from an explicit government distinction, nor even from the special adverse effects of burdens intended to apply to everyone. Instead, it resulted from:

(i) the administration of legislation;
(ii) the differential impact of "facially neutral" administration on people in Ms. Eldridge's situation; and
(iii) the inability of people in Ms. Eldridge's situation to benefit from services extended to everyone.

The second feature of Ms. Eldridge's claim made it a claim of "adverse effects" discrimination. She was arguing that the lack of sign language interpreters prevented people in her situation from communicating adequately with hospital doctors. Note the relationship between the forms of permitted discrimination and the issues considered in Chapter 8 about the scope of the *Charter*. In cases of adverse effects discrimination, action by the state provides only the trigger for the *Charter* ground; the remainder of the ground depends on special features of non-state claimants.

EXTRACT

[LA FOREST J. for himself, LAMER C.J., and L'HEUREUX-DUBÉ, SOPINKA, GONTHIER, CORY, McLACHLIN, IACOBUCCI, and MAJOR JJ.:]

[34] ... [T]he fact that the *Hospital Insurance Act* does not expressly mandate the provision of sign language interpretation does not render it constitutionally vulnerable. The Act does not, either expressly or by necessary implication, forbid hospitals from exercising their discretion in favour of providing sign language interpreters. Assuming the correctness of the appellants' s. 15(1) theory, the *Hospital Insurance Act* must thus be read so as to require that sign language interpretation be provided as part of the services offered by hospitals whenever necessary for effective communication. As in the case of the *Medical and Health Care Services Act*, the potential violation of s. 15(1) inheres in the discretion wielded by a subordinate authority, not the legislation itself.

. . . .

[54] In the case of s. 15(1), this Court has stressed that it serves two distinct but related purposes.

---

† [1997] 3 S.C.R. 624; rev'g. (1995), 125 D.L.R. (4th) 323 (B.C.C.A.); aff'g. (1992), 75 B.C.L.R. (2d) 6, [1992] B.C.J. No. 2229 (QL) (B.C.S.C.). [Commentary note by David W. Elliott.]

First, it expresses a commitment — deeply ingrained in our social, political and legal culture — to the equal worth and human dignity of all persons.... Secondly, it instantiates a desire to rectify and prevent discrimination against particular groups "suffering social, political and legal disadvantage in our society." ... While this Court has confirmed that it is not necessary to show membership in a historically disadvantaged group in order to establish a s. 15(1) violation, the fact that a law draws a distinction on such a ground is an important *indicium* of discrimination....

[55] As deaf persons, the appellants belong to an enumerated group under s. 15(1) — the physically disabled....

.   .   .   .

[56] It is an unfortunate truth that the history of disabled persons in Canada is largely one of exclusion and marginalization. Persons with disabilities have too often been excluded from the labour force, denied access to opportunities for social interaction and advancement, subjected to invidious stereotyping and relegated to institutions....

.   .   .   .

[58] ... While this Court has not adopted a uniform approach to s. 15(1), there is broad agreement on the general analytic framework.... A person claiming a violation of s. 15(1) must first establish that, because of a distinction drawn between the claimant and others, the claimant has been denied "equal protection" or "equal benefit" of the law. Secondly, the claimant must show that the denial constitutes discrimination on the basis of one of the enumerated grounds listed in s. 15(1) or one analogous thereto. Before concluding that a distinction is discriminatory, some members of this Court have held that it must be shown to be based on an irrelevant personal characteristic; see *Miron*, *supra* (per Gonthier J.), and *Egan*, *supra* (*per* La Forest J.) Under this view, s. 15(1) will not be infringed unless the distinguished personal characteristic is irrelevant to the functional values underlying the law, provided that those values are not themselves discriminatory. Others have suggested that relevance is only one factor to be considered in determining whether a distinction based on an enumerated or analogous ground is discriminatory; see *Miron*, *supra* (*per* McLachlin J.), and *Thibaudeau* v. *Canada*, [1995] 2 S.C.R. 627 (*per* Cory and Iacobucci JJ.).

[59] In my view, in the present case the same result is reached regardless of which of these approaches is applied.... There is no question that the distinction here is based on a personal characteristic that is irrelevant to the functional values underlying the health care system. Those values consist of the promotion of health and the prevention and treatment of illness and disease, and the realization of those values through the vehicle of a publicly funded heath care system. There could be no personal characteristic less relevant to these values than an individual's physical disability.

[60] The only question in this case, then, is whether the appellants have been afforded "equal benefit of the law without discrimination" within the meaning of s. 15(1) of the *Charter*. On its face, the medicare system in British Columbia applies equally to the deaf and hearing populations. It does not make an explicit "distinction" based on disability by singling out deaf persons for different treatment....

[61] This Court has consistently held that s. 15(1) of the *Charter* protects against this type of discrimination. In *Andrews*, *supra*, McIntyre J. found that facially neutral laws may be discriminatory. "It must be recognized at once," he commented, at p. 164, "... that every difference in treatment between individuals under the law will not necessarily result in inequality and, as well, that identical treatment may frequently produce serious inequality"; see also *Big M Drug Mart Ltd.*, *supra*, at p. 347. Section 15(1), the Court held, was intended to ensure a measure of substantive, and not merely formal equality.

.   .   .   .

[64] Adverse effects discrimination is especially relevant in the case of disability. The government will rarely single out disabled persons for discriminatory treatment. More common are laws of general application that have a disparate impact on the disabled....

.   .   .   .

[66] Unlike in *Simpsons-Sears* and *Rodriguez*, in the present case the adverse effects suffered by deaf persons stem not from the imposition of a burden not faced by the mainstream population, but rather from a failure to ensure that they benefit equally from a service offered to everyone. It is on this basis that the trial judge and the majority of the Court of Appeal found that the failure to provide medically related sign language interpretation was not discriminatory. Their analyses presuppose that there is a

categorical distinction to be made between state-imposed burdens and benefits, and that the government is not obliged to ameliorate disadvantage that it has not helped to create or exacerbate....

. . . .

[68] Having determined that sign language interpretation is a discrete, non-medical "ancillary" service, the courts below were able to conclude that the appellants were not denied a benefit available to the hearing population. As the majority of the Court of Appeal explained, prior to the introduction of a universal medicare system, deaf and hearing persons were each required to pay their doctors. When necessary for effective communication, deaf persons were also obliged to pay for sign language translators. The Medical Services Plan, the court observed, removes the responsibility of both hearing and deaf persons to pay their physicians. Deaf persons, of course, remain responsible for the payment of translators in order to receive equivalent medical services as hearing persons, as they would be in the absence of the legislation. In the court's view, however, any resulting inequality exists independently of the benefit provided by the state.

[69] While this approach has a certain formal, logical coherence, in my view it seriously mischaracterizes the practical reality of health care delivery. Effective communication is quite obviously an integral part of the provision of medical services. At trial, the appellants presented evidence that miscommunication can lead to misdiagnosis or a failure to follow a recommended treatment. This risk is particularly acute in emergency situations, as illustrated by the appellant Linda Warren's experience during the premature birth of her twin daughters. That adequate communication is essential to proper medical care is surely so incontrovertible that the Court could, if necessary, take judicial notice of it....

. . . .

[71] If there are circumstances in which deaf patients cannot communicate effectively with their doctors without an interpreter, how can it be said that they receive the same level of medical care as hearing persons? ...

. . . .

[73] ... It has been suggested that s. 15(1) of the *Charter* does not oblige the state to take positive actions, such as provide services to ameliorate the symptoms of systemic or general inequality; see

Thibaudeau, *supra*, at para. 37 (per L'Heureux-Dubé J.). Whether or not this is true in all cases, and I do not purport to decide the matter here, the question raised in the present case is of a wholly different order....

. . . .

[77] This Court has consistently held ... that discrimination can arise both from the adverse effects of rules of general application as well as from express distinctions flowing from the distribution of benefits. Given this state of affairs, I can think of no principled reason why it should not be possible to establish a claim of discrimination based on the adverse effects of a facially neutral benefit scheme. Section 15(1) ... makes no distinction between laws that impose unequal burdens and those that deny equal benefits. If we accept the concept of adverse effect discrimination, it seems inevitable, at least at the s. 15(1) stage of analysis, that the government will be required to take special measures to ensure that disadvantaged groups are able to benefit equally from government services.... [I]f there are policy reasons in favour of limiting the government's responsibility to ameliorate disadvantage in the provision of benefits and services, those policies are more appropriately considered in determining whether any violation of s. 15(1) is saved by s. 1 of the *Charter*.

. . . .

[80] In my view, therefore, the failure of the Medical Services Commission and hospitals to provide sign language interpretation where it is necessary for effective communication constitutes a *prima facie* violation of the s. 15(1) rights of deaf persons. This failure denies them the equal benefit of the law and discriminates against them in comparison with hearing persons.

. . . .

[82] This is not to say that sign language interpretation will have to be provided in every medical situation. The "effective communication" standard is a flexible one, and will take into consideration such factors as the complexity and importance of the information to be communicated, the context in which the communications will take place and the number of people involved; see 28 C.F.R. [section] 35.160 (1997). For deaf persons with limited literacy skills, however, it is probably fair to surmise that sign language interpretation will be required in most cases; see *Chilton*, *supra*, at p. 886, and the many studies there cited.

[83] Finally, I note that it is not in strictness necessary to decide whether, according to this standard, the appellants' s. 15(1) rights were breached. This Court has held that if claimants prove that the equality rights of members of the group to which they belong have been infringed, they need not establish a violation of their own particular rights....

[La Forest J. held that the failure to provide for sign language interpreters was an unjustified denial of *Charter* equality. He directed the provincial government to administer the legislation in a manner consistent with the requirements of *Charter* s. 15(1).]

(e) *Vriend v. Alberta*†

NOTE

Mr. Vriend was dismissed from his laboratory coordinator job at a private religious college in Alberta on the ground that he was a homosexual. The Alberta Human Rights Commission told Vriend he could not file a discrimination complaint under the provincial *Individual's Rights Protection Act* (*IRPA*), because the *IRPA* did not prohibit discrimination on the basis of sexual orientation.

Vriend challenged this omission in the *IRPA* as a violation of the *Charter* guarantee of equality before the law. He succeeded in the Alberta Court of Queen's Bench, lost in the Alberta Court of Appeal, and won in the Supreme Court of Canada. The Supreme Court said the omission of the sexual orientation provision was an unjustified breach of section 15 of the *Charter*. The majority of the Court ordered that the words "sexual orientation" be read into the provincial Act as a prohibited ground of discrimination.

The Supreme Court's decision provoked controversy in Alberta. Gay and lesbian rights activists hailed it as long overdue justice. Some others

called on the provincial government to undo the effects of the decision by invoking the override provision.

Although *Vriend* was labelled as "activist", it is important to identify which aspect of the decision and of activism one has in mind. Arguably, the protection of sexual orientation was not unexpected. Earlier analogous grounds jurisprudence had been moving in this direction. Although the Court's decision to "read in" a legislative provision not enacted by the legislature was striking, it followed the approach set down in *Schachter* and already applied in *Eldridge*.

On the other hand, *Vriend* took a rigorous approach to the "pressing and substantial" objective part of the *Oakes* test[1] for section 1 of the *Charter*[2] — an approach that affects virtually all *Charter* cases. Substantively, *Vriend*'s impact went well beyond its specific facts. Only three weeks later, for example, the Ontario Court of Appeal cited *Vriend* in holding that a federal law restricting tax advantages to opposite-sex couples' pension plans was unjustified discrimination contrary to the *Charter*.[3] Within Alberta, as a result of the scope of

---

† [1998] 1 S.C.R. 493, aff'g. (1996), 132 D.L.R. (4th) 595 (A.C.A.), rev'g. [1994] 6 W.W.R. 414 (A.Q.B.), finding the omission of sexual orientation protection in the Alberta *Individual's Rights Protection Act* to be an unjustified violation of s. 15(1) of the *Charter*. (Major J. dissenting in part.) [Commentary note by David W. Elliott.]

[1] From *R. v. Oakes*, [1986] 1 S.C.R. 103. At para. 108 of his reasons in *Vriend*, Iacobucci J. quoted the restatement of the *Oakes* test in *Egan v. Canada*, [1995] 2 S.C.R. 513 at para. 182:

> A limitation to a constitutional guarantee will be sustained once two conditions are met. First, the objective of the legislation must be pressing and substantial. Second, the means chosen to attain this legislative end must be reasonable and demonstrably justifiable in a free and democratic society. In order to satisfy the second requirement, three criteria must be satisfied: (1) the rights violation must be rationally connected to the aim of the legislation; (2) the impugned provision must minimally impair the *Charter* guarantee; and (3) there must be a proportionality between the effect of the measure and its objective so that the attainment of the legislative goal is not outweighed by the abridgement of the right. In all s. 1 cases the burden of proof is with the government to show on a balance of probabilities that the violation is justifiable.

[2] In applying the *Oakes* test, Iacobucci J. indicated that courts should focus on the objective *of the limitation on equality* (para. 110), not on the objective of the statute or provision as a whole. He said the latter are relevant, but in a more general way: they help provide the context in which the objective of the limitation is determined: para. 111.

[3] *Rosenberg v. Canada (A.G.)*, [1998] O.J. No 1627 (QL) (Ont. C.A.), 23 April 1998.

the *IRPA*, the decision in *Vriend* affected not only government but also large segments of the private sector. It is not surprising, then, that the Court chose this decision in which to comment at length on the legitimacy of the judicial role under the *Charter*.

EXTRACT

[CORY and IACOBUCCI JJ (LAMER C.J. and GONTHIER, McLACHLIN, and BASTARACHE JJ. concurring):]

[1] ... In these joint reasons Cory J. has dealt with the issues pertaining to standing, the application of the *Canadian Charter of Rights and Freedoms*, and the breach of s. 15(1) of the *Charter*. Iacobucci J. has discussed s. 1 of the *Charter*, the appropriate remedy, and the disposition.

. . . .

[CORY J. referred to the relevant provisions of the *IRPA*, including the following:]

7(1) No employer shall
(a) refuse to employ or refuse to continue to employ any person, or
(b) discriminate against any person with regard to employment or any term or condition of employment, because of the race, religious beliefs, colour, gender, physical disability, mental disability, marital status, age, ancestry, place of origin, family status or source of income of that person or of any other person.

10 No trade union, employers' organization or occupational association shall
(a) exclude any person from membership in it,
(b) expel or suspend any member of it, or
(c) discriminate against any person or member, because of the race, religious beliefs, colour, gender, physical disability, mental disability, marital status, age, ancestry, place of origin, family status or source of income of that person or member.

[Cory J. said that Mr. Vriend and the three other appellants had standing to challenge not only the employment provisions of the *IRPA*, but its other discrimination protection provisions as well.]

. . . .

[56] It is suggested that this appeal represents a contest between the power of the democratically elected legislatures to pass the laws they see fit, and the power of the courts to disallow those laws, or to dictate that certain matters be included in those laws. To put the issue in this way is misleading and erroneous. Quite simply, it is not the courts which limit the legislatures. Rather, it is the Constitution, which must be interpreted by the courts, that limits the legislatures....

. . . .

[60] The relevant subsection, s. 32(1)(b), states that the *Charter* applies to "the legislature and government of each province in respect of all matters within the authority of the legislature of each province." There is nothing in that wording to suggest that a <u>positive act</u> encroaching on rights is required; rather the subsection speaks only of <u>matters within the authority of the legislature</u>....

. . . .

[65] The respondents further argue that the effect of applying the *Charter* to the *IRPA* would be to regulate private activity. Since it has been held that the *Charter* does not apply to private activity (*RWDSU* v. *Dolphin Delivery Ltd.*, [1986] 2 S.C.R. 573; *Tremblay* v. *Daigle*, [1989] 2 S.C.R. 530; McKinney, supra), it is said that the application of the *Charter* in this case would not be appropriate. This argument cannot be accepted. The application of the *Charter* to the *IRPA* does not amount to applying it to private activity. It is true that the *IRPA* itself targets private activity and as a result will have an "effect" upon that activity. Yet it does not follow that this indirect effect should remove the *IRPA* from the purview of the *Charter*. It would lead to an unacceptable result if any legislation that regulated private activity would for that reason alone be immune from *Charter* scrutiny.

. . . .

[69] It is easy to say that everyone who is just like "us" is entitled to equality. Everyone finds it more difficult to say that those who are "different" from us in some way should have the same equality rights that we enjoy. Yet so soon as we say any enumerated or analogous group is less deserving and unworthy of equal protection and benefit of the law all minorities and all of Canadian society are demeaned. It is so deceptively simple and so devastatingly injurious to say that those who are handicapped or of a different race, or religion, or colour or sexual orien-

tation are less worthy. Yet, if any enumerated or analogous group is denied the equality provided by s. 15 then the equality of every other minority group is threatened. That equality is guaranteed by our constitution. If equality rights for minorities had been recognized, the all too frequent tragedies of history might have been avoided. It can never be forgotten that discrimination is the antithesis of equality and that it is the recognition of equality which will foster the dignity of every individual.

. . . .

[74] In this case, as in *Eaton, Benner* and *Eldridge*, any differences that may exist in the approach to s. 15(1) would not affect the result, and it is therefore not necessary to address those differences. The essential requirements of all these cases will be satisfied by enquiring first, whether there is a distinction which results in the denial of equality before or under the law, or of equal protection or benefit of the law; and second, whether this denial constitutes discrimination on the basis of an enumerated or analogous ground.

. . . .

[75] The respondents have argued that because the *IRPA* merely omits any reference to sexual orientation, this "neutral silence" cannot be understood as creating a distinction. They contend that the *IRPA* extends full protection on the grounds contained within it to heterosexuals and homosexuals alike, and therefore there is no distinction and hence no discrimination....

[76] These arguments cannot be accepted. They are based on that "thin and impoverished" notion of equality referred to in *Eldridge* (at para. 73). It has been repeatedly held that identical treatment will not always constitute equal treatment (see for example *Andrews* v. *Law Society of British Columbia*, [1989] 1 S.C.R. 143, at p. 164)....

[77] ... Lesbian and gay individuals are ... denied protection [on] the ground that may be the most significant for them, discrimination on the basis of sexual orientation.

. . . .

[81] It is clear that the *IRPA*, by reason of its underinclusiveness, does create a distinction. The distinction is simultaneously drawn along two different lines. The first is the distinction between homosexuals, on one hand, and other disadvantaged groups which are protected under the Act, on the

other. Gays and lesbians do not even have formal equality with reference to other protected groups, since those other groups are explicitly included and they are not.

[82] The second distinction, and, I think, the more fundamental one, is between homosexuals and heterosexuals.... [T]he exclusion of the ground of sexual orientation, considered in the context of the social reality of discrimination against gays and lesbians, clearly has a disproportionate impact on them as opposed to heterosexuals. Therefore the *IRPA* in its underinclusive state denies substantive equality to the former group....

. . . .

[83] This case is similar in some respects to the recent case of *Eldridge, supra*. There the *Charter's* requirement of substantive, not merely formal, equality was unanimously affirmed. It was, as well, recognized that substantive equality may be violated by a legislative omission....

. . . .

[84] Finally, the respondents' contention that the distinction is not created by law, but rather exists independently of the *IRPA* in society, cannot be accepted.... [But] it is not necessary to find that the legislation creates the discrimination existing in society in order to determine that it creates a potentially discriminatory distinction.

. . . .

[87] It is apparent that the omission from the *IRPA* creates a distinction. That distinction results in a denial of the equal benefit and equal protection of the law. It is the exclusion of sexual orientation from the list of grounds in the *IRPA* which denies lesbians and gay men the protection and benefit of the Act in two important ways. They are excluded from the government's statement of policy against discrimination, and they are also denied access to the remedial procedures established by the Act.

[88] Therefore, the *IRPA*, by its omission or underinclusiveness, denies gays and lesbians the equal benefit and protection of the law on the basis of a personal characteristic, namely sexual orientation.

. . . .

[90] In *Egan*, it was held, on the basis of "historical social, political and economic disadvantage suffered

by homosexuals" and the emerging consensus among legislatures (at para. 176), as well as previous judicial decisions (at para. 177), that sexual orientation is a ground analogous to those listed in s. 15(1)....

. . . .

[104] In excluding sexual orientation from the *IRPA*'s protection, the Government has, in effect, stated that "all persons are equal in dignity and rights," except gay men and lesbians. Such a message, even if it is only implicit, must offend s. 15(1), the "section of the *Charter*, more than any other, which recognizes and cherishes the innate human dignity of every individual" (*Egan*, at para. 128). This effect, together with the denial to individuals of any effective legal recourse in the event they are discriminated against on the ground of sexual orientation, amount to a sufficient basis on which to conclude that the distinction created by the exclusion from the *IRPA* constitutes discrimination.

. . . .

[107] In summary, this Court has no choice but to conclude that the *IRPA*, by reason of the omission of sexual orientation as a protected ground, clearly violates s. 15 of the *Charter*. The *IRPA* in its underinclusive state creates a distinction which results in the denial of the equal benefit and protection of the law on the basis of sexual orientation, a personal characteristic which has been found to be analogous to the grounds enumerated in s. 15. This, in itself, would be sufficient to conclude that discrimination is present and therefore there is a violation of s. 15. The serious discriminatory effects of the exclusion of sexual orientation from the Act reinforce this conclusion. As a result, it is clear that the *IRPA*, as it stands, violates the equality rights of the appellant Vriend and of other gays and lesbians. It is therefore necessary to determine whether this violation can be justified under s. 1. This analysis will be undertaken by my colleague.

[IACOBUCCI J.:]

. . . .

[109] ... In my view, where, as here, a law has been found to violate the *Charter* owing to underinclusion, the legislation as a whole, the impugned provisions, and the omission itself are all properly considered.

[Iacobucci J. said the objective of the statute or section as a whole is relevant to s. 1 analysis in the sense that it can provide a context for understanding the objective of the limitation.]

[110] Section 1 of the *Charter* states that it is the limits on *Charter* rights and freedoms that must be demonstrably justified in a free and democratic society. It follows that under the first part of the *Oakes* test, the analysis must focus upon the objective of the impugned limitation, or in this case, the omission....

. . . .

[115] ... In the absence of any submissions regarding the pressing and substantial nature of the objective of the omission, the respondents have failed to discharge their evidentiary burden, and thus, I conclude that their case must fail at this first stage of the s. 1 analysis.

[116] ... In my view, where, as here, a legislative omission is on its face the very antithesis of the principles embodied in the legislation as a whole, the Act itself cannot be said to indicate any discernible objective for the omission that might be described as pressing and substantial so as to justify overriding constitutionally protected rights. Thus, on either analysis, the respondents' case fails at the initial step of the *Oakes* test.

. . . .

[Iacobucci J. said that, on the assumption that there was a pressing and substantial objective for the legislative omission, the means chosen to implement failed the proportionality test laid down in *Oakes*.]

. . . .

[130] Much was made in argument before us about the inadvisability of the Court interfering with or otherwise meddling in what is regarded as the proper role of the legislature, which in this case was to decide whether or not sexual orientation would be added to Alberta's human rights legislation. Indeed, it seems that hardly a day goes by without some comment or criticism to the effect that under the *Charter* courts are wrongfully usurping the role of the legislatures. I believe this allegation misunderstands what took place and what was intended when our country adopted the *Charter* in 1981–82.

[131] When the *Charter* was introduced, Canada went, in the words of former Chief Justice Brian Dickson, from a system of Parliamentary supremacy to constitutional supremacy....

[132] We should recall that it was the deliberate choice of our provincial and federal legislatures in adopting the *Charter* to assign an interpretive role to the courts and to command them under s. 52 to declare unconstitutional legislation invalid.

[133] However, giving courts the power and commandment to invalidate legislation where necessary has not eliminated the debate over the "legitimacy" of courts taking such action.... [J]udicial review, it is alleged, is illegitimate because it is anti-democratic in that unelected officials (judges) are overruling elected representatives (legislators)....

[134] To respond, it should be emphasized again that our *Charter*'s introduction and the consequential remedial role of the courts were choices of the Canadian people through their elected representatives as part of a redefinition of our democracy. Our constitutional design was refashioned to state that henceforth the legislatures and executive must perform their roles in conformity with the newly conferred constitutional rights and freedoms. That the courts were the trustees of these rights insofar as disputes arose concerning their interpretation was a necessary part of this new design.

[135] So courts in their trustee or arbiter role must perforce scrutinize the work of the legislature and executive not in the name of the courts, but in the interests of the new social contract that was democratically chosen. All of this is implied in the power given to the courts under s. 24 of the *Charter* and s. 52 of the *Constitution Act, 1982*.

[136] Because the courts are independent from the executive and legislature, litigants and citizens generally can rely on the courts to make reasoned and principled decisions according to the dictates of the constitution even though specific decisions may not be universally acclaimed. In carrying out their duties, courts are not to second-guess legislatures and the executives; they are not to make value judgments on what they regard as the proper policy choice; this is for the other branches. Rather, the courts are to uphold the Constitution and have been expressly invited to perform that role by the Constitution itself. But respect by the courts for the legislature and executive role is as important as ensuring that the other branches respect each [other's] role and the role of the courts.

[137] This mutual respect is in some ways expressed in the provisions of our constitution as shown by the wording of certain of the constitutional rights themselves. For example, s. 7 of the *Charter* speaks of no denial of the rights therein except in accordance with the principles of fundamental justice, which include the process of law and legislative action. Section 1 and the jurisprudence under it are also important to ensure respect for legislative action and the collective or societal interests represented by legislation. In addition, as will be discussed below, in fashioning a remedy with regard to a *Charter* violation, a court must be mindful of the role of the legislature. Moreover, s. 33, the notwithstanding clause, establishes that the final word in our constitutional structure is in fact left to the legislature and not the courts....

[138] As I view the matter, the *Charter* has given rise to a more dynamic interaction among the branches of governance. This interaction has been aptly described as a "dialogue" by some.... In reviewing legislative enactments and executive decisions to ensure constitutional validity, the courts speak to the legislative and executive branches. As has been pointed out, most of the legislation held not to pass constitutional muster has been followed by new legislation designed to accomplish similar objectives.... By doing this, the legislature responds to the courts; hence the dialogue among the branches.

[139] To my mind, a great value of judicial review and this dialogue among the branches is that each of the branches is made somewhat accountable to the other. The work of the legislature is reviewed by the courts and the work of the court in its decisions can be reacted to by the legislature in the passing of new legislation (or even overarching laws under s. 33 of the *Charter*). This dialogue between and accountability of each of the branches have the effect of enhancing the democratic process, not denying it.

[140] There is also another aspect of judicial review that promotes democratic values. Although a court's invalidation of legislation usually involves negating the will of the majority, we must remember that the concept of democracy is broader than the notion of majority rule, fundamental as that may be. In this respect, we would do well to heed the words of Dickson C.J. in *Oakes* [*R. v. Oakes*, [1986] 1 S.C.R. 103], at p. 136:

> The Court must be guided by the values and principles essential to a free and democratic society which I believe to embody, to name but a few, respect for the inherent dignity of the human person, commitment to social justice and equality, accommodation of a wide variety of beliefs, respect for cultural and group identity, and faith in social and political institutions which

enhance the participation of individuals and groups in society.

[141] So, for example, when a court interprets legislation alleged to be a reasonable limitation in a free and democratic society as stated in s. 1 of the *Charter*, the court must inevitably delineate some of the attributes of a democratic society....

[142] Democratic values and principles under the *Charter* demand that legislators and the executive take these into account; and if they fail to do so, courts should stand ready to intervene to protect these democratic values as appropriate. As others have so forcefully stated, judges are not acting undemocratically by intervening when there are indications that a legislative or executive decision was not reached in accordance with the democratic principles mandated by the *Charter*....

[After considering the remedial principles articulated in *Schachter v. Canada*, [1992] 2 S.C.R. 679, Iacobucci J. concluded that the ground of sexual orientation should be read into the relevant provisions of the *IRPA*.] In separate reasons, L'Heureux-

Dubé J. agreed with this result. She stressed that equality analysis should emphasize the factors of social vulnerability, human dignity, and personhood. Major J., dissenting, agreed that there was unjustified discrimination contrary to section 15 of the *Charter*. However, he felt the appropriate remedy was to declare the employment-related provisions of the *IRPA* to be invalid, and to suspend the declaration of invalidity in order to give the legislature an opportunity to rectify them.

A year after *Vriend*, people in same-sex relationships won another major victory in the highest Court. *M. v. V.*, [1999] 2 S.C.R. 3 concerned an Ontario law that made provision for spousal support to members of unmarried opposite-sex couples, but failed to give the same right to same-sex couples. The Supreme Court held that this omission was an unjustified violation of equality before the law. To give Ontario time to rectify the problem, the Court suspended its declaration of invalidity for six months. Because of the breadth of the ruling, many other Canadian provincial governments had to act quickly too, to change their own law.]

(f) *Law v. Canada (Minister of Employment and Immigration)*†

NOTE

After her husband died, 30-year-old Mrs. Nancy Law was denied survivor's benefits under the *Canada Pension Plan*. The CPP did not allow survivor's benefits for able-bodied claimants who are younger than 35 and have no dependent children. It allowed only partial benefits, on an ascending scale, from age 35 to 45. The Pension Plan Review Tribunal found that this distinction discriminated against Mrs. Law on the basis of age, contrary to section 15(1) of the *Charter*. However, a majority of the Tribunal held that the discrimination was justified under section 1. The Pension Appeals Board held that there was no discrimination. Its decision was upheld by the Federal Court of Appeal and a unanimous

Supreme Court of Canada. The Supreme Court of Canada concluded that the age distinction did not constitute discrimination contrary to section 15. Its decision is notable for Iacobucci J.'s wide-ranging effort to synthesize and summarize s. 15 interpretation principles.

When you read the Extract below, consider the following questions: (1) What is differential treatment? (2) What criteria determine the relevant comparator groups (i.e., the claimant's group and the group with which the claimant's group is to be compared)? (3) What are enumerated or analogous grounds? (4) What are the main contextual factors used to determine if there has been discrimination that demeans human dignity? (5) In considering whether human dignity has been demeaned, to

---

† [1999] 1 S.C.R. 497, aff'g. (1996), 135 D.L.R. (4th) 293 (F.C.A.), dismissing an application to set aside a decision of the Pension Appeals Board (1995), C.E.B. & P.G.R. 8574, finding certain age distinctions in the *Canada Pension Plan* constitutional. [Commentary note by David W. Elliott.]

what extent do courts consider the perspective of the claimant? (6) Does *Law* answer all these questions?

EXTRACT

[IACOBUCCI J. for the Court:]

[88] ... I believe it would be useful to summarize some of the main guidelines for analysis under s. 15(1) to be derived from the jurisprudence of this Court, as reviewed in these reasons.... [T]hese guidelines should not be seen as a strict test, but rather should be understood as points of reference.... [A]s our s. 15 jurisprudence evolves it may well be that further elaborations and modifications will emerge.

General Approach

(1) It is inappropriate to attempt to confine analysis under s. 15(1) of the *Charter* to a fixed and limited formula. A purposive and contextual approach to discrimination analysis is to be preferred, in order to permit the realization of the strong remedial purpose of the equality guarantee, and to avoid the pitfalls of a formalistic or mechanical approach.

(2) The approach adopted and regularly applied by this Court to the interpretation of s. 15(1) focuses upon three central issues:

(A) whether a law imposes differential treatment between the claimant and others, in purpose or effect;

(B) whether one or more enumerated or analogous grounds of discrimination are the basis for the differential treatment; and

(C) whether the law in question has a purpose or effect that is discriminatory within the meaning of the equality guarantee.

The first issue is concerned with the question of whether the law causes differential treatment. The second and third issues are concerned with whether the differential treatment constitutes discrimination in the substantive sense intended by s. 15(1).

(3) Accordingly, a court that is called upon to determine a discrimination claim under s. 15(1) should make the following three broad inquiries:

(A) Does the impugned law (a) draw a formal distinction between the claimant and others

on the basis of one or more personal characteristics, or (b) fail to take into account the claimant's already disadvantaged position within Canadian society resulting in substantively differential treatment between the claimant and others on the basis of one or more personal characteristics?

(B) Is the claimant subject to differential treatment based on one or more enumerated and analogous grounds?

and

(C) Does the differential treatment discriminate, by imposing a burden upon or withholding a benefit from the claimant in a manner which reflects the stereotypical application of presumed group or personal characteristics, or which otherwise has the effect of perpetuating or promoting the view that the individual is less capable or worthy of recognition or value as a human being or as a member of Canadian society, equally deserving of concern, respect, and consideration?

Purpose

(4) In general terms, the purpose of s. 15(1) is to prevent the violation of essential human dignity and freedom through the imposition of disadvantage, stereotyping, or political or social prejudice, and to promote a society in which all persons enjoy equal recognition at law as human beings or as members of Canadian society, equally capable and equally deserving of concern, respect and consideration.

(5) The existence of a conflict between the purpose or effect of an impugned law and the purpose of s. 15(1) is essential in order to found a discrimination claim. The determination of whether such a conflict exists is to be made through an analysis of the full context surrounding the claim and the claimant.

Comparative Approach

(6) The equality guarantee is a comparative concept, which ultimately requires a court to establish one or more relevant comparators. The claimant generally chooses the person, group, or groups with whom he or she wishes to be compared for the purpose of the discrimination inquiry. However, where the claimant's characterization of the comparison is insufficient, a court may, within the scope of the ground or grounds pleaded, refine the comparison

presented by the claimant where warranted. Locating the relevant comparison group requires an examination of the subject-matter of the legislation and its effects, as well as a full appreciation of context.

Context

(7) The contextual factors which determine whether legislation has the effect of demeaning a claimant's dignity must be construed and examined from the perspective of the claimant. The focus of the inquiry is both subjective and objective. The relevant point of view is that of the reasonable person, in circumstances similar to those of the claimant, who takes into account the contextual factors relevant to the claim.

(8) There is a variety of factors which may be referred to by a s. 15(1) claimant in order to demonstrate that legislation demeans his or her dignity. The list of factors is not closed. Guidance as to these factors may be found in the jurisprudence of this Court, and by analogy to recognized factors.

(9) Some important contextual factors influencing the determination of whether s. 15(1) has been infringed are, among others:

(A) Pre-existing disadvantage, stereotyping, prejudice, or vulnerability experienced by the individual or group at issue. The effects of a law as they relate to the important purpose of s. 15(1) in protecting individuals or groups who are vulnerable, disadvantaged, or members of "discrete and insular minorities" should always be a central consideration. Although the claimant's association with a historically more advantaged or disadvantaged group or groups is not per se determinative of an infringement, the existence of these pre-existing factors will favour a finding that s. 15(1) has been infringed.

(B) The correspondence, or lack thereof, between the ground or grounds on which the claim is based and the actual need, capacity, or circumstances of the claimant or others. Although the mere fact that the impugned legislation takes into account the claimant's traits or circumstances will not necessarily be sufficient to defeat a s. 15(1) claim, it will generally be more difficult to establish discrimination to the extent that the law takes into account the claimant's actual situation in a manner that respects his or her value as a human being or member of Canadian society, and less difficult to do so where the law fails to take into account the claimant's actual situation.

(C) The ameliorative purpose or effects of the impugned law upon a more disadvantaged person or group in society. An ameliorative purpose or effect which accords with the purpose of s. 15(1) of the *Charter* will likely not violate the human dignity of more advantaged individuals where the exclusion of these more advantaged individuals largely corresponds to the greater need or the different circumstances experienced by the disadvantaged group being targeted by the legislation. This factor is more relevant where the s. 15(1) claim is brought by a more advantaged member of society.

and

(D) The nature and scope of the interest affected by the impugned law. The more severe and localized the consequences of the legislation for the affected group, the more likely that the differential treatment responsible for these consequences is discriminatory within the meaning of s. 15(1).

(10) Although the s. 15(1) claimant bears the onus of establishing an infringement of his or her equality rights in a purposive sense through reference to one or more contextual factors, it is not necessarily the case that the claimant must adduce evidence in order to show a violation of human dignity or freedom. Frequently, where differential treatment is based on one or more enumerated or analogous grounds, this will be sufficient to found an infringement of s. 15(1) in the sense that it will be evident on the basis of judicial notice and logical reasoning that the distinction is discriminatory within the meaning of the provision.

. . . .

[Applying these criteria, Iacobucci J. said that although the CPP did draw a distinction between Mrs. Law and others on the basis of age, this differential treatment did not violate Mrs. Law's human dignity because (i) she was not a member of a discrete and insular minority, (ii) the distinction does not reflect or promote the notion that younger people are less capable or less deserving of consideration, but instead takes account of the fact that younger people have a greater prospect of long-term income replacement; and (iii) the purpose of the pension scheme is to allocate funds to those with the weakest ability to overcome need. He observed that:]

[101] "It seems to me that the increasing difficulty with which one can find and maintain employment as one grows older is a matter of which a court may appropriately take judicial notice. Indeed, this Court has often recognized age as a factor in the context of labour force attachment and detachment.

. . . .

[Iacobucci J. concluded that:]

[108] In these circumstances, recalling the purposes of s. 15(1), I am at a loss to locate any violation of human dignity. The impugned distinctions in the present case do not stigmatize young persons, nor can they be said to perpetuate the view that surviving spouses under age 45 are less deserving of concern, respect or consideration than any others. Nor do they withhold a government benefit on the basis of stereotypical assumptions about the demographic group of which the appellant happens to be a member. I must conclude that, when considered in the social, political, and legal context of the claim, the age distinctions in ss. 44(1)(d) and 58 of the CPP are not discriminatory.

(g) *R. v. Kapp*†

NOTE

When the federal government decided to provide a 24-hour communal licence to fish for salmon to three Aboriginal bands, the appellants, mainly non-Aboriginal commercial fishers, held a protest fishery and were charged with fishing at a prohibited time: *R. v. Kapp*, 2008 SCC 41 at para. 1. At trial they argued that the communal fishing licence discriminated against them on the basis of race, contrary to the equality provisions found in section 15(1) of the *Charter*. The Provincial Court found that the licence granted to the Aboriginal bands did indeed discriminate against the appellants under section 15(1); the court also determined that the licence was not justifiable in a free and democratic society and, therefore, could not be saved pursuant to section 1 of the *Charter*: *ibid*. at para. 2. On appeal this finding was reversed, and convictions were entered against the appellants.

The Supreme Court of Canada dismissed the appellants' claim, concluding that the communal fishing licence was protected by section 15(2) of the *Charter*, which establishes, in part, that not every "law, program or activity that has as its object the amelioration of conditions of disadvantaged individuals or groups" based on race, among other factors, is precluded by section 15(1): *ibid*. at para. 3. In the view of the Court, one of the objects of the communal fishing licence was to improve the conditions of the Aboriginal bands subject to the one-day fishing licence so that section 15(2) protected the licence from a finding that it was discriminatory pursuant to section 15(1) of the *Charter*: *ibid*. In addition to *Kapp* becoming a leading case on the interpretation of section 15(2) of the *Charter*, it commented on the development of equality jurisprudence under section 15(1) and responded to academic criticism regarding the approach of the Court to such questions. In an aside, not necessary to determine the case before them, the Supreme Court acknowledged the difficulty of the human dignity criterion it first established in *Law v. Canada*, [1999] 1 S.C.R. 497, and that it was both "abstract and subjective", and "confusing and difficult to apply": *R. v. Kapp*, at para. 22. McLachlin C.J. and Abella J. indicated that human dignity was not meant to burden an equality claim but was rather a "philosophical enhancement"; therefore, it was not to be "read literally as if [a] legislative disposition[], but as a way of focussing on the central concern of s. 15 identified in *Andrews* — combatting discrimination....": *ibid*. at 24. When reading the case excerpt below, ask yourself what the present test for discrimination under section 15(1) of the *Charter* is if *Law* mandated factors to be applied by way of a binding precedent and then *Kapp*, in non-binding comments, limited the effect of that precedent. Do claimants still need to formally establish the human dignity criterion in order to satisfy the requirements

---

† 2008 SCC 41, [2008] 2 S.C.R. 483 [Notes omitted.].

of a section 15(1) analysis, or does *Kapp* do away with such questions entirely? Finally, does *Kapp* require an additional element that claimants must now prove relating to the perpetuation of disadvantage or stereotyping in order to found a discrimination allegation under the *Charter*? (See Peter Hogg, *Constitutional Law of Canada*, 2011 Student Edition (Toronto: Carswell, 2001) at 55-31–55-32.) What do the Court's comments in *Kapp* do to the stability and predictability of equality jurisprudence going forward, given the questions it raises in relation to *Law v. Canada*?

EXTRACT

[McLACHLIN C.J. and ABELLA J. (Binnie, LeBel, Deschamps, Fish, Charron, and Rothstein JJ. concurring):]

1. The Purpose of Section 15

[14] Nearly 20 years have passed since the Court handed down its first s. 15 decision in the case of *Andrews v. Law Society of British Columbia*, [1989] 1 S.C.R. 143. *Andrews* set the template for this Court's commitment to substantive equality — a template which subsequent decisions have enriched but never abandoned.

[15] Substantive equality, as contrasted with formal equality, is grounded in the idea that: "The promotion of equality entails the promotion of a society in which all are secure in the knowledge that they are recognized at law as human beings equally deserving of concern, respect and consideration": *Andrews*, at p. 171, per McIntyre J., for the majority on the s. 15 issue. Pointing out that the concept of equality does not necessarily mean identical treatment and that the formal "like treatment" model of discrimination may in fact produce inequality, McIntyre J. stated (at p. 165):

> To approach the ideal of full equality before and under the law — and in human affairs an approach is all that can be expected — the main consideration must be the impact of the law on the individual or the group concerned. Recognizing that there will always be an infinite variety of personal characteristics, capacities, entitlements and merits among those subject to a law, there must be accorded, as nearly as may be possible, an equality of benefit and protection and no more of the restrictions, penalties or burdens imposed upon one than another. In other words, the admittedly unattainable ideal should be that a law expressed to bind all should not because of

irrelevant personal differences have a more burdensome or less beneficial impact on one than another.

While acknowledging that equality is an inherently comparative concept (p. 164), McIntyre J. warned against a sterile similarly situated test focussed on treating "likes" alike. An insistence on substantive equality has remained central to the Court's approach to equality claims.

[16] Sections 15(1) and 15(2) work together to promote the vision of substantive equality that underlies s. 15 as a whole. Section 15(1) is aimed at preventing discriminatory distinctions that impact adversely on members of groups identified by the grounds enumerated in s. 15 and analogous grounds. This is one way of combatting discrimination. However, governments may also wish to combat discrimination by developing programs aimed at helping disadvantaged groups improve their situation. Through s. 15(2), the *Charter* preserves the right of governments to implement such programs, without fear of challenge under s. 15(1). This is made apparent by the existence of s. 15(2). Thus s. 15(1) and s. 15(2) work together to confirm s. 15's purpose of furthering substantive equality.

[17] The template in *Andrews*, as further developed in a series of cases culminating in *Law v. Canada (Minister of Employment and Immigration)*, [1999] 1 S.C.R. 497, established in essence a two-part test for showing discrimination under s. 15(1): (1) Does the law create a distinction based on an enumerated or analogous ground? (2) Does the distinction create a disadvantage by perpetuating prejudice or stereotyping? These were divided, in *Law*, into three steps, but in our view the test is, in substance, the same.

[18] In *Andrews*, McIntyre J. viewed discriminatory impact through the lens of two concepts: (1) the perpetuation of prejudice or disadvantage to members of a group on the basis of personal characteristics identified in the enumerated and analogous grounds; and (2) stereotyping on the basis of these grounds that results in a decision that does not correspond to a claimant's or group's actual circumstances and characteristics. *Andrews*, for example, was decided on the second of these concepts; it was held that the prohibition against non-citizens practising law was based on a stereotype that non-citizens could not properly discharge the responsibilities of a lawyer in British Columbia — a view that denied non-citizens a privilege, not on the basis of their merits and capabilities, but on the basis of what the Royal Commission Report on *Equality in Employment* (1984),

referred to as "attributed rather than actual characteristics" (p. 2). Additionally, McIntyre J. emphasized that a finding of discrimination might be grounded in the fact that the impact of a particular law or program was to perpetuate the disadvantage of a group defined by enumerated or analogous s. 15 grounds. In this context, he said (at p. 174):

> I would say then that discrimination may be described as a distinction, whether intentional or not but based on grounds relating to personal characteristics of the individual or group, which has the effect of imposing burdens, obligations, or disadvantages on such individual or group not imposed upon others, or which withholds or limits access to opportunities, benefits, and advantages available to other members of society.

[19] A decade later, in *Law*, this Court suggested that discrimination should be defined in terms of the impact of the law or program on the "human dignity" of members of the claimant group, having regard to four contextual factors: (1) pre-existing disadvantage, if any, of the claimant group; (2) degree of correspondence between the differential treatment and the claimant group's reality; (3) whether the law or program has an ameliorative purpose or effect; and (4) the nature of the interest affected (paras. 62–75).

[20] The achievement of *Law* was its success in unifying what had become, since *Andrews*, a division in this Court's approach to s. 15. *Law* accomplished this by reiterating and confirming *Andrews'* interpretation of s. 15 as a guarantee of substantive, and not just formal, equality. Moreover, *Law* made an important contribution to our understanding of the conceptual underpinnings of substantive equality.

[21] At the same time, several difficulties have arisen from the attempt in *Law* to employ human dignity as a legal test. There can be no doubt that human dignity is an essential value underlying the s. 15 equality guarantee. In fact, the protection of all of the rights guaranteed by the *Charter* has as its lodestar the promotion of human dignity. As Dickson C.J. said in *R. v. Oakes*, [1986] 1 S.C.R. 103:

> The Court must be guided by the values and principles essential to a free and democratic society which I believe embody, to name but a few, respect for the inherent dignity of the human person, commitment to social justice and equality, accommodation of a wide variety of beliefs, respect for cultural and group identity, and faith in social and political institutions which enhance the participation of individuals and groups in society. [p. 136]

[22] But as critics have pointed out, human dignity is an abstract and subjective notion that, even with the guidance of the four contextual factors, cannot only become confusing and difficult to apply; it has also proven to be an *additional* burden on equality claimants, rather than the philosophical enhancement it was intended to be.[1] Criticism has also accrued for the way *Law* has allowed the formalism of some of the Court's post-*Andrews* jurisprudence to resurface in the form of an artificial comparator analysis focussed on treating likes alike.[2]

[23] The analysis in a particular case, as *Law* itself recognizes, more usefully focusses on the factors that identify impact amounting to discrimination. The four factors cited in *Law* are based on and relate to the identification in *Andrews* of perpetuation of disadvantage and stereotyping as the primary indicators of discrimination. Pre-existing disadvantage and the nature of the interest affected (factors one and four in *Law*) go to perpetuation of disadvantage and prejudice, while the second factor deals with stereotyping. The ameliorative purpose or effect of a law or program (the third factor in *Law*) goes to whether the purpose is remedial within the meaning of s. 15(2). (We would suggest, without deciding here, that the third *Law* factor might also be relevant to the question under s. 15(1) as to whether the effect of the law or program is to perpetuate disadvantage.)

[24] Viewed in this way, *Law* does not impose a new and distinctive test for discrimination, but rather affirms the approach to substantive equality under s. 15 set out in *Andrews* and developed in numerous subsequent decisions. The factors cited in *Law* should not be read literally as if they were legislative dispositions, but as a way of focussing on the central concern of s. 15 identified in *Andrews* — combatting discrimination, defined in terms of perpetuating disadvantage and stereotyping.

[25] The central purpose of combatting discrimination, as discussed, underlies both s. 15(1) and s. 15(2). Under s. 15(1), the focus is on preventing governments from making distinctions based on the enumerated or analogous grounds that: have the effect of perpetuating group disadvantage and prejudice; or impose disadvantage on the basis of stereotyping. Under s. 15(2), the focus is on enabling governments to pro-actively combat existing discrimination through affirmative measures.

[26] Against this background, we turn to a more detailed examination of s. 15(2) and its role in this appeal.

2. Section 15(2)

[27] Under *Andrews*, as previously noted, s. 15 does not mean identical treatment. McIntyre J. explained that "every difference in treatment between individuals under the law will not necessarily result in inequality", and that "identical treatment may frequently produce serious inequality" (p. 164). McIntyre J. explicitly rejected identical treatment as a *Charter* objective, based in part on the existence of s. 15(2). At p. 171, he stated that "the fact that identical treatment may frequently produce serious inequality is recognized in s. 15(2)".

[28] Rather than requiring identical treatment for everyone, in *Andrews*, McIntyre J. distinguished between difference and discrimination and adopted an approach to equality that acknowledged and accommodated differences. McIntyre J. proposed the following model, at p. 182:

> [I]n assessing whether a complainant's rights have been infringed under s. 15(1), it is not enough to focus only on the alleged ground of discrimination and decide whether or not it is an enumerated or analogous ground. The effect of the impugned distinction or classification on the complainant must be considered. Once it is accepted that not all distinctions and differentiations created by law are discriminatory, then a role must be assigned to s. 15(1) which goes beyond the mere recognition of a legal distinction. A complainant under s. 15(1) must show not only that he or she is not receiving equal treatment before and under the law or that the law has a differential impact on him or her in the protection or benefit accorded by law but, in addition, must show that the legislative impact of the law is discriminatory.

In other words, not every distinction is discriminatory. By their very nature, programs designed to ameliorate the disadvantage of one group will inevitably exclude individuals from other groups. This does not necessarily make them either unconstitutional or "reverse discrimination". *Andrews* requires that discriminatory conduct entail more than different treatment. As McIntyre J. declared at p. 167, a law will not "necessarily be bad because it makes distinctions".

[29] In our view, the appellants have established that they were treated differently based on an enumerated ground, race. Because the government argues that the program ameliorated the conditions of a disadvantaged group, we must take a more detailed look at s. 15(2).

[30] The question that arises is whether the program that targeted the aboriginal bands falls under s. 15(2) in the sense that it is a "law, program or activity that has as its object the amelioration of conditions of disadvantaged individuals or groups". As noted, the communal fishing licence authorizing the three bands to fish for sale on August 19–20 was issued pursuant to an enabling statute and regulations — namely the ACFLR. This qualifies as a "law, program or activity" within the meaning of s. 15(2). The more complex issue is whether the program fulfills the remaining criteria of s. 15(2) — that is, whether the program "has as its object the amelioration of conditions of disadvantaged individuals or groups".

[31] Even before the enactment of the *Charter*, this Court in *Athabasca Tribal Council v. Amoco Canada Petroleum Co.*, [1981] 1 S.C.R. 699, recognized that ameliorative programs targeting a disadvantaged group do not constitute discrimination. The issue in the case was whether the Energy Resources Conservation Board had jurisdiction to require an "affirmative action" program for the hiring of aboriginal people as a condition of its approval of a tar sands plant. The Court unanimously concluded that there was no such jurisdiction, but Ritchie J., writing for four of the judges (Laskin C.J., himself, Dickson J. and McIntyre J.), addressed the affirmative action aspect of the case, concluding that a program designed to benefit the aboriginal community was not discrimination within the meaning of *The Individual's Rights Protection Act* of Alberta, S.A. 1972, c. 2:

> In the present case what is involved is a proposal designed to improve the lot of the native peoples with a view to enabling them to compete as nearly as possible on equal terms with other members of the community who are seeking employment in the tar sands plant. With all respect, I can see no reason why the measures proposed by the "affirmative action" programs for the betterment of the lot of the native peoples in the area in question should be construed as "discriminating against" other inhabitants. The purpose of the plan as I understand it is not to displace non-Indians from their employment, but rather to advance the lot of the Indians so that they may be in a competitive position to obtain employment without regard to the handicaps which their race has inherited. [p. 711]

[32] The Royal Commission Report on *Equality in Employment*, whose mandate was to determine whether there should be affirmative action in Canada and on which McIntyre J. relied to develop his theories of discrimination and equality, set out the principles underlying s. 15(2), at pp. 13–14:

In recognition of the journey many have yet to complete before they achieve equality, and in recognition of how the duration of the journey has been and is being unfairly protracted by arbitrary barriers, section 15(2) permits laws, programs, or activities designed to eliminate these restraints. While section 15(1) guarantees to individuals the right to be treated as equals free from discrimination, section 15(2), though itself creating no enforceable remedy, assures that it is neither discriminatory nor a violation of the equality guaranteed by section 15(1) to attempt to improve the condition of disadvantaged individuals or groups, even if this means treating them differently.

Section 15(2) covers the canvas with a broad brush, permitting a group remedy for discrimination. The section encourages a comprehensive or systemic rather than a particularized approach to the elimination of discriminatory barriers.

Section 15(2) does not create the statutory obligation to establish laws, programs, or activities to hasten equality, ameliorate disadvantage, or eliminate discrimination. But it sanctions them, acting with statutory acquiescence.

[33] In essence, s. 15(2) of the *Charter* seeks to protect efforts by the state to develop and adopt remedial schemes designed to assist disadvantaged groups. This interpretation is confirmed by the language in s. 15(2), "does not preclude".

[34] This Court dealt explicitly with the relationship between s. 15(1) and s. 15(2) in *Lovelace v. Ontario*, [2000] 1 S.C.R. 950, 2000 SCC 37. The Court, per Iacobucci J., appeared unwilling at that time to give s. 15(2) independent force, but left the door open for that possibility, at para. 108:

> [A]t this stage of the jurisprudence, I see s. 15(2) as confirmatory of s. 15(1) and, in that respect, claimants arguing equality claims in the future should first be directed to s. 15(1) since that subsection can embrace ameliorative programs of the kind that are contemplated by s. 15(2). By doing that one can ensure that the program is subject to the full scrutiny of the discrimination analysis, as well as the possibility of a s. 1 review. <u>However ... we may well wish to reconsider this matter at a future time in the context of another case.</u> [Emphasis added.]

[35] Iacobucci J. in Lovelace perceived two possible approaches to the interpretation of s. 15(2). He believed that the Supreme Court could either read s. 15(2) as an interpretive aid to s. 15(1) (the approach adopted in Lovelace) or read it as an exception or exemption from the operation of s. 15(1).

[36] He favoured the interpretive aid approach, while acknowledging that the exemption approach had some support. In particular, he cited Mark A. Drumbl and John D. R. Craig for the proposition that s. 15(2) should defend against a s. 15(1) violation because otherwise the provision becomes redundant and does not encourage the government to combat discrimination pro-actively through ameliorative programs ("Affirmative Action in Question: A Coherent Theory for Section 15(2)" (1997), 4 Rev. Const. Stud. 80, at para. 102).

[37] In our view, there is a third option: if the government can demonstrate that an impugned program meets the criteria of s. 15(2), it may be unnecessary to conduct a s. 15(1) analysis at all. As discussed at the outset of this analysis, s. 15(1) and s. 15(2) should be read as working together to promote substantive equality. The focus of s. 15(1) is on preventing governments from making distinctions based on enumerated or analogous grounds that have the effect of perpetuating disadvantage or prejudice or imposing disadvantage on the basis of stereotyping. The focus of s. 15(2) is on enabling governments to pro-actively combat discrimination. Read thus, the two sections are confirmatory of each other. Section 15(2) supports a full expression of equality, rather than derogating from it. "Under a substantive definition of equality, different treatment in the service of equity for disadvantaged groups is an expression of equality, not an exception to it": P.W. Hogg, *Constitutional Law of Canada* (5th ed. Supp. 2007), vol. 2, at p. 55-53.

[38] But this confirmatory purpose does not preclude an independent role for s. 15(2). Section 15(2) is more than a hortatory admonition. It tells us, in simple clear language, that s. 15(1) cannot be read in a way that finds an ameliorative program aimed at combatting disadvantage to be discriminatory and in breach of s. 15.

[39] Here the appellants claim discrimination on the basis of s. 15(1). The source of that discrimination — the very essence of their complaint — is a program that may be ameliorative. This leaves but one conclusion: if the government establishes that the program falls under s. 15(2), the appellants' claim must fail.

[40] In other words, once the s. 15 claimant has shown a distinction made on an enumerated or analogous ground, it is open to the government to show that the impugned law, program or activity is ameliorative and, thus, constitutional. This approach has the advantage of avoiding the symbolic problem

of finding a program discriminatory before "saving" it as ameliorative, while also giving independent force to a provision that has been written as distinct and separate from s. 15(1). Should the government fail to demonstrate that its program falls under s. 15(2), the program must then receive full scrutiny under s. 15(1) to determine whether its impact is discriminatory.

[41] We would therefore formulate the test under s. 15(2) as follows. A program does not violate the s. 15 equality guarantee if the government can demonstrate that: (1) the program has an ameliorative or remedial purpose; and (2) the program targets a disadvantaged group identified by the enumerated or analogous grounds. In proposing this test, we are mindful that future cases may demand some adjustment to the framework in order to meet the litigants' particular circumstances. However, at this early stage in the development of the law surrounding s. 15(2), the test we have described provides a basic starting point — one that is adequate for determining the issues before us on this appeal, but leaves open the possibility for future refinement.

[42] We build our analysis of s. 15(2) and its operation around three key phrases in the provision. The subsection protects "any law, program or activity that <u>has as its object</u> the <u>amelioration</u> of conditions of <u>disadvantaged</u> individuals or groups"....

(h) *Reference re Same-Sex Marriage*†

NOTE

For evidence of the apparent influence of the Canadian judiciary, few subjects can compare with the evolving *Charter* law on equality and sexual orientation. In *Egan v. Canada*, [1995] 2 S.C.R. 513, a majority of the Supreme Court said that federal legislation that limited spousal benefits to heterosexual couples discriminated against same-sex couples. Although the Court concluded that the discrimination was justified, it reached this result by a majority of only one, and the determining judge said that his view was only provisional. In *Vriend*, the Court held unanimously that human rights legislation that failed to protect against discrimination on grounds of sexual orientation was an unjustifiable violation of section 15 of the *Charter*. Then in *M. v. H.* [1999] 2 S.C.R. 3, a majority of the Court struck down a provincial law that excluded same-sex couples from spousal support benefits available to heterosexual couples. Across the country, legislatures were required to end discriminatory provisions in these and similar social benefits programs.

Attention started to focus on the definition of marriage itself. The relevant law here was the common law definition of "the voluntary union for life of one man and one woman, to the exclusion of all others" (from the leading decision in *Hyde v. Hyde* (1866), L.R. 1 P. & D. 130, at 133). Parliament seemed reluctant to change this situation. In 1999, for example, a large majority of the House of Commons passed a resolution to re-affirm the traditional definition of marriage as the union of one man and one woman to the exclusion of all others. Section 1.1 of the *Modernization of Benefits and Obligations Act*, S.C. 2000, c. 12, stated that recent federal amendments in favour of same-sex couples did not affect the definition of marriage as "the lawful union of one man and one woman to the exclusion of all others."

In the courts, though, the momentum that started in *Egan, Vriend*, and *M. v. H.* continued at the provincial level. In 2002 and 2003, a superior court in Quebec and appellate courts in British Columbia and Ontario held that the common law definition was an unjustified violation of the *Charter*'s equality guarantee: *Hendricks v. Québec (Procureur général)*, [2002] R.J.Q. 2506 (C.S.); *EGALE Canada Inc. v. Canada (Attorney General)*

† *Reference re Same-Sex Marriage (IN THE MATTER OF Section 53 of the Supreme Court Act, R.S.C. 1985, c. S-26, AND IN THE MATTER OF a Reference by the Governor in Council concerning the Proposal for an Act respecting certain aspects of legal capacity for marriage for civil purposes, as set out in Order in Council P.C. 2003-1055, dated July 16, 2003)*, [2004] 3 S.C.R. 698. [Commentary note by David W. Elliott.]

(2003), 13 B.C.L.R. (4th) 1; and *Halpern v. Canada (Attorney General)*, (2003) 65 O.R. (3d) 161 (C.A.).

Meanwhile, public opinion appeared to be shifting. In 2003, the federal government drafted legislation to extend the right to civil marriage to same-sex couples and then referred the question of its validity to the Supreme Court. Between the referral and the reference hearing, lower courts made same-sex marriages legal in four more jurisdictions, so when the highest court rendered its decision on December 9, 2004, the effect may have seemed anti-climactic. On July 20, 2005, after many months of heated debate, the federal bill became law, making Canada one of only three countries in the Western world to legalize same-sex marriages.

When looking at the reference, consider how the Court addressed the tension between equality and freedom of religion, and why the Court refused to answer the fourth reference question. Were it not for the judiciary, would same-sex marriages be legal in Canada today? Are the judiciary better able to rule on matters such as these than politicians?

EXTRACT

[THE COURT:]

I. INTRODUCTION

[1] On July 16, 2003, the Governor in Council issued Order in Council P.C. 2003-1055 asking this Court to hear a reference on the federal government's Proposal for an *Act respecting certain aspects of legal capacity for marriage for civil purposes* ("Proposed Act"). The operative sections of the Proposed Act read as follows:

1. Marriage, for civil purposes, is the lawful union of two persons to the exclusion of all others.
2. Nothing in this Act affects the freedom of officials of religious groups to refuse to perform marriages that are not in accordance with their religious beliefs. It will be noted that s. 1 of the Proposed Act deals only with civil marriage, not religious marriage.

[2] The Order in Council sets out the following questions:

1. Is the annexed Proposal for an Act respecting certain aspects of legal capacity for marriage for civil purposes within the exclusive legislative authority of the Parliament of Canada? If not, in what particular or particulars, and to what extent?
2. If the answer to question 1 is yes, is section 1 of the proposal, which extends capacity to marry to persons of the same sex, consistent with the *Canadian Charter of Rights and Freedoms*? If not, in what particular or particulars, and to what extent?
3. Does the freedom of religion guaranteed by paragraph 2(a) of the *Canadian Charter of Rights and Freedoms* protect religious officials from being compelled to perform a marriage between two persons of the same sex that is contrary to their religious beliefs?

[3] On January 26, 2004, the Governor in Council issued Order in Council P.C. 2004-28 asking a fourth question, namely:

4. Is the opposite-sex requirement for marriage for civil purposes, as established by the common law and set out for Quebec in section 5 of the *Federal Law — Civil Law Harmonization Act, No. 1*, consistent with the *Canadian Charter of Rights and Freedoms*? If not, in what particular or particulars and to what extent?

[The Court held that the Proposed Act fell under Parliament's jurisdiction in relation to "Marriage and Divorce" in section 91(26) of the *Constitution Act, 1867*, not provincial jurisdiction in relation to "[t]he Solemnization of Marriage in the Province" in section 92(12).]

[45] Some interveners submit that the mere legislative recognition of the right of same-sex couples to marry would have the effect of discriminating against (1) religious groups who do not recognize the right of same-sex couples to marry (religiously) and/or (2) opposite-sex married couples. No submissions have been made as to how the Proposed Act, in its effect, might be seen to draw a distinction for the purposes of s. 15, nor can the Court surmise how it might be seen to do so. It withholds no benefits, nor does it impose burdens on a differential basis. It therefore fails to meet the threshold requirement of the s. 15(1) analysis laid down in *Law v. Canada (Minister of Employment and Immigration)*, [1999] 1 S.C.R. 497.

[46] The mere recognition of the equality rights of one group cannot, in itself, constitute a violation of

the rights of another. The promotion of *Charter* rights and values enriches our society as a whole and the furtherance of those rights cannot undermine the very principles the *Charter* was meant to foster.

(b) Section 2(a): Religion

[47] The question at this stage is whether s. 1 of the proposed legislation, considered in terms of its effects, is consistent with the guarantee of freedom of religion under s. 2(a) of the Charter. It is argued that the effect of the Proposed Act may violate freedom of religion in three ways: (1) the Proposed Act will have the effect of imposing a dominant social ethos and will thus limit the freedom to hold religious beliefs to the contrary; (2) the Proposed Act will have the effect of forcing religious officials to perform same-sex marriages; and (3) the Proposed Act will create a "collision of rights" in spheres other than that of the solemnization of marriages by religious officials.

[48] The first allegation of infringement says in essence that equality of access to a civil institution like marriage may not only conflict with the views of those who are in disagreement, but may also violate their legal rights. This amounts to saying that the mere conferral of rights upon one group can constitute a violation of the rights of another. This argument was discussed above in relation to s. 15(1) and was rejected.

[49] The second allegation of infringement, namely the allegation that religious officials would be compelled to perform same-sex marriages contrary to their religious beliefs, will be addressed below in relation to Question 3.

[50] This leaves the issue of whether the Proposed Act will create an impermissible collision of rights. The potential for a collision of rights does not necessarily imply unconstitutionality. The collision between rights must be approached on the contextual facts of actual conflicts. The first question is whether the rights alleged to conflict can be reconciled : *Trinity Western University v. British Columbia College of Teachers*, [2001] 1 S.C.R. 772, 2001 SCC 31, at para. 29. Where the rights cannot be reconciled, a true conflict of rights is made out. In such cases, the Court will find a limit on religious freedom and go on to balance the interests at stake under s. 1 of the Charter: *Ross v. New Brunswick School District No. 15*, [1996] 1 S.C.R. 825, at paras. 73–74. In both steps, the Court must proceed on the basis that the Charter does not create a hierar-

chy of rights (*Dagenais v. Canadian Broadcasting Corp.*, [1994] 3 S.C.R. 835, at p. 877) and that the right to religious freedom enshrined in s. 2(a) of the Charter is expansive.

[51] Here, we encounter difficulty at the first stage. The Proposed Act has not been passed, much less implemented. Therefore, the alleged collision of rights is purely abstract. There is no factual context. In such circumstances, it would be improper to assess whether the Proposed Act, if adopted, would create an impermissible collision of rights in as yet undefined spheres. As we stated in *MacKay v. Manitoba*, [1989] 2 S.C.R. 357, at p. 361:

> Charter decisions should not and must not be made in a factual vacuum. To attempt to do so would trivialize the Charter and inevitably result in ill-considered opinions. The presentation of facts is not, as stated by the respondent, a mere technicality; rather, it is essential to a proper consideration of Charter issues.

. . . .

[56] Against this background, we return to the question. The concern here is that if the Proposed Act were adopted, religious officials could be required to perform same-sex marriages contrary to their religious beliefs. Absent state compulsion on religious officials, this conjecture does not engage the Charter. If a promulgated statute were to enact compulsion, we conclude that such compulsion would almost certainly run afoul of the Charter guarantee of freedom of religion, given the expansive protection afforded to religion by s. 2(a) of the Charter.

[57] The right to freedom of religion enshrined in s. 2(a) of the Charter encompasses the right to believe and entertain the religious beliefs of one's choice, the right to declare one's religious beliefs openly and the right to manifest religious belief by worship, teaching, dissemination and religious practice: *Big M Drug Mart*, *supra*, at pp. 336–37. The performance of religious rites is a fundamental aspect of religious practice.

[58] It therefore seems clear that state compulsion on religious officials to perform same-sex marriages contrary to their religious beliefs would violate the guarantee of freedom of religion under s. 2(a) of the Charter. It also seems apparent that, absent exceptional circumstances which we cannot at present foresee, such a violation could not be justified under s. 1 of the Charter.

[59] The question we are asked to answer is confined to the performance of same-sex marriages by

religious officials. However, concerns were raised about the compulsory use of sacred places for the celebration of such marriages and about being compelled to otherwise assist in the celebration of same-sex marriages. The reasoning that leads us to conclude that the guarantee of freedom of religion protects against the compulsory celebration of same-sex marriages, suggests that the same would hold for these concerns.

[60] Returning to the question before us, the Court is of the opinion that, absent unique circumstances with respect to which we will not speculate, the guarantee of religious freedom in s. 2(a) of the Charter is broad enough to protect religious officials from being compelled by the state to perform civil or religious same-sex marriages that are contrary to their religious beliefs.

D. Question 4: Is the Opposite-Sex Requirement for Marriage for Civil Purposes, as Established by the Common Law and Set Out for Quebec in Section 5 of the *Federal Law — Civil Law Harmonization Act, No. 1*, Consistent With the Charter?

. . . .

[64] A unique set of circumstances is raised by Question 4, the combined effect of which persuades the Court that it would be unwise and inappropriate to answer the question.

[65] The first consideration on the issue of whether this Court should answer the fourth question is the government's stated position that it will proceed by way of legislative enactment, regardless of what answer we give to this question. In oral argument, counsel reiterated the government's unequivocal intention to introduce legislation in relation to same-sex marriage, regardless of the answer to Question 4. The government has clearly accepted the rulings of lower courts on this question and has adopted their position as its own. The common law definition of marriage in five provinces and one territory no longer imports an opposite-sex requirement. In addition, s. 5 of the *Federal Law — Civil Law Harmonization Act, No. 1*, S.C. 2001, c. 4, no longer imports an opposite-sex requirement. Given the government's stated commitment to this course of action, an opinion on the constitutionality of an opposite-sex requirement for marriage serves no legal purpose.

On the other hand, answering this question may have serious deleterious effects, which brings us to our next point.

[66] The second consideration is that the parties to previous litigation have now relied upon the finality of the judgments they obtained through the court process. In the circumstances, their vested rights outweigh any benefit accruing from an answer to Question 4. Moreover, other same-sex couples acted on the finality of *EGALE*, *Halpern* and *Hendricks* to marry, relying on the Attorney General of Canada's adoption of the result in those cases. While the effects of the *EGALE and Hendricks* decisions were initially suspended, the suspensions were lifted with the consent of the Attorney General. As a result of these developments, same-sex marriages have generally come to be viewed as legal and have been regularly taking place in British Columbia, Ontario and Quebec. Since this reference was initiated, the opposite-sex requirement for marriage has also been struck down in the Yukon, Manitoba, Nova Scotia and Saskatchewan: *Dunbar v. Yukon*, [2004] Y.J. No. 61 (QL), 2004 YKSC 54; *Vogel v. Canada (Attorney General)*, [2004] M.J. No. 418 (QL) (Q.B.); *Boutilier v. Nova Scotia (Attorney General)*, [2004] N.S.J. No. 357 (QL) (S.C.); and *N.W. v. Canada (Attorney General)*, [2004] S.J. No. 669 (QL), 2004 SKQB 434. In each of those instances, the Attorney General of Canada conceded that the common law definition of marriage was inconsistent with s. 15(1) of the Charter and was not justifiable under s. 1, and publicly adopted the position that the opposite-sex requirement for marriage was unconstitutional.

[67] As noted by this Court in Nova Scotia (*Attorney General*) *v. Walsh*, [2002] 4 S.C.R. 325, 2002 SCC 83, at para. 43:

> The decision to marry or not is intensely personal and engages a complex interplay of social, political, religious, and financial considerations by the individual. The parties in *EGALE*, *Halpern* and *Hendricks* have made this intensely personal decision. They have done so relying upon the finality of the judgments concerning them. We are told that thousands of couples have now followed suit. There is no compelling basis for jeopardizing acquired rights, which would be a potential outcome of answering Question 4.

[68] There is no precedent for answering a reference question which mirrors issues already disposed of in lower courts where an appeal was available but not pursued. Reference questions may, on occasion, pertain to already adjudicated disputes: see, e.g., *Reference re Truscott*, [1967] S.C.R. 309; *Reference re*

Regina v. Coffin, [1956] S.C.R. 191; *Reference re Minimum Wage Act of Saskatchewan*, [1948] S.C.R. 248; and *Reference re Milgaard (Can.)*, [1992] 1 S.C.R. 866. In those cases, however, no appeal to the Supreme Court was possible, either because leave to appeal had been denied (*Truscott* and *Milgaard*) or because no right of appeal existed (*Coffin* and *Minimum Wage Act of Saskatchewan*). The only instance that we are aware of where a reference was pursued in lieu of appeal is *Reference re Newfoundland Continental Shelf*, [1984] 1 S.C.R. 86. That reference is also distinguishable: unlike the instant reference, it was not a direct response to the findings of a lower appellate court and the parties involved in the prior proceedings had consented to the use of the reference procedure.

[69] The final consideration is that answering this question has the potential to undermine the government's stated goal of achieving uniformity in respect of civil marriage across Canada. There is no question that uniformity of the law is essential. This is the very reason that Parliament was accorded legislative competence in respect of marriage under s. 91(26) of the *Constitution Act, 1867*. However, as discussed, the government has already chosen to address the question of uniformity by means of the Proposed Act, which we have found to be within Parliament's legislative competence and consistent with the Charter. Answering the fourth question will not assist further. Given that uniformity is to be addressed legislatively, this rationale for answering Question 4 fails to compel.

[70] On the other hand, consideration of the fourth question has the potential to undermine the uniformity that would be achieved by the adoption of the proposed legislation. The uniformity argument succeeds only if the answer to Question 4 is "no". By contrast, a "yes" answer would throw the law into confusion. The decisions of the lower courts in the matters giving rise to this reference are binding in their respective provinces. They would be cast into doubt by an advisory opinion which expressed a contrary view, even though it could not overturn them. The result would be confusion, not uniformity.

[71] In sum, a unique combination of factors is at play in Question 4. The government has stated its intention to address the issue of same-sex marriage by introducing legislation regardless of our opinion on this question. The parties to previous litigation have relied upon the finality of their judgments and have acquired rights which in our view are entitled

to protection. Finally, an answer to Question 4 would not only fail to ensure uniformity of the law, but might undermine it. These circumstances, weighed against the hypothetical benefit Parliament might derive from an answer, convince the Court that it should exercise its discretion not to answer Question 4.

(2) The Substance of Question 4

[72] For the reasons set out above, the Court exercises its discretion not to answer this question.

III. CONCLUSION

[73] The Court answers the reference questions as follows:

1. Is the annexed Proposal for an Act respecting certain aspects of legal capacity for marriage for civil purposes within the exclusive legislative authority of the Parliament of Canada? If not, in what particular or particulars, and to what extent?

   Answer: With respect to s. 1: Yes. With respect to s. 2: No.

2. If the answer to question 1 is yes, is section 1 of the proposal, which extends capacity to marry to persons of the same sex, consistent with the *Canadian Charter of Rights and Freedoms*? If not, in what particular or particulars, and to what extent?

   Answer: Yes.

3. Does the freedom of religion guaranteed by paragraph 2(a) of the *Canadian Charter of Rights and Freedoms* protect religious officials from being compelled to perform a marriage between two persons of the same sex that is contrary to their religious beliefs?

   Answer: Yes.

4. Is the opposite-sex requirement for marriage for civil purposes, as established by the common law and set out for Quebec in section 5 of the *Federal Law — Civil Law Harmonization Act, No. 1*, consistent with the *Canadian Charter of Rights and Freedoms*? If not, in what particular or particulars and to what extent?

   Answer: The Court exercises its discretion not to answer this question.

11   Group Rights

(a)   Individual and Group Rights

David W. Elliott

In the 1986 *Ontario Education Act* reference, the Ontario Court of Appeal distinguished between group and individual rights as follows:

> ... [G]roup rights ... are asserted by individuals or groups of individuals because of their membership in the protected group. Individual rights are asserted equally by everyone despite membership in certain ascertainable groups.[1]

It may be useful to refine this distinction a little, as *everyone* belongs to groups of various kinds. Individual rights are claimed by individuals as human beings or as members of the general community. Group rights are claimed by individuals or groups because of their connection with particular groups *within* the general population or community. An individual right, then, would include an individual's right to freedom of conscience or speech, or his or her right to vote, or to equality without discrimination on grounds such as race or sex. Examples of group rights are Aboriginal rights, official language rights, and collective bargaining rights.

Implicit in this distinction is the existence of a third set of interests, the general interests of the community as a whole. These interests, set by government policy, could include such things as national defence, safety regulations, health and unemployment insurance, and education programs.

Individual rights might appear to have one major advantage over group rights: that of universality. In the words of the Ontario Court of Appeal, they are "asserted equally by everyone". In contrast, rights of particular groups in the community are necessarily selective, claimed by one part of society and not by another. Perhaps, because of this, individual rights are often regarded as self-evident, needing no more justification than the basic fact of human dignity. Since group rights are selective, society often expects special justification before offering them legal protection.

Collective bargaining rights, for example, give unique powers to trade unions, and supporters justify them with the need to protect the interests of individual workers in the face of the superior economic power of large corporate employers. Aboriginal rights are based on the fact that the Aboriginal peoples were here first. Rights of English and French speaking minorities in Canada are claimed under an implied Confederation bargain that gave French-speaking minorities certain rights at the federal level in return for English-speaking minority rights inside Quebec. Another Confederation bargain recognized certain denominational school rights existing in 1867.

But individual rights must be treated with caution too, and may need to be subordinated to pressing community needs. The enjoyment of some individual rights may interfere with the enjoyment of others, requiring adjustments to each. In appropriate cases, they will also have to be balanced against justified group rights.[2] Michael Mac Neil argues that since individuals are not just self-contained units but are also the products of relations with others, community interests — both general interests and special group rights — should be accorded equal importance with individual rights.[3] Moreover, individuals in some groups are less able than others to enjoy their individual rights, and may require help — through progressive taxation, affirmative action, and other group efforts — to be able to do so.

233

Two important group rights in Canada are collective bargaining rights and Aboriginal rights. Collective bargaining rights were directly involved in the *Dolphin Delivery* decision,[4] but are also relevant to *Metropolitan Life*,[5] *S.E.P.Q.A.*,[6] and the tragic *Westray* story.[7] They are discussed in the Mac Neil article below. Aboriginal rights are among the oldest and newest of group rights in Canada — oldest, because they pre-date recorded history, and newest, because only recently have courts, legislatures, and constitution makers begun to deal with them explicitly. They are considered in the remaining extracts in this chapter.

Notes

1. *Re Bill 30, An Act to Amend the Education Act (Ont.)*, (1986), 25 D.L.R. (4th) 1, 54–55; aff'd. in [1987] 1 S.C.R. 1148.
2. In *Re Bill 30, An Act to Amend the Education Act (Ont.)*, (1986), 25 D.L.R. (4th) 1, 54–55; aff'd. in [1987] 1 S.C.R. 1148, the courts held that certain collective rights

(denominational school rights guaranteed in the *Constitution Act, 1867*) should prevail over individual rights (equality rights guaranteed in the *Charter*). The government of Ontario proposed to extend full funding to Roman Catholic high schools beyond grade 10. In response to concerns that this would violate s. 15 of the *Charter*, Ontario referred the constitutionality of the proposed funding bill to the courts. A majority of the Ontario Court of Appeal, and the Supreme Court of Canada, upheld funding under the denominational school rights provisions. The Supreme Court of Canada held that the opening words of s. 93 combined with s. 93(3) authorized the province to grant new rights or privileges to denominational schools as contemplated in the bill, and that this power to provide for new special arrangements for denominational schools could not have been intended to be subject to the *Charter*. Five judges felt that special denominational rights in 1867 and the possibility of new special denominational rights after 1867 were "a fundamental part of the Confederation compromise." Two other judges said that s. 93(3) expressly contemplated the special treatment being attacked here.

3. "Courts and Liberal Ideology" by Mac Neil below.
4. Chapter 8, above.
5. Chapter 5, above.
6. Chapter 5, above.
7. Chapter 2, above.

(b) Labour and the *Charter*: An Evolving Narrative[†]

David W. Elliott

Do guarantees such as freedom of expression and freedom of association protect groups as well as individuals? If so, should section 1 of the *Charter* apply as rigorously to groups as to individuals? How should courts apply the *Charter* in important economic areas such as labour relations? These questions were all relevant to the Supreme Court's decision in the *Dolphin Delivery* case.[1]

In fact, this case was one of four early decisions that caused much concern to the labour movement. In *Dolphin Delivery*, the Supreme Court refused to invalidate a common law-based injunction that was directed against secondary picketing. In *obiter* comments, the main majority accepted that picketing can be a constitutionally protected form of expression under section 2(c) of the *Charter*. However, what the Court gave with one hand, it took away with the other. It required little specific evidence to conclude that secondary picketing restrictions can be justified under section 1. It was

enough to show an intent to prevent the labour dispute from escalating beyond the actual parties.[2]

Accompanying *Dolphin Delivery* was the controversial "Labour Trilogy" of 1987. In each of these cases, a majority of the Court declined to apply the constitutional guarantee of freedom of association to protect other collective bargaining interests. In the *Alberta Labour* reference,[3] the Court refused to apply the guarantee of freedom of association to invalidate an Alberta statute that banned public sector strikes. In the *Saskatchewan Dairy Workers* case,[4] the Court refused to use it to invalidate a statute requiring striking dairy workers to return to work. In the *Public Service Alliance* case,[5] it refused to use this provision to invalidate legislation imposing wage freezes and similar restrictions on federal public servants.

In the last two cases, the majority repeated the majority views in the *Alberta Labour* reference, especially those of McIntyre J. In that reference, McIntyre J. said that freedom of association is an individual's

---

† Revised and updated by Nick E. Milanovic.

right.[6] In his view, it cannot give greater constitutional protection to people when they act collectively than when they act alone.[7] Hence, freedom of association protects the right to join groups, and to carry out in groups those activities that are constitutional and lawful for individuals.[8] Since the right to cease work is not lawful for individuals acting on their own, section 2(d) of the *Charter* cannot guarantee a right to strike for unions.

McIntyre J. supported this rationale by saying that the right to strike was a relatively recent legislative creation and not a longstanding philosophical tradition, and that to constitutionalize a right to strike could interfere with a delicate balance between employers and employees that is better handled by expert administrative tribunals than courts:[9]

> If the right to strike is constitutionalized, then its application, its extent and any questions of its legality, become matters of law. This would inevitably throw the courts back into the field of labour relations and much of the value of specialized labour tribunals would be lost.[10]

In contrast, the dissenting judges in the *Alberta Labour* reference stressed the fundamental nature of the right to work and the importance of freedom of association to modern labour relations. Dickson C.J., dissenting, said that some associational activity has no analogies with individual activity.[11] He said that freedom of association is most important in situations where an individual is vulnerable to prejudice in the actions of a larger entity such as an employer or the government.[12] Accordingly, he felt that freedom of association should protect some collective labour activities that cannot be performed lawfully by individuals, such as the right to bargain collectively and the right to strike.

In the first two cases of the Trilogy, a majority concluded that the freedom of association does *not* include a right to strike (*Alberta Labour* reference and the Saskatchewan dairies case); or bargain collectively (the Saskatchewan dairies case); in the third (the *Professional Institute* case), the Court failed to find that freedom of association includes a right to bargain collectively.[13] In the last case, Sopinka J. said the *Alberta Labour* reference established four propositions:

> ... [F]irst, that s. 2(d) protects the freedom to establish, belong to and maintain an association; second, that s. 2(d) does not protect an activity solely on the ground that the activity is a foundational or essential purpose of an association; third, that s. 2(d) protects the exercise

in association of the constitutional rights and freedoms of individuals; and fourth, that s. 2(d) protects the exercise in association of the lawful rights of individuals.[14]

What do you think of McIntyre J.'s reasons for refusing to extend constitutional protection to the right to strike or bargain collectively? Has the Court taken a similar approach to the economic rights of corporations?[15] Has the Court's approach to the latter affected the former? In a 1989 article, Michael J. MacNeil argued that the reasoning in *Dolphin Delivery* and the Trilogy is a good example of traditional liberal theory, emphasizing individual interests and neglecting important group and communitarian concerns.[16] See also the Hutchinson and Monahan article, "A Democratic Approach to Civil Liberties", in Chapter 7. Can collective rights be reconciled with traditional liberal theory?[17]

However, the early individualist orientation of the Supreme Court began to moderate on these matters. In a 2002 article, Diane Pothier described the Supreme Court's impact on labour relations as "marginal".[18] Yet, as Pothier acknowledged,[19] there have been some countercurrents. For example, in *Lavigne* in 1991, the Supreme Court rejected an individualist freedom *from* association argument attack on union rights. The Court held that individual workers cannot prevent unions from levying compulsory dues on all employees in a bargaining unit, including those who are not union members. One set of majority judges held that although a requirement of compulsory dues payment violates an individual worker's right to freedom of — and from — association, the restriction is justified because it is necessary to the important role of unions in democratizing the workplace and promoting democratic principles in society as a whole.[20] Another set of majority judges held that section 2(d) did not apply, as it cannot include freedom from association.[21] A seventh judge agreed that section 2(d) can protect freedom from association, but said that there was no violation here, since the compulsory association did not involve compulsory ideological conformity.[22]

In the 2001 *Advance Cutting* decision,[23] the Supreme Court continued its narrow approach to freedom from association. Three majority judges said that compulsory association alone is insufficient to attract s. 2(d) protection.[24] There must be something more, such as ideological coercion, as required by McLachlin J. in *Lavigne*.[25] Another majority judge rejected the notion that there is a clear freedom from association.[26] The fifth majority judge held that although compulsory association alone can merit s. 2(d) protection, the restriction on s. 2(d) rights was justified in this case.[27] This judge stressed the need for some deference to legislative judgment in a case like this.[28] Clearly, the narrower the scope of freedom from association, or the more lenient the test for s. 1 justification, the wider the potential scope for collective labour rights.

Two months later, in its 2001 *Dunmore* decision,[29] the Court indicated that it might be retreating from the approach in the *Alberta Labour* reference. In *Dunmore*, agricultural workers argued that a provincial law that prevented them from forming unions violated their freedom of association under the *Charter*. Bastarache J. for the majority referred[30] to the four-part summary of the *Alberta Labour* reference quoted above,[31] and said that it was not a comprehensive statement of the scope of freedom of association. In particular, Bastarache J. suggested that section 2(d) may protect some collective activities that (a) are not lawful when carried out individually or (b) *cannot be* carried out individually, and (c) are not protected by other fundamental freedoms.[32] Although Bastarache J. repeated the Labour Trilogy finding that the right to bargain collectively is not constitutionally protected, he found that this law went further and prevented the workers from forming unions and carrying on lawful union activities short of full collective bargaining.[33] Hence, there was a breach of the agricultural workers' right to freedom of association. Bastarache J. found the breach to be unjustified, and gave the legislature 18 months in which to extend to the workers the statutory freedom to organize, together with:

> ... protections judged essential to its meaningful exercise, such as freedom to assemble, to participate in the lawful activities of the association and to make representations, and the right to be free from interference, coercion and discrimination in the exercise of these freedoms.[34]

Bastarache J. left it up to the legislature to decide if the agricultural workers should also be included in a full bargaining regime.

Dunmore creates a paradoxical situation. On one hand, it upholds the Labour Trilogy result that section 2(d) does not protect collective bargaining. On the other hand, it undermines a key rationale for this result — the proposition that section 2(d) protects only those activities that can be carried out by individuals. If freedom of association can now protect activities that cannot be carried out individually, why not the right to bargain collectively and the right to strike?

Then, in its *Pepsi-Cola* decision of 2002,[35] the Supreme Court qualified the finding in *Dolphin Delivery* that government could justify restricting secondary picketing to prevent a labour conflict from escalating beyond the actual parties. The Court said that McIntyre J.'s comments in *Dolphin Delivery* "should not be read as suggesting that third parties should be completely insulated from economic harm arising from labour conflict".[36] The Court held that government may not be justified in restricting forms of secondary picketing that cause no undue harm[37] to others.

Five years after *Pepsi-Cola*, the Supreme Court reversed course and extended the fundamental freedoms to labour relations.[38] When the provincial government in British Columbia legislated important changes to health care workers' collective agreement without meaningfully consulting their labour unions beforehand, the bargaining agents challenged that action in the courts. In *Health Services and Support — Facilities Subsector Bargaining Assn. v. British Columbia*, [2007] 2 S.C.R. 391, a majority of the Supreme Court found that a procedural right to collective bargaining was an associational activity protected by section 2(d) of the *Charter*.[39] The Court explained that the constitutional right to collective bargaining protects the ability of workers to engage in associational activity in order to jointly achieve shared goals concerning the terms and conditions of work. The Court held that section 2(d) did not guarantee the particular goals of workers, but it did guarantee them a process through which those goals could be pursued.[40] In other words, employees have a right to unite collectively, press their demands to government employers, and engage in negotiations in an attempt to achieve their workplace objectives. The procedural right to collective bargaining also placed corresponding duties on government employers to meet and discuss these matters in good faith with their employees.[41] The Court found that the right to collective bargaining was limited to "substantial interference" with the activity of collective bargaining that involved action that seriously undermined the activity of workers joining together to pursue their common goals and negotiate the terms and conditions of work with their employer.[42] Only where a matter is important to the process of collective bargaining and had been imposed in violation of the duty of good faith negotiations can section 2(d) be violated.[43] As the legislation in question substantially interfered with key collective agreement terms, such as the lay-offs clause and the exercise of seniority rights,[44] the impugned statute breached the *Charter* and was not saved by section 1 as the statute in question did not minimally impair the employee's s. 2(d) rights.[45]

Labour unions and their supporters were jubilant upon receiving the Supreme Court's decision overturning the labour trilogy, but their celebration was short-lived. Just four years later, the Supreme Court decided a new labour rights case, which had its origins in *Dunmore v. Ontario*, emerged. As a result of the ruling in *Dunmore*, the government of Ontario passed new legislation that gave farmworkers the right to organize unions but was devoid of many of the protections normally found in labour legislation that ensure collective bargaining. The new law essentially required that their employers must hear or read the representations made to them by the union. When a mushroom farm refused to bargain with a group of unionized farmworkers, their labour union challenged the suspect statute, claiming that section 2(d) permits workers to unionize and bargain through those unions. In a unanimous decision, the Ontario Court of Appeal agreed with the unions and required minimal statutory protections, such as a mechanism for resolving bargaining impasses, to be included in the legislation in order to pass constitutional muster.

A five-member majority of the Supreme Court in *Ontario (Attorney General) v. Fraser*, [2011] 2 S.C.R. 3, concluded that to require that legislation consist of minimum labour-relations-styled protections for unionized workers was an endorsement of a particular kind of statutory model of collective bargaining. In the Court's view, that finding stretched the parameters of the right to associate found in section 2(d) of the *Charter*.[46] Among other things, the Court's decision clarified that no particular kind of collective bargaining regime is required by section 2(d), and in each case the court will consider whether the impugned statute or action makes it impossible for workers to act collectively to achieve workplace goals.[47] The Supreme Court interpreted the requirement, found in the farmworker statute, of employers to listen or to read the union's proposals as imposing a duty to negotiate in good faith.[48] Even though the farmworkers attempted to engage the employer in bargaining and the employer refused to recognize or to meet and bargain with the employee's representative,[49] the Supreme Court decided that the challenge was premature.[50] It indicated that the union did not make a significant attempt to make the law work, and the process provided by the statute was left largely unexplored. However, the Court did again confirm that section 2(d) does include a right to

collective bargaining and affirmed that Ontario's farmworkers "are entitled to meaningful processes by which they can pursue workplace goals."[51] The Supreme Court upheld the appeal of the Ontario government and reversed the Court of Appeal.

The obvious question for critics of this decision, which saw Justices Rothstein and Charron call for a reversal of the *ratio* in *Heath Services*, is whether the Supreme Court has fashioned a right that can meaningfully assist workers to pursue their workplace goals? What use is a procedural right to collective bargaining when vulnerable workers in the agricultural sector cannot access the right, after years of litigation, to ensure meetings with their employer to simply discuss their proposals? If the Supreme Court limited the procedural right to collective bargaining in *Fraser*, because it seemingly endorsed a particular kind of labour regime, what hope is there that the Supreme Court will recognize a right to strike under section 2(d)? Would constitutionalizing the right to strike bolster the ability of workers to achieve their goals through collective bargaining? If it does, do you expect the Court to do so, or will it claim that would constitutionalize a particular labour relations regime and therefore decline to do so? In overruling the B.C. government's attempt to unilaterally alter its collective agreement with its workers, did the Supreme Court in *Health Services* elevate the collective agreement above statutes and grant them a similar status to the *Charter* itself?[52] Is there a real danger in constitutionalizing labour rights that courts, who have no particular expertise in labour relations, will now be invited to interfere with labour law in a way that will damage the existing social arrangement between employers and unions? After reading about the development of labour rights in the *Charter*, do you believe there is, or will be, a robust right to collective bargaining for workers protected by section 2(d)?

Notes

1. *Retail, Wholesale and Department Store Union, Local 580 v. Dolphin Delivery Ltd.* (1987), 33 D.L.R. (4th) 174 (S.C.C.), in Chapter 8, above.
2. *Ibid.* at para. 23.
3. *Re Public Service Employee Relations Act (Alberta)*, [1987] 1 S.C.R. 313 (S.C.C.).
4. *Government of Saskatchewan v. Retail, Wholesale and Department Store Union*, [1987] 1 S.C.R. 460 (S.C.C.).
5. *Public Service Alliance of Canada v. The Queen in Right of Canada*, [1987] 1 S.C.R. 424.
6. *Re Public Service Employee Relations Act (Alberta)*, [1987] 1 S.C.R. 313 at para. 155. McIntyre J. said that most of the *Charter* is concerned to protect rights of individuals, rather than groups: para. 155.
7. *Ibid.* at para. 171.
8. *Ibid.* at paras. 175–76.

9. *Ibid.* at paras. 181–83.
10. *Ibid.* at 183. In a very brief judgment, Le Dain J., for himself, Beetz and La Forest JJ., agreed with the result reached by McIntyre J., but stressed the need for restraint in applying s. 2(d) protection, in light of the wide variety of associations it could affect, and the need for judicial restraint in light of the balance and specialized expertise required in the collective bargaining area: *ibid.* at paras. 142–44.
11. *Ibid.* at para. 89.
12. *Ibid.* at para. 87.
13. In *Professional Institute of the Public Service of Canada v. Northwest Territories*, [1990] 2 S.C.R. 367, a majority of the Court said unequivocally that freedom of association does not encompass a right to bargain collectively.
14. *Ibid.* at para. 183.
15. See, for example, early decisions on fundamental freedoms of companies such as *R. v. Big M Drug Mart Ltd.*, [1985] 1 S.C.R. 295 and *Ford v. Quebec (Attorney General)*, [1988] 2 S.C.R. 712 (both in Chapter 9, above).
16. Michael J. Mac Neil, "Courts and Liberal Ideology: An Analysis of the Application of the *Charter* to Some Labour Law Issues" (1989), 34 McGill Law J. 87. Mac Neil identifies four key concepts of liberal ideology: individual autonomy, formal equality, state neutrality, and a public/private boundary that creates a wide sphere for private activity.
17. Writing about collective cultural rights, Will Kymlicka has answered "yes". Kymlicka has argued that the special concerns of minority cultural groups can and should be incorporated into liberal theories of justice: see *Liberalism, Community and Culture* (New York: Oxford University Press, 1989); and *Multi-Cultural Citizenship: A Liberal Theory of Minority Rights* (Toronto: Clarendon Press, 1995). Are Kymlicka's arguments applicable to workers' rights? For a commentary on Kymlicka, see E. Metcalfe, "Illiberal Citizenship? A Critique of Will Kymlicka's Liberal Theory of Minority Rights" (1996) 22 Queens L.J. 167. Compare Kymlicka's approach to group diversity with that in Neil Bissoondath, *Selling Illusions: The Cult of Multiculturalism in Canada* (Toronto: Penguin, 1994) and Todd Gitlin, *The Twilight of Common Dreams* (New York: Henry Holt, 1995).
18. Dianne Pothier, "Twenty Years of Labour Law and the *Charter*" (2002) 40 Osgoode Hall L.J. 369 at 370.
19. Pothier said that the *Dunmore*, *Advance Cuttings*, and *Pepsi-Cola* decisions referred to below had "created the potential for a more significant impact", but added — quite correctly — that it was too early to determine their full significance: *ibid.*
20. La Forest J., for three judges. McLachlin J. concurred.
21. Wilson J., for three judges.
22. McLachlin J.
23. *R. v. Advance Cutting & Coring Ltd.*, [2001] 3 S.C.R. 206.
24. LeBel J., for three judges.
25. *Ibid.* at para. 206.
26. L'Heureux-Dubé J.
27. Iacobucci J.
28. Iacobucci J., *ibid.* at paras. 267–69.
29. *Dunmore v. Ontario (Attorney General)*, [2001] 3 S.C.R. 1016.
30. Bastarache J. at para. 14.
31. *Supra* note 14.
32. *Ibid.* at para. 16.
33. *Ibid.* at paras. 34–48.
34. *Ibid.* at paras. 67–68.
35. *R.W.D.S.U., Local 558 v. Pepsi-Cola Canada Beverages (West) Ltd.*, [2002] 1 S.C.R. 156.
36. *Ibid.* at para. 44. The judgment of the Court was delivered by McLachlin C.J. and LeBel J.
37. The Court held that secondary picketing that causes undue harm should be defined as picketing that involves tortious or criminal conduct: *ibid.* at para. 66. Since the secondary picketing in this case was tortious, it was illegal: para. 117.
38. For some further reading, see Roy J. Adams, "The Revolutionary Potential of Dunmore" (2003) 10 C.L.E.I.J. 117; Jamie Cameron, "The Second Labour Trilogy: A Comment on *R. v. Advance Cutting, Dunmore v. Ontario, and R.W.D.S.U. v. Pepsi Cola*" (2002) 16 Sup. Ct. L. Rev. (2d) 67; Ken Norman, "Freedom of Association (Section 2(d))" in Gérald A. Beaudoin and Errol Mendez, eds., *The Canadian Charter of Rights and Freedoms*, 4th ed. (Markham, Ont.: LexisNexis Butterworths, 2005).
39. *Health Services and Support — Facilities Subsector Bargaining Assn. v. British Columbia*, [2007] 2 S.C.R. 391 at para. 66.
40. *Ibid.* at para. 89.
41. *Ibid.* at para. 91.
42. *Ibid.* at para. 92.
43. *Ibid.*
44. *Ibid.* at para. 127–128.
45. *Ibid.* at para. 141.
46. *Ontario (Attorney General) v. Fraser*, [2011] 2 S.C.R. 3 at para. 45.
47. *Ibid.* at para. 46.
48. *Ibid.* at para. 54.
49. *Ibid.* at para. 9–10.
50. *Ibid.* at para. 146.
51. *Ibid.* at para. 117.
52. See Peter Hogg, *Constitutional Law of Canada*, 2011 Student Edition (Toronto: Carswell, 2011) at pp. 44–49, who contends as much; but note the Court has not formally enunciated this contention, and it has not been so held in any other Supreme Court judgement since the decision in *Health Services* was released.

(c) Aboriginal Rights†

David W. Elliott

Aboriginal rights is a very big subject, but in some ways it symbolizes a bigger paradox about Canadian public law.

One measure of civilized society is how well it treats its less fortunate members. By many criteria, the more than one million Aboriginal peoples

---

† Updated by Nick E. Milanovic.

of Canada are among the least fortunate.[1] We have all seen statistics on poor native housing, disease, infant mortality, unemployment, school dropout rates, and teen-aged suicides. We also know that the ancestors of many non-Aboriginal Canadians helped contribute to this situation. White settlers, mainly from Europe, took over much of the land, reducing the native population to the margins. In northern North America, large numbers of Aboriginal peoples were killed, less by European guns than by European germs. Then came alcohol, the extermination of the buffalo, roads, television, residential schools, logging, dams, and mercury poisoning.

But help for Aboriginal peoples goes beyond equality concerns and paying old debts. If Aboriginal peoples can contribute more actively to society as a whole, the rest of us benefit too. These people bring cultures thousands of years old, a huge diversity of languages and traditions, and philosophies that could temper the non-Aboriginal obsessions with consumerism and competition.

What mechanisms can Canadian public law offer to deal with this? What non-legal alternatives are there?

To begin to answer these questions we must start by identifying the Aboriginal peoples in Canada. They are the descendants of the first known inhabitants of the northern part of North America. They include the Inuit, who have traditionally lived north of the treeline, and Indians and Métis people to the south. Traditionally, there were six main native culture areas, 11 main language families, and a large number of sub-groups. Indeed, over 50 native languages are still spoken in Canada today.[2] The term Indians generally describes people who are eligible to be registered under the federal *Indian Act*.[3] This more than a century-and-a-third-old federal statute used to determine eligibility to live on reserves. It still provides the framework for reserve government and certain federal benefits. The term Métis describes people of mixed Aboriginal and non-Aboriginal ancestry. Used more specifically, it describes people in this group whose ancestors lived in settlements on the Prairies. There are more than 850,000 Indians, almost 60,000 Inuit, and over 450,000 Métis people.

The main legal mechanisms available for addressing the situation of Canadian Aboriginal peoples are (1) treaties; (2) legislative change; (3) constitutional change; (4) court change through interpretation of the concept of Aboriginal rights; and (5) land claims agreements. Non-legal mechanisms include devoting more government money and effort to improving such things as housing, education, and skills of native administrators.

The story of the traditional treaties is deplorable. Whether they were peace treaties or land cession treaties, these agreements were one-sided affairs that promised Aboriginal peoples little and delivered even less. The spirit of the old treaties is still very important, and courts today try to interpret them generously. Often, though, there isn't much to be generous with, and the result has been some highly activist judicial interpretation. In the 1999 *Marshall* case,[4] for example, a 239-year-old treaty was cited in support of a right to fish for eels. The treaty text contained little more than a trade restriction, but the Court relied on oral evidence of prior treaty negotiations and on its interpretation of British policy to conclude that the treaty guaranteed an ongoing right to hunt, fish, and trade, for a "moderate livelihood".[5]

How about legislative change? Plans and efforts to reform the *Indian Act* have been part of federal government policy for decades. That Act has been criticized as repressive, paternalistic, and discriminatory. Aboriginal groups have complained of restrictions on self-government, while government has been concerned about a lack of effective accountability for its annual expenditures of billions of dollars for status Indians.

Some of the Act's bigger problems have already been tackled. After the *Drybones* case,[6] the Act's alcohol restrictions were removed. Most of the Act's sex discrimination was removed in 1985. Control of the right to live on reserves was given to almost 600 First Nation band councils. These changes highlighted a need for reform of *Indian Act* election procedures and related administrative structures.

Indeed, as Aboriginal peoples continue to demand more self-government, real control of reserve life has been passing from government departments to these band councils. For example, the Sechelt Band in British Columbia negotiated a legislative structure that replaced the *Indian Act* for them. Still, there are limits to what can be done by legislation. For some, the problem with legislative changes is that they are not guaranteed in the Constitution. The *Indian Act* itself is still connected with some benefits, such as tax exemptions, health benefits, and post-secondary education assistance, that many Indians would like to keep. Finally, *Indian Act* changes affect only the 700,000 registered Indians, not all Canadian Aboriginal peoples.[7]

Let us consider the next possible legal route to change: amendments to the Constitution of Canada. Negotiated formal constitutional change has been tried in four main phases in recent Canadian history: first in regard to the *Constitution Act, 1982*; second in the four constitutional conferences authorized by the *Constitution Act, 1982*, in 1983, 1984, 1985, and 1987; third, in regard to the Meech Lake Accord; and fourth, in regard to the Charlottetown Accord.

The 1982 changes produced a constitutional provision that recognized and affirmed Aboriginal rights, and a non-derogation provision to protect Aboriginal and other native rights against the *Charter*. The 1983 conference produced other constitutional guarantees, including special protection for Aboriginal gender equality and a constitutional requirement of consultation before governments make changes to constitutional provisions involving Aboriginal peoples.

By the mid-1980s, though, most Aboriginal spokespeople were seeking a constitutionally entrenched Aboriginal right of self-government. Although this goal was debated at three post-1983 Aboriginal constitutional conferences, neither they nor the Meech Lake Accord achieved it. Indeed, all the Meech Lake Accord contained on Aboriginal rights was a non-derogation provision to protect Aboriginal constitutional rights against the proposed new distinct society provision.

By way of contrast, Aboriginal peoples won massive constitutional protections in the proposed Charlottetown Accord. These included an entrenched right to Aboriginal self-government, to be enforced by the courts if negotiations did not produce results in five years' time; a high priority for Aboriginal self-government in the Canada clause; guaranteed representation in the new Senate; possible guaranteed representation in the House of Commons; the right to veto constitutional changes affecting Aboriginal peoples; the right to participate in future First Ministers Conferences; special Métis rights; and still more First Ministers Conferences to deal exclusively with Aboriginal constitutional concerns. However, these proposals went up in smoke when the Charlottetown Accord was rejected in October 1982.

How about the court route? Unquestionably, there has been dramatic movement in this forum. Back in 1973, the big question was whether Aboriginal rights could be recognized at common law. In the *Calder* case of that year, the Supreme Court of Canada suggested that they probably could.[8] Before *Calder*, it had been recognized that Aborigi-

nal people had some kind of land rights acknowledged in the Royal Proclamation of 1763. In *Calder*, the Nisga'a of northern B.C. argued that even if the boundaries of the Proclamation did not extend to B.C., their rights could be recognized at common law. Three judges agreed; three other judges said that whatever rights the Nisga'a might have had had since been terminated or extinguished; and a seventh judge dismissed the Nisga'a's claim on a technicality. Nevertheless, the Nisga'a still had cause to celebrate. Even the judges who said there had been extinguishment suggested that the rights might have existed originally at common law, by virtue of the Nisga'a's occupation and use of land. This suggestion had far-reaching effects. On this basis, all Aboriginal peoples in Canada who had not signed land cession treaties might still be able to claim Aboriginal rights.

For two decades after *Calder*, the courts had little luck in defining Aboriginal rights and the general Aboriginal interest in land, referred to as Aboriginal title. Then the 1982 constitutional changes made it important not only to provide more definition for Aboriginal rights, but also to say just what their new constitutional status was. Section 35(1) of the *Constitution Act, 1982* says, "The existing aboriginal and treaty rights of the aboriginal peoples of Canada are recognized and affirmed." It defines Aboriginal peoples of Canada as including Indians, Inuit, and Métis people, but it provides no further definition. Were these rights now entrenched? If so, were Aboriginal rights entrenched in their original form, or subject to whatever restrictions had been placed on them by legislation or treaties? If they were entrenched, how would this affect other interests, such as the government's interest in conservation?

The Supreme Court answered some of these questions in *Sparrow*.[9] It took an activist approach, and opened the door to extensive judicial involvement in Aboriginal rights. Mr. Sparrow was convicted of fishing in the Fraser River with a net longer than permitted by a licence under federal legislation. He defended himself by saying he had an Aboriginal right to fish in the area, because it was part of his peoples' traditional fishing ground. He argued that the Aboriginal right to fish was guaranteed against government legislation because of section 35(1) of the *Constitution Act*. Although Mr. Sparrow lost before the trial judge, the Supreme Court accepted the argument that his right was guaranteed by section 35(1) of the *Constitution Act, 1982*. However, the Court said there were some limits to the scope of this guarantee.

Since it did not have sufficient evidence to determine if the limits applied in this case, the Court sent the matter back to the trial court. The matter never did come back to trial. Since then, the federal government has increased and broadened its special guaranteed quotas for Indian food fishing throughout the country.

The Court considered several options[10] before holding that section 35(1) does entrench Aboriginal rights. It said that if these rights have not been ended by 1982, all pre-1982 restrictions on them are removed. The Court construed extinguishment narrowly. It required government to show a clear and plain intention to extinguish. If there is no extinguishment, Aboriginal rights are guaranteed against infringement. The Court defined "infringement" as an unreasonable interference that causes undue hardship or interferes with Aboriginal peoples' preferred means of exercising their rights. If there is an infringement, government may be able to justify it. To provide justification, the government must show that:

(i) the infringement has a valid legislative objective, such as conservation;

(ii) the Aboriginal interest is given first priority after this objective; and

(iii) there have been other safeguards, such as consultation and fair compensation for any expropriation.

These were subjective criteria. Arguably, they had the potential to cast Canadian courts in the role of a constitutional fisheries department, determining and monitoring permitted fish catches around the country, with different results for different rivers, Aboriginal groups, and months of the year. Compounding the challenge was the fact that the criteria for the proof, content, and general nature of Aboriginal rights were still uncertain.

The Supreme Court addressed these issues in its 1996 *Van der Peet* decision.[11] The question here was whether the Sto:lo people of British Columbia had an Aboriginal right to sell, barter, or trade salmon they had caught in the Fraser River, and whether this right was protected by section 35(1) of the *Constitution Act, 1982*. To answer this, the Court discussed the basis of Aboriginal rights, considered the purpose of section 35(1), and propounded a test for identifying and proving Aboriginal rights in specific situations. Lamer C.J. said Aboriginal rights are based on the fact that when the Europeans came, Aboriginal peoples were already occupying the land and participating in distinctive cultures. He said section 35(1) is intended to reconcile this fact with the Crown's assertion of sovereignty. For identifying and proving specific Aboriginal rights, the Chief Justice said a claimant must demonstrate that the activity in question is "an aspect of a practice, custom or tradition integral to a distinctive Aboriginal culture". He suggested that the activity in question must be precise and specific, central to the traditional culture, and relatively continuous from traditional to present times.

Applying these criteria, the Court concluded that selling, bartering, or trading salmon had not been sufficiently integral to Sto:lo traditional culture to meet the criteria. Although this approach filled in some gaps, notions of what is "integral" or "distinctive" are subjective. They will require yet more discretionary judgment on the part of the courts.

Subsequent cases addressed other aspects of Aboriginal and treaty rights and their protection under section 35(1).[12] Often, though, resolution of one problem raised others. In *Gladstone*,[13] for example, the Court amended the section 35(1) test for justification to accommodate situations involving Aboriginal rights that are not "self-limiting".[14] It called for a range of preferences that involved less than absolute priority. This was a reasonable approach, but it made the justification concept still more complex. Then the Court added "economic and regional fairness" and historical non-Aboriginal resource use to the list of factors that might help justify that infringement of Aboriginal rights — further broadening the justification test. In another decision, the Court rightly considered safety needs, but did so as an aspect of infringement rather than justification.[15]

In the 1997 *Delgamuukw* decision,[16] considered below, the Court clarified the link between Aboriginal rights and land. It said that Aboriginal rights lie along a spectrum in regard to their relationship to land. Rights associated with land but not tied to any particular location lie at one end, while Aboriginal title lies at the other. Despite this, the challenge of identifying these rights in specific cases seems little easier than before *Delgamuukw*. Post-*Delgamuukw* case law must now field difficult questions about oral proof, extent of occupancy, and government liability to compensation. Other questions, such as the nature of Aboriginal self-government and the impact of competing Aboriginal claims, were postponed partly or wholly to a later day. The result in *Delgamuukw* was relatively typical. The Court ordered a re-trial, but it urged the parties to try negotiation instead.

In *Mitchell*[17] in 2001, there were signs that the Court was restricting its position on Aboriginal evidence a little. The main majority rejected a Mohawk claim to an Aboriginal right to trade across the Canada–U.S. border, on the basis of insufficient evidence. McLachlin C.J. said that although courts should apply Aboriginal evidence sensitively, this should not lead them to accept a claim on the basis of evidence that is "[s]parse, doubtful and equivocal".[18]

Can section 35(1) protect mere claims to Aboriginal rights before they have been proven and defined? In the 2004 *Haida Nation* decision,[19] the Supreme Court said yes. If government knows, or should have known, of an Aboriginal rights claim, courts may require it to consult with the claimants and — in some cases — to try to accommodate their claims. The Court said that this duty, and the duty to conclude treaties, derive from the underlying notion of the honour of the Crown.

Another important dimension of Aboriginal rights is the question of whether and how they apply to Métis people in Canada. In its 2003 *Powley* decision, the Supreme Court of Canada said that Métis people can claim Aboriginal rights and formulated a modified approach for identifying Métis Aboriginal rights.[20]

The potential for Aboriginal and treaty rights litigation seems unlimited. Is this the best use of the resources of courts? Would Canadians, including Aboriginal Canadians, benefit from a similar judicial decision on self-government? Should fishing policy and governmental powers be litigated in courtrooms and then imposed from on high, by way of constitutional edict? Can we litigate our way to a fairer relationship with Canada's Aboriginal peoples?

In this area, as in others, there are alternatives. We have mentioned traditional treaties, constitutional negotiations, and legislative changes. Another possibility — which even the judges are advocating — is the land claims process. Approximately 20 land claims agreements have been concluded to date, including the high profile Nisga'a Final Agreement, and many more await resolution.[21] This process has the merit of involving the Aboriginal peoples concerned directly in the negotiating process, together with people authorized by our political representatives. It is slow, but it can provide complex compromises in a non-adversarial context, qualities lacking in litigation. Not all Aboriginal peoples have Aboriginal land claims, but most have treaties that could and should be re-negotiated under the fairer conditions of the early 21st century. On the other hand, land claims agreements can result in legal and constitutional accords so complex that they cannot be applied without constant legal interpretation.

We should be careful not to overlook non-legal or less legal forms of action. It will take more than courtroom battles or constitutional victories to help provide more Aboriginal peoples with decent housing, fight disease, cut infant mortality, reduce unemployment on reserves, improve school drop-out rates, and stop glue-sniffing and teen-aged suicides.[22] These grass-roots challenges won't be won by lawyers at the building on Wellington Street. They require money, carefully directed government money, not for Canada clauses, entrenched rights, and notwithstanding clauses, but for indoor plumbing and a chance at a job.[23] They require education, not just general education in non-Aboriginal values, but practical training for future Aboriginal administrators and politicians, and more education for Aboriginal peoples themselves. They require greater awareness by all Canadians of what Aboriginal cultures and philosophies have to offer to the rest of society.

The Aboriginal peoples of Canada are distinct in many ways, but in one sense their situation is the situation of all less fortunate members of this country. For the rest of us to sit back and expect courts to look after oppressed minorities and those at the bottom of the economic ladder would be unfair, both to the courts and those they are expected to help. The courts have a role, but a finite role, in advancing social fairness and equality. Arguably, the main responsibility for the really big social challenges should fall on elected politicians, and on you and me, the people who elect them and who decide, ultimately, how our tax dollars are spent. The paradox of Canadian public law is that despite our increasing reliance on specialists, lawyers, judges, courts, and charters, many issues are just too important to be left to the legal experts. There is still a role for the citizen in Canadian public law.

Notes

1. See, generally, J. Silman, ed., *Enough is Enough: Aboriginal Women Speak Out* (Toronto: The Women's Press, 1987); G. York, *The Dispossessed: Life and Death in Native Canada* (Toronto: Lester, 1989); P. Comeau and A. Santin, *The First Canadians: A Profile of Canada's Native People Today* (Toronto: James Lorimer & Company, 1990); R. Hunter and R. Calihoo, *Occupied Canada: A Young White Man Discovers His Unsuspected Past* (Toronto: McClelland & Stewart, 1991); L. Krotz, *Indian*

Country: Inside Another Canada (Toronto: McClelland & Stewart, 1992); M. Boldt, *Surviving as Indians: The Challenge of Self-Government* (Toronto: University of Toronto Press, 1993); D. Smith, *The Seventh Fire: The Struggle for Aboriginal Government* (Toronto: Key Porter Books, 1993); *Report of the Royal Commission on Aboriginal Peoples* (Ottawa: Canada Communications Group, 1996); J. Sawchuk, "Native People, Social Conditions" in J.H. Marsh, ed., *The Canadian Encyclopedia*, Year 2000 ed. (Toronto: McClelland & Stewart, 1999), at 1594–96; H. McCue, "Native People, Education," *ibid.* at 1581–82; J.A. Price, rev'd. F. Trovato and M. Mills, "Native People, Economic Conditions," *ibid.* at 1580–81; T.K. Young, "Native People, Health," *ibid.* at 1584–85.

2. Unfortunately, many of these languages are now in danger of extinction — a measure of the force of the dominant language cultures.
3. R.S.C. 1985, c. I-5.
4. *R. v. Marshall*, [1999] 3 S.C.R. 456.
5. *Ibid.*, paras. 4 and 59. The case occurred at a time when East Coast Aboriginal and non-Aboriginal people were struggling desperately to maintain their own shares of a declining harvest of lobster, eel, and other natural resources. There was heated controversy about the scope of the decision. A non-Aboriginal fishing group applied for a rehearing to clarify, *inter alia*, whether the ruling applied to the lobster fishery and whether it allowed continued government regulation. *A month after its first Marshall* decision, the Supreme Court rendered a 43-paragraph decision in *R. v. Marshall*, [1999] 3 S.C.R. 533. It refused the rehearing application but said no to the first question above and yes to the second. Government attempted to negotiate lobster and other fishery agreements with East Coast First Nations, amid continued controversy as to how much government regulation the *Marshall* decisions permitted.
6. *R. v. Drybones*, [1970] S.C.R. 282.
7. For another, more specific legislative reform, see s. 718.2(e) of *Criminal Code*. This provides that "all available sanctions other than imprisonment that are reasonable in the circumstances should be considered for all offenders, with particular attention to the circumstances of aboriginal offenders." The provision was implemented in 1996 as part of a reform package to combat overincarceration, especially overincarceration of Aboriginal peoples. In *R. v. Gladue*, [1999] 1 S.C.R. 688, the Supreme Court said that overrepresentation of Aboriginal peoples in Canadian prisons is one aspect of widespread systemic discrimination against them (para. 61) and required that s. 718.2(e) be given a broad, remedial interpretation.
8. *Calder v. A.G.(B.C.)*, [1973] S.C.R. 313.
9. *R. v. Sparrow*, [1990] 1 S.C.R. 1075. See W.I.C. Binnie, "The Sparrow Doctrine: Beginning of the End or End of the Beginning" (1990) 15 Queen's L.J. 217; D.W. Elliott, "In the Wake of Sparrow: A New Department of Fisheries?" (1991) 40 U.N.B.L.J. 23.
10. The court was confronted with several sets of potential choices about the status of Aboriginal rights. First, it had a choice between holding that s. 35(1) creates a *presumption* in favour of Aboriginal rights and holding that it entrenches Aboriginal rights. Second, if it went the entrenchment route, it had a choice between construing "existing" as referring to original Aboriginal rights, unextinguished Aboriginal rights, or unextinguished and unrestricted rights. Third, it had a choice between accepting inconsistent legislation as sufficient to extinguish Aboriginal rights and requiring something more. Fourth, it

had a choice between upholding a simple rights guarantee, and attempting to develop a complex calculus of factors for balancing between Aboriginal rights and other needs.

11. *R. v. Van der Peet*, [1996] 2 S.C.R. 507. See D.W. Elliott, "Fifty Dollars of Fish: A Comment on R. v. Van der Peet" (1997) 35 Alta. L. Rev. 759.
12. *R. v. Badger*, [1996] 1 S.C.R. 771; *R. v. Pamajewon* [*R. v. Jones; R. v. Gardner*], [1996] 2 S.C.R. 821; *R. v. Lewis*, [1996] 1 S.C.R. 921; *R. v. Nikal*, [1996] 1 S.C.R. 1013; *R. v. Gladstone*, [1996] 2 S.C.R. 723; *R. v. Smokehouse*, [1996] 2 S.C.R. 672; *R. v. Adams*, [1996] 3 S.C.R. 101; *R. v. Côté*, [1996] 3 S.C.R. 139; *St. Mary's Indian Band v. Cranbrook City*, [1997] 2 S.C.R. 657. See also *Dick v. The Queen*, [1985] 2 S.C.R. 309 (division of federal and provincial powers and Indians) and *Guerin v. The Queen*, [1984] 2 S.C.R. 335 and *Blueberry River Indian Band v. Canada (Department of Indian Affairs and Northern Development)*, [1995] 4 S.C.R. 344 (Crown's special fiduciary obligations to Aboriginal peoples).
13. *Ibid.*
14. For example, an Aboriginal right to fish for food is limited by the food needs of the Aboriginal people in question. In contrast, an Aboriginal right to fish commercially has no such limit. Hence, requiring government to give the latter right "priority" over other rights could exclude all other rights.
15. *R. v. Badger*, [1996] 1 S.C.R. 771 at para. 89.
16. [1997] 3 S.C.R. 1010.
17. *Mitchell v. Canada (Minister of National Revenue — M.N.R.)*, [2001] 1 S.C.R. 911.
18. *Ibid.* at para. 51. McLachlin C.J., seven judges. Two other judges agreed, but went on to say that any further claim to an Aboriginal right to move and trade across international borders was inconsistent with the sovereignty of the Canadian Crown.
19. *R. v. Powley*, [2003] 2 S.C.R. 207. The Supreme Court said that Métis status can be demonstrated by self-identification, a connection with a traditional Métis society, and evidence of acceptance into the corresponding modern Métis society. As well, the Court said that the activity in question must have been exercised by the traditional Métis society prior to the date of effective control by the Europeans.
20. *R. v. Haida Nation*, [2004] 3 S.C.R. 511.
21. See D.W. Elliott, *Law and Aboriginal Peoples in Canada*, 5th ed. (North York, Ont.: Captus Press, 2005) Ch. 11.
22. Some of these social problems are documented in the five-volume *Report of the Royal Commission on Aboriginal Peoples* (Ottawa: Canada Communication Group, 1996), discussed in *Law and Aboriginal Peoples in Canada*, *ibid.*, Ch. 12.
23. This practical emphasis was evident in a *First Ministers and National Aboriginal Leaders Meeting* held in Kelowna, B.C. on November 24 and 25, 2005. This two-day conference ended with a federal commitment to spend $5.1 billion over a five-year period for improving Aboriginal housing and infrastructure, including water treatment systems; reducing Aboriginal infant mortality rates, youth suicide, childhood obesity and diabetes; increasing the number of Aboriginal health professionals; bringing the Aboriginal high school graduation rate to parity with that for non-Aboriginal students; and improving Aboriginal vocational and training opportunities. Unfortunately, this ambitious plan was short on detail. In 2006, a newly-elected federal government said that aspects of the plan would need further work.

(d)   Extracts from Aboriginal Constitutional Provisions

CONSTITUTION ACT, 1867[1]

91. It shall be lawful for the Queen, by and with the Advice and Consent of the Senate and House of Commons, to make Laws for the Peace, Order, and good government of Canada, in relation to all matters not coming within the Classes of Subjects by this Act assigned exclusively to the Legislatures of the Provinces; and for greater Certainty, but not so as to restrict the Generality of the foregoing Terms of this Section, it is hereby declared that (notwithstanding anything in this Act) the exclusive Legislative Authority of the Parliament of Canada extends to all Matters coming within the Classes of Subject next hereinafter enumerated, that is to say, —

.   .   .   .

(24) Indians, and Lands reserved for the Indians.

CONSTITUTION ACT, 1982[2]

Aboriginal rights and freedoms not affected by Charter

25. The guarantee in this Charter of certain rights and freedoms shall not be construed so as to abrogate or derogate from any aboriginal, treaty or other rights or freedoms that pertain to the aboriginal peoples of Canada including

(a) any rights or freedoms that have been recognized by the Royal Proclamation of October 7, 1763; and

(b) any rights or freedoms that now exist by way of land claims settlements or may be so acquired.

Recognition of existing aboriginal and treaty rights

35.(1) The existing aboriginal and treaty rights of the aboriginal peoples of Canada are hereby recognized and affirmed.

Definition of "aboriginal peoples of Canada"

(2) In this Act, "aboriginal peoples of Canada" includes the Indian, Inuit and Métis peoples of Canada.

Land claims agreements

(3) For greater certainty, in subsection (1) "treaty rights" includes rights that now exist by way of land claims agreements or may be so acquired.

Aboriginal and treaty rights are guaranteed equally to both sexes

(4) Notwithstanding any other provision of this Act, the aboriginal and treaty rights referred to in subsection (1) are guaranteed equally to male and female persons.

Commitment to participation in constitutional conference

35.1. The government of Canada and the provincial governments are committed to the principle that, before any amendment is made to Class 24 of section 91 of the *Constitution Act, 1867*, to section 25 of this Act or to this Part,

(a) a constitutional conference that includes in its agenda an item relating to the proposed amendment, composed of the Prime Minister of Canada and the first ministers of the provinces will be convened by the Prime Minister of Canada, and

(b) the Prime Minister of Canada will invite representatives of the aboriginal peoples of Canada to participate in the discussions on that item.

References

61. A reference to the *Constitution Acts, 1867 to 1982* shall be deemed to include a reference to the *Constitution Amendment Proclamation, 1983*.

---

[1]   *Constitution Act, 1867* (U.K.), 30 & 31 Vict., c. 3, s. 91(24).

[2]   *Constitution Act, 1982*, being Schedule B to the *Canada Act 1982* (U.K.), 1982, c. 11. [Commentary note by David W. Elliott.]

[Section 37, providing for a constitutional conference to include participation by Aboriginal peoples and territorial leaders, was repealed on April 17, 1983. Section 37.1, providing for at least two more such constitutional conferences, was repealed on April 17, 1987. Between 1983 and 1987, four constitutional conferences were held. The first resulted in the *Constitution Amendment Proclamation, 1983*, which amended sections 25 and 35 of the *Constitution Act, 1982*, and added sections 35.1, 37.1 and 61.]

(e) *Delgamuukw v. British Columbia*†

NOTE

About 7,000 Gitksan and Wet'suwet'en people claimed full ownership and Aboriginal self-government, or other Aboriginal rights, in regard to over 22,000 square miles (or 58,000 kilometres) of west central British Columbia. The British Columbia Supreme Court rejected the ownership and self-government claims, and declared that the claimants' Aboriginal rights of occupation and use had been extinguished by the Crown prior to British Columbia's entry into Confederation.[1] The Court assigned no independent weight to oral Aboriginal histories offered in support of the claimed rights, and limited the use of other Aboriginal evidence.[2] However, the Court said the Crown owed the Aboriginal people a fiduciary duty to let them use unoccupied Crown lands in the territory, subject to laws of general application and to adverse Crown needs.[3]

The Gitksan and Wet'suwet'en appealed this decision, except the fiduciary duty finding. A majority of the British Columbia Court of Appeal rejected the claim to full ownership because of lack of evidence of exclusive occupation and clear boundaries.[4] They said that any Aboriginal self-government — in the sense of sovereign legislative powers — had been ended by British sovereignty or by the exhaustive division of legislative powers in the *Constitution Act, 1867*. On the other hand, the majority upheld the claimed Aboriginal rights of occupation and use of land and said that these rights had not been extinguished. Lambert and Hutcheon JJ.A., dissenting in part, agreed with the majority in regard to rights of occupation and use. However, they would have also accepted the claim to ownership and to Aboriginal self-government (which Hutcheon J.A. regarded as a non-sovereign right of internal regulation).

The Gitksan and Wet'suwet'en appealed the Court of Appeal's decision to the Supreme Court of Canada. They replaced their original claims to ownership and jurisdiction with claims to Aboriginal title and self-government. They also replaced their claim to many separate parcels of land with a claim to two large parcels that occupied the same area. The Supreme Court dismissed the appeal, partly on the ground that government might have been prejudiced by being unable to respond in the lower courts to this new description of the claim. The Court went on to address five sets of key questions:

1. What evidentiary weight should be given to oral Aboriginal histories in Aboriginal rights cases?
2. How does Aboriginal title relate to Aboriginal rights, what is the content of Aboriginal title, and what is required to prove it?
3. How is Aboriginal title protected under section 35(1) of the *Constitution Act, 1982*?
4. Had the Gitksan and Wet'suwet'en made out a claim to guaranteed Aboriginal self-government rights in this case?
5. Can a province extinguish Aboriginal rights after its entry into Confederation, either on its

---

† [1997] 3 S.C.R. 1010, rev'g. in part and dismissing a cross-appeal from (1993), 104 D.L.R. (4th) 470 (B.C.C.A.), varying an order in (1991), 79 D.L.R. (4th) 185 (B.C.S.C.). [Commentary note by David W. Elliott.]

[1] (1991), 79 D.L.R. (4th) 185 (B.C.S.C.).

[2] *Ibid.*, and *Uukw v. R.*, [1987] 6 W.W.R. 155 (B.C.S.C.).

[3] *Ibid.* at 487–90.

[4] (1993), 104 D.L.R. (4th) 470 (B.C.C.A.).

own authority or through the operation of section 88 of the *Indian Act?*

Note the disposition of this decision [para. 184] and Lamer C.J.'s concluding remarks [paras. 185–86]. Extracts from Lamer C.J.'s main majority opinion are reproduced here. McLachlin J. said she was also "in substantial agreement"[5] with the separate majority reasons of La Forest J. (for himself and L'Heureux-Dubé J.).

EXTRACT

[LAMER C.J. for himself, CORY, McLACHLIN and MAJOR JJ.:]

[1. Oral Aboriginal Histories]

. . . .

[80] ... As I said in *R.* v. *Van der Peet*, [1996] 2 S.C.R. 507, at para. 68:

> In determining whether an aboriginal claimant has produced evidence sufficient to demonstrate that her activity is an aspect of a practice, custom or tradition integral to a distinctive aboriginal culture, *a court should approach the rules of evidence, and interpret the evidence that exists*, with a consciousness of the special nature of aboriginal claims, and of the evidentiary difficulties in proving a right which originates in times where there were no written records of the practices, customs and traditions engaged in. *The courts must not undervalue the evidence presented by aboriginal claimants simply because that evidence does not conform precisely with the evidentiary standards that would be applied in, for example, a private law torts case.* [Emphasis added.]

. . . .

[82] ... [A]lthough the doctrine of aboriginal rights is a common law doctrine, aboriginal rights are truly *sui generis*, and demand a unique approach to the treatment of evidence which accords due weight to the perspective of aboriginal peoples. However, that accommodation must be done in a manner which does not strain "the Canadian legal and constitutional structure" (at para. 49)....

. . . .

[107] The trial judge's treatment of the various kinds of oral histories did not satisfy the principles I laid down in *Van der Peet*. These errors are particularly worrisome because oral histories were of critical importance to the appellants' case. They used those histories in an attempt to establish their occupation and use of the disputed territory, an essential requirement for aboriginal title. The trial judge, after refusing to admit, or giving no independent weight to these oral histories, reached the conclusion that the appellants had not demonstrated the requisite degree of occupation for "ownership." Had the trial judge assessed the oral histories correctly, his conclusions on these issues of fact might have been very different.

[108] In the circumstances, the factual findings cannot stand. However, given the enormous complexity of the factual issues at hand, it would be impossible for the Court to do justice to the parties by sifting through the record itself and making new factual findings. A new trial is warranted, at which the evidence may be considered in light of the principles laid down in *Van der Peet* and elaborated upon here. In applying these principles, the new trial judge might well share some or all of the findings of fact of McEachern C.J.

. . . .

[2a. Content of Aboriginal Title]

[117] ... [T]he content of aboriginal title can be summarized by two propositions: first, that aboriginal title encompasses the right to exclusive use and occupation of the land held pursuant to that title for a variety of purposes, which need not be aspects of those aboriginal practices, customs and traditions which are integral to distinctive aboriginal cultures; and second, that those protected uses must not be irreconcilable with the nature of the group's attachment to that land....

. . . .

[125] The content of aboriginal title contains an inherent limit that lands held pursuant to title cannot be used in a manner that is irreconcilable with the nature of the claimants' attachment to those lands. This limit on the content of aboriginal title is a manifestation of the principle that underlies the various

---

[5] See para. 209.

dimensions of that special interest in land — it is a *sui generis* interest that is distinct from "normal" proprietary interests, most notably fee simple.

. . . .

[127] ... [T]he relationship of an aboriginal community with its land] should not be prevented from continuing into the future. As a result, uses of the lands that would threaten that future relationship are, by their very nature, excluded from the content of aboriginal title.

[128] Accordingly, in my view, lands subject to aboriginal title cannot be put to such uses as may be irreconcilable with the nature of the occupation of that land and the relationship that the particular group has had with the land which together have given rise to aboriginal title in the first place....

[129] It is for this reason also that lands held by virtue of aboriginal title may not be alienated. Alienation would bring to an end the entitlement of the aboriginal people to occupy the land and would terminate their relationship with it....

. . . .

[131] ... [W]hat I have just said regarding the importance of the continuity of the relationship between an aboriginal community and its land, and the non-economic or inherent value of that land, should not be taken to detract from the possibility of surrender to the Crown in exchange for valuable consideration. On the contrary, the idea of surrender reinforces the conclusion that aboriginal title is limited in the way I have described. If aboriginal peoples wish to use their lands in a way that aboriginal title does not permit, then they must surrender those lands and convert them into non-title lands to do so.

. . . .

[2b. Relationship between Aboriginal Rights and Aboriginal Title]

. . . .

[138] ... [T]he aboriginal rights which are recognized and affirmed by s. 35(1) fall along a spectrum with respect to their degree of connection with the land. At the one end, there are those aboriginal rights which are practices, customs and traditions that are integral to the distinctive aboriginal culture of the group claiming the right. However, the "occupation

and use of the land" where the activity is taking place is not "sufficient to support a claim of title to the land" (at para. 26). Nevertheless, those activities receive constitutional protection. In the middle, there are activities which, out of necessity, take place on land and indeed, might be intimately related to a particular piece of land. Although an aboriginal group may not be able to demonstrate title to the land, it may nevertheless have a site-specific right to engage in a particular activity....

. . . .

... [A]boriginal title confers more than the right to engage in site-specific activities which are aspects of the practices, customs and traditions of distinctive aboriginal cultures. Site-specific rights can be made out even if title cannot. What aboriginal title confers is the right to the land itself.

[139] Because aboriginal rights can vary with respect to their degree of connection with the land, some aboriginal groups may be unable to make out a claim to title, but will nevertheless possess aboriginal rights that are recognized and affirmed by s. 35(1), including site-specific rights to engage in particular activities....

. . . .

[2c. Proof of Aboriginal Title]

[140] In addition to differing in the degree of connection with the land, aboriginal title differs from other aboriginal rights in another way. To date, the Court has defined aboriginal rights in terms of activities. As I said in *Van der Peet* (at para. 46):

> [I]n order to be an aboriginal right an *activity* must be an element of a practice, custom or tradition integral to the distinctive culture of the aboriginal group claiming the right. [Emphasis added.]

Aboriginal title, however, is a <u>right to the land</u> itself. Subject to the limits I have laid down above, that land may be used for a variety of activities, none of which need be individually protected as aboriginal rights under s. 35(1). Those activities are parasitic on the underlying title.

[141] This difference between aboriginal rights to engage in particular activities and aboriginal title requires that the test I laid down in *Van der Peet* be adapted accordingly....

. . . .

Since the purpose of s. 35(1) is to reconcile the prior presence of aboriginal peoples in North America with the assertion of Crown sovereignty, it is clear from this statement that s. 35(1) must recognize and affirm both aspects of that prior presence — first, the occupation of land, and second, the prior social organization and distinctive cultures of aboriginal peoples on that land. To date the jurisprudence under s. 35(1) has given more emphasis to the second aspect. To a great extent, this has been a function of the types of cases which have come before this Court under s. 35(1) — prosecutions for regulatory offences that, by their very nature, proscribe discrete types of activity.

[142] The adaptation of the test laid down in *Van der Peet* to suit claims to title must be understood as the recognition of the first aspect of that prior presence. However, as will now become apparent, the tests for the identification of aboriginal rights to engage in particular activities and for the identification of aboriginal title share broad similarities. The major distinctions are first, under the test for aboriginal title, the requirement that the land be integral to the distinctive culture of the claimants is subsumed by the requirement of occupancy, and second, whereas the time for the identification of aboriginal rights is the time of first contact, the time for the identification of aboriginal title is the time at which the Crown asserted sovereignty over the land.

. . . .

[143] In order to make out a claim for aboriginal title, the aboriginal group asserting title must satisfy the following criteria: (i) the land must have been occupied prior to sovereignty, (ii) if present occupation is relied on as proof of occupation pre-sovereignty, there must be a continuity between present and pre-sovereignty occupation, and (iii) at sovereignty, that occupation must have been exclusive.

. . . .

[3. Aboriginal Title and Section 35(1) of Constitution Act, 1982]

[Note: At para. 133, Lamer J. said that Aboriginal title was included in the common law rights that were constitutionalized by section 35(1) of the *Constitution Act, 1982*. As such, Aboriginal title was protected against infringements by federal or pro-

vincial governments, unless these infringements could be justified. Later, Lamer C.J. considered how the existing test for justification applied to Aboriginal title:]

[161] The test of justification of section 35(1) aboriginal or treaty] rights has two parts, which I shall consider in turn. First, the infringement of the aboriginal right must be in furtherance of a legislative objective that is compelling and substantial....

. . . .

The conservation of fisheries [is one compelling and substantial objective].... But legitimate government objectives also include "the pursuit of economic and regional fairness" and "the recognition of the historical reliance upon, and participation in, the fishery by non-aboriginal groups" (para. 75). By contrast, measures enacted for relatively unimportant reasons, such as sports fishing without a significant economic component (*R. v. Adams*, [1996] 3 S.C.R. 101), would fail this aspect of the test of justification.

[162] The second part of the test of justification requires an assessment of whether the infringement is consistent with the special fiduciary relationship between the Crown and aboriginal peoples. What has become clear is that the requirements of the fiduciary duty are a function of the "legal and factual context" of each appeal (*R. v. Gladstone*, [1996] 2 S.C.R. 723, at para. 56).

. . . .

[165] The general principles governing justification laid down in *R. v. Sparrow*, [1990] 1 S.C.R. 1075, and embellished by *Gladstone*, operate with respect to infringements of aboriginal title. In the wake of *Gladstone*, the range of legislative objectives that can justify the infringement of aboriginal title is fairly broad.... In my opinion, the development of agriculture, forestry, mining, and hydroelectric power, the general economic development of the interior of British Columbia, protection of the environment or endangered species, the building of infrastructure and the settlement of foreign populations to support those aims, are the kinds of objectives that are consistent with this purpose and, in principle, can justify the infringement of aboriginal title. Whether a particular measure or government act can be explained by reference to one of those objectives, however, is

ultimately a question of fact that will have to be examined on a case-by-case basis.

[166] The manner in which the fiduciary duty operates with respect to the second stage of the justification test — both with respect to the standard of scrutiny and the particular form that the fiduciary duty will take — will be a function of the nature of aboriginal title. Three aspects of aboriginal title are relevant here. First, aboriginal title encompasses the right to <u>exclusive</u> use and occupation of land; second, aboriginal title encompasses <u>the right to choose</u> to what uses land can be put, subject to the ultimate limit that those uses cannot destroy the ability of the land to sustain future generations of aboriginal peoples; and third, that lands held pursuant to aboriginal title have an inescapable <u>economic component</u>.

[167] The exclusive nature of aboriginal title is relevant to the degree of scrutiny of the infringing measure or action. For example, if the Crown's fiduciary duty requires that aboriginal title be given priority, then it is the altered approach to priority that I laid down in *Gladstone* which should apply. What is required is that the government demonstrate (*Gladstone*, at para. 62) "both that the process by which it allocated the resource and the actual allocation of the resource which results from that process reflect the prior interest" of the holders of aboriginal title in the land. By analogy with *Gladstone*, this might entail, for example, that governments accommodate the participation of aboriginal peoples in the development of the resources of British Columbia, that the conferral of fee simples for agriculture, and of leases and licences for forestry and mining reflect the prior occupation of aboriginal title lands, that economic barriers to aboriginal uses of their lands (e.g., licensing fees) be somewhat reduced. This list is illustrative and not exhaustive....

[168] Moreover, the other aspects of aboriginal title suggest that the fiduciary duty may be articulated in a manner different than the idea of priority.... First, ... [since Aboriginal title involves a discretion as to how land is used, the fiduciary relationship may be satisfied by consulting aboriginal peoples about the uses to which their land is put.] There is always a duty of consultation ... [whose nature and scope] will vary with the circumstances....

[169] Second, aboriginal title, unlike the aboriginal right to fish for food, has an inescapably economic aspect, particularly when one takes into account the modern uses to which lands held pursuant to aboriginal title can be put.... In keeping with the duty of honour and good faith on the Crown, fair compensation will ordinarily be required when aboriginal title is infringed. The amount of compensation payable will vary with the nature of the particular aboriginal title affected and with the nature and severity of the infringement and the extent to which aboriginal interests were accommodated. Since the issue of damages was severed from the principal action, we received no submissions on the appropriate legal principles that would be relevant to determining the appropriate level of compensation of infringements of aboriginal title. In the circumstances, it is best that we leave those difficult questions to another day.

[4. Self-Government]

[170] In the courts below, considerable attention was given to the question of whether s. 35(1) can protect a right to self-government, and if so, what the contours of that right are. The errors of fact made by the trial judge, and the resultant need for a new trial, make it impossible for this Court to determine whether the claim to self-government has been made out. Moreover, this is not the right case for the Court to lay down the legal principles to guide future litigation. The parties seem to have acknowledged this point, perhaps implicitly, by giving the arguments on self-government much less weight on appeal. One source of the decreased emphasis on the right to self-government on appeal is this Court's judgment in *R. v. Pamajewon*, [1996] 2 S.C.R. 821. There, I held that rights to self-government, if they existed, cannot be framed in excessively general terms. The appellants did not have the benefit of my judgment at trial. Unsurprisingly, as counsel for the Wet'suwet'en specifically concedes, the appellants advanced the right to self-government in very broad terms, and therefore in a manner not cognizable under s. 35(1).

[171] The broad nature of the claim at trial also led to a failure by the parties to address many of the difficult conceptual issues which surround the recognition of aboriginal self-government. The degree of complexity involved can be gleaned from the *Report of the Royal Commission on Aboriginal Peoples*, which devotes 277 pages to the issue. That report describes different models of self-government, each differing with respect to their conception of territory, citizenship, jurisdiction, internal government organization, etc. We received little in the way of submissions that would help us to grapple with these difficult and central issues. Without assistance from the parties, it

would be imprudent for the Court to step into the breach. In these circumstances, the issue of self-government will fall to be determined at trial.

. . . .

[5. Capacity of Province to Extinguish Aboriginal Title]

[175] ... [A]lthough on surrender of aboriginal title the province would take absolute title, jurisdiction to accept surrenders lies with the federal government. The same can be said of extinguishment — although on extinguishment of aboriginal title, the province would take complete title to the land, the jurisdiction to extinguish lies with the federal government.

. . . .

[178] ... Laws which purport to extinguish [the rights that are recognized and affirmed by s. 35(1)] ... touch the core of Indianness which lies at the heart of s. 91(24), and are beyond the legislative competence of the provinces to enact. The core of Indianness encompasses the whole range of aboriginal rights that are protected by s. 35(1). Those rights include rights in relation to land; that part of the core derives from s. 91(24)'s reference to "Lands reserved for the Indians." But those rights also encompass practices, customs and traditions which are not tied to land as well; that part of the core can be traced to federal jurisdiction over "Indians." Provincial governments are prevented from legislating in relation to both types of aboriginal rights.

. . . .

[183] ... I see nothing in the language of [s. 88 of the Indian Act] which even suggests the intention to extinguish aboriginal rights. Indeed, the explicit reference to treaty rights in s. 88 suggests that the provision was clearly not intended to undermine aboriginal rights.

. . . .

[6. Disposition and Concluding Remarks]

[184] For the reasons I have given above, I would allow the appeal in part, and dismiss the cross-appeal. Reluctantly, I would also order a new trial.

[185] I conclude with two observations. The first is that many aboriginal nations with territorial claims that overlap with those of the appellants did not intervene in this appeal, and do not appear to have done so at trial. This is unfortunate, because determinations of aboriginal title for the Gitksan and Wet'suwet'en will undoubtedly affect their claims as well. This is particularly so because aboriginal title encompasses an <u>exclusive</u> right to the use and occupation of land, i.e., to the <u>exclusion</u> of both non-aboriginals and members of other aboriginal nations. It may, therefore, be advisable if those aboriginal nations intervened in any new litigation.

[186] Finally, this litigation has been both long and expensive, not only in economic but in human terms as well. By ordering a new trial, I do not necessarily encourage the parties to proceed to litigation and to settle their dispute through the courts....

[In separate reasons (with which McLachlin J. expressed substantial agreement), La Forest J. (for himself and L'Heureux-Dubé J.) agreed with the Chief Justice's conclusion. However, La Forest J. said, "I disagree with various aspects of his reasons and in particular, with the methodology he uses to prove that aboriginal peoples have a general right of occupation of certain lands (often referred to as 'aboriginal title')": para. 187. La Forest J. felt that courts should refrain from trying to define Aboriginal title in detail. For him, it is sufficient to say that Aboriginal title (i) is based on traditional use and occupation of the land; (ii) is inalienable except to the Crown; and (iii) attracts a fiduciary obligation which is owed by the Crown: para. 190. La Forest J. said that the *Van der Peet* test for proof of Aboriginal rights requires "precision, specificity, continuity, and centrality": para. 193. For him, proof of occupancy should not subsume the requirements of precision, specificity, and centrality. Instead, occupancy should be taken as proof of the latter. La Forest J. agreed generally with the Chief Justice on the issues of justification for infringement of Aboriginal title, self-government, provincial extinguishment either independently or under section 88 of the *Indian Act*, and the desirability of addressing cases of this kind through negotiation.]

(f)   *Haida Nation v. British Columbia (Minister of Forests)*†

NOTE

The Haida people claimed Aboriginal rights and title to Haida Gwai (the Queen Charlotte Islands). They argued that the provincial government had a legal duty to consult with them before transferring a tree farm licence on Haida Gwai from one logging company to another. This argument failed in the trial court, but the British Columbia Court of Appeal held that both the provincial Crown and the transferee logging company had a fiduciary (trust-like) duty to consult.

The Supreme Court of Canada upheld the consultation requirement in regard to the province. It said that a duty to consult can arise wherever the Crown knows or should have known of a credible claim to Aboriginal rights. It added that this duty is sometimes accompanied by a duty to accommodate — an obligation to minimize harm. However, the Court said that the duty to consult is not a fiduciary duty and does not bind parties other than the Crown.

Note how the Supreme Court based this duty to consult on the concept of the "honour of the Crown". It said that this concept is also the foundation of the Crown's obligation to negotiate and uphold Aboriginal treaties, and of the Crown's fiduciary obligations to Aboriginal peoples. What is the origin of this concept? What do you think of it as a legal foundation for government's dealings with Aboriginal peoples? What factors govern the scope and content of the duty to consult and accommodate?

The Crown must now consult and accommodate some Aboriginal rights claims even before these claims have been proven in court. Can you see any practical problems with (a) having a prior consultation requirement, and (b) having no such requirement? How did the Court address these problems?

Do you think the duty to consult is likely to advance or to impede the conclusion of Aboriginal land claims agreements?

EXTRACT

[McLACHLIN C.J. for the Court:]

[11] This case is the first of its kind to reach this Court. Our task is the modest one of establishing a general framework for the duty to consult and accommodate, where indicated, before Aboriginal title or rights claims have been decided. As this framework is applied, courts, in the age-old tradition of the common law, will be called on to fill in the details of the duty to consult and accommodate.

. . . .

[16] The government's duty to consult with Aboriginal peoples and accommodate their interests is grounded in the honour of the Crown. The honour of the Crown is always at stake in its dealings with Aboriginal peoples: see for example *R. v. Badger*, [1996] 1 S.C.R. 771, at para. 41; *R. v. Marshall*, [1999] 3 S.C.R. 456. It is not a mere incantation, but rather a core precept that finds its application in concrete practices.

. . . .

[18] The honour of the Crown gives rise to different duties in different circumstances. Where the Crown has assumed discretionary control over specific Aboriginal interests, the honour of the Crown gives rise to a fiduciary duty: *Wewaykum Indian Band v. Canada*, [2002] 4 S.C.R. 245, 2002 SCC 79, at para. 79. The content of the fiduciary duty may vary to take into account the Crown's other, broader obligations. However, the duty's fulfilment requires that the Crown act with reference to the Aboriginal group's best interest in exercising discretionary con-

---

† [2004] 3 S.C.R. 511, dismissing an appeal by the Crown and allowing an appeal by Wayerhaeuser Co. from [2002] 6 W.W.R. 243 (B.C.C.A.) with supplementary reasons in (2002), 10 W.W.R. 587 (B.C.C.A.) rev'g [2001] 2 C.N.L.R. 83 (B.C.S.C.). See also the companion decision of *Taku River Tlingit First Nation v. British Columbia (Project Assessment Director)*, 2004 SCC 74. The NOTE on Haida Nation is adapted from D.W. Elliott, *Law and Aboriginal Peoples in Canada*, 5th ed. (Concord, Ont.: Captus Press Inc., 2005) at 378. [Commentary note by David W. Elliott.]

trol over the specific Aboriginal interest at stake. As explained in *Wewaykum*, at para. 81, the term "fiduciary " does not connote a universal trust relationship encompassing all aspects of the relationship between the Crown and Aboriginal peoples:

> ... "fiduciary duty" as a source of plenary Crown liability covering all aspects of the Crown-Indian band relationship.... overshoots the mark. The fiduciary duty imposed on the Crown does not exist at large but in relation to specific Indian interests.

Here, Aboriginal rights and title have been asserted but have not been defined or proven. The Aboriginal interest in question is insufficiently specific for the honour of the Crown to mandate that the Crown act in the Aboriginal group's best interest, as a fiduciary, in exercising discretionary control over the subject of the right or title.

[19] The honour of the Crown also infuses the processes of treaty making and treaty interpretation. In making and applying treaties, the Crown must act with honour and integrity, avoiding even the appearance of "sharp dealing" (*Badger*, at para. 41). Thus in *Marshall*, *supra*, at para. 4, the majority of this Court supported its interpretation of a treaty by stating that "nothing less would uphold the honour and integrity of the Crown in its dealings with the Mi'kmaq people to secure their peace and friendship...."

[20] Where treaties remain to be concluded, the honour of the Crown requires negotiations leading to a just settlement of Aboriginal claims: *R. v. Sparrow*, [1990] 1 S.C.R. 1075, at pp. 1105–6. Treaties serve to reconcile pre-existing Aboriginal sovereignty with assumed Crown sovereignty, and to define Aboriginal rights guaranteed by s. 35 of the *Constitution Act, 1982*. Section 35 represents a promise of rights recognition, and "[i]t is always assumed that the Crown intends to fulfil its promises" (*Badger, supra*, at para. 41). This promise is realized and sovereignty claims reconciled through the process of honourable negotiation. It is a corollary of s. 35 that the Crown act honourably in defining the rights it guarantees and in reconciling them with other rights and interests. This, in turn, implies a duty to consult and, if appropriate, accommodate.

. . . .

[32] The jurisprudence of this Court supports the view that the duty to consult and accommodate is part of a process of fair dealing and reconciliation that begins with the assertion of sovereignty and continues beyond formal claims resolution. Reconciliation is not a final legal remedy in the usual sense. Rather, it is a process flowing from rights guaranteed by s. 35(1) of the *Constitution Act, 1982*. This process of reconciliation flows from the Crown's duty of honourable dealing toward Aboriginal peoples, which arises in turn from the Crown's assertion of sovereignty over an Aboriginal people and de facto control of land and resources that were formerly in the control of that people. As stated in *Mitchell v. M.N.R.*, [2001] 1 S.C.R. 911, 2001 SCC 33, at para. 9, "[w]ith this assertion [sovereignty] arose an obligation to treat aboriginal peoples fairly and honourably, and to protect them from exploitation ..." (emphasis added).

[33] To limit reconciliation to the post-proof sphere risks treating reconciliation as a distant legalistic goal, devoid of the "meaningful content" mandated by the "solemn commitment" made by the Crown in recognizing and affirming Aboriginal rights and title: *Sparrow, supra*, at p. 1108. It also risks unfortunate consequences. When the distant goal of proof is finally reached, the Aboriginal peoples may find their land and resources changed and denuded. This is not reconciliation. Nor is it honourable.

. . . .

[36] This leaves the practical argument. It is said that before claims are resolved, the Crown cannot know that the rights exist, and hence can have no duty to consult or accommodate. This difficulty should not be denied or minimized. As I stated (dissenting) in *Marshall, supra*, at para. 112, one cannot "meaningfully discuss accommodation or justification of a right unless one has some idea of the core of that right and its modern scope." However, it will frequently be possible to reach an idea of the asserted rights and of their strength sufficient to trigger an obligation to consult and accommodate, short of final judicial determination or settlement. To facilitate this determination, claimants should outline their claims with clarity, focussing on the scope and nature of the Aboriginal rights they assert and on the alleged infringements. This is what happened here, where the chambers judge made a preliminary evidence-based assessment of the strength of the Haida claims to the lands and resources of Haida Gwaii, particularly Block 6.

. . . .

[37] There is a distinction between knowledge sufficient to trigger a duty to consult and, if appropriate, accommodate, and the content or scope of the duty in a particular case. Knowledge of a credible but unproven claim suffices to trigger a duty to consult and accommodate. The content of the duty, however, varies with the circumstances, as discussed more fully below. A dubious or peripheral claim may attract a mere duty of notice, while a stronger claim may attract more stringent duties. The law is capable of differentiating between tenuous claims, claims possessing a strong *prima facie* case, and established claims. Parties can assess these matters, and if they cannot agree, tribunals and courts can assist. Difficulties associated with the absence of proof and definition of claims are addressed by assigning appropriate content to the duty, not by denying the existence of a duty.

. . . .

[39] The content of the duty to consult and accommodate varies with the circumstances. Precisely what duties arise in different situations will be defined as the case law in this emerging area develops. In general terms, however, it may be asserted that the scope of the duty is proportionate to a preliminary assessment of the strength of the case supporting the existence of the right or title, and to the seriousness of the potentially adverse effect upon the right or title claimed.

. . . .

[43] Against this background, I turn to the kind of duties that may arise in different situations. In this respect, the concept of a spectrum may be helpful, not to suggest watertight legal compartments but rather to indicate what the honour of the Crown may require in particular circumstances. At one end of the spectrum lie cases where the claim to title is weak, the Aboriginal right limited, or the potential for infringement minor. In such cases, the only duty on the Crown may be to give notice, disclose information, and discuss any issues raised in response to the notice. "'[C]onsultation' in its least technical definition is talking together for mutual understanding": T. Isaac and A. Knox, "The Crown's Duty to Consult Aboriginal People" (2003), 41 Alta. L. Rev. 49, at p. 61.

[44] At the other end of the spectrum lie cases where a strong *prima facie* case for the claim is established, the right and potential infringement is of high significance to the Aboriginal peoples, and the risk of non-compensable damage is high. In such cases deep consultation, aimed at finding a satisfactory interim solution, may be required. While precise requirements will vary with the circumstances, the consultation required at this stage may entail the opportunity to make submissions for consideration, formal participation in the decision-making process, and provision of written reasons to show that Aboriginal concerns were considered and to reveal the impact they had on the decision. This list is neither exhaustive, nor mandatory for every case. The government may wish to adopt dispute resolution procedures like mediation or administrative regimes with impartial decision-makers in complex or difficult cases.

[45] Between these two extremes of the spectrum just described, will lie other situations....

. . . .

[47] When the consultation process suggests amendment of Crown policy, we arrive at the stage of accommodation. Thus the effect of good faith consultation may be to reveal a duty to accommodate. Where a strong *prima facie* case exists for the claim, and the consequences of the government's proposed decision may adversely affect it in a significant way, addressing the Aboriginal concerns may require taking steps to avoid irreparable harm or to minimize the effects of infringement, pending final resolution of the underlying claim. Accommodation is achieved through consultation, as this Court recognized in *R. v. Marshall*, [1999] 3 S.C.R. 533, at para. 22: "... the process of accommodation of the treaty right may best be resolved by consultation and negotiation".

[48] This process does not give Aboriginal groups a veto over what can be done with land pending final proof of the claim. The Aboriginal "consent" spoken of in *Delgamuukw* is appropriate only in cases of established rights, and then by no means in every case. Rather, what is required is a process of balancing interests, of give and take.

. . . .

(g) *Tsilhqot'in Nation v. British Columbia*†

NOTE

On December 18, 1998, Chief Roger William launched a claim on behalf of himself and the Xeni Gwet'in First Nations Government, eventually adding the Tsilhqot'in Nation, for Aboriginal title for a large swath of land southwest of Williams Lake in the interior of British Columbia. Prior to this, the provincial government had permitted a lumber company to harvest trees on land that was claimed by these First Nations. On November 20, 2007, the Supreme Court of British Columbia ruled that the claim established occupation of the land for the purpose of proving regular and exclusive use of the land in question: *Tsilhqot'in Nation v. British Columbia*, 2014 SCC 44 at paras. 5–7. In 2012, the Court of Appeal rejected the claim, leaving open the possibility of granting limited use of the land over specific sites: *ibid.* at para. 8.

In a unanimous decision, the Supreme Court of Canada overturned that decision and granted a declaration of Aboriginal title over 1,750 square kilometers of land for the first time in Canadian history. Among other things, this landmark case (i) clarifies the requirement for proving sufficient occupation of disputed land in order to establish title, explaining that claims can extend beyond specific sites to surrounding territory and (ii) declared that the province breached the duty to consult, which was owed to the appellants: *ibid.* at para. 153. It explicitly endorses an approach to deciding occupancy that extends beyond the common law to include an Aboriginal perspective: *ibid.* at paras. 32–34. Further, the decision sets out the benefits conferred with Aboriginal title (*ibid.* at para. 70) to the land for Aboriginal communities and refines the duty to consult and accommodate (*ibid.* at paras. 78, 87–88) Aboriginal people involved in such claims.

When you read the passage below, ask yourself whether the duty to consult has been elevated by the Supreme Court? Does this decision provide greater certainty to provincial and federal governments, as well as third parties such as corporations, concerning their requirement to consult with Aboriginal people in non-treaty areas when deciding to undertake a project on disputed land? Does the decision place a regulatory chill on land and natural resource development, delaying or denying future projects such as mining, oil and gas exploration, and the construction of pipelines? If so, why is that so? Alternatively, has the Supreme Court's decision renewed the relationship between Aboriginal people and the provincial and federal governments, forcing them to all rethink basic governance issues in order to kick-start the process of concluding outstanding land claims?

EXTRACT

[McLACHLIN C.J. (for the Court):]

V.   IS ABORIGINAL TITLE ESTABLISHED?

A.   The Test for Aboriginal Title

· · · ·

1. *Sufficiency of Occupation*

[33] The first requirement — and the one that lies at the heart of this appeal — is that the occupation be *sufficient* to ground Aboriginal title. It is clear from *Delgamuukw* that not every passing traverse or use grounds title. What then constitutes *sufficient* occupation to ground title?

[34] The question of sufficient occupation must be approached from both the common law perspective and the Aboriginal perspective (*Delgamuukw*, at para. 147); see also *R. v. Van der Peet*, [1996] 2 S.C.R. 507.

[35] The Aboriginal perspective focuses on laws, practices, customs and traditions of the group (*Delgamuukw*, at para. 148). In considering this perspective for the purpose of Aboriginal title, "one must take into account the group's size, manner of life, material resources, and technological abilities, and the character of the lands claimed": B. Slattery,

---

† 2014 SCC 44.

"Understanding Aboriginal Rights" (1987), 66 Can. Bar Rev. 727, at p. 758, quoted with approval in *Delgamuukw*, at para. 149.

[36] The common law perspective imports the idea of possession and control of the lands. At common law, possession extends beyond sites that are physically occupied, like a house, to surrounding lands that are used and over which effective control is exercised.

. . . .

[38] To sufficiently occupy the land for purposes of title, the Aboriginal group in question must show that it has historically acted in a way that would communicate to third parties that it held the land for its own purposes. This standard does not demand notorious or visible use akin to proving a claim for adverse possession, but neither can the occupation be purely subjective or internal. There must be evidence of a strong presence on or over the land claimed, manifesting itself in acts of occupation that could reasonably be interpreted as demonstrating that the land in question belonged to, was controlled by, or was under the exclusive stewardship of the claimant group. As just discussed, the kinds of acts necessary to indicate a permanent presence and intention to hold and use the land for the group's purposes are dependent on the manner of life of the people and the nature of the land. Cultivated fields, constructed dwelling houses, invested labour, and a consistent presence on parts of the land may be sufficient, but are not essential to establish occupation. The notion of occupation must also reflect the way of life of the Aboriginal people, including those who were nomadic or semi-nomadic.

. . . .

[41] In summary, what is required is a culturally sensitive approach to sufficiency of occupation based on the dual perspectives of the Aboriginal group in question — its laws, practices, size, technological ability and the character of the land claimed — and the common law notion of possession as a basis for title. It is not possible to list every *indicia* of occupation that might apply in a particular case. The common law test for possession — which requires an intention to occupy or hold land for the purposes of the occupant — must be considered alongside the perspective of the Aboriginal group which, depending on its size and manner of living, might conceive of possession of land in a somewhat different manner than did the common law.

[42] There is no suggestion in the jurisprudence or scholarship that Aboriginal title is confined to specific village sites or farms, as the Court of Appeal held. Rather, a culturally sensitive approach suggests that regular use of territories for hunting, fishing, trapping and foraging is "sufficient" use to ground Aboriginal title, provided that such use, on the facts of a particular case, evinces an intention on the part of the Aboriginal group to hold or possess the land in a manner comparable to what would be required to establish title at common law.

. . . .

2. Continuity of Occupation

[45] Where present occupation is relied on as proof of occupation pre-sovereignty, a second requirement arises — continuity between present and pre-sovereignty occupation.

[46] The concept of continuity does not require Aboriginal groups to provide evidence of an unbroken chain of continuity between their current practices, customs and traditions, and those which existed prior to contact (*Van der Peet*, at para. 65). The same applies to Aboriginal title. Continuity simply means that for evidence of present occupation to establish an inference of pre-sovereignty occupation, the present occupation must be rooted in pre-sovereignty times. This is a question for the trier of fact in each case.

3. Exclusivity of Occupation

[47] The third requirement is *exclusive* occupation of the land at the time of sovereignty. The Aboriginal group must have had "the <u>intention and capacity to retain exclusive control</u>" over the lands (*Delgamuukw*, at para. 156, quoting McNeil, *Common Law Aboriginal Title*, at p. 204 (emphasis added)). Regular use without exclusivity may give rise to [usufructuary] Aboriginal rights; for Aboriginal title, the use must have been exclusive.

[48] Exclusivity should be understood in the sense of intention and capacity to control the land. The fact that other groups or individuals were on the land does not necessarily negate exclusivity of occupation. Whether a claimant group had the intention and capacity to control the land at the time of sovereignty is a question of fact for the trial judge and depends on various factors such as the characteristics of the claimant group, the nature of other groups in the area, and the characteristics of the land in question. Exclusivity can be established by proof that

others were excluded from the land, or by proof that others were only allowed access to the land with the permission of the claimant group. The fact that permission was requested and granted or refused, or that treaties were made with other groups, may show intention and capacity to control the land. Even the lack of challenges to occupancy may support an inference of an established group's intention and capacity to control.

[49] As with sufficiency of occupation, the exclusivity requirement must be approached from both the common law and Aboriginal perspectives, and must take into account the context and characteristics of the Aboriginal society. ...

. . . .

VI. WHAT RIGHTS DOES ABORIGINAL TITLE CONFER

. . . .

A. The Legal Characterization of Aboriginal Title

[69] The starting point in characterizing the legal nature of Aboriginal title is Justice Dickson's concurring judgment in *Guerin*, discussed earlier. At the time of assertion of European sovereignty, the Crown acquired radical or underlying title to all the land in the province. This Crown title, however, was burdened by the pre-existing legal rights of Aboriginal people who occupied and used the land prior to European arrival. The doctrine of *terra nullius* (that no one owned the land prior to European assertion of sovereignty) never applied in Canada, as confirmed by the *Royal Proclamation (1763)*, R.S.C. 1985, App. II, No. 1. The Aboriginal interest in land that burdens the Crown's underlying title is an independent legal interest, which gives rise to a fiduciary duty on the part of the Crown.

[70] The content of the Crown's underlying title is what is left when Aboriginal title is subtracted from it: s. 109 of the *Constitution Act, 1867*; *Delgamuukw*. As we have seen, *Delgamuukw* establishes that Aboriginal title gives "the right to exclusive use and occupation of the land ... for a variety of purposes", not confined to traditional or "distinctive" uses (para. 117). In other words, Aboriginal title is a beneficial interest in the land: *Guerin*, at p. 382. In simple terms, the title holders have the right to the benefits associated with the land — to use it, enjoy it and profit from its economic development. As such,

the Crown does not retain a beneficial interest in Aboriginal title land.

[71] What remains, then, of the Crown's radical or underlying title to lands held under Aboriginal title? The authorities suggest two related elements — a fiduciary duty owed by the Crown to Aboriginal people when dealing with Aboriginal lands, and the right to encroach on Aboriginal title if the government can justify this in the broader public interest under s. 35 of the *Constitution Act, 1982*. The Court in *Delgamuukw* referred to this as a process of reconciling Aboriginal interests with the broader public interests under s. 35 of the *Constitution Act, 1982*.

[72] The characteristics of Aboriginal title flow from the special relationship between the Crown and the Aboriginal group in question. It is this relationship that makes Aboriginal title *sui generis* or unique. Aboriginal title is what it is — the unique product of the historic relationship between the Crown and the Aboriginal group in question. Analogies to other forms of property ownership — for example, fee simple — may help us to understand aspects of Aboriginal title. But they cannot dictate precisely what it is or is not. As La Forest J. put it in *Delgamuukw*, at para. 190, Aboriginal title "is not equated with fee simple ownership; nor can it be described with reference to traditional property law concepts".

B. The Incidents of Aboriginal Title

[73] Aboriginal title confers ownership rights similar to those associated with fee simple, including: the right to decide how the land will be used; the right of enjoyment and occupancy of the land; the right to possess the land; the right to the economic benefits of the land; and the right to pro-actively use and manage the land.

[74] Aboriginal title, however, comes with an important restriction — it is collective title held not only for the present generation but for all succeeding generations. This means it cannot be alienated except to the Crown or encumbered in ways that would prevent future generations of the group from using and enjoying it. Nor can the land be developed or misused in a way that would substantially deprive future generations of the benefit of the land. Some changes — even permanent changes — to the land may be possible. Whether a particular use is irreconcilable with the ability of succeeding generations to benefit from the land will be a matter to be determined when the issue arises.

[75] The rights and restrictions on Aboriginal title flow from the legal interest Aboriginal title confers, which in turn flows from the fact of Aboriginal occupancy at the time of European sovereignty which attached as a burden on the underlying title asserted by the Crown at sovereignty. Aboriginal title post-sovereignty reflects the fact of Aboriginal occupancy pre-sovereignty, with all the pre-sovereignty incidents of use and enjoyment that were part of the collective title enjoyed by the ancestors of the claimant group — most notably the right to control how the land is used. However, these uses are not confined to the uses and customs of pre-sovereignty times; like other land-owners, Aboriginal title holders of modern times can use their land in modern ways, if that is their choice.

[76] The right to control the land conferred by Aboriginal title means that governments and others seeking to use the land must obtain the consent of the Aboriginal title holders. If the Aboriginal group does not consent to the use, the government's only recourse is to establish that the proposed incursion on the land is justified under s. 35 of the *Constitution Act, 1982*.

C.   Justification of Infringement

[77] To justify overriding the Aboriginal title-holding group's wishes on the basis of the broader public good, the government must show: (1) that it discharged its procedural duty to consult and accommodate, (2) that its actions were backed by a compelling and substantial objective; and (3) that the governmental action is consistent with the Crown's fiduciary obligation to the group: *Sparrow*.

[78] The duty to consult is a procedural duty that arises from the honour of the Crown prior to confirmation of title. Where the Crown has real or constructive knowledge of the potential or actual existence of Aboriginal title, and contemplates conduct that might adversely affect it, the Crown is obliged to consult with the group asserting Aboriginal title and, if appropriate, accommodate the Aboriginal right. The duty to consult must be discharged prior to carrying out the action that could adversely affect the right.

[79] The degree of consultation and accommodation required lies on a spectrum as discussed in *Haida*. In general, the level of consultation and accommodation required is proportionate to the strength of the claim and to the seriousness of the adverse impact the contemplated governmental action would have on the claimed right. "A dubious or peripheral claim may attract a mere duty of notice, while a stronger claim may attract more stringent duties" (para. 37). The required level of consultation and accommodation is greatest where title has been established. Where consultation or accommodation is found to be inadequate, the government decision can be suspended or quashed.

[80] Where Aboriginal title is unproven, the Crown owes a procedural duty imposed by the honour of the Crown to consult and, if appropriate, accommodate the unproven Aboriginal interest. By contrast, where title has been established, the Crown must not only comply with its procedural duties, but must also ensure that the proposed government action is substantively consistent with the requirements of s. 35 of the *Constitution Act, 1982*. This requires both a compelling and substantial governmental objective and that the government action is consistent with the fiduciary duty owed by the Crown to the Aboriginal group.

.   .   .   .   .

[86] First, the Crown's fiduciary duty means that the government must act in a way that respects the fact that Aboriginal title is a group interest that inheres in present and future generations. The beneficial interest in the land held by the Aboriginal group vests communally in the title-holding group. This means that incursions on Aboriginal title cannot be justified if they would substantially deprive future generations of the benefit of the land.

[87] Second, the Crown's fiduciary duty infuses an obligation of proportionality into the justification process. Implicit in the Crown's fiduciary duty to the Aboriginal group is the requirement that the incursion is necessary to achieve the government's goal (rational connection); that the government go no further than necessary to achieve it (minimal impairment); and that the benefits that may be expected to flow from that goal are not outweighed by adverse effects on the Aboriginal interest (proportionality of impact). The requirement of proportionality is inherent in the *Delgamuukw* process of reconciliation and was echoed in *Haida's* insistence that the Crown's duty to consult and accommodate at the claims stage "is proportionate to a preliminary assessment of the strength of the case supporting the existence of the right or title, and to the seriousness of the potentially adverse effect upon the right or title claimed" (para. 39).

[88] In summary, Aboriginal title confers on the group that holds it the exclusive right to decide how the land is used and the right to benefit from those uses, subject to one carve-out — that the uses must be consistent with the group nature of the interest and the enjoyment of the land by future generations. Government incursions not consented to by the title-holding group must be undertaken in accordance with the Crown's procedural duty to consult and must also be justified on the basis of a compelling and substantial public interest, and must be consistent with the Crown's fiduciary duty to the Aboriginal group.

D. Remedies and Transition

[89] Prior to establishment of title by court declaration or agreement, the Crown is required to consult in good faith with any Aboriginal groups asserting title to the land about proposed uses of the land and, if appropriate, accommodate the interests of such claimant groups. The level of consultation and accommodation required varies with the strength of the Aboriginal group's claim to the land and the seriousness of the potentially adverse effect upon the interest claimed. If the Crown fails to discharge its duty to consult, various remedies are available including injunctive relief, damages, or an order that consultation or accommodation be carried out: *Rio Tinto Alcan Inc. v. Carrier Sekani Tribal Council*, 2010 SCC 43, [2010] 2 S.C.R. 650, at para. 37.

[90] After Aboriginal title to land has been established by court declaration or agreement, the Crown must seek the consent of the title-holding Aboriginal group to developments on the land. Absent consent, development of title land cannot proceed unless the Crown has discharged its duty to consult and can justify the intrusion on title under s. 35 of the *Constitution Act, 1982*. The usual remedies that lie for breach of interests in land are available, adapted as may be necessary to reflect the special nature of Aboriginal title and the fiduciary obligation owed by the Crown to the holders of Aboriginal title.

[91] The practical result may be a spectrum of duties applicable over time in a particular case. At the claims stage, prior to establishment of Aboriginal title, the Crown owes a good faith duty to consult with the group concerned and, if appropriate, accommodate its interests. As the claim strength increases, the required level of consultation and accommodation correspondingly increases. Where a claim is particularly strong — for example, shortly before a court declaration of title — appropriate care must be taken to preserve the Aboriginal interest pending final resolution of the claim. Finally, once title is established, the Crown cannot proceed with development of title land not consented to by the title-holding group unless it has discharged its duty to consult and the development is justified pursuant to s. 35 of the *Constitution Act, 1982*.

[92] Once title is established, it may be necessary for the Crown to reassess prior conduct in light of the new reality in order to faithfully discharge its fiduciary duty to the title-holding group going forward. For example, if the Crown begins a project without consent prior to Aboriginal title being established, it may be required to cancel the project upon establishment of the title if continuation of the project would be unjustifiably infringing. Similarly, if legislation was validly enacted before title was established, such legislation may be rendered inapplicable going forward to the extent that it unjustifiably infringes Aboriginal title.

E. What Duties Were Owed by the Crown at the Time of the Government Action?

[93] Prior to the declaration of Aboriginal title, the Province had a duty to consult and accommodate the claimed Tsilhqot'in interest in the land. As the Tsilhqot'in had a strong *prima facie* claim to the land at the time of the impugned government action and the intrusion was significant, the duty to consult owed by the Crown fell at the high end of the spectrum described in *Haida* and required significant consultation and accommodation in order to preserve the Tsilhqot'in interest.

[94] With the declaration of title, the Tsilhqot'in have now established Aboriginal title to the portion of the lands designated by the trial judge with the exception as set out in para. 9 of these reasons. This gives them the right to determine, subject to the inherent limits of group title held for future generations, the uses to which the land is put and to enjoy its economic fruits. As we have seen, this is not merely a right of first refusal with respect to Crown land management or usage plans. Rather, it is the right to proactively use and manage the land.

VII. BREACH OF THE DUTY TO CONSULT

. . . .

[97] I add this. Governments and individuals proposing to use or exploit land, whether before or after a declaration of Aboriginal title, can avoid a charge of infringement or failure to adequately consult by obtaining the consent of the interested Aboriginal group.

Public International Law

(a) Note on Nature and Sources of Public International Law

David W. Elliott

Most of the materials we have considered so far involve the law of Canada or of other individual states. Law of this kind is sometimes described as municipal law. Public international law,[1] in contrast, is the law governing relations between states. This, in turn, is sometimes contrasted with private international law, the law about relations between non-governmental organizations and citizens of different states. It is preferable, though, not to draw too sharp a boundary. In the international world, as in nation-states, the difference between "governmental" and "non-governmental" is often more one of degree than kind.

In a world of ongoing ethnic and religious conflict, and of continuous confrontation over trade, resources, and boundaries, public international law may seem like a pale shadow of its municipal counterparts, at the mercy of power politics. Rich nations, capped by a single economic and military superpower, can set their own agendas. Some local populations are oppressed by rogue states; many others are torn by civil war. Meanwhile, global terrorist rings and drug cartels do their deadly business in the shadows. International law seems ill-prepared to cope. It has no central legislative body or set of binding norms comparable to those of municipal law systems, and lacks a standing international police force.[2]

On the other hand, there is a world deliberative body, the United Nations,[3] and two international judicial bodies: the International Court of Justice[4] and the International Criminal Court.[5] As most Canadians know, the United Nations can make provision for *ad hoc* peacekeepers.[6] More-over, international law has norms that are followed generally by most nations, important multinational treaties such as the *Law of the Sea Convention*,[7] and high-profile trade and finance regulatory bodies such as the World Trade Organization[8] and the World Bank.[9] Although international law norms tend to be less well defined than their municipal counterparts, and are less certain of enforcement, most states usually find it in their own interest to comply.[10]

The main sources of international law — and public international law — are international treaties, international customs, recognized general principles of international law, judicial decisions, and academic writings.[11] Treaties bind only the states that agree to them, but many large modern treaties carry additional weight because they codify international customary law. International law's dependence on custom provides both flexibility and instability: national positions that lack full international support can now sometimes gain general acceptance in a matter of decades.[12]

Despite its imperfections, public international law is more than a matter of ideals or convenience. When combined with tolerance, diplomacy, and assistance to those in less fortunate nations, it is a vital defence against mutual destruction.

Notes

1. For general works on public international law, see the Select Bibliography at the end of this sourcebook.
2. On the imperfections of public international law, see H.J. Morgenthau and K.W. Thompson, *Politics Among Nations: The Struggle for Power and Peace*, 6th ed. (New York: Alfred Knopf, 1985) Ch. 18; Leslie Claude Green, *Interna-*

tional Law: A Canadian Perspective, 2d ed. (Toronto: Carswell, 1988) at 52–53.

3. See P. Sands and P. Klein, *Blowett: The Law of International Institutions*, 5th ed. (London: Sweet and Maxwell, 2001) Ch. 3, the extracts below from the *United Nations Charter*, below, and the extracts below from E. Childers, "The United Nations System" in E. Childers, ed., *United Nations: Building a Safer World* (New York: St. Martin's Press, 1994), and *Globalization, Governance and the State*, below. As seen, although the United Nations performs a vital role in some areas, it is significantly underutilized in others.

4. See S. Rosenne, *The World Court: What it Is and How it Works* (Boston: M. Nijoff, 1989); E. LeGresly, Law and Government Division, Research Branch, Library of Parliament, *The World Court* (Ottawa: Library of Parliament, 1992); and extract from the *Statute of International Court of Justice*, below. Note, though, that this is not a busy institution. In areas related to trade, the focus is on bodies such as the World Trade Organization: see *Globalization, Governance and the State*, below.

5. *Rome Statute of the International Court*, adopted July 17, 1998 by 120 countries, in force July 1, 2002. The ICC is not part of the United Nations.

6. See Senate Standing Committee on Foreign Affairs, *Meeting New Challenges: Canada's Response to a New Generation of Peace Keeping (Report)* (Ottawa: Queen's Printer, 1993); J.T. Jockel, *Canada and International Peacekeeping* (Washington, D.C.: Center for Strategic and International Studies, 1994).

7. *United Nations Convention on the Law of the Sea*, April 30, 1982, opened for signatures December 10, 1982, entered into force November 16, 1994, UN Doc. A/CONF. 62/122 (1982), reprinted in (1982), 21 *International Legal Materials* 1261.

8. The WTO is a relatively new international organization. It was created pursuant to the *World Trade Agreement*, signed on April 15, 1994 by over 100 countries, and started operating on January 1, 1995. See further, *Globalization, Governance and the State*, below.

9. See *Globalization, Governance and the State*, below.

10. See H.J. Morgenthau and K.W. Thompson, *Politics Among Nations: The Struggle for Power and Peace*, 6th ed. (New York: Alfred Knopf, 1985) at 312–13.

11. See Ian Brownlie, *Principles of Public International Law*, 6th ed. (Oxford, England: Oxford University Press, 2003) Ch. 1; Hugh M. Kindred, general ed., *International Law: Chiefly as Interpreted and Applied in Canada*, 6th ed. (Toronto: Emond Montgomery, 2000) Ch. 3.

12. Note the speed with which state practice on exclusive fishing and economic zones became rules of international law: see Kindred, *International Law, supra* note 11 at 849–52.

(b)   The United Nations†[1]

David W. Elliott

On June 26, 1945, representatives of 50 countries looked beyond six years of global destruction to a brave new world of planned peace. They signed the *Charter of the United Nations*, and brought into being an international association dedicated to war *against* human conflict and suffering.[2] According to Article 1 of the UN Charter, the United Nations was to serve as a centre to harmonize state action for maintaining "international peace and security"; for developing "friendly state relations based on the principle of equal rights and self-determination of peoples"; for solving international "economic, social, cultural, or humanitarian" problems; and for encouraging respect for basic human rights and freedoms.

Today, this association has 191 members, comprising almost every nation-state on earth.[3] It is the town hall of the world, a central hub of diplomacy and cooperative efforts, a forum for global conferences on human rights, population, sustainable development, women, and the environment,[4] and the birthplace of international treaties.[5] In 2006, the United Nations had 15 peacekeeping and peacemaking missions in more than a dozen regions of the world, United Nations agencies and affiliated associations were involved in coordination and humanitarian work in fields as diverse as agriculture, refugee concerns, and labour standards, and the United Nations Secretary-General continued to play a major role on the world stage.

On the other hand, there have been many calls for UN reform.[6] Often, this body has seemed marginal or ineffectual in a world of instant political crises, shrinking natural resources, and non-governmental crime, weapons, and terror. In recent years, the world's most powerful country has strongly criticized the United Nations, has repeatedly withheld its UN dues, and has preferred unilateral or U.S.-led initiatives to those of the UN. In 2003, the United States and Great Britain invaded Iraq, despite lack of express approval from the Security Council.[7] Meanwhile, important states such

---

† Revised and updated by Nick E. Milanovic.

as Japan and India call for permanent seats on the Security Council.

What is the United Nations? Is it still the world's best hope for peace? Or is it a relic from generations past, ill-suited to the problems of the 21st century? If reforms are needed, what should these be?[8] These questions cannot be fully answered here, but a few introductory comments are in order.

The structure of the United Nations "system"[9] can be represented by three concentric circles, each linked or related to the central constitutional document, the UN Charter. In the core circle are the six main organs of the United Nations, a deliberative body called the General Assembly,[10] a political executive body called the Security Council,[11] the departments and offices of an administrative body called the Secretariat, a research and coordination unit called the Economic and Social Council, a judicial tribunal, the International Court of Justice,[12] and a now-inactive agency for assisting newly independent colonies, the Trusteeship Council. In the second circle is a collection of United Nations funds, programs, councils, and commissions that are also within the Secretariat, but have some degree of operating independence. Further out, in a third circle, are more than a dozen specialized agencies, such as the International Labour Organization, the UN Educational, Scientific, and Cultural Organization, and the World Health Organization.[13] These are relatively autonomous members of the United Nations that report directly to the General Assembly or (in the case of the International Atomic Energy Agency) the Security Council. At the outer edge of this circle, because of their very high level of autonomy, are the International Atomic Energy Agency, the World Bank group, and the International Monetary Fund.[14] Other international bodies, such as the World Trade Organization, interact with the United Nations system but are independent of it.

Some of the key institutions in the core circle merit a second look. The General Assembly is based on the principle of representation and universality. Each United Nations member state, no matter how small, is entitled to one vote in the General Assembly. Important issues require a two-thirds vote from members who are present; otherwise, a simple majority vote is sufficient. The Assembly meets in one session per year, or when it is convened by the Security Council or by a request of a majority of the members. The Assembly's responsibilities include overseeing the budget of the United Nations. Contrary to the situation in a parliamentary system, though, the General Assembly has no power to control the political executive — the Security Council — through no-confidence motions. Instead, much of the Assembly's time is devoted to debating and passing non-binding resolutions on world issues. Some of these, such as the *Millennium Declaration* of 2000, may carry considerable moral weight, despite their non-compulsory nature.[15]

In contrast to the General Assembly, the Security Council is based on the principles of representation *and* power, with an emphasis on the latter. It includes five permanent members who have a veto over all Security Council decisions, including any Council decision to amend the UN Charter. These are the United States, Russia (formerly the U.S.S.R.), China, Great Britain, and France, the most powerful victor nations of the Second World War, and still five of the most powerful states today. The other 10 members of the Security Council are elected from among the main geographical regions of the world. They serve for terms of only two years, and have no veto. Although the non-permanent members are in the majority, the real decision-making power is with the permanent holders of the veto. The Security Council has the main responsibility for matters affecting world security and peace. This includes the direction of UN peacekeeping and peacemaking forces, and the authorization of military and economic sanctions. As well, it recommends candidates for UN membership and for the position of UN Secretary General. The Security Council's security resolutions are binding on all UN members.

The other major core organ, the Secretariat, is an international executive staff of about 9,000 people in departments and offices and another approximately 16,000 people in the more independent UN funds, programs, councils, and commissions.[16] These people administer the policies of the main organs of the United Nations, under the general direction of the Secretary General. The Secretary General is appointed by the General Assembly for a five-year renewable term, on the recommendation of the Security Council. Although the Secretariat headquarters are in New York, it has offices around the world. Secretariat members take an oath of loyalty to the United Nations, agreeing not to take instructions from member state governments.

Where, then, are some of the key substantive and administrative challenges that confront this organization? No comprehensive answer is possible here, but one or two areas stand out.

A central challenge is the goal of preventing and resolving conflict. Subject to a right of self-defence, Article 2(4) prohibits the unilateral use of force, and requires member states to settle their disputes "by peaceful means". These means may include "negotiation, enquiry, mediation, conciliation, arbitration, judicial settlement, resort to regional agencies or arrangements, or other peaceful means of their own choice".[17] They can lead to specific peace settlements and to longer-term agreements on topics such as disarmament.

One of these mechanisms is the organ for addressing international legal disputes, the International Court of Justice.[18] The ICJ comprises 15 permanent judges, who are elected to nine-year renewable terms.[19] All member states of the United Nations are parties before the Court. On the other hand, the Court's jurisdiction is voluntary. The Court must depend on the Security Council to enforce its decisions against uncooperative parties. This could pose a special problem if the uncooperative party were a permanent member of the Council. Because of its veto, a permanent member can block the enforcement of any ICJ judgment against it.[20] The Court has rendered some significant decisions on subjects such as the law of the sea.[21] However, its overall caseload has been light.[22]

The only exception to the UN Charter's prohibition against force is Article 51. This authorizes a right of individual or collective self-defence. However, this right is available only in response to an armed attack, and only pending action by the Security Council.[23] The Charter envisaged that the prohibition against force would be balanced by a UN military force, directed by a committee acting under the Security Council. In return for agreeing to limit unilateral force to short-term defensive measures, member states would enjoy the collective security of the United Nations. Unfortunately, this goal was not met.

Cold War and post-Cold War rivalries and perceptions of self-interest discouraged member states from making the agreements needed to establish the UN force, and the military committee does virtually nothing. Instead, UN conflict resolution has centred on more *ad hoc* mechanisms, such as peacekeeping and peacemaking[24] missions and specific disarmament and peace settlements.[25] Although the number of UN peacekeeping and peacemaking initiatives increased significantly after the Cold War, the 1990s brought a series of high-profile failures. For example, UN forces failed to prevent ethnic cleansing of Muslims in Bosnia, to end the civil war in Somalia, and to stop the massacre of more than 800,000 people in Rwanda. An inquiry into the Rwanda tragedy said that UN staff mismanagement was partly responsible, but it also blamed the failure of Security Council and other United Nations members to commit sufficient resources to the United Nations peacekeeping force.[26]

Lacking a conflict resolution force of its own, the UN must rely on voluntary participation by its more important members. As a result, field operations tend to be controlled largely by the countries who supply the troops. For example, most aspects of the UN-approved wars in Korea, Bosnia,[27] Afghanistan, and Iraq-Kuwait (in 1991) were controlled by the United States and (in Bosnia and Afghanistan) NATO.[28]

Within the UN, it is the Security Council that has primary responsibility for peace and security.[29] However, when there are calls for intervention to resolve conflict, the Council tends to be slow to respond. Council members have diverse interests, and some may not feel sufficiently threatened to agree to measures that could require them to contribute their own troops. Others may be reluctant to authorize intervention against an ally. Because of the veto power, a single "no" vote from a permanent member can close the door to action by the Council as a whole.

Slowness or impasse in the Security Council, combined with the preponderant military power of the United States, has sometimes encouraged that country to take the initiative. For example, in October 2001, the United States invaded Afghanistan under NATO — and not directly under UN Security Council — auspices.[30] Although the Security Council had supported strong measures against terrorism,[31] it had not expressly authorized armed force. Several months later, the Security Council passed a resolution to support action against the Taliban in Afghanistan,[32] and the United States remained in control of the military mission.[33] The United States took the initiative again in 2003. By the spring of that year, the Security Council had supported progressively stronger measures against Iraq, which continued to impede inspectors looking for weapons of mass destruction.[34] On the other hand, the Security Council did not expressly authorize armed force in this context.[35] Instead, most members preferred to further strengthen the inspection system. However, this route was closed, as the United States and Britain concluded that force was justified. In March 2003, the United States, Britain, and other members of a "coalition of the willing" invaded Iraq. In cases such as these, the UN seems caught between ratifying the security agenda of its strongest member and failing to act at all.

Nevertheless, there is a more positive side to the UN's balance sheet on conflict. The problems in Bosnia, Somalia, and Rwanda should be considered in the context of more successful UN peacekeeping and peacemaking efforts, in places such as East Timor, El Salvador, Namibia, Cambodia, and Mozambique.[36] Since its inception in 1945, the United Nations has negotiated more than 170 settlements to regional conflicts.[37] It has provided a forum for more than 300 international treaties, some directed at conflict prevention and disarmament.[38] Examples of the latter are the nuclear weapons *Non-Proliferation Treaty*, concluded in 1968 and in force in 1970,[39] and *Mine Ban Treaty*, concluded in 1997 and in force in 1999.[40] In December 2005, the General Assembly and Security Council addressed an urgent need by authorizing a new ongoing Peacebuilding Commission for helping countries to rebuild after conflicts.

Another major challenge for the United Nations is to play an effective positive role in regard to the global economic order.[41] There is an enormous gulf between the small number of rich nations and the overwhelming majority of impoverished "developing" countries. Not surprisingly, the latter press the United Nations for economic aid and redistributive programs. For their part, most of the wealthier nations prefer measures that support stable and liberalized world trade. For this, they tend to go outside the core United Nations institutions, and to focus on independent UN affiliates such as the World Bank Group and the International Monetary Fund, on wholly separate international entities such as the World Trade Organization, and on regional economic alliances.[42] The international banking and trading institutions are dominated by the richest nations. They have been accused of favouring short-term market interests over the needs of poorer countries.[43] Richer nations may feel a less direct interest in supporting United Nations' efforts to widen the economic base of developing countries, and to strengthen their social framework.

The United Nations has tried hard to target social development programs that have economic implications — providing humanitarian relief and social development funds for purposes such as assisting refugees, alleviating poverty and hunger, combatting disease, crime, and illegal drugs, and setting standards for human rights. Unfortunately, though, the budget here is limited. Apart from

funding for World Bank loans, the UN Development Programme and related agencies have about $6.5 billion annually to spend on the kind of social development programs described above.[44] Depending on the size of donations, they have about $1.4 billion annually to spend on humanitarian relief.[45] If these sums seem generous, it is helpful to note that world military expenditures amount to about $800,000 billion per year![46]

Some of the United Nations' biggest challenges are not substantive, but administrative, in nature, and a perennial administrative problem is the challenge of financing. The United Nations system has an overall budget of between[47] $15 billion and $20 billion,[48] divided mainly between an assessed budget, a voluntary budget, and a largely voluntary peacekeeping budget. The core UN organization has a regular assessed budget of between $1 billion and $2.5 billion (U.S.) per year, determined for two-year terms, in addition to funding from voluntary donations.[49] Regular budget payments are assessed on the basis of the population and economic ability of individual members to pay; military expenses are met partly from the regular budget and partly by voluntary contributions from participating states.[50] The voluntary portion of the budget is unpredictable, and depends on donors' goodwill.

Because of the extreme differences in the wealth of member counties, the richest countries bear by far the largest share of the financing bill. In 2013, for example, over half of the regular UN budget came from contributions from the United States, Japan, Germany, and France.[51] The United States has long been dissatisfied with the size of its assessed contribution. In the face of American demands and withheld payments, the United States' regular budget assessment was reduced in 2000 from 25% of the total to 22%, and its peacekeeping contribution was reduced from 30% to a target of 25%.[52] The United States has called for further reductions, and has threatened to withhold future contributions if its desired reforms are not implemented.[53] Meanwhile, many countries are in arrears in their payments. In 2005, members' arrears amounted to $333 million, of which $252 million was owed by the United States.[54]

Whether present UN financing is seen as too much or too little depends on whether a state regards the UN as a vital part of world peacekeeping, economic, and social efforts, or as a costly and inefficient obstacle to the achievement of national objectives. The wealthier and more powerful a country, the greater the possibility of the latter perspective.[55] Under pressure from the United States, the UN has reduced staff, merged units, closed information offices, and made personnel changes, but demands for further changes and efficiencies continue.[56]

Other administrative problems have included controversies over representation in UN organs and agencies and over processes for selecting executive heads, lack of transparency, lack of coordination between agencies, and alleged inefficiency and corruption in some administrative units. The permanent representation and veto powers of the United States, Great Britain, France, Russia, and China in the Security Council have given rise to demands for permanent member status by other large countries such as Japan, India, Germany, and Brazil. These demands were not supported by permanent members such as the United States and China, although the United States indicated a willingness to consider permanent member status for Japan *after* the implementation of reforms sought by the United States.[57] Non-governmental organizations have sought representation at the General Assembly, thus far without success. Another critical structural question — which is not mentioned in the UN Charter — involves the process for selecting the Secretary General. As well, countries such as Canada have pressed for a more open nomination procedure in the Security Council.

A persistent theme from UN critics has been the need for greater openness, and the organization has made some attempts to respond. The United Nations established its own website[58] in 1994. In 1997, it began to make a large store of official UN documents available on the Internet, first by password and then (in 2004) to the general public.

On the question of management, in the late 1990s the Secretary General made several efforts to merge overlapping administrative units and to improve coordination within the UN system. In 2004, a more serious administrative problem emerged when an inquiry uncovered corruption on the part of some UN staff officials in the administration of the 1996–2003 oil-for-food program for Iraq.[59] On another front, a defective selection process allowed member states with poor human rights records to sit on the former UN Commission on Human Rights.[60] In 2006, in response to its 2005 Millennium +5 Summit on UN reform, the General Assembly replaced the Commission with a new Human Rights Council and a better regulated selection process. However, apart from the Peacekeeping Commission referred to earlier, most other major recommendations of the Millennium +5 Summit[61] were abandoned as a result of objections from the United States.[62]

As the account above suggests, there are some major accomplishments and notable reforms[63] on the positive side of the ledger. However, the pressure for reform continues, and so does the controversy over the direction it should take. In one sense, this is understandable, as reform is a necessary response to changing circumstances. There have been significant changes since the creation of the United Nations about 70 years ago. The Cold War has come and gone; the superpowers are now overshadowed by a single superpower. Conventional conflicts share the stage with terrorism, global pandemics, environmental degradation, and wide access to weapons of mass destruction. The new threats are urgent, ongoing, and complex.

However, reform of any kind requires consensus, and many controversies about the United Nations and its future are still strongly shaped by two longstanding and opposing perspectives — that of the rich and that of the poor. Poorer developing nations[64] tend to want universal representation in an active international body that promotes generous economic redistribution and effective humanitarian help.[65] Wealthy nations[66] tend to prefer a more modest international organization that focuses on maintaining political and military stability, and leaves most of the economic field to bodies that are designed especially to promote and maintain free international trade.[67] Within the latter group, the government of the most powerful nation of all has been pressing for a more modest UN role in virtually all areas,[68] generally subordinate to U.S.-led or U.S.-dominated international organizations and alliances or to unilateral initiatives.[69]

To reach agreement on United Nations reform, both the poor and the rich will have to yield. The former should recognize that a member state who contributes proportionately more to resources and personnel should be entitled to a special voice in allocation decisions. Conversely, though, the richer and more powerful nations should appreciate the value of legitimacy that comes only from the majority support of a universal organization. The price for this legitimacy is effective economic redistribution, humanitarian help, and multilateralism. Finally, all nations should remember that human suffering goes beyond national borders.[70] It may be insoluble outside a common world forum. For all its failings, the United Nations provides that forum.

Arguably, it is as necessary today as it was on June 26, 1945.

Notes

1. See generally, UN Website: <http://un.org>. *Yearbook of the United Nations* (The Hague/Boston/London: Martinus Nijhoff, annual); Erskine Childers, ed., *United Nations: Building a Safer World* (New York: St. Martin's Press, 1994); Dimitris Bourantonis and Jarrod Wiener, eds., *The United Nations in the New World Order: The World Organization at Fifty* (Basingstoke, Hampshire: Macmillan, 1995); H. von Margoldt et al., *The United Nations System and Its Predecessors* (Oxford, England; New York, N.Y.: Oxford University Press, 1997), 2 vols.; Brian Urquhart and Erskine Childers, *A World in Need of Leadership: Tomorrow's United Nations*, rev. 2d ed. (New York: Ford Foundation [distributor], 1996); W. Andy Knight, *A Changing United Nations: Multilateral Evolution and the Quest for Global Governance* (New York: Palgrave, 2000); Nigel D. White, *The United Nations System: Toward International Justice* (Boulder, Colorado: Lynne Rienner, 2002); Jean E. Krasno, ed., *The United Nations: Confronting the Challenges of a Global Society* (Boulder, Colorado: Lynne Rienner, 2004); Thomas G. Weiss, David P. Forsythe, and Roger A. Coate, *The United Nations and Changing World Politics* (Boulder, Colorado: Westview Press, 2004); Paul Heinbecker and Patricia Goff, eds., *Irrelevant or Indispensable?: The United Nations in the Twenty-first Century* (Waterloo, Ont.: Wilfrid Laurier University Press, 2005); Courtney B. Smith, *Politics and Process at the United Nations: the Global Dance* (Boulder, Colorado: Lynne Rienner, 2006).

2. On the origins of the United Nations, see Robert C. Hilderbrand, *Dumbarton Oaks — The Origins of the United Nations and the Search for Postwar Security* (Chapel Hill: University of North Carolina Press, 1990); Stephen C. Schlesinger, *Act of Creation: The Founding of the United Nations: A Story of Superpowers, Secret Agents, Wartime Allies and Enemies, and Their Quest for a Peaceful World* (Boulder, Colorado: Westview Press, 2003); Adam Chapnick, *The Middle Power Project: Canada and the Founding of the United Nations* (Vancouver: UBC Press, 2005).

    For other historical accounts of the United Nations, see Newton R. Bowles, *The Diplomacy of Hope: The United Nations Since the Cold War* (London; New York: I. B. Tauris, 2004); Charles Patterson, *The Oxford 50th Anniversary Book of the United Nations* (New York and London: Oxford, 1995).

3. Two non-members of the United Nations are Taiwan and the Vatican City. Although Taiwan possesses some of the features of an independent state, it is not recognized as such by a majority of the countries of the world. The Vatican City can be regarded as an independent state, but it has not applied for UN membership. The International Court of Justice has held that the United Nations itself can be regarded as an international person, but not a state: see *Regulations Case*, Adv. Op. [1949] I.C.J. 174.

4. On UN conferences, see Michael G. Schechter, ed., *United Nations-sponsored World Conferences: Focus on Impact and Follow-up* (New York: United Nations Press, 2001); Michael G. Schechter *United Nations Global Conferences* (New York, NY: Routledge, 2005).

5. For example, the Kyoto Protocol of 1997 (in force, 2005): see <http://unfccc.int/resource/docs/convkp/kpeng.html>. This treaty is based on the *United Nations Framework Convention on Climate Change*, signed by 154 countries, including Canada, in 1992. The Kyoto Protocol sets mandatory target limits for greenhouse emissions, a major problem in industrialized nations. The United States signed the protocol but has refused to ratify it on the ground that its targets would be harmful to the American economy. Canada was a strong supporter of the protocol at the beginning. However, there was strong opposition from interest groups such as the Canadian oil and gas industry. In May 2006, the Canadian government indicated that it might not continue to support the protocol.

6. For some of the main developments since 1992, see Global Policy Forum, *UN Reform Chronology: 1992 — Present* <http://www.globalpolicy.org/reform/intro/chronology.htm>.

7. The Saddam Hussein regime in Iraq was suspected of accumulating an illegal stockpile of weapons of mass destruction, contrary to numerous Security Council resolutions. On November 8, 2002, the Security Council passed Resolution 1441 of 8 October 2002, UNSCOR, 57th Year, UN Doc. S.C. S/RES/1441 (2002) requiring Iraq to comply with its disarmament obligations or face "serious consequences". Weapons declarations by Iraq in December 2002 failed to show that the weapons had been destroyed. The United States maintained that Iraq's noncompliance with Resolution 1441 and earlier resolutions justified the use of force. Security Council members France, Germany, Russia, and China disagreed, arguing that the weapons inspection process in Iraq should be given more time. Nevertheless, on March 19, 2003, the United States and British forces attacked Iraq, and invaded the country the following day. Although nearly all the occupying forces were American and British, the war was supported by about 35 other countries, described by the American government as "the coalition of the willing." Canada did not support the war. See Jean E. Krasno and James S. Sutterlin, *The United Nations and Iraq: Defanging the Viper* (Westport, CT: Praeger, 2003), on UN efforts to eliminate weapons of mass destruction in Iraq, from 1991–1998); Hans Blix, *Disarming Iraq* (London: Bloomsbury, 2005), on the UN weapons inspection efforts in Iraq prior to the American and British invasion; and Irwin Abrams, ed., *The Iraq War and its Consequences: Thoughts of Nobel Peace Laureates and Eminent Scholars* (River Edge, New Jersey; London: World Scientific, 2003). For the specific content of some of the key Security Council resolutions before the invasion, see *infra*, note 34.

8. On some existing and proposed reforms, see Edward C. Luck, "Reforming the United Nations: Lessons from a History in Progress", in Jean E. Krasno, ed., *The United Nations: Confronting the Challenges of a Global Society* (Boulder, Colorado: Lynne Rienner, 2004) Ch. 11; Joachim Müller, ed. *Reforming the United Nations: the Quiet Revolution* (Boston: Kluwer Law International, 2001); UN Commission on Global Governance, *Our Global Neighbourhood Report of the Commission on Global Governance* (New York: Oxford University Press, 1995).

9. See United Nations, *The United Nations: Principle Organs* <http://www.un.org/aboutun/chartlg.html> and United Nations, *The UN in Brief* <http://www.un.org/Overview/brief.htm>. The latter site indicates that the UN system comprises about 30 affiliated organizations altogether.

10. See M.J. Peterson, *The General Assembly* (London; New York: Routledge, 2005); Smith, *Politics and Process at the United Nations, supra* note 1 at 147–62.

11. See Pascal Teixeira, *The Security Council at the Dawn of the Twenty-first Century: To What Extent Is it Willing and Able to Maintain International Peace and Security?* (Geneva: UNIDIR, 2003); Neil Fenton, *Understanding the UN Security Council: Coercion or Consent?* (Aldershot, Hampshire, England; Burlington, VT: Ashgate, 2004); David M. Malone, ed., *The UN Security Council: from the Cold War to the 21st Century* (Boulder, Colorado: Lynne Rienner, 2004); Dimitris Bourantonis, *the History and Politics of UN Security Council Reform* (London; New York: Routledge, 2005); Max Hilaire, *United Nations Law and the Security Council* (Aldershot, England; Burlington, VT: Ashgate, 2005); Courtney Smith, *ibid.* at 162–77.

12. Terry D. Gill, ed., with the assistance of Harm Dotinga, Erik Jaap Molenaar, and Alex Oude Elferink, *Rosenne's the World Court: What It Is and How It Works* (Leiden; Boston: Martinus Nijhoff, 2003); Mohamed Sameh M. Amr, *The Role of the International Court of Justice as the Principal Judicial Organ of the United Nations* (The Hague; New York: Kluwer Law International, 2003).

13. See United Nations, "The Specialized Agencies" in *The UN in Brief*, <http://www.un.org/Overview/brief6.html>. The International Atomic Energy Agency is not technically a specialized agency, but has funding and other arrangements similar to those of the specialized agencies.

14. See, for example, section 2 of the *Agreement Governing the Relationship Between the United Nations and the International Atomic Energy Agency*, which describes the Agency as "an autonomous international organization in the working relationship with the United Nations established by this Agreement": IAEA link in <http://www.iaea.org/Publications/Documents/Conventions/index.html>.

15. See *United Nations Millennial Declaration*, G.A. Res. A/55/L.2, Agenda Item 60(b), UN GAOR, 55th Sess., UN Doc. A/Res/55/2 (2000). The declaration was supported by 147 member states, and articulated objectives for the new century in the following areas: "peace"; "security and disarmament"; "development and poverty eradication"; "protecting our common environment"; "human rights", "democracy and good governance"; "protecting the vulnerable"; "meeting the special needs of Africa"; and "strengthening the United Nations".

16. Precise figures vary from year to year, and according to whether temporary and state-loaned personnel are taken into account.

17. Article 33.

18. See International Court of Justice, *General Information: The Court at a Glance*, in <http://www.icj-cij.org/icjwww/igeneralinformation.htm>; Terry D. Gill, ed., with the assistance of Harm Dotinga, Erik Jaap Molenaar, and Alex Oude Elferink, *Rosenne's the World Court: What It Is and How It Works* (Leiden; Boston: Martinus Nijhoff, 2003); Mohamed Sameh M. Amr, *The Role of the International Court of Justice as the Principal Judicial Organ of the United Nations* (The Hague; New York: Kluwer Law International, 2003).

19. A party to a dispute may also appoint an *ad hoc* judge for that dispute, if the state in question has no representation among the permanent judges.

20. For example, Nicaragua attempted to have the Security Council enforce the ICJ's judgment against the United States in *The Republic of Nicaragua v. The United States of America*, 1984 ICJ REP. 392 June 27. However, the United States had withdrawn from the Court's jurisdiction in regard to Central American disputes, and refused to comply with the judgment. Because of the American veto power at the Security Council, the Council was unable to act.

21. See, for example, the *Anglo-Norwegian Fisheries* case: 1951 ICJ REP. 116 (Dec. 18); and the *Continental Shelf* cases: *North Sea Continental Shelf Cases* (FRG/Den.; FRG/Neth.), 1969 ICJ REP. 3 (Feb. 20); *Continental Shelf* (Tunis./Libya), Judgment, 1982 ICJ REP. 18 (Feb. 24); and *Continental Shelf* (Libya/Malta), 1985 ICJ REP. 13 (June 3).

22. Since its creation in 1946, the Court has delivered 92 judgments and given 25 advisory opinions: see International Court of Justice, *General Information: The Court at a Glance*, in <http://www.icj-cij.org/icjwww/igeneralinformation.htm>. This is an average of about two decisions per year.

23. Need a state wait until an attack has occurred before it can resort to self-defence measures? In 2002, President Bush asserted a right of preemptive self-defence, which was presumably intended to apply to situations similar to the those in Afghanistan and Iraq: see U.S. White House,

National Security Council, *The National Security Strategy of the United States* (17 September 2002) <http://www.whitehouse.gov/nsc/nss.html>. UN High-Level Panel on Threats, Challenges and Change said that unilateral defensive military action should be limited to threats that were "imminent", and that other threats should be referred to the Security Council: "A More Secure World: Our Shared Responsibility": United Nations, *Report of the High-Level Panel on Threats, Challenges and Change*, UN GAOR, 2004, 59th Sess., UN Doc. A/59/565 (2004). <http://www.un.org/secureworld/>. [Compare this with the classical statement in the letter from Mr. Daniel Webster to Mr. Fox of April 24, 1841. Webster said that to invoke a right of self-defence, a state must demonstrate a "necessity of self-defence [that] is instant, overwhelming, and leaving no choice of means, and no moment for deliberation": 29 British and Foreign State Papers 1129, 1138 (1857), in regard to *The Caroline* case, (1937), 2 Moore, 409, quoted in Hugh M. Kindred, general ed., *International Law: Chiefly as Interpreted and Applied in Canada* (Toronto: Emond Montgomery, 2000) at 1125.] See also Thomas Franck, suggesting that although self-defence should be possible in response to an imminent armed attack, the question as to whether an attack is imminent should be decided by the Security Council, not the defending state: Thomas M. Franck, "Centennial Essay: the Power of Legitimacy and the Legitimacy of Power: International Law in an Age of Power Disequilibrium" (2006) 100 A.J.I.L. 88 at 101–105.

24. Technically, the term "peacekeeping" is limited to supervising peace settlements, at the invitation of the states whose territories are affected. Peacemaking and enforcement action involves intervention between warring parties, in an attempt to bring conflict to an end. Peacekeeping depends on the consent of the parties; peacemaking and enforcement requires the authorization of the Security Council. The latter role may sometimes be more effective in military terms, but can carry greater risk to the perceived neutrality of a UN force, and — in some situations — to the safety of its troops.

25. On peacemaking and peacekeeping, see generally Fen Osler Hampson and David M. Malone, eds., *From Reaction to Conflict Prevention: Opportunities for the UN System* (Boulder, Colorado: Lynne Rienner, 2002); Mohamed Awad Osman, *The United Nations and Peace Enforcement: Wars, Terrorism and Democracy* (Burlington, VT: Ashgate, 2002); James S. Sutterlin, foreword by Bruce Russett, *The United Nations and the Maintenance of International Security: A Challenge to Be Met* (Westport, Conn.: Praeger, 2003); Max Hilaire, *United Nations and the Security Council* (Aldershot, Hants, U.K.: Ashgate Publishing, 2005); Stephen M. Hill, *United Nations Disarmament Processes in Intra-state Conflict* (Houndmills, Basingstoke, Hampshire; New York: Palgrave Macmillan, 2004); William J. Lahnemanm, *Military Intervention: Cases in Context for the Twenty-first Century* (Oxford, England: Rowen & Littlefield, 2004); Richard M. Price and Mark W. Zacher, *The United Nations and Global Security* (New York; Houndmills, England: Palgrave Macmillan, 2004); Alex Conte, *Security in the 21st Century: the United Nations, Afghanistan, and Iraq* (Aldershot, Hants, England; Burlington, VT: Ashgate, 2005); John Terence O'Neill and Nicholas Rees, *United Nations Peacekeeping in the Post-cold War Era* (London; New York: Routledge, 2005); Nina M. Serafino, *Peacekeeping and Related Stability Operations* (New York: Novinka Books, 2005).

26. United Nations Security Council, *Report of the Independent Inquiry into the actions of United Nations during the 1994 Genocide in Rwanda* (United Nations Security Council, Document S/1999/1257, 15 December 1999) <http://www.un.org/Docs/journal/asp/ws.asp?m=S/1999/1257>. For example, having suffered casualties to its UN peacekeeping contingent in Somalia, the United States

was reluctant to authorize any but the most limited military measures in Rwanda. See, further, Michael N. Barnett, *Eyewitness to a Genocide: The United Nations and Rwanda* (Ithaca: Cornell University Press, 2002); Romeo Dallaire with Brent Beardsly, *Shake Hands With The Devil: The Failure Of Humanity In Rwanda* (Toronto: Random House Canada, 2003).

27. For Bosnia, see Marie Isabelle Palacios-Hardy, International Civil-Military Relations: UN and NATO Interventions in the Former Yugoslavia (M.A. Research Essay, Carleton University, 2001) [unpublished].

28. In Afghanistan, for example, the main international military mission is Operation Enduring Freedom (OEF), authorized but not specifically created by the United Nations (see *infra* note 30). It comprises NATO troops led by the United States. Since 2003 Canada has contributed about 2000 troops to this force. The other main international military mission in the country is the International Security Assistance Force (ISAF). This is a smaller security and reconstruction force, originally for the Kabul and surrounding areas. It was specifically mandated by UN Security Resolutions 1386 (2001), 1413 (2002), and 1444 (2002). It has been led by the United States and comprises troops from NATO, the Euro-Atlantic Partnership Council (a NATO partnership organization), and New Zealand.

In May 2006, the Canadian government agreed to extend its contribution for another five years. After the summer of 2006, the Canadian and other non-American components of OEF were to be transferred to ISAF, which would continue to be controlled by NATO. However, the direction of ISAF in NATO would be transferred from the United States to Canada, and ISAF's area of responsibility would expand to include all Afghanistan except the southeastern quarter patrolled by OEF: see Paul Koring, "New NATO role leaves U.S. force largely in charge", *The Globe and Mail* (14 May 2006) A14.

29. See UN Charter, Article 24(1).

30. After the tragic September 11, 2001 attack on people and buildings in the United States, the UN Security Council passed *Anti-terrorism Resolution* 1373 (2001) of September 28, 2001, UNSCOR 56th Sess., UN Doc. S/RES/1373 (2001). This resolution was broadly worded, and called upon states to "[t]ake the necessary steps to prevent the commission of terrorist acts ...": para. 2 [b]: see <http://www.un.org/docs/scres/2001/sc2001.htm>; United Nations Press Release SC/5178 <http://www.un.org/News/Press/docs/2001/sc7158.doc.htm>. (UNSCOR, 56th Year, S/RES/1373 (2001)). To support its invasion, the United States relied in part on this and other Security Council resolutions, on the notion of self-defence in Article 51 of the UN Charter, and on Article 5 of the NATO treaty, which treats an attack on one NATO member as an attack on the others as well.

31. See, for example, Security Council Resolution 1378 of November 14, 2001, UNSCOR, 56th year, S/RES 1378 (2001), and the resolutions referred to in it.

32. United Nations, *Security Council Resolution 1390 (2002)* of January 16, 2002, UNSCOR, 57th Year, UN Doc. S/RES/1390 (2002).

33. Not until after the invasion did the United States speak of a United Nations role, limited mainly to reconstructing Afghanistan after the conflict: see, for example, Government of the United States: The White House, Office of the Press Secretary, *President Holds Prime Time News Conference* (11 October 2001), <http://www.whitehouse.gov/news/releases/2001/10/20011011-7.html>; Government of the United States: The White House, Office of the Press Secretary, *Remarks by the President to United Nations General Assembly* (November 10, 2001), <http://bratislava.usembassy.gov/cis/cisen016.html>.

34. For example, Security Council Resolution 660 of August 2, 1990, UNSCOR, 48th Year, U.N. Doc. S/RES/660

(1990), issued on the day of Iraq's invasion of Kuwait, ordered Iraq to withdraw from Kuwait; Security Council Resolution 678 of November 29, 1990, UNSCOR, 48th Year, U.N. Doc. S/RES/678 (1990), authorized states "to use all necessary means to uphold and implement resolution 660 (1990) and all subsequent relevant resolutions and to restore international peace and security in the area"; Resolution 687 of April 3, 1991, UNSCOR, 49th Year, UN Doc. S/RES/687 (1991) required Iraq to destroy or remove all weapons of mass destruction and missiles with a range of over 150 kilometres; and Resolution 1441 of October 8, 2002, UNSCOR, 57th Year, UN Doc. S.C. S/RES/1441 (2002) ordered Iraq to provide UN inspectors and the International Atomic Energy Authority with "immediate, unimpeded, unconditional, and unrestricted access" to suspected weapons sites, and repeated its earlier warnings that Iraq would face "serious consequences" if it did not comply. For further background on the circumstances of the invasion, see *supra* note 7.

35. See the resolutions cited, *ibid.* Resolution 678 of 1990 had authorized the use of "all necessary means", but it was issued in the context of Iraq's invasion of Kuwait.

36. See, for example, cases discussed in William J. Lahnemanm, *Military Intervention: Cases in Context for the Twenty-first Century* (Oxford, England: Rowen & Littlefield, 2004); Max Hilaire, *United Nations and the Security Council* (Aldershot, Hants, U.K.: Ashgate Publishing, 2005). Of course, the concept of "success" is itself complex, and depends on the nature of the mission and the particular criteria used: see Daniel Druckman and Paul Stern, "Perspectives on Evaluating Peacekeeping Missions" (1999) 4 *The International Journal of Peace Studies* <http://www.gmu.edu/academic/ijps/vol4_1/druckman.htm>. In East Timor, the United Nations force was effective once it was introduced, but unfortunately there were several months of mass violence against civilians before the Security Council agreed to deploy the mission: Hilaire, 149–54. Another UN mission, the Cambodian peacekeeping operation of 1992–1993, proceeded smoothly and enabled Cambodia to hold democratic elections, but did not result in long-term stability: *ibid.* at 39–40.

37. Global Policy Forum, *The United Nations: A Snapshot of Accomplishments* <http://www.globalpolicy.org/finance/action/whyun$.htm>. Of course, these settlements have had widely varying effects in ending or lessening conflict.

38. United Nations, *Major Achievements of the United Nations* <http://www.un.org/aboutun/achieve.htm>.

39. *Treaty on the Non-proliferation of Nuclear Weapons* (NPT): <http://disarmament.un.org/TreatyStatus.nsf>. Canada is a party to this treaty. Non-signatories include India, Pakistan, and Israel. See also Jayantha Dhanapala with Randy Rydell, *Multilateral Diplomacy and the NPT: An Insider's Account* (Geneva, Switzerland: UNIDIR, 2005).

40. *Convention on the Prohibition of the Use, Stockpiling, Production and Transfer of Anti-personnel Mines and on their Destruction (Mine Ban Treaty)*: <http://www.un.org/Depts/mine/UNDocs/ban_trty.htm>. Canada is a party to this treaty. Non-signatories include China, India, and the United States.

41. See generally, Mahfuzur Rahman, *World Economic Issues at the United Nations: Half a Century of Debate* (Boston: Kluwer Academic, 2002); United Nations, Office for the Coordination of Humanitarian Affairs, *The Humanitarian Decade: Challenges for Humanitarian Assistance in the Last Decade and Into the Future* (New York: United Nations, Office for the Coordination of Humanitarian Affairs, 2004); John Toye and Richard Toye, *The UN and Global Political Economy: Trade, Finance, and Development* (Bloomington: Indiana University Press, 2004).

42. See *Globalization, Governance, and the State* in this chapter, and the sources referred to in it.

43. See, for example, Joseph E. Stiglitz, *Globalization and its Discontents* (New York: W.W. Norton, 2002).

44. United Nations, *How Does the UN Handle Emergency Relief?*, in Questions and Answers ... Image and Reality ... About the United Nations <http://www.un.org/geninfo/ir/ch3/ch3.htm>.

45. United Nations, *What Does the UN Do to Promote Development?*, in Questions and Answers ... Image and Reality ... About the United Nations <http://www.un.org/geninfo/ir/ch3/ch3.htm>.

46. United Nations, *What Does the UN Do to Promote Development?*, in Questions and Answers ... Image and Reality ... About the United Nations <http://www.un.org/geninfo/ir/ch3/ch3.htm>.

47. Specific budget figures depend on the year and specific institutions that are included. For example, although the World Bank and International Monetary Fund are regarded as part of the United Nations system, their funding is administered independently of this system. Conversely, although the International Atomic Energy Agency is not formally classified as a UN specialized agency, its funding is raised through the United Nations system.

48. UN General Assembly, *Budgetary and financial situation of organizations of the United Nations system*, G.A. Prov. Agenda Item 113, UN GAOR, 59th Sess., UN Doc. A/C.59/315 (2004), Table 1, indicates that the regular budget for the UN system in 2005 was $3.7 billion ($1.4 billion for the core UN departments, offices and other units) and $2.3 billion for 12 other specialized agencies and the International Atomic Energy Agency). Table 7 of this document indicates that the voluntary budget for the UN system in 2003 (the latest year for which complete figures were available) was about $10 billion. For peacekeeping, United Nations, *United Nations Peacekeeping* http://www.un.org/Depts/dpko/dpko/index.asp>, says that "[t]he approved DPKO [Department of Peacekeeping Operations] budget for the period from July 1, 2005 to June 30, 2006 is approximately $5 billion."

49. Leon Gordenker, *The UN Secretary-General and Secretariat* (Abingdon, U.K.: 2005), 31. For the General Assembly draft resolution proposal for the 2006–2007 year, see UN General Assembly, *Proposed Programme Budget for the Biennium 2006–2007*, G.A. Draft Res., Agenda Item 60(b), UN GAOR, 60th Sess., 5th Committee, UN Doc. A/C.5/60/L.26 (2006).

50. Gordenker, *ibid.*

51. In 2006, the total assessment of the United States, Japan and Germany amounted to 50.13% of the U.N. regular budget: see Congressional Research Service, Foreign Affairs, Defense, and Trade Division, "United Nations System Funding: Congressional Issues", *CRS Issue Brief for Congress* (updated March 30, 2006), online: U.S. Department of State <http://fpc.state.gov/documents/organization/64942.pdf>; see also United Nations, Department of Management, "Programme Planning, Budget and Accounts" <http://www.un.org/en/hq/dm/budget.shtml>.

52. *Ibid.* and Government of the United States, Congressional Research Services, Foreign Affairs, Defense, and Trade Division, *CRS Issue Brief: United Nations System Funding: Congressional Issues*, updated March 26, 2006, <www.betterworldfund.org/pdf/crsun.pd>. Under the terms of the 2000 agreement, the proportion of U.S. peacekeeping contributions would fall over a number of years. By 2006, the proportion had fallen to 26.5%: *CRS Issue Brief*.

    In 1985–1988, American arrears in UN dues payments and threats to withhold future contributions brought the United States close to insolvency. The crisis was averted when the United Nations agreed to spending and staff cuts and to greater informal U.S. input into the approval of UN budgets: Jeffrey Laurenti in "Financing the United Nations", *The United Nations*, supra note 1 at 282–83.

53. Most of these reforms are intended to drastically cut UN — and therefore U.S. — costs.

54. See Global Policy Forum, *UN Financial Crisis* <http://www.globalpolicy.org/finance/index.htm>; UN General Assembly, *Budgetary and financial situation of organizations of the United Nations system*, G.A. Prov. Agenda Item 113, UN GAOR, 59th Sess., UN Doc. A/C.59/315 (2004), Table 5 (figures for 2002 and 2003).

55. As suggested by Jeffrey Laurenti in "Financing the United Nations", *The United Nations*, supra note 1 at 275, "the major dividing line [on the issue of increased or decreased UN spending] at the start of the twenty-first century, as it had been for three decades, is between the industrialized countries and the developing countries."

56. See, for example, Global Policy Forum, *UN Reform Chronology: 1992 — Present* <http://www.globalpolicy.org/reform/intro/chronology.htm>; John R. Crook, ed., "U.S. Views on UN Reform, Security Council Expansion" (2005) 99 A.J. I.L. 906.

57. See John R. Crook, ed., "U.S. Views on UN Reform, Security Council Expansion" (2005) 99 A.J. I.L. 906.

58. See <http://www.unsystem.org/>.

59. In the course of this program, a number of UN officials apparently permitted the Iraq government to spend money on programs other than food in exchange for oil vouchers to benefit the officials themselves. See the very critical account in Joshua Muravchek, *The Future of the United Nations* (New York: The AEI Press, 2005) at 49–56.

60. *Ibid.* at 59.

61. UN General Assembly, *Draft resolution referred to the High-level Plenary Meeting of the General Assembly by the General Assembly at its fifty-ninth session 2005 World Summit Outcome* (G.A. Draft Res., Prov. Agenda Items 48 and 121, UN GAOR, 60th Sess., UN Doc. A/60/L.1 (2005).

62. See Global Policy Forum, *UN Reform Chronology: 1992 — Present* (for year 2005) <http://www.globalpolicy.org/reform/intro/chronology.htm>.

63. The major recent reforms — and attempted reforms — are summarized in *UN Reform Chronology: 1992 — Present, ibid.*

64. This is a loose grouping often represented by the "Group of 77", a group of 77 developing countries who formed a block in 1964 to voice the interests of developing countries. The group, which currently has 132 members, focuses mainly on questions of economic development and aid: Group of Seventy-seven at the United Nations website: <http://www.g77.org/main/main.htm>. Another group that represents developing countries is the 112-member Non-Aligned Movement, which tends to stress political issues such as disarmament as well as economic development. See further, "Groups and Blocs", in Smith, *Politics and Process at the United Nations*, supra note 1, Ch. 3.

65. See, for example, *Commentary on "Renewing the United Nations: A Programme for Reform": A policy brief prepared by the South Centre at the request of the Group of 77 (circa 1997)* <http://www.g77.org/Docs/policy%20brief.htm>; Ministers of Foreign Affairs of the Group of 77, *Ministerial Statement*, New York (22 September 2005), <http://www.g77.org/main/docs.htm>.

66. "Wealthy" and "industrialized" are of course relative terms. Many of the richest countries are part of the 30-member Organization for Economic Co-operation and Development (OECD website: <http://www.oecd.org/home/0,2605,en_2649_201185_1_1_1_1,00.html>). The focus of the OECD is on liberalizing trade and increasing economic competitiveness and productivity.

67. For example, the World Trade Organization, the OECD, the World Bank Group, and the International Monetary Fund. See, for example, Nigel D. White, *The United Nations System: Toward International Justice* (Boulder, Colorado: Lynne Rienner, 2002) Ch. 11. As with poorer and developing nations, wealthier states take differing approaches to UN reform, so the tendencies noted here may not be present in all cases, or at all times.

68. Notable exceptions are U.S. support for a new human rights body and peacebuilding commission, a "democracy fund", and combatting terrorism. In regard to the latter, though, the United States affirms the right to preemptive action: e.g., U.S. National Security Strategy of 2002, elaborated in <http://www.whitehouse.gov/news/releases/2002/10/20021001-6.html>.

69. For examples, see Paul Rogers, "If it's good for America, it's good for the world", The Observer World Today Essay", *The Observer* (27 January 2002); Clyde Prestowitz, *Rogue Nation: American Unilateralism and the Failure of Good Intentions* (New York: Basic Books, 2003).

70. For example, high-speed modern transportation can carry SARS and avian flu viruses from one country to another, in a matter of months or, even, days. Aids has spread to much of Africa and has reached most corners of the world. Conflicts, poverty, and natural disasters in one country generate refugee pressure elsewhere in the world. Close trade ties can be a source of weakness as well as strength. Coca crops in Colombia and poppy fields in Afghanistan feed consumer addicts in rich industrial states. Drought in low-income food producing countries can cause starvation at home and high prices abroad. Environmental degradation in one region can deprive other regions of clean air or water, ozone layer protection, or safe marine and migratory food sources. Instant electronic communications can spread details of weapon-making as well as knowledge of a more benign character.

(c) *Charter of the United Nations*†

WE THE PEOPLE OF THE UNITED NATIONS DETERMINE

to save succeeding generations from the scourge of war, which twice in our lifetime has brought untold sorrow to mankind, and

to reaffirm faith in fundamental human rights, in the dignity and worth of the human person, in the equal rights of men and women and of nations large and small, and

to establish conditions under which justice and respect for the obligations arising from treaties and other sources of international law can be maintained, and to promote social progress and better standards of life in larger freedom,

AND FOR THESE ENDS

to practice tolerance and live together in peace with one another as good neighbors, and

to unite our strength to maintain international peace and security, and

to ensure, by the acceptance of principles and the institution of methods, that armed force shall not be used, save in the common interest, and

to employ international machinery for the promotion of the economic and social advancement of all peoples,

HAVE RESOLVED TO COMBINE OUR EFFORTS TO ACCOMPLISH THESE AIMS

Accordingly, our respective Governments, through representatives assembled in the City of San Francisco, who have exhibited their full powers found to be in good and due form, have agreed to the present Charter of the United Nations and do hereby establish an international organization to be known as the United Nations.

PURPOSES AND PRINCIPLES

Article 1

The Purposes of the United Nations are:

1. To maintain international peace and security, and to that end: to take effective collective measures for the prevention and removal of threats to the peace, and for the suppression of acts of aggression or other breaches of the peace, and to bring about by peaceful means, and in conformity with the principles of justice and international law, adjustment or settlement of international disputes or situations which might lead to a breach of the peace;

2. To develop friendly relations among nations based on respect for the principle of equal rights and self-determination of peoples, and to take other appropriate measures to strengthen universal peace;

† From International Court of Justice Website: Basic Documents, <www.icj-cij.org/documents/index.php?p1=4&p2=1&p3=0>.

3. To achieve international co-operation in solving international problems of an economic, social, cultural, or humanitarian character, and in promoting and encouraging respect for human rights and for fundamental freedoms for all without distinction as to race, sex, language, or religion; and

4. To be a center for harmonizing the actions of nations in the attainment of these common ends.

Article 2

The Organization and its Members, in pursuit of the Purposes stated in Article 1, shall act in accordance with the following Principles:

1. The Organization is based on the principle of the sovereign equality of all its Members.

2. All Members, in order to ensure to all of them the rights and benefits resulting from membership, shall fulfil in good faith the obligations assumed by them in accordance with the present Charter.

3. All Members shall settle their international disputes by peaceful means in such a manner that international peace and security, and justice, are not endangered.

4. All Members shall refrain in their international relations from the threat or use of force against the territorial integrity or political independence of any State, or in any other manner inconsistent with the Purposes of the United Nations.

5. All Members shall give the United Nations every assistance in any action it takes in accordance with the present Charter, and shall refrain from giving assistance to any State against which the United Nations is taking preventive or enforcement action.

6. The Organization shall ensure that States which are not Members of the United Nations act in accordance with these Principles so far as may be necessary for the maintenance of international peace and security.

7. Nothing contained in the present Charter shall authorize the United Nations to intervene in matters which are essentially within the domestic jurisdiction of any state or shall require the Members to submit such matters to settlement under the present Charter; but this principle shall not prejudice the application of enforcement measures under Chapter VII.

. . . .

THE GENERAL ASSEMBLY

. . . .

Article 13

1. The General Assembly shall initiate studies and make recommendations for the purpose of:

(a) promoting international co-operation in the political field and encouraging the progressive development of international law and its codification;

(b) promoting international co-operation in the economic, social, cultural, educational, and health fields, and assisting in the realization of human rights and fundamental freedoms for all without distinction as to race, sex, language, or religion.

. . . .

ACTION WITH RESPECT TO THREATS TO THE PEACE, BREACHES OF THE PEACE, AND ACTS OF AGGRESSION

Article 39

The Security Council shall determine the existence of any threat to the peace, breach of the peace, or act of aggression and shall make recommendations, or decide what measures shall be taken in accordance with Articles 41 and 42, to maintain or restore international peace and security.

Article 40

In order to prevent an aggravation of the situation, the Security Council may, before making the recommendations or deciding upon the measures provided for in Article 39, call upon the parties concerned to comply with such provisional measures as it deems necessary or desirable. Such provisional measures shall be without prejudice to the rights, claims, or position of the parties concerned. The Security Council shall duly take account of failure to comply with such provisional measures.

Article 41

The Security Council may decide what measures not involving the use of armed force are to be employed to give effect to its decisions, and it may call upon the Members of the United Nations to apply such measures. These may include complete or partial interruption of economic relations and of rail, sea, air, postal, telegraphic, radio, and other means of communication, and the severance of diplomatic relations.

Article 42

Should the Security Council consider that measures provided for in Article 41 would be inadequate or have proved to be inadequate, it may take such action by air, sea, or land forces as may be necessary to maintain or restore international peace and security. Such action may include demonstrations, blockade, and other operations by air, sea, or land forces of Members of the United Nations.

Article 43

1. All Members of the United Nations, in order to contribute to the maintenance of international peace and security, undertake to make available to the Security Council, on its call and in accordance with a special agreement or agreements, armed forces, assistance, and facilities, including rights of passage, necessary for the purpose of maintaining international peace and security.

2. Such agreement or agreements shall govern the numbers and types of forces, their degree of readiness and general location, and the nature of the facilities and assistance to be provided.

3. The agreement or agreements shall be negotiated as soon as possible on the initiative of the Security Council. They shall be concluded between the Security Council and Members or between the Security Council and groups of Members and shall be subject to ratification by the signatory States in accordance with their respective constitutional processes.

Article 44

When the Security Council has decided to use force it shall, before calling upon a Member not represented on it to provide armed forces in fulfilment of the obligations assumed under Article 43, invite that Member, if the Member so desires, to participate in the decisions of the Security Council concerning the employment of contingents of that Member's armed forces.

Article 45

In order to enable the United Nations to take urgent military measures, Members shall hold immediately available national air-force contingents for combined international enforcement action. The strength and degree of readiness of these contingents and plans for their combined action shall be determined, within the limits laid down in the special agreement or agreements referred to in Article 43, by the Security Council with the assistance of the Military Staff Committee.

Article 46

Plans for the application of armed force shall be made by the Security Council with the assistance of the Military Staff Committee.

Article 47

1. There shall be established a Military Staff Committee to advise and assist the Security Council on all questions relating to the Security Council's military requirements for the maintenance of international peace and security, the employment and command of forces placed at its disposal, the regulation of armaments, and possible disarmament.

2. The Military Staff Committee shall consist of the Chiefs of Staff permanent members of the Security Council or their representatives. Any Member of the United Nations not permanently represented on the Committee shall be invited by the Committee to be associated with it when the efficient discharge of the Committee's responsibilities requires the participation of that Member in its work.

3. The Military Staff Committee shall be responsible under the Security Council for the strategic direction of any armed forces placed at the disposal of the Security Council. Questions relating to the command of such forces shall be worked out subsequently.

4. The Military Staff Committee, with the authorization of the Security Council and after consultation with appropriate regional agencies, may establish regional sub-committees.

Article 48

1. The action required to carry out the decisions of the Security Council for the maintenance of international peace and security shall be taken by all the Members of the United Nations or by some of them, as the Security Council may determine.

2. Such decisions shall be carried out by Members of the United Nations directly and through their action in the appropriate international agencies of which they are members.

Article 49

The Members of the United Nations shall join in affording mutual assistance in carrying out the measures decided upon by the Security Council.

Article 50

If preventive or enforcement measures against any state are taken by the Security Council, any other state, whether a Member of the United Nations or not, which finds itself confronted with special economic problems arising from the carrying out of those measures shall have the right to consult the Security Council with regard to a solution of those problems.

Article 51

Nothing in the present Charter shall impair the inherent right of individual or collective self-defense if an armed attack occurs against a Member of the United Nations, until the Security Council has taken measures necessary to maintain international peace and security. Measures taken by Members in the exercise of this right of self-defense shall be immediately reported to the Security Council and shall not in any way affect the authority and responsibility of the Security Council under the present Charter to take at any time such action as it deems necessary in order to maintain or restore international peace and security.

. . . .

Article 55

With a view to the creation of conditions of stability and well-being which are necessary for peaceful and friendly relations among nations based on respect for the principle of equal rights and self-determination of peoples, the United Nations shall promote.... [Such goals as better standards of living; solutions to social, health, and related problems; cultural and educational co-operation; and universal respect for human rights.]

. . . .

PACIFIC SETTLEMENT OF DISPUTES

Article 33

1. The parties to any dispute, the continuance of which is likely to endanger the maintenance of international peace and security, shall, first of all, seek a solution by negotiation, enquiry, mediation, conciliation, arbitration, judicial settlement, resort to regional agencies or arrangements, or other peaceful means of their own choice.

2. The Security Council shall, when it deems necessary, call upon the parties to settle their dispute by such means.

. . . .

THE INTERNATIONAL COURT OF JUSTICE

Article 92

The International Court of Justice shall be the principal judicial organ of the United Nations. It shall function in accordance with the annexed Statute, which is based upon the Statute of the Permanent Court of International Justice and forms an integral part of the present Charter.

Article 93

1. All members of the United Nations are *ipso facto* parties to the Statute of the International Court of Justice.

2. A state which is not a Member of the United Nations may become a party to the Statute of the International Court of Justice on conditions to be determined in each case by the General Assembly upon the recommendation of the Security Council.

Article 94

1. Each Member of the United Nations undertakes to comply with the decision of the International Court of Justice in any case to which it is a party.

2. If any party to a case fails to perform the obligations incumbent upon it under a judgment rendered by the Court, the order party may have recourse to the Security Council, which may, if it deems necessary, make recommendations or decide upon measures to be taken to give effect to the judgment.

Article 95

Nothing in the present Charter shall prevent Members of the United Nations from entrusting the solution of their difference to other tribunals by virtue of agreements already in existence or which may be concluded in the future.

Article 96

1. The General Assembly or the Security Council may request the International Court of Justice to give an advisory opinion on any legal question.

2. Other organs of the United Nations and specialized agencies, which may at any time be so authorized by the General Assembly, may also request advisory opinions of the Court on legal questions arising within the scope of their activities.

(d) *Statute of the International Court of Justice*†

Article 1

The International Court of Justice established by the Charter of the United Nations as the principal judicial organ of the United Nations shall be constituted and shall function in accordance with the provisions of the present Statute.

. . . .

Article 3

1. The Court shall consist of fifteen members, no two of whom may be nationals of the same state.

. . . .

Article 36

1. The jurisdiction of the Court comprises all cases which the parties refer to it and all matters specially provided for in the Charter of the United Nations or in treaties and conventions in force.

2. The States parties to the present Statute may at any time declare that they recognize as compulsory *ipso facto* and without special agreement, in relation to any other state accepting the same obligation, the jurisdiction of the Court in all legal disputes concerning:

(a) the interpretation of a treaty;
(b) any question of international law;
(c) the existence of any fact which, if established, would constitute a breach of an international obligation;

(d) the nature or extent of reparation to be made of the breach of an international obligation.

3. The declarations referred to above may be made unconditionally or on condition of reciprocity on the part of several or certain States, or for a certain time.

4. Such declarations shall be deposited with the Secretary-General of the United Nations, who shall transmit copies thereof to the parties to the Statute and to the Registrar of the Court.

5. Declarations made under Article 36 of the Statute of the Permanent Court of International Justice and which are still in force shall be deemed, as between the parties to the present Statute, to be acceptances of the compulsory jurisdiction of the International Court of Justice for the period which they still have to run and in accordance with their terms.

6. In the event of a dispute as to whether the Court has jurisdiction, the matter shall be settled by the decision of the Court.

. . . .

Article 38

1. The Court, whose function is to decide in accordance with international law such disputes as are submitted to it, shall apply:

(a) international conventions, whether general or particular, establishing rules expressly recognized by the contesting states;

---

† From International Court of Justice Website: Basic Documents, <www.icj-cij.org/documents/index.php?p1=4&p2=2&p3=0>.

(b) international custom, as evidence of a general practice accepted as law;

(c) the general principles of law recognized by civilized nations;

(d) subject to the provisions of Article 59, judicial decisions and the teachings of the most highly qualified publicists of the various nations, as subsidiary means for the determination of rules of law.

. . . .

Article 59

The decision of the Court has no binding force except between the parties and in respect of that particular case.

(e) *Canada (A.G.)* v. *Ontario (A.G.)*†

NOTE

Treaties — formal agreements between two or more sovereign states — are an important source of international law obligations. However, a treaty that is validly concluded between Canada and other signatory states does not automatically bind individual citizens as a part of the municipal law of this country. Treaties that would alter Canadian law, affect individuals' rights, or extend existing governmental powers must be implemented in legislation. Hence the legislature as well as the executive must normally participate in the Canadian treaty-making process.

The *Constitution Act, 1867* did not specifically allocate an independent treaty-making power to either the federal or provincial levels of government. The federal government was expressly empowered (s. 132) to make treaties that Canada entered into as a member of the British Empire, but the Constitution said nothing of *non*-British Empire treaties. If the federal government's treaty-making power extended to these, could it use it to legislate in relation to subjects otherwise within provincial jurisdiction? On the other hand, if treaty-making were split between Parliament and the provincial legislatures, would Canada as a nation be able to discharge effectively its international responsibilities?

These were some of the questions in the background to the *Labour Conventions* case. In 1935, Parliament enacted three labour law statutes to ensure minimum standards for working conditions and minimum wages. These were intended to implement labour conventions drafted by the International Labour Organization. Although the ILO was itself a product of the Treaty of Versailles (a British Empire Treaty), that treaty had not required Canada to sign the conventions.

When the Judicial Committee considered the validity of these statutes, they said that since Canada had signed the conventions on its own, and not in compliance with any requirement in the Treaty of Versailles, the statutes were not enacted pursuant to a British Empire Treaty. Thus there was no specific power in the *Constitution Act, 1867* to govern the case.

In the 1932 *Radio* reference, [1932] A.C. 304, the Judicial Committee had suggested that the power to make treaties independently of the British Empire might itself constitute "new" subject matter not envisaged in 1867, and thus falling under the residual sense of Peace, Order, and good Government. Given the strict approach to the division of powers that had characterized Judicial Committee decisions since the beginning of the century, this was a radical proposition. The Judicial Committee rejected it here, using the "watertight compartments" analogy contained at the end of the extract.

When reading the extract below, consider (i) the different legal effects of treaties in international and Canadian municipal law; (ii) the respective roles of the executive and legislative branches in treaty-making; and (iii) the respective treaty-making roles of Parliament and the legislatures. Would the result in this reference be affirmed by

---

† *Canada (Attorney General)* v. *Ontario (Attorney General)*: *Reference re Weekly Rest in Industrial Undertakings Act, Minimum Wages Act and Limitation of Hours of Work Act*, [1937] 1 D.L.R. 673 (J.C.P.C.), aff'g. [1936] 3 D.L.R. 673 (S.C.C.). [Commentary note by David W. Elliott.]

the Supreme Court of Canada today, in light of cases such as *R.* v. *Crown Zellerbach Canada* (1988), 49 D.L.R. (4th) 161 (S.C.C.)? Is the effect of the reference affected by decisions such as *Baker* v. *Canada (Minister of Citizenship and Immigration)*, [1999] 2 S.C.R. 817, and *Suresh* v. *Canada (Minister of Citizenship and Immigration)*, [2002] S.C.J. No. 3 (S.C.C.)?

EXTRACT

[LORD ATKIN for the Judicial Committee (comprising Lord Atkin, Lord Thankerton, Lord MacMillan, Lord Wright M.R., and Sir Sidney Rowlatt):]

... It will be essential to keep in mind the distinction between the formation and the performance, of the obligations constituted by a treaty, using that word as comprising any agreement between two or more sovereign States. Within the British Empire there is a well-established rule that the making of a treaty is an executive act, while the performance of its obligations, if they entail alteration of the existing domestic law, requires legislative action. Unlike some other countries, the stipulations of a treaty duly ratified do not within the Empire, by virtue of the treaty alone, have the force of law. If the national executive, the government of the day, decided to incur the obligations of a treaty, which involved alteration of law, they have to run the risk of obtaining the assent of Parliament, an expression of approval. But it has never been suggested, and it is not the law, that such an expression of approval operates as law, or that in law it precludes the assenting Parliament, or any subsequent Parliament, from refusing to give its sanction to any legislative proposals that may subsequently be brought before it. Parliament, no doubt, as the Chief Justice points out, has a constitutional control over the executive; but it cannot be disputed that the creation of the obligations undertaken in treaties and the assent to their form and quality are the function of the executive alone. Once they are created, while they bind the State against the other contracting parties, Parliament may refuse to perform them and so leave the State in default. In a unitary State, whose Legislature possesses unlimited powers, the problem is simple. Parliament will either fulfil or not treaty obligations imposed upon the State by its executive. The nature of the obligations does not affect the complete authority of the Legislature to make them law if it so chooses. But in a State where the Legislature does not possess absolute authority, in a federal State where legislative authority is limited by a constitutional document, or is divided up between different Legislatures in accordance with the classes of subject-matter submitted for legislation, the problem is complex. The obligations imposed by treaty may have to be performed, if at all, by several Legislatures; and the executive have the task of obtaining the legislative assent not of the one Parliament to whom they stand, to whom they may be responsible, but possibly of several Parliaments to whom they stand in no direct relation. The question is not how is the obligation formed, that is the function of the executive; but how is the obligation to be performed, and that depends upon the authority of the competent Legislature or Legislatures....

. . . .

For the purposes of ss. 91 and 92, i.e., the distribution of legislative powers between the Dominion and the Provinces, there is no such thing as treaty legislation as such. The distribution is based on classes of subjects; and as a treaty deals with a particular class of subjects so will the legislative power of performing it be ascertained. No one can doubt that this distribution is one of the most essential conditions, in the inter-provincial compact to which the British North America Act gives effect. If the position of Lower Canada, now Quebec, alone were considered, the existence of her separate jurisprudence as to both property and civil rights might be said to depend upon loyal adherence to her constitutional right to the exclusive competence of her own Legislature in these matters. Nor is it of less importance for the other Provinces, though their law may be based on English jurisprudence, to preserve their own right to legislate for themselves in respect of local conditions which may vary by as great a distance as separates the Atlantic from the Pacific. It would be remarkable that while the Dominion could not initiate legislation, however desirable, which affected civil rights in the Provinces, yet its Government [is] not responsible to the Provinces nor controlled by Provincial Parliaments need only agree with a foreign country to enact such legislation, and its Parliament would be forthwith clothed with authority to affect Provincial rights to the full extent of such agreement. Such a result would appear to undermine the constitutional safeguards of Provincial constitutional autonomy.

It follows from what has been said that no further legislative competence is obtained by the Dominion from its accession to international status, and the consequent increase in the scope of its executive functions. It is true, as pointed out in the judgment of the Chief Justice, that as the executive is now clothed with the powers of making treaties, so the Parliament of Canada, to which the executive is responsible, has imposed upon it responsibilities in connection with such treaties, for if it were to disapprove of them, they would either not be made or the Ministers would meet their constitutional fate. But this is true of all executive functions in their relation to Parliament. There is no existing constitutional ground for stretching the competence of the Dominion Parliament, so that it becomes enlarged to keep pace with enlarged functions of the Dominion executive. If the new functions affect the classes of subjects enumerated in s. 92, legislation to support the new functions is in the competence of the Provincial Legislatures only. If they do not, the competence of the Dominion Legislature is declared by s. 91 and existed *ab origine*. In other words, the Dominion cannot, merely by making promises to foreign countries, clothe itself with legislative authority inconsistent with the constitution which gave it birth.

But the validity of the legislation under the general words of s. 91 was sought to be established not in relation to the treaty-making power alone, but also as being concerned with matters of such general importance as to have attained "such dimensions as to affect the body politic," and to have "ceased to be merely local or provincial," and to have "become matter of national concern." It is interesting to notice how often the words used by Lord Watson in *Attorney-General for Ontario* v. *Attorney-General for the Dominion* have unsuccessfully been used in attempts to support encroachments on the Provincial legislative powers given by s. 92. They laid down no principle of constitutional law, and were cautious words intended to safeguard possible eventualities which no one at the time had any interest or desire to define. The law of Canada on this branch of con-

stitutional law has been stated with such force and clarity by the Chief Justice in his judgment in the reference concerning the Natural Products Marketing Act dealing with the six Acts there referred to, that their Lordships abstain from stating it afresh. The Chief Justice, naturally from his point of view, excepted legislation to fulfil treaties. On this, their Lordships have expressed their opinion. But subject to this, they agree with and adopt what was there said. They consider that the law is finally settled by the current of cases cited by the Chief Justice on the principles declared by him. It is only necessary to call attention to the phrases in the various cases, "abnormal circumstances" "exceptional conditions," "standard of necessity" (*Board of Commerce* case), "some extraordinary peril to the national life of Canada," "highly exceptional," "epidemic of pestilence" (*Snider's* case), to show how far the present case is from the conditions which may override the normal distribution of powers in ss. 91 and 92. The few pages of the Chief Justice's judgment will, it is to be hoped, form the locus classicus of the law on this point, and preclude further disputes.

It must not be thought that the result of this decision is that Canada is incompetent to legislate in performance of treaty obligations. In totality of legislative powers, Dominion and Provincial together, she is fully equipped. But the legislative powers remain distributed, and if in the exercise of her new functions derived from her new international status Canada incurs obligations they must, so far as legislation be concerned, when they deal with Provincial classes of subjects, be dealt with by the totality of powers, in other words by co-operation between the Dominion and the Provinces. While the ship of state now sails on larger ventures and into foreign waters, she still retains the watertight compartments which are an essential part of her original structure.

(f) Globalization, Governance, and the State[†]

David W. Elliott

INTRODUCTION

Invisible webs are squeezing the earth. A fuel order travels from London to Riyadh . . . in seconds. A manufacturer in Seoul imports metal parts from four continents, then sells them back as cars. A panel ruling in Geneva transforms trade patterns in Indonesia. Debt problems in Argentina chill stock

† Updated by Nick E. Milanovic.

markets in New York. Arctic schoolchildren discuss hamburgers with e-pals in Australia. Asian child workers make designer outfits for Mediterranean windsurfers. Terrorists in desert headquarters use jetliners to devastate cities. World newsgroups debate topics from weight loss to Habermas. Non-governmental groups accuse multinationals of environmental degradation. Protesters clash with police at international trade meetings. This is all happening at a faster and faster pace. It is driven by extraordinary developments in communications technology. Welcome to the world of INGOs, the Internet, the WTO, and McDonald's. Welcome to globalization.

DEFINITIONS AND DIMENSIONS

In its broadest sense, globalization is the increasing interconnection and integration of world economies and populations.[1] This phenomenon intensified during the last two decades of the 20th century, and its heightened pace continues. Although globalization has many dimensions,[2] four are especially significant: economic globalization, communications globalization, cultural globalization, and institutional globalization.

Economic globalization is marked by the rise of multinational corporations and a corresponding philosophy in favour of enhancing market competition and reducing barriers to international trade.[3] This phenomenon has been spurred by the emergence of a dominate state superpower, the United States, which has a strong pro-market orientation. A second dimension, communications globalization, involves the rapid world-wide exchange of information, facilitated by revolutionary changes in Internet and other communications technology.[4] A third dimension is cultural globalization. Arguably, its diverse features include American-influenced entertainment and consumer preferences,[5] a constitutional "rights" revolution,[6] world-wide non-governmental interest groups,[7] and a widespread belief in pluralism of choice and social group affiliation.[8]

A fourth dimension is political globalization. This phenomenon includes the development of new regional or world organizations in response to globalization. It also encompasses the evolving relationship between globalization and existing international organizations and actors. These agents of "globalization governance" are one aspect of general international governance. The latter phenomenon is the sum of institutions, processes, and arrangements that contribute to the regulation or organization of the international community.[9] Indeed, some of the key institutions of general international governance — such as the United Nations and its agencies — also have a significant role to play in governance responses to globalization. However, globalization has other governance tools as well.

All these dimensions are closely interrelated.[10] For example, communications, cultural, and political globalization shape economic globalization and *vice versa*. Globalization can also be affected by deviant forms, such as global crime and terrorism.[11]

The discussion here focuses on economic and political globalization. We will look at some general challenges and problems, at some globalization "governance" structures, and at implications of globalization for the nation-state and for governance in general.

SOME GLOBALIZATION CHALLENGES

Much of the debate about globalization centres on its economic dimension. Supporters of economic globalization[12] argue that wider and freer world trade benefits consumers across the world. Economies of scale, pressures from increased competition, and the potential for greater resource-based specialization in individual regions will result in more efficient production of goods and services. Supporters may also argue that increased economic interdependence can reduce the likelihood of military conflict. For their part, critics of economic globalization[13] argue that globalization widens the gap between rich and poor people and nations, contributes to global environmental degradation, human and labour rights abuses, and political tensions, and undermines the capacity of nation-states to carry out public interest and public welfare obligations to their citizens. Critics say the processes of globalization are dominated by large corporations, and are secretive and undemocratic.

What is your view of these opposing arguments? Will it be possible to democratize and control globalization, keeping and distributing the benefits while containing the burdens? Is this a problem of governance? Can the breakthroughs in communications globalization be applied to harness economic globalization? Is there a grain of truth in the arguments of both the supporters and the critics, one that varies with the context at hand? Certainly there are many different forms of globalization, even in its economic aspect, and not all people, nations, and other organizations are as dramatically affected as others. What is indisputable is that the phenomenon is here and shows no signs of losing momentum.

GLOBALIZATION GOVERNANCE INSTITUTIONS[14]

United Nations

The United Nations[15] is the leading institution for general global governance. It also plays a role in the governance of globalization. Created in 1945 to maintain and promote world peace, human rights, and humanitarian goals, the UN has many organs and agencies devoted to trade and interconnection issues. These include the Economic and Social Council, the United Nations Conference on Trade and Development, and the United Nations Commission on International Trade Law. During the 1990s, the UN convened several world conferences on environmental and other issues affected by globalization.[16] For several decades, the International Labour Organization has been concerned with the social responsibilities of liberalized global business. It has issued a code to guide labour activities of multinational enterprises.[17] The UN World Health Organization is trying to cope with global transmission of infectious diseases, an old problem aggravated by modern high-speed, long-distance movement of people. The UN Office for Drug Control and Crime is dealing with a greatly expanded world trade in drugs and human migrants, and with the globalization of terrorism and other crime.[18] The United Nations Environmental Program is active in persuading states and other international organizations to put a high priority on environmental considerations.[19] Other UN organizations involved in globalization governance include the International Telecommunication Union, an international organization for the coordination of public and private sector global telecommunication networks and services;[20] the Universal Postal Union, based in Berne;[21] the International Civil Aviation Organization, based in Montreal;[22] and the World Intellectual Property Organization, based in Geneva.[23]

Despite its vital presence, the UN is not the only governance forum for globalization issues. In some cases, as with the World Bank and the International Monetary Fund, other existing organizations have taken on this role.[24] In other cases, as

with the World Trade Organization, new institutions have been created. They may have been considered more suited to the needs of the multinational trading corporations and their main host countries.[25] As a result, some UN agencies have been left in the position of addressing the humanitarian and environmental consequences attributed to globalization, rather than directing its application in the first place.[26]

World Bank Group

The World Bank Group[27] consists of five organizations whose main purpose is to provide development loans to poorer countries. The Group, which was created in 1944, has more than 180 shareholder-member countries and a staff of about 9,300 employees. The Bank's headquarters are in Washington, D.C. By tradition, the Bank's president is a citizen of the United States. Votes at the World Bank are in proportion to a state's share of world trade. This gives dominant voting power to the United States (with about 28% of world trade) and to the G7 group of countries that includes the United States (with about half of world trade). Although there has been some recent attention to environmental and social considerations, the World Bank's loan conditions generally require national fiscal restraint and dismantling of state trade barriers. Generally speaking, then, World Bank governance is dominated by the richest nations, is directed at developing nations, and is focused mainly on government restraint and trade liberalization.

International Monetary Fund

The International Monetary Fund is the main international body for managing the world's monetary system. Typically, it lends money to countries experiencing balance of payments crises. The IMF has a voluntary membership comprising most of the world's states, a 24-member executive board, and a Washington D.C.-based secretariat of about 2,700 people. As at the World Bank, voting is weighted according to a country's share of world trade. This gives a predominant position to the G7 nations, and to the United States in particular.[28] Like the World Bank, the IMF generally imposes financial restraint and trade liberalism conditions in return for its assistance. Recipients of IMF aid are generally members of the developing world.

World Trade Organization

One result of globalization is that states are focusing more and more on international trade issues, and less on more traditional international concerns. The leading international trade governance organization today is the World Trade Organization. The WTO was created in 1995 to administer the 1994 General Agreement on Tariffs and Trade (GATT) and over a dozen other world trade accords.[29] The WTO has a General Council of representatives of more than 160 nations, accounting for most of the world's trade, a ministerial conference of representatives of members, and a Geneva-based Secretariat of about 640 people.[30]

Membership in the WTO is voluntary, but the alternative is exclusion from the world's largest trading regime. Although every member country of the WTO has an equal vote,[31] WTO trade agreements are generally negotiated by the leading supplier of a product and the leading purchaser. They are then applied — if approved — to all members.[32] Because the United States and the European Union account for a major share of world trade, they are directly involved in the negotiation of most WTO agreements.

A key condition of belonging to the WTO is that members are subject to its dispute resolution process. The WTO's ongoing governing body, the General Assembly, meets as a Dispute Settlement Body to address trade disputes between members. The DSB appoints a panel to investigate an individual dispute, and the panel then makes a report that may or may not be appealed to the WTO's Appellate Body. Proceedings of DSB panels and the Appellate Body are closed to the public.[33] The losing party must either implement the recommendations of the panel or Appellate Body, or negotiate compensation. Otherwise, the losing party faces retaliatory measures authorized by the DSB. Because of the reciprocal nature of most world trade, the latter prospect is usually sufficient to encourage compliance, especially by smaller states. Conversely, larger economic powers may feel less pressure to comply.

Sectoral Governance Institutions

Numerous international organizations set standards for specific aspects of global economic activity. These bodies include the Bank for International Settlements, an international financial organization comprising the central banks or monetary authorities of 50 countries, which formulates financial supervision standards and provides banking services for its member organizations;[34] the International Centre for Settlement of Investment Disputes, a body that provides facilities for conciliation and arbitration of international investment disputes between member states or nationals;[35] the Permanent Court of Arbitration, created in 1899 for the peaceful arbitration of inter-state disputes, and located in the same building as the International Court of Justice in the Hague;[36] the International Organization of Securities Commissions, a "non-governmental" association of national securities commissions, based in Madrid;[37] Intelsat Ltd., an international corporation owned by satellite telecommunications providers;[38] and the Internet Corporation for Assigned Names and Numbers.[39] Many of these are essentially self-governing regulatory bodies with extensive private sector participation.[40]

Regional and Related Cooperative Institutions

Globalization is also subject to governance structures and processes at the regional level. Two of the most important of these are the European Union[41] and its associated institutions, and the North American Free Trade Agreement. The main decision-making organ of the EU is the Council of the Economic Union, which is served by an executive called the European Commission, the European Court of Justice, a court of auditors, and a central bank. Unlike most international associations, the European Union has its own democratically elected representative body, the 750-plus-member European Parliament.[42]

The European Union is a customs and monetary union with the goal of becoming — in some degree — a political union. Its rules already have supranational authority in many trade areas. In the *Factortame* case, for example, the British House of Lords held that parts of a British shipping act were invalid because they were contrary to European Community law.[43]

The North American Free Trade Agreement creates a free trade area between Canada, the United States, and Mexico.[44] NAFTA has a supervisory commission of political representatives from the member countries, a small secretariat,[45] and *ad hoc* dispute resolution panels. The panels operate when issues cannot be resolved by consensus. They are the key governance institutions of NAFTA. Once the disputing states have made representations before a panel, it issues a report. Panel reports are not enforceable in domestic law; but if a member state refuses to comply, the other party affected is authorized to withdraw benefits under the Agreement. Negotiations have sought to expand NAFTA's scope to all the Americas except Cuba. Other regional trade organizations include the Asia-Pacific Economic Community (APEC);[46] the ASEAN Free Trade Area (AFTA);[47] and the Southern Cone Common Market (MERCOSUR), a customs union comprising Brazil, Argentina, Uruguay, and Paraguay.[48]

Two older agreements that involve Canada directly are the Canada-Israel Free Trade Agreement (CIFTA)[49] and the Canada-Chile Free Trade Agreement (CCFTA)[50]. Both agreements came into force in 1997, and both are patterned on NAFTA.

One of the most important sub-global cooperative institutions is based less on common geography than on common economic interests. The Organization for Economic Co-operation and Development (OECD) is not a regional trade or tariff union. It is an association of 30 of the most developed or industrialized countries, formed to exchange information and develop agreements on issues of special concern to producers of goods and services, such as trade liberalization.[51] Membership requires a commitment to a market economy and to "pluralistic democracy". The OECD has a Secretariat in Paris of about 2000 people, and conducts its research in more than 200 committees.

In 1976, the OECD adopted a Declaration on International Investment and Multinational Enterprises. As well as committing members to encourage investment, the declaration contains suggested guidelines for multinationals on disclosure of information, labour relations, and related matters.[52]

International Non-governmental Organizations (INGOs)

There are now thousands of international non-governmental organizations, such as Greenpeace International, the World Wildlife Fund, CARE, World Vision International, Save the Children International, Amnesty International, the International Red Cross, Oxfam, MSF (Médecins Sans Frontières), and CIDSE (Coopération Internationale pour le Développement et la Solidarité). With the help of the Internet, INGOs are able to mobilize large bodies of public opinion on specific issues. In 1998, for example, a coalition of over 600 non-govern-

mental organizations played a key role halting plans for Multilateral Agreement on Investment in the Organization for Economic Co-operation and Development.[53] INGOs might be seen as voices of a growing "international civil society" of individuals and private groups with concerns about world issues such as globalization.[54] On the other hand, even the strongest INGOs have only persuasive powers at best. Moreover, many INGOs are topic-specific, and most lack the broad accountability of democratic nation-states.

Globalization Governance by Nation States

Arguably, individual nation-states and groups of nation-states are still the ultimate agents of globalization governance. The world has no supranational global government. Most international associations enjoy powers agreed to and delegated by their individual member countries. The largest and richest states have significant power to influence these associations and other international actors, and to act unilaterally.

Paramount here is the United States, the only military superpower, and the leading economic superpower. The home state of most multinationals,[55] the United States has played a key role in encouraging trade expansion and liberalization. As a result of its economic size and voting strength, the United States has a dominant position in key international financial institutions such as the WTO, the IMF, and the World Bank (in addition to its veto in the United Nations' Security Council).

Because of its collective influence, the most important informal economic and political group of individual states today is the G8.[56] The G8 comprises Britain, Canada, France, Germany, Italy, Japan, the United States, and Russia, which has been suspended due to its recent military adventures. In each of these groupings, the United States is the most powerful single participant. This power is enhanced by the capacity of the United States to act on its own if joint efforts fail to achieve its goals. On the other hand, because of the interdependent nature of world trade and security, it is normally in the interest of even the most powerful state to consider the interests of the others. Although members of the group do not always agree, they achieved considerable consensus in completing the dismantling of the cold war and in coordinating responses to global economic problems such as the 1997–98 Asian financial crisis.[57] More as a process or forum than an institution,[58] the G8 convenes annual summits of the leaders of its member countries. Recently, these summits have included meetings with other world leaders and with the leaders of the IMF, the IBRD, the WTO, and the UN.[59]

GLOBALIZATION, THE NATION STATE, AND GOVERNANCE

Are globalization and its governance reducing the relative importance of the traditional nation-state? Traditionally, a key feature of a nation-state is a high level of exclusive sovereignty or control over a defined territory.[60] For example, Chapter 1 of this sourcebook refers to Max Weber's famous description of the state as a social organization with a monopoly on the legitimate use of force in a particular territory.[61] By virtue of this control — and usually through democratic accountability mechanisms as well — the traditional nation-state purports to act on behalf of the people who live in its territory. Many writers feel that globalization has weakened the capacity of the nation-state to control its population and territory internally, and to act on behalf of its population internationally.[62]

Self-imposed Restrictions

Several factors support these views. The organizing philosophies of globalization — enhancing market competition, liberalizing all trade, and reducing government restrictions on trade — have taken firm hold in richer nations. Thus, while some governments are *required* to reduce redistributive or public welfare policies that affect trade, others tend to do so voluntarily. In the interests of general productivity and efficiency, most governments have deliberately privatized, deregulated, and downsized in a wide range of areas, leaving more space for private competition and companies.[63] Even in developed nations, then, globalization has tended to restrict state power and to enhance that of private multinational corporations.[64]

Main Globalization Governance Restrictions

In a number of areas, globalization governance can limit the capacity of nation-states to carry out specific health, environmental, and other policies. For example, the WTO Agreement requires laws, regulations, and administrative procedures of member countries to comply with WTO trade agree-

ments.[65] Other members can refer complaints of violations to WTO panels. WTO panels have ruled that an EU ban on hormone-injected beef was contrary to WTO agreements, despite health concerns about the practice.[66] A WTO panel ruled against a US ban on imports of shrimp caught in ways that endangered shrimp and turtles.[67] A panel ruled against Canadian efforts to protect Canadian culture by subsidizing Canadian magazines.[68] A panel ruled against India's efforts to restrict imports so as to combat a balance of payments crisis.[69] Another panel enforced limits on the licensing of generic drugs.[70] As seen, WTO panel rulings are enforceable by sanctions if necessary. Note, though, that the weight of WTO rulings is uneven. Although some of the WTO rulings have gone against major states or groups of states, the cost and time of WTO proceedings, and the nature of its sanctions for non-compliance (WTO-authorized retaliation by the winning party) all favour more powerful states.[71] Moreover, as seen, the WTO trade agreement negotiation process ensures the United States and the European Community countries a major role in formulating trade agreements in the first place.

For its part, NAFTA has also generated significant limits to the scope of national power. For example, Chapter 11 of NAFTA permits private companies to sue governments in the event of "expropriation". In 1998, American-based Ethyl Corp. filed a Chapter 11 NAFTA claim against Canada, arguing that a Canadian ban on the import of MMT constituted unlawful expropriation. MMT is a gasoline additive considered by many to be a health hazard. The Canadian government settled the matter before it was decided by a NAFTA panel. It withdrew its ban, and paid Ethyl $13 million in compensation.[72] In a more recent Chapter 11 proceeding, a NAFTA panel held that its procedural rules against disclosure prevail over the *Canadian Access to Information Act*.[73]

However, NAFTA (and WTO) determinations are not always very conclusive. For many years, American lumber producers claimed that Canadian government forest management ("stumpage") programs provided Canadian lumber exporters with a subsidy that gave an unfair advantage in export markets. A series of NAFTA rulings and World Trade Organization reports were generally in favour of Canada, but failed to end the dispute.[74]

The dispute was finally resolved by negotiations.[75] In other situations, as with the World Bank and the IMF, recipients are generally required to adhere to strict financial austerity and trade liberalization conditions before receiving assistance. Here, too, though, some countries (poorer countries) tend to be on the receiving end of the rules, while the United States and other G8 members have a dominant role in influencing the formulation of the rules.

Potentially, the United Nations and its agencies could be central agents of globalization governance. Their mandates address international trade as well as other concerns. They offer the possibility of a single coordinated economic and social forum. However, as seen above, in some important economic areas leading industrial nations and multinationals have by-passed the United Nations, perhaps preferring institutions tailored more closely to their conception of their own interests.

Other Globalization Governance Restrictions

Beyond the institutions discussed above and other regional arrangements, such as the European Community,[76] globalization "governance" is limited mainly to international responses to globalization problems; self-regulation by multinationals or national trading authorities; and to lobbying by international non-governmental organizations. Although these actions are generally persuasive rather than coercive, they can influence the policies of nation-states.[77]

Countercurrents

There are exceptions to globalization's tendency to limit state power. As seen, the highly industrialized countries can significantly influence the course of economic globalization. Moreover, INGOs in these and other countries are often committed to preserving or reclaiming public power in areas such as environmental controls, health protection, and human rights. Global criminal and terrorist activities tend to result in expanded state police power. For example, the September 11, 2001 terrorist attacks on the World Trade Center and the Pentagon in the United States prompted many national governments to enact sweeping new anti-terrorist legislation,[78] and to re-think policies that delegate security controls to private companies. On the other hand, these developments forced resources away from other national priorities, and were accompanied by strong pressure to harmonize domestic security and security information systems with those of other states.

CONCLUSION

Globalization is a combination of developments that are integrating and transforming the world at a pace that would have been unimaginable three decades ago. Globalization is not subject to compulsory control by a single government comparable to a nation-state. However, globalization is affected by varying degrees of regulation or organization that can be referred to as governance. Especially in the economic area, globalization governance is significantly influenced by the world's rich nations, especially the dominant superpower, and a number of key trade bodies, such as the World Trade Organization.[79] Their governance imposes liberalized trade, mainly for the benefit of developed nations and large multinational corporations. In many ways it is governance of the poor, by the rich. Yet in order to further the free-market goals of globalization, developed nations tend to impose similar voluntary restrictions on themselves. Moreover, however imperfectly, new quasi-legislative, quasi-executive, and quasi-judicial bodies are emerging in international economic relations. So are new protagonists (greatly expanded multinationals), new threats (such as international criminal and terrorist associations), new "opposition" (such as international non-governmental interest groups and movements, e.g., Occupy Wall Street), and new forums for cross-border public discussion (social media). Thus, although globalization limits some states much more than others, it tends to limit them all.

Does this trend include an emerging international governance system that is comprehensive, coherent, balanced, and democratic? From the survey above, the answer is a resounding no! There is still a hope, though, that the rich and powerful will recognize that their own welfare and stability — political and personal, as well as economic — depends on improving that of their neighbours.[80] Ensuring this will require a wider, more coordinated, more even-handed, and more accountable system of global governance than the world has today.[81] Globalization in some form is with us to stay, but so is the broader phenomenon of increasing global interdependence.

Notes

1. This definition is offered tentatively, as descriptions of globalization vary widely. The ILO describes globalization as "a process of growing interdependence between all people of this planet. People are linked together economically and socially by trade, investments and governance. These links are spurred by market liberalization and information, communication and transportation technologies":

International Labor Organization, Bureau for Workers' Activities <http://www.ilo.org/actrav>. The IMF describes globalization as "the increasing integration of economies around the world, particularly through trade and financial flows" (referring to economic globalization): International Monetary Fund Staff, "Globalization: Threat or Opportunity?" (12 April 2000), online: <http://www.imf.org/external/np/exr/ib/2000/041200.htm#III>. John Nye, Jr. and John Donahue define globalism as "a state of the world involving networks of interdependence at multicontinental distances," and describe "globalization" as "the increase ... of globalism": Joseph Nye, Jr. and John D. Donahue, eds. *Visions of Governance for the 21st Century* (Washington, D.C.: Brookings Institution Press, 2000) at 2. See generally David Held and Anthony McGrew, eds. *The Global Transformations Reader: An Introduction to the Globalization Debate* (Cambridge, England: Polity Press, 2000) at Part 1.

2. See D. Held et al., *Global Transformations: Politics, Economics, and Culture* (Stanford, Calif.: Stanford University Press, 1999); *Visions of Governance for the 21st Century*, *supra* note 1, esp. at 3–7; David Held and Anthony McGrew, *Globalization / Anti-globalization* (Cambridge, England: Polity Press, 2002); Manfred Steger, *Globalization: A Very Short Introduction* (New York: Oxford University Press, 2003); Jürgen Osterhammel and Niels P. Peterson, *Globalization: A Short History*, trans. by Dona Geyer (Princeton, N.J.: Princeton University Press, 2005). Two other important dimensions are military globalization (*Global Transformations* Ch. 2 and *Visions* Ch. 3) and environmental globalization (*Global Transformations* Ch. 8 and *Visions* Ch. 4). Not all international corporations and economic ventures are lawful.

3. On the rise and power of giant multinational corporations, see R. J. Barnet and J. Cavanagh, *Global Dreams: Imperial Corporations and the New World Order* (New York: Simon & Schuster, 1994); Naomi Klein, *No Logo: Taking Aim at the Brand Bullies* (Toronto: A. Knopf Canada, 2000); Noreena Hertz, *The Silent Takeover* (London: Heinemann, 2000); David C. Korten, *When Corporations Rule the World*, 2d ed. (West Hartford, Conn.: Kumarian Press, 2001).

4. Thomas L. Friedman, *The Lexus and the Olive Tree: Understanding Globalization* (London, England: Harper Collins, 2000); Thomas Homer-Dixon, *The Ingenuity Gap* (London: Jonathan Cape, 2000); and V. Mayer-Schönberger and D. Hurley, "Globalization of Communication" in *Visions of Governance for the 21st Century*, *supra* note 1, Ch. 6.

5. "... [G]lobalization has a distinctly American face. It wears Mickey Mouse ears, it eats Big Macs, it drinks Coke or Pepsi and it does its computing on an IBM or Apple laptop, using Windows 98, with an Intel Pentium processor and a network link from Cisco systems": Friedman, *The Lexus and the Olive Tree: Understanding Globalization*, *ibid.* at 309.

6. See Mortimer N.S. Sells, *The New World Order: Sovereignty, Human Rights, and the Self-Determination of Peoples* (Washington, D.C.: Berg, 1996); Michael Ignatieff, *The Rights Revolution* (Toronto: Anansi Press, 2000).

7. See "International non-governmental organizations" section below.

8. Cf. A. Appadurai, *Modernity at Large: Cultural Dimensions of Modernization* (Minneapolis: University of Minnesota, 1998); John Thomlinson, *Globalization and Culture* (Chicago: University of Chicago Press, 1999); and M.M. Suárez Orozco and D.B. Qin-Hilliard, eds., *Globalization Culture and Education in the New Millennium* (Berkeley, CA: University of California Press, 2004).

9. Cf. Michel Foucault's definition of governance as an institutional arrangement that "structures the possible fields of actions of others": "The Subject and Power," in H. Dreyfus and P. Rabinow, eds., *Beyond Structuralism and Hermeneutics* (Chicago: University of Chicago Press, 1982) at 21, cited by P.M. Haas, "Social Constructivism," in Aseem P. Prakash and Jeffrey A. Hart, eds., *Globalization and Governance* (New York: Routledge, 1999) at 104. This broad concept of governance is much looser than the more systematic, centralized, and binding power of "government" exercised by most domestic nation-states. In these respects, only a regional international body such as the European Community comes close to the nation-state paradigm.

10. See *Visions of Governance for the 21st Century*, *supra* note 1 at 9–11.

11. On global crime, see H.R. Friman and P. Andreas, *The Illicit Global Economy and State Power* (Lanham, Maryland: Rowman & Littlefield Publishers, 1999); E.C. Viano, *Global Organized Crime and International Security* (Aldershot, Hants, England and Brookfield, Vermont: Ashgate, 1999); and D. Kyle and R. Koslowski, eds., *Global Human Smuggling: Comparative Perspectives* (Baltimore: Johns Hopkins University Press, 2001). On global terrorism, see R. Higgins and M. Flory, eds., *Terrorism and International Law* (London and New York: Routledge, 1997); C. Harmon, *Terrorism Today* (Portland, Oregon: Frank Cass, 2000); and I.D. Onwudiwe, *The Globalization of Terrorism* (Aldershot and Burlington, U.S.A.: Ashgate, 2001).

     Global terrorism can be seen as both an offshoot and a shaper of non-violent forms of globalization. In *The Cult of Efficiency* (Toronto: Anansi, 2001) at 229, Janice G. Stein has pointed out that "[w]ithout global markets and communications, the widespread mobility of people, and multicultural, diverse societies, these networks of terror could not survive, much less succeed." Conversely, an example of the influence of global terrorism on other aspects of globalization can be seen in actions of the al-Qaeda network. Al-Qaeda has opposed the Western and American cultural, trade, and military presence in Middle East Moslem countries such as Saudi Arabia. The September 11, 2001 terrorist killings in the United States, attributed to al-Qaeda, led to a shift in global political relations, including a closer relationship between the United States and Russia. Arguably, it also helped contribute to a world economic recession, including a drop in world trade.

12. See, for example, V. Cable, The Royal Institute of International Affairs, *Globalization and Global Governance* (New York: The Royal Institute of International Affairs, 1999); International Monetary Fund Staff, *Globalization: Threat or Opportunity?*, International Monetary Fund, April 12, 2000; Friedman, *The Lexus and the Olive Tree, supra* note 4; online: <http://www.imf.org/external/np/exr/ib/2000/041200.htm#II>; "Globalisation and its Critics: A Survey of Globalisation," *The Economist*, 360:8241 (29 September–5 October 2001), special supplement after 52; and M. Wolf, *Why Globalization Works* (New Haven, CT: Yale University Press, 2004).

13. See, for example, J. Gray, *False Dawn: The Delusions of Global Capitalism* (London: The New Press, 1998); Richard Falk, *Predatory Globalization: A Critique* (New Jersey: Princeton University Polity Press, 1999); Klein, *No Logo*, *supra* note 3; *The Silent Takeover*, *supra* note 3; D.C. Korten, *When Corporations Rule the World*, 2d ed. (West Hartford, Conn.: Kumarian Press, 2001). See also the websites of leading anti-globalization INGOs such as Greenpeace <http://www.greenpeace.org>; Amnesty International <http://www.amnesty.ca>; Global Policy Forum <http://www.globalpolicy.org>; and the International Council on Social Welfare <http://www.icsw.org>.

14. See generally N.D. White, *The Law of International Organisations* (New York: Manchester University Press, 1996).

15. The United Nations is the most important of the traditional international organizations. The UN includes a General Assembly of delegates from most nations of the world, a

Security Council of five permanent members with vetos, and 10 non-permanent members; a Secretariat of approximately 10,000 people, a 15-member International Court of Justice (which tends to address international political, territorial, and human rights issues rather than those of a strictly financial or economic nature: see ICJ website at <http://www.icj-cij.org>); a 54-member state elected Economic and Social Council to make studies and recommendations on economic, social, and related matters; a Trusteeship Council for administering trust territories; and a host of other specialized organizations, such as the Office of the UN High Commissioner for Refugees and the World Health Organization. See further E. Childers, "The United Nations System" in E. Childers, ed., *United Nations: Building a Safer World* (New York: St. Martin's Press, 1994) at 14, and Chapter 12, above.

16. E.g., the 1992 UN Conference on Environment and Development in Rio De Janeiro. See generally, Michael G. Schechter, ed., *United Nations-sponsored World Conferences: Focus on Impact and Follow-up* (New York, United Nations Press, 2001).

17. The 1977 ILO *Tripartite Declaration of Principles Concerning Multinational Enterprises*, relating to employment, industrial relations, and settlement of labour disputes: <http://www.itcilo.it/english/actrav/telearn/global/ilo/multinat/multinat.htm>.

18. See <www.und.cp.org>.

19. See P.M. Haas, "Social Constructivism," in *Globalization and Governance, supra* note 9. See UNEP website: <http://www.unep.org>.

20. ITU website: <http://www.itu.int/home/index.html>.

21. UPU website: <http://www.upu.int>.

22. ICAO website: <http://www.icao.org/cgi/goto.pl?icao/en/structure.htm>

23. See <www.wipo.org>.

24. The World Bank, the International Monetary Fund, and the General Agreement on Tariffs and Trade (now administered by the World Trade Association) were originally subject to the general supervision of the Economic and Social Council of the United Nations. Moreover, the WB and IMF are still affiliated formally with the UN. However, in 1947 the General Assembly approved an agreement giving the IMF, the World Bank, and GATT operational autonomy from the UN, and they act free of UN control today.

25. Some UN economic agencies have tended to focus on concerns in the developing world. Some of these concerns are at odds with the priorities of the multinational corporations. Others are aimed at advancing economic governance: see S. Ostry, "Convergence and Sovereignty" in Aseem P. Prakash and Jeffrey A. Hart, eds., *Coping with Globalization* (New York: Routledge, 2000) 53 at 56–57, quoting a speech by the chairman and CEO of Pfizer about the role of the World Intellectual Property System; and N. Adams, "The UN's Neglected Brief: The Advancement of All Peoples" in E. Childers, ed., *Challenges to the United Nations: Building a Safer World* (London, Catholic Institute for International Relations, 1994) 26 at 32–33 and 42–43 about the role of the United Nations Conference on Trade and Development. In Adams' view, "the United Nations has been losing its role as a forum for discussion of global economic policy issues": 43.

26. It is unclear how UN agencies might best regain the initiative. A report commissioned for the ITU recommended that this organization make provision for private sector representation, saying that "[t]he decision-making functions of the ITU should reflect the modern, competitive telecommunications environment in which the private sector plays the lead role while the regulatory agencies act as an arbitrator for the wider public interest": ITU Reform Advisory Panel *Observations and Recommendations for Reform*, <http://www.itu.int/home/index.html>, recommendation #1.

27. See World Bank Group Home Page, <http://www.worldbank.org>.

28. See M.R. Hodges et al., *The G8's Role in the New Millennium* (Aldershot, U.K.: Ashgate, 1999).

29. The WTO had 144 member countries as of January 1, 2002, with dozens more applying for membership. See *The WTO*, online: <http://www.wto.org/english/thewto_e/thewto_e.htm>.

30. See generally, World Trade Organization, *What is the World Trade Organization?: Fact File* <http://www.wto.org/english/thewto_e/whatis_e/whatis_e.htm>; Gary P. Sampson, *The Role of the World Trade Organization in Global Governance* (Tokyo: United Nations University, 2001). Also see <http://www.wto.org/english/thewto_e/secre_e/intro_e.htm>

31. The one technical exception to the one-member-one-vote rule is the European Community, whose voting strength is equal to the number of its own members. See Agreement Creating the World Trade Organization (WTO Agreement), April 15, 1994 (Dobbs Ferry, N.Y.: Oceana Publications, 1997); <http://www.wto.org/english/docs_e/legal_e/04-wto.pdf> art. IX, para. 1.

32. F. McGillivray, *Democratizing the World Trade Organization*, Hoover Institution Essays in Public Policy, <http://www-hoover.stanford.edu/publications/epp/105/105a.html>.

33. See Article 14 (for panels) and Article 17 (for the Appellate Body process) of the *Understanding on Rules and Procedures Governing the Settlement of Disputes*, Annex 2 to Agreement Creating the World Trade Organization, <http://www.wto.org/english/docs_e/legal_e/04-wto.pdf>.

   However, panel and Appellate Body reports are available to the public on the Internet: <http://docsonline.wto.org/gen_browseDetail.asp?preprog=2#Procedure> and <http://www.wto.org/english/tratop_e/dispu_e/distab_e.htm>. On WTO efforts to increase public access, see M. Moore, Director-General of WTO, "The WTO Door is Open, to a Point", *The Globe and Mail* (12 June 2002) A15.

34. See BIS website at <http://www.bis.org/about/proforgan.htm>.

   Created in 1930, the BIS is the world's oldest international financial institution. Eight of its 17-member Board of Governors are heads of the central banks or main financial authorities of the leading industrial nations. The BIS has a staff of nearly 600 people, based in Basel, Switzerland.

35. The ICSID was created in 1966. It has an Administrative Council chaired by the World President of the World Bank, and its own Secretariat. See ICSID description at <http://www.worldbank.org/icsid/about/main.htm>.

36. See the PCA website at: <http://www.pca-cap.org>. Note that the PCA is independent of the United Nations.

37. IOSCO website: <http://www.iosco.org/gen-info.html>.

38. INTELSAT website: <http://www.intelsat.int>.

39. See ICANN website: <http://www.icann.org>. ICANN assumes responsibility at the international level for assigning domain names for Web addresses on the Internet. Complaints of infringement of names held by registered trademark owners can be heard by arbitration in a variety of forums, including (in Canada) the World Intellectual Property Organization, the National Arbitration Forum, eResolution Inc. of Montreal, and the CPR Institute for Dispute Resolution.

40. For example, on July 18, 2001 Intelsat changed from its former status as an international treaty-based organization to that of a private company with shareholders in 145 countries: see INTELSAT website, <http://www.intelsat.int>. Should global resource allocation be controlled mainly by private interests? In regard to ICANN, *ibid.*: see M. Geist, "Public's Role in Net Gover-

nance Threatened", *The Globe and Mail* (13 June 2002) B21.

41. See European Union: *EU Institutions and Other bodies* <http://europa.eu/institutions/index_en.htm>.

42. See European Union: *Europa: The EU at a Glance* <http://europa.eu/abc/index_en.htm>.

43. *R.* v. *Secretary of State for Transport ex parte Factortame Ltd.*, [1990] 1 A.C. 603 (H.L.).

44. North American Free Trade Agreement, 17 December 1992, Can. T.S. 1994 No. 2 and *North American Free Trade Agreement Implementation Act*, S.C. 1993, c. 44. NAFTA is based largely on the Canada-United States Free Trade Agreement, which was in effect 1989 and 1993. NAFTA came into force on January 1, 1994. See <http://www.nafta-sec-alena.org/DefaultSite/Index_e.aspx?CategoryId=42>.

45. See *About the NAFTA Secretariat* <http://www.nafta-sec-alena.org/DefaultSite/index_e.aspx>.

46. Created in 1989.

47. AFTA was created in 1992. ASEAN itself was established in 1967.

48. MERCOSUR was created in 1991.

49. In force January 1, 1997, see <http://www.international.gc.ca/tna-nac/cifta-en.asp>.

50. In force July 5, 1997, see <http://www.international.gc.ca/tna-nac/cda-chile/menu-en.asp>.

51. OECD website: <http://www.oecd.org/EN/home>. Compare the OECD with the Organization of the Petroleum Exporting Countries (OPEC), the powerful 11-country oil suppliers' cartel: see OPEC website: <http://www.opec.org>.

52. See International Labour Organization, Bureau for Workers' Activities, *Multinational Corporations*: <http://www.itcilo.it/english/actrav/telearn/global/ilo/multinat/multinat.htm>.

53. S. Kobrin, "Neomedievalism and the Postmodern Economy" in *Globalization and Governance*, *supra* note 9 at 174.

54. For a study of these individuals and groups in the Canadian context, see T. Falconer, *Watchdogs and Gadflies: Activism from Marginal to Mainstream* (Toronto: Penguin Canada, 2001).

55. In 1996, 162 of the 500 largest companies in the world, in revenue terms, were from the United States. Another 126 of these were from Japan. American and European-based companies were the largest in terms of foreign assets. Among these companies were General Motors, Ford, Exxon, Shell, and Mitsui: International Labour Organization, Bureau for Workers' Activities, *Multinational Corporations*: <http://www.itcilo.it/english/actrav/telearn/global/ilo/multinat/multinat.htm>.

56. M.R. Hodges et al., eds., *The G8's Role in the New Millennium* (Aldershot, U.K.: Ashgate, 1999); J. Kirton et al. *Guiding Global Order: G8 Governance in the Twenty First Century* (Aldershot, U.K.: Ashgate, 2001).

57. *The G8's Role in the New Millennium*, *ibid.* at 54–56.

58. M.R. Hodges, "The G8 and the New Political Economy," *ibid.* at 69. The G8 has no formal secretariat.

59. J.J. Kirton, "Explaining G8 Effectiveness," *ibid.* at 48.

60. On the modern state and nation-state before the late 20th century, see G. Poggi, *The Development of the Modern State* (London: Hutchinson, 1978); G. McLellan et al., *The Idea of the Modern State* (Milton Keynes: Open University Press, 1984); and M. Horseman and A. Marshall, *After the Nation State* (London: Harper Collins, 1994) (also addressing the effect of globalization). For works stressing the relatively low degree of sovereignty in the traditional state and nation-state, see Paul Hirst and Grahame Thompson, *Globalization in Question* (Cambridge, England: Polity Press, 1996) Ch. 8; and Y.L. Ferguson and R.W. Mansbach, "History's Revenge and Future Shock" in M. Hewson and T.J. Sinclair, *Approaches to Global Gov-*

ernance Theory (Albany: State University of New York Press, 1999) Ch. 10.

61. See *Note on Social Goals, Techniques, and the State*, referring to Max Weber, *Economy and Society: An Outline of Interpretive Sociology* [from German 4th ed., 1956], ed. and trans. by G. Roth et al. (New York: Bedminster Press, 1968) at 54; and the reference to these features in *Globalization in Question*, *supra* note 60, Ch. 8.

62. See, for example, K. Ohmae, *The End of the Nation-State: The Rise of Regional Economies* (New York: The Free Press, 1995); Susan Strange, *The Retreat of the State: The Diffusion of Power in the World Economy* (Cambridge, Mass.: Cambridge University Press, 1996); S. Sassen, *Losing Control? Sovereignty in an Age of Globalization* (New York: Columbia University Press, 1996); Kenichi Ohmae, *The Borderless World: Power and Strategy in the Interlinked Economy* (New York: Harper Business, 1999); Gordon Smith and Moisés Naím, *Altered States: Globalization, Sovereignty, and Governance* (Ottawa: International Development Research Centre, 2000).

Not all take this view. For the view that the impact of globalization on national power has been exaggerated include Paul Hirst and Grahame Thompson, *Globalization in Question*, *supra* note 60, Ch. 8; W. Watson, *Globalization and the Meaning of Canadian Life* (Toronto: University of Toronto Press, 1998), T. Purvis, "Regulation, Governance and The State: Reflections on the Transformation of Regulatory Practices in Late-Modern Liberal Democracies" in Michael Mac Neil et al., eds., *Law, Regulation, and Governance* (Don Mills, Ont.: Oxford University Press, 2002) at 28, and B. Wright, *The Legal Regulation of Politics*, *ibid.* at 78. However, even those who assert that the nation-state still plays a significant role tend to concede some weakening in certain areas. See further, *The Global Transformations Reader*, *supra* note 1, Part 2.

63. In A. Farazmand, ed., *Privatization or Public Enterprise Reform* (Westport, Conn.: Greenwood Press, 2001) at 8, Farazmand argues that "[g]lobalization requires massive privatization and pushing the role of the state out of economic, social, and public sector governmental activities, and turning these activities totally over to the private market dominated by business corporations." See also D.J. Gayle and J.N. Goodrich, eds., *Privatization and Deregulation in Global Perspective* (Westport, Conn.: Quorum Books, 1990); International Labour Organization, Bureau for Workers' Activities, *National Framework for Globalization*, May 1999, <http://www.itcilo.it/english/actrav/telearn/global/ilo/frame/national.htm#Sectoral Developments>; Friedman, *The Lexus and the Olive Tree*, *supra* note 4, Ch. 5. In the area of agriculture, however, wealthy countries tend to apply massive trade preferences to their own products: see Joseph E. Stiglitz, *Globalization and its Discontents* (New York: W.W. Norton, 2002). In Canada, government cutbacks have included deregulation in fields such as energy, transportation, communications, and electricity sectors; privatizing of functions such as air traffic control; public sector layoffs and contracting-out; and attempts to reduce the number of individual regulations. See also S. McBride and J. Shields, *Dismantling a Nation: The Transition to Corporate Rule in Canada*, 2d ed. (Halifax: Fernwood, 1997); and J. Shields and B.M. Evans, *Shrinking the State: Globalization and Public Administration Reform* (Halifax: Fernwood, 1998). For a perceptive look at the broader impact of globalization in Canada, see D. Coyne, *Why Canada?* (Ottawa: unpublished, November 2000).

64. Even the GATT/WTO Agreement on Trade-related Intellectual Property Rights (TRIPS), which amounts to trade protection rather than liberalization, provides direct corporate benefits. TRIPS safeguards existing intellectual property rights, such as drug patents. This is especially beneficial for the largest holders of these rights, multinational cor-

porations. Multinational corporations had a key role in helping shape TRIPS: S. Ostry, "Convergence and Sovereignty" in *Coping with Globalization, supra* note 25, 53 at 56–57.

65. Agreement Establishing the World Trade Organization (WTO Agreement), 15 April 1994 <http://www.wto.org/english/docs_e/legal_e/04-wto.pdf>, art. XVI, para. 4.

66. *Beef Hormone Case: Challenge by the U.S. and Canada against the European Union*, WTO Case WT/DS26, 1997 and WT/DS48, 1998. Although the European Union cited scientific evidence of a *possibility* of cancer from the hormone treatment, the WTO rulings required scientific evidence of the *certainty* of cancer or other harmful health effects. The European Union refused to comply with the report, and the WTO authorized trade sanctions. Thus the strict WTO evidentiary requirement leaves national governments (or the EU) with the alternative of (a) failing to act against possible — but technically unproven — health risks within their borders, or (b) facing retaliatory sanctions for taking positive action.

67. *Shrimp-Turtle Case: Challenge by India, Malaysia, Pakistan and Thailand against the U.S.*, WTO Case WT/DS58, 1998. The U.S. *Endangered Species Act* (ESA) banned import of shrimp products from countries that did not use turtle excluder devices to protect endangered sea turtles from being caught in shrimp nets. A WTO panel held that the application of this law violated WTO trade rules, such as the principle of National Treatment. This principle prohibits trade embargoes that discriminate against specific countries.

68. *Canadian Magazines Case: Challenge by the U.S. against Canada*: WTO Case WT/DS31, 1997. (Canada eliminated the subsidies, which were in the form of postal rates and a tax.)

69. *India Quantitative Restrictions Case: Challenge by the U.S. against India*: WTO Case WT/DS90, adopted by Dispute Settlement Body, September 22, 1999. The Appellate Body upheld a panel ruling that India's restrictions on its balance of payments violated Article XI of the General Agreement on Tariffs and Trade.

70. *Generic Drug Case: Challenge by the U.S. against Canada*, WTO Case WT/DS 170, 2001. Canadian law protected only some drug patents for 20 years. A WTO panel held that this was contrary to the WTO agreement on Trade-related Intellectual Property Rights (TRIPS), which requires a protection period of 20 years for all patents. There were concerns that the long protection period hampers the ability of national governments to make available low-cost drugs to deal with problems such as AIDS.

71. *The Role of the World Trade Organization in Global Governance, supra* note 30.

72. The events are described in Baker & McKenzie, <http://www.bakerinfo.com/Publications/Documents/771_tx.htm>.

73. See Decision and Order by the Arbitral Tribunal in *NAFTA UNCITRAL Investor-State Claim: Pope & Talbot, Inc. and Government of Canada*, March 11, 2002.

74. In 2001 and 2002, for example, the WTO held that export restraints do not constitute a countervailable subsidy. From 2003 to 2005, NAFTA panels found — among other things — that American countervailing duty determinations on Canadian softwood lumber were illegal. In August 2005, a NAFTA Extraordinary Challenge Committee again ruled in favour of Canada. Meanwhile, a WTO panel ruled against Canada in 2004, but in April 2006, the WTO

Appellate Body decided in favour of Canada. The United States continually appealed the NAFTA panel rulings, and continued to levy countervailing duties on Canadian softwood lumber exports. Finally, in the face of the 2006 WTO decision, and of a Canadian appeal to the U.S. Court of International Trade to enforce the NAFTA panel decisions, Canada and the United States negotiated a settlement in late April 2006, which took effect in October 2006. See Canada, Department of Foreign Affairs and International Trade, *Softwood Lumber* <http://www.dfait-maeci.gc.ca/eicb/softwood/menu-en.asp>.

75. See Canada, Department of Foreign Affairs and International Trade, *Basic Terms of a Canada United States Agreement on Softwood Lumber* (announced April 27, 2006) <http://www.dfait-maeci.gc.ca/eicb/softwood/basic-terms-en.asp>.

76. As seen above, the European Union does involve clear supranational restrictions on the powers of its member states.

77. E.g., the 1998 success of international non-government organizations in helping halt OECD negotiations on the Multilateral Agreement on Investment.

78. In Canada, see S.C. 2001, c. 41; and *Proceeds of Crime (Money Laundering) and Terrorist Financing Act*, S.C. 2002, c. 17. Cf. B. Wright, "The Legal Regulation of Politics" in Michael Mac Neil et al., eds., *Law, Regulation, and Governance* (Don Mills, Ont.: Oxford University Press, 2002) 28 at 91–93, arguing that recent developments only intensify the Canadian state's ongoing preoccupation with state security.

79. Cf. Stephen Gill, identifying those with the greatest power over globalization governance as "globalizing elites": S. Gill, "Structural Change and Global Political Economy: Globalizing Elites and the Emerging World Order," in Y. Sakamoto, *Global Transformation: Challenges to the State System* (Tokyo: United Nations University Press, 1994); and Gramsci's concept of hegemony discussed in Chapter 1, above.

80. As noted earlier, the webs of globalization carry trade, potential prosperity, and enhanced communication past national borders, but they also transport such baggage as pollution, drugs, disease, crime, and terrorism. Not only are these problems not self-contained, but they are generally beyond the capacity of one country to combat effectively. For example, after the September 11, 2001 airliner attacks on the United States, the world's only superpower found it desirable to try to mobilize worldwide support for its efforts to eradicate global terrorism. On the other hand, the United States insisted that it, rather than international bodies, should direct these efforts. Here, as elsewhere, global governance had a long way to go.

As well as being self-destructive in the senses above, globalization that neglects its weaker and poorer subjects could risk encouraging globally based forces of resistance: see, for example, M. Hardt and A. Negri, *Empire* (Cambridge, MA: Harvard University Press, 2000).

81. An obvious candidate for this role would be a reinvigorated United Nations. See the UN Commission on Global Governance, *Our Global Neighbourhood Report of the Commission on Global Governance* (New York: Oxford University Press, 1995), and the International Council on Social Welfare, *Sustainable Social Progress: A Three-Point Plan for Strengthening International Cooperation: Strengthening Governance* <http://www.icsw.org>.

(g) *Reference Re Secession of Quebec*†

NOTE

In a referendum on October 30, 1995, Quebecers rejected by only 50.6% a provincial government proposal that Quebec be able to secede[1] unilaterally from Canada.[2] Afterward, the sovereigntist Quebec government spoke of holding another similar referendum as soon as it seemed likely to win. On September 30, 1996, acting pursuant to section 53 of the *Supreme Court Act*, the Governor in Council submitted the following reference questions to the Supreme Court of Canada:[3]

- Under the Constitution of Canada, can the National Assembly, legislature, or government of Quebec effect the secession of Quebec from Canada unilaterally?
- Does international law give the National Assembly, legislature, or government of Quebec the right to effect the secession of Quebec from Canada unilaterally? In this regard, is there a right to self-determination under international law that would give the National Assembly, legislature, or government of Quebec the right to effect the secession of Quebec from Canada unilaterally?
- In the event of a conflict between domestic and international law on the right of the National Assembly, legislature, or government of Quebec to effect the secession of Quebec from Canada unilaterally, which would take precedence in Canada?

The reference was argued before the Supreme Court of Canada from February 16 to February 19, 1998.[4] Because the government of Quebec refused to participate in the proceedings, an *amicus curiae* was appointed to argue the secessionist case before the Court. Also represented were the federal government, several provincial and territorial governments, a number of Aboriginal organizations, and Mr. Guy Bertrand, whose own court challenge to the Quebec referendum bill had preceded the federal reference.

On the last day of the hearings, the Court asked for, and subsequently received, written clarification from the parties on some of the issues.[5]

The Court addressed the parties' arguments on jurisdictional and domestic constitutional matters first.[6] The Court held that it had jurisdiction to hear these references. On Question 1, the Court said that unilateral secession would violate a constitutional requirement to negotiate, and would be contrary to the underlying constitutional principles of federalism, constitutionalism and the rule of law, protection of individual and minority rights, and democracy (in Canada as a whole and outside Quebec).[7] However, the Court also found that the principle of democracy would be satisfied within Quebec if a clear majority of the population of Quebec voted on a clear referendum question to pursue secession. In this situation, said the Court, the federal government and the other provincial governments would be required to participate in negotiating constitutional changes to respond to that desire.

The second and third of the reference questions are of special interest in international law. Sovereigntist supporters had argued that the population of Quebec has an international law right of self-determination. They claimed that this right entitles Quebecers to freely choose their own political future, by secession if necessary.[8]

The *amicus* didn't rely much on these self-determination arguments.[9] Moreover, he argued that international law issues are beyond the jurisdiction of the Supreme Court.[10] However, he did claim that secession is quite legitimate in international law where it reflects the democratically expressed will of the seceding people, and where the secessionist government establishes its effective control of the population and territory in question.[11]

The federal government argued that self-determination has both an "internal" and an "external" aspect. In its internal aspect, self-determination gives a people the right to full participation in the government of a state. In its external aspect, self-determination gives a people the right to determine

---

† [1998] 2 S.C.R. 217 (*IN THE MATTER OF Section 53 of the Supreme Court Act, R.S.C., 1985, c. S-26; AND IN THE MATTER OF a Reference by the Governor in Council concerning certain questions relating to the secession of Quebec from Canada, as set out in Order in Council P.C. 1996-1497, dated the 30th day of September, 1996*), 20 August 1998. [Commentary note by David W. Elliott.]

their own form of government and their international status. The federal government said that in non-colonial situations, this does not involve a right of secession, except perhaps for a people who are subject to alien domination or to gross oppression — i.e., to a people who have been denied the capacity to enjoy "internal" self-determination. Otherwise, the rights of a people within an existing state are subject to that state's right to maintain its territorial integrity.[12] In regard to state practice, the federal government argued that there have been very few modern situations of successful unilateral secession.[13]

Finally, Aboriginal groups in Quebec argued that *they* have a self-determination right, which would entitle them to remain within Canada in the event of a secession.[14]

As to whether Canadian domestic law or international law prevails in the event of a conflict, as noted, the *amicus* argued that international law issues are beyond the jurisdiction of the Supreme Court. The federal government argued that in the event of a conflict, under general common law principles, domestic law prevails.[15]

Assuming that under some circumstances a right of self-determination can give rise to a right to secede, is this a legal or a moral right in international law? If it is the latter, is recognition by the international community required to give practical effect to statehood? If the answers here are yes, who is a "people" with a right to self-determination? When does this right give rise to a moral right to secede? What requirements are needed to give practical legal effect to a secession in international law? Can a Canadian court answer these questions authoritatively? If international law recognizes a moral or legal right to secede and Canadian law does not, which prevails? These are only some of the questions to look for in the international law portions of the Supreme Court's decision.

In its opinion of August 20, 1998, the Supreme Court of Canada answered "no" to Questions 1 and 2 (both parts) that had been submitted to it. It was therefore unnecessary to answer Question 3.

At the end of its decision, the Court (Lamer C.J. and L'Heureux-Dubé, Gonthier, Cory, McLachlin, Iacobucci, Major, Bastarache, and Binnie JJ.) summarized the reasons for its answers to Questions 1 and 2. The following extract is from the part of the summary that relates especially to international law. What role does the Court envisage for the international community in regard to the conduct of secession negotiations and the viability of a unilateral attempt at secession?

EXTRACTS FROM THE REFERENCE[16]

[152] The negotiation process [that would be required in the event of a clear expression of the will of the people of Quebec to secede] would require the reconciliation of various rights and obligations by negotiation between two legitimate majorities, namely, the majority of the population of Quebec, and that of Canada as a whole. A political majority at either level that does not act in accordance with the underlying constitutional principles we have mentioned [federalism, democracy, the rule of law and constitutionalism, and the protection of minority and individual rights] puts at risk the legitimacy of its exercise of its rights, and the ultimate acceptance of the result by the international community.

. . . .

[154] We have also considered whether a positive legal entitlement to secession exists under international law in the factual circumstances contemplated by Question 1, i.e., a clear democratic expression of support on a clear question for Quebec secession. Some of those who supported an affirmative answer to this question did so on the basis of the recognized right to self-determination that belongs to all "peoples." Although much of the Quebec population certainly shares many of the characteristics of a people, it is not necessary to decide the "people" issue because, whatever may be the correct determination of this issue in the context of Quebec, a right to secession only arises under the principle of self-determination of peoples at international law where "a people" is governed as part of a colonial empire; where "a people" is subject to alien subjugation, domination or exploitation; and possibly where "a people" is denied any meaningful exercise of its right to self-determination within the state of which it forms a part. In other circumstances, peoples are expected to achieve self-determination within the framework of their existing state. A state whose government represents the whole of the people or peoples resident within its territory, on a basis of equality and without discrimination, and respects the principles of self-determination in its internal arrangements, is entitled to maintain its territorial integrity under international law and to have that territorial integrity recognized by other states. Quebec does not meet the threshold of a colonial people or an oppressed people, nor can it be suggested that Quebecers have been denied meaningful access to government to pursue their political, economic, cultural and social development. In the circumstances, the National Assembly, the legislature or the government of

Quebec do not enjoy a right at international law to effect the secession of Quebec from Canada unilaterally.

[155] Although there is no right, under the Constitution or at international law, to unilateral secession, that is secession without negotiation on the basis just discussed, this does not rule out the possibility of an unconstitutional declaration of secession leading to a *de facto* secession. The ultimate success of such a secession would be dependent on recognition by the international community, which is likely to consider the legality and legitimacy of secession having regard to, amongst other facts, the conduct of Quebec and Canada, in determining whether to grant or withhold recognition. Such recognition, even if granted, would not, however, provide any retroactive justification for the act of secession, either under the Constitution of Canada or at international law.

[156] The reference questions are answered accordingly.

Notes

1. Secession is the withdrawal of a political unit of an existing state to form a new state.
2. Although the proposal was framed in language of partnership and negotiation, it clearly contemplated the option of unilateral withdrawal from Canada.
3. P.C. 1996-1497. (The order in council also included a six-paragraph preamble.)
4. For the positions of the parties and key intervenors and the reference decision itself, see Anne F. Bayefsky, ed., *Self-determination in International Law: Quebec and Lessons Learned* (The Hague: Kluwer Law International, 2000). See also Warren J. Newman, *The Quebec Secession Reference: The Rule of Law and the Position of the Attorney General of Canada* (Toronto: York University, 1999), summarizing the federal position and the reference; and David Schneiderman, *The Quebec Decision: Perspectives on the Supreme Court Ruling on Secession* (Toronto: James Lorimer & Company, 1999).

5. See *Self-determination in International Law, ibid.* at 405–52 for the Court's supplementary questions and the responses and replies of the parties.
6. On jurisdiction, the *amicus curiae* argued that the issues should not be before the Court for a variety of reasons, such as their hypothetical nature. On the first reference question, the *amicus* argued that secession was possible because it was not expressly prohibited in the formal procedure for amending the Constitution of Canada, and that the free expression of the will of Quebecers was supported by a principle of democracy implicit in the preamble to the *Constitution Act, 1867*. Counsel for the Attorney General for Canada argued that the Court should hear the reference, and that the answer to the first question was governed exclusively by the amending procedure in Part V of the *Constitution Act, 1982*. He said that under Part V, the secession of a province requires the consent of the House of Commons and Senate and of the legislatures of at least two-thirds or, possibly, all of the provinces. See further *Self-determination in International Law, ibid.* at 307–31 and 371–77 (federal factum and reply) and at 333–42 and 379–86 (factum and reply of *amicus curiae*).
7. See further, D.W. Elliott, *Introduction to Public Law: Sourcebook*, 7th ed. (North York, Ont.: Captus Press, 2006) Chs. 2, 3, and 12.
8. See, for example, D. Turp, "Quebec's Democratic Right to Self-Determination: A Critical and Legal Reflection, in *Tangled Web: Legal Aspects of Deconfederation* (Toronto: C.D. Howe Institute, 1992).
9. For the main discussion of this issue by the *amicus*, see his factum at paragraphs 92–112, in *Self-determination in International Law, supra* note 4 at 339–42. The *amicus* saw the right as a supporting and secondary factor in his general international law secession argument.
10. Factum of *amicus*, paragraphs 46–53, referred to in *Self-determination in International Law, ibid.* at 423.
11. Factum of *amicus*, paragraphs 75–90, *ibid.* at 334–38.
12. Factum of Attorney General for Canada, paragraphs 120–98, *ibid.* at 309–31.
13. *Ibid.*, paragraphs 165–71, at 322–23.
14. See, for example, factum of the Grand Council of the Crees (Eeyou Istchee), paragraphs 78–99, *ibid.* at 354–61.
15. Factum of the Attorney General for Canada, paragraphs 199–211.
16. *Reference Re Secession of Quebec*, [1998] 2 S.C.R. 217, pursuant to s. 53 of the *Supreme Court Act*, concerning the secession of Quebec from Canada.

(h) Is Kosovo's Unilateral Declaration of Independence in Accordance with International Law?†

NOTE

On February 17, 2008, for the second time in almost twenty years, the Assembly of Kosovo unilaterally declared its independence from the Republic of Serbia. This unilateral declaration of independence (UDI) of the former Socialist Autonomous Province of Kosovo from Serbia followed much internal civil strife and a brief war that was triggered by the dissolution of the former Socialist

† *Accordance with International Law of Unilateral Declaration of Independence in Respect of Kosovo, Advisory Opinion of 22 July 2010*, [2010] I.C.J. Rep. 403 at 436–438.

Federal Republic of Yugoslavia in 1991. Serbia challenged the UDI as being illegal and requested a non-binding advisory opinion from the International Court of Justice (ICJ) based in The Hague, Netherlands. The Court ruled by a vote of 10–4 that the declaration did not violate international law. This decision led directly to talks that created the *Brussels Agreement* in 2013, which saw Kosovo separate from Serbia. When reading the excerpt below, ponder whether this decision sets a precedent for other independence movements around the globe. Closer to home, does the reasoning presented by the ICJ challenge the ruling of the Supreme Court of Canada in 1998 that there is no right to unilateral secession at international law?: *Reference re Secession of Quebec*, [1998] 2 S.C.R. 217 at para. 155. Can Quebec separatist supporters use the ICJ decision to properly cast doubt on the legitimacy of the Supreme Court's *Quebec Secession Reference* (*ibid.*) as a political device to re-ignite the debate concerning the province's status in Canada? Will the ICJ ruling encourage separation in places like Scotland or Catalonia in Spain? If so, will the international community see more states splintering into their sub-units because of precedents like the ICJ decision? Finally, can a decision like the ICJ ruling be used to destabilize a weak state and provide credence to individuals that claim legal secession in order to join a neighbouring state? Does it matter if the neighbouring state provided monetary, military, or other aid for the declaration of independence to be issued as is alleged in the Ukraine and Georgia?

EXTRACT

[THE COURT (President Owada; Vice-President Tomka; Judges Koroma, Al-Khasawneh, Buergenthal, Simma, Abraham, Keith, Sepúlveda-Amor, Bennouna, Skotnikov, Cançado Trindade, Yusuf, Greenwood; Registrar Couvreur) gives the following Advisory Opinion:]

. . . .

79. During the eighteenth, nineteenth and early twentieth centuries, there were numerous instances of declarations of independence, often strenuously opposed by the State from which independence was being declared. Sometimes a declaration resulted in the creation of a new State, at others it did not. In no case, however, does the practice of States as a whole suggest that the act of promulgating the declaration was regarded as contrary to international law. On the contrary, State practice during this period points clearly to the conclusion that international law contained no prohibition of declarations of independence. During the second half of the twentieth century, the international law of self-determination developed in such a way as to create a right to independence for the peoples of non–self-governing territories and peoples subject to alien subjugation, domination and exploitation.... A great many new States have come into existence as a result of the exercise of this right. There were, however, also instances of declarations of independence outside this context. The practice of States in these latter cases does not point to the emergence in international law of a new rule prohibiting the making of a declaration of independence in such cases.

80. Several participants in the proceedings before the Court have contended that a prohibition of unilateral declarations of independence is implicit in the principle of territorial integrity. The Court recalls that the principle of territorial integrity is an important part of the international legal order and is enshrined in the Charter of the United Nations, in particular in Article 2, paragraph 4, which provides that:

> "All Members shall refrain in their international relations from the threat or use of force against the territorial integrity or political independence of any State, or in any other manner inconsistent with the Purposes of the United Nations."

In General Assembly resolution 2625 (XXV), entitled "Declaration on Principles of International Law concerning Friendly Relations and Co-operation among States in Accordance with the Charter of the United Nations", which reflects customary international law... the General Assembly reiterated "[t]he principle that States shall refrain in their international relations from the threat or use of force against the territorial integrity or political independence of any State". This resolution then enumerated various obligations incumbent upon States to refrain from violating the territorial integrity of other sovereign States. In the same vein, the Final Act of the Helsinki Conference on Security and Co-operation in Europe of 1 August 1975 (the Helsinki Conference) stipulated that "[t]he participating States will respect the territorial integrity of each of the participating States" (Art. IV). Thus, the scope of the principle of territorial integrity is confined to the sphere of relations between States.

81. Several participants have invoked resolutions of the Security Council condemning particular declarations of independence: see, *inter alia*, Security Council resolutions 216 (1965) and 217 (1965), concerning Southern Rhodesia; Security Council resolution 541 (1983), concerning northern Cyprus; and Security Council resolution 787 (1992), concerning the Republika Srpska. The Court notes, however, that in all of those instances the Security Council was making a determination as regards the concrete situation existing at the time that those declarations of independence were made; the illegality attached to the declarations of independence thus stemmed not from the unilateral character of these declarations as such, but from the fact that they were, or would have been, connected with the unlawful use of force or other egregious violations of norms of general international law, in particular those of a peremptory character (*jus cogens*). In the context of Kosovo, the Security Council has never taken this position. The exceptional character of the resolutions enumerated above appears to the Court to confirm that no general prohibition against unilateral declarations of independence may be inferred from the practice of the Security Council.

82. A number of participants in the present proceedings have claimed, although in almost every instance only as a secondary argument, that the population of Kosovo has the right to create an independent State either as a manifestation of a right to self-determination or pursuant to what they described as a right of "remedial secession" in the face of the situation in Kosovo. The Court has already noted (see paragraph 79 above) that one of the major developments of international law during the second half of the twentieth century has been the evolution of the right of self-determination. Whether, outside the context of non–self-governing territories and peoples subject to alien subjugation, domination and exploitation, the international law of self-determination confers upon part of the population of an existing State a right to separate from that State is, however, a subject on which radically different views were expressed by those taking part in the proceedings and expressing a position on the question. Similar differences existed regarding whether international law provides for a right of "remedial secession" and, if so, in what circumstances. There was also a sharp difference of views as to whether the circumstances which some participants maintained would give rise to a right of "remedial secession" were actually present in Kosovo.

83. The Court considers that it is not necessary to resolve these questions in the present case. The General Assembly has requested the Court's opinion only on whether or not the declaration of independence is in accordance with international law. Debates regarding the extent of the right of self-determination and the existence of any right of "remedial secession", however, concern the right to separate from a State. As the Court has already noted (see paragraphs 49 to 56 above), and as almost all participants agreed, that issue is beyond the scope of the question posed by the General Assembly. To answer that question, the Court need only determine whether the declaration of independence violated either general international law or the *lex specialis* created by Security Council resolution 1244 (1999).

84. For the reasons already given, the Court considers that general international law contains no applicable prohibition of declarations of independence. Accordingly, it concludes that the declaration of independence of 17 February 2008 did not violate general international law....

(i) Other Extracts on International Law and Secession†

David W. Elliott

For provisions of the UN Charter[1] that are relevant to self-determination and territorial integrity, see articles 1(2), 2(4), and 55, reproduced earlier in this chapter.

---

† See also the following primary materials: *Legal Consequences for States of the Continued Presence of South Africa in Namibia (South West Africa) Notwithstanding Security Council Resolution 276 (1970)*, International Court of Justice Advisory Opinion, [1971] I.C.J. Rep. 16 at 31–32 (self-determination); *Western Sahara, International Court of Justice Advisory Opinion*, [1975] I.C.J. Rep. 12 at 31–32 (self-determination); *Bertrand* v. *Quebec (Procureur General)* (1995), 127 D.L.R. (4th) 408 (Quebec Superior Court) (recognition of new states; relationship between domestic and international law; also domestic Canadian law: this is the most extensive of several decisions involving secession litigation by M. Bertrand); Ian Brownlie, ed., *Basic Documents in International Law*, 5th ed. (Oxford, England: Clarendon Press, 2002)

1960 United Nations General Assembly Declaration on the Granting of Independence to Colonial Countries and Peoples[2] (Colonial Peoples Declaration)

2. All peoples have the right to self-determination; by virtue of that right they freely determine their political status and freely pursue their economic, social and cultural development.

...

4. All armed action or repressive measures of all kinds directed against dependent peoples shall cease in order to enable them to exercise peacefully and freely their right to complete independence, and the territorial integrity of their national territory shall be respected.

...

6. Any attempt aimed at the partial or total disruption of the national unity and the territorial integrity of a country is incompatible with the purposes and principles of the United Nations.

7. All States shall observe faithfully and strictly the provisions of the Charter of the United Nations, the Universal Declaration of Human Rights and the present Declaration on the basis of equality, non-interference in the internal affairs of all States, and respect for the sovereign rights of all peoples and their territorial integrity.

1966 International Covenant on Economic, Social and Cultural Rights[3] and the 1966 International Covenant on Civil and Political Rights[4]

Article 1 of both covenants:

(1) All peoples have the right of self-determination. By virtue of that right they freely determine their political status and freely pursue their economic, social and cultural development.

(2) All peoples may, for their own ends, freely dispose of their natural wealth and resources without prejudice to any obligations arising out of international economic co-operation, based upon the principle of mutual benefit and international law. In no case may a people be deprived of its own means of subsistence.

(3) The States Parties to the present Covenant, including those having responsibility for the administration of Non-Self-Governing and Trust Territories, shall promote the realization of the right of self-determination, and shall respect that right, in conformity with the provisions of the Charter of the United Nations.

1970 United Nations General Assembly Declaration on Principles of International Law concerning Friendly Relations and Co-operation among States in accordance with the Charter of the United Nations[5] (Declaration on Friendly Relations)

By virtue of the principle of equal rights and self-determination of peoples enshrined in the Charter of the United Nations, all peoples have the right freely to determine, without external interference, their political status and to pursue their economic, social and cultural development, and every State has the duty to respect this right in accordance with the principles of the Charter.

Every State has the duty to promote, through joint and separate action, realization of the principle of equal rights and self-determination of peoples, in accordance with the provisions of the Charter, and to render assistance to the United Nations in carrying out the responsibilities entrusted to it by the Charter regarding the implementation of the principle, in order:

(a) To promote friendly relations and co-operation among States; and

(b) To bring a speedy end to colonialism, having due regard to the freely expressed will of the peoples concerned; and bearing in mind that subjection of peoples to alien subjugation, domination and exploitation constitutes a violation of the principle, as well as a denial of fundamental human rights, and is contrary to the Charter.

...

The establishment of a sovereign and independent State, the free association or integration with an independent State or the emergence into any other political status freely determined by a people constitute modes of implementing the right of self-determination by that people.

...

Nothing in the foregoing paragraphs shall be construed as authorizing or encouraging any action which would dismember or impair, totally or in part, the territorial integrity or political unity of sovereign and independent States conducting themselves in compliance with the principle of equal rights and self-determination of peoples as described above and thus possessed of a government representing the whole people belonging to the territory without distinction as to race, creed or colour. Every State shall refrain from any action aimed at the partial or total disruption of the national unity and territorial integrity of any other State or country.

1993 Vienna Declaration and Programme of Action[6] (Vienna Declaration)

The Declaration affirms the principle of self-determination, and continues:

In accordance with the Declaration on Principles of International Law concerning Friendly Relations and Cooperation Among States in accordance with the Charter of the United Nations, *[the right of self-determination]* shall not be construed as authorizing or encouraging any action which would dismember or impair, totally or in part, the territorial integrity or political unity of sovereign and independent States conducting themselves in compliance with the principle of equal rights and self-determination of peoples and thus possessed of a government representing the whole people belonging to the territory without distinction of any kind.

Convention on the Rights and Duties of States[7] (Montevideo Convention)

Article 1

The State as a person of international law should possess the following qualifications: (a) a permanent population; (b) defined territory; (c) government; and (d) capacity to enter into relations with other States.

Madzimbamuto[8]

In 1965, a breakaway régime headed by Ian Smith unilaterally declared its independence of Britain. Britain actively opposed the régime, and in *Madzimbamuto*, the Judicial Committee of the Privy Council refused to recognize its validity. Majority Judge Lord Reid referred to earlier decisions affirming the validity of revolutionary governments which had succeeded in establishing themselves in effective control of their territories.[9] He continued:

Their lordships would not accept all the reasoning in these judgments but they see no reason to disagree with the results.... It would be very different if there had been still two rivals contending for power ... because that would mean that by striving to assert its lawful right the ousted legitimate government was opposing the lawful ruler.[10]

Chung Chi Cheung[11]

It must always be remembered that, so far, at any rate, as the Courts of this country are concerned, international law has no validity save in so far as its principles are accepted and adopted by our own domestic law. There is no external power that imposes its rules upon our own code of substantive law or procedure. The Courts acknowledge the existence of a body of rules which nations accept amongst themselves. On any judicial issue they seek to ascertain what the relevant rule is, and, having found it, they will treat it as incorporated into the domestic law, so far as it is not inconsistent with rules enacted by statutes or finally declared by their tribunals.

Notes

1. 26 June 1945, Can. T.S. 1945 No. 7.
2. G.A. Res. 1514 (XV), U.N. GAOR, 15th Sess., Supp. No. 16, U.N. Doc. A/4684 (1961) at 66, paras. 2, 4, 6, 7.
3. 16 December 1966, Can. T.S. 1976 No. 46, art. 1.
4. 19 December 1966, Can. T.S. 1976 No. 47, art. 1.
5. G.A. Res. 2625 (XXV), U.N. GAOR, 25th Sess., Supp. No. 28, U.N. Doc. A/8028 (1970) (adopted by consensus).
6. *Vienna Declaration and Programme of Action*, United Nations World Conference on Human Rights, U.N. GAOR, U.N. Doc. A/CONF.157/24 (Part I) (1993) 20 at 22.
7. 49 Stat. 3097, T.S. 881, 165 L.N.T.S. 19 (signed at Montevideo, Uruguay, on December 26, 1933, entered into force on December 26, 1934), article 1.
8. *Madzimbamuto* v. *Lardner-Burke*, [1968] 3 All E.R. 561 (J.C.P.C.).
9. *State v. Dosso*, [1958] P.L.D. 533 (Supreme Court of Pakistan); and *Uganda* v. *Commissioner of Prisons ex parte Matovu*, [1966] E. Africa L.R 514 (High Court of Uganda).
10. *Madzimbamuto v. Lardner-Burke*, [1968] 3 All E.R. 561 at 574 (J.C.P.C.).
11. *Chung Chi Cheung v. The King*, [[1939] A.C. 160 at 167–68 (J.C.P.C., Lord Atkin). See also *Reference Re Powers of Ottawa (City) and Rockcliffe Park (Foreign Legations Reference)*, [1943] S.C.R. 208 at 213–14.

Select Bibliography

[This Select Bibliography represents a compilation of citations of published sources related to Law, State, and Citizen. The works are grouped into sub-topics to assist readers/researchers in selecting appropriate works for their particular areas of study. Readings are listed in chronological order with the most recently published works first]

I. Law and the State

Terrance Ball et al., *Political Ideologies and the Democratic Ideal*, 9th ed. (Boston, Mass.: Pearson, 2014).

Mark O. Dickerson, Thomas Flanagan, and Brenda O'Neill, *An Introduction to Government and Politics: A Conceptual Approach*, 9th ed. (Toronto: Nelson Canada, 2013).

Terrance Ball et al., *Political Ideologies and the Democratic Ideal*, Third Canadian ed. (Toronto: Pearson Education Canada, 2012).

Alan Haworth, *Understanding the Political Philosophers: From Ancient to Modern Times*, 2d ed. (New York: Routledge, 2012).

Neil Craik et al., *Public Law: Cases, Materials, and Commentary* (Toronto: Emond Montgomery, 2011).

Mitchell Dean, *Governmentality: Power and Rule in Modern Society*, 2d ed. (London, England: Sage, 2010).

H.B. McCullough, *Political Ideologies* (Toronto: Oxford University Press, 2010).

Logan Atkinson and Neil Sargent, *Private Law, Social Life: An Introduction*, 2d ed. (Markham, Ont.: LexisNexis Canada, 2007).

Steven Lukes, *Power: A Radical View*, 2d ed. (New York: Palgrave Macmillan, 2005).

Michael Mac Neil et al., eds., *Law, Regulation, and Governance* (Don Mills, Ont.: Oxford University Press, 2002).

Alan Cairns, *Citizens Plus; Aboriginal Peoples and the Canadian State* (Vancouver: UBC Press, 2000).

Nickie Charles et al., *Feminism, the State, and Social Policy* (Basingstoke: Macmillan, 2000).

J.L. Finlay and D.N. Sprague, *The Structure of Canadian History*, 6th ed. (Scarborough, Ont.: Prentice Hall Allyn and Bacon Canada, 2000).

Nöel O'Sullivan, *Political Theory in Transition* (London, England: Routledge, 2000).

Jene M. Porter, *Classics in Political Philosophy*, 3d ed. (Scarborough, Ont.: Prentice-Hall Canada, 2000).

Scott Gordon, *Controlling the State: Constitutionalism From Ancient Athens to Today* (Cambridge, Mass.: Harvard University Press, 1999).

Patricia Monture-Angus, *Journeying Forward: Dreaming First Nations' Independence* (Halifax, N.S.: Fernwood, 1999).

Robert Benewick and Philip Green, *The Routledge Dictionary of Twentieth-Century Political Thinkers*, 2d ed. (New York: Routledge, 1998).

Jürgen Habermas, *Between Facts and Norms: Contributions to a Discourse Theory of Law and Democracy* (Cambridge, Mass.: MIT Press, 1998).

John A. Hall, ed., *The State of the Nation; Ernest Gellner and the Theory of Nationalism* (New York: Cambridge University Press, 1998).

Alan Hunt and Gary Wickham, *Foucault and Law: Towards a Sociology of Law as Governance* (London, England: Pluto, 1994).

Mark O. Dickerson, Thomas Flanagan, and Neil Nevitte, eds., *Introductory Readings in Government and Politics*, 4th ed. (Toronto: Nelson Canada, 1995).

Roger Cotterrell, *The Sociology of Law: An Introduction*, 2d ed. (London, England: Butterworths, 1992).

Catharine A. MacKinnon, *Toward a Feminist Theory of the State* (Cambridge, Mass.: Harvard University Press, 1989).

John Locke, *Two Treatises of Government* (Cambridge, England: Cambridge University Press, 1988 [1698]).

J. Rick Ponting, ed., *Arduous Journey: Canadian Indians and Decolonization* (Toronto: McClelland & Stewart, 1986).

Gordon T. Stewart, *The Origins of Canadian Politics: A Comparative Approach* (Vancouver: UBC Press, 1986).

Bill Jordon, *The State: Authority and Autonomy* (Oxford, England: Blackwell, 1985).

B. Russell, *A Contemporary History of Western Philosophy* (London, England: Unwin Paperbacks, 1984 [1946]).

David Held, "Central Perspectives on the Modern State" in David Held et al., *States and Societies* (Oxford, England: Oxford University Press, 1983).

Christine Buci-Glucksmann, *Gramsci and the State*, trans. of Gramsci et l'état (London, England: Lawrence, 1980).

Quentin Hoare and Geoffrey Nowell-Smith, *Selections from the Prison Notebooks of Antonio Gramsci*, trans. from Italian (London, England: Lawrence, 1971).

Max Weber, *Economy and Society: An Outline of Interpretive Sociology*, ed. and trans. by G. Roth and C. Wittich et al. (New York: Bedminster Press, 1968 [from German 4th ed., 1956]).

Albert Venn Dicey, *An Introduction to the Study of the Law of the Constitution*, 10th ed. (London, England: Macmillan, 1965 [1885, last edition by Dicey: 1915]).

Karl Marx, *Preface to Contribution to Critique of Political Economy* and *German Ideology*, ed. and trans. by T.B. Bottomore, *Selected Writings in Sociology and Social Philosophy* (New York: McGraw-Hill, 1964 [1859] and [1845–46], respectively).

Westel Woodbury Willoughby, *The Political Theories of the Ancient World* (Freeport, N.Y.: Books for Libraries, 1964 [1903]).

John Stuart Mill, *Considerations on Representative Government* (New York: Liberal Arts Press, 1962 [1861]).

———, *Utilitarianism and Other Writings* (Cleveland: Meridian Books, 1962 [1859]).

Thomas Hobbes, *Leviathan*, ed. by M. Oakshott (Oxford, England: Basil Blackwell Ltd., 1947 [1651]).

Hans Kelsen, *General Theory of Law and State* (New York: Russell and Russell, 1945).

II. Administrative Law

A. Administrative Process

Rand Dyck and Christopher Cochrane, *Canadian Politics: Critical Approaches*, 7th ed. (Toronto: Nelson Education, 2014) Ch. 21.

Heather MacIvor, ed., *Parameters of Power: Canada's Political Institutions*, 5th ed. (Toronto: Nelson Education, 2010) Chs. 8 and 9.

John Swaigen, *Administrative Law: Principles and Advocacy*, 2d ed. (Toronto: Emond Montgomery Publications, 2010).

Michael Mac Neil et al., eds., *Law, Regulation, and Governance* (Don Mills, Ont.: Oxford University Press, 2002).

Janice G. Stein, *The Cult of Efficiency* (Toronto: Anansi, 2001).

Kenneth Kernaghan and David Siegel, *Public Administration in Canada*, 4th ed. (Scarborough, Ont.: ITP Nelson, 1999) Part III.

John C. Strick, *The Public Sector in Canada: Programs, Finance and Policy* (Toronto: Thompson Educational Publishing, 1999).

Michael Taggart, ed., *The Province of Administrative Law* (Oxford, England: Hart Publishing, 1997).

John C. Strick, *The Economics of Government Regulation: Theory and Canadian Practice*, 2d ed. (Toronto: Thompson Educational, 1994).

René Dussault and Louis Borgeat, *Administrative Law: A Treatise*, vol. 1, 2d ed., trans. by Murray Rankin (Toronto: Carswell, 1985).

Henry Hart Jr. and Albert Sacks, *The Legal Process, Basic Problems in the Making and Application of Law* (Westbury, N.Y.: Library Foundation Press, 1984 [original, unpublished, 1958]).

B. Judicial Control

David Phillip Jones and Anne S. de Villars, *Principles of Administrative Law*, 6th ed. (Toronto: Carswell, 2014).

Sara Blake, *Administrative Law in Canada*, 5th ed. (Toronto: LexisNexis Canada, 2011).

Gus Van Harten, Gerald Heckman, and David J. Mullan, *Administrative Law: Cases, Text, and Materials*, 6th ed. (Toronto: Emond Montgomery, 2010).

Donald J.M. Brown and J.M. Evans, *Judicial Review of Administrative Action in Canada*, looseleaf (Toronto: Carswell, 2009– [annual updates]).

David J. Mullan, *Administrative Law* (Toronto: Irwin Law, 2001).

Robert Kligman, *Bias* (Markham, Ont.: LexisNexis Butterworths, 1998).

David J. Mullan, *Administrative Law*, 3d ed. (Toronto: Carswell, 1996).

Philip Anisman and Robert F. Reid, *Administrative Law* (Toronto: Carswell, 1995).

III. Basic Values, Rights, and the *Charter*

A. General Aspects

Brian Peckford, *Some Day the Sun Will Shine and Have Not Will Be No More* (St. John's, NL: Flanker Press, 2012)

Antonia Maioni, *Parting at the Crossroads: The Emergence of Health Insurance in the United States and Canada* (Princeton, N.J.: Princeton University Press, 1998).

James W. St. G. Walker, *Race, Rights and the Law in the Supreme Court of Canada Historical Case Studies* (Waterloo, Ont.: Wilfred Laurier University Press, 1997).

Maggie Siggins, *Riel: A Life of Revolution* (Toronto: Harper Collins, 1994).

Thomas R. Berger, *Fragile Freedoms: Human Rights and Dissent in Canada* (Toronto and Vancouver: Clarke, Irwin & Company, 1981).

Ken Adachi, *The Enemy that Never Was: A History of the Japanese Canadians* (Toronto: McClelland & Stewart, 1976).

M. James Penton, *Jehovah's Witnesses In Canada — Champions of Freedom of Speech and Worship* (Toronto: MacMillan Company of Canada, 1976).

Isaiah Berlin, *Two Concepts of Liberty: An Inaugural Lecture Delivered Before the University of Oxford on 31 October 1958* (Oxford, England: Clarendon Press, 1958).

B. Constitutional and *Charter* Protection

Peter W. Hogg, *Constitutional Law of Canada*, 2013 student ed. (Toronto, Ont.: Carswell, 2013).

Errol Mendes and Stéphane Beaulac, *Canadian Charter of Rights and Freedoms*, 5th ed. (Markham, Ont.: LexisNexis Canada, 2013).

Kent Roach and Robert J. Sharpe, *The Charter of Rights and Freedoms*, 5th ed. (Toronto: Irwin Law, 2013).

W.A. Bogart, *Good Government? Good Citizens?: Courts, Politics, and Markets in a Changing Canada* (Vancouver: UBC Press, 2005).

James B. Kelly, *Governing with the Charter: Legislative and Judicial Activism and Framers' Intent* (Vancouver: UBC Press, 2005).

Robert I. Martin, *The Most Dangerous Branch: How the Supreme Court of Canada Has Undermined Our Law and Our Democracy* (Montreal & Kingston: McGill-Queen's University Press, 2003).

Robert H. Bork, *Coercing Virtue: The Worldwide Rule of Judges* (Toronto: Random House Vintage Canada, 2002).

Janet L. Hiebert, *Charter Conflicts: What is Parliament's Role?* (Montreal & Kingston: McGill-Queen's University Press, 2002).

Paul Howe and Peter H. Russell, eds., *Judicial Power and Canadian Democracy* (Montreal & Kingston: McGill-Queen's University Press, 2001).

Kent Roach, *The Supreme Court on Trial: Judicial Activism or Democratic Dialogue* (Toronto: Irwin Law, 2001).

Christopher P. Manfredi, *Judicial Power and the Charter: Canada and the Paradox of Liberal Constitutionalism*, 2d ed. (Don Mills, Ont.: Oxford University Press, 2000).

Michael Ignatieff, *The Rights Revolution* (Toronto: Anansi, 2000).

F.L. Morton and Rainer Knopff, *The Charter Revolution and the Court Party* (Peterborough: Broadview Press, 2000).

Joel Bakan, *Just Words: Constitutional Rights and Social Wrongs* (Toronto: University of Toronto Press, 1997).

David Schneiderman and Kate Sutherland, eds., *Charting the Consequences: The Impact of Charter Rights on Canadian Law and Politics* (Toronto: University of Toronto Press, 1997).

Allan C. Hutchinson, *Waiting for Coraf: A Critique of Law and Rights* (Toronto: University of Toronto Press, 1995).

W.A. Bogart, *Courts and Country: The Limits of Litigation and the Social and Political Life of Canada* (Toronto: Oxford University Press, 1994).

Michael Mandel, *The Charter of Rights and the Legalization of Politics in Canada*, rev. ed. (Toronto: Thompson Educational, 1994).

David M. Beatty, *Talking Heads and the Supremes: The Canadian Production of the Constitutional Review* (Toronto: Carswell, 1990).

Ian Greene, *The Charter of Rights* (Toronto: James Lorimer & Company, 1989).

Patrick Monahan, *Politics and the Constitution: The Charter, Federalism, and the Supreme Court of Canada* (Toronto: Carswell, 1987).

John Hart Ely, *Democracy and Distrust: A Theory of Judicial Review* (Cambridge, Mass.: Harvard University Press, 1980).

C. Collective Security and Terrorism

Noam Chomsky, *Hegemony or Survival: America's Quest for Global Dominance* (New York: Owl Books, 2004).

Michael Ignatieff, *The Lesser Evil: Political Ethics in an Age of Terror* (Toronto: Penguin Canada, 2004).

Jennifer Welsh, *At Home in the World: Canada's Global Vision for the 21st Century* (Toronto: Harper Perennial, 2004).

Benjamin R. Barber, *Fear's Empire: War, Terrorism and Democracy in an Age of Interdependence* (New York: Norton, 2003).

Kent Roach, *September 11: Consequences for Canada* (Montreal & Kingston: McGill-Queen's University Press, 2003).

Noam Chomsky, *Pirates and Emperors, Old and New: International Terrorism in the Real World* (Toronto: Between the Lines, 2002).

Karim-Aly Kassam, George Melynk, and Lynne Perras, eds., *Canada and Sept. 11: Impact and Responses* (Calgary: Detselig Enterprises, 2002).

Ronald J. Daniels, Patrick Macklem, and Kent Roach, eds., *The Security of Freedom: Essays on Canada's Anti-Terrorism Bill* (Toronto: University of Toronto Press, 2001).

IV. Group Rights

A. Collective Bargaining and Labour Relations

Morton Mitchnick and Brian Etherington, *Leading Cases on Labour Arbitration*, 2d ed., looseleaf (Toronto: Lancaster House, 2011– [regular updates]).

Donald J.M. Brown and David M. Beatty, *Canadian Labour Arbitration*, 4th ed. (looseleaf) (Aurora, Ont.: Canada Law Book, 2006– [annual updates]).

Michael Mac Neil et al., *Trade Union Law in Canada*, looseleaf (Aurora, Ont.: Canada Law Book, 1994– [annual updates]).

CCH Canadian Limited, *Canadian Labour Law Reporter*, looseleaf (Toronto: CCH Canadian, 1946– [Bi-weekly updates]).

Labour Law Casebook Group, *Labour and Employment Law: Cases, Materials, and Commentary*, 8th ed. (Toronto: Irwin Law, 2011).

J.F.W. Weatherill, *A Practical Guide to Labour Arbitration Procedure*, 2d ed. (Aurora, Ont.: Canada Law Book, 1998).

B. Aboriginal Rights and Related Issues

David Milward, *Aboriginal Justice and the Charter* (Vancouver: UBC Press, 2012).

Olive Patricia Dickason and David T. McNab, *Canada's First Nations: A History of Canada's Founding Peoples from Earliest Times*, 4th ed. (Don Mills, Ont.: Oxford University Press, 2009).

Law Commission of Canada, ed., *Indigenous Legal Traditions* (Vancouver: UBC Press, 2007).

David W. Elliott, *Law and Aboriginal Peoples of Canada*, 5th ed. (North York, Ont.: Captus Press, 2005).

John Burrows, *Recovering Canada: The Resurgence of Indigenous Law* (Toronto: University of Toronto Press, 2002).

Alan C. Cairns, *Citizens Plus: Aboriginal Peoples and the Canadian State* (Vancouver: UBC Press, 2000).

Ken S. Coates, *The Marshall Decision and Native Rights* (Montreal & Kingston: McGill-Queen's University Press, 2000).

Thomas Flanagan, *First Nations? Second Thoughts* (Montreal & Kingston: McGill-Queen's University Press, 2000).

Canada, Royal Commission on Aboriginal Peoples, *Report of the Royal Commission on Aboriginal Peoples* (Ottawa: Royal Commission on Aboriginal Peoples, 1996).

Robert Alan Reiter, *The Law of First Nations* (Edmonton: Juris Analytica Publishing, 1996).

V. Public International Law

A. General Aspects

Hugh M. Kindred and Phillip M. Saunders, general eds., *International Law: Chiefly as Interpreted and Applied in Canada*, 8th ed. (Toronto: Emond Montgomery, 2014).

J.-Maurice Arbour and Geneviève Parent, *Droit international public*, 6e édiition (Cowansville, Qué.: Éditions Yvon Blais, 2012).

Clyde Sanger, *Ordering the Oceans: The Making of the Law of the Sea* (Toronto: University of Toronto Press, 1987).

David G. Haglund, *Canada and the Law of the Sea* (Kingston, Ont.: Centre for International Relations, Queen's University, 1986).

United Nations, *United Nations Convention on the Law of the Sea*, opened for signature 10 December 1982, UN Doc. A/CONF.62/122 (1982), reprinted in United Nations, *Official Text of the United Nations Convention on the Law of the Sea with Annexes and Index*, UN Sales. No. E.83.V.5 (1983), and U.S. Senate Treaty Doc. 103-39 (1994).

E. Secession

Chantal Hebert, *The Morning After: The 1995 Quebec Referendum and the Day that Almost Was* (Toronto: Knopf Canada, 2014).

James Crawford, *The Creation of States in International Law*, 2d ed. (Oxford, England: Oxford University Press, 2007).

Marcelo G. Kohen, ed., *Secession: International Law Perspectives* (Cambridge, England: Cambridge University Press, 2006).

David Carment et al., *The International Politics of Quebec Secession: State Making and State Breaking in North America* (Westport, Conn.: Praeger, 2001).

Anne F. Bayefsky, ed., *Self-determination in International Law: Quebec and Lessons Learned* (The Hague: Kluwer Law International, 2000).

Warren J. Newman, *The Quebec Secession Reference: The Rule of Law and the Position of the Attorney General of Canada* (Toronto: York University, 1999).

David Schneiderman, *The Quebec Decision: Perspectives on the Supreme Court Ruling on Secession* (Toronto: James Lorimer & Company, 1999).

Michael W. Hughey, ed., *New Tribalism: The Resurgence of Race and Ethnicity* (New York: New York University Press, 1998).

Will Kymlicka, *Finding our Way: Rethinking Ethnocultural Relations in Canada* (Don Mills, Ont.: Oxford University Press, 1998).

Hurst Hannum, *Autonomy, Sovereignty, and Self-Determination: The Accommodation of Conflicting Rights*, rev. ed. (Philadelphia: University of Pennsylvania Press, 1996).

Patrick J. Monahan et al., *Coming to Terms with Plan B: Ten Principles Governing Secession* (Toronto: C.D. Howe Institute Commentary, June 1996).

Mortimer N.S. Sellers, *The New World Order: Sovereignty, Human Rights and the Self-Determination of Peoples* (Oxford: Berg, 1996).

Antonio Cassese, *Self-Determination of Peoples: A Legal Reappraisal* (Cambridge, England: Cambridge University Press, 1995).

Grand Council of the Crees, *Sovereign Injustice: Forcible Inclusion of the James Bay Crees and Cree Territory in a Sovereign Quebec* (Nemaska, Québec: Grand Council of the Crees, 1995).

Robert A. Young, *The Secession of Quebec and the Future of Canada* (Montreal & Kingston: McGill-Queen's University Press, 1995).

Sharon A. Williams, *International Legal Effects of Secession by Quebec* (North York, Ont.: York University Centre for Public Law and Public Policy, 1992).

Allen E. Buchanan, *Secession: The Morality of Political Divorce from Fort Sumter to Lithuania and Quebec* (Boulder: Westview, 1991).

Lee C. Buchheit, *Secession: The Legitimacy of Self-Determination* (New Haven: Yale University Press, 1978).

301